CW01546525

FABRICATE 2020
MAKING RESILIENT
ARCHITECTURE

JANE BURRY / JENNY SABIN / BOB SHEIL / MARILENA SKAVARA

The Bartlett
School of
Architecture

UCL
THE BARTLETT

Cornell AAP
Architecture Art Planning

SWiN
BUR
NE

SWINBURNE
UNIVERSITY OF
TECHNOLOGY

CONTENTS

FOREWORD

FABRICATE 2020 is the latest in a series of triennial conferences that, over the last decade, have creatively engaged emerging issues in architecture and design, particularly in relation to confluences of technology and making. This year's emphasis on 'making resilient architecture' is significant and timely. First, the conference theme signals the rise of resilience as a priority across architectural education, research and practice in response to accelerating climate change. In an age of wildfire, rising seas, proliferating plastic, habitat loss, forced migration, and food insecurity – to name just a few pressing issues – architecture has a responsibility to seek out the design innovations that make it possible for communities to survive and thrive under growing conditions of risk. In doing so, it is important that architecture promotes forms of resilience that reduce social-spatial inequalities, rather than extending them. Second, the conference theme of 'making resilient architecture' can be taken as a provocation to attend to the vitality of the discipline/profession in the face of transforming practice. New technologies and materials, shifting economic conditions, emerging models of interdisciplinary (and inter-professional) collaboration, and changing political imperatives are all posing questions about the place and value of architecture, design and construction in the world. FABRICATE 2020 offers a unique opportunity to rearticulate the centrality of critical and creative making to building a more resilient and just future.

Professor Christoph Lindner
Dean of The Bartlett Faculty of the Built Environment, UCL

Material and process are inextricably linked. Matter is getting up to things all of the time, at varying scales of time and space, in order to exist and generate the world of objects. The process of crystallisation, by which a liquid metal becomes a solid, is as important to the successful functioning of a tubular steel framed chair as the processes of extrusion or welding are. A spectacular view across London from the 72nd floor viewing-platform of The Shard, is as much to do with the subatomic structure and behaviour of silica atoms that cause glass to be a transparent solid, as it is the result of the invention of the float glass process and differing densities of molten glass on liquid tin, or the modern construction techniques employed to build extremely tall buildings.

Making, in all its gloriously broad variants, is ultimately the relationship between materials and processes. The diversity of practices that are involved with, part of and born from traditions of making, be they described as engineering, architecture, craft, cookery or ceramics, have at their heart a shared passion for materiality, a delight in the transformative potential of stuff and an appreciation of the potential of tools. We, the communities of makers, are bound by our shared endeavours to play with materials, to try things out and subsequently see what happens. Bring it on!

Dr Zoe Laughlin
Director of the Institute of Making
Faculty of Engineering, UCL

Now in its fourth edition, FABRICATE 2020 confirms the importance of an event that has examined and mapped the deployment of manufacturing processes linked to the expansion of digital technologies and applications; a development that has now become an authentic industrial domain known as Design for Manufacture and Assembly. In less than 25 years, computational design platforms – first designed as representation instruments, then as integrated solid modelling tools – have opened manufacturing capability to the designer, establishing new digital production chains through the notion of 'file to factory'.

Such new methods of computationally-assisted design have followed the transfer of proven technologies from automotive and aviation fields, as pioneered by Gehry Partners, LLP and Gehry Technologies on experimental projects using Catia (Dassault Systems). Now the trajectory is mainstream and occupied by large international agencies, first in the form of prototype elements, and finally opened up to off-site prefabrication of large-scale elements. At the same time, the generalisation of Building Information Modelling has definitively transcribed all of the disciplines of architectural design in the digital field, multiplying the interrelationships between design, structural engineering, materials science, control systems and robotics.

Today, technologies such as 3D printing and robotics are the subject of heavy investment by large construction companies, confirming the mainstream adoption of digital design and manufacturing tools in public works. Experiments developed by universities or laboratories have opened the way to new forms of industrialisation of architecture, combining off-site and on-site robotisation and automation techniques, prefabrication systems, and serial automated production. By asserting itself as an observatory of digital manufacturing and the technologies associated with it, FABRICATE set out to report on the advent of new prototypes imposing innovative forms of industrialisation of architecture, but also reported on alternative and critical forms of construction.

The implementation of 3D printing using local materials, assisted by virtual and augmented reality, offers new construction ecologies that can reduce cost and waste, as well as rationalise transport logistics. Augmented Digital Fabrication has become a vital alternative to economies of architectural production on a global scale. The selected themes proposed by FABRICATE 2020 bring together a wide diversity of challenging research projects from academia and industry and introduce us to a variety of new possibilities when using multiple materials and bio-technologies, through unprecedented experiments on complex and composite structures, and applications in a wide variety of contexts.

Professor Frédéric Migayrou
Bartlett Professor of Architecture
Chair, The Bartlett School of Architecture, UCL

ACKNOWLEDGEMENTS

JANE BURRY / JENNY SABIN / BOB SHEIL / MARILENA SKAVARA
EDITORS OF FABRICATE: MAKING RESILIENT ARCHITECTURE

As the editors of FABRICATE 2020, we have many people to thank. We received over 250 submissions from 45 countries; we would like to thank everyone who responded to the call for works, for the extraordinary breadth, depth and quality of the work submitted that made the exacting process of review, selection and curatorship so challenging. We are grateful to all authors and collaborators on every selected project, and everyone who generously agreed to present their work.

We are indebted to more than 50 distinguished peer reviewers, listed below, who fulfilled their duties with impeccable professionalism and care during the early northern hemisphere summer/southern hemisphere winter 2019. Thank you also to our wonderful 2020 keynote presenters and 2017 keynote presenters, not only for your respective provocative orations, but also for your generosity in participating in the considered in-depth conversations published in this book, often at strange hours of the night; and to Chairs of our 2011, 2014, and 2017 outings for their counsel.

For its fourth iteration, the FABRICATE conference has returned to The Bartlett, UCL, where it is co-chaired by Jane Burry and Jenny Sabin with Bob Sheil, a partnership between three universities on three continents: UCL, Swinburne University of Technology, and the College of Architecture, Art, and Planning (AAP) at Cornell University. As Chairs we would like to express our sincere gratitude to all three institutions for their support for this great enterprise, including our Deans and Chairs, and to the entire local FABRICATE team at The Bartlett. First and foremost, thank you to co-editor Marilena Skavara who has been involved in every event and production since 2011 and whose astute strategic judgement and impeccable

management brings each to life as though it were the work of a much larger team. None of this would be possible without Marilena's key role and contribution.

Our thanks to Ruth Evison, Dragana Krsic, Chee-Kit Lai, Christopher Leung, Andy O'Reilly, Julie Richardson, Rosie Riordan, David Shanks, Emily Stone, Paul Weston, and Alice Whewell, as well as 2011 Co-Founder of FABRICATE Ruairi Glynn, who have contributed extensively to planning and delivery. In addition, thank you to all the researchers and students who helped with the wide range of aspects that needed to be taken care of for such a major event. We are lacking the space here to mention all contributions in detail but, again, FABRICATE would not have been possible without the tremendous effort and passion of this fantastic group of people. Thanks, too, to The Bartlett, B-made and Here East for providing an excellent context for our research activities, which included making it possible for us to host such a remarkable event and exhibition.

The editorial team of four wish to thank the following people, who have helped us to assemble this wonderful publication. We offer sincere thanks to Clare Hamman and Patrick Morrissey, our meticulous copy-editor and designer respectively, both of whom have executed their tasks with elegance, patience and beauty. Thank you to Lara Speicher, Publishing Manager at UCL Press, and her team; as well as our US co-publishers, Riverside Architectural Press, for their support. Thanks to Laura Cherry for her guidance and coordination with remarkable professionalism and patience. And our thanks to those responsible for the tactile experience that you, as reader, are enjoying now. To Tom Maes and Hugh Jolly of Albe de Coker printers: we salute your passion for craft and detail, and deeply appreciate your kindness and tolerance – qualities that are vital in the making of well-made things.

From The Bartlett, Swinburne and Cornell AAP, we extend our sincere thanks to all our sponsors, as it is their support and partnership that enables FABRICATE to be disseminated widely. Thank you to our Platinum sponsor Autodesk, Gold sponsors Arup, Happold Foundation, Perkins + Will, Boston Dynamics and Here East, our Silver sponsors Blumer Lehmann and Bollinger + Grohmann and our Bronze sponsors Hawkins\ Brown, LLDC and ABB. A special thank you to Boston Dynamics, Harvard University, Australian Research Council, Fologram and KADK for their support and coordination of cutting-edge and innovative workshops. We would also like to thank UCL Engineering, CEGE and Loughborough University for their contributions and ongoing support.

Finally, we would like to thank all our fellow peer reviewers for their invaluable contribution to the FABRICATE 2020 selection process: Sean Ahlquist, Francis Aish, Phil Ayres, Ehsan Baharlou, Martin Bechthold, Mirco Becker, Philip Beesley, Nick Callicott, Canhui Chen, Brandon Clifford, Dana Cupkova, Moritz Dörstelmann, Evan Douglis, Stylianos Dritsas, Nick Dunn, Stephen Gage, David Gerber, Volker Helm, Axel Kilian, Nathan King, Toni Kotnik, Oliver Krieg, Julian Lienhard, Areti Markopoulou, Wes McGee, Achim Menges, Philippe Morel, Caitlin Mueller, Catie Newell, Paul Nicholas, Brady Peters, Marshall Prado, Dagmar Reinhardt, Gilles Retsin, Matthias Rippmann, Christopher Robeller, Stanislav Roudavski, Virginia San Fratello, Simon Schleicher, Tobias Schwinn, Asbjørn Søndergaard, Lauren Vasey, Kathy Velikov, Tobias Wallisser, Michael Weinstock, Mark West, Nicholas Williams, Jan Willmann and Dylan Wood.

INTRODUCTION
FABRICATE 2020: MAKING RESILIENT ARCHITECTURE

PROFESSOR JANE BURRY
DEAN OF THE SCHOOL OF DESIGN, FACULTY OF HEALTH ARTS AND DESIGN, SWINBURNE UNIVERSITY OF TECHNOLOGY
ASSOCIATE PROFESSOR JENNY E. SABIN
ASSOCIATE DEAN FOR DESIGN, DEPARTMENT OF ARCHITECTURE / AAP, CORNELL UNIVERSITY

Welcome to FABRICATE 2020! Almost a decade since the inaugural event 'Making Digital Architecture', chaired by Ruairi Glynn and Bob Sheil at The Bartlett School of Architecture, UCL, London, the event has returned 'home'; but how home has transformed in the interim. In 2020, the FABRICATE community meets at the new UCL Campus at Here East in the emerging creative heart of London in Stratford where the space and facilities have been developed to think big, think collectively, and act in a multitude of spheres. Digital fabrication and making have been placed at the core, the metaphorical hearth around which the academic disciplines of architecture, design, engineering, materials science and biology are gathering, with practice and industry partners, to uncover and explore creative solutions to the biggest and most pressing questions of our day. Congratulations to The Bartlett on the vision and realisation of the new campus. It is emblematic of the core value of making in research and education in contemporary architecture, design and construction.

Since the first event in 2011, FABRICATE has travelled to other fabrication hotspots. In 2014, it was Chaired by Fabio Gramazio and Matthias Kohler at ETH Zurich, hub to science and technology, and coincided with their launch of the National Centre of Competence in Research for Digital Fabrication (NCCR DFAB). The editorial team of Gramazio, Kohler and Langenberg wrote in their introduction that their focus in 2014 was to bring the new technological developments, still concentrated in research institutes and young specialist start-ups, into early design within mainstream practice; a social and cultural shift. For them, FABRICATE was 'Negotiating Design and Making'.

FABRICATE 2017, chaired by Achim Menges and Bob Sheil, brought the FABRICATE community into the industrial heartland of Germany, to the Institute for Computational Design and Construction, University of Stuttgart; world leader in linking manufacturing industry to design for construction, and now home to the German Excellence Cluster: Integrative Computational Design for Architecture and Construction. Already there was a noted shift in the scale and level of realisation of projects submitted for review and selected for presentation and publication. There was greater collaboration with industry, and participation from practice and industry – the field of players had expanded. Digital fabrication was on the move out of the lab and into the world, increasingly impacting construction at real scale. In 2017, FABRICATE was 'Rethinking Design and Construction'.

Each event has hosted academia, practice and industry and taken on particular characteristics and concerns of the host institution and chairs, whilst building on both the unfolding questions and the developing state of knowledge across the domain over the three intervening years. Each has called for an abstract on works in progress close to a year out from the conference, reaching out to practice and industry as well as academia. After blind review, selected project authors are then invited to submit a full paper, understanding that the work is still in development. A further selection of half of the projects for publication are invited to present at the conference. In 2020, of 250 initial submissions, 32 were selected for publication in this book, with 20 conference presentations, representing 20 projects.

Every FABRICATE conference has spawned a highly regarded and cited book with over 100,000 collective downloads in more than 120 nations, a record of the highest level of investigative making, thinking and writing in digital fabrication of the time. 2020 is no exception. Yet Bob Sheil has called FABRICATE 'a work in progress about works in progress'. The aim remains to both capture and generate investigative making,

1

thinking, and dialogue live, *in vivo*, to feed an active culture of research of, and through, new ways of designing and building. This book itself should be regarded as a living, resilient and interactive testament to active endeavour and discourse.

In the nine years since the first event, we have received over 830 submissions from institutions and practices across more than 45 countries. From this pool, we have selected 128 papers for publication and 68 for presentation, alongside 16 highly distinguished keynote lectures. A team of 7 conference chairs, 9 editors, 16 panel chairs and over 70 peer reviewers have been intimately involved throughout. FABRICATE is now widely regarded as the leading international forum on the topic in which centres of excellence in architecture, design, engineering and manufacturing can engage, collaborate and create. It has become a unique public platform for open debate on how these disciplines exchange and evolve their design and making expertise.

In FABRICATE 2020, the conference chairs come from three continents and three schools: The College of Architecture, Art, and Planning at Cornell University; Swinburne University of Technology; and The Bartlett School of Architecture, UCL. We are joined by academic partners: The Faculty of Engineering at UCL, including its departments of Civil,

Environmental and Geomatic Engineering (CEGE), and Computer Science; the Institute of Making; The Bartlett Faculty, including the Institute for Environmental Design and Engineering (IEDE); and neighbouring institutions at Here East, Loughborough University, and the Building Crafts College. Always a global event by virtue of its participating community, the submissions and published works in this iteration volubly address challenges that are also of a global nature. A beleaguered planet in climate emergency is now central to current research. Construction waste; big data; migration; metal smelting and processing; The Great Pacific Garbage Patch; new forms of communication; augmented reality and artificial intelligence; extreme environments; urban air quality; catastrophic natural disasters; climate change; all of these topics and more demand that we embrace change and cultivate new research models to comprehend key social, material, environmental, pedagogical and technological issues in the context of 'making resilient architecture'.

More specifically, challenges of diminishing resource, the carbon footprint of the construction industry and of key construction materials are either explicit or implicit in most, if not all, of the FABRICATE 2020 work. Questions of how to build lighter and cheaper, and optimise the structural and environmental performance of architecture have been there

1. A corner of Protolab, School of Design, Swinburne University, completed and opened in 2019 in response to the addition of new under- and post-graduate architecture programs within Design in 2018/19. Photo by Doris Dai.

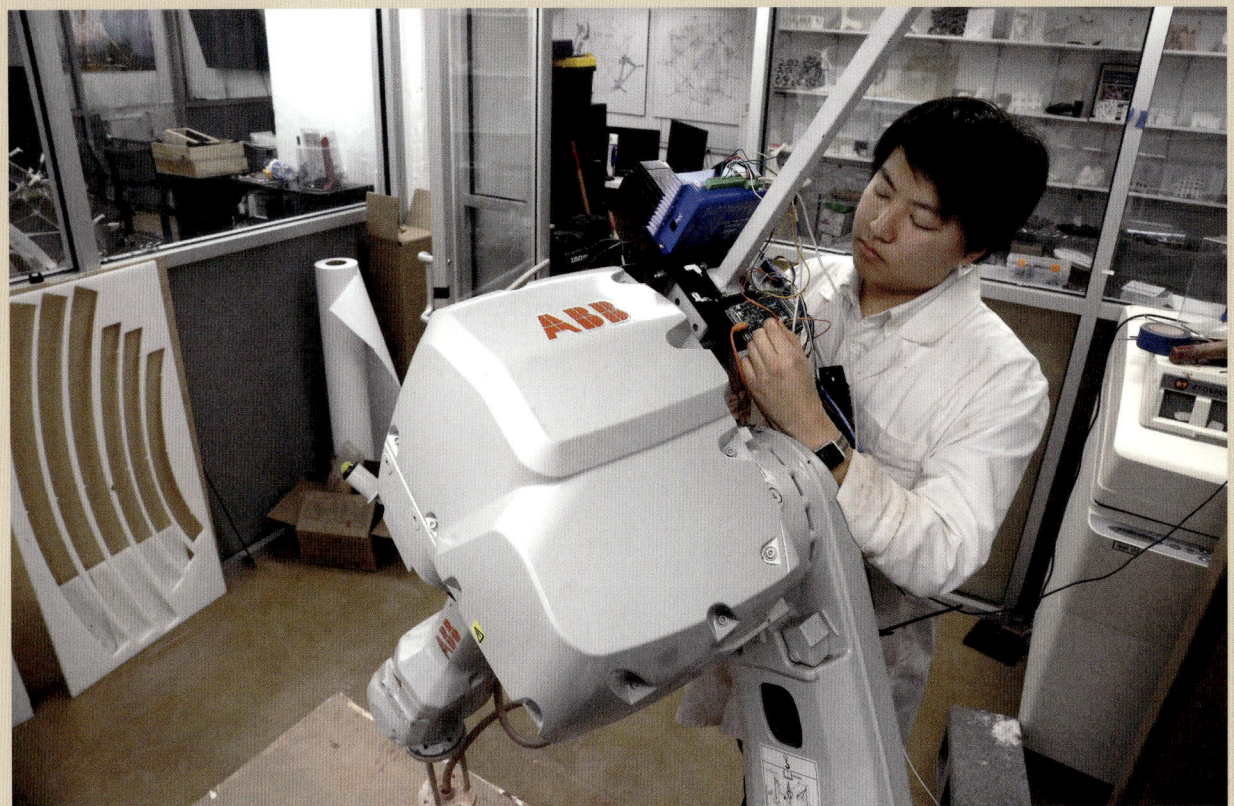

2

from the start. As the urgency ramps up, the approaches to addressing these challenges become even richer and more diverse, tapping into the biological and transient, mineralogical and enduring, and opening up new seams of questioning, making and evaluating. The cultural, aesthetic, human and experiential goals entwine with the search for new and responsible paradigms. This heightening awareness, and action through making, is not wasted on us as invited FABRICATE 2020 conference co-chairs, operating as we do in two of the countries that have not responded to climate change at the necessary speed, where land is already burning in predicted but unprecedented ways in response to the changes.

At Swinburne, we have had the opportunity to create and curate a completely new suite of architecture courses within an established design school (first intake 2018). It is no coincidence that the single greatest capital investment has been into *Protolab*, a vastly expanded and enhanced digital fabrication workshop that not only hosts very real-world research with industry partners, but can accommodate up to 100 students simultaneously. In architecture, making is no longer an elective option for the enthusiasts, or occasional recourse, the workshop is now the kitchen in the house. The boundaries between the computational, virtual, augmented, machined and grown are still not seamless but much less

discussed than the high-level creative objectives. Fabrication is key to education and an essential way to plumb the depths of the questions of materiality and assembly, performance and real cost and lifecycle. It is a vital component of exploring not only the art of design but new systems for translation into industry. Digital Fabrication is one of three high level streams of enquiry in Swinburne Design, the others, deeply impacted and implicated in it, are Human Health and Wellbeing and Urban Ecology.

At Cornell University in the Department of Architecture at the College of Architecture, Art, and Planning, we launched a new advanced research degree in the winter of 2017, the Master of Science in Matter Design Computation. A kick-off event of the same name brought together key pioneers in digital fabrication from around the globe, many of whom are featured in this publication or have chaired FABRICATE in the past. The new programme affords students of architecture and alternate disciplines to expand their creative design potential by increasing their critical knowledge and understanding of material and computational design, digital fabrication, and emerging materials and technologies at the nexus of biology, materials science, ecology and architecture. Last year, we welcomed our new Dean, J. Meejin Yoon, who has brought her expertise and vision at the intersections between architecture,

2. Sabin Design Lab at Cornell College of Architecture, Art, and Planning, Cornell University. Research Associate Kevin Guo working on a clay extruder and end effector. Photo by William Staffeld for Cornell AAP.

technology and the public realm to a multitude of exciting and ground-breaking initiatives across our college and the university. We recently formed new teaching partnerships and research collaborations with Cornell Tech, our technology innovation hub in New York City, to work on some of the most pressing challenges in areas of urban and health tech, transportation, sustainable architecture, big data, K-12 technology education and beyond. Our recent faculty hires hail from many of the incredible institutions represented in this book to implement cutting-edge research and teaching agendas in areas of bio-informed adaptive materials, robotic construction, the reuse and reconfiguration of building materials, energy modelling and passive climate control, performance-driven design workflows, and urbanisation and mass-customised robotic construction methods. At Cornell Architecture, and through the leadership of chair, Andrea Simitch, making has always been central to our teaching and research; where informed form and the role of context are central to our critical thinking, and increasingly expanded awareness of our role and responsibility to address climate change and implement action in multivalent ways in our labs, studios, practices and through our collaborations.

The theme and subtitle of FABRICATE 2020 is 'Making Resilient Architecture'. It is a message that has emerged from both the submitted work and from the lively dialogues between the co-chairs and past and present keynote presenters. The contributed work within the book falls naturally into four sections. The first of these, 'Bio-Materiality', engages a breadth of material systems consciously and creatively embraced for their contribution to a biologically-led, zero-net carbon future of design and construction, and tested to various levels of demonstrator including finely crafted buildings. All these works are generalisable, applied to appropriate scales and design contexts. The second section, 'Synthesising Design and Production', explores a different level of translation of ideas into contemporary construction practice and collaboration with industry, at greater scale ranging up to the majestic. All reflect the thoughtful development of systems of structure and construction that embrace powerful and novel ideas, new approaches to light-weighting to low waste production of componentry. The third section, 'Optimisation for a Changing World', explores the latest developments in shape, structural and material optimisation: eloquent results from economy of means working with a panoply of organic and non-organic materials. The fourth and final section, 'Polemical Performative Practice', groups projects that exemplify singular practices in which the living and generative process of making overtakes the made. It enters the uncanny world of artificially living architecture, ground-breaking AI and interactivity, discrete architecture, simulated life, floating and balancing follies.

FABRICATE 2020 refocuses the conversation around creative exploration at the nexus of computation and making in architecture and construction in an atmosphere of increasing urgency. The work in this volume, to be read as a flourishing conversation-in-progress, breathes new and inspiring life into the familiar adage that necessity is the mother of invention. In an era where we are witnessing one of the biggest paradigm shifts in the conceptualisation, making and construction of buildings, FABRICATE 2020 celebrates and debates the most cutting-edge innovations in digital fabrication to impact architectural pedagogy, trans-disciplinary research, and applied professional practice in a changing world.

FROM MAKING DIGITAL ARCHITECTURE TO MAKING RESILIENT ARCHITECTURE

PROFESSOR BOB SHEIL
DIRECTOR OF THE BARTLETT SCHOOL OF ARCHITECTURE, UCL

This text is written in a manner that offers a series of contexts and overviews in parallel to notes on a series of incorporated images. Central to this approach is a belief that both design and making are complex non-linear operations in constant dialogue with one another on themes that navigate shifting contexts over time. Both designers and makers, increasingly reunited as core hybrid disciplines, respond to a myriad of imposed or selected parameters, some that are practical, others that are philosophical, with skill and knowledge that are both explicit and tacit. On this basis this text begins with the image of a now extinct form that requires more than a glance.

Figure 1. Frozen Relic (2012). Founded and led by Matt Shaw and Will Trossell on graduating from The Bartlett School of Architecture in 2010, ScanLAB Projects are a firm who specialise in 3D capture and visualisation. One of their first commissions was to scan every display in the shipping gallery at London's Science Museum, configured in an exhibition layout that had not changed since the 1960s. The digital twin they generated allowed the institution to regard the highly reputable display as preserved, thus permitting its replacement by displays of other less familiar objects in the collection in unconventional ways.

As a new form of practice, akin to Factum Arte in Madrid and Forensic Architecture in London, ScanLAB Projects have utilised the agency of digital technology to rethink the status of the physical. Their work has evolved in scale and scope to include the scanning of buildings and cities, both ancient and new, allowing geometrical relationships, structures and timescales to be understood in entirely new ways. They have also explored 3D scanning as a way of understanding the stacking of time through experiments in choreography and dance, landscape, and vehicular motion, in particular rethinking Ansel Adams' work in Yosemite Valley, and the eyes of the autonomous car in London and other cities.

On landscape, they have progressed from capturing topography as a one-off freeze frame into the meticulous measurement of change upon place and condition through repetition and layering. In this regard, their work illustrated here, on board Greenpeace's ice-breaker *Arctic Sunrise*, with scientists from Cambridge University, has been seminal in translating numerical data into visualisations that communicate the complexity of ice formation and behaviour over time, offering an understanding and literacy that the data alone cannot. The latest work by the research-based enterprise that emanates from a background in

architectural design is entitled FRAMERATE. Drawing on a year of daily data capture of selected environments such as forests, gardens and coastlines, it generates the world's largest temporal pointcloud model for scrutiny via animation and virtual reality. Some of ScanLAB Projects' earliest models were published in FABRICATE 2011 and, in the short decade that has passed since, their rapid trajectory into a new hybrid discipline that is part-archaeological and part-propositional, part-temporal and part-literal identifies a key shift in what we understand digital architecture to be, and what it can become.

All Change Please

In the half-century preceding 2016 approximately nine trillion tonnes of ice melted from the earth's glaciers (Zemp et al., 2019). Current estimates suggest that half a trillion tonnes of ice are now melting annually, and the surface areas of both the Arctic and Antarctic ice caps are at the lowest on record since accurate surface and subsurface monitoring began. Global weather patterns and air quality are changing; biodiversity is both diminishing and altering its profile; agricultural production is proliferating in scale and reducing in diversity; ancient species and habitats, and non-renewable resources, are expiring; and world human population is increasing by over 20,000 per day (United Nations, 2019).

Ecological change has happened on this and greater scales before, but not under similar conditions to our present where the consequences are so stark and where the potential to repair is so slim. Our rising aspirations on the quantity, quality and origin of the things we produce, consume, digest, accumulate, need and utilise, including those curious things we seek firmness, commodity and delight from, are behind many of these unprecedented transformations. These and the many further startling observations that are defining the pretext of a post-human age challenge all disciplines, cultures, and domains of

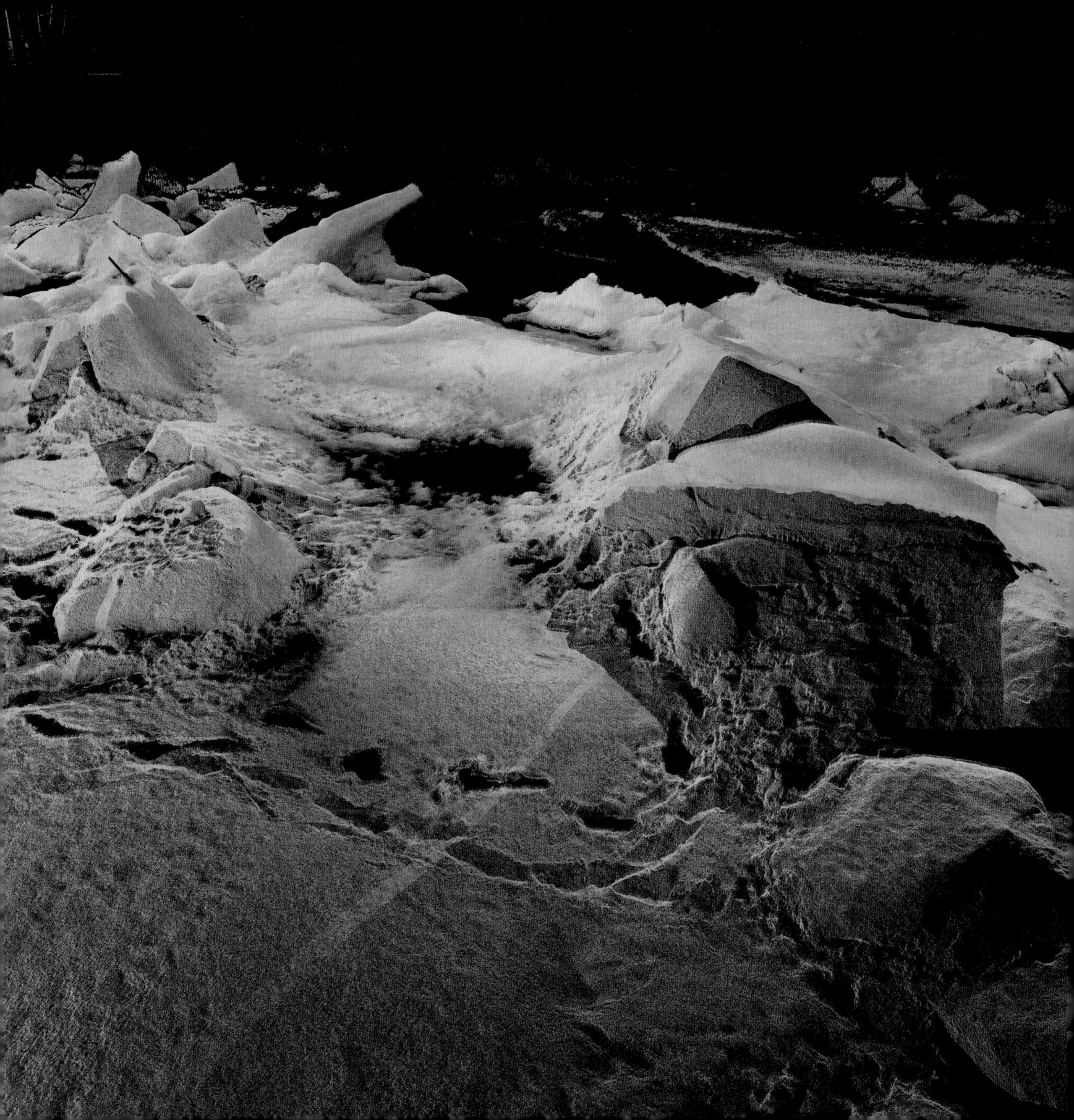

knowledge to act in synchronicity, simultaneously and collaboratively, to prepare to cope for such an occurrence, let alone slow it down, halt it, or reverse it.

Architectural and engineering research and practice, together occupy vital roles in preparing for a changed world by rethinking how the built environment is designed, made, used and operates, including its location on this and other planets (Sheil et al., 2020). They are but only two forces in a constellation that spans a disparate industry charged with addressing grand challenges. They operate within vast logistical equations: from the supply and processing of materials, to the organisation of necessary infrastructures; the functionality of software and its integration with manufacture and assembly, to deployed energy systems used in the production of construction; from the pace and integrity that project and legal management set for procurement, to monitoring stock and the data it captures, to how and from where built environment projects are financed; and where, in all this, ethical principles are agreed upon and followed through.

The role of design research is to forward plan, to read the turbulence and potential that surrounds perpetual progression and regression across humanities and sciences, with both insight and foresight, offering a pathway for better things ahead. Its core agency is its capacity to cut through barriers, including disciplinary boundaries, many of which are still constrained by professional and cultural definitions that were formed almost two centuries ago. The Royal Institute of British Architects (RIBA) for instance, was established by around a dozen privileged males in 1834 when world population was 12% (US Census Bureau) of what it is today and only three cities had populations greater than 1 million: London, Beijing, and Paris. Today it is estimated that over 50% of the world's population live in cities, 50% of the world's population also live in poverty, and 7% of the world's population holds a degree.

On chronic housing needs, not exclusive to only those living in poverty, current rates of world population growth alone require that we build double the quantity of living space over the next 30 years that currently exists (Knippers et al., 2020). The expertise for this task resides with possibly less than 0.5% of the world's population. This focus must further mobilise the understanding that design research is far more than what is defined by the talents of the individual designer alone, and thus is not a form of practice operating in isolation. Here it is argued that design research is an ecology of both forms and systems of practice, where industry and academia oscillate with one another on a mission of advancing prosperity,

eliminating inequality, and improving the lives and experiences of citizens. For some, the goal is an existence that is biophilic for current and future generations, underpinned by stock that is fit for purpose in conditions that are uncertain, unknown, and unstable.

Figure 2. The Eco-Visionaries (2015). Established at the Architectural Association London in 2010 by Kate Davies (The Bartlett School of Architecture, 2007) and Liam Young (University of Queensland, 2002), Unknown Fields soon evolved into a forum for artists, writers and scientists, including architects, filmmakers, bloggers, performers and activists. Their work involves the organisation, choreography, execution and documentation of group field studies in areas of particular vulnerability and popular narrative such as Chernobyl, the Galapagos Islands, Southeast Asian seas, and the Australian outback. As well as drawing mass attention to the visible, albeit largely in remote, difficult to access and cordoned off areas, Unknown Fields also draw attention to unseen matters such as air quality, logistics, human infrastructure, and both the distribution and ultimately the wastage of irreplaceable resources. In this regard, their recent monitoring of lithium mines in Bolivia draws attention to the vast acquisition of land and minerals that are harvested to generate batteries for billions of portable devices, as well as future millions of electric-powered vehicles.

Figure 3. Black Oak (3000BC and 2019). A recently found length of bog oak, estimated to have been preserved for 5000 years, is prepared for conversion into a ceremonial table for Ely Cathedral by staff and students at The Building Crafts College London (BCC). Over 13m in length, the exceptionally large trunk was found in 2012 as a farmer ploughed his fields in the Fenland District, on the Isle of Ely, Cambridgeshire. No more than 10m above sea level, the fens are steeped in geological, environmental and cultural history, and at the time of writing are underwater following Storms Ciara and Dennis. Ten boards were produced from the trunk, each weighing around 300kg; it took 18 people to lift each one into a 14m kiln especially built for the purpose where they stayed for 10 months during which moisture content was reduced to 18% with 2000 litres of water extracted.

The BCC was founded in 1893 by the Worshipful Company of Carpenters, a City livery company, to educate in a range of construction crafts. The first Chairman of the College was Professor Sir Banister 'Flight' Fletcher of University College London, co-author with his father Banister Fletcher of *A History of Architecture on the Comparative Method*, first published in 1896 (Fraser (ed.), 2019).[1] Founded at almost exactly the same time (1894) by the arts and crafts designer, architect, and social reformer, Charles Robert Ashbee, The Survey of London (SoL) seeks to capture in meticulous detail London's built environment fabric borough by borough, brick by brick. In 2013, and for the first time in its history, SoL was subsumed into an academic institution, The Bartlett School of Architecture, UCL, where technologies such as 3D scanning have extended their established methods, which are now components of a new Master's programme, Architecture and Historic Urban Environments. Likewise, BCC is but a walk away from the school's new facilities at Here East, where the availability of advanced design and manufacture technologies offer rich scope for exchange, set against the rigorous demands of traditional working methods in stone and wood, where varying quality of the latter in particular presents challenges for developing craft skill at its highest level.

Evolving Forms of Design Practice

Unlike their pre-industrial ancestors, generations of architects and engineers have not actually made buildings, rather they have made information that is used in the making of buildings. Information that is subsequently cloned or amended, adopted or erased, extended or misread, stored or discarded. Intentions and concepts are frequently lost, entirely misunderstood, or deliberately removed. These transgressions can occur

1. Frozen Relic: Arctic Works – Snow covered sea ice in the Fram Strait 2012. © ScanLAB Projects.

2. The Eco-Visionaries: 'We Power our Future with the Breastmilk of Volcanoes'. © Unknown Fields (2015) at 'Eco-Visionaries' Royal Academy of Arts, London.

3. Preparing to make the Fenland Black Oak Table at Building Crafts College London. © Christopher Leung (2019).

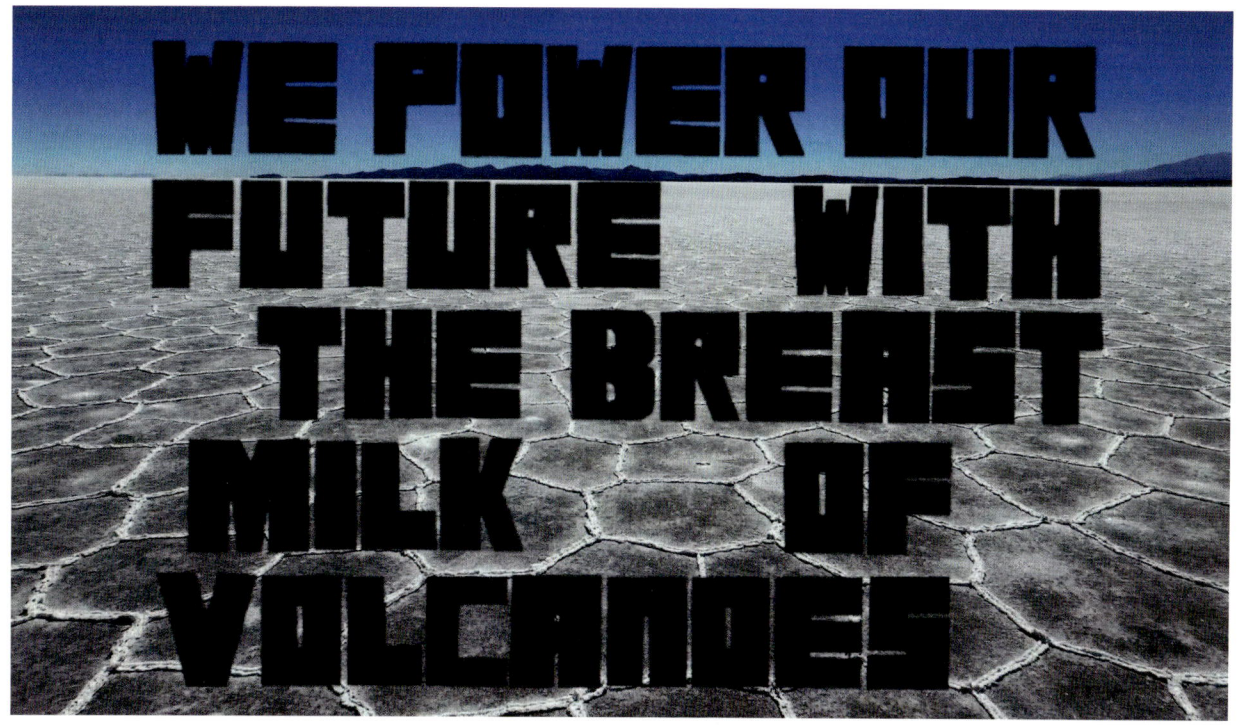

2

3

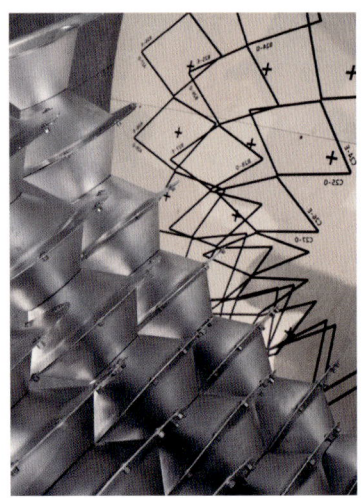

4

5

6

at any time from sudden amputations to imperceptibly slow transformations over a lifetime. While Liam Young asserts that an 'architect's skills are completely wasted on making buildings', the polemic relates to the wastage of their skill in knowing how buildings were, are, and could be made, both by others who don't recognise by whom such knowledge is owned, and by those who don't maintain it (Young, 2014). Such core knowledge underpins many forms of architectural practice that are contingent on the knowledge of how buildings are made, engineered, and spatially organised, such as the historical work of The Survey of London, and the investigatory work of Forensic Architecture.

Central to progressing knowledge in the making of buildings is the maintenance of an extended talent pipeline. The first leg of which is to rechannel the role that design research plays in the architectural and engineering professions, including its partnership and overlap with academia, and the second is to extend that channel towards academic research and education. On the former, certainly in the UK at least, long-term substantial underfunding for design must be corrected where authorities (central and local governments, research councils, banks and industry partners) must invest in ambitious interdisciplinary innovation for the built environment at its earliest stages where design, as an embedded component ensuring holistic and contextual thinking, is routinely adopted.

In this regard, the outlook for making resilient architecture must merge from the strengths of all quarters in associated design research, in particular that of innovative technology and computation. This is reflected in all four volumes of FABRICATE, the first of

which was published almost a decade ago as technologies of automated production were entering the mainstream and being awakened by pioneering design researchers for their potential to address variation, specificity, assembly, craft, structural performance and architectural language. In 2011, 'Making Digital Architecture' forecast that such processes would have powerful significance in design and making operations, and they have. In 2020 'Making Resilient Architecture' declares these processes to be central in our response to the climate and ecological emergency. Running core to this mission is the capability to harness vast potential for precision measurement, complex modelling, and synthesised manufacturing, including machine learning and artificial intelligence, using renewable materials, optimised and autonomous methods, with ethically-minded and generous design creativity.

Figure 4. Advancing Metrology. Professor Stuart Robson is Co-Investigator on 'Robotic Teleoperation for Multiple Scales: Enabling Exploration, Manipulation and Assembly Tasks in New Worlds Beyond Human Capabilities', supported by a £2.4m EPSRC award. Recent industrial-focused work includes: aircraft wing structural testing (Airbus); wind tunnel and space structure photogrammetry (NASA); optimising metrology for jet engine manufacture (Rolls Royce); optical inspection of beryllium tile surfaces for the nuclear industry (UKAEA); optimising deformation monitoring for the railway industry (Network Rail); and the creation of standards artefacts and metrology best practice (NPL).

With established collaborations with NASA, NPL, Airbus, Philips, Network Rail, Leica Geosystems, EFTA JET, Faro, Nikon, Arius3D and with KTP-supported technology transfer with SMEs, 3DImpact research is also embodied in 3D imaging and digital recording for heritage, medical, earth science, fisheries and the creative industries including The Bartlett School of Architecture. Adjacency of 3DImpact research to speculative architectural design research not only offers a platform for mutual collaboration, but provokes challenging reflections at the scale each partner views the world. 1:1 to an architect does not generate the same perspective as 1:1 for a metrologist. One might see the wing as a complex and mass produced lightweight structure, the other as a complex assembly of parts in search of the smoothest datum array. The common research trajectory here is the impact of measurement in design, between the drawn and the made.

4. Advancing Metrology. The unique 2.5m snake arm robot developed by OC Robotics for 3DImpact Research Group at UCL Here East, led by Professor Stuart Robson. Image: © Bob Sheil 2018.

5. Spot® robot. © Image provided courtesy of Boston Dynamics, Inc.

6. IncreMENTAL. A collaboration between ARUP and B-made (The Bartlett Manufacturing and Design Exchange). Arup team: Fernando Ruiz, Vincenzo Reale, Chris Clark, Henry Unterrenier, Danny Steadman and Cristina Garza. B-made: Peter Scully and Vincent Huyghe. © Image provided courtesy of ARUP.

7

8

Figure 5. Spot® (2019). Boston Dynamics were established in 1992 as a spin-out from MIT. In 2019, Spot mini became commercially available, following the evolution of its predecessors: Big Dog (2004), Little Dog (2009), Alpha Dog (2011), LS3 (2012), Cheetah (2012), Petman (2013), Atlas (2013) and Spot (2015). What this form of robotics, and other parallel approaches, represents for design research is the transformation of construction through autonomy: from the safe and synchronised distribution of materials across building sites; to the assembly, installation and maintenance of components; to the monitoring of building performance through time and use; and the inhabitation of non-human occupied architectures. Here the research trajectory is between machine learning and artificial intelligence. The existence of such a company of robust shepherds and regulators not only alters the designer's strategy, it will become a design informer.

Figure 6. IncreMENTAL (2019). Prompted by emerging research from The Bartlett's Design for Manufacture MArch programme, this work develops propositions for low cost production of bespoke durable building components, utilising robotically-controlled incremental sheet forming techniques. While generically formed sheet metal occupies a significant volume of market provision, it is in how such generic components deal with unique and complex geometries – often dictated by site conditions, performance standards, and integration with opposing components, openings and junctions – that challenge its versatility.

Figure 7. Large Additive Subtractive Integrated Modular Machine (2019). Built as a technology demonstrator for a Horizon 2020 research project developed collaboratively between Foster + Partners (Design), Autodesk, Cranfield University, Vestas, BAE Systems, Global Robots, Loxin, Helmholtz-Zentrum Geesthacht (HZG), Instituto Superior Tecnico (IST), and the European Federation for Welding, Joining and Cutting (EWF). Central to this international and multidisciplinary research project is to establish combined manufacturing methods within singular machining configurations. LASIMM achieved three core aims: to develop a large modular self-contained platform with Technology Readiness Level (TRL) 6; a multi-phase software package for design and production that enables parallel manufacturing; to fabricate demonstrator parts to show the machine's capabilities and opportunities for the aerospace, energy and construction sectors.

Figure 8. Design and Production in Augmented Reality (2019). Layered upon the idea that design and making come into being through dialogue as well as instruction and documentation, so too is the matter of where things are designed and where things are made. Cutting across the agendas and outcomes of the works discussed here is the contribution that the environment in which design and making take place has upon the work. An example of this is how furniture makers were encouraged to take prototypes out of their workshops to be 'fitted' in their destined location,

in order to judge scale. Through the work of organisations like fologram (an example of their assisted reality bricklaying illustrated here), we are witnessing an evolution of this principle where the place of design, production and installation have become interchangeable and cross-referred. The remote abstraction of the digital has been harnessed by the physical as a means to verify, guide and prompt.

Evolving Forms of Design Research

Central to the need to re-approach the knowledge and talent pipeline by rethinking the relationships between education, academic research and practice-based research is the necessity to redefine our disciplines around greater flexibility and exchange. This is a matter beyond the point of urgency, and with growing impatience with regulatory protocol, new breeds of interdisciplinary study and practice are emerging with fervent student support demanding more. Posted in 2019, an open letter from Architecture Education Declares stated that *'We are concerned that at present our education does not give sufficient weight to the inherently ecological and political basis of architecture, nor to our responsibility to meet our uncertain future with socially and environmentally informed practice'.*[2]

Echoed by many practitioners and academics around the world, these concerns also challenge too narrow an emphasis on the protection and regulation of professional boundaries and definitions that became outdated long ago and fail to offer the flexibility and hybridity that is so urgently required today. Drawing to a conclusion, this essay turns to the work of a new breed of design researcher, one that is fascinated by the intellectual, ethical and entrepreneurial opportunities afforded by new forms of education. Design for Manufacture MArch was launched in UCL's new experimental facility for design and engineering in 2017-18, alongside new programmes

7. Hybrid manufacture of an optimised 2m steel cantilever beam using wire-and-arc additive manufacturing (WAAM, i.e. 3D metal printing) and CNC-subtractive machining. © Image provided courtesy of Foster + Partners.

8. Design and Production in Augmented Reality. © Image provided courtesy of Fologram.

in Design for Performance and Interaction, Bio-Integrated Design, Situated Practice, and Engineering and Architectural Design. Offering state-of-the-art resources to acquire new skills and knowledge, the impetus of these courses to address core challenges on both how and why architecture is made is raw and unhindered. Driving many of the projects on these fledgling programmes is a critical thread seeking connection with material processes and selections that offer constructive responses to the decay of environment conditions, where making things digital is seen as a core route to making things resilient.

Figure 9. Viscous Catenary (2019). This investigation explores the challenges and opportunities in fabricating a free-form architectural glass assembly. At once resilient and fragile, transparent and substantial, thin membrane and amorphous matter, the essence of glass as a material remains elusive to most designers, despite its major presence in the built environment. By analysing traditional techniques of craftsmanship along with contemporary industrial manufacturing standards, new approaches are demonstrated through a series of prototypes that explore geometry, assembly, alignment, adhesives and lamination in glass structures.

Figure 10. Point to Point (2018). A triangulated structure is developed as a site to evolve an uninterrupted workflow for the design and production of timber elements. Robotic control strategies (through tooling and manipulation) become a fundamental part of the synthesis as they influence the shapes of the connections from the beginning of the design process. A single software platform, containing all geometric, structural and fabrication properties and constraints, choreographs the complete design to production process where an additional tracking system is tested to minimise the time of production and maximise precision by updating data with regard to material deviations.

Figure 11. Sloppy Topologies – Precise Datums (2018). This project involving hydroforming, 3D scanning and robotic plasma cutting, explores the relationship between a manufacturing process that produces a formed surface with a significant degree of uncertainty and non-repeatability, and how it joins and coordinates with precise components, as well as building planning and structural grids. The resulting 'sloppy topology' is laser scanned at high resolution to allow bespoke brackets and junctions to be precisely modelled and 3D printed, to compensate for the underlying geometric uncertainty.

Figure 12. Spatial Felted Structure (2018). By exploring advanced felting strategies, this project develops a process that allows wool fibres to be embedded into sheet materials using water pressure. The technique enables bonding between materials and produces a novel composite with numerous qualities. The working area of the waterjet machine defines the component width and depth, but not its length. Utilising water pressure as a means to bind different materials as well as to repurpose discarded materials could be further explored.

Figure 13. Reflective Geometries (2019). This project focuses on the exploration of subtractive manufacturing technologies and their effects on material behaviour. It aims to predict and design visual light transmission of machined surfaces using virtual simulation, enabling new material responses and qualities to be programmed into conventional materials such as aluminium. Material performance is largely dependent on physical properties where manufacturing processes are guided by imposed formal geometry. In contrast, these prototypes intend to define the optical performance of aluminium through carefully selected fabrication parameters that uncover inherent metaproperties. By integrating feedback data loops between the multiple stages of digital fabrication, novel ways of making become possible.

Towards Resilient Architecture

"Historically, architecture and engineering skills were indivisible – entirely symbiotic". Norman Foster (2018)

Educational, academic, practice, and industry-based design research across the field of computation and manufacture has a fundamental role to play in addressing the ongoing ecological emergency. Beginning with the tools we choose to use, and within a single generation, architects and engineers have been served with unprecedented and abundant capability. Yet there remains a critical skills shortage in how these tools are fully deployed, which includes critique of their appropriate use. From forecasting scenarios, to simulating methods, to optimising and creating materials, to tracking and tracing resources (see the work of Certain Measures), the bind between making digital architecture and making resilient architecture must be secured. In this regard, devising new hybrid disciplines and operations between design and science that advance the prospect of establishing future biophilic environments, synthesising design and production methods, optimising the capability of intelligence in systems, and remaining speculative about the potential for design to invent and generate beauty, is an essential scaffold for holistic and sustainable outcomes.

References

Knippers, J., Sheil, R., and Ramsgaard Thomsen, M. 2020. 'Innochain: A Template for Innovative Collaboration', in Sheil, R. Ramsgaard Thomsen, M., Tamke, M., Hanna, S. (eds.), *Design Transactions: Information Modelling for a New Material Age*, London: UCL Press, pp.14–21.

Sheil, R. Ramsgaard Thomsen, M., Tamke, M., Hanna, S. (eds). 2020. *Design Transactions: Information Modelling for a New Material Age*, London: UCL Press.

Trossell, W. and Shaw, M. 2011. 'ScanLAB', in Sheil, B and Glynn, R (eds), *FABRICATE*, London: Riverside Architectural Press, pp. 61–68.

United Nations. 2019. *World Population Prospects 2019: Highlights*. United Nations Department of Economic and Social Affairs, June 2019.

United States Census Bureau, https://www.census.gov/en.html

Young, L. 2014. 'Liam Young', *Tank magazine*, *The City Limits Issue*, 61. Autumn 2014. https://tankmagazine.com/issue-61/talk/liam-young. [Accessed 22 February 2020]

Zemp, M., Huss, M., Thibert, E. et al. 2019. 'Global glacier mass changes and their contributions to sea-level rise from 1961 to 2016'. *Nature* 568, pp. 382-386. doi: 10.1038/s41586-019-1071-0

Notes

1. The 21st edition, with the revised title of *Sir Banister Fletcher's Global History of Architecture*, was published in 2019 by Bloomsbury Visual Arts, edited by Murray Fraser.

2. Architecture Education Declares: https://www.architectureeducationdeclares.com

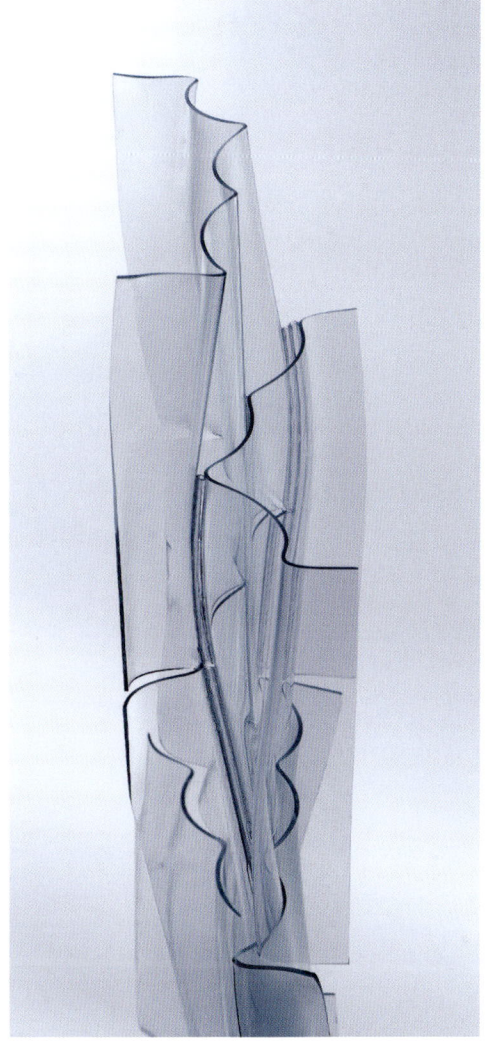

9

10

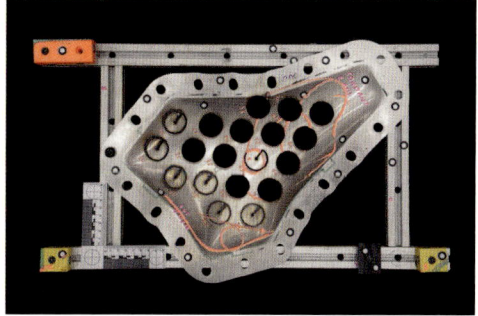

11

12

13

9. Viscous Catenary by
Gosia Pawłowska, MArch
Design for Manufacture
2018-19. Photo: Sarah Lever.

10. Point to Point by Lin Yu
Chieh and Marielena
Papandreou, MArch Design
for Manufacture 2017-18.
Photo: B-made.

11. Sloppy Topologies –
Precise Datums by
Matthew Ferguson, MArch
Design for Manufacture
2017-18. Photo: B-made.

12. Spatial Felted Structure
by Chun-Nien Ou Yang and
Anat Uziely, MArch Design
for Manufacture 2017-18.
Photo: B-made.

13. Reflective Geometries
by Mariana Rivera Berrios
and Sara Zaidan MArch
Design for Manufacture
2017-18. Photo: B-made.

BIO–
MATERIALITY

1

MUD FRONTIERS

VIRGINIA SAN FRATELLO
EMERGING OBJECTS / SAN JOSE STATE UNIVERSITY
RONALD RAEL
EMERGING OBJECTS / THE UNIVERSITY OF CALIFORNIA BERKELEY

During the last 35 years, additive manufacturing has become commonplace within the realm of academic research as a tool for creating models and full scale working prototypes and, in very rare instances, it is used as a method of manufacture by specialists to fabricate custom componentry for buildings. However, additive manufacturing is still not close to being a commonplace method of manufacture within the construction industry due to the expense associated with the purchase of large, industrial 3D printers and robot arms. Additionally, many materials such as resins, bulk filament and pellets, and proprietary powders are expensive when used for large format printing and in instances where these materials must be shipped long distances. Finally, additive manufacturing requires expertise in 3D modelling and coding, which means additional costs and time must be spent mastering advanced software applications. For many end users, these obstacles have precluded the use of additive manufacturing as a way of building. This research aims to overcome these three obstacles through the development of a lightweight, inexpensive, and mobile robotic setup capable of 3D printing. The use of ubiquitous and free materials such as local soil for 3D printing, and the scripting of an easy to use g-code generator for developing 3D printable files, enables a more accessible, portable and ecological approach to additive manufacturing at the architectural scale (Fig. 1).

Context

The construction industry is one of the largest sectors in the world economy, representing up to 13% of global GDP and employing 7% of the world's population (World Economic Forum, 2016). It is also an industry with very low annual productivity increases, only 1% per year over the past 20 years, where less than 1% of revenues is invested in R&D, remarkably poor in comparison to other sectors such as the automotive or retail supply chain industries (Barbosa et al., 2017). Additionally, only 0.2% of all robots worldwide are sold to the construction industry compared to 55% sold to the automotive industry (Executive Summary World Robotics, 2018). To date, there are only a few examples where robots are predominantly used in the construction of entire buildings; some examples include: the Canal House Cabin by DUS Architects; the DFAB House by Gramazio and Kohler Research; and the Flotsam and Jetsam Pavilion by Branch Technologies. The mobile robot used as part of the MUD Frontiers project is designed to extrude traditional formulations of adobe

2

and cob, made from clay, sand, silt, aggregate and chopped straw, with the capacity to print cement-based formulations as well. Other existing examples of robotic paste extrusion that can be found in the construction industry include: the Gaia 3D printed earth house by WASP; the Batiprint House, made of foam and cement; and several extruded cement 'showcase homes' by WinSun, ApisCor, and ICON. All of these buildings require specialised software knowledge by the designer and the builder. If more buildings are to be constructed using technologies such as 3D printing and robotics in the future, the industry will require either highly skilled digital talent to migrate to that sector, or a reduction in the skills required to use the requisite software and programming applications necessary to drive such new technologies.

The construction industry is the largest global consumer of raw materials, and accounts for 25 to 40% of the world's total carbon emissions (World Economic Forum, 2016). A return to mud as a building material attempts to correct the errors of a wasteful, polluting and consumptive industry. Ecological and sustainable issues are at the forefront of conversations surrounding the future of construction, and soil-based construction materials are the most 'earth friendly' materials that exist (Rael, 2009). Earth is a ubiquitous material and buildings made of local soils can be found in almost every region of the world. However, traditional and indigenous earth building knowledge is being lost in many parts of the world due,

in part, to a shift from agrarian to capitalist societies. For the past 10,000 years until only recently, earth was the most widely used building material on the planet; but it has now been replaced by cement which is a contributor to 8% of the world's carbon dioxide emissions in its production (World Business Council for Sustainable Development, 2002). Nevertheless, there has been a worldwide movement to continue to build using unstabilised soils, in the form of rammed earth, adobe, cob, and the numerous other earth-based building technologies. A large number of earthen building codes, guidelines and standards have appeared around the world over the past two decades, based upon a considerable amount of research and field observations regarding the seismic, thermal and moisture durability performance of earthen structures opening the door for the nascent revival of building with earth.

Mobility: Portable Robotic 3D Printing

The MUD Frontier project is addressing the challenge of creating accessible robotics for construction through the development of a mobile and lightweight 3D printing set-up that can be transported easily to the field or jobsite. The scara robotic 3D printer that was developed for this endeavour is combined with a continuous flow hopper that can print wall sections and enclosures of up to 2200mm diameter circle and 2500 mm tall, structures considerably larger than the printer itself. The set up can be carried by 1-2 people and relocated in order to continue printing.

1. The fabrication setup.

2. High alpine 3D printing with local soils.

3. The fabrication setup.

3

The robotic arm was developed for approximately $16,000, considerably less than the average price of a new industrial robot arm that costs $50,000 to $80,000 at this time, however it uses much of the same mechanical technology used in industrial robots.

Ubiquity: Local Earthen Materials

The printer is able to 3D print local soils directly from the work site in order to demonstrate the possibilities of sustainable and ecological construction in a two-phase project that explores traditional material craft at the scale of both architecture and pottery. The clays harvested for the projects are free, as they can be dug directly from the ground or surrounding region where the walls, enclosures and pottery are being printed. The material undergoes no chemical transformation, nor are any stabilisers, such as cement, added to the mixture.

Phase I of the MUD Frontier project took place along the U.S.-Mexico border in El Paso, Texas and Ciudad Juarez, Chihuahua, where earthen architecture and clay pottery of the Mogollon culture (A.D. 200-1450) define the archaeological history of the region. Excavated pit houses and above ground adobe structures defined the historic architecture of the region, and by A.D. 400 this region witnessed the development of a distinctive, indigenous coil-and-scrape pottery tradition known as Brownware.

Local, 'wild' clays were gathered from eight sites throughout the region and used to 3D print 170 ceramic vessels by local potters from both countries, reflecting current craft skills and recalling the coil pottery through additive manufacturing. A large 3D-printed adobe

structure was also manufactured using largely the same material as the pots, but with the introduction of sand. The vessels reveal the nature of the local geology and the creativity of local ceramic artisans from the contemporary Jornada Mogollon region. The fired earthenware exposes a range of clay complexions: greens, browns, purples, wheat, pink and red colours that speak to the nature of mono, bi, and polychrome traditions that developed over time. The structure and vessels were produced with the intent of connecting the forefront of digital manufacturing with the traditional coiled pottery techniques, and subterranean and adobe architecture of the borderland regions between Texas and New Mexico in the United States and the state of Chihuahua in Mexico.

During Phase I, the robotic setup for printing the large structure was installed at the Rubin Center Gallery. The gallery was maintained at a constant temperature of approximately 20°C. A mixture of five parts locally sourced clay and three parts sand was mixed with chopped straw and water and pumped through the printer. The layer height of each mud coil is 30mm and each coil is between 40 and 60mm wide. The overall structure is 213cm tall and 180cm wide and took seven days to print at approximately 300mm per day.

Phase II of the MUD Frontier project took place in the high alpine desert of the San Luis Valley which spans southern Colorado and northern New Mexico in the United States (Fig. 2). The second phase of the research reflects the earthen construction of the Indo-Hispano settlers of the valley and the local Rio-Grande pueblo culture. The 3D-printed and fired earthenware vessels from phase II take advantage of locally sourced, wild micaceous clay dug directly from the nearby mountains. The clay is used directly from the ground as both the clay body for printing and as a slip on top of the 3D-printed clay vessels. The vessels are fired in the 3D-printed kiln.

During phase II, the robotic setup was installed outside in the alpine desert of the San Luis Valley, Colorado (Fig. 3). The temperature of the valley floor fluctuated from a high of 30°C during the day to 6°C at night. The desert environment was sunny, windy with some rain over the sixty days of printing. It was observed that printing was most successful when the weather conditions were dry, sunny and most importantly, windy. The mud mixture used was wild, dug directly from the ground, sieved to a particle size of less than 6mm, and mixed with chopped straw and water. The clay/sand/loam mixture in this region has historically been used to make mud bricks and mud plaster for local buildings and there is a tacit understanding among the community about where to dig

4

5

for the mud and how moist it should be. The mixture proved to be very well suited for 3D printing coiled mud structures. The layer height of each mud coil is on average 30mm and each coil is between 40 and 60mm wide. Four structures were printed of varying dimensions, however it was observed that under ideal weather conditions an average of 400mm in height could be printed every 24-hour period.

The research during phase II was conceptualised under four themes: The Hearth, Beacon, Lookout, and Kiln. The Hearth explores the decorative aspects of structure (Fig. 4). The structural reinforcement of double-layer earthen walls creates a simple interior environment and an exterior that has structural expressiveness. The thin mud wall construction is reinforced using local, rot-resistant juniper wood to hold the interior and exterior coiled walls together. The wood sticks extend beyond the walls of the structure on the outside, and are flush on the inside, referencing the cultural differences between the architectural traditions of Pueblo and Indo-Hispano buildings. It also recalls traditional African architecture such as the Mosque in Djenne, where the wood sticks protruding from the building are not only decorative but also used as scaffolding. The interior holds a 3D-printed *tarima*, or mud bench, surrounding a fireplace that burns the aromatic juniper (Fig. 5).

The Beacon is a study in lightness, both illumination and weight. It explores how texture and the undulation of the 3D-printed coil of mud can produce the thinnest possible structural solution for enclosure. These coils are then illuminated at night, contrasting the difference between the concave and convex curves that create the mud walls.

The Lookout is an exploration in structure; the 3D-printed staircase and mezzanine are made entirely of mud. A dense network of undulating mud coils is laid out to create a structure that can be walked on. This also demonstrates how wide yet airy walls can create interior enclosures that represent possibilities for insulation, especially in the harsh climate of the San Luis Valley which can drop below -29°C in winter (Figs 6, 7).

The Kiln explores several of the techniques discussed, including undulating/interlocking mud deposition to create structural and insulative walls. The Kiln is also used to enclose an area that draws in oxygen and keeps in heat to fire locally sourced clay with a juniper wood fire, which burns hot (Fig. 8).

Democracy: Software

Custom software, called Potterware, was created to be the underlying control for the 3D printer. In its most accessible form, it is used to design the ceramic vessels. A more robust version is employed to design the walls and enclosures created by the robotic 3D printer. The software is an intuitive design application for 3D printing, that runs in the cloud from a typical web browser, such as Google Chrome; it features easy-to-use sliders and automatically generates printable g-code files, alleviating the need to learn 3D modelling software, meaning instead that a novice user can quickly begin to create complex g-code to 3D print functional pottery or earthen environments. Objects, walls and enclosures, at the scale of rooms, can be designed and ready for printing within minutes.

4. The Hearth exterior viewed from the east.

5. The Hearth interior.

6. 3D printing The Lookout substructure.

7. The Lookout stair during construction.

8. The 3D printed kiln.

Conclusion

The MUD Frontiers project re-examines and conceptually unearths traditional indigenous building traditions and materials using 21st century technology and craft coupled with local labour to explore new possibilities for ecological and local construction techniques. Based on the research so far, the robotic printing of local soils shows promise for the rapid creation of robotically-crafted, geometrically complex, buildings that are durable and structural, using wild clays that have historically proven successful in building construction. Further research is needed to understand how the surface of the 3D-printed mud will weather over time, but by studying traditional earthen buildings in the region, these structures' longevity will require only a roof and occasional maintenance to be viable as long-term enclosures. The current size limitation of the printer is a drawback and the creation of a new printer, with a longer arm, that can print larger 'rooms' is desirable. Next steps include creating 3D-printed mud buildings that can be fully sealed which means addressing how elements such as roofs and doors can be factored into the printing process. Upon their 40th anniversary, the *Smithsonian Magazine* announced the 40 most important things they believed one should know about the next 40 years. Number one on their list was that 'Sophisticated Buildings will be made of mud'. MUD Frontiers aims to see this prediction become a reality.

References

Barbosa, E., Woetzel, ,Mischke, J., Ribeirinho, M., Sridhar, M., Parsons, M., Bertram, N. and Brown, S. 2017. *Reinventing Construction: A route to higher productivity*. Technical report, McKinsey Global Institute.

International Federation of Robotics. 2017. 'Executive Summary World Robotics 2017 Service Robots.' Technical report, International Federation of Robotics, pp. 12–19, https://ifr.org/downloads/press/Executive_Summary_WR_Service_Robots_2017_1.pdf (Accessed 23 December 2019)

Rael, R. 2009. *Earth Architecture*, New York: Princeton Architectural Press.

Renz, A. and Solas, M. Z. 2016. *Shaping the Future of Construction. A Breakthrough in Mindset and Technology*. Technical report, World Economic Forum.

Smithsonian Magazine. 2010. 'Smithsonian 40th Anniversary: 40 Things You Need to Know About the Next 40 Years' in *Smithsonian Magazine*, http://microsite.smithsonianmag.com/content/40th-Anniversary/ (Accessed 23 December 2019)

World Business Council for Sustainable Development. 2002. 'Climate Protection', in *The Cement Sustainability Initiative: Our agenda for action*, Geneva: World Business Council for Sustainable Development, p. 20, https://web.archive.org/web/20070714085318/http://www.wbcsd.org/DocRoot/1IBetslPgkEie83rTa0J/cement-action-plan.pdf (Accessed 23 December 2019)

6

7

8

THE DESIGN AND FABRICATION OF CONFLUENCE PARK

ANDREW KUDLESS
MATSYS
JOSHUA ZABEL
KREYSLER & ASSOCIATES
CHUCK NAEVE
ARCHITECTURAL ENGINEERS COLLABORATIVE
TENNA FLORIAN
LAKE|FLATO ARCHITECTS

Aspirations for an Iconic Park

This paper focuses on the design, engineering and fabrication of an innovative tilt-up concrete structure using fibreglass composite moulds. The design was produced through a small but multidisciplinary team that valued the integration of form, fabrication and performance through the application of biomimetic principles, computational design/fabrication, and original construction logics.

The BHP Pavilion is located in San Antonio, Texas and is the central outdoor classroom and community hub of Confluence Park (Fig. 1). There were three primary project objectives that the pavilion needed to satisfy that were driven by the needs of the client, a local non-profit foundation that leads educational and artistic projects along the San Antonio River. The first objective was to create an educational venue that would integrate the architecture of the pavilion into the mission of the park which was to educate the community on the critical role of water in the regional ecosystems. The second objective was to create a unique and inspiring iconic pavilion that helped catalyse a new identity to this historically under-appreciated part of the city. Due to the relatively

limited budget of the project, the final objective was to use innovative fabrication technologies and methods to lower the overall project costs while meeting the client's ambitious educational and aesthetic vision.

Tactics for Integrated Design

When the final design team first met, the client had already spent several years working on the project and was eager for it to be completed as soon as possible. With time already invested, the client was committed to creating a unique educational and community venue but was also cognisant of their limited budget and compressed construction schedule. Faced with these challenges, the design team focused on pre-rationalising the geometry of the pavilion. That is, rather than initially proposing a form that would need to be rationalised in order to be produced, the team focused on several geometric forms and fabrication strategies that already had an inherently rational basis.

During the first week of the design, the team had developed an initial proposal that used a toroidal surface patch to generate a series of timber beams of varying lengths but with identical curvatures. These beams could

all be developed from the same glulam mould and then CNC milled to different lengths. This strategy was inspired by a number of projects developed at Foster + Partners that used toroidal patches to rationalise seemingly free-form surfaces (Peters, 2008). Although the design quickly moved away from using this specific technique, the project team continued to think through the material and construction implications early in the design process in order to better integrate the form, material and fabrication logics, and hopefully reduce construction time and budget.

At this point in the schematic design, several tensions became apparent to the team. The first was the great need in the project for the central pavilion to reflect the primary mission of the client, but the initial design of a large timber shell structure did not clearly communicate this mission since the primary stance most architecture has to water is repulsion. Typically, structures are made to push

water away from architecture as quickly as possible in order to keep the structures (and the inhabitants and materials within) dry. However, in the context of San Antonio's climate (long dry spells periodically punctuated by heavy rain storms) and the specific context of a park devoted to the educational mission of reconnecting the community with the vital importance of water, it seemed that accepting water into the structure was a more productive strategy. After all, the park was being designed to collect and recycle all groundwater for use in the toilets and irrigation system so the pavilion could be used to highlight this process. The decision was made to use the pavilion to celebrate the collection of rainwater and to make the form of the pavilion a pedagogical device for the park's employees and visiting teachers.

The form that emerged from this process was based on the doubly curved fronds of many local plant species that cantilever out to collect and redirect dew and rainwater

2

1. Aerial view of Confluence Park showing the smooth fibreglass finish and broom-finished concrete surfaces. The namesake of the park, the confluence of the San Antonio River and San Pedro Creek, is shown in the background. Credit: Rialto Studio.

2. The BHP Pavilion at Confluence park is a 550m² outdoor classroom and community hub at the centre of the park overlooking the San Antonio River. Credit: Casey Dunn.

back to their root stem. The double curvature not only gives these cantilevers more strength, but the curvature also creates a channel on the top surface for the efficient flow of water. Within days, the project had moved from a singular large shell pushing water towards the structure's fringes to several funnel-like doubly-curved forms that directed the water to an underground cistern for storage and eventual reuse throughout the site (Fig. 2).

From Funnels to Petals

The second tension that emerged at this point was the client's desire for an 'iconic' and unique pavilion in relation to the budgetary need for simplicity and modularity. Although the new doubly-curved funnels aligned with the pedagogical mission of the client, the complexity of making these forms initially resisted easy construction strategies. Early designs for the funnels involved complex steel and cable-net structures which, even if each was identical, were beyond the modest budget. At this point, inspired by the work of Felix Candela, Heinz Isler, Robert Maillart and many others who had investigated the use of concrete to create complex forms that aligned with structural forces, the team quickly moved to concrete as the primary material (Nordenson, 2008).

As the team shifted to concrete, it became necessary to begin to divide the funnel shapes into discrete parts in order to break the forms into manageable parts while also allowing views into the interior of the funnel. A rationalised solution emerged which paired each discrete funnel part with a symmetric element to create a complete arch. This represented a major conceptual shift in the structural organisation of the project. Rather than several structurally independent funnel-like forms, each discrete section of the funnel was paired with another section from an adjacent funnel to create a structural arch.

The resulting arch is the simplest of structures: the statically determinate three-hinged arch. An arched structure plays to concrete's significant compressive strength while minimising its limited tensile strength. Referring back to the biomimetic inspiration for the funnels, each half-arch was nicknamed a 'petal'. By separating the petals with pinned connections at the top of each arch, the team greatly simplified the scope by producing matching petal shapes with the expressed pins transferring the horizontal stabilising force between adjoining petals.

An additional benefit to this new organisation of petals or half-arches was the idea of using a modified tilt-up concrete fabrication technique. Tilt-up concrete construction is defined by concrete panels being cast flat on the ground on site and then lifted (or tilted) into place and connected to the foundation and adjacent panels. It is a common fabrication technique in the region as it has a very low cost due to the lack of significant formwork. The technique was invented in the U.S. in the early 20th century by Robert Aiken and popularised by Thomas Edison who, in 1908, stated, 'tilt-up construction eliminates the costly, cumbersome practice of erecting two wooden walls to get one concrete wall' (Kayler, 2006). By the late 20th century, some tilt-up concrete fabricators had begun producing curved concrete panels by casting against curved forms dug from the ground or wooden forms built up through multiple layers of plywood (Hurd, 2005). In the context of Confluence Park, tilt-up had a distinct advantage over cast-in-place concrete as it allowed reusable moulds to be utilised which could be erected in one place on-site throughout construction.

Irregular Tiling

Now that the team had settled on the half-arch or 'petal' concept and an initial material and fabrication strategy, the next task was to determine the exact shape, position and number of petals. Returning to the objective of creating a unique and iconic pavilion for the park, the team wanted to make sure that the need for modularity due to the budget constraints did not create a system that was too geometrically rigid or monotonous. Several organising grids were developed that explored the implications of overall petal quantity, petal module quantity, and how repetitive the deployment of these petals within the grid appeared. The goal was to simultaneously use as few modules as possible in order to reduce the number of petal moulds and increase the casts from each mould while also obscuring the modularity of the entire project. This tension between a strict modularity of parts and the overall desire for an informal organisation of the whole led to the use of an irregular tiling grid.

After exploring uniform triangular, rectangular, and hexagonal grids, an irregular pentagonal tiling grid was developed. While regular pentagons do not tile the plane (and these gaps would create large unshaded areas for the pavilion), there are fifteen types of irregular pentagons that tile the plane (Pottmann, 2007). One of those, 'type 4' (also known as the Cairo Tile after several streets in Cairo, Egypt paved with this shape), has four long edges of the same length and one short side and vertex angles of 120°, 90°, 120°, 90°, and 120°. When this pentagon is subdivided into five triangles by connecting the pentagon's centre with each vertex, it results in only 3 unique triangles: A(2),

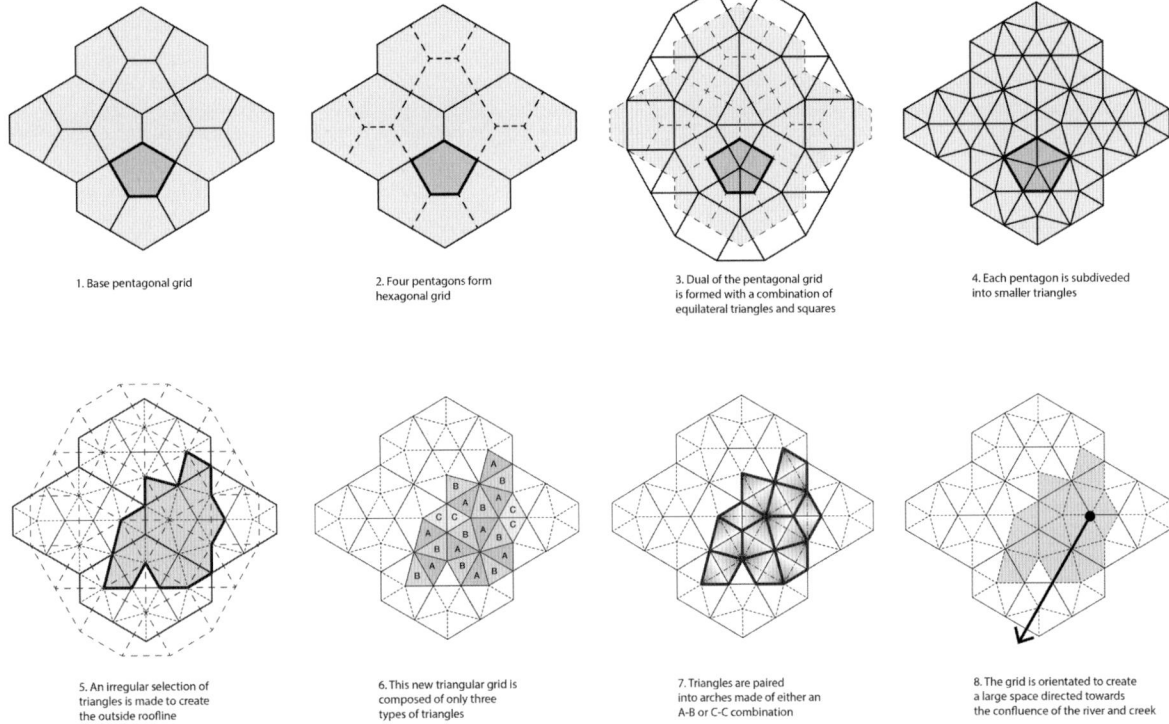

1. Base pentagonal grid

2. Four pentagons form hexagonal grid

3. Dual of the pentagonal grid is formed with a combination of equilateral triangles and squares

4. Each pentagon is subdiveded into smaller triangles

5. An irregular selection of triangles is made to create the outside roofline

6. This new triangular grid is composed of only three types of triangles

7. Triangles are paired into arches made of either an A-B or C-C combination

8. The grid is orientated to create a large space directed towards the confluence of the river and creek

3

B(2), and C(1). Triangles A and B are mirrors of each other and each have internal angles of 75°, 60°, 45° while triangle C is equilateral (all angles are 60°) (Fig. 3).

The centre of each pentagon represented a funnel drain and the edges of the pentagon represented the apex of each arch. Each A triangle is paired with a B triangle from an adjacent pentagon to produce a full arch. Similarly, each C triangle is paired with a C triangle from an adjacent pentagon to create a full arch. In order to produce the final pavilion plan, various selections of A-B and C-C arches were explored and analysed for the amount of shade produced as well as the informality of the arches when seen in perspective. That is, the design team tried multiple options of arch arrangements to produce a pattern that, although completely modular, appeared not to line up and only one full pentagon (funnel) was formed (Fig. 4).

Flowing Form

There were three primary objectives in developing the sections and curvature of the petals. First, for both structural reasons and water flow capture, the petals had to retain a double curvature. Second, the thickness of each petal needed to change from bottom to top in accordance to its structural demand, building codes and rebar placement. Third, the surface curvature should be continuous from petal to petal.

In order to test how water would flow on the top surface of the petals, a rainwater simulation script was developed that sampled points on the surface and then iteratively found the steepest downhill direction. If the paths of the rainwater flowing on the surface ran into the gaps between petals instead of into the valley of each petal, the petal parameters were modified until the rainwater flows all ended at the central drains (Fig. 5).

The panel thicknesses were largely driven by building code requirements for concrete clear cover over reinforcement. The concept for reinforcement was to place the rebar in a fan-like pattern from the column base emerging into the outer thinning field with reinforcement on inside and outside faces. This placement of the reinforcement resisted tension wherever it might occur within a shell. Within the column section, the full structural demand of gravity, wind and live loading was concentrated and reinforced appropriately. In the field beyond the column, stresses were lower and the panel

3. Plan diagrams showing the geometric logic of the organisational grid made of irregular pentagons subdivided into 3 unique triangles. Credit: Andrew Kudless/Matsys.

4. Diagram showing all concrete petal configurations to form structurally independent three-hinged arches. Petals MC were cast using the C forms with an insert to shorten the column by 3m for the smaller satellite pavilions. Credit: Andrew Kudless/Matsys.

5. In order to validate the flow of rainwater on the roof surface, a particle simulation was used where particles sought the steepest downhill direction on the surface. Credit: Andrew Kudless/Matsys.

6. The positives for the fibreglass mould were milled using a combination of 5-axis and 7-axis robotic machines. Credit: Cade Bradshaw and Stuart Allen.

correspondingly became thinner as the demand lessened. Ultimately the top edges were resolved within a 100mm edge, the code minimum for adequate coverage of reinforcement.

A Turning Point

Once the design team had moved towards the use of concrete, it was assumed that the formwork would need to be digitally fabricated to be able to achieve the necessary construction tolerances. In addition, it was assumed that fibreglass composites would be the ideal material for the formwork as it was not only strong but very durable and could withstand multiple castings.

However, due to the contractual relationships between contractors and architects in the United States where the contractor is responsible for determining the ways and means of a project, the project's contractor, unfamiliar with digital fabrication or fibreglass composites, wanted to first get bids for traditional wooden formwork made from layered up plywood. The only bid received from a traditional formwork fabricator was far more than the budget allowed so the general contractor agreed to contact the suggested fibreglass composite fabricator and their bid was well within the budget.

This is an interesting example of a turning point within the industry. Historically, digital fabrication has been used in some of the largest and most expensive projects while less expensive projects used traditional techniques. However, in this case, the traditional technique was far more expensive than the digitally-fabricated fibreglass mould. In addition, the fibreglass mould was not only less expensive, but it was stronger, more durable and more accurate.

The three formwork modules (A, B, and C) were fabricated from five- and seven-axis CNC milled EPS foam forms (Fig. 6). After milling the forms, a 50mm thick composite structure composed of inner and outer layers of fibreglass composite with a central core of balsa wood was applied (Fig. 7). One of the biggest advantages of using this method was that the milled surface of the foam positive was highly accurate and that all accumulation errors inherent to fabrication were offset from this surface instead of working towards it as would have been the case if a traditional plywood formwork system had been used.

Due to the size of each full petal formwork (roughly 9m wide x 8m tall), each of the modules had to be subdivided into three primary sub-sections in addition to several side forms that could be transported to Texas by lorry (Fig. 8).

4

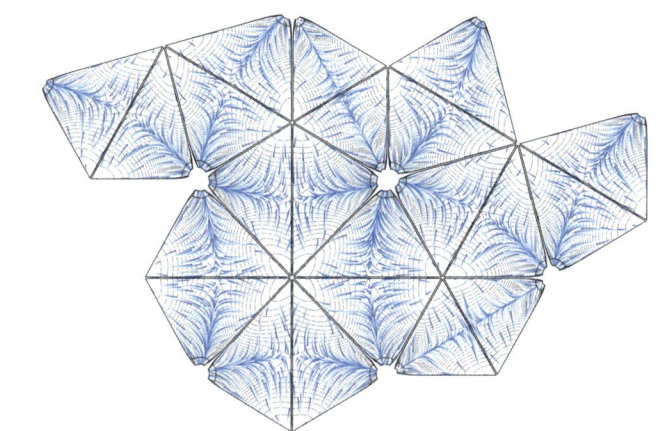

5

6

Although the joints between these sections were nearly seamless due to excellent casting of the fibreglass, sanding, and a small amount of caulk that was applied between pours, the seams were still designed to accentuate the undulating curvature of the concrete petals. If one looks closely at the underside of each petal, two thin seams can be seen swooping up and down from side to side on the surface.

The fact that the bottom surface of each petal was cast against the smooth fibreglass while the top surface was cast open to the air allowed the two sides of the petal to have radically different finishes (Figs 9, 10). In order to have the petals resonate with the flow of water, even when it was not raining, the open top side of each petal was broom-finished with the direction of the broom strokes aligning with the flow direction of the water. In effect, the top surface of each petal is one giant valley covered with a network of small valleys produced by the bristles of the broom. Over time, this textured surface of the broom-finished concrete will reveal the flow of water as various airborne matter such as pollen, dust and bird droppings collect in the broom finish and stain the concrete as water runs across the texture.

Conclusion

Having completed the project nearly two years ago, there are various things the team has learned in the process and have begun to speculate about how they might do similar projects in the future differently. In terms of material, higher strength concrete with improved tensile capacity and uniform disbursement of reinforcement might be considered. Building codes limitations could be challenged to allow thinner shells. However, the interest in this project from the public and AEC community demonstrates a longing for the beauty of simple forms, well executed. When a diverse team focuses on the smart application of new technologies and concentrates on the integration of form, fabrication and performance throughout the design process, innovative projects that meet the client's missions are possible even within modest project budgets.

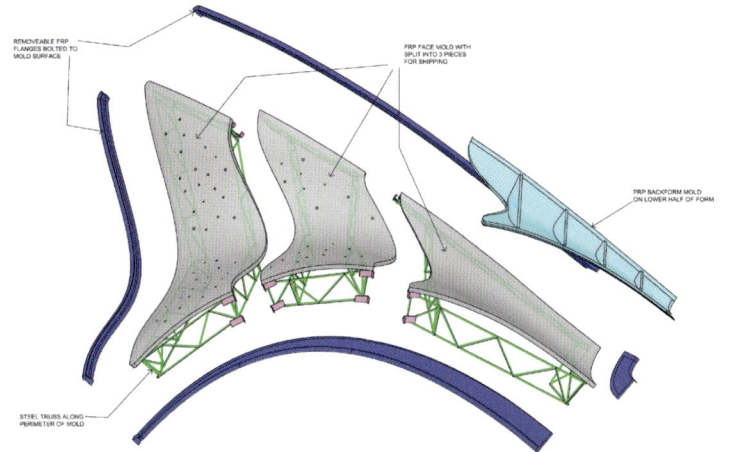

References

Hurd, M. K. 2005. *Formwork for Concrete*, Michigan: American Concrete Institute.

Kayler, K. 2006. 'The History of TCA', *Tilt-Up Today*. Vol 14(2). Available at: https://tilt-up.org/tilt-uptoday/2006/04/01/the-history-of-tca/. (Accessed 23 December 2019)

Nordenson, G. 2008. *Seven Structural Engineers: The Felix Candela Lectures*. New York: Museum of Modern Art.

Peters, B. 2008. 'Copenhagen Elephant House: A Case Study of Digital Design Processes', in Swackhamer, M., Kudless, A. and Oxman, N. (eds), *ACADIA 2008: Silicon + Skin – Biological Processes and Computation, Proceedings of the 28th Annual Conference of the Association for Computer Aided Design in Architecture*, Minneapolis, United States: ACADIA, pp.134-141.

Pottmann, H., Asperl, A., Hofer, M. and Kilian, A. 2007. *Architectural Geometry*, Exton, Penn.: Bentley Institute Press.

8

9

10

7. One of the three fibreglass composite moulds in the workshop. Credit: Cade Bradshaw and Stuart Allen.

8. Exploded axonometric diagram showing the various parts of one of the petal mould. Each mould needed to be divided up for transportation limitations, assembly/disassembly logics, and efficient use of materials. Credit: Kreysler & Associates.

9 & 10. Views of the formwork before rebar placement, after rebar placement, and after casting. Credit: Andrew Kudless/Matsys.

THE ROLE OF ROBOTIC MILLING IN THE RESEARCH AND DEVELOPMENT OF THE CORK CONSTRUCTION KIT

OLIVER WILTON
THE BARTLETT SCHOOL OF ARCHITECTURE, UCL
MATTHEW BARNETT HOWLAND
CSK ARCHITECTS
PETER SCULLY
B-MADE, THE BARTLETT SCHOOL OF ARCHITECTURE, UCL

Aims and Objectives

The aim of this research was to develop a viable robotic cork milling method that could contribute to the development of the Cork Construction Kit, a radically simple new form of cork and timber construction developed under a broader research project and subsequently refined further and used in Cork House, the first of its type.

Research Context

Cork is the outer bark of *Quercus suber*, the cork oak tree, harvested around once a decade using traditional methods in a process that does not harm the tree. It has been used in construction for several millennia, including documented use as a roofing material in Roman times (Pereira, 2007). The material used in this research is pure expanded cork agglomerate (expanded cork), accidently invented by John Smith in New York and patented in 1891 (Thomas, 1928; Smith, 1891). Expanded cork was widely used in construction in the 20th century, mostly as thermal insulation board, and has been resurgent in recent years, in part due to its strong environmental sustainability profile and also its rich experiential character when used as an internal or external finish.

The specific material used for this work is manufactured by research partner Amorim in Portugal using granulated cork, the by-product from forestry and other cork industries, which is cooked with pressurised steam in autoclaves at around 350°C using heat from waste biomass (Fig. 2). The result is a 100% plant-based cork billet with a very particular combination of properties, bonded with the suberin resin naturally present in the cork. It is thermally insulative (its principle use is as an insulation board), vapour permeable, aromatic, and has some load bearing capacity, as indicated by some of its historical uses, for example self-supporting partitions (Thomas, 1928). It is also carbon-negative owing to the absorption of atmospheric carbon during the growth of the tree bark (refer to Environmental Product Declaration number DAP 002:2016 for specific figures).

Due to its particular combination of properties, expanded cork was identified as a suitable material for use in the development of a radically simple new form of construction, the Cork Construction Kit. This combines large format monolithic cork blocks with engineered timber and aims to fulfil all of the performance requirements of the contemporary building envelope and deliver exceptional whole life performance. The aim was that the interlocking

2

Work was undertaken in 2015 with research partners to develop a custom grade of expanded cork for use in the project. A range of sample blocks of differing densities was produced by Amorim. Alongside existing production grade samples, these were all characterised using lab tests at the University of Bath and were then reviewed by Arup. The outcome was that an existing grade of cork, MD Façade, was selected due to its suitable characteristics and because of the broader applicability benefits for the system of using a readily available product that did not require a special production run to manufacture. MD Façade has a density of around 150kg/m^2, with cork granules selected with care in order to give a good quality surface finish.

cork block assemblies, dry jointed with no glue or mortar, would provide structural enclosure, thermal and acoustic insulation, and rain and air tightness. This work was undertaken in three interrelated and overlapping stages, with initial hypothesising and prototyping being undertaken from 2014 to 2015, the major research project being undertaken from 2015 to 2018 and Cork House being constructed from 2017 to the start of 2019.

Initial prototyping work undertaken at The Bartlett utilised traditional woodworking machine tools to shape the cork billets into blocks of relatively simple geometry, which slotted and locked together when combined with timber profiles. Expanded cork is relatively straightforward to machine using these tools. This initial system utilised lime mortar to bond each course of cork blocks together to form walls and a corbelled roof in a construction method that had some similarities with traditional masonry and was used to make a very small first prototype building in late 2014, the Cork Casket.

The Reasons for Selecting Robotic Milling and the Questions Arising

Evaluation of the system used in the Cork Casket determined that the timber profiles and lime mortar used to connect the cork blocks were building in unnecessary technical challenges and significant whole life complexity to the structure. A decision was made to pursue the development of a simpler form of wall and roof assembly using only expanded cork blocks, without any additional elements. Tongue and grooved block geometries were developed that interlocked in plan and section with an interference fit, a bit like a giant plant-based toy construction kit. The development of a dry-jointed assembly method was of particular interest in relation to ease of assembly, and ease of disassembly enabling ready recovery of the blocks at the end of a building's life. Initial block prototypes cut using a table saw and spindle moulder showed promise (Fig. 3).

1. View of Cork House from the garden, 2019. Image: David Grandorge.

2. Freshly cooked expanded cork billets emerging from the autoclave at Amorim, Portugal, 2015. Image: Matthew Barnett Howland and Oliver Wilton.

3. Interlocking tongue and groove roof blocks fabricated with a spindle moulder and table saw, The Bartlett, 2015. Image: Matthew Barnett Howland and Oliver Wilton.

4. Left, model of early Cork Cabin design in SolidWorks. Right, roof block toolpath development in PowerMill Robot. 2015. Images: Matthew Barnett Howland and Oliver Wilton.

3

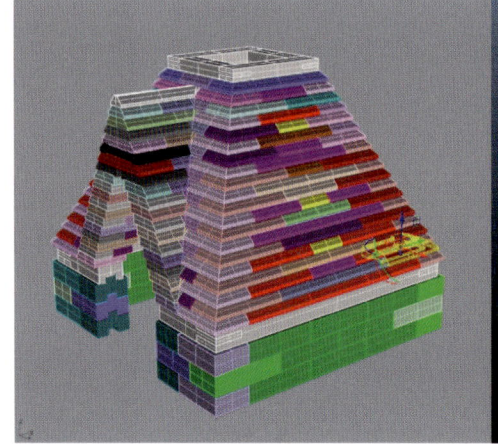

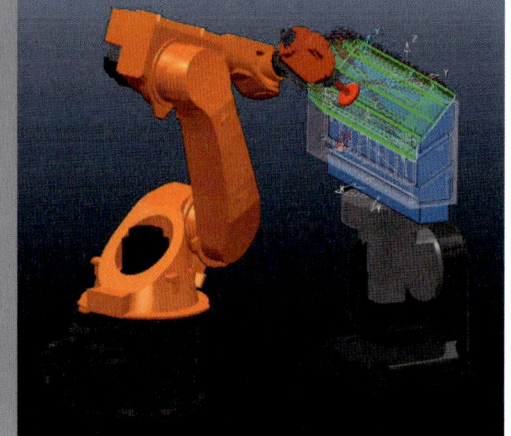

4

5

With these challenges in mind, the robotic cell was identified as being well placed to play host for design development, as an unfinished machine awaiting purpose. Whilst the research and design of the Cork Construction Kit was in its plastic phase, the specifics of the manufacturing process evolved concurrently with the component design. This enabled a gradual reduction in uncertainty for local and global design decision-making relating to fabrication. It presented procedural constraints and opportunities that could have only occurred in a manufacturing process whose particular attributes were open to change, allowing design and fabrication processes to co-evolve. This activity was made possible by access to The Bartlett's robotics facilities, and the work proceeded to address the following questions:

- What robotic milling set-up is suitable for milling large format 1000 x 500 x 220mm expanded cork billets into tongue and grooved blocks of the required geometries?
- What design and fabrication workflow will be effective for this?
- Is it possible to cut all blocks with a single cutter in order to minimise cutting time (using an industrial robot with no automatic cutter changer)?
- If so, then how will this constrain and inform block geometry, and what will the resultant milling time per block be?

The Robotic Milling Method and Its Influence on Design Development

A tailored robotic milling method was developed to cut the expanded cork billets into the blocks for the construction kit, with a target cutting time of 10 minutes per block. The method utilised a six-axis Kuka KR60 HA industrial robot with a high-volume cutter held by a bespoke spindle in a milling end effector. Cork billets were held in place by a bespoke vacuum bed fitted to a two-axis positioner. The vacuum bed was designed to hold both full size 1000 x 500 x 220mm billets and also those of shorter lengths from which shorter modules of the wall and roof blocks were milled. The cork proved to be relatively simple to mill, with cutter speed and rpm adjusted to higher speeds when removing bulk cork to form the block and to lower speeds for finer cutting of the finished block surfaces.

The design and fabrication workflow utilised SolidWorks modelling of blocks and assemblies as part of the design development process, in combination with hand sketching and scaled physical prototyping including creating a 1:5 constructional model of the second prototype building, Cork Cabin. Individual block geometries were then

5. Cork Cabin blocks being transported from The Bartlett to the site in Eton, UK, 2016. Image: Magnus Dennis.

Using traditional machine tools has the advantage of maximising broader applicability, with the potential for the cork block system to be readily machined by any joinery workshop. However, while there is a simplicity in asking one material to perform all of the functions of a building envelope, as design hypotheses developed so the resultant block geometries became more complex due to the multiple roles required from the blocks, and this in turn was time consuming to manually machine. Also, in order to give a positive connection and to meet the hypotheses for a dry-jointed system with air and rain-tightness, relatively low tolerance machining was needed in the region of +/-0.5mm to give a satisfactory interference fit between blocks. Accounting for these matters, proceeding with the current tools was deemed unviable as it was too time consuming – potentially over an hour to machine each full-size block even when using a range of jigs – and with too high a risk of unacceptable resultant block tolerances.

6

exported from SolidWorks to PowerMill Robot to generate cutting paths (Fig. 4). Some challenges were encountered in controlling transitions between cuts with this set up, and the use of Rhino with Grasshopper using a script developed in-house to generate the g-code was also trialled. Another challenge that emerged was some initial off-tolerance block cutting and this was eventually identified as being caused by insufficient calibration of the robot, with this particular application requiring a high calibration accuracy due to the tolerances needed to give a satisfactory block-to-block interference fit.

All blocks were cut with a single, high-volume, 125mm diameter by 14mm thick cutter in order to keep fabrication as quick and simple as possible, using the available robot that did not have a tool autochanger. The use of this configuration with the single cutter was enabled by developing the design of the cork blocks to fit within this particular set of geometric parameters, allowing the cutter geometry to play a role in determining the final block geometries for the construction kit. This was a negotiated outcome between what was desirable and what was possible under the chosen constraints, with the possible range of cutting geometries sitting alongside other constraints, considerations and strategies when designing the blocks. Other considerations for each block and its contribution to the construction kit, and buildings made with it, included the need for sufficient airtightness and rain tightness, a suitable structural block-to-block

interlock, and block geometries that allowed them to be combined into assemblies in all cases.

The resultant milling process enabled the cork blocks to be formed in around 10 to 15 minutes cutting time for a wall block and 15 to 20 minutes for a roof block. During milling, up to around 20% of the cork billet is cut away while forming a roof block, less for a wall block. So, the milling process generated large quantities of cork granules as by-product, requiring a suitable enclosure for the robot and regular clean ups between milling blocks. As part of the broader work, an investigation was undertaken by research partner Ty Mawr into using these granules for a range of purposes. This included use as an additive to lime mortar to give texture and improve insulation level (something they already use cork granules for), for more novel cork granule and lime formulations including a form of Terrazzo, and to form cork fuel briquettes for use in their on-site biomass boiler.

Contribution to the Broader Research

The robotic milling process was used to fabricate all 202 cork blocks for the prototype Cork Cabin, including 10 different types, some with multiple lengths. It was also used to fabricate all blocks for subsequent lab tests, including wall and roof assemblies subjected to structural, fire and rain tightness testing. The cabin walls and roof were assembled at The Bartlett after fabrication, to ensure

6. Cork Cabin being assembled on site in Eton, UK, 2017. Image: Matthew Barnett Howland and Oliver Wilton.

7. The last roof block in a course ready to be pressed into place on Cork House, demonstrating the interference fit using no glue or mortar, Eton, UK, 2018. Image: Matthew Barnet Howland and Oliver Wilton.

7

for the duration of the project, with cork billets shipped from Amorim in Portugal direct to site for fabrication in the correct sequence and then assembly. There are a number of interesting aspects to this, including the potential to evolve self-build and also to broaden the applicability of the construction kit by reducing cost. Robot-assisted self-build was ultimately not selected in this instance for reasons including the prohibitive cost of installing 3-phase power on this particular site, necessary for the specific robot that was available.

The 1268 cork blocks used in Cork House were milled on a large format five-axis CNC machine with automatic tool changer by Wup Doodle. The blocks were then transported to site for assembly by hand with no glue or mortar. This was a relatively clean and simple exercise, with each block weighing around 12 to 13kg and being easy to manipulate. The house was completed in early 2019 (Fig. 7) and post-occupancy evaluation is now commencing.

Conclusion

Robotic milling has played a key role in enabling this research to directly address its key aims. It has lowered the barriers to developing this uncommonly simple plant-based form of construction, developed to fully meet contemporary building performance standards, while delivering outstanding whole life performance. This is an example of work combining historical and emerging methods to form a tailored research, design and making methodology that uses digital tools to serve broader architectural, habitation and environmental sustainability aims, with their use enabling and also subtly informing the resultant architectural language.

Acknowledgements

The robotic milling work described here formed part of a broader research project with partners MPH Architects, The Bartlett School of Architecture, UCL, University of Bath, Amorim, and Ty Mawr, with Arup and BRE acting as sub-consultants. The research was part-funded under the Building Whole-Life Performance competition by Innovate UK grant number 102474 and EPSRC grants numbers EP/N509048/1 and EP/N50905X/1. It also benefited from a Bartlett Architecture Project Fund grant.

References

Pereira, H. 2007. *Cork: Biology, Production and Uses*. Amsterdam: Elsevier Science B.V.

Smith, J. T. 1891. *Process of Treating Cork*. USD456068. https://patentimages. storage.googleapis.com/1a/86/34/e967599b6e528a/US456068.pdf. (Accessed 14 November 2019)

Thomas, P. E. 1928. *Cork insulation: A complete illustrated Textbook*. Chicago: Nickerson & Collins Co.

the assembly was correct, before being disassembled and shipped to site in Berkshire for re-assembly. This also served to test and demonstrate the readiness of the system for disassembly, a key part of the design allowing the cork blocks to be readily recovered for re-use at the end of the building's life.

The cabin was assembled on site by hand, with no glue or mortar (Fig. 6). The CLT floor plate was laid within the bolted oak ring beam and raised off the ground on wheels. Cork block walls were laid on the floor platform, acting in structural compression and capped by oak eave-beams that take lateral loading. The corbelled cork block roof was built off this, also acting in compression. The completed structure is capped by a rooflight, mounted on a timber ring beam, which lets in daylight and also adds some weight to the top of the structure, acting a bit like a giant paperweight. The completed cabin was then subjected to air tightness testing and temperature and humidity monitoring over several months, which informed further design development of the construction kit.

At this point in 2017, the Cork Construction Kit was sufficiently developed and de-risked to apply an evolved version to its first live architecture project – Cork House. Options were appraised for fabricating the cork blocks required for the house design. These included robot-assisted self-build, where an industrial robot similar to that used to fabricate the cabin would be installed on site

PULP FACTION
3D PRINTED MATERIAL ASSEMBLIES THROUGH MICROBIAL BIOTRANSFORMATION

ANA GOIDEA / **DIMITRIOS FLOUDAS** / **DAVID ANDRÉEN**
LUND UNIVERSITY

The world is currently facing an ecological crisis of unprecedented scale and urgency and, as the building sector is a significant contributor to the current state, it must look towards radical change to achieve a sustainable practice. The most destructive environmental impact is found in material extraction, processing and discharge. This paper presents an alternative to industrially mined and synthesised materials by utilising biological growth processes as passive engines for the transformation of renewable materials. This is achieved through fungal-lignocellulosic composites which have been developed along with the design and fabrication processes that are necessary for their application in the construction industry.

Plant-derived materials are abundantly and sustainably available on both local and global scales, particularly in the form of by-products and recycled waste. Additive fabrication provides an opportunity to create high value products from this material, but comes with its own challenges. In particular, most of the strength of the wood is lost as fibres are ground down so that the material can pass through the extrusion nozzle. Rather than relying on thermosetting plastics or synthetic binders, this project explores the controlled growth of fungal mycelium within the printed material post-extrusion as a binder of lignocellulosic biomass.

Fungal-lignocellulosic materials inherit properties from both wood and mycelium, resulting in lightweight and strong bio-composites. Generally, they exhibit good insulative performance for both heat and sound, are hydrophobic, and have good tension and compression resistance (Yang et al., 2017; Elsacker, 2019). In addition, the raw materials for such composites are low in cost, locally sourced, renewable, and able to capture and store carbon dioxide.

Mycelium Bio-Composites

The main components of mycelium composites are the biopolymers cellulose and chitin, followed by lignin and hemicellulose. Mycelium is the vegetative part of a fungus, made up from a dense network of long, branching filamentous structures termed hyphae. The cell wall of the hyphae is made of chitin – a tough, resilient, inert and non-water-soluble modified polysaccharide that has promising potential in biotechnology (Latgé and Calderon, 2006). When the fungus colonises a substrate, it first grows on the surface and gradually, depending on

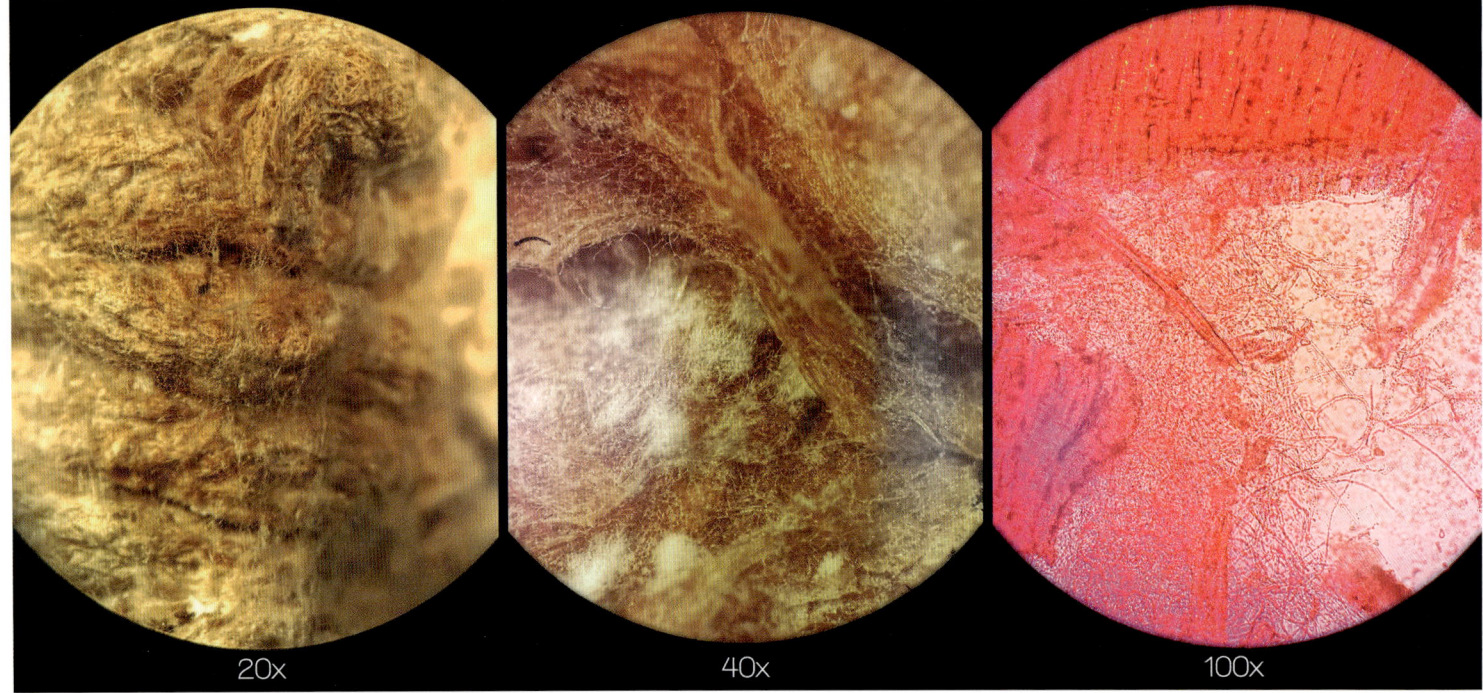

2

the properties of the material, it spreads its mycelium throughout it in a complex three-dimensional binding matrix (Boyce and Andrianopoulos, 2006) (Fig. 4). During growth, the fungus secretes extracellular polymeric substances (EPS), which are mainly composed of polysaccharides and proteins (Gazzé et al., 2013). Their role is to facilitate growth and allow the anchoring of the cells on the substrate, acting as a glue between the hyphae and the substrate. Moreover, EPS allow for the conglomeration of particles around the hyphae, resulting in an irreversible fusing of the material (Fig. 2).

3D Bio-Printing

Most precedents using lignocellulosic substrate and mycelial growth for creating bio-composites use casting as the means of production, for example: The Living's Hy-Fi Tower (Nagy et al., 2015); Block Research Group's MycoTree (Heisel et al., 2018); Mogu panels (Appels et al., 2019). Such methods are relatively straightforward and therefore well-suited for industrial mass-production. However, the casting process limits the customisation of the products as well as geometrical complexity that can be employed for functional performance. In addition, the strength of the material is markedly determined by the extent of the mycelium coverage (Yang et al., 2017). As this is dependent on oxygen, growth is limited to the material surface. When cast in solid volume, the mycelium covers a smaller percentage of the total volume, limiting the potential strength of the composite.

These limitations can be overcome through the use of digital additive fabrication which allows for a complex meso-scale structure, radically increasing the surface area within a given volume and thus ensuring maximum distribution of hyphae within the composite.

The strategy of additively fabricating mycelium composites is not unprecedented in nature. Mound-building macrotermites have evolved to a symbiotic existence together with fungus of the genus *Termitomyces*. The termites harvest plant-based material and carry it back to the mound where the regulated internal climate is suitable for fungi. The fungus processes the plant matter, turning it into nutrients that both the termites and fungus live on (Turner, 2005). The fungal combs (Fig. 3) have a particular geometry which, on the one hand provides access to the termites for managing the comb, and on the other enable a convective flow of air and respiratory gases near the comb surfaces. This flow is facilitated by vertical channels and assisted by the thermal buoyancy generated by the metabolic heat of the fungus. The combs are constructed as an intricately folded and interconnected sheet with an even thickness of approximately 4mm, likely corresponding to the depth at which the mycelium can effectively grow while maintaining access to oxygen. The

1. Section of a column showing an assembly of the fungal-lignocellulosic components. Bonding between the segments is proposed to be achieved by extrusion of a connective tissue consisting of a modified version of the live pulp.

2. Substrate under microscope. The different magnifications showing: (1) The print layers covered in mycelium. (2) The fusion of mycelium and substrate. (3) The partial decomposition of the cellulose and lignin fibres by the fungus.

3

4

fungus comb provided an initial set of assumptions for a design that could provide a suitable balance of parameters in the project.

Integrated Research Protocols

The research presented in this article concerns the finding of a set of processes for additive fabrication of fungal-lignocellulosic materials and the evaluation of their suitability for architectural fabrication. The primary intent was to address the questions that arise from the interdependencies between these processes through a transdisciplinary approach. Focus has been on testing feasibility, building a protocol, and establishing a foundation for informed speculation.

The research was guided by the following questions: How can a process of bio-fabrication best be structured to achieve desirable artefacts? How does the introduction of fungal mycelium affect the material properties? And how could the developed processes be utilised for fabrication at architectural scales?

To answer these questions, the presented work explored the interconnections between (1) the living system, (2) the digital fabrication, and (3) the computational design strategy. Subsequently, a number of material performance tests were carried out on the resulting samples. The protocol presented here led to the most successful outcomes with regards to rate of growth, extrudability, stability and resulting material properties.

Live Pulp

The pulp consists of a substrate that has been inoculated with fungus. The substrate was developed to comply with two primary criteria: its ability to support the growth and development of the fungus, and its suitability for fabrication which includes both extrudability and the stability of the material in the print and growth phases. The main components of the substrate are fine woodchips, paper pulp, and kaolin clay, which are mixed with water. Wood and paper pulp compose the bulk of the material and provide the nutrients for the fungus; during incubation, these are partially transformed into fungal biomass. As the substrate doesn't have an immediate bonding agent, it remains unstable during printing. Therefore, clay was added to the mixture to provide stability during the fabrication and incubation phases. The substrate also contains a thickening agent which allows the solid and liquid components to form a coherent aggregate (Fig. 10).

Two fungal strains were used in the experiments, a strain of *Byssomerulius corium* and a strain of *Gloeophyllum* sp. They are both wood decomposers, but follow different strategies of wood decomposition termed white rot and brown rot, respectively. Both fungal strains were propagated on a malt-yeast medium. When the mycelial growth was sufficient, the fungus was introduced into the autoclaved substrate. The inoculated substrate was left for an incubation period of one week, in which the mycelium propagated through the substrate and adapted to the new environment, enabling it to resist contaminants introduced when sterile conditions were no longer maintained.

3. *Termitomyces* fungus comb. This symbiotic structure is additively assembled by macrotermites from dead plant matter inoculated with fungal spores. The fungus slowly digests the plant matter into components which the termites can ingest as food, while it simultaneously acts to regulate the humidity of the mound's internal climate.

4. Living printed composite after two weeks of incubation.

Following the initial incubation, the pulp was 3D printed, after which it went through a second and longer incubation period. This allowed the mycelium to grow through the printed artefacts and transform the substrate into the desired bio-composite. Once the growth had reached the target state, the printed component was desiccated to reach its final and stable form, stopping the decomposition process.

Fabrication Strategy

The live pulp was 3D printed using Vormvrij Lutum v4, which relies on a combination of pressurised air and a rotating auger to extrude material. A nozzle diameter of 3.5mm was used in combination with a layer height of 1.5mm, which provided a working balance of resolution, stability, and print speed.

Several factors influence the stability of the print, and the ability to produce artefacts with the desired geometric variation. A larger nozzle and consequently greater wall thickness make for more stable prints, but have the drawback of lower resolution and decrease in surface to volume ratio, which reduces the amount of mycelial growth on the material. Straight vertical walls are prone to both deformation and collapse. To reduce this, the curvatures have been maximised and additional interconnections between walls were introduced.

During desiccation, the material contracts in volume by approximately 30%. In order to minimise the resulting distortion, a set of aluminium meshes with vertical channels were used as print base and cover. These secure the position of the first and last layers, thereby constraining the contraction to the Z-axis. Mesh-print adhesion was improved by the explorative growth of the mycelium. The meshes allow vertical airflows through the print, supporting biological growth by ensuring even moisture levels and the circulation of respiratory gases, and eventually facilitate rapid and even desiccation.

Design Strategy

In addition to the architectural scale constraints, the design of the components had to accommodate both the biological requirements of the fungus and the mechanical constraints of the printing process. A reaction-diffusion simulation based on the the Gray-Scott model generated the basis for the form-finding of the fabricated geometries. The scale of the pattern was derived from the fungus comb reference. This generative model has been developed by increasing the feed rate along the vertical axis. The boundaries of the geometry have been created at the

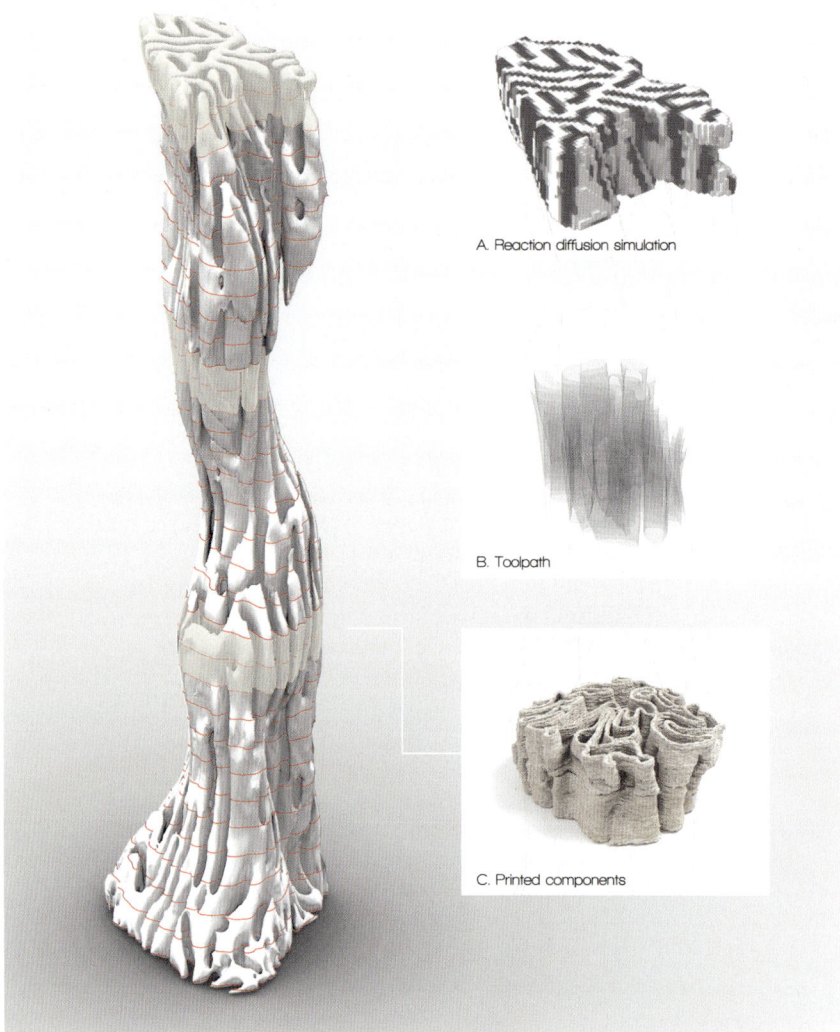

A. Reaction diffusion simulation

B. Toolpath

C. Printed components

5

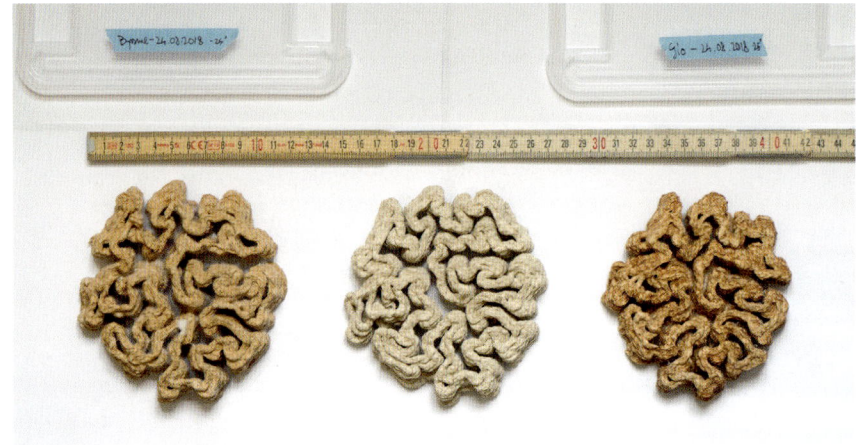

6

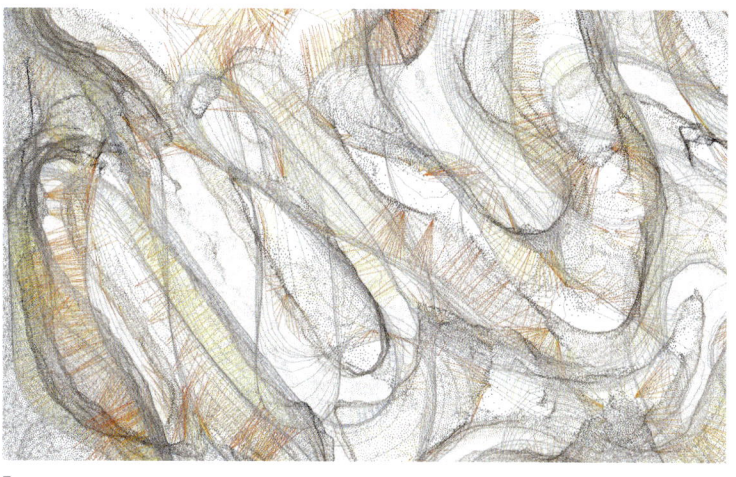

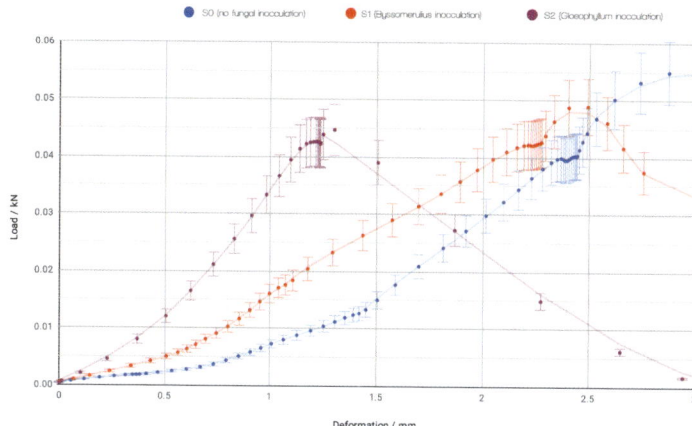

7

8

transition points between the two simulated substances. Subsequently, the resulting geometry consists of two (internal and external) interwoven volumes that never converge, lending itself to functional use in the architectural outcome. Similar to the structure found in fungus combs, the model ensures significant vertical continuity that is beneficial to flows of both air and structural forces. (Fig. 5)

The curves that constitute the print layers are taken through a secondary algorithmic transformation which connects all curves into a single curve on a per-layer basis. This transformation allows for a continuous extrusion rate along an uninterrupted toolpath which improves speed, stability and precision in the print process. This also ensures that the entire printed component is cohesive and that additional stabilising cross-bracings are created without disturbing the continuity and separation of the two sets of volumes. In order to maintain thin extrusions while increasing the print height, the design strategy combined vertical continuity with recurring interconnections, while strengthening through double curvature.

Results

Three different material samples (designated *S0*, *S1*, and *S2*) were tested for the resulting material properties and their suitability for architectural application. S0 was printed substrate with no fungal inoculation, S1 was pulp with the fungal species *Byssomerulius corium*, and S2 was pulp with a *Gloeophyllum* sp. (Fig. 6). Three tests were carried out: a bending test to evaluate stiffness, a test for dispersion in water, and a test for water absorption properties. Since the results from these tests indicated that the *Gloeophyllum* pulp composite has the most desirable properties, additional samples were produced and further scanned to

characterise the distortion of the material during drying (Fig. 7). This is notable since most other mycelium-based materials use white rot fungus, while here is was found that the brown rot fungus, *Gloeophyllum*, gave the better result.

Mechanical Performance

The bending test showed that the samples with more extensive hyphae distribution exhibited significantly higher stiffness than the mycelium-free sample and afforded a slightly higher force before failure (Fig. 8). The deformation before failure was twice as high for S0 as S2, with S1 falling in between. The hardness of the material as perceived when cutting the samples with a sharp knife was significantly higher with increased hyphae coverage (S2 > S1 > S0).

Dispersion in Water

The resilience of the material bond when wet was tested by submerging the samples in water for a period of 10 hours. After this period, the water and samples were stirred (Fig. 9). The sample without mycelium (S0) quickly swelled and completely disintegrated upon agitation. S1 and S2 remained intact during stirring.

Hydrophobicity

A droplet of water was placed on each of the surfaces of the three samples, and the subsequent absorption was observed. The droplets on S0 and S1 were quickly absorbed, while the droplet placed on S2 did not absorb but maintained its shape, indicating strong hydrophobicity on the material surface (Fig. 11). The samples' capacity for buffering water in vapour form was also measured, and remained equally high in all three samples.

5. Column assemblage: design to fabrication.

6. Dessicated printed sample comparison. From left: S1, S0, S2.

7. Detail of the 3D scanned prototype. Analysis of deviation from the toolpath sent for fabrication, after printing, growth and desiccation. Although there is considerable distortion, it is locally distributed throughout the height of each module and therefore not global, the tolerances not penalising the current design application.

8. Mechanical performance: bending test.

Bio-Integrated Design:
Architecture as Multi-Scalar Interfaces

The printed prototypes and tests conducted on the resulting bio-composite demonstrate some of the advantages of the proposed approach. The resulting components were highly hydrophobic with a retained capacity of moisture buffering, and remained stable even when exposed to prolonged submersion in water. The transformation of the material by the fungus resulted in improved stiffness and hardness, and eliminated the tendency of the samples to delaminate between printed layers. The surface hardness of the resulting material was markedly different from many other reported mycelium-based materials. This may be due to the use of a brown rot fungus instead of white rot, and this strain's interaction with the substrate. However, further studies are required to investigate these relationships.

The ability to fabricate larger scale elements relies on navigating the requirements in the design space, and the stability and predictability of the printed components in the growth and desiccation phases. The robustness of the process was improved by the inclusion of clay to the substrate as well as the use of stabilising meshes. Equally, the component design is of critical significance, both in terms of enabling the growth of the mycelium and stabilising the material during and after fabrication. This resulted in a requirement for a high surface area, high curvature form.

When engaging with the agency of microorganisms as well as with highly responsive and interdependent materials, significant constraints are placed on the design. These constraints require integration between the multiple scales of the project, from the microscopic scale of microbial behaviour, through the material arrangement at the centimetre scale, all the way to the component and assembly, and eventually human scales. Rather than considering these constraints as limitations, they present an opportunity for responsive and functional architectures.

The demonstrated components (Fig. 1) assemble into a column that retains several of the properties that allow the fungus to thrive: it has a high surface area ratio, the vertical interstitial spaces allow for convective flow, and the material exhibits an active interaction with air and water vapour. These properties remain after the element is constructed, and can be utilised to affect and modulate the environment in direct proximity to the column. Rather than a passive load-carrying element, such a structure should be considered a part of a building's vascular

t=0

t=10 min

t=10 hr

S0 S1 S2

10

11

Acknowledgements

This research has been funded by The Crafoord Foundation and Boverket, the Swedish National Board of Housing, Building and Planning. We would also like to extend our gratitude to Eva Frühwald Hansson and Maria Fredriksson at Lund University for their assistance with the material testing.

References

Appels, F.V.W., Camere, S., Montalti, M., Karana, E., Jansen, K.M.B., Dijksterhuis, J., Krijgsheld, P. and Wösten, H.A. 2019. 'Fabrication factors influencing mechanical, moisture- and water-related properties of mycelium-based composites', *Materials & Design*, 161, pp. 64-71.

Boyce, K.J. and Andrianopoulos, A. 2006. 'Morphogenesis: Control of Cell Types and Shape', in Kües U., Fischer R. (eds), *Growth, Differentiation and Sexuality vol 1: The Mycota (A Comprehensive Treatise on Fungi as Experimental Systems for Basic and Applied Research)*, Berlin, Heidelberg: Springer, pp. 3-20.

Elsacker, E., Vandelook, S., Brancart, J., Peeters, E. and De Laet, L. 2019. 'Mechanical, physical and chemical characterisation of mycelium-based composites with different types of lignocellulosic substrates', *PLoS ONE* 14(7), p. e0213954. (doi: 10.1371/journal.pone.0213954)

Gazzè, S.A., Saccone, L., Smits, M.M., Duran, A.L., Leake, J.R., Banwart, S.A., Ragnarsdottir, K.V. and McMaster, T.J. 2013. 'Nanoscale Observations of Extracellular Polymeric Substances Deposition on Phyllosilicates by an Ectomycorrhizal Fungus', *Geomicrobiology Journal*, 30(8), pp. 721-730.

Heisel, F., Lee, J., Schlesier, K., Rippmann, M., Saeidi, N., Javadian, A., Nugroho, A., Mele, T., Block, P. and Hebel, D. 2018. 'Design, Cultivation and Application of Load-Bearing Mycelium Components: The MycoTree at the 2017 Seoul Biennale of Architecture and Urbanism', *International Journal of Sustainable Energy Development*, 6(1), pp. 296-303.

Latgé, J. P. and Calderone, R. 2006. 'The Fungal Cell Wall', in Kües U., Fischer R. (eds), *Growth, Differentiation and Sexuality vol 1: The Mycota (A Comprehensive Treatise on Fungi as Experimental Systems for Basic and Applied Research)*, Berlin, Heidelberg: Springer, pp. 73-104.

Nagy, D., Locke, J. and Benjamin, D. 2015. 'Computational Brick Stacking for Constructing Free-Form Structures', in Thomsen M., Tamke M., Gengnagel C., Faircloth B. and Scheurer F. (eds), *Modelling Behaviour*, Cham: Springer, p. 203-212.

Turner, J. S. 2005. 'Extended physiology of an insect-built structure', *American Entomologist*, 51(1), pp. 36–38.

Yang, Z., Zhang, F., Still, B., White, M. and Amstislavski, P. 2017. 'Physical and Mechanical Properties of Fungal Mycelium-Based Biofoam', *Journal of Materials in Civil Engineering*, 29(7). (doi: 10.1061/(ASCE)MT.1943-5533.0001866)

system, mediating and enabling flows that drive an active modulation of the micro-climates which the occupants inhabit.

Conclusion

The project demonstrates both the challenges and the potential of additive fabrication of mycelium composites. The introduction of fungus improves the properties of the resulting material in multiple ways, resolving difficulties associated with wood printing through improved water resistance and increased stiffness and hardness. Compared to previous fungus composites which are typically fabricated through casting, additive fabrication can improve the conditions for fungus growth, enabling faster growth rates and more complete coverage. This can result in better material performance and more efficient manufacturing. The process enables complex and customised form beyond what can be achieved through casting, opening up new functional potential in the resulting products.

The biologically active process adds constraints, such as the need for sterile material processing and the prolonged wet state. However, it was demonstrated how a combination of material composition, design integration and fabrication processes can be used to overcome these challenges, potentially enabling the use of such materials in the construction industry. If implemented at large scales, such a shift could radically reduce the building industry's ecological footprint by lessening the need for extraction of non-renewable minerals and for energy intense chemical processing, while ensuring environmentally safe and biodegradable properties.

9. Dispersion in water. The fungus-free sample disintegrates completely, while the two fungal composites exhibit minimal swelling and remain intact after stirring.

10. Substrate development prototype, here without fungus. The substrate was tested for extrudability, as well as for the design – material compatibility.

11. Hydrophobicity. From left: S0, S1, S2.

FROM MACHINE CONTROL TO MATERIAL PROGRAMMING
SELF-SHAPING WOOD MANUFACTURING OF A HIGH PERFORMANCE CURVED CLT STRUCTURE – URBACH TOWER

DYLAN WOOD[1] / **PHILIPPE GRÖNQUIST**[2,3] / **SIMON BECHERT**[4] / **LOTTE ALDINGER**[4] / **DAVID RIGGENBACH**[5] / **KATHARINA LEHMANN**[5] / **MARKUS RÜGGEBERG**[2,3] / **INGO BURGERT**[2,3] / **JAN KNIPPERS**[4] / **ACHIM MENGES**[1]

[1] INSTITUTE FOR COMPUTATIONAL DESIGN AND CONSTRUCTION, UNIVERSITY OF STUTTGART
[2] LABORATORY FOR CELLULOSE & WOOD MATERIALS, EMPA
[3] INSTITUTE FOR BUILDING MATERIALS, ETH ZURICH
[4] INSTITUTE FOR BUILDING STRUCTURES AND STRUCTURAL DESIGN, UNIVERSITY OF STUTTGART
[5] BLUMER LEHMANN AG

Research Aims and Objectives

Computational design and digital fabrication for architecture focuses increasingly on advanced robotic machine control for the shaping and assembly of pre-engineered building materials to produce structures with complex functional geometries. Intelligent digital planning methods and machine material feedback make processes of additive, subtractive and formative manufacturing incrementally more efficient and tuneable. However, complex shaping is still achieved by combinations of pre-shaped formwork, application of brute mechanical force, robotic manipulation, and subtractive machining from larger stock. In the shaping process, powerful innate material behaviour that influences shape is either viewed as problematic or ignored. In the quest for infinitely more axes, and endlessly more sophisticated end effectors, it's clear we have overlooked the useful capacities found within the structures and tissues of the materials we fabricate with.

This research presents a paradigm shift towards a material-driven self-shaping fabrication method for full scale timber building components. Here the 3D geometry emerges from the designed material arrangement in flat 2D parts that are exposed to an external stimulus (Fig. 2). By utilising the unique capacity of the material to act as an integrated, shaping actuator and the final load-bearing structure, elaborate external forming equipment is eliminated. This simple yet informed material programming replaces typically material, energy and labour intensive shaping process. Using wood, which exhibits strong anisotropic dimensional instability in response to changes in moisture, we developed a material-specific predictive model, and a physical material programming routine that allows for a self-shaping manufacturing process for high curvature Cross Laminated Timber (CLT) building components.

Surface active structures benefit tremendously from curvature in both the overall structural geometry and individual building components. For wooden shell structures, curvature is, however, expensive to produce in terms of costs, material, and environmental impact. In this research, the manufacturability of high curvature CLT components enabled by self-shaping is paired with the development of performative geometry and structural analysis for folded plate cylindrical shell structures. The concept is demonstrated with the design, engineering, manufacture, and construction of a 14m tall thin shell

tower structure (Fig. 1). Architecturally, the tower serves as a shelter and landmark, showcasing the potentials of innovative high performance and sustainable timber construction.

Research Context

Manufacturing of structural building components can be conducted by combinations of additive, subtractive and forming processes. Advanced digitally-controlled robotic manufacturing builds upon these processes through automation and increased precision but fundamentally still relies on machines to provide the shaping force and logic. Self-shaping systems where shape is generated from physical material programming to actuate based on external stimuli have already been developed at much smaller scales for medical applications, micro robotic applications, and meso-scale mechanisms with a wide range of functions (Studart and Erb, 2014; Tibbits, 2014; Duro-Royo and Oxman, 2015; Wang et al., 2017; Kara et al., 2018; Kotikian et al., 2019). In architecture, similar principles have been applied for self-regulating façade systems that respond continuously to changes in the environment such as temperature and moisture (Correa et al., 2013; Reichert et al., 2014; Holstov et al., 2015; Sung, 2016; Correa and Menges, 2017; Vailati et al., 2017, 2018; Poppinga et al., 2018). Most shape-morphing structures are limited in scale due to the reduced stiffness of the material required for actuation and high costs of the material and processes to produce them. Wood, however, exhibits the natural ability to change shape without electrical input and with incredibly high forces combined with high stiffness, making it ideal for self-shaping large parts (Rüggeberg and Burgert, 2015; Wood et al., 2016, 2018; Grönquist et al., 2018; Grönquist et al., 2019). It is therefore possible to build high strength shape-changing parts; however with increased volume comes reduced actuation speeds (Mannes et al., 2009).

Timber is a readily available and highly sustainable building material undergoing a renaissance in the face of an increased focus on the environmental impact of building construction. CLT, which is comprised of overlapping layers of solid boards with alternating fibre directions, is one of the fastest growing construction markets worldwide. CLT production is efficient and standardised for flat panels. Despite the inherent structural and architectural advantages of curved parts, they are exponentially more expensive to produce. Even with advancements in digital design and fabrication, use of curved wood components is universally limited by the physical forming process (Robeller et al., 2014; Stecher et al., 2016; Svilans et al., 2017). Parts are produced by first

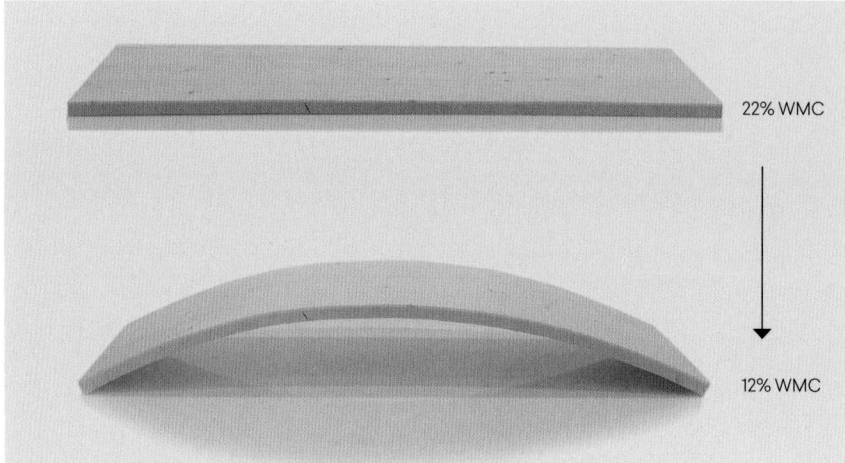

22% WMC

12% WMC

2

constructing either adaptable jigs, or solid formwork on top of which layers of lamella are iteratively screwed or vacuum laminated. The bending stiffness and cross section of the wood lamella limit the possible curvature. In contradiction, larger numbers of thinner lamella allow higher curvature, while lower quantities of thicker lamella would be preferred for production and material efficiency. While extreme curvatures can be manufactured for specialty projects, 10mm is the lower limit for standard sawmill production of lamella with 3.5-4.0m radius the highest known curvature for standard industrial production curved CLT.

Research Questions

The challenge of applying self-shaping technologies for the building industry is how to upscale basic principles to a size that is suitable for the manufacture of building components while ensuring that both material and building structure are maintained. The fundamental research question centres on how known shape-changing properties of a building material can be used purposely to generate shape. Programming of the shape changes requires an advanced understanding of the underlying mechanisms of deformation, which can only be gained by employing simulations based on specific material models coupled with experimental testing. Critical to manufacturing innovation is the development of a materially-informed digital design methodology that could be used to predict and tune the final shape and translate a design geometry to the material information required for production. To be effective, the predictive model must be accurate using material input parameters and sorting ranges that can be collected and implemented in an industrial context.

1. The Urbach Tower, a high performance timber structure utilising self-shaping wood manufacturing for curved CLT. (Rolland Halbe).

2. The basic self-shaping wood manufacturing process in which curvature is generated from loss of wood moisture content in a designed bilayer structure. A sample 1.2m x 0.6m x 40mm thick spruce wood bilayer cut from the larger production parts, shown in the flat high moisture (22 % WMC) production state and curved dry (12% WMC) actuated state (bottom). (ICD/ITKE- University of Stuttgart).

3. Integration and upscaling of the self-shaping manufacturing process to produce high curvature CLT components for the tower structure. Bilayer design, actuation, combining/ stacking, edge finishing, and connection detailing. (ICD/ITKE- University of Stuttgart).

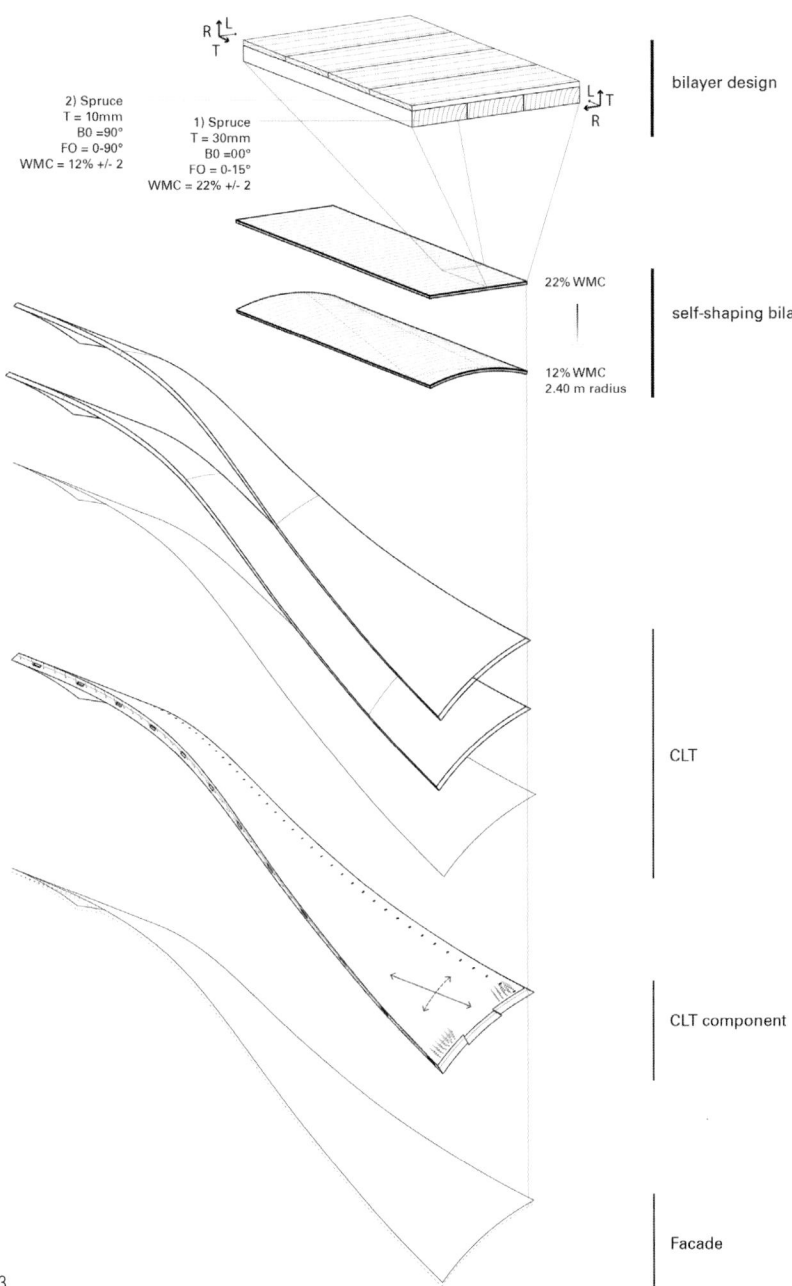

2) Spruce
T = 10mm
B0 = 90°
FO = 0-90°
WMC = 12% +/- 2

1) Spruce
T = 30mm
B0 = 00°
FO = 0-15°
WMC = 22% +/- 2

bilayer design

22% WMC

self-shaping bilayers

12% WMC
2.40 m radius

CLT

CLT component

Facade

3

In addition to the manufacturing process, the curved CLT must be designed and assessed for load-bearing construction. Where and in what types of structures can increased curvature and directional build-ups of the parts be best used? Lastly, what types of materially-driven architecture and construction emerge from a new class of self-shaping processes?

Research Methods

The project has been conducted as an inter-disciplinary collaboration bridging better the raw material entering the sawmill to the completed structure. Feasibility was tested in the laboratory before integration and adaptation to industry for production of components for the Urbach Tower as part of the Remstal Gartenschau, 2019.

Material Programming and Modelling

Wood bilayers are the basic part for the self-shaping process (Fig. 2). A bilayer is constructed from elements: active and restrictive layers of boards oriented at 90° to each other and glued together to create a cross ply plate (Fig. 3). When harvested, wood exhibits a high Wood Moisture Content (WMC). Producing bilayers with a high WMC in the active layer and then drying them creates curvature perpendicular to the longitudinal (L-) direction of the active layer. The curvature achieved is dependent on inputs such as wood species, quality, type of cut (which determines the angle of the transversal or radial (T/R) plane known as end grain), the thickness ratio between the layers, and the change of WMC below fibre saturation point induced in the manufacturing. First a sensitivity analysis was conducted using a digital simulation to determine how the input parameters influence the curvature (Grönquist et al., 2018). Next, a rheological model of wood was used in combination with numerical simulations based on the Finite Element Method (FEM), which takes into account all possible strain mechanisms of wood in a fully coupled time- and moisture-dependent model. Data for expansion coefficient, density and moisture-dependent stiffness was collected from physical samples to supplement literature values in the numerical simulations. A range of bilayer configurations was tested physically in the laboratory with two commonly used species, European beech and Norway spruce, using 0.6m x 0.6m x 10-45mm total thickness to verify the accuracy of the model (Grönquist et al., 2019). From the simulation, a database of build-ups and associated curvature and structural capacity was produced within the range of feasible production thickness of lamellas and drying ranges.

4

In parallel, a computational design model was developed to parametrically interface between the geometric curvature of the component represented as a trimmed cylindrical NURBS (Non-Uniform Rational B-Splines) surface, the simulated bilayer database for material build and actuation ranges, the overall structural engineering model which includes the CLT buildup and connection detailing, and back to the wood FEM model for tuning and verification (Fig. 6). Simple material information for the flat build-ups was sent to the sawmill for material selection and production, while the geometric model could be continuously adapted to deviations during the process.

Industry Manufacturing Integration

From the integrative design approach, a bilayer made of Norway spruce sourced locally from Switzerland (FSC and HSH certified) with an active layer thickness of 30mm and a restrictive layer of 10mm was chosen. Active layer boards with starting WMC of 22% (+/-2%) and R/T angles in a range of 0-15° were semi-automatically selected and sorted in the sawmill using inline WMC measurement and visual grading. Restrictive layer boards were sourced from a standard 10mm thick wood product with 12% WMC. Active layer boards were planed and edge-glued to create a continuous plate on which restrictive layer boards were press laminated with one component (1 C) PUR adhesive, resulting in a bilayer plate 5.0m x 1.2m x 40mm thick. Bilayers were placed in racks and kiln-dried in an adapted kiln-drying programme lowering the WMC to 12% and shaping to the targeted curvature of 2.4m radius (Fig. 2). To achieve form stability under changing relative humidity, two curved bilayers were stacked together with an elastically bent spruce locking layer and again press laminated using the same 1 C PUR adhesive (Fig. 3). Moisture content and curvature were documented per board at two depths in each production step. Structural capacity of the resulting experimental CLT was verified through testing in a three-point bending test (rolling shear), shear block testing (glue bond strength), and long-term outdoor tests for form stability and delamination.

Building Demonstrator – Urbach Tower

The architectural and structural potentials for high curvature CLT were demonstrated with the design of a 14.2m tall thin shell wood structure that serves as a look-out point and shelter for hikers in the Remstal in southern Germany. The unique design is based on the co-intersection of 12 cylindrical surfaces. Curvature in the individual components increases the bending stiffness of the tower surface, similar to a corrugated sheet, while the primary fibre orientation within the CLT matches the vertical load-bearing direction (Aldinger et al., 2020) computational design, and digital fabrication, as well as a growing awareness for sustainable construction, have led to a renaissance of structural timber in architecture. Its favourable elastic properties allow bending of timber for use in free-form curved beam structures. Such complex geometries necessitate a high degree of pre-fabrication enabled by the machinability of timber and established digital fabrication methods. In parallel, cross-laminated timber (CLT).

To produce the tower, self-shaping bilayers were used to manufacture curved rohlings from which four of the twelve components were trimmed and detailed using a five-axis CNC machine (Fig. 4). As a benchmark, the remaining eight components were produced using a conventional form-bending process requiring a negative formwork and thinner layers. The component-to-component connections are aligned using beech wood blocks and joined using crossed full-thread screws that are structurally optimised in their arrangement and specific angle (Li and Knippers, 2015). Components were preassembled in assembly groups of three components each and a 10mm thick glue-laminated larch wood façade was added (Fig. 5). A metal oxide coating (UVood®) for UV protection treatment was applied to create a surface that will lighten over time (Guo et al., 2017). On site, groups were placed and connected in eight hours (Fig. 7). A curved steel and polycarbonate roof was added to enclose the structure. Over the planned 10- to 15-year lifetime, the structure will be monitored continuously with integrated WMC sensors, climate sensors and iterative laser scanning to detect deformations.

4. Completed curved CLT rohling after the stacking and combining of bilayer panels to create 5-layer, 90mm thick CLT. Shown mounted on a large scale 5-axis CNC machine used for lightly machining the edges and adding the crossing screw connection detailing.

5. Completed prefabrication of assembly groups prepared for transport following in the connection of three components and addition of the Larch wood façade with UVood® surface treatment. (ICD/ITKE- University of Stuttgart).

6. FEA modelling of the structural design aspects for the thin shell structure. Global deformations of the structure due to wind loads (left), CLT utilisation including intra component joints (centre) and the range of connection angles for fine-tuning of crossing screen angles per building regulations and fabrication constraints (right). (ICD/ITKE- University of Stuttgart).

Research Evaluation

On a technical level, self-shaping enables the production of high curvature parts (<3.0m radius). This can be accomplished with fewer, thicker boards, which reduces waste in processing and labour. A CLT build-up with a radius of 2.4m was achieved with 2 bilayers of 10/30mm and a 10mm locking layer resulting in a 5-layer, 90mm thick CLT cross section. While mechanically possible, the equivalent form-bending to this radius is outside normal production ranges determined through initial industry research for using solid wood lamella; this would have required 9 layers of 10-15mm lamella. Using the self-shaping method provides up to a 40% reduction in the number of layers. While curved guides and sorting are still needed to even the curvature variation when gluing the curved bilayers to CLT, the amount is significantly reduced as the pre-shaping of the parts is within 10% of the predicted curvature. Initial observations show a reduction in spring-back after forming, substantially reducing corrective measures and surface finishing. From a manufacturing perspective, these design methods combined with the reduction in custom formwork makes the process highly adaptable, where the bilayer build-up and input parameters can be adjusted to shape different radii in each part. However, in the current state it requires a more careful selection of higher grade wood than used in standard CLT. Testing of structural behaviour of self-shaped parts did not indicate the need for additional safety factors.

From a design perspective, the use of multiple connected curved CLT parts in surface-active structures allows a new architectural language to emerge from the natural capacity of the material. In the Urbach Tower, the concave curvature of the exterior surfaces results in sharp lines

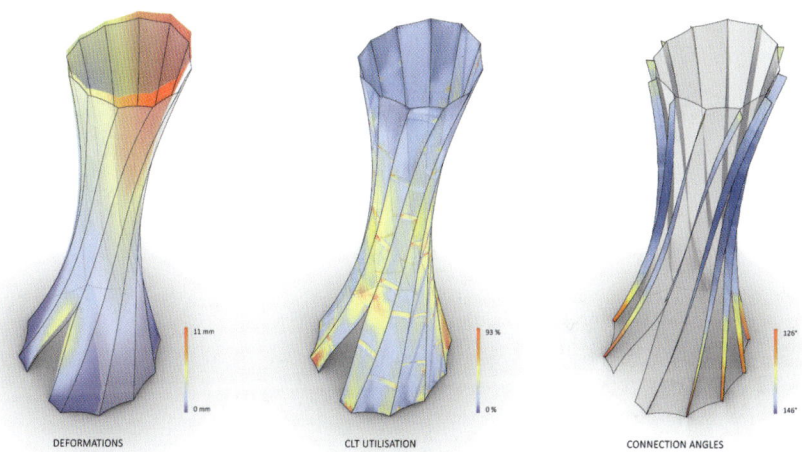

DEFORMATIONS   CLT UTILISATION   CONNECTION ANGLES

6

and crisp surfaces, while the convex interior surfaces are invitingly soft, evoking an unexpected tactile material experience within a load-bearing structure (Fig. 8). The integration of structure and skin as well as the hidden detailing of the curved parts results in an elegant expression of form and force. This is backed quantitatively by the relative lightweight and slender nature of the structure (slenderness ratio of 160 to 1). In addition, the structure can be fully disassembled and recycled at the end of use. Combined, these aspects contribute to create a striking landmark and a space of internal reflection that simultaneously reframes our perception of the material and surroundings (Fig. 9).

Conclusion

The construction of the tower demonstrated self-shaping manufacturing for industry level production of curved load-bearing building components. As the same material is both the shaping mechanism and the final structure, the need of larger machines and formwork is greatly reduced. The current process is directly applicable for the solid wood production of lightweight curved roof components, curved vertical shear walls for multi-storey timber construction and cylindrical structures such as silos or turbine towers. It presents an ecological option for performative curved geometries that are often produced with malleable yet energy intensive materials such as concrete, plastic or metals.

A designed self-shaping process is a new approach to digital fabrication at the scale of building components. Rather than outputting machine codes to communicate a position for additive or subtractive shaping, the self-shaping process means geometry is communicated through the specific characteristic and arrangement of material, providing an implicit understanding of the resulting physical transformation. As the scale of parts increase, the self-shaping processes become inherently more valuable as the force and coordination required to bend the parts increase. Similarly, self-shaping enables adaptable and parallel manufacturing within a standard setup, which is valuable for large quantity and high variation production.

Rethinking materials' active role in construction leads to new architectural opportunities as well as increased sustainability in the production and operation of buildings. As our understanding and control of materials become increasingly sophisticated, their symbiotic relationship with the digitally-controlled fabrication machines of the future is brought into question, productively inverting and blurring the relationship between material and machine. Perhaps in the future the materials will do the fabricating and the machines as we know them will rest.

Acknowledgments

The research was funded by: The Swiss Innovation Agency – InnoSuisse (grant number 25114.2), GETTYLAB, The Deutsche Bundesstiftung Umwelt DBU (German Federal Environmental Foundation) (grant number DBU Az. 34714/01), Blumer Lehmann AG, the University of Stuttgart, Deutsche Forschungsgemeinschaft (DFG, German Research Foundation) under Germany's Excellence Strategy – EXC 2120/1 – 390831618, Gemeinde Urbach, Remstal Gartenschau 2019 GmbH, Carlisle-CCM Europe, and Scanntronik Mugrauer GmbH. The demonstrator with completed with the support of Ramon Weber, Robert Faulkner, Christo van der Hoven, Denista Kolvea, Monika Monika Göbel , Urs Basalla,Stefan Bischof, Markus Fitzi, Peter Trittenbass, Josua Preisig ,Kai Strehlke, Martin Antemann, Urban Jung, Richard Jussel, and Huizhang Guo.

7

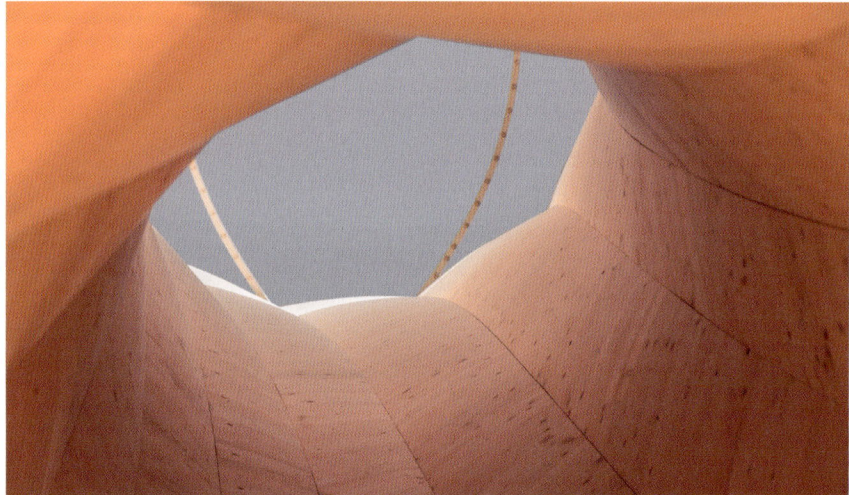

8

9

References

Aldinger, L., Bechert, S., Wood, D., Knippers, J. and Menges, A. 2020. 'Design and Structural Modelling of Surface-Active Timber Structures Made from Curved CLT – Urbach Tower, Remstal Gartenschau 2019', in Gengnagel, C., Baverel, O., Burry, J., Ramsgaard Thomsen, M. and Weinzierl, S. (eds), *Impact: Design With All Senses*, Cham: Springer International Publishing, pp. 419-432. (doi: 10.1007/978-3-030-29829-6_33)

Correa, D., Krieg, O. D., Menges, A. and Reichert, S. 2013. 'HYGROSKIN: A Climate Responsive Prototype Project Based on the Elastic and Hygroscopic Properties of Wood', in Beesley, P., Kahn, O. and Stacey, M. (eds), *ACADIA 2013: Adaptive Architecture*, Cambridge: ACADIA, pp. 33-42.

Correa, D. and Menges, A. 2017. 'Fused Filament Fabrication for Multi-Kinematic-State Climate Responsive Aperatures', i in Menges, A., Sheil, B., Glynn, R. and Skavara M. (eds), *Fabricate 2017: Rethinking Design and Construction*, London: UCL Press, pp. 190-195.

Duro-Royo, J. and Oxman, N. 2015. 'Towards Fabrication Information Modeling (FIM): Four Case Models to Derive Designs informed by Multi-Scale Trans-Disciplinary Data', *MRS Proceedings*, 1800, p. 294. (doi: 10.1557/opl.2015.647)

Grönquist, P., Wittel, F. K. and Rüggeberg, M. 2018. 'Modeling and design of thin bending wooden bilayers', *PLoS ONE*, 13(10), e0205607. (doi: 10.1371/journal.pone.0205607)

Grönquist, P., Wood, D., Hassani, M. M., Wittel, F. K., Menges, A. and Rüggeberg, M. 2019. 'Analysis of hygroscopic self-shaping wood at large scale for curved mass timber structures', *Science Advances*, 5(9), eaax1311. (doi: 10.1126/sciadv.aax1311)

Guo, H., Klose, D., Hou, Y., Jeschke, G. and Burgert, I. 2017. 'Highly Efficient UV Protection of the Biomaterial Wood by A Transparent TiO2/Ce Xerogel', *ACS Applied Materials & Interfaces*, 9(44), pp. 39040-39047. (doi: 10.1021/acsami.7b12574)

Holstov, A., Bridgens, B. and Farmer, G. 2015. 'Hygromorphic materials for sustainable responsive architecture', *Construction and Building Materials*, 98, pp. 570-582. (doi: 10.1016/j.conbuildmat.2015.08.136)

Kara, L. B., Yan, Z., Gu, J., Tao, Y., Gecer Ulu, N., Yao, L., Wang, G. and Yang, H. 2018. '4DMesh – 4D Printing Morphing Non-Developable Mesh Surfaces', *UIST '18: The 31st Annual ACM Symposium on User Interface Software and Technology*, pp. 623-635. (doi: 10.1145/3242587.3242625)

Kotikian, A., McMahan, C., Davidson, E. C., Muhammad, J. M., Weeks, R. D., Daraio, C. and Lewis, J. A. 2019. 'Untethered soft robotic matter with passive control of shape morphing and propulsion', *Science Robotics*, 4(33), p. eaax7044. (doi: 10.1126/scirobotics.aax7044)

Li, J.-M. and Knippers, J. 2015. 'Structures, Segmental Timber Plate Shell for the Landesgartenschau Exhibition Hall in Schwäbisch Gmünd – the Application of Finger Joints in PlateNo Title', *International Journal of Space Structures*, 30(2), pp. 123-139. (doi: 10.1260/0266-3511.30.2.123)

Mannes, D., Sonderegger, W., Hering, S., Lehmann, E. and Niemz, P. 2009. 'Non-destructive determination and quantification of diffusion processes in wood by means of neutron imaging', *Holzforschung*, 63(5), pp. 589-596. (doi: 10.1515/HF.2009.100)

Poppinga, S., Zollfrank, C., Prucker, O., Rühe, J., Menges, A., Cheng, T. and Speck, T. 2018. 'Toward a New Generation of Smart Biomimetic Actuators for Architecture', *Advanced Materials* – Special Issue: Bioinspired Materials, 30(19), p. e1703653. (doi: 10.1002/adma.201703653)

Reichert, S., Menges, A. and Correa, D. 2014. 'Meteorosensitive architecture: Biomimetic building skins based on materially embedded and hygroscopically enabled responsiveness', *Computer-Aided Design*, 60, pp. 50-69. (doi: 10.1016/j.cad.2014.02.010)

Robeller, Christopher; Nabaei, Seyed Sina; Weinand, Y. 2014. 'Design and Fabrication of Robot-Manufactured Joints for a Curved-Folded Thin-Shell Structure Made from CLT', in McGee, W. and Ponce de Leon, M. (eds), *Robotic Fabrication in Architecture*, Cham: Springer, pp. 67-81. (doi: 10.1007/978-3-319-04663-1_5)

Rüggeberg, M. and Burgert, I. 2015. 'Bio-Inspired Wooden Actuators for Large Scale Applications', *Plos One*, 10(4), p. e0120718. (doi: 10.1371/journal.pone.0120718)

Stecher, G., Maderebner, R., Zingerle, P., Flach, M. and Kraler, A. 2016. 'Curved Cross Laminated Timber Elements', *World Conference of Timber Engineering (WCTE) 2016*. Available at: https://www.researchgate.net/publication/308304297_CURVED_CROSS-LAMINATED_TIMBER_ELEMENTS. (Accessed 23 December 2019)

Studart, A. R. and Erb, R. M. 2014. 'Bioinspired materials that self-shape through programmed microstructures', *Soft matter*, 10(9), pp. 1284-1294. (doi: 10.1039/c3sm51883c)

Sung, D. 2016. 'Smart Geometries for Smart Materials: Taming Thermobimetals to Behave', *Journal of Architectural Education*, 70(1), pp. 96-106. (doi: 10.1080/10464883.2016.1122479)

Svilans, T., Poinet, P., Tamke, M. and Thomsen, M. R. 2017. 'A Multi-scalar Approach for the Modelling and Fabrication of Free-Form Glue-Laminated Timber Structures', in De Rycke, K., Gengnagel, C., Baverel, O., Burry, J., Mueller, C., Nguyen, M. M., Rahm, P. and Thomsen, M. R. (eds), *Humanizing Digital Reality, Design Modelling Symposium 2017*. Singapore: Springer, pp. 247–257. (doi: 10.1007/978-981-10-6611-5_22)

Tibbits, S. 2014. '4D printing: Multi-material shape change', *Architectural Design*, 84(1), pp. 116-121. (doi: 10.1002/ad.1710)

Vailati, C., Bachtiar, E., Hass, P., Burgert, I. and Rüggeberg, M. 2018. 'An autonomous shading system based on coupled wood bilayer elements', *Energy and Buildings*, 158, pp. 1013-1022. (doi: doi:10.1016/j.enbuild.2017.10.042)

Vailati, C., Hass, I., Burgert, I. and Rüggeberg, M. 2017. 'Upscaling of wood bilayers: design principles for controlling shape change and increasing moisture change rate', *Materials and Structures*, 50, pp. 250-262. (doi: doi:10.1617/s11527-017-1117-4)

Wang, W., Yao, L., Zhang, T., Cheng, C.-Y., Levine, D. and Ishii, H. 2017. 'Transformative Appetite', in Mark, G., Fussell, S., Lampe, C., Schraefel, M. C., Hourcade, J. P., Appert, C. and Wigdor, D. (eds), *CHI '17: Proceedings of the 2017 CHI Conference on Human Factors in Computing Systems*, New York, NY: ACM Press, pp. 6123-6132. (doi: 10.1145/3025453.3026019)

Wood, D. M., Correa, D., Krieg, O. D. and Menges, A. 2016. 'Material computation – 4D timber construction: Towards building-scale hygroscopic actuated, self-constructing timber surfaces', *International Journal of Architectural Computing*, 14(1), pp. 49-62. (doi: 10.1177/1478077115625522)

Wood, D., Vailati, C., Menges, A. and Rüggeberg, M. 2018. 'Hygroscopically actuated wood elements for weather responsive and self-forming building parts – Facilitating upscaling and complex shape changes', *Construction and Building Materials*, 165, pp. 782-791. (doi: 10.1016/S0950061817325394)

7. On-site assembly of the prefabricated groups highlighting the slenderness of the load bearing structural CLT (90cm). (ICD/ITKE-University of Stuttgart).

8. Upward interior view with the locally convex curvature creating a soft billowing aesthetic from fully load bearing structural components with hidden connection details. (ICD/ITKE- University of Stuttgart).

9. The sharp edges at the intersections of the concave geometry catching the light as the 14.2m-tall structure stands in the natural landscape. (Roland Halbe).

BENDING THE LINE
ZIPPERED WOOD CREATING NON-ORTHOGONAL ARCHITECTURAL ASSEMBLIES USING THE MOST COMMON LINEAR BUILDING COMPONENT (THE 2X4)

BLAIR SATTERFIELD / ALEXANDER PREISS / DEREK MAVIS / GRAHAM ENTWISTLE
THE UNIVERSITY OF BRITISH COLUMBIA
MARC SWACKHAMER
HOUMINN PRACTICE
MATTHEW HAYES
UNIVERSITY OF COLORADO

Research Aims and Objectives

Light frame wood construction is flexible, adaptable, cheap, renewable, and requires very little skill to assemble. It is a dominant system in North America for good reason and has changed little in over a century. The authors believe that the introduction of their Zippered Wood research to the conventional stick framing approach will revolutionise this construction method, rendering it more situationally adaptable and resource responsible.

The research team developed a pair of experimental prototypes that challenge conventional wall construction through the free modification of its most basic component: the standard 2x4. Their investigation works at the scales of wood grain, wood member, software interface and tool development to liberate the architect to fluidly conceptualise formal strategies and deliver more sophisticated wood framed buildings. The authors aim to empower the architect by amplifying her control over material-forming strategies, introducing adaptability into the forming process, and finally reducing the cost of shaping materials in time, measure and setup. Even in the context of normative, orthogonal and flat wall construction, Zippered Wood offers significant material savings over standard stud wall construction without sacrificing strength. Through increases in wood member strength afforded by an introduced twisting geometry, the typical stud wall maintains its original length, height, and thickness through a smaller material investment.

Thus, the objective of the Zippered Wood project is twofold. On one hand, it positions the standard 2x4 lumber unit as a more flexible, adaptable and mutable building component, capable of wildly varied geometric manipulation with little added cost. On the other hand, it offers material efficiencies to standard wall construction, significantly reducing the volume of wood required to build an otherwise conventional wall. In both cases, the research advantages used, off-cut and discarded lumber, amplifying its sophistication through a precise yet economical set of cutting and reassembly procedures. The authors have installed a wall prototype and, subsequently, a small, temporary pavilion, to test the strategy. Most recently, through the development of custom saws capable of cutting members with little or no waste, the authors are further streamlining the process of hacking the standard 2x4.

Research Context

At times, it seems as though architects have remarkably little agency over how the buildings they design are fabricated and constructed. The fiscal power and market politics of global capital conspire to diminish their influence. The voices of academic researchers feel even fainter when railing against the forces of asset urbanism. In a city like Vancouver, Canada, issues of 'materiality and methodology' in architecture, while present and important, are far from the heart of public conversations about buildings, construction and city making. Discourse veers towards marketability, housing availability and workflow efficiency. The challenge for 21st-century architects is finding places to apply effective pressure to an immaterial body of economic forces. Where can architects make any meaningful impact in this space? The authors decided to look for material opportunities in the wake of global capital.

Metro Vancouver is one of the fastest growing and most expensive real estate markets on the planet. Existing neighbourhoods accommodate most of its growth through the demolition of older single-family houses and other light frame buildings. An outcome of this is, and will continue to be, an abundance of construction waste. In 2015 alone, the construction industry in metro Vancouver produced approximately 218,000 tons of waste wood, including 29% untreated dimensional lumber (Fulton, 2016). Throughout North America, it is estimated that roughly 20% of all materials that enter landfill come from construction and demolition waste. Put more bluntly, in Vancouver and across North America, the effects of a series of abstractions (soaring land values, lax oversight on real estate speculation, and construction undertaken to shelter and launder money) contribute to the destruction and disposal of nearly 1000 single-family homes annually (City of Vancouver, 2018). These older buildings contain wood that is serviceable and in many cases superior in quality to new timber members. Salvaged dimensional lumber is often from older growth trees, is dry and dimensionally stable, and may be longer and more robust than today's standard eight-foot stock. Much of this waste material is still viable for light wood frame construction.

Research Questions

Considering the massive volumes of waste wood produced by the construction industry through both leftover, surplus materials during building assembly, and discarded materials during demolition of existing buildings, the authors developed two primary research questions which yielded a number of secondary and

2

tertiary research questions. The first driving research question was: can strategically-modified used and discarded 2x4s, with specific geometries (joints in the form of teeth), be mated to generate predictable, specific bent forms, inexpensively and with little waste? This, of course, opened other questions like: can the assembly of these members form predictable bends and twists without the use of formwork? Can custom, computer numerically-controlled tools cut members to minimise or even eliminate waste?

The second driving research question was: can manipulations to used and discarded 2x4s provide performance benefits and an economic use of material? For example, can the complex bends and twists in the wood members offer not just formal novelty, but also geometrically-derived strength advantages? If it is true that the bent and twisted lumber is stronger, can one construct a standard wall, floor, or roof structure using less material than is typically expended through conventional stick frame construction?

To help answer these questions, the authors first examined three primary precedents. First, they looked at boat building, which is common in the Pacific Northwest. They investigated the work of John Lockwood, the founder of Pygmy Sea Kayaks in Port Townsend, Washington. His technique for boat building uses no formwork. He developed proprietary software to digitally mill wood sheets, then he sews the sheets together, forcing the wood into shape. Once sewn, glue fixes the assembly, and upon removal of the stitching, the boat is finished (Lockwood, 2018).

Lockwood's edge-formed compound geometries are useful examples of leveraging material behaviour and geometry

1. One Bay Prototype – A single bay of a larger proposed performance/ teaching space was executed as a proof of concept. The structure performed well and has led to a larger proposition. The recognisable building form is intended to remind occupants of conventional construction as it subverts the logic of the stud-wall. The zippered members translate between a planer logic (roof) and a columnar logic.

2. Tooth and Twist. Through trial, error and, finally, strategic modelling and milling, the research team generated a strategy for predictably bending and twisting 2x4s using only geometry.

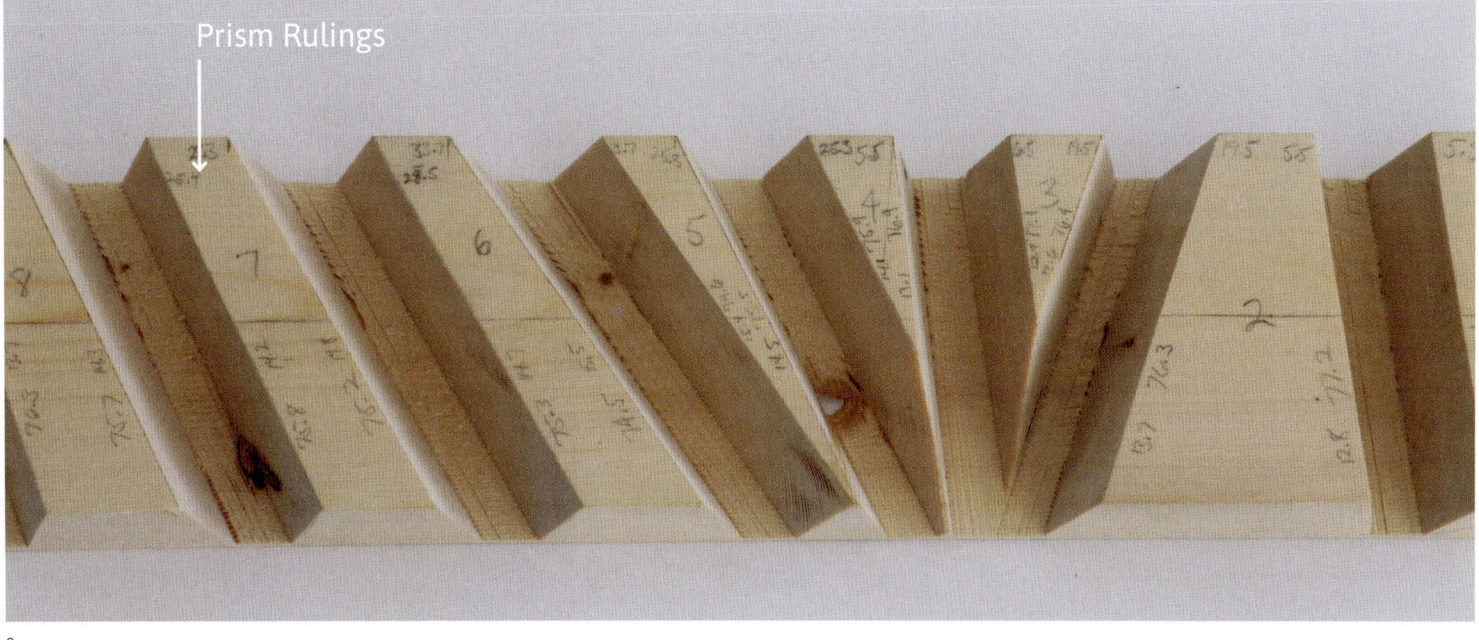

Prism Rulings

3

3. Manually Cut Teeth – Researchers worked on two tasks concurrently. One team was assigned physical prototypes and the other virtual models. The two teams worked in parallel and communicated often. The first attempt at a physical zippered wood prototype was generated using a cross-cut saw and a pencil. This version was measured and fed back into the computer.

to make form. However, the Pygmy example is not a template for transforming 2x4s. For clues on how to transform solid block, the team looked to a method called 'ZipShape' developed in Germany by Christoph Schindler. Schindler's digital kerfing strategy uses 3D-modelling software and six-axis robots to generate meshing panels that, when locked together, form undulating surfaces. Schindler applies his technique to furniture, cutting his kerfs out of a soft core faced with wood laminate. While his techniques were deployed primarily to generate planar curves along a single axis, an example of a developed surface twist was also present in an earlier paper (Shindler, 2011). Kennedy and Violich Architecture advance this technique with 'Smart Rockers', a clever public furniture project that uses small Kuka robots to mill MDF cores (Kennedy and Violich, 2011). When assembled, the sheets of laminated MDF achieve sweeping axial bends.

All three precedents offer valuable insights into the generation of form using material behaviour and smart geometry, but work was still necessary to create more ambitious deformation and to answer the initial research questions outlined above.

Research Methods

A 'kerf' is a groove made by removing material with a cutting tool (saw, torch, bit, etc.). Kerfing is the act of making repeated parallel cuts most of the way through

a solid block, allowing it to bend. Kerfing can make a standard 2x4 remarkably flexible, but the bending is unpredictable and the resulting board is structurally weak. These complications prompted a decision to change direction and focus on controlling the cut. The kerf cuts in the research transitioned from parallel to eccentric. They then morphed into modified finger joints and eventually evolved into continuous topographies, capable of predictably deforming material (Fig. 2).

A deliberate division of labour informed this evolution. One research team focused on physical prototyping and the other on developing virtual models. The material team started with hand-measured and milled 2x4 prototypes, cut with a compound mitre saw to produce examples with polyhedral teeth (Fig. 3). When trained together, the resulting compound formed bends and twists. The other team's task, bending 2x4s virtually using Rhino and Grasshopper, was more straightforward. The gap in the process resided in the translation from physical to virtual. To bridge it, the authors developed Grasshopper scripts to analyse simulated shapes and generate toolpaths required by a CNC mill to produce viable tooth patterns (Fig. 4).

Outputting the digital model revealed new challenges. First, the depth of the cuts affected the wood's ability to bend. Too much wood left at the thinnest point of a given 'valley' cracked due to material stiffness. Too little wood failed due to weakness. To find an optimal thickness, the research team iteratively cut a series of physical

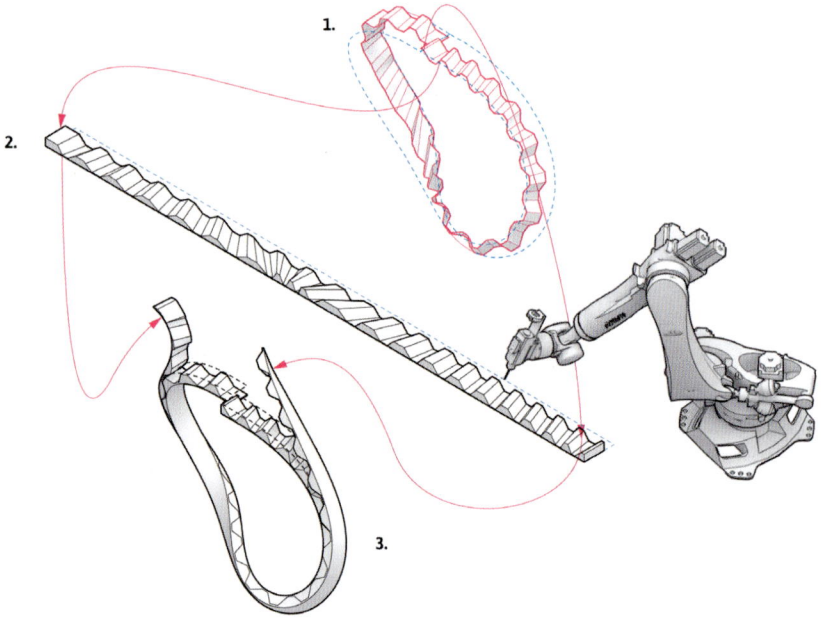

1.

2.

3.

4

4. From Virtual to Physical – This illustration shows a virtual mobius strip. (1) Rule lines generated through analysis create a tooth pattern that manifests the desired curve. (2) The virtual tool pattern is unrolled to allow a CNC mill or robot to cut the pattern into a 2x4. (3) That pattern is mated to a second milled board to form the designed curvature in the 2x4.

5. One Hundred Thirty-five Degrees – Team members demonstrate the bending of a two-by-four prepared for use in the pavilion prototype. No steaming or soaking was required to bend the member. Members are glued and vacuum-bagged.

6. Scan Test – The research team scanned multiple test members to verify tolerances. The composite image shows one progression. The purple 'board' was in the correct position.

prototypes using a consistent tooth pattern. They started with a 6mm maximum depth and decreased through subsequent millruns. The most successful test prototypes left a minimum of 3mm of wood along the flat face of the milled board. When tested, this piece was both flexible enough to bend yet proved very stiff once glued. The assembled member was able to resist twisting and bending forces. The second challenge was the gluing surface itself. The faceted cuts exposed too much end grain, which is poor for gluing, and the interior corners of the faceted teeth were prone to cracking under loading.

The solution to this problem was to smooth the tooth profile. The authors developed an undulating sinusoidal pattern that generated a continuous gluing surface. The glued bond was much better than anything the team had achieved with faceted cuts. The sinusoidal strategy showed that the geometry embedded in the angle of the teeth was the defining factor in predictably bending wood (not the shape of the tooth). The authors have been progressing a modified planar strategy to replace the sinusoidal work. The planar approach dramatically reduces milling time and breakage in early prototypes has been eliminated. Finally, the team applied more traditional dovetail joints to end join already formed boards (Fig. 5). The combination of these techniques meant they could take breakage and off-cuts and theoretically generate articulated boards at any length, be they straight, twisted, curved, or bent. This could be done with relative accuracy (Figs 6, 7).

Research Evaluation

To date, the team has developed two full-scale, physical prototypes, and a third virtual analysis, to evaluate the Zippered Wood research. The first full-scale prototype, called Stick Formed Wall is a variation on a traditional stud wall (Fig. 8). By curving the 2x4 bottom plate of a traditionally framed wall, the team transformed a portion of a normally planar wall into a volumetric hyperbolic paraboloid. Another design 'delaminates' to create a modest covered space for the display of didactic boards explaining the Zippered Wood project. The goal of this proposal was to demonstrate that while Zippered Wood can be used in all members of a structural system (yielding highly complex forms), the system's lasting value might be found in its compatibility with existing light wood framing techniques. Our virtual analysis, explained below, expands on the capacity of the research to integrate with existing wood frame construction processes and in-place trade skills.

The second Zippered Wood prototype is more ambitious. It explores the formal capacity of the research through the production of a modified bay of a larger outdoor pavilion designed to house student performances and impromptu teaching (Fig. 1). The team fabricated the structure using repurposed timber. It sits on four temporary footings and features bundled columns built from salvaged 2x4s. Each bundle springs from a footing, bending and fanning inward using four unique profiles that meet to create cover. The zippered members translate between the columnar supports and an overhead truss strategy that meets at a ridge beam. The pavilion serves as a test of the repeatability of the zippered geometry and whether the Zippered Wood members embody the structural capacity required for the larger version of the pavilion. It successfully demonstrates that customisation in stick framing can be achieved without significantly greater fabrication time or material cost.

The third prototype, a virtual analysis of the research, explores the capacity of the Zippered Wood system to fit seamlessly into existing wood frame construction standards, drastically increasing the material efficiency of the typical stud wall. The team virtually tested over 150 Zippered Wood stud wall variants. The findings were encouraging. Because a typical Zippered Wood stud is significantly stronger than a standard 2x4 stud (a conclusion the team has drawn from anecdotal physical testing, but one that the team is in the process of testing through finite analysis software), less material produces the same length and height of wall. Stud spacing and wall

5

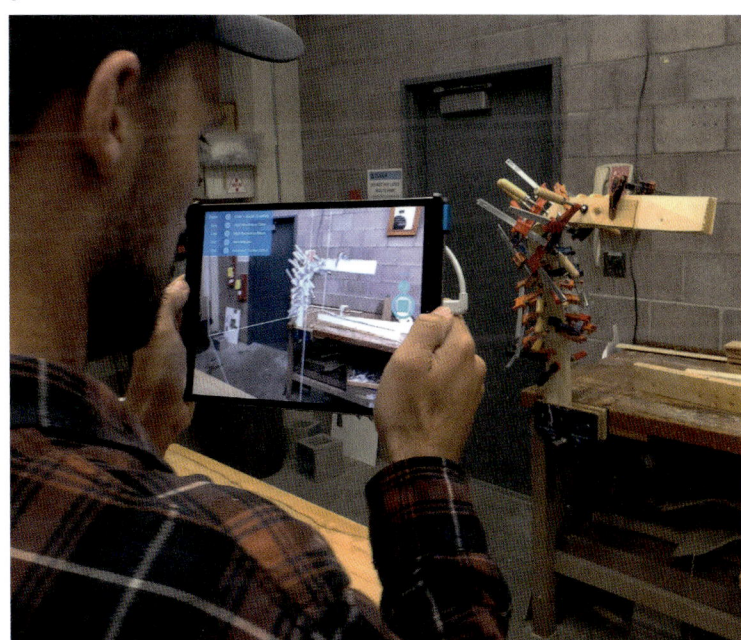

6

thickness can grow without sacrificing strength or adding more material. Further, a Zippered Wood stud wall with a thickness of 15cm or more can accommodate runs of electrical, plumbing, and mechanical conduit without on-site cutting of studs (Fig. 9).

The team sees these prototypes as incremental research steps and provocations. The intent of the work is to demonstrate the potential of Zippered Wood and to find optimal locations for its application.

Conclusion

It is impossible to know how architecture will weather the coming decades. The world is facing massive change, including increasingly turbulent market forces, diminishing resource availability, a transition from computerisation to computational work, and inevitable automation. Perhaps automation will save us, freeing the architect to refocus on inherited roles as auteurs of form and meaning. Maybe we are already lost, the proverbial 'frogs in the pot', unaware we are doomed as we yield to algorithms and robots. Most likely, architecture will evolve, our techniques merging with technology, blurring the boundaries between design and building, policy and culture, material and programming. Whatever the scenario, it is clear that we can no longer be content to simply refine our methods. We must enter the black box and program it, disrupt it, and redirect its output. The Zippered Wood process is offered as an example of how. This research offers a novel approach to wood joinery and material deformation, deployed to convert standard 2x4s into formally sophisticated building components. The approach generates form using material behaviour and geometry, advancing techniques from analogue production to digital (and back), and from precision fitting to precision displacement. It also recognises that this process results in the loss of material in modified pieces. Despite this loss, Zippered Wood promotes the use of reclaimed material and off-cuts, thus extending the life of otherwise compromised wood members destined for landfill and giving life to those parts previously deemed inadequate for use in conventional construction methods. Zippered Wood could generate a new vocabulary of built form using readily accessible stock material (the 2x4) and waste material (salvaged lumber). This process emerged out of the constraints of existing dimensional lumber, specifically the 2x4's parallel edges, standard dimensions, and orthogonality. These same attributes are what make the Zippered Wood process possible. Parallel longitudinal edges make the surface rulings much easier to locate. Near continuous face grain allows for bending to occur. The system re-imagines reclaimed lumber as an

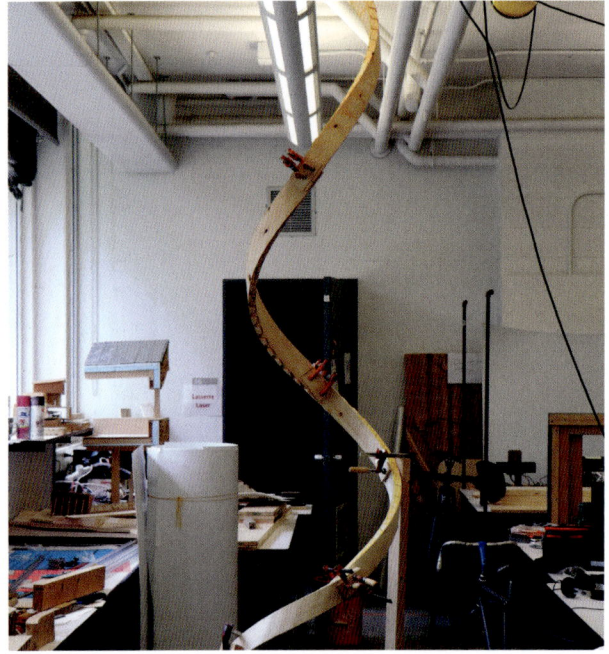

7

opportunity for sustainable construction that is not bound to the orthogonal status quo, but also renders that status quo, the existing conventional wood frame systems that are in place, as lighter and more efficient. The authors hope that by challenging the limits of recycling, and engaging that territory with new digital and computational tools, architects might create a new urgency for reuse in the building industry.

Specifically, the research demonstrates that the millions of tons of discarded wood stud framing, from both new construction and demolished existing buildings, can be the exclusive source for new construction that is formally dynamic and adaptable, more efficient, and yet still rooted in existing labour skillsets. Through the development of increasingly faster cutting approaches and streamlined algorithms for determining tooth geometry, the process of moving from conceptual design to fabrication is economic and seamless. The concept of scarcity and abundance is essential to positioning the research in relation to current discourse around resilience and building construction. Where there is an increasing scarcity of first-source materials for building construction (materials that are mined, extracted or harvested aggressively through invasive processes), there is an abundance of existing and, most commonly, discarded materials. There is also emerging an abundance of accessible, sophisticated and intelligent technologies to strategically adapt those abundant existing materials for new and more sophisticated uses.

7. Cylinder Test – It took time for the team to generate consistent outcomes. This test mated multiple zipped 2x4s together around an implied cylinder. The success of this piece gave the team enough confidence to attempt a small structure.

8. Hyperbolic Paraboloid Stud Wall – The team radically deformed a conventional wall by replacing the base-plate with a single Zippered Wood element. A hyperbolic paraboloid wall is generated using traditional framing labour and technique.

9. Increased efficiency through Zippering – This series of diagrams illustrate the potential material savings possible if zippered wood is applied to standard structural assemblies.

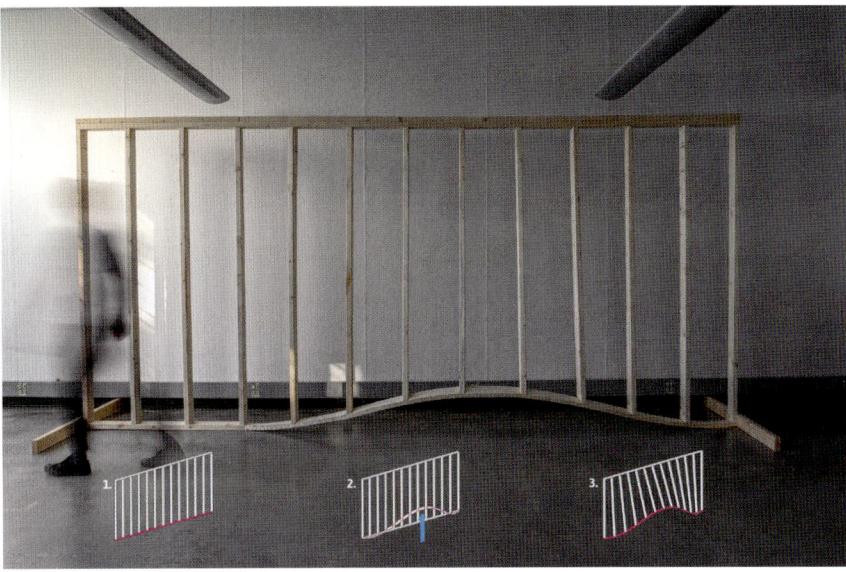

Zippered Wood is a designed contagion that is productively disruptive precisely because it simultaneously takes responsibility for the black box logics of material production and programming as it seamlessly adapts to standard construction practices. The project could be part of a larger strategy that radically changes the building industry's relationship with wood products and sustainable wood use. The goal of Zippered Wood is nothing short of affecting wooden architecture as profoundly as the straight 2x4 did over a century ago.

References

City of Vancouver. 2018. Statistic based on demolition permits issued by the City of Vancouver over the last six years.

Fulton, T. 2016. '2015 Demolition, Land-clearing, and Construction Waste Composition Monitoring Program', *Metro Vancouver*, http://www.metrovancouver.org/services/solid-waste/SolidWastePublications/2015DLCWasteCompositionMonitoring.pdf. (Accessed 16 February 2019)

Kennedy, S. and Violich, J. 2011. 'Soft Rockers', *Kennedy & Violich Architecture, Ltd.*, http://www.kvarch.net/projects/95 . (Accessed 18 February 2019)

Liu, Y., Pottman, H., Wallner, J., Yang, Y.-L. and Wang, W. 2006. 'Geometric Modeling with Conical Meshes and Developable Surfaces', *ACM Transactions on Graphics* 25(3), pp. 681-689.

Lockwood, J. 2018. *About Pygmy Boats,* https://www.pygmyboats.com/about-pygmy-boats.html. (Accessed 12 August 2018)

Nettelbladt, M. 2013. *The Geometry of Bending.* Stockholm: Mårten Nettelbladt.

Piker, D. 2013. 'Kangaroo: Form Finding with Computational Physics', *Computation Works: The Building of Algorithmic Thought – Architectural Design, Special Issue,* 83(2), pp. 136-7.

Rabinovich, M., Hoffmann, T. and Sorkine-Hornung O. 2018. 'Discrete Geodesic Nets for Modeling Developable Surfaces', *ACM Transaction on Graphics* 37(2), pp. 16:1-16:17.

Shindler, C. and Espinoza, M. 2011. 'ZipShape Mouldless Bending II: A Shift from Geometry to Experience', *Respecting Fragile Places: 29th aCAADe Conference Proceedings*, pp. 477-484.

WOOD VOLUME COMPARISONS
TYPICAL STUD WALL VERSUS ZIPPERED WOOD WALL

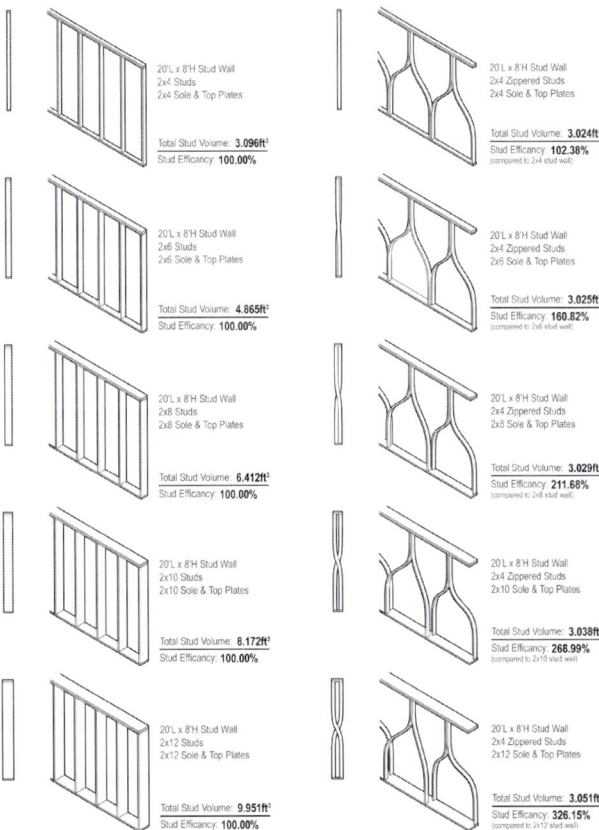

BIOCOMPOSITES FROM ANNUALLY RENEWABLE RESOURCES DISPLAYING VISION OF FUTURE SUSTAINABLE ARCHITECTURE
DESIGN AND FABRICATION OF TWO 1:1 DEMONSTRATORS

HANAA DAHY
BIOMAT AT ITKE- FACULTY OF ARCHITECTURE- UNIVERSITY OF STUTTGART /
FEDA (FACULTY OF ENGINEERING, DEPARTMENT OF ARCHITECTURE), AIN SHAMS UNIVERSITY
JAN PETRS / **PIOTR BASZYŃSKI**
BIOMAT AT ITKE- FACULTY OF ARCHITECTURE- UNIVERSITY OF STUTTGART

Introduction

The paper aims to demonstrate through two research pavilions sustainable alternatives to traditional building materials and methods. Natural materials were used, especially natural fibre reinforced polymer composites (NFRP) which are also referred to as *Biocomposites* (Dahy, 2019c) as a structural material in a non-linear design process in which the material defines the final design following the design philosophy: 'Materials as a design tool' (Dahy, 2019b).

The building industry consumes more than 40% of global resources, around 50% of non-recyclable waste, and more than 35% of energy. Until now, aggregate materials and concrete are the predominant materials used in building in the EU (UN Environment and International Energy Agency, 2017). These serious facts of the building industry highlight the crucial need to change to more sustainable methods of building in the near future.

In this paper, the potential to replace traditional materials comes from the field of fibre-reinforced polymer composites (FRP), composed of fibres and binders. In the last decade, fibre composites sparked interest mostly in aerospace, automotive or sports industries which later started to influence architecture in lightweight structures. Although fibre composites significantly reduce weight, they offer high structural performance. The fibres are mostly made of non-renewable fossil-based materials such as carbon or glass. In this paper, annually-renewable natural fibres applied as biocomposite are proposed in lightweight structural applications.

Biocomposites are materials where at least one component is biomass-based. The first applications in the building industry date back to the 1990s, mostly through Wood Polymer Composites (WPC) from wood and agricultural residues bonded by thermoplastics. By contrast, bio-composites with lignocellulose fibres were being used in the automotive industry by Henry Ford in the 1940s. Very few examples of using biocomposites as a structural component in the building industry have been developed. One example is a pedestrian bridge made by the Eindhoven University of Technology where the girder is a biocomposite of hemp and flax fibres attached to a Polylactic Acid (PLA)-based foam core (Blok et al., 2019).

In this paper, two approaches are presented through two different research 1:1 demonstrators: BioMat Pavilion 2018;

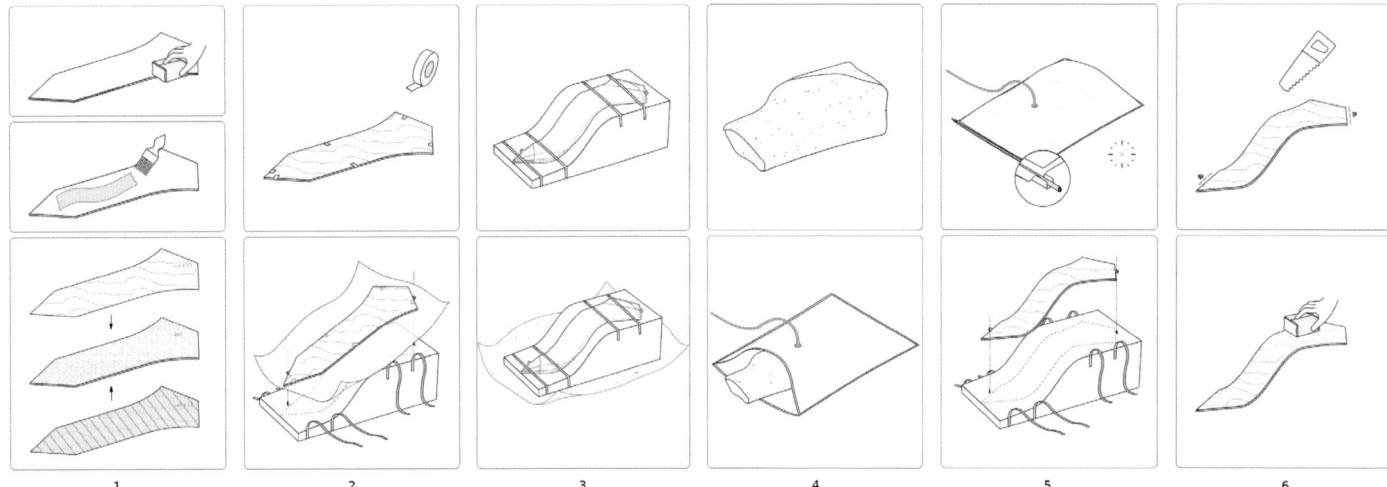

2

| 1 | 2 | 3 | 4 | 5 | 6 |

and Tailored Biocomposite Mock-up 2019. BioMat Pavilion 2018 is based on the use of sandwich elements where a flexible semi-elastic lignocellulosic fibre core from agricultural residues is sandwiched between semi-elastic lignocellulosic biocomposite fibreboards on both sides, reinforced by veneer. In the second example, The Tailored Biocomposite Mock-up 2019, continuous flax fibres were tailored using additive manufacturing techniques into the desired geometries before being impregnated by the resin binder.

Case Study 1: BioMat Pavilion 2018, Segmented Shell of Biocomposites and Wood

The task was to design the pavilion in semi-elastic lignocellulosic oriented fibreboards (Dahy, 2017; 2019a; 2019b). Architecture students within an academic design studio conceptualised their designs depending on three factors: geometrical variations; fabrication limitations; and mechanical properties of the newly developed biocomposite material.

Design Optimisation
The selected design was based on a complex 3D textile-like structure, chosen to represent new innovative design but mainly for structural reasons. The structure was composed of two interconnected layers that provide the spatial rigidity which was found necessary for the used material.

For such a complex structure, a parametric model was necessary. The structure of the pavilion consisted of 360 segments. The global design was designed according to size limits of flexible boards, mechanical properties and building site limitations. The model was also used for

smart numbering, structural optimisation and fabrication control. Through optimisation, only four moulds for vacuum-assisted fabrication described in figure 2 were used to produce the 360 different segments. The design was constantly updated by feedback from material tests and structural calculations provided through international cooperation with colleagues from the Technical University Eindhoven and KE institute of the University of Stuttgart.

Biocomposite Material Development
A semi-elastic lignocellulosic biocomposite, which was developed in a parallel research project lead by the first author, was used. It is a high-density fibreboard consisting of up to 90% annually renewable natural agricultural fibres like wheat straw. In parallel, a second lignocellulose biocomposite sandwich panel has been developed and applied. These fibreboards enabled the possibility of being freely adjusted into the desired double-curved geometry once both sides have been reinforced with a special wood-veneer type, namely 3D veneer, in a closed vacuum moulding process.

Fabrication
Off-site fabrication of large free-form biocomposite segments were mass-produced by the architectural students through a digital fabrication setup of CNC (Computer Numeric Control) – milling and closed-moulding using a vacuum appliance – of around 360 segments. Later, these items were assembled to form 120 larger individual elements, each composed of 3 segments. On-site assembly started by erecting three supporting laminated arches positioned precisely according to the 3D scan model of the site made in cooperation with a geodesic team from IIGS Institute at the University of Stuttgart. Successive 3D scanning of the site before,

1. Biomat Research Pavilion 2018.

2. Closed-moulding vacuuming process of c. 360 segments.

3. (1) Off-site fabrication of individual segments. (2) On-site connection of elements into 4 groups. (3) Lifting of interconnected groups on arches.

4. (1) Parametric model. (2) 3D scanned building site. (3) Comparison between 3D scanned completed pavilion and parametric model.

5. Biomat Research Pavilion 2018.

All photos: © BioMat at ITKE/ University of Stuttgart

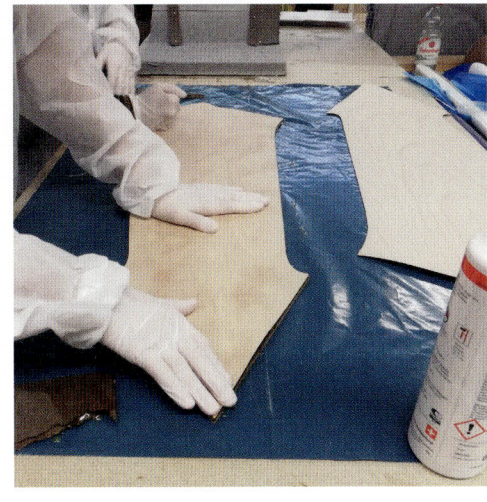

3

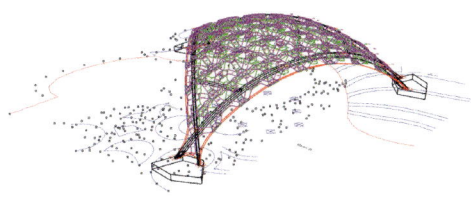
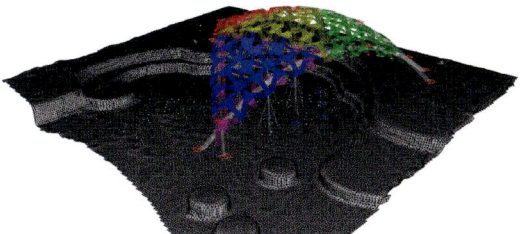
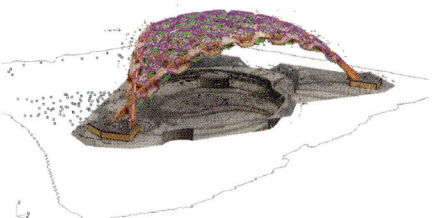

4

5

6

Like BioMat Pavilion 2018, this pavilion was integrated into a Design Studio course where 10 bachelor architecture students worked together for four months on design, testing, fabrication and erection of a small mock-up of BioMat 2019. From the start, the selected fabrication system was TFP (Tailored Fibre Placement) (Boehler et al., 2015) of annual industrial natural fibres like hemp or flax fibres.

Design Optimisation

The Mock-up is a single-curved canopy, generatively designed as a lightweight structure of 225cm high and 125cm width (Fig. 7). The initial geometry was form-found by Rhinoceros plugins Grasshopper + Galapagos + Millipede where the geometry performing the smallest deformation was chosen. The selected design was later topologically optimised to reduce the amount of unnecessary material to achieve optimum lightness. Parameters from the topology optimisations that took place using Matlab were later used as constraints for an agent-based system (code in processing using Plethora plugin) to simulate the optimum smooth direction of the continuous flax fibres. The different tracks coming from individual agents were post-processed into the mesh geometry and the most feasible design was selected accordingly. The whole design process is described in figure 8.

Biocomposite Material Development

The focus, in this case, was to develop and apply continuous natural fibres as a reinforcement agent for the developed biocomposite, instead of the short fibres used in the first case study. The selected fabrication method was Tailored Fibre Placement (TFP) of 1cm wide flax fibres and tape placement of 40cm wide flax tapes, where both fibre types were later impregnated with epoxy resin matrix in a closed vacuum resin process.

In this case, non-wood lignocellulose bast fibres were also used. Because of their annual renewability (each 90-100 days), comparable properties to glass fibres (GF), and minimum waste, they are considered a sustainable alternative to synthetic fibres. (Peças et al., 2018). The greatest advantage, however, is their significant low density and damping as well as vibration absorption properties in comparison to synthetic fibres such as carbon and glass fibres (CF) and (GF). For our development, flax fibres were selected due to their high tensile strength and availability in central Europe.

throughout and after erection enabled guaranteed high precision of the arches to reach the accuracy for assembling the 120 biocomposite elements. The elements were first interconnected through plywood plates and bolts into four triangular groups on the ground, then lifted on to the beams and fixed in position as shown in figure 3. After completion, repetitive 3D scanning took place and was compared with the parametric model (Fig. 4). The differences between the digital model and after-erection were in the allowed tolerance range.

Results and Reflection

The selected global design and the applied connection system allowed the possibility of reusing the individual elements for other applications, for example façade elements and shading structures. This was set as the main criterion at the beginning of the designing process to reach a closed-material cycle. After the completion of the pavilion (Figs 5, 6), it stayed under real weather conditions for six months which proved the applicability of the concept. The biocomposite was able to meet the structural requirements in terms of stiffness and weathering. However, the high quality of fabrication, especially coating of individual components, was crucial. Future research will investigate the long-term behaviour (degradation, moisture, etc.) and further automatisation of the fabrication and assembly. A high focus of the design in a similar lifetime application will be on how to design the connections to enable quicker re-assembly and stable weathering resistance.

In fibre composites, especially upon application of continuous fibres, the orientation and position of the fibres in the composite are crucial. Therefore the TFP method was specially selected. TFP is a digitally-controlled embroidery technology that enables the fabrication of complex textile preforms. Individual continuous fibres were stitched to a matrix according to a predefined vector pattern that followed an unrolled surface of the desired geometry. This allowed the fabrication of precise 2D and 3D fibre structures with an accuracy of fibres up to ±0.3mm.

Fabrication and Erection
Fabrication was divided into three stages as shown in figure 9: TFP fabrication, mould preparation, and placement on the mould with vacuum assistance.

For most of the fibre composites using placement methods, the mould is needed. For the mock-up, a reusable mould was developed. The mould components were CNC cut and later assembled to a waffle structure, which saved material consumption in comparison with the most common mould types.

The mock-up structure consisted of four layers of TFP preforms. The initial geometry had to be divided into pieces of no more than 1.0 x 1.4m, due to the limitations of the TFP machine. The layers were designed to overlap to avoid any cracks on the edges between the preforms. For every single preform, a Computer-Aided Design (CAD) model was generated for the tailoring path, as shown in the last two pictures of figure 8, in cooperation with the Institute of Aircraft Design (IFB) at the University of Stuttgart. The ready-made preforms were afterwards impregnated with epoxy resin then moulded in a closed vacuum-assisted moulding process. After the structure was removed, additional reinforcement from two layers of TFP preforms was applied. After the curing time, final post-processing took place including sanding and coating.

Results
The mock-up showcases automatised fabrication of a canopy structure from continuous natural fibres using the TFP technique. This was investigated as a single canopy with no connections. The fabrication method seems very feasible for the production of precise shell or panel structures with controlled fibre-orientation according to

7

6. Detail of connection.

7. Tailored Biocomposite Mock-up.

All photos: © BioMat at ITKE/University of Stuttgart

predominant tension forces. In future research, the mould will be optimised to minimise the amount of resin used and to eliminate manual moulding processes.

Outcome and Discussion

Both demonstrators express new aesthetic architectural features of bio-based materials using digital manufacturing technologies and generative design methods. The research showcases alternative sustainable material selections when even wood can be partially replaced. Contrary to wood, biocomposite can achieve very complex structures with minimum waste from fabrication.

Both pavilions showed different design and fabrication methods that followed the philosophy 'Materials as a design tool'. A different scale of the pavilion is not considered in the comparison. The goal of the Biomat pavilion 2018 was to fabricate and erect a reusable segmented shell. The design was influenced by the size of lignocellulosic composite fibreboards which could be fabricated under limited dimensions during their production. Compared to the use of continuous natural fibres, the fibreboards are not feasible to use over the whole structure without any segmentation. Segmentation needs connections, holes for bolts have to be optimised so that they do not compromise the integrity of the composite in ways that can have a negative influence on, for example, its humidity protection. The advantages in comparison to the mock-up are the elimination of big moulds and a relatively simple fabrication set-up which doesn't depend on non-standard fabrication techniques like TFP. The Tailored Biocomposite Mock-up 2019 focuses more on the digital fabrication of the canopy

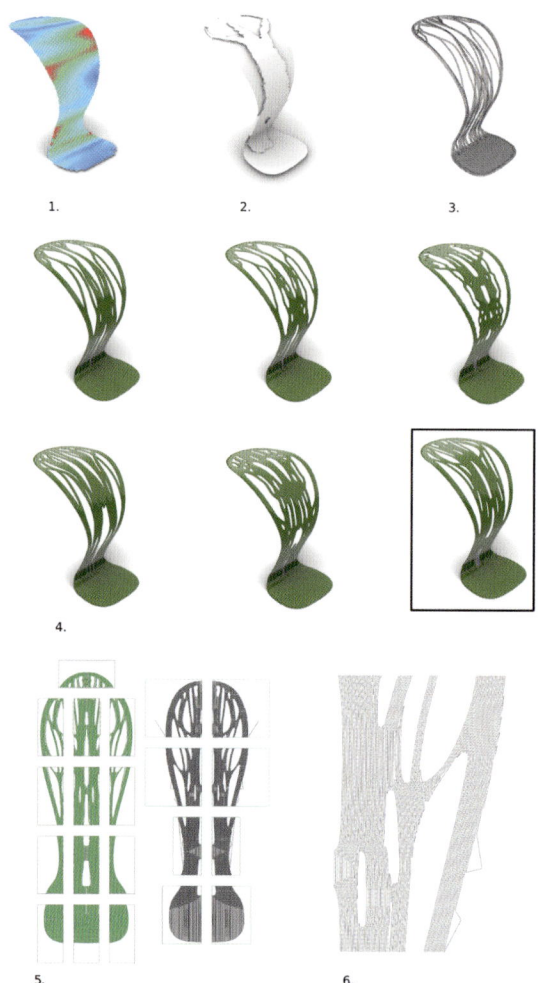

8

1.   2.   3.

4.

5.   6.

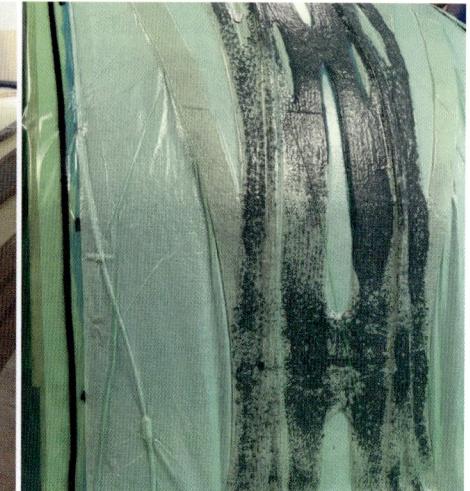

without any segmentation. The used TFP technique allows precise control of the direction and position of the fibres which positively influence load distribution, material efficiency and weight. TFP minimises the amount of redundancy which, in comparison to CNC cutting of fibreboards, is significantly smaller. TFP preforms allow highly flexible bending in both directions which allows a greater range of possible geometries compared to fibreboards reinforced by 3D veneer which can be shaped only in one direction. The mock-up uses more digital fabrication which significantly reduces the manufacture effort and time. Generally, it is not possible to state which fabrication method is better, it depends on the application, scale, and available tools.

The integration of sustainable approaches, which are already in architectural education, is important for the next generation of architects who will have to deal with alternative materials, digitally-driven fabrication and effective life cycles of future buildings. The selected methodology, 'Materials as a design tool', can help students experience the whole architectural process from design to completion within a very short time, which is different from classical architectural educational models. In both case-studies, architecture students practiced a different philosophy for the design process, physically experimenting up to erection within the same semester and using newly developed alternative biocomposite materials.

Acknowledgments

The authors would like to thank all students, employees, technicians, and agencies who participated in both projects.

The BioMat Pavilion 2018 was the result of cooperation between around 40 architecture students of (Flexible Forms) Design Studio(WS17/18 and SS18) supported by University of Stuttgart and the Baden-Württemberg Foundation, financially supported by German Agency for Renewable Resources (FNR) under the Ministry of Food and Agriculture (BMEL), scientifically supported by Fraunhofer-Institut für Holzforschung (Fraunhofer WKI), and industrial partners Mathias Stange ETS and Profine GmbH in the framework of the research Project (BioProfile) FKZ 22021516 with assistance of BioMat employees including Michaela Mey. International collaboration with the Technical University Eindhoven in the Netherlands (TU/e) – Department of Built Environment (Prof. Dr-Ing. Patrick Teuffel, Arjan Habraken, and Derk Bos). The local collaboration took place with: Institute of Construction and Structural Design (KE, Faculty 02: Civil and Environmental Engineering) - Prof. Urlike Kuhlmann and Janusch Töpler; Institute of Engineering Geodesy (IIGS, Faculty 06: Aerospace Engineering and Geodesy) - Prof. Volker Schwieger and Gabriel Kerekes. Wooden beams were fabricated and supported by Burgbacher Holztechnologie GmbH with the assistance of Mr. Steffen Haller.

The Tailored Biocomposite mock-up was a result of cooperation between: 10 architectural students of (Pavilion Design and Fabrication: Multifunctional Biocomposite Building Elements) Design Studio in SS 2019; Institute of Aircraft Design (Faculty 06: Institute of Aircraft Design) – Prof. Dr-Ing. Peter Middendorf, Dr Stefan Carosella and Benjamin Wolfinger; Czech Technical University in Prague (CTU, Department of Mechanics, Faculty of Civil Engineering and Experimental Centre, Faculty of Civil Engineering); Dr Jan Novák and Marek Tyburec.

Natural Flax fibres were provided by company Groupe Depestele. EcoTechnilin provided natural flax tapes.

For both projects, the authors would like to thank the technical support from Andreas Kulla, Michael Preisack, Michael Schneider and Michael Tondera. And Frieder Schwarz from Hexion Inc., who provided resins and weathering resistant coatings.

The project was partially supported by the Deutsche Forschungsgemeinschaft (DFG, German Research Foundation) under Germany's Excellence Strategy EXC 2120/1-390831618.

References

Blok, R., Smits, J., Gkaidatzis, R. and Teuffel, P. 2019. 'Bio-Based Composite Footbridge: Design, Production and In Situ Monitoring', *Structural Engineering International*, 29(3), pp. 453-465. (doi: 10.1080/10168664.2019.1608137)

Bohler, P., Carosella, S., Goetz, C. and Middendorf, P. 2015. 'Path Definition for Tailored Fiber Placement Structures Using Numerical Reverse Draping Approach', *Key Engineering Materials*, 651–653, pp. 446-451. (doi: 10.4028/www.scientific.net/KEM.651-653.446)

Dahy, H. 2017. 'Biocomposite materials based on annual natural fibres and biopolymers – Design, fabrication and customized applications in architecture', *Construction and Building Materials*, 147, pp. 212-220. (doi: 10.1016/j.conbuildmat.2017.04.079)

Dahy, H. 2019a. 'Efficient Fabrication of Sustainable Building Products from Annually Generated Non-wood Cellulosic Fibres and Bioplastics with Improved Flammability Resistance', *Waste and Biomass Valorization*, 10, pp. 1167–1175. (doi: 10.1007/s12649-017-0135-3)

Dahy, H. 2019b. '"Materials as a design tool" design philosophy applied in three innovative research pavilions out of sustainable building materials with controlled end-of-life scenarios', *Buildings*, 9(3), p. 64. (doi: 10.3390/buildings9030064)

Dahy, H. 2019c. 'Natural fibre-reinforced polymer composites (NFRP) fabricated from lignocellulosic fibres for future sustainable architectural applications, case studies: Segmented-shell construction, acoustic panels, and furniture', *Sensors*, 19(3), p.738. (doi: 10.3390/s19030738)

Peças, P., Carvalho, H., Salman, H. and Leite, M. 2018. 'Natural Fibre Composites and Their Applications: A Review', *Journal of Composites Science*, 2(4), p. 66. (doi: 10.3390/jcs2040066)

UN Environment and International Energy Agency. 2017. *Towards a zero-emission, efficient, and resilient buildings and construction sector. Global Status Report 2017*, https://www.worldgbc.org/sites/default/files/UNEP%20188_GABC_en%20%28web%29.pdf. (Accessed 23 December 2019)

8. Design process:
(1) Basic shell optimisation.
(2) Topology optimisation of a single-curved canopy.
(3) Generated structure by agents attracted by results from topology optimisation.
(4) Selection of the final design from generated variants. (5) CAD paths of individual preforms.
(6) Detail of path for tailoring.

9. Fabrication: (1) TFP preforms. (2) Mould preparation. (3) Vacuum-assisted moulding process.

All photos: © BioMat at ITKE/University of Stuttgart.

CELLULOSIC BIOCOMPOSITES FOR SUSTAINABLE MANUFACTURING

STYLIANOS DRITSAS / YADUNUND VIJAY / SAMUEL HALIM / RYAN TEO / NARESH SANANDIYA / JAVIER G. FERNANDEZ
SINGAPORE UNIVERSITY OF TECHNOLOGY AND DESIGN

Overview

The aim of this research work is to create a general-purpose manufacturing technology considering foremost its sustainability characteristics. Our approach is bio-inspired in that we attempt to replicate some of the principles of natural synthesis, characterised by exclusive use of locally available resources, utilising material ingredients which are often insignificant by themselves, performing assembly of complex hierarchical structures in low-energy environments and producing artefacts integrally embedded within their ecological cycles.

We implement those principles with the development of a new family of biocomposites combining cellulose and chitin, the first and second most abundant biopolymers on earth, and assembling spatial artefacts by selective deposition of materials through additive manufacturing at room temperature. The technology developed can produce large-scale objects at low-cost that are fully bio-sourced and biodegradable. Applications investigated within the building industry range from: interiors such as furniture and fittings; to construction such as insulated panels, pre-finished building members and recyclable moulds; even to restoration of timber elements and ornamentations in heritage buildings.

Objectives

Biological polymers produced by plants and animals are in the realm of billions of tonnes annually. A key feature of biological materials is in their innate embedding within ecological cycles. This offers an untapped opportunity for a fundamentally sustainable approach to manufacturing, if we manage to control their synthesis and assembly.

The constraints guiding the design of our bio-material process include: (a) use of ingredients ubiquitous in every natural ecosystem aiming to promote regional as opposed to transcontinental production and transport; (b) ensuring available material component sourcing at low-cost from renewable resources and even industrial by-products or waste recovery, aiming to enable scalability for general manufacturing that competes with commodity plastics and potentially supports circular models of production and consumption; (c) low-energy fabrication process at room temperature without thermoforming or high-pressure processes to achieve a small environmental footprint in production; and (d) ecologically embedded material synthesis avoiding material transformation by chemical modification, as for each intervention an additional reversing step is required and one away from natural recovery.

1

Materials

Cellulose is the most abundant biological material on earth (Reiterer, 1999). It is the main component of timber and plant matter in general. Chitin is also a highly abundant bio-material encountered mainly in the animal kingdom, in the exoskeleton of arthropods such as shrimps, crabs and lobsters as well as in insects including bees, grasshoppers and maggots. Despite their molecular similarity and being some of the most common bio-polymers on earth, cellulose and chitin rarely appear in the same organism.

Composition of these two ingredients gives rise to a family of lightweight biocomposites named fungal-like adhesive materials (FLAM), after oomycotes or egg-shaped fungi, a species of eukaryotic organisms, historically misclassified as fungi, whose cell walls contain cellulose and chitin. Experiments with different ratios of the two components were performed to determine the best mechanical but also rheologic parameters suitable for manufacture. One may consider cellulose as the fibrous reinforcement within a chitinous matrix in a conventional composite materials sense. Therefore, too high cellulose to chitin ratio produces viscuous materials which are difficult to extrude and dry to become brittle, while too high chitin produces materials that slump too much and shrink uncontrollably. Surprisingly, the same ratio as in the cell-walls of oomycota (1:8) produced both strong, extrudable and controllable composites. A unique aspect of FLAM is their ability to adhere to themselves even after drying which allows for infinitely restorable objects. Before drying, they can also be rehydrated and reused. To protect them from water after curing, they require coating like natural timbers.

FLAMs can be produced from either industrial grade, pure cellulose, used as fillers or wood fibre waste from timber manufacturing. The properties of FLAM (370 kg/m3 density | 0.26GPa Young's modulus) are in the range of high-density synthetic foams, such as machinable polyurethanes, and low-density natural timbers such as balsa and cedar. Using pure cellulose, the material appears as compressed paper while using wood fibre, its appearance is similar to particle boards. However, unlike common cellulosic materials and composites such as cellophane, plywood, particle boards and wood-plastics, FLAMs involve no petrochemical adhesives or toxic chemical substances such as strong solvents. In addition, unlike conventional 3D printing materials such as wood particulate plastics and bio-plastics such as PLA, it is 100% biodegradable without requiring specialised composting or recovery processes. In the eyes of nature, FLAMs are no different from mushrooms or timbers. Additional information pertaining the materials science of FLAMs, including extensive study of material characterisations, was first presented by Sanandiya et al. (2018), and precursor research on chitinous biocomposites – on which this project builds – by Fernandez (2009) and Fernandez and Ingber (2014).

Manufacturing

Fabricating with organic composites is vastly different from working with inorganic or inert materials such as plastics or concrete. Foremost it requires understanding and addressing issues which spring from the innate variability of its constituent components. Just as no two pieces of wood are ever the same, inevitable variation of its cellulosic content produces material property changes, such as viscosity for instance, which affect both assembly as well as curing. Moreover, the composite in its wet state is an adhesive which makes it very difficult to handle as it is highly tacky and shear thinning. Therefore, co-evolution of the material formulation alongside its manufacturing method was integral.

The digital fabrication system is comprised of an industrial robot equipped with a volumetric auger dispenser for sealants and adhesives, a bulk material supply (15 litre batches) and a programmable control logic controller for flow rate modulation. Details on the setup are presented by Dritsas et al. (2018). Early implementations follow the canonical material extrusion AM principles, where objects are built by filament layers arranged vertically, not unlike Fused Deposition Modelling of rapid prototyping or Direct Ink Writing of tissue engineering. The material is dispensed as a viscous paste and fuses with consecutive layers.

3D printing FLAM is a low-energy process compared with FDM and SLS as it does not require thermal input. Filaments are directly printed at room temperature and by evaporation at ambient conditions water is removed from the colloid as objects transform to rigid solids. Working with a broad range of nozzle diameters (1 to 7mm) motivated departing from conventional three-axis printing to leverage production time and resolution. We investigated fusion of fabrication paradigms, namely five-axis dispensing to coat over scaffolds, subtractive techniques to introduce features below the nozzle diameter, and forming operations displacing material while in a wet-state with net-zero material change.

Space-filling algorithms were developed to maximise surface to volume ratios for accelerating evaporative hardening. Production of large objects in a single printing

1. Natural composite pillar overall photography and details. Photo: Frank Pinckers.

2. Fungus-like adhesive material with cellulosic waste from timber manufacturing at wet-state.

3. Detail of large-diameter nozzle extrusion in canonical 3-axis mode.

2

3

session gave its place to understanding how to segment for improved throughput: as the process is not bottlenecked by thermo-dispensing such as in large diameter FDM, printing can be much faster, for example 50mm/sec at 7mm diameter, while curing takes place separately. It became evident that it was thus more meaningful to consider scaling in terms of time, within a heterogenous sequence of production steps, instead of targeting physical scale using additive manufacturing exclusively.

Challenges

FLAMs are suspensions of fibres (chitin to cellulose 1:8) in an organic matrix comprised of chitosan and water (3%). The uncured composite's properties are in the class of non-Newtonian viscoelastic materials. The material behaviour, both during extrusion and while curing, is highly non-linear as properties including density, viscosity and elasticity depend on both the shear force applied during extrusion as well as time. Challenges pertaining to fabrication with shrinkage anisotropy being the highest (5% along the extrusion direction, 12% in the transverse and 32% vertically), are presented in detail by Dritsas et al. (2019).

To overcome these issues, instead of a mechanistic, such as transient multi-physics computational fluid dynamics, we employed experimental modelling methods leveraging the ease of 3D printing to collect data via optical metrology and 3D scanning, for statistical analysis. This approach allowed us to absorb the variability of controllable but also the uncontrollable design parameters related to material and environmental conditions and to bypass the highly involved development of an analytical CFD model which would incorporate material state transition, moisture convection-diffusion, and transient forces affecting the 3D printed geometry.

Control of the extrusion process parameters such as the robot's feed rate, material flow rate and layer height, presented by Vijay et al. (2019), were modelled through a face-centred Central Composite Design of Experiment (Montgomery, 2009) to associate the resulting filament dimensions and their mechanical properties. The model is expressed as a set of multiple quadratic equations that capture not only the main parameters but also all the possible combinations of their interactions. To derive desirable operating points from the response surface models, we employed multi-response optimisation methodology (Derringer and Suich, 1980).

Interestingly, the study shows that we can retain constant filament dimensions whilst controlling their tensile strength dynamically via motion-flow rate modulation. This implies that the material process has innate functionally-graded characteristic potential, beyond conventional geometric density modulation by 3D printing, such as variably-sized spatial lattices. Non-linear regression models using machine-learning techniques were employed to relate notional-to-resultant geometries and enable prediction-correction of object deformation during curing. We call the process pre-set modelling which is equivalent to elongating structural members in building design in anticipation of progressive compression deformation during construction.

Evaluation

The necessity for statistical data to develop predictive models resulted in numerous early prototypes of simple measurable geometries. Single filaments were printed to assess filament profile uniformity against feed and flow rates; pairs of adjacent filaments determined the requisite overlapping fraction sufficient for adhesion; straight walls measured vertical compaction rate and intralayer fusion; square profiles determined shrinkage anisotropy; and surfaces were printed to collect curvature and deflection features.

The first large-scale prototype was an airfoil (NACA 0015) printed in two halves (50% infill, 1 hour printing time each), fused and coated with the same material and hand polished (1.2m length, 5kg weight). Its objective was to demonstrate the versatility of the material used for 3D printing, its self-adhesive properties past curing, and compatibility with conventional casting and wood-working techniques. While the material's surface characteristics are not suitable for airfoil applications, it may be an alternative to current core designs using natural materials such as balsa.

To demonstrate the free-form fabrication capability, material strength, assess the reliability of the extrusion system and understand the workflow, we developed an architectural-scale prototype pillar of 0.6-1.0m diameter and 5m height. The form was split into 50 vertical segments of 250mm height, taking 30-120min each to print. Segments are comprised of two adjacent filaments with wall thickness of 25mm. Alternative wall structures were tested such as incorporating buttress fins or an internal web pattern for increased stiffness but the double filament wall design was the most time efficient. The amount of time required for printing was 60 hours with total wet material weight c. 480kg and cured weight 105kg. The cost of materials was c. £220 | £2.1/kg.

4

5

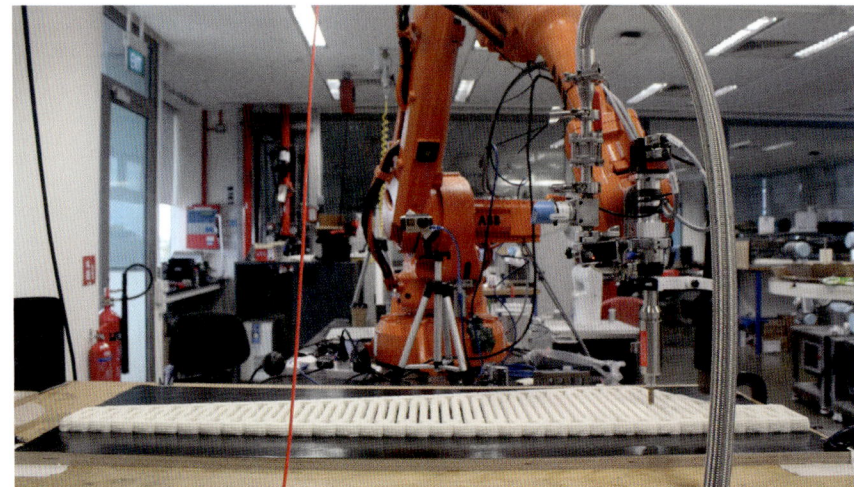

6

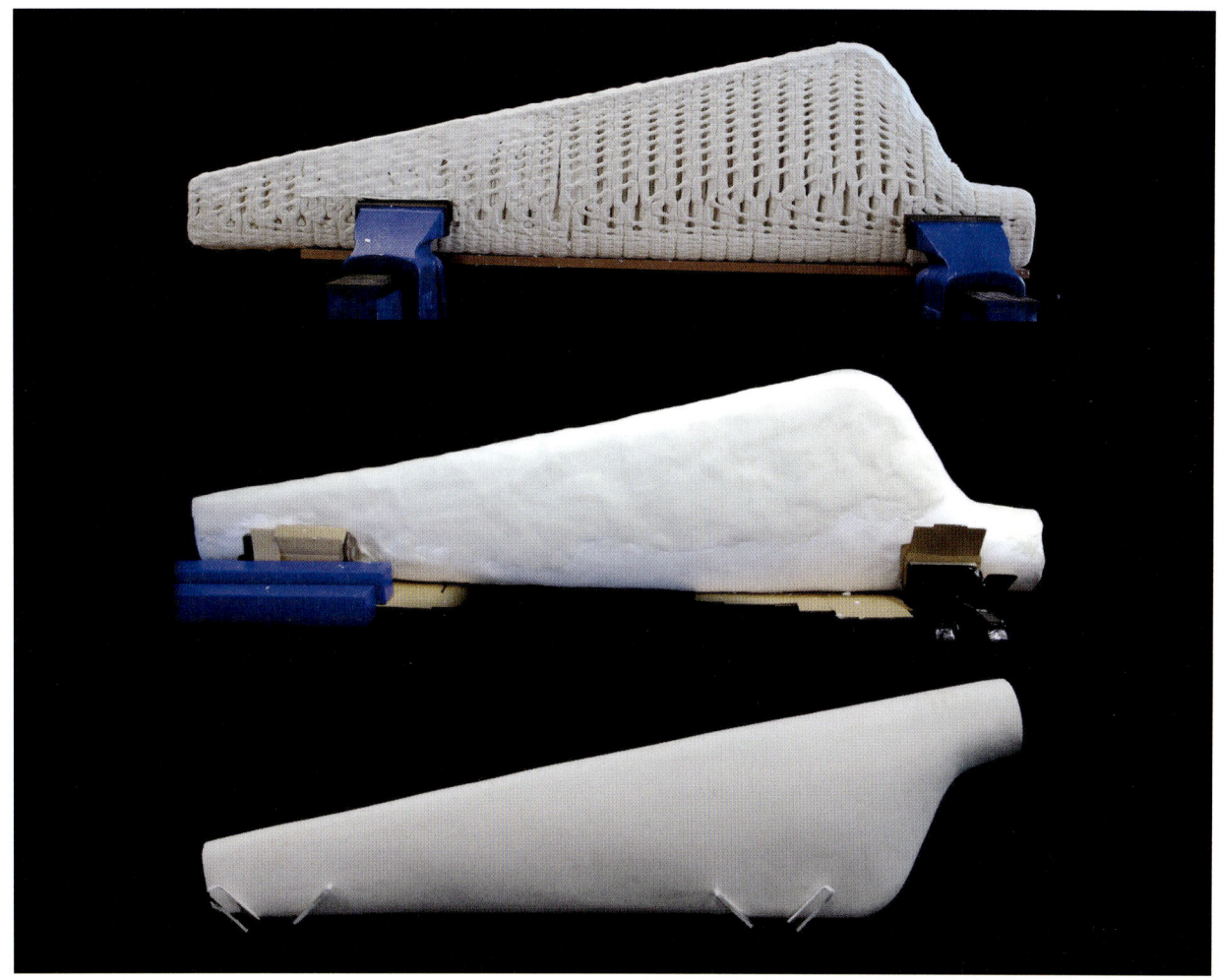

7

4. Prediction correction
non-linear regression
modeling for shrinkage
compensation.

5. Prediction correction
non-linear regression
modelling for shrinkage
compensation.

6. Printing half of the airfoil
prototype required
approximately one hour.

7. Two halves bonded with
FLAM, coated and sanded
using woodworking
methods.

Apart from human-related operating errors that required recycling the material and reprinting two segments, the process was highly robust. The predictive-corrective models used to adjust notional geometry to account for shrinkage gave overall good results, but additional work is required to reduce error over the diameter of segments to be under 1% or 5mm. Nevertheless, if segments are assembled within the first 48 hours after 3D printing while the material is still moist, parts can be fused seamlessly. The artefact suggests direct applications for non-load bearing interior fittings as well as an approach for free-form structural element mould-making, perhaps even pre-finished as it can be easily sanded and/or coated.

Conclusions

Additive manufacturing became the dominant paradigm during the past few decades representing the future of industrial production (Thompson et al., 2016) and even building construction. Despite unmatched benefits such as rapid design-to-production, capability for free-form geometry, design customisation and efficient material use (Tofail et al., 2018), challenges in materiality, scalability, sustainability, affordability and reliability still persist (Royal Academy of Engineers, 2013). Sustainability in additive manufacturing (Baumers et al., 2011) is a domain that only recently came to the foreground (Gebler et al., 2014).

We presented a new technology addressing several of those challenges. Its significance is in an approach which departs from optimising resource uptake within current production workflows or developing eco-friendly materials that suit existing modes of production, such as injection moulding and 3D printing PLA, currently the most popular bioplastic sourced from agricultural food sources which nevertheless requires specialised composting recovery.

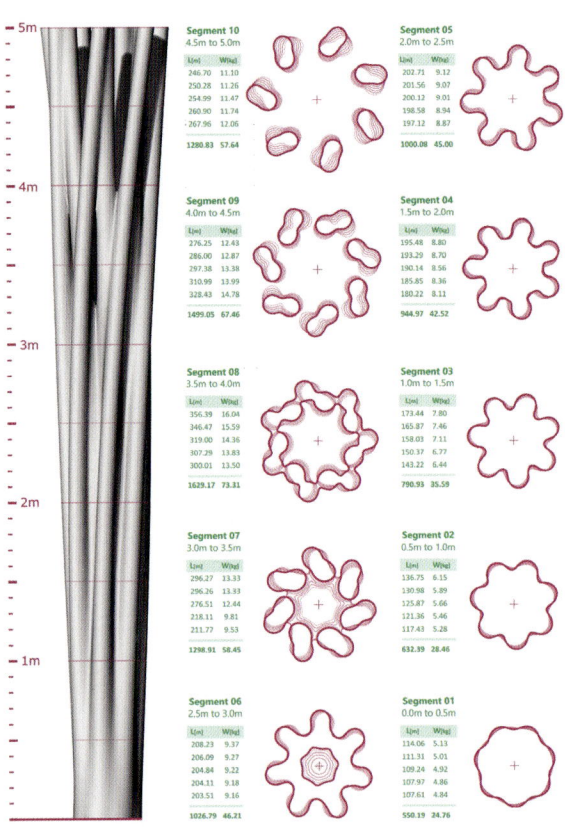

Instead, the work is informed by biology and the life-sciences where materials are understood as being embedded within their production and consumption cycles. FLAMs are produced by widely available natural bio-materials: both cellulose and chitin are sourced from waste of the timber and fishing industries and most importantly they remain unmodified, meaning they are natural. Nevertheless, precisely because they were not designed with priority on ease of manufacture, they require development of a specialised approach for their fabrication and control.

Digital methods of modelling and fabrication offer a level of precision that was impossible to achieve in the past. Additional research work is currently underway in both material characterisation including thermal, acoustical and fire properties, as well as process-control simulation and optimisation to enable adoption and use in construction and general-manufacturing. We believe the use of ubiquitous natural materials and digital fabrication may offer an environmentally-benign manufacturing and design paradigm towards a circular and sustainable society.

8

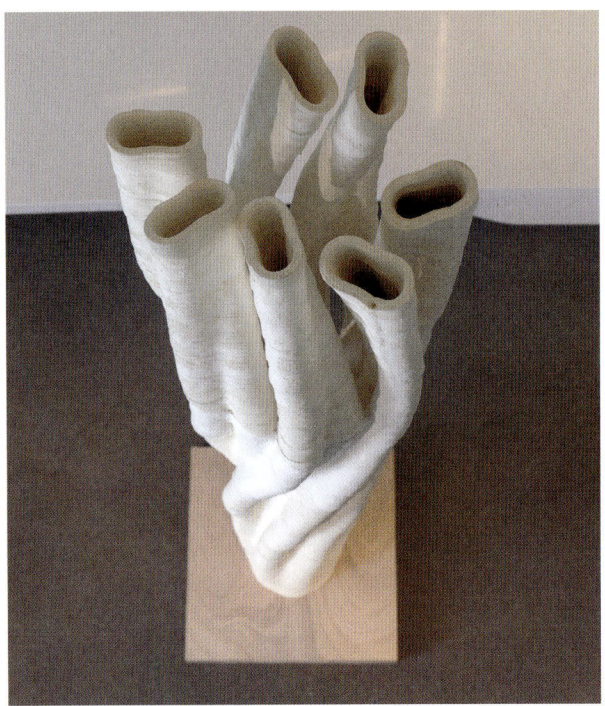

9

8. The design of the natural composite pillar is comprised of seven arcs fused using implicit surface distance field methodology producing a geometrically- and topologically-complex surface model.

9. Prototype of natural composite pillar reinforced with convetional rebar cage and cast with concrete.

10. Natural composite pillar. Photo: Frank Pinckers.

Acknowledgements

The research was supported by the SUTD-MIT International Design Centre (IDG21600101), the National Additive Manufacturing Innovation Cluster (NAMIC2016026), Digital Manufacturing and Design Centre (RGDM1620303).

References

Baumers, M., Tuck, C., Bourell, D.L., Sreenivasan, R. and Hague, R. 2011. 'Sustainability of additive manufacturing: measuring the energy consumption of the laser sintering process', Proceedings of the Institution of Mechanical Engineers, Part B: *Journal of Engineering Manufacture*, 225(12), pp. 2228-2239. (doi: 10.1177/0954405411406044)

Derringer, G. and Suich, R. 1980. 'Simultaneous Optimization of Several Response Variables', *Journal of Quality Technology*, 12(4), pp. 214-219.

Dritsas, S., Halim, E.P.S., Vijay, Y., Sanandya, G.N. and Fernandez, G. J. 2018. 'Digital Fabrication with Natural Composites', *Journal of Construction Robotics*, 2, pp. 41-51.

Dritsas, S., Vijay, Y., Halim, E.P.S., Teo, R., Sanandya, N. and Fernandez, J. 2019. 'Additive Manufacturing with Natural Composites', in *Intelligent & Informed, Proceedings of the 24th International Conference of the Association for Computer-Aided Architectural Design Research in Asia (CAADRIA)*, Vol. 2, Hong Kong: CAADRIA, pp. 263-272.

Fernandez, J. G., Mills, C. A. and Samitier, J. 2009. 'Complex Microstructured 3D Surfaces Using Chitosan Biopolymer', *Small*, 5(5), pp. 614-620. (doi: 10.1002/smll.200800907)

Fernandez, J. G. and Ingber, D. E. 2014. 'Manufacturing of Large-Scale Functional Objects Using Biodegradable Chitosan Bioplastic', *Macromolecular Materials and Engineering*, 299(8), pp. 932-938. (doi: 10.1002/mame.201300426)

Gebler, M., Anton, J.M., Uiterkamp, S. and Visser, C. 2014. 'A global sustainability perspective on 3D printing technologies', *Energy Policy*, 74(C), pp. 158-167.

Montgomery, C.D. 2009. *Introduction to Statistical Quality Control*, (sixth edition), Hoboken, N.J: Wiley.

Reiterer, A., Lichtenegger, H., Tschegg, S., Fratzl, P. 1999. 'Experimental evidence for a mechanical function of the cellulose microfibril angle in wood cell walls', *Philosophical Magazine* A, 79(9), pp. 2173-2184.

Sanandiya, N., Dimopoulou, M., Vijay, Y., Dritsas, S. and Fernandez, J. 2018. 'Large-Scale Additive Manufacturing with Bioinspired Cellulosic Materials', *Scientific Reports*, 8: p. 8642. (doi: 10.1038/s41598-018-26985-2)

Thompson, M.K., Moroni, G., Vaneker, T., Fadel, G., Campbell, I., Gibson, I., Bernard, A., Schulz, J., Graf, P., Ahuja, B. and Martina, F. 2016. 'Design for Additive Manufacturing: Trends, opportunities, considerations, and constraints', *CIRP Annals*, 65(2), pp. 737-760.

The Royal Academy of Engineering. 2013. 'Additive manufacturing: Opportunities and Constraints'. Available from *The Royal Academy of Engineering*, https://www.raeng.org.uk/publications/reports/additive-manufacturing. (Accessed 23 December 2019).

Tofail, S.A.M., Koumoulos, E., Bandyopadhyay, A., Bose, S., O'Donoghue, L. and Charitidis, C. 2018. 'Additive Manufacturing: Scientific and Technological Challenges, Market uptake and Opportunities', *Materials Today*, 21(1), pp. 22-37.

Vijay, Y., Sanadiya, G.N., Dritsas, S. and Fernandez, J. 2019. 'Control of Process Settings for Large-Scale Additive Manufacturing with Sustainable Natural Composites', *Journal of Mechanical Design, American Society of Mechanical Engineers*, 141(8), pp. 081701 (doi: 10.1115/1.4042624).

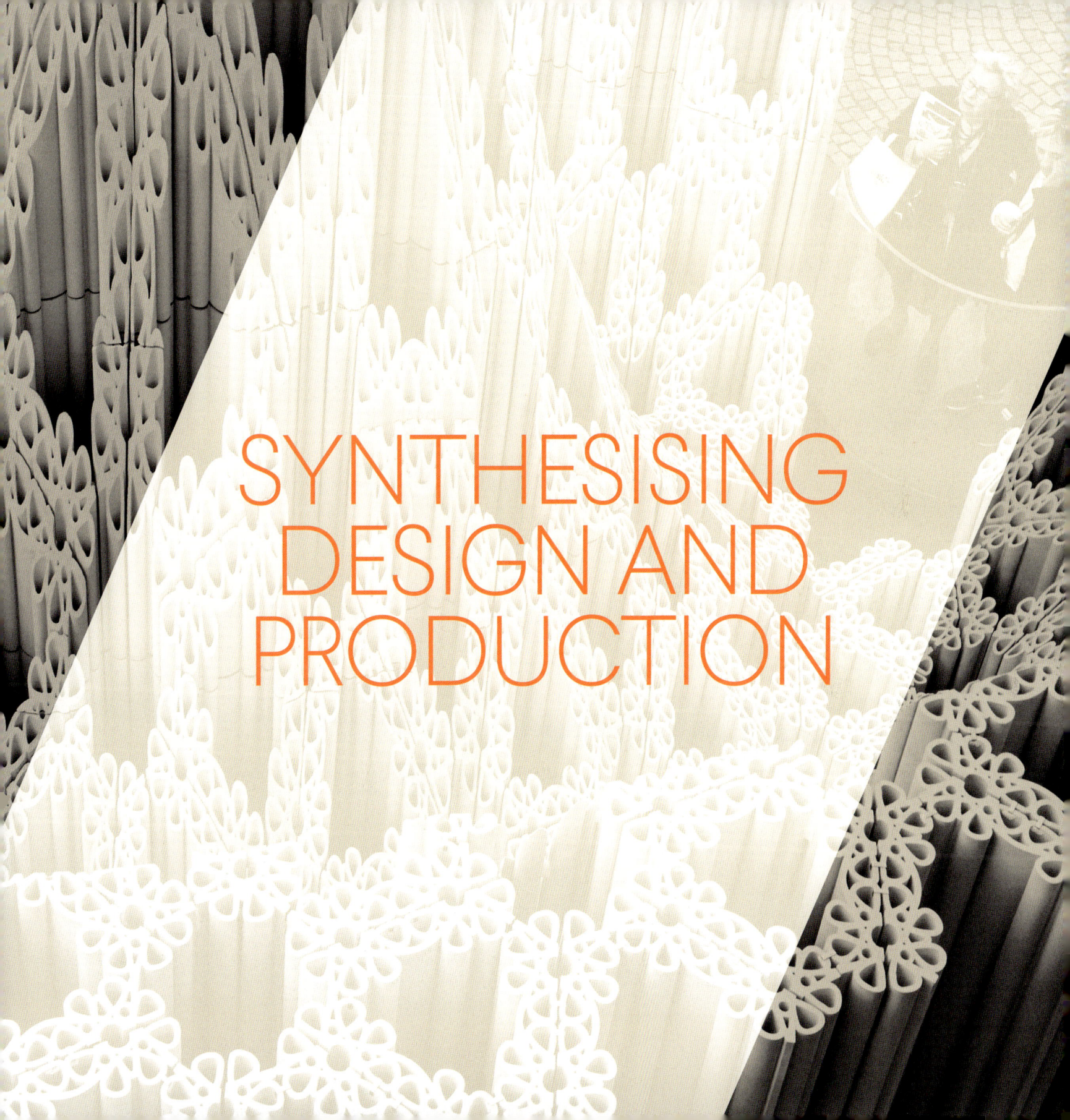

SYNTHESISING DESIGN AND PRODUCTION

KUWAIT INTERNATIONAL AIRPORT TERMINAL 2
ENGINEERING AND FABRICATION OF A COMPLEX PARAMETRIC MEGASTRUCTURE

LUCIO BLANDINI / GUIDO NIERI
WERNER SOBEK AG

Introduction

In order to increase the capacity of Kuwait International Airport, a new state-of-the-art terminal building is currently under construction (Fig. 1). The roof of the new terminal was conceived as a continuous free-form shell structure with a surface of approximately 320,000m² (Josefsson, 2013). This shell is – in conjunction with a pre-stressed concrete arch system – the terminal's principal structure. It is also one of the driving architectural elements of the building. This functional interdependence between structure and design differs significantly from the practice typical for projects characterised by a complex iconic geometry, namely, that of treating the main structure and the cladding as separate entities (Winterstetter et al., 2015).

Reinforced concrete shells are an excellent tool to realise fascinating wide-span structures with a complex geometry. Activating their membrane behaviour through the definition of a shape that harmonises in the best possible manner with the acting forces allows for large open spaces with a minimum use of material. In the past engineers like Nervi, Torroja, Candela and Isler successfully explored the structural and creative potential of shells. However, given

the time-consuming formwork and in situ works usually required, cost turned out to be a critical point for these types of structures. Extensive research was carried out over the past decades, among others at the Universities of Stuttgart (Sobek, 1987; Bögle et al., 2003), Delft (Schipper, 2015), and Graz (Peters et al., 2017) to reduce formwork costs and to allow for a resurgence of these impressive structures – the overall objective being to avoid intensive formwork installation by using innovative fabrication methods. Despite these efforts, there are only a few projects (for instance Stuttgart's new railway station S21 (Blandini et al., 2011) that have gone beyond an experimental character (Kovaleva et al., 2019; Popescu et al., 2019). Kuwait International Airport Terminal 2 defines a turning point with regard to the large-scale use of wide-span reinforced concrete shells. As described in the present paper, the extensive use of prefabrication and design-to-fabrication processes made it possible to build geometrically complex reinforced concrete shells without complex formwork or expensive scaffolding systems.

The authors of the present paper were in charge of engineering the roof structures and façades after the tender phase (Munro et al., 2018). Their scope of work included structural calculation, design development

and detailing of all roof structures and façades as well as the preparation and coordination of the BIM models (up to LOD 400). In addition to that, for some special components (such as the shell structure or the complex steel embeds) the authors also developed the digital models used for production.

The present paper describes the process and the challenges linked to this project, outlining among other things the difficulties encountered in addressing different aspects (geometry, calculation, production, etc.) and in developing specific engineering methods, and interfaces between various software platforms, as well as the integration of cutting edge fabrication technologies (i.e. adaptive moulding) within the constraints of such a megastructure.

General Description and Adopted Methodology

The terminal has a trefoil plan comprising three symmetrical wings each with a length of 1.2km; the height varies between 25 and 50m. The structure spans up to 120m and cantilevers up to 50m, thus allowing for a

naturally shaded entrance area and a spectacular, flexible interior space. An hierarchical organisation of each part of the building, using a project-specific naming convention and element numbering was adopted for all documents, digital models and drawings. This was the first measure to generate an automatised and organised workflow and to allow for a correct data control. The macro system subdivision of the structures and façades are: the main roof structure (group 100), the composite shell structure (steel structure: group 200, reinforced concrete panels: group 800), the trusses (groups 400, 500 and 600), the secondary roof structure (group 700), and the façades (glass façade: group 300, roof envelope: group 900). The first two of these groups make up the principal roof structure. They were the most challenging ones; therefore, they are the main point of interest of this paper.

The main roof structure (group 100) is composed of 90 in situ columns and a complex system of prefabricated and pre-stressed arches, with a free span of up to 120m. The arch system is composed of 823 single prefabricated mega-elements, which present a maximum weight of 340 tonnes each (Fig. 2). Each prefabricated element is

2

1. Aerial view of the central area. © Foster + Partners.

2. Aerial view. © Foster + Partners.

a complex assembly of its own, due to the intricate arrangement of longitudinal rebars on multiple rows, stirrups, local reinforcements, tendons ducts, as well as a large amount of embedded plates. These are the main interfaces between the reinforced concrete and all other structural elements. For this reason they were subject to a specific design process, including customised design tools and parametric models.

At a macro level, the shell structure (groups 200/800) is a static highly indeterminate composite structure devoid of any expansion joints (Nieri et al., 2018), (Blandini et al., 2019). At a micro level, the shell is a parametric modular system presenting high *topological* modularity (almost all the elements present the same quantity of edges, corners, etc.) but only reduced *geometrical* modularity (most of the elements are only repeated three times). Two major prefabricated modular systems could be identified: the 37,000 shell elements named 'cassettes', and the 41,000 connection nodes. Each cassette is composed of four steel side plates and a 160mm thick double-curved reinforced concrete panel. Based on a specific parametric description, the depth of the plates varies between 560mm in the middle and 1,300mm at the edge zones. Depending on the structural utilisation, the wall thickness of the side plates was optimised by the authors within a range from 10 to a maximum of 20mm. The corner nodes are a cruciform element composed of 40mm thick steel plates. The vertical and horizontal angles between fin plates depend on the shell geometry, while the depth and length of the fins were optimised according to the arising forces. The connection between the corner nodes and the side plates is made by slip-resistant bolted connections. Depending on the structural demands, the number of bolts per connection varies between 9 and 30.

Given the sheer scale of the project and the geometrical variation of the different components, the authors invested a considerable amount of time and energy in the development of a semi-automatised process. Starting from a parametric geometrical model, this process allowed for structural calculations of the different components and led to modular detailing driven by forces and geometry. This was a particular challenge for computers and human beings alike. Model size and complexity were pushed to the limit of what current FE and BIM models can handle within the building construction field. Each task needed to be first parametrically defined, then automatised and finally optimised. For this reason, the scope of the engineer was not only to design and develop individual structural elements. The task was rather the definition of methods and rules that could be applied to large groups of elements presenting common characteristics

(like topology, function or geometry). The result was a dual digital model containing the information for fabrication and for the structural analysis.

In order to better understand the challenges of this project, it can be compared to a six-dimensional puzzle. On top of the tri-dimensional geometrical complexity, there is a fourth dimension defined by the highly demanding structural requirements, which are linked to the geometry itself. For example, the geometry of the side plates is a function of both the shell curvature and the structural utilisation of the element itself. The fifth dimension is represented by the specific conditions of fabrication and installation, and the sixth dimension is defined by time and cost constraints.

The Engineering Workflow

The overall objective of the authors was the establishment of an 'Integrated Design Approach' connecting geometry, engineering, and digital modelling from design to fabrication. The workflow was therefore based on a single source of input. This was the only way to provide the efficiency and the flexibility needed and to overcome the lack of interdisciplinary communication between specialised software, like for example between FEM, BIM, and CAD/CAM software. The 'Central Data Model' containing all the important information (dimensions, material, etc.) of each component (beams, cables, connections, etc.) was based on the software McNeel Rhinoceros. Within this platform almost all the elements were defined by scripting (C++, C# and Grasshopper). Using specific interfaces (some of which were developed in-house by the authors). This unique source was employed to share information with other software programs (FEM, BIM, CAD, etc.) and to develop sub-models.

For example, the shell engineering workflow was as follows: First, geometrical and structural information was imported into the FE model. Subsequently calculations were carried out. Arising forces and related geometrical information on each single structural element were then exported into a database. All necessary engineering checks and iterative optimisation processes (minimisation of the amount of steel and bolts used, etc.) were carried out via a project-specific automatic design tool. Finally, the optimised elements were exported to a model-for-production.

Such an approach was particularly challenging in the initial part of the project. It required breaking down the complexity and defining the relationship between geometrical and structural parameters. This was an essential prerequisite in order to set up the correct workflow. It was not always easy for the client to understand why this process required a large amount of time and needed to be well prepared. Thanks to this approach, late changes – which may always happen, for example due to difficulties with regard to logistics or procurement, special wishes by the client, etc.) – could be addressed with a reasonable effort. The authors thus overcame one of the limits of traditional approaches used in the past. Furthermore, it was possible to define a fully coordinated package constituted of structural models (SOFiSTik, and custom structural design tools), BIM coordination models (Revit, Rhinoceros, Navisworks, etc.), BIM models for production (Tekla, Rhinoceros, Allplan, etc.) and CAD drawings (overview drawings, formwork drawings, rebar drawings, etc.).

Production and Quality Control

Given the variety of materials, sizes and structural components of the main roof structure, several fabrication approaches were developed and implemented. All approaches had one characteristic in common, namely the extensive use of prefabrication and automatised production. Except for the main columns and foundations (which were cast in situ) all other elements were produced through a semi-automatic process which took place in temporary factories built next to the construction site. This approach led not only to a high level of precision, but also to a remarkable speed of fabrication, despite the complexity and geometrical variety of the individual elements. The production of each precast element used for the arches can be divided into five phases:

1. Production of embedment plates and automatised cut and bend of the reinforcing bars.
2. Preparation of a segmented formwork based on hinged modular systems, which can be adapted, hence reused, to cast geometrically different concrete segments.
3. Manual assembly of the rebar cage and placement of additional elements (e.g. embedment plates, tendon ducts, etc.).
4. Pouring of the concrete.
5. Transportation and installation of the elements on site.

As in comparable reinforced concrete constructions (Blandini et al., 2011), it was not yet possible to implement a fully automated production process. For this reason, a shared digital platform based on different 3D software programs (Allplan Nemetschek, Revit and Tekla) as well as more traditional manual work based on 2D drawings was required. For example, embeds were produced using CNC machines on the basis of Tekla parametric custom

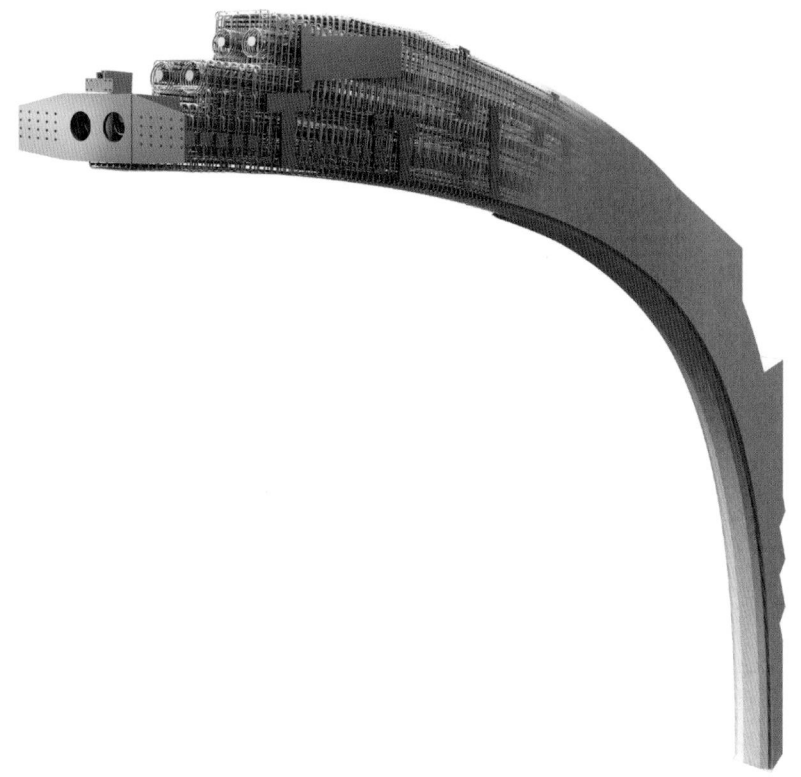

3

components, whereas inspections and approvals of rebar cages were still based on the control of 2D drawings. The production of the modular shell elements presented higher levels of automatisation and a more complex integration of production into the digital workflow. Very few overview 2D drawings were prepared; the production was completely based on 3D parametric models (Fig. 3). The production of the cassettes required five subsequent steps:

1. Production of the steel elements and their coating.
2. Assembly of the steel plates building the edge and the setting of the adaptive mould.
3. Geometrical and quality control.
4. Installation of rebars.
5. Pouring of the concrete.

The first step consisted in the production of the side plates, the welding of the connectors for shear transfer, and the application of the Thermal Spray Aluminium (TSA) coating. The whole process was mostly, but not fully, automated: the cutting and bevelling was done by means of CNC machines, the application of coatings by multiaxial KUKA robots. Nonetheless a certain amount

3. 3D model of precast rebars and embeds. © Werner Sobek AG.

4. Pre-cast element production: assembly of rebars and embedment plates. © LIMAK.

5. Pre-cast element production: adaptive formwork. © LIMAK.

4

5

of human supervision and refining was still necessary. In order to produce the 37,000 cassettes (with a total of almost 13,000 different geometries), 85 adaptive moulds were used (Raun et al., 2015). The cassettes were cast on a reconfigurable surface which could be adapted according to the information from the CAD model. Contrary to the common way of producing moulds for double curved geometries (namely manufacturing them by CNC milling foam materials (Schipper, 2015; Raun et al., 2015), an automatic process was developed, thus avoiding labour-intensive operations and waste production. The surface achieved was so smooth that no manual post-treatment was required.

In order to achieve the given design shape and the required structural performance, the steel structure had to match exactly the reinforced concrete panels; both elements were connected mechanically by means of so-called 'rebar edge trusses' (Figs 4, 5). In general, the fabrication of the shell elements required extreme precision of the fabrication tools as well as a tightly coordinated digital workflow (file-to-production method). In order to ensure this, once the adaptive moulds were shaped with the exact geometry, the corresponding side

plates were positioned on it based on laser projected reference edges; then the reinforcing bars were installed, and finally the concrete was poured. The corner nodes also followed a semi-automated process. The fin plates were produced on a CNC laser cutting machine and then welded together by an automated Electroslag welding process (ESW), thus generating the different angles that result from the architectural geometry. 3D scans of the areas built up so far confirmed that the deviation from the reference geometry is minimal.

Conclusion

The methodologies, workflows and tools developed by the authors together with the contractor show that complex concrete megastructures can be built on a large scale even within tight constraints with regard to time and budget. The tools that were developed do not only allow for a high degree of prefabrication within the tight frame defined by budget and time, they also allow for a parametric variation of the different bays. This is a clear step forward in comparison with classic shell structures of the 20th century. Moreover, the development and integration of automatised processes and a direct chain of control from design to fabrication were fundamental to guarantee the high level of precision required. It has to be admitted that the shell structures realised at Kuwait International Airport do not have the same slenderness ratio as the more experimental shell structures built by Nervi, Torroja, et al. This is due to the architects' design intent of working without any expansion joints, therefore thermal movement had to be accounted for in different ways. However, the methods developed in the context of this challenging project can also be used for other – more slender – applications in the future.

Despite the progress achieved, the authors believe that there is still a long way to go before a fully integrated digital workflow between design and fabrication can be achieved in the building industry. The tools and methods presented in this article show how planners can significantly increase the quality and cost-effectiveness of large-scale projects. It will hopefully push for further development of the interchangeability of software platforms in the future – the authors had to overcome several interface issues by developing their own customised tools and scripting. Moreover, certain consolidated contractual processes such as approvals – which are generally still based on 2D drawings – as well as the overall understanding for a parametric and digital approach in engineering should be further enhanced in the future.

Last but not least, the extensive use of digital models opens the way for a more holistic approach to the building sector, thus considering the entire life cycle of the building materials. Considering the reduced amount of resources available, as well as still growing demand for ever more buildings and infrastructure, it is mandatory to consider dismantling and recycling strategies from the start of the (digital) planning and execution process.

Project participants

Client: Ministry of Public Works, Kuwait
Architects: Foster + Partners, London / United Kingdom
Construction company: Limak Insaat Kuwait
Structural and Facade Design (to tender): Arup, London / United Kingdom; Gulf Consult, Kuwait
Structural and Facade Engineering (from tender): Werner Sobek AG / Germany
Consulting on construction phases: Robert Bird Group, Brisbane / Australia

References

Blandini, L., Schuster, A. and Sobek, W. 2011. 'The Railway Station Stuttgart 21 – Structural Modelling and Fabrication of Double Curved Concrete Surfaces,' in: *Proceedings of the Design Modelling Symposium Berlin 2011*, Berlin: Springer Edition, pp. 217-224.

Blandini, L., Nieri, G. and Sobek, W. 2019. 'Das Schalentragwerk des Kuwait International Airport Terminal 2 – Bemessung und Ausführung einer komplexen Megastruktur in Zeiten der Digitalisierung'. *Stahlbau*, 88(3), pp. 194-202.

Bögle, A.P. Cachola Schmal, I. Flagge (eds). 2004. *Light Structures*, London: Prestel Edition, pp. 86-93.

Josefsson, K., 2013. 'Symmetry as Geometry Kuwait International Airport,' *Architectural Design 83* (2), pp. 28-31.

Kovaleva, D., Gericke, O., Kappes, J., Tomovic, I. and Sobek, W. 2019. 'Rosenstein Pavilion – Design and Structural Analysis of a functionally graded Concrete Shell'. *Structures*, 18, pp. 91-101.

Munro, D., Arkinstall, M. and Carfrae, T. 2018. 'Kuwait International Airport Terminal II: the development of a new form of precast composite shell', *Proceedings of IASS Annual Symposium 2018, Boston*, 16-20 July 2018.

Nieri, G., Blandini, L. and Sobek, W. 2018. 'Kuwait International Airport Terminal 2: Detailed Design and Fabrication of a Large-Span Composite Shell'. *Proceedings of the IASS Annual Symposium 2019 – Structural Membranes 2019*, 7-10 October 2019, Barcelona, Spain.

Peters, S., Trummer, A., Amtsberg, F. and Parmann G. 2017. 'Precast Concrete Shells: a structural challenge', in Menges, A., Sheil, B., Glynn, R. and Skavara M. (eds), *Fabricate 2017: Rethinking Design and Construction*, London: UCL Press, pp. 250-257.

Popescu, M., Rippmann, M., Liew, A., Van Mele, T. and Block, P. 2018. 'KnitCandela – A flexibly formed thin Concrete Shell at MUAC, Mexico City, 2018'. Press Release, ETH Zurich.

Raun, C. and Kirkegaard, P. H. 2015. 'Adaptive mould – A cost-effective mould system linking design and manufacturing of double-curved GFRC panels'. GRCA 2015, Dubai.

Schipper, H. R. 2015. 'Double-curved precast concrete elements Research into technical viability of the flexible mould method'. PhD Thesis, TU Delft. Sobek. W. 1987. 'Auf pneumatisch gestützten Schalungen hergestellte Betonschalen'. PhD Thesis, University Stuttgart.

Winterstetter, T., Alkan, M., Berger, R., Watanabe, M., Toth, A. and Sobek, W. 2015. 'Engineering complex geometries – The Heydar Aliyev Centre in Baku'. *Steel Construction*, 8(1), pp. 65-71.

6. Construction site: Main roof structure. © Werner Sobek AG.

A FACTORY ON THE FLY
EXPLORING THE STRUCTURAL POTENTIAL OF CYBER-PHYSICAL CONSTRUCTION

ASBJØRN SØNDERGAARD / RADU BECUS / GABRIELLA ROSSI
ODICO FORMWORK ROBOTICS
KYLE VANSICE / RAHUL ATTRAYA / AUSTIN DEVIN
SKIDMORE OWINGS & MERRIL LLP

Research Aim

Concrete construction – in particular the production and calcination of cement – represented in 2015 8% of global, anthropogenic emissions of CO_2 (PBL Netherlands Environmental Assessment Agency, 2015). As such, the global use of cement – at material volumes superseded only by human consumption of fresh water – represents a significant source of greenhouse gas production, four times the emissions associated with combined global aviation traffic (Graver, 2019). At a time when efforts to arrest and reverse the continued increase in atmospheric carbon dioxide is deemed critical for the mitigation of disruptive climate change, the imperative to devise new measures of reducing the carbon footprint of the international concrete industry – projected to more than triple by 2050 due to increasing global consumption – is at an all-time high.

Among the plurality of measures proposed to achieve this target, one lies at the heart of construction engineering: reducing material consumption through structural optimisation and doing more with less. In this vein, numerous studies have identified a significant potential for increasing the performance of current structural designs, measuring feasible reductions of up to 70% of the concrete volume, compared to massive equivalents (Kulkarni et al., 2016; Søndergaard & Dombernowsky, 2012; Adriaenssens et al., 2014). A primary measure in achieving these reductions is the computational optimisation of the structure's size, shape or topology, to which end a comprehensive body of methodological work has been developed (Rozvany, 2009; HSU, 1994). In the context of construction, however, any sophistication of shape or morphology is faced with the following dilemma: the material price of concrete and reinforcement comprise only a fraction of the cumulative cost of concrete construction. The vast majority – depending on application and national markets – is constituted by the cost of formwork which, particularly in the case of non-standard designs, can represent up to 75% of the construction total (Lab, 2007; Sarma & Adeli, 1998). In this context, wide scale deployment of any structural optimisation strategy is foreseeable only under the assumption of a radical innovation in construction technology that significantly reduces the cost of advanced formwork. Here, the defining scalability metric is the ability to achieve cost-neutrality between increased expenditure arising from manufacturing complexity, and the marginal decrease in material cost stemming from reduced consumption.

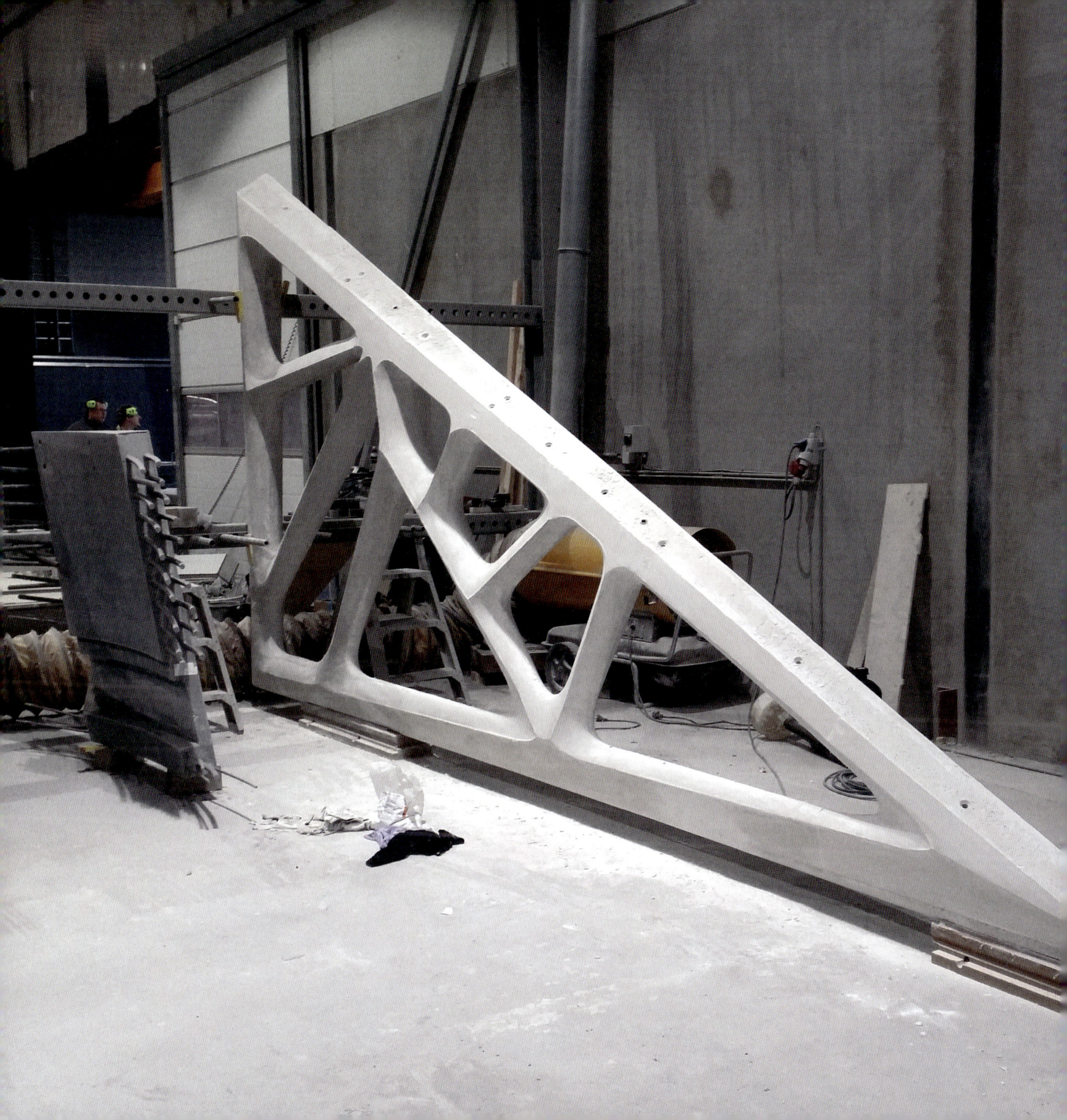

Experiment R

In pursuit of this target, the authors of this paper initiated – in conjunction with an innovation consortium of the Danish construction industry – a multi-year research effort to develop new means of high-speed construction manufacturing of advanced concrete formwork. Instigated at the lunchbreak of the Fabricate 2011 conference in a dialogue between two presenters, initial academic research focused on robotic hot-wire cutting of EPS moulds. This method holds the prospect of significantly increasing production speed over comparable CNC or manual formwork production. A commercial body, Odico Construction Robotics, was established to test the viability of the approach at industrial scale. Having demonstrated, as an international first, the feasibility of the approach in large scale construction in the Fjordenhus Kirk Kapital HQ project [10], Odico's technology R&D refocused on a novel mechanical concept to further this advantage. By replacing the thermal cutting process with an abrasive wire, rotated on flywheels through electrical propulsion, an increase in production speed of 1500% over comparable technologies was achieved (Fig. 2) (Søndergaard et al., 2018). To test the feasibility of this novel approach, research efforts were undertaken to develop a topology-optimised, ultra-high performance concrete prototype through integrated geometry rationalisation and advanced wire-cutting of EPS formwork. At the time of construction, the 21m prototype, comprising 6 pre-cast components assembled on site at the bay of Aarhus and composed through a generative scheme of hyperbolic paraboloid sections and linear extrusions, represented the most advanced concrete structure erected in a national Danish context (Figs 3–5).

Factory on the Fly

From the experiences gained in Experiment R, a roadmap to achieve cost parity for realisation of topology-optimised concrete structures versus established designs was developed. This map entails two measures: create an easily deployable, robotic pop-up formwork factory to alleviate logistical overheads in on-site manufacturing; and devise simplified formwork design approaches. The public listing of Odico as the first Danish robotic company created the basis for achieving the first target, resulting in the development of a system prototype, the Factory on the Fly X11 (FotF). The system entails an IRB 6700 manipulator equipped with a proprietary, abrasive wire-cutting end-effector consisting of a carbon-frame

2

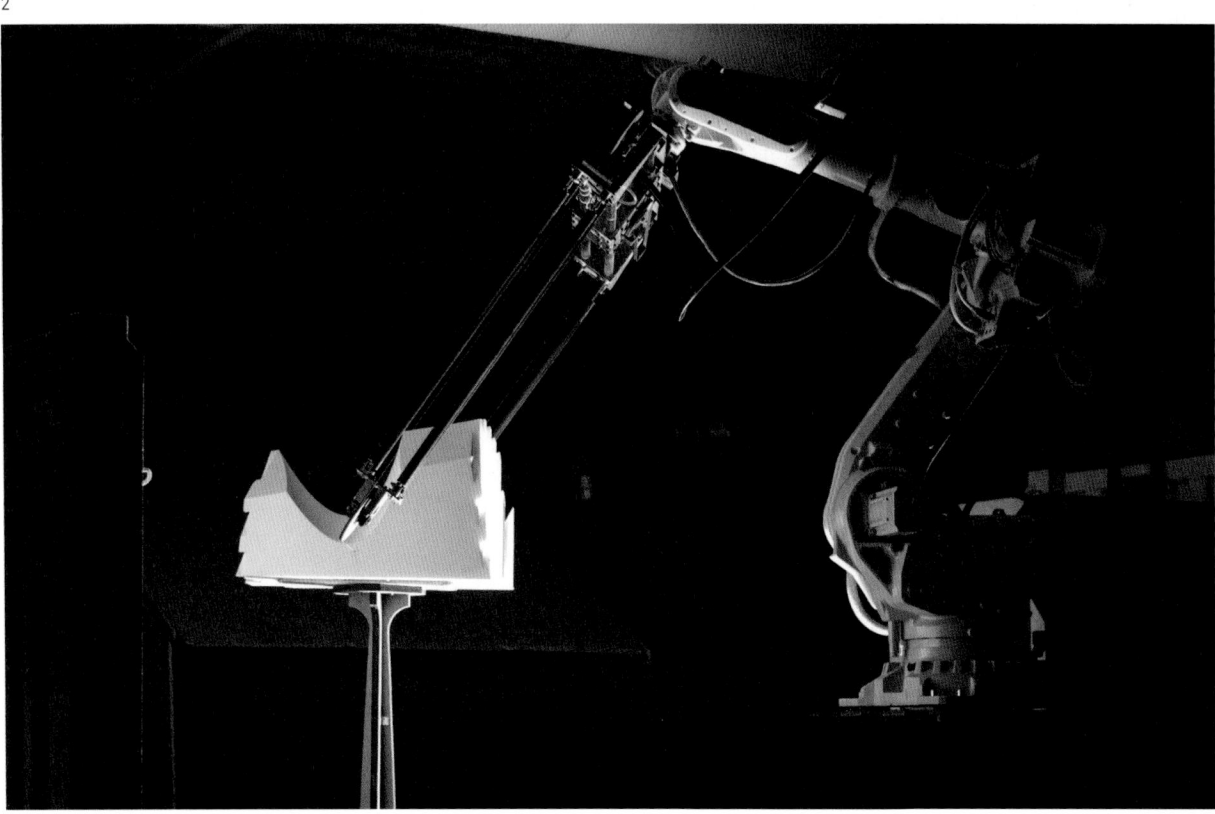

1. The formwork pieces are assembled to form the casting moulds for 6 precast elements of variable design.

2. Robotic Abbrasive Wire Cutting Station at Odico with an IRB 6700 manipulator and external rotary axis.

3. The precast components are cast using Ultra High Performance Concrete mix in order to acheive structural cross-sectional dimensions as llow as 50 x 50mm.

4. As a result of the topological optimisation, the structural design morphology exhibits high degrees of topological non-uniformity between components.

5. The perforations embody a semi-enclosure, framing the surrounding marina at each point of observation.

3

4

5

mounted flywheel and electric propulsion of an industrial diamond wire. The entire configuration is boarded on a containerised structural frame for plug-in on-site deployment, hereby enabling wire-cutting of a plurality of construction materials, including EPS, hard plastics, natural stone, aerated autoclaved concrete and timber. In a global first, commercial deployment of FotF units began in 2019, ushering in a new availability of localised, cyber-physical construction.

Stereoform Slab

The second road map target was envisioned as a series of commercial project collaborations, exploring the realisation of optimised concrete structures. The first such collaboration to take place was initiated from dialogue between Odico, American design practice Skidmore, Owings & Merril LLP, and leading Chicago-based contractor, James McHugh Construction.

Stereoform Slab is the result of a year-long research effort to re-think the design of conventional high-rise office buildings from the perspective of materialisation and embodied carbon. The office building is one of the most prevalent typologies among all new construction, situated in an industry with a large embodied carbon footprint. Of the principal structural components, the concrete floor slab is the largest contributor to carbon emissions – typically comprising 40-60% of total project emissions. Hence this component typology must constitute a principal optimisation target for efforts to curb emissions from realisation of multi-story office designs.

Further, the lifecycle of a constructed design represents a significant component in the analysis of its carbon footprint. Building designs exhibiting greater flexibility in their use and functional programming have a longer operational life, capable of accommodating the multitude of demands placed upon them by continuously shifting economic and societal conditions. For example, open floor plans with minimal constraints imposed by structural members, such as functional cores and columns, provides a maximum of flexibility in this regard. As such, the design of the principal structural system additionally impacts the carbon footprint through the implied constraints imposed by it on the floor plan layout.

Exploring the potential of the design freedom enabled by the availability of low-cost formwork production through robotic wire-cutting, Stereoform Slab outlines a future building system that replicates and abstracts the single-storey bay found in high-construction. Materialised through a full-scale prototype erected

6

in West Loop, Chicago, as part of the 2019 Chicago Architecture Biennial (Fig. 6), Stereoform envisions a more sustainable mode of construction by lowering material consumption through structural shape optimisation. Extending the conventional concrete span by 50% – without the use of post-tension reinforcing – it simplifies spatial programming and adaptions of the spaces hosted on the slab between floors.

Shape Optimisation

The shape of Stereoform follows the moment diagram of a simply supported, pin-pin beam with backspans on both sides. Anticipating its realisation via robotic wire-cutting, the design is formed as compositions of single ruled surfaces. The analysis follows the Working Stress Method for reinforced concrete. However, instead of designing for sections at the mid-span and end conditions, they were completed at 30cm intervals. This increase in analytical resolution allowed for a refinement of the global shape. Single-Objective Optimisation was then applied to fit a ruled surface to the resulting analytical geometry envelope. The result is an optimal beam shape that also reduces slab thickness from the 25cm in a conventional flat-plate, to 15cm. As a result, when implemented at the building scale as designed, the total concrete quantity is approximately 39m³ per unit. Compared to a conventional system where total concrete quantity is approximately 49m³ per unit, a reduction of 21% is achieved. Further, a reduction of 14% in total flexural steel reinforcing was achieved. In the United States, most reinforcing steel is recycled, while concrete is not. Thus, when their respective carbon contributions are calculated within the slab overall, the total carbon reduction is approximated at 20%.

7

Fabrication

To simplify overseas shipping and on-site assembly, the beam formwork was conceptualised as one singular EPS body mounted on a rigid, lattice-reinforced flooring plate. The structure was divided in two sections of 11.2m each for transportation in standard 40-foot shipping containers.

In order to ensure high-precision continuity of the formwork surfaces, the two halves were produced via three continuous swiping cuts, each of 12,000-15,000mm lengths, leveraging the unique 24 x 4 x 3m work envelope of Odico's long range, robotic hot-wire cutting system. Deploying a custom end-effector, designed and manufactured for the project for maximum reachability relative to the designed toolpaths, the cuts were conducted by an ABB IRB 6400 manipulator mounted on a 24m IRT X004 external axis in a low-density, work object body of EPS S80 measuring 12 x 2.4 x 1.2m. To achieve a durable and walkable surface for subsequent handling and reinforcement works, the casting surfaces were coated with a high-strength, two-component isocyanate compound dispensed through a Graco E-10hp reactor.

To allow for the evaluation of the constructability for large scale implementation, the construction of the pavilion was planned to mimic the construction process of high rise erection as closely as possible. Conventional falsework was set to support the robotically-crafted, EPS formwork that was craned into place in two pieces. Conventional formwork was then placed around the EPS form to cast the slab. The column formwork was also conventional, and all three elements – columns, beam, slab – were cast in one monolithic pour (Fig. 7).

Remaining Challenges to Full Scale Adoption in High-Rise Construction

The current digitisation of design practice has enabled intelligent Building Information Modelling workflows throughout the entire project detailing phase, hereby providing parametric and fully specified, three-dimensional CAD data on all construction details. However, there currently is no precedence for an equivalent commercial, digital construction practice, capable of directly consuming this data and translating it into machine instructions.

With the plurality of approaches for robotic manufacturing in a construction and architectural context that has been proposed in recent years, a future of file-to-factory manufacturing of building components and on-site construction is anticipated. However, to break the barrier into large scale, commercial operations and demonstrate self-sustained growth on market terms, significant advances are required in the areas of deployment methodology, system design and robotic process innovation. On the observation that commercial construction must constitute the final testing ground for realistically assessing the relevance and feasibility of experimental construction methodologies, the developments outlined in this paper entail the following prospect.

While a plurality of existing digital methods for structural optimisation enable the conceptualisation of high-performing structural concrete designs, their realisation is generally prohibited in main stream construction by the high-cost of non-standard formwork. In the city of

6. The Stereoform slab formwork being cut in two, single EPS work objects of 11 x 1.2 x 1.5m on Odico's 7-axis robotic hotwire station with 24m linear external axis.

7. Stereoform Slab exhibition for the Chicago Architecture Biennial.

8 & 9. Of particular importance to the geometry of the formwork re-use over multi-storey construction is the mould release and casting surface durability ensured though high-durability coating, resulting in the concrete surface smoothness.

9

Chicago, these economics accordingly favour reducing the complexity of formwork to limit labour costs – resulting in a formwork system that is as 'flat' as possible. Resulting layouts are typically square, 9m x 9m bays; however, beams can be introduced at a cost premium to increase spans. The formwork systems employed for flat slabs, and flat slabs with beams, are composed of simple plywood panels that sit on falsework. The robotically-crafted formwork deployed in the Stereoform prototype is compatible within this more conventional horizontal casting system. This makes its use comparable to current practices, hereby reducing the learning curve for adoption by those constructing in the field.

In this context, the deployment of large scale robotic wire-cutting of EPS formwork is successfully demonstrated to enable the realisation of structurally optimised designs at near cost-neutrality when compared to conventional realisation, hereby paving the way, at principle, for at-scale high-rise construction deployment. The flexibility of this approach is significantly enhanced through the availability of adaptive, on-site manufacturing of formwork, enabled by Factory-On-the-Fly, pop-up workstations.

Towards Building Scale Optimisation

Further work to streamline the process of demoulding and re-using the formwork – as well as enhancing formwork durability for high levels of repeated casting – is necessary to meet the level of standardisation consistent construction cycle times require. Increased customisation of formwork moulds is also necessary in order to ensure the multitude of design conditions within a given building can be accommodated.

At the moment of closure of this paper, Odico A/S has undertaken prototyping work for development of topology-optimised load-bearing structures for an undisclosed, multi-storey building project in central Copenhagen, Denmark. The project, slated for realisation in spring 2020 will, at its inauguration, constitute the first example internationally of a commercial-scale implementation of a topology-optimised, load-bearing concrete structure realised with robotic wire-cutting of EPS formwork.

Acknowledgements

Experiment R was funded by the Mærsk McKinney Møller Foundation, Dreyer Foundation and the Danish Art Foundation. The project was led by Aarhus School of Architecture, in collaboration with Odico Construction Robotics A/S, Søren Jensen Consulting Engineers A/S, Hi-con A/S, Brunsgaard A/S, Aarsleff A/S, Aarhus Tech and TU Delft.

The Stereoform Slab was kindly funded by Autodesk and conducted by Skidmore Owings Merril LLP, Odico A/S, Sterling Bay and James McHugh Construction, all providing in-kind contributions.

References

Trends in global CO_2 emissions: 2015. Report. PBL Netherlands Environmental Assessment Agency. The Hague, 2015, https://www.pbl.nl/sites/default/files/downloads/pbl-2015-trends-in-global-co2-emisions_2015-report_01803_4.pdf. (Accessed 23 December 2019)

Graver, B., Zhang, K., Rutherford. D. 2019. 'CO2 emissions from commercial aviation, 2018' in *The International Council on Clean Transportation*, 2019.

Kulkarni, A. R. and Bhusare, M. V. 2016. 'Structural Optimization of Reinforced Concrete Structures', *International Journal of Engineering and Technical Research*, 5(7), pp. 123-127.

Søndergaard A. and Dombernowsky, P. 2012. 'Design, analysis and realization of topology optimized concrete structures', *International Association of Shell Spatial Structures Journal*, 53(4), pp. 209-216.

Adriaenssens, S., Block, P., Veenendaal, D. and Williams, C. (eds). 2014. *Shell Structures for Architecture: Form finding and optimization*. London: Routledge.

ROZVANY, G. 2009. 'A critical review of established methods of structural topology optimization', *Structural and multidisciplinary optimization*, 37(3), pp. 217-237.

HSU, Y-L. 1994. 'A review of structural shape optimization', Computers in Industry, 25(1), pp. 3-13.

Lab, R. H. 2007. 'Think Formwork - Reduce Cost', *Structural Practice*, April 2007, pp. 14-16.
Sarma, K. C. and Adeli, H. 1998. 'Cost optimization of concrete structures', *Journal of Structural Engineering*, 124(5), pp. 570-578.

Søndergaard A., Feringa, J. 2017. 'Scaling Architectural Robotics—Realisation of The Kirk Kapital Headquarters', In Menges, A., Sheil, B., Glynn, R. and Skavara, M. (eds), *Fabricate 2017: Rethinking Design and Construction*. London: UCL Press, pp. 264-271.

Søndergaard, A., Feringa, J., Mihai-Stan, F. and Maier, D. 2018. 'Robotic abrasive wire cutting of polymerized styrene formwork systems for cost-effective realization of topology-optimized concrete structures', *Construction Robotics*, 2(1-4), pp. 81-92. (doi: 10.1007/s41693-018-0016-8).

DIRECT-TO-DRAWING
AUTOMATION IN EXTRUDED TERRACOTTA FABRICATION

**SCOTT OVERALL / JOHN PAUL RYSAVY / CLINTON MILLER / WILLIAM SHARPLES /
CHRISTOPHER SHARPLES / SAMEER KUMAR / ANDREA VITTADINI / VICTOIRE SABY**
SHoP ARCHITECTS

The computer enables a paradigm of design thinking, including processes and outcomes, that past methods of practice were unable to conceive. The emergence of computation in project delivery allows digitisation of material craft. It empowers the designer to simultaneously determine material, space, form and fabrication procedures. Through computational design rigour, each component can be digitally configured as a constructible part, creating new responsibilities for the designer to develop and manage fabrication with unprecedented involvement, commonly referred to as 'direct-to-fabrication'. Where communication between an architect and contractor is conventionally facilitated through shop drawings as a confirmation of understanding and capacity to produce an intended product, direct-to-fabrication leverages the architect's involvement through management and output from a coordinated digital model. This relationship creates potential for new efficiencies, shortening the distance between design thinking and fabrication processes, and removing the divide between the architect and fabricator that often complicates communication and separates the design of buildings and building systems (SHoP Architects, 2002).Recognising the opportunities for increased collaboration and precision of direct-to-fabrication, SHoP Architects explored new workflows

with the WAVE/CAVE installation in Milan, Italy, as part of *Interni* Magazine's Material Immaterial exhibition at the 2017 FuoriSalone (Fig. 1). WAVE/CAVE was developed as an extended architectural experience of fabrication, material and form. The installation drew upon examples over the past decade including SHoP's Barclays Center in New York City, and Gramazio & Kohler's Gantenbein Winery in Fläsch, Switzerland, projects designed to deliver models and machine code for production machinery which removes the intermediary of a tradesperson from the process. WAVE/CAVE provides a case study in how computation delivers a complex project through direct-to-fabrication, incorporating the craft knowledge of tradespersons and leveraging learned experience without isolating design production through computer-controlled fabrication methodologies alone.

Research Context

WAVE/CAVE is a 55m² topographic composition of 1,670 unglazed terracotta blocks. The blocks are extruded through a custom die and CNC (Computer Numerical Control) cut into 797 individual profiles. Stacked in three tiers, the interior faces of the blocks reveal a surprising ornamental richness, described by a smoothly curved

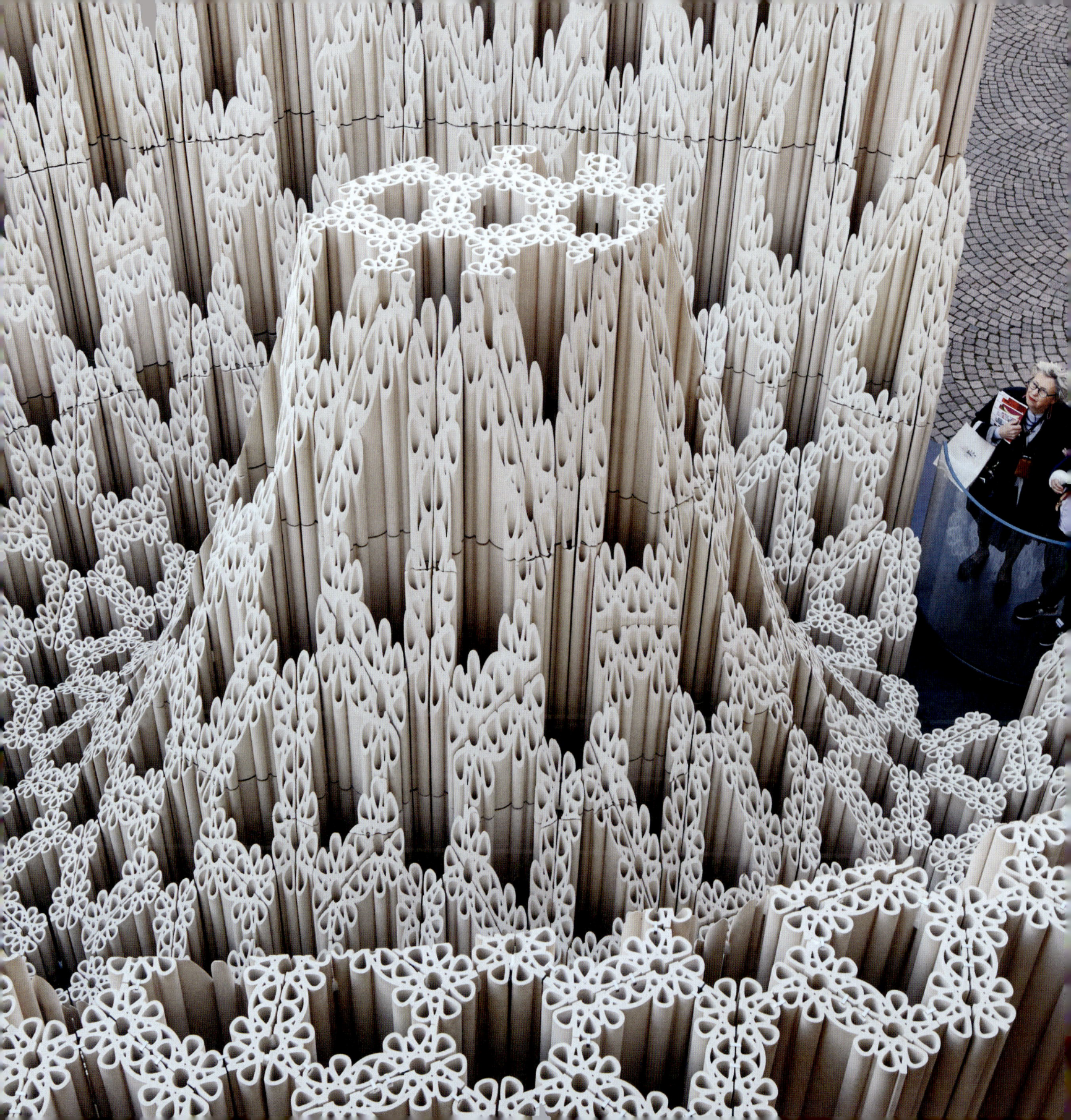

surface inscribed within a 3.6m high perimeter wall (Fig. 2). Developed in collaboration with skilled artisans and tradespersons, unique terracotta extrusions feature regularly fluted exterior faces and a webbed cross-section, exposed when cut at various inclinations (Fig. 3).

Terracotta relies on the knowledge and mastery of fabrication, including extrusion tolerances, cutting processes and required wall thicknesses. Through a geometry that reveals, pushes to the breaking point, and is itself defined by these characteristics, WAVE/CAVE investigates the embodied knowledge and genius of the material's production, supported by computational design and automation (Fig. 4).

In recent years, the use of terracotta has had a resurgence as a surface treatment, frequently in rain screen applications. A wet material traditionally manufactured in batch quantities as a cut extrusion, terracotta affords perceived depth through linear surface variation. At the WAVE/CAVE installation, SHoP furthered its investigation of the material, expanding from previous projects such as 111 West 57th Street, where the appearance of a non-linear surface was achieved

through the assembly of arrayed tiles of varied profiles within a panel assembly. At the WAVE/CAVE Pavilion, digital technology was further integrated to augment the design and manufacturing of each individual tile as both a formal and ornamental construct.

By leveraging SHoP's experience in direct-to-fabrication processes, the architectural team took the responsibility of documenting and managing each terracotta tile according to the scripted design. Expanding on the office's previous design and fabrication research – including at Dunescape, Camera Obscura, Barclays Center, and Botswana Innovation Hub – the office set out to fully realise an entirely automated workflow of design and documentation, previously performed semi-manually. This brought the benefits of total automation to a traditional fabrication and production process.

At the Barclays Center and Botswana Innovation Hub, CATIA – a 3D CAD (Computer Aided Drafting) and PLM (Project Lifecycle Management) software – was used to manage fabrication. CATIA's parametric modelling and documentation capabilities were leveraged to facilitate system modelling. This allowed modelled elements to handle variable global geometry. CATIA could easily

1. Completed pavilion from above. © Tom Harris, 2020.

2. Pavilion perimeter wall. © Delfino Sisto Legnani, 2020.

3. Pavilion tile detail. © Delfino Sisto Legnani, 2020.

4. Interior of completed pavilion. © Delfino Sisto Legnani, 2020.

3

4

adapt to variation in element dimension, but the software was not well-suited to manage variable quantities of elements. If the number of parts or tooling requirements change based on system design or input changes, the designer was typically responsible for modelling those changes through analogue procedures. Additionally, scripting the dimensioning of 2D documentation was limited; only very simple dimension resizing can be performed. At WAVE/CAVE, an opportunity was presented to reconsider direct-to-fabrication workflow, allowing efficient fabrication and construction of complex, unique geometries though custom workflows built to overcome past challenges.

Research Questions

Direct-to-fabrication has been enabled by continued development of CNC and CAD technologies as a means of determining cut angles, tool paths, and bend angles directly from CAD files using computer-aided manufacturing (CAM) software as the intermediary with limited to no human intervention. With the means to manufacture from 3D models, the architect works within a fully model-based environment, where a design model is developed and refined into a deliverable fabrication model. This bypasses the architectural drawing process, save for regulatory and legal systems predicated on paper documentation. While direct-to-fabrication offers efficiencies, the process also raises several questions concerning contemporary architectural production. Specifically, how is the embodied knowledge of skilled tradespersons in contemporary building practice leveraged through digital fabrication? And how does the knowledge and craft of design scripting translate and support the work of established building trades?

In a crucial step of the terracotta fabrication process – the cutting of terracotta extrusions – a CAM software to directly convert models to a CNC saw at WAVE/CAVE was not available. This necessitated the production of detailed paper fabrication drawings. The scale of a pavilion allowed for reduced model complexity, leading to a hypothesis that the necessary fabrication and paper documentation for assembly could be fully automated, releasing a bottleneck present in past projects of drawing production via CAD drafting or BIM modelling. With a fully automated documentation process, the design model and fabrication model were no longer detached, allowing the design to develop alongside documentation rather than through a separate procedure.

While it may be that the 3D model is a future paradigm of practice, a great deal of change is necessary for the construction and fabrication industries, as well as the legal environment, to phase out the 2D drawing set. The WAVE/CAVE pavilion is unique not just in the creation of parametric 3D geometry, but also in delivery of a fully parametric, measured 2D fabrication drawing set.

Design Script

To execute the vison of automating the architects' direct-to-fabrication responsibilities, it was necessary to develop a suite of new digital tools that create high-resolution geometry and accurate documentation, achieving total automation of both the design and documentation. A model and output script were built within Grasshopper for Rhinoceros 5, taking advantage of its capacity to quickly prototype and construct geometric scripts, allowing the ability to integrate C# programming for more sophisticated and computationally-efficient code, interfacing directly with Rhino's back-end API (Application Programming Interface) for custom processes. The entire script required minimal design input, and once in place would run until all model and drawing documentation was output. Using Grasshopper as the basis for the script allowed quick isolation of portions of the definition to perform design studies and revise segments of the process as needed. Three primary modules describe the design script: conceptual design, geometry development and organisation, and documentation.

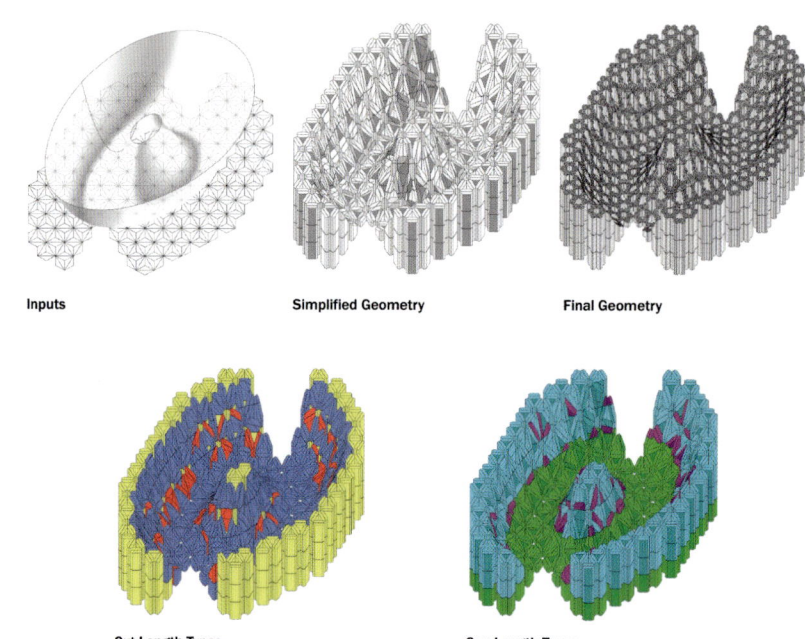

Inputs   **Simplified Geometry**   **Final Geometry**

Cut Length Types   **Cap Length Types**

5

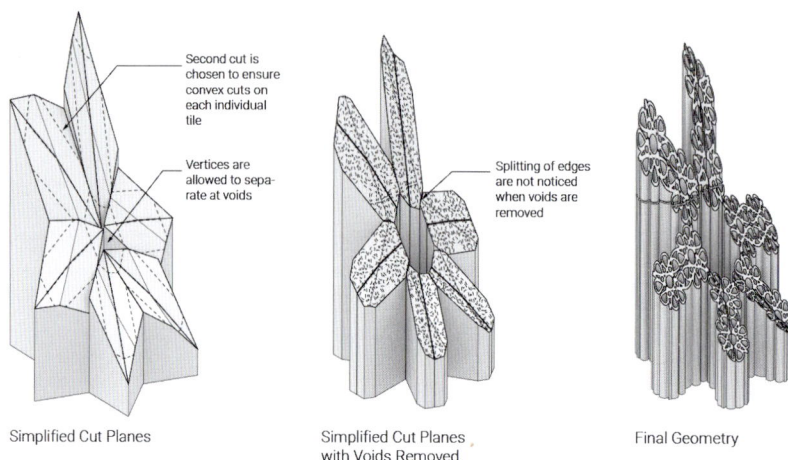

Second cut is chosen to ensure convex cuts on each individual tile

Vertices are allowed to separate at voids

Splitting of edges are not noticed when voids are removed

Simplified Cut Planes

Simplified Cut Planes with Voids Removed

Final Geometry

6

5. Inputs and geometry development. © SHoP Architects, 2020.

6. Simplified tiles. © SHoP Architects, 2020.

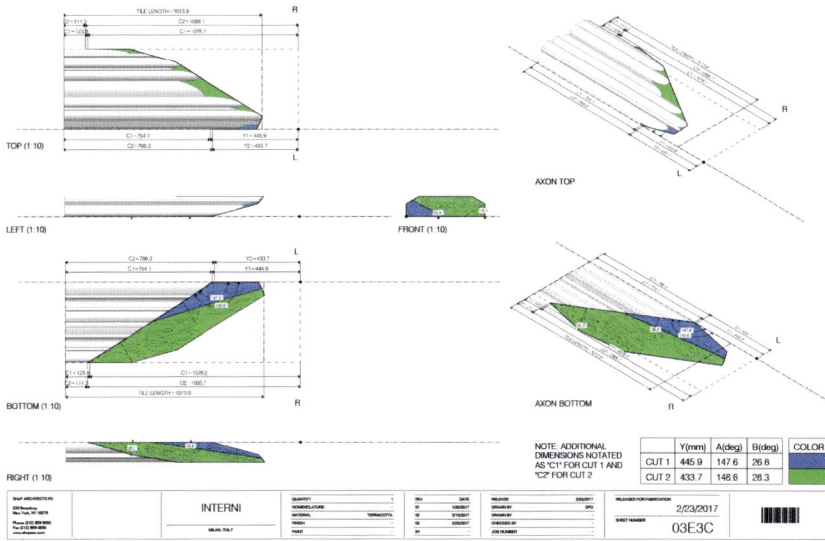

7

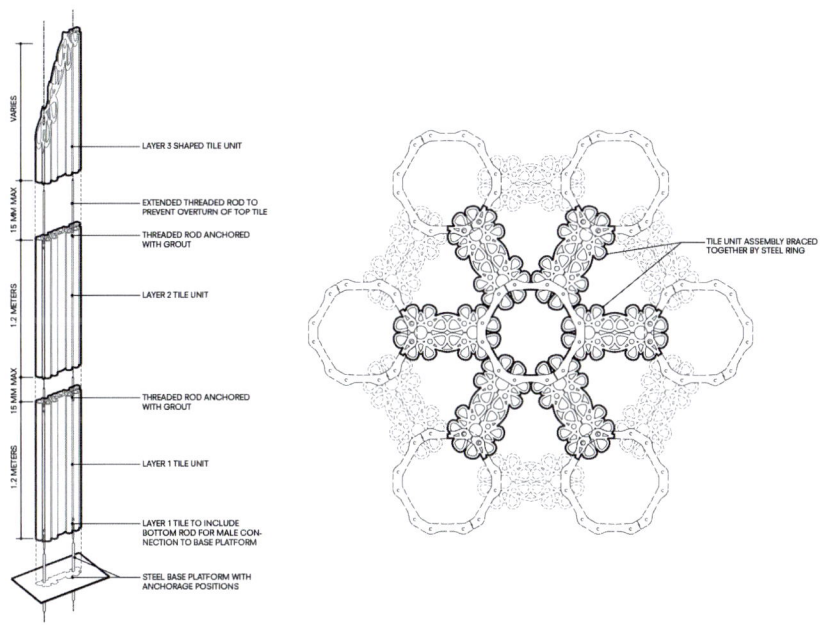

8

7. Typical fabrication ticket
© SHoP Architects, 2020.

8. Tile assembly.
© SHoP Architects, 2020.

The conceptual design portion operates on a set of three inputs: a plan layout, tile profile, and design surface. The plan layout was a regular grid positioned manually to define the extents of the terracotta in plan. The design surface was a simplified version of the space carved out from the terracotta form, creating sculptural figuration proposed in the design concept (Fig. 5).

Through the script, the base grid was projected on to the design surface. A custom Grasshopper node was used to achieve proper faceting of the tiles, taking the projected grid and simplifying the form as a set of two convex cuts. If the angle between planes was less than 1°, the average plane was used instead, giving the tile just one cut.

Geometry Simplification

A simplified bounding geometry of convex planar faces represented the final tile geometry in the design and organisation segments of the script. A description of the geometry was maintained as mathematical planes rather than boundary representations, constructing a depiction when necessary through a convex hull algorithm, resulting in a more responsive script (Fig. 6).

The convex hull implementation was unique in that it uses infinite planes rather than points. The script operated by finding the intersection of all sets of three planes, discarding all points with a negative relative z-coordinate to any of the planes. Additionally, 15mm joints were added to accommodate structure required for lateral bracing. Host surfaces partitioned the remaining planes, and a boundary was built with 2D 'gift wrapping', or Jarvis march algorithm, providing each face of the final geometry (Jarvis, 1972). Performing a 2D convex hull operation was feasible because the host plane was known, allowing the design team to forego implementing a more complex 3D convex hull algorithm. Each face of the geometry was created and joined into one single closed convex planar solid for visualisation and further analysis. The benefit of this method, in addition to calculation time, was that existing convex planar solids could be easily defined as a series of planes by finding a tangent plane to each face. A simplified geometry was built, divided and organised in preparation for fabrication.

Output Geometry and Organisation

With the design geometry established, a second script module generated geometry in preparation for documentation and output. First, the script created a system of organisation and identification of named tile units based on each tile's horizontal and vertical location in the construction grid. The tiles were then tagged with an identifying name within a 3D naming grid to assist in locating them during construction. For example, a tile tagged 07D1B would indicate it was to be placed in location B within the grid at row 7 column D level 1. If the design inputs were changed and tiles were added or subtracted, names were associated dynamically without renaming other tiles, facilitating geometry alterations late into the documentation process. Within the data structure, all geometry was indexed within a three-dimensional array corresponding to the naming grid so that geometry associated with the tile could be easily retrieved.

Detailed tile geometry requiring the use of solid Boolean operations not defined as a convex hull alone was created after sorting simplified geometry and locating connection hardware (Fig. 8). Due to the complexity of the composition, it proved computationally prohibitive to generate full detailed geometry all at once. Instead, a custom system was created to iteratively construct each tile one unit at a time, 'baking' each tile into the Rhino model as datum geometry, then moving to the next tile, rather than holding the entire construction process for each tile in memory. 'Baked' tiles were paired with their connection hardware using a system of instancing, identifying and copying duplicate tiles rather than creating unique sets of identical geometry.

Following the completion of WAVE/CAVE, new strategies were developed to generate fully detailed fabrication geometry in parallel rather than iteratively. This reduced computation times, leveraging parallel computing on high thread-count CPUs to eliminate the need for iteratively 'baking' geometry and holding all geometry in memory instead. Grasshopper's built in parallel computing was bypassed in the process to more efficiently allocate tasks to threads when working with large amounts of data. Custom solid Boolean components were also built to quickly check for common edge cases and prevent excess calculations, preventing unnecessary overhead.

Drawing Production

The final portion of the script generated fabrication drawings using the geometry as scripted. Four measured drawings and one 3D DXF model were produced for each tile. Three of the drawings were required to locate measured cuts per tile (Fig. 7). Due to constraints of the saw, each tile was oriented on the cutting bed on its back, left, or right side depending on the nature of the cut. For each orientation, a measured drawing was produced. An additional set of drawings was likewise delivered for quality control, locating discrete points describing each

9

10

geometry and verifying dimensional accuracy. The 3D DXF model set was provided for three-dimensional reference. All outputs were integrated into the parametric model and, when enabled, produced the entire set of fabrication documents as the design progressed.

Each of the cut drawings was produced automatically by dimensioning to set points defined by the intersection of the plane of the mitred face and the edge of the cut bed. Double mitre angles were defined by a pair of angles relative to the edge of the cut bed, with each tile receiving one or two mitre cuts. Quality control documents were produced by dimensioning set identifiable points along the lengths of the tile relative to a work point located on the cut bed.

Research Evaluation

The scripted automation process was invaluable to completion of the project ahead of schedule. Modifications to the design were possible the day before delivery of documentation as new information regarding fabrication constraints or site conditions arrived without disrupting the project schedule. When the fabricator began cutting (Fig. 9) and required additional dimensions or other information, the project team could quickly input data to the script and re-issue documentation.

Tools and workflows for handing fabrication-ready fully parametric geometry developed in WAVE/CAVE likewise proved scalable to larger-scale projects currently in construction. It is bringing similar, fully computational models to traditional practice and fabrication, successfully executed within traditional design teams without deploying full virtual design and construction teams in managing the process. Projects include a 1980m² architectural feature wall containing 12,200 timber elements and 135,200 hardware elements, successfully applying scalability of parametric and automated model production and documentation to projects over ten times the model size of WAVE/CAVE.

The transferability of the WAVE/CAVE process has been possible as the strategies developed for handling convex planar geometries were not tied to terracotta as a material, but instead to the machining processes associated with materials modified through cutting, including extruded metals and timber. Further strategies for efficiently handling non-convex and non-planar geometries have been developed based on the challenges encountered with the fully detailed geometry of WAVE/CAVE. Many snippets of code developed from WAVE/CAVE can be found in Sasquatch, an open-source plugin for Grasshopper,

including methods for handling convex hulls and Boolean operations for efficient handling of solid geometries.

Conclusion

The completion of WAVE/CAVE over a nine-month period from project inception to completion – with a small part-time design team and an extremely tight production and installation schedule of four weeks – demonstrated the value of automating measured drawings leading up to the beginning of production. Scripting the output of documentation describing complex geometry and assemblies minimised human error and facilitated fabrication of a complex customised assembly. The 1,670 fluted terracotta tiles arranged as a soaring sculptural enclosure is a study in material and technological innovations leveraged by a strong collaboration between the design team operating through computation and skilled fabricators with an extensive understanding of their trade (Fig. 10).

WAVE/CAVE is a critical case study considering the automation of 2D drawings. The project serves as a model for bridging the distance between computational design and analogue forms of contemporary construction. Direct-to-drawing provides a means of communication with traditionally skilled artisans and trades. Until such time that project delivery is fully 3D, the direct-to-drawing paradigm provides architectural precedence for meaningful collaboration and change within current contract structures and fabrication constraints in the building industry.

Acknowledgements

WAVE/CAVE was made possible thanks to Michelangelo Giombini of Interni – Mondadori and our collaborators Klaus Bayer and Maik Bluhm of NBK Keramik; Flavio Tunesi, Adriano Capuozzo, Carlo Geddo, Daniele Ruboni, and Paolo Branca of Metalsigma Tunesi; Elena Massignan, Monica D'Emidio, and Luca Cusinato of Luce&Light; Beatriz Fernandez of Cricursa; Peiheng Tsai of PHT Lighting Design; and Daniela Azzaro, Federico Lorenzon, Paolo Cresci, and Nicola Carofano of Arup as well as Gregg Pasquarelli, Corie Sharples, John Cerone, Angelica Baccon, and Dana Getman for their leadership, Philip Nobel for his advice, and the rest of the SHoP team for their continued support of the project.

References

Jarvis, R. A. 1972. 'On the Identification of the Convex Hull of a Finite Set of Points in the Plane.' *Information Processing Letters*, 2(1), pp. 18–21.

SHoP Architects. 2002. 'Eroding the Barriers', in SHoP Architects, (ed.). *Versioning: Evolutionary Techniques in Architecture – Architectural Design, Special Issue*, 72(5), pp. 90–100.

Sharples, C. and Cerone, J. 2016. 'bigBIM', in Briscoe, D. (ed.), *Beyond BIM: Architecture Information Modeling*. London: Routledge, pp. 211–36.

9. Cutting process at NBK fabrication shop in Emmerich am Rhein, Germany. © SHoP Architects, 2020.

10. Pavilion exterior, night. © Tom Harris, 2020.

THE TIDE [PHASE 1]
GREENWICH PENINSULA, LONDON

EMMANUEL VERKINDEREN
AKT II
BRYCE SUITE
DILLER SCOFIDIO + RENFRO
RYAN NEIHEISER
NEIHEISER ARGYROS
EDOARDO TIBUZZI / **JEG DUDLEY**
AKT II P.ART

Introduction

'The Tide' is envisioned as a 5km long linear park – shaped like a figure '8' – that will encircle and criss-cross Greenwich Peninsula, one of the most actively developed regions in East London. This project was conceived by designers Diller Scofidio + Renfro (DS+R) and the international development firm Knight Dragon, with the intent of connecting the varied elements of their Peninsula masterplan to one another and to the surrounding river landscape, while also generating a series of unique event spaces.

Diller Scofidio + Renfro describe the scheme as a *'productive linear park [that] acts as a kind of flexible infrastructure, hosting a legible network of social and cultural hubs across the Peninsula, while also thickening the public ground, blurring the boundary between built and green spaces, and creating a rich three-dimensional landscape of social interactions.'* (Diller, Scofidio, Renfro, 2016)

The three-dimensional aspect of the route is emphasised at regular intervals along its length as it lifts away from the ground and rises into the air, supported by clusters of sculptural columns, or 'islands', connected by elegant tapered 'link' bridges (Fig. 1). These vertical shifts offer users branching routes that pass under, around, and on top of the walkway, activating the public realm on multiple levels and creating a series of unique spaces, such as a cantilevered promenade that overlooks the river, a public café nestled under one island, and terraced seating formed by an oversized island adjacent to the central plaza. By incorporating elevated routes within the linear park, this scheme also has the significant advantage of being able to sail over, instead of obstruct, the busy network of pedestrian thoroughfares and vehicular routes that service and connect the O2 venue, Greenwich Underground station, and the encompassing Peninsula district.

For the first phase of The Tide to be built, a section was chosen that runs East-West between the central plaza and the Eastern riverside. This portion is almost entirely elevated, and so composed of 29 sculptural islands, each set between 6 and 10m above the ground. These islands are arranged into seven clusters of between three and eight islands, connected to one another by six tapering link bridges. During this phase, the core design team of DS+R and Neiheiser Argyros were supported by structural engineers AKT II, MEP engineers AECOM, and landscape architects Gross Max.

1

Context to Construction System

One of the earliest challenges for the design team was to generate an architectural language for the islands that was systematic in its structural solution and method of construction while remaining flexible and responsive to the differing site conditions, both within the phase one boundary and for future phases located beyond and across the Peninsula (Fig. 2). During concept development, an expressive form for the islands emerged – one that is in fact dictated by stringent site, programmatic, and structural constraints: a sloping column negotiates complex ground conditions, allowing the supports to avoid the existing infrastructure below; while a tapered stem provides, at its highest point, the necessary width and volume to encase the root ball of mature trees supported above. Lastly, the rapid expansion and 'flare' in the soffit provides a generous upper surface for the walkway and its attendant landscape, while avoiding any structurally-redundant depth.

To inform this evolving concept, several different material options were considered for the islands. Initial studies focused on forming them as either monolithic in-situ cast concrete elements, or assembling them from precast concrete segments, or even encasing a steel core in a spray-applied concrete shell. However, the complex spatial and geotechnical characteristics of the site – which has substantial sub-surface infrastructure and services, including a London Underground station, train tunnels and a car park – led to all of these options being ruled out. The site is too constrained to allow the placement and choreography of necessary temporary works and formwork for any scheme involving substantial in-situ casting and, most critically, the Underground station that runs underneath much of the site allows only limited loading capacity due to the highly variable infill layered above it.

For these reasons, a comparatively lightweight prefabricated steel structural system was chosen instead. Steel has an inherently high strength-to-weight ratio that ensured each island would be structurally robust yet remain light enough to be transported and erected swiftly on site. Sheet steel is also a more cost-effective material than either precast or in-situ concrete in producing unique variants of a core design-type – a critical factor, given the divergence in island forms.

Furthermore, by utilising a thicker gauge for the outer envelope, this 10-20mm surface could double as both architectural finish and load-transmitting element, negating the need for a duplicative layer of cladding, and instead creating a structurally efficient, fully mobilised stressed-skin assembly. This system has the additional benefit of being sealed watertight against the harsh riverside environment. Environmental durability was further assured by specifying weathering steel coated in a multi-layer spray-applied acrylic polyurethane paint finish.

The effect achieved is therefore of complex flowing forms and 'dancing' columns – yet they are formed almost entirely of economical planar surfaces, with just one type of singly-curved surface present in the 'flare' that efficiently blends between the radically different upper and lower column cross sections.

Having established this formal and structural language for the islands, which clearly expresses the structural and programmatic constraints embedded within, this concept was repeated for the link bridges. The result is a simple external form and elevation that are a pure expression of the bending moment forces acting on them under uniform loading, supported by an efficient internal skeleton of longitudinal and transverse stiffeners.

2

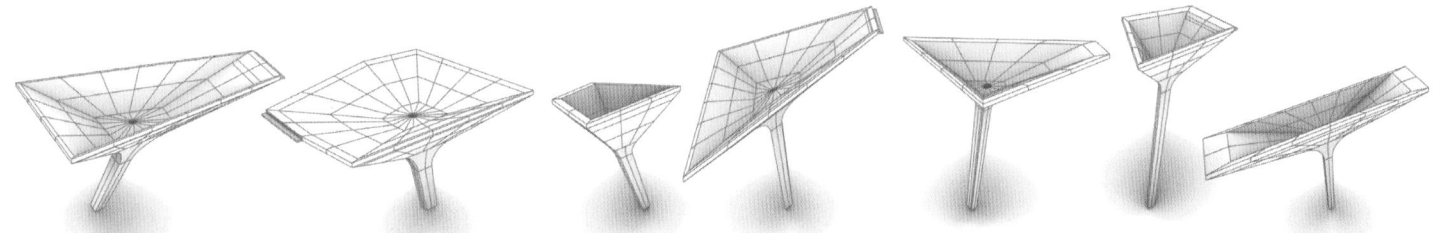

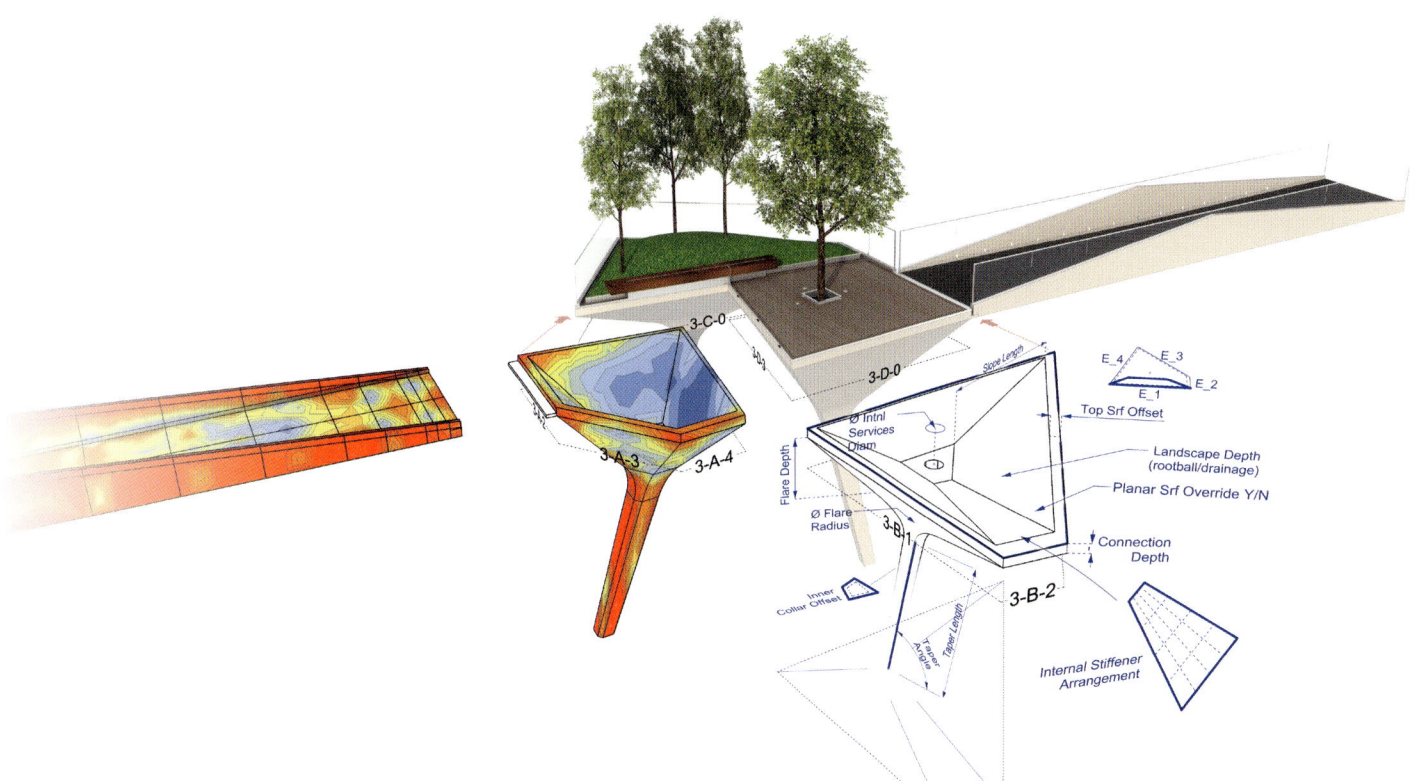

Labels within figure:
3-C-0, 3-D-0, 3-A-3, 3-A-4, 3-B-1, 3-B-2, E_4, E_3, E_1, E_2, Slope Length, Top Srf Offset, Landscape Depth (rootball/drainage), Planar Srf Override Y/N, Connection Depth, Ø Intnl Services Diam, Flare Depth, Ø Flare Radius, Inner Collar Offset, Taper Angle, Taper Length, Internal Stiffener Arrangement

Computational Design and Structural Optimisation

Although all of the islands share a consistent typology, each one was iteratively adjusted and refined by the design team into a unique variant in order to respond most efficiently to its own specific combination of programmatic, environmental and structural parameters. For example, certain islands support more trees and deeper landscapes, so must transfer larger loads, while others cantilever further or are more irregular in plan in order to negotiate the dense infrastructure below – and all of the islands sit on legs of differing length.

This wide variety was only possible due to the interdisciplinary 'master' parametric model jointly created by DS+R, Neiheiser Argyros and AKTII. Developed throughout the project, this model merged architectural, structural and production workflows together within the visual programming environment of Rhino and Grasshopper, and was supported by the Reakt interoperability platform developed at AKTII. Reakt has previously been successfully implemented on a number of built projects to accelerate collaboration and design coordination, as shown in Tibuzzi (2016) and

Kingman (2017). This project significantly expanded the capability of Reakt as it necessitated the introduction of detailed dynamic assessment and refinement processes.

Using this master model, the design team was able to rapidly iterate through potential configurations for both individual islands, and the parent clusters they sat within. On a geometric level, it allowed the evaluation of numerous parameters, including (but not limited to): the number and position of islands within each cluster; the unique angles and lengths of supporting stems; as well as the area, shape regularity, flare depth, offset and cantilever that defines the flat walkable zone atop each island (Fig. 3).

The master model was also vital in automatically generating both global and local frame, and shell Finite Element (FE) models for structural analysis by the engineering team that were verified using principles established in Beg (2011). The islands utilise semi-rigid moment connections at their base, so it was critical to optimise leg positions and angles to reduce these moments in order to create self-stable island clusters that placed minimal overturning forces on the interrelated network of pile, pad and transfer foundations.

1. View of the completed project from Greenwich Peninsula plaza. Photograph by Ben Luxmoore. © DS+R.

2. Each Island is a unique expression of site, programme and structural constraints. © AKT II.

3. A 'master' digital model was used to coordinate architectural, structural and fabrication development. © AKT II.

In contrast, the link bridges were designed with elastomeric pad bearings at both ends that act as sliding pinned connections. This allows thermal expansion while avoiding the onerous transfer of moment forces into the clusters. The critical structural behaviour to analyse and resolve in these elements was therefore the vertical deflection under live and wind loads, and dynamic behaviour. Numerous configurations of profile shape, internal plate spacing and plate thickness were tested for each link, in order to find combinations that efficiently limited deflections to less than 1/250 of the unsupported spans.

The non-linear buckling behaviour was also analysed for each plate within both the islands and links, and used to inform the size and arrangement of parametrically-generated steel skin stiffeners.

Dynamic Assessment

The design team was aware that due to the low mass, limited surface finishes and fully-welded construction system chosen, the natural damping of many of the Tide's long-span link bridges and large cantilevered islands is very low, which could make them susceptible to footfall-induced vibration and potentially resulting structural fatigue.

To determine whether this was an issue, AKTII carried out several time history footfall analyses in which digital FE models were subjected to combinations of sinusoidally-pulsating dynamic and irregular live loadings that simulate the forces induced by pedestrians jogging and walking across the link bridges. The density and rhythm of these forces was derived by treating the link bridges as 'C' class bridges, with their attendant high volume and variation in foot traffic. This study discovered approximately 500 modes in frequencies ranging from 0.5-6.0Hz (using 0.01Hz increments) before reaching a mass participation above 90%, which enabled the design team to generate non-linear time histories. They confirmed that complex dynamic responses would occur along the full length of the Tide, even as a result of single excitation actions within one link bridge (Figs 4, 5). Additionally, the studies highlighted vibration-sensitive locations where accelerations would be induced more easily, and the corresponding locations where these accelerations would be most perceivable.

Before the human perception of this default dynamic performance could be quantified though, it was necessary for AKTII to create a bespoke dynamic design criteria that reflected the atypical programmatic requirements of the

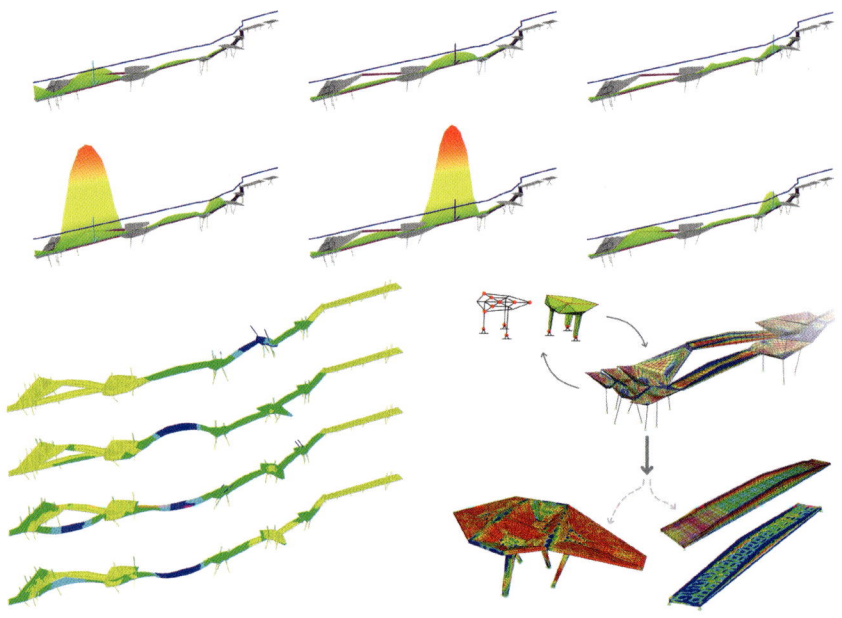

4

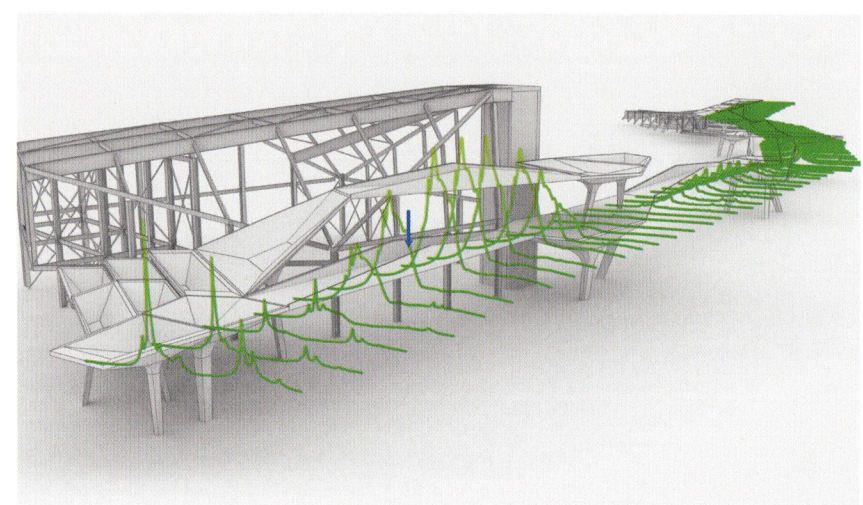

5

4. The master digital model generated numerous local and global models – critical in analysing the dynamic behaviour. © AKT II.

5. Dynamic response of the entire structure to a singular excitation event. © AKTII.

links and islands. Since the structure is both building and walkway, some visitors will be jogging rapidly and thus less sensitive to structural movement, while others will be sitting or immobile for longer periods, thus more aware of vibration and structural motion. Additionally, there are a wide range of acceleration limits documented as acceptable for human occupants (Zivanovic, 2005), and many are lower than the Eurocode limits, for example the $0.5m/s^2$ recommended in Bachmann (1987). The solution to these intertwined factors was to merge criteria from the multiple sources – the National Annex to Eurocode 1 (NA EN1991-2 footbridge), HIVOSS footbridge and Steel Construction Institute publications – into a new hybrid design criteria that captured all of these varied situations to ensure maximum user comfort.

Comparing the digitally-simulated response factors against this new design criteria revealed that certain longer link bridges would be perceived as uncomfortably 'bouncy' by users, and therefore the design team moved on to second phase simulations that tested the response with various sizes of Tuned Mass Dampers (TMDs) installed within either the Link Bridge floor or vertical balustrade cavities. These studies established that small 750kg TMDs located within the balustrade would be sufficient to considerably lower response factors, and ensure none exceeded the criteria. At the same time, this analysis also determined the optimum frequency band for

each mechanism to be tuned to during installation on site, in order to be most effective.

Fabrication and Assembly

During the detailed design phase, the specialist steelwork fabricators Cimolai joined the design team. With their help, the prefabrication strategy was refined further to streamline the construction process that would be undertaken at their Porto Nogaro factory in Italy.

Physical mock-ups were built for part of an island and link bridge, as well as several plate mock-ups that tested different spacings of internal supports (Fig. 8). These were used in concert with the prior digital analyses to reduce certain plate thicknesses and remove specific internal stiffeners, lowering weight and cost. A similar exercise enabled some weld categories to be switched from continuous to intermittent, thus accelerating fabrication, further reducing cost and limiting buckling through heat distortion.

The design team also found a plate assembly sequence for the islands that minimised plug and slot welds from the exterior, thereby limiting the number of external penetrations into the structure and increasing corrosion resistance. In fact, both the islands and links were designed to limit post-installation processes that might

6. Cimolai fabricators welding internal stiffeners. For kind concession of Cimolai S.p.A.

7. Radial internal plate distribution. © AKT II.

8

9

compromise their sealed external envelopes. Landscape drainage, electrical conduits, lifting connections, and minimally-dimensioned access hatches were all integrated within their prefabrication (Figs 6, 7, 9).

As each cluster was completed, it was preassembled and tested for construction tolerance and assumed lifting and installation processes. Afterwards they were separated back into individual islands, loaded onto boats and shipped from the North Adriatic Sea to Tilbury Dock at the mouth of the Thames, before being offloaded to barges for the 30km journey up the Thames to the Peninsula. Working together, Cimolai and Mace implemented a bespoke lifting scheme to safely and rapidly unload the barges on to shore. This task was particularly onerous, due to the unique shape and internal weight distribution of each island, as well as the short tidal windows that determined offloading (Figs 10, 11).

In the final stage, the elements were manoeuvred across the Peninsula and delivered to site on the back of remotely-controlled self-propelled modular transporters, before being erected on site using minimal temporary works (Fig. 12). The islands were connected to their foundations with calibrated torque post-tensioned bolts to extend design fatigue life, and they were completed by fitting secondary elements and finishes: low-iron glass balustrades, the Resysta decking and its support structure, and the trees and landscape.

With the islands in place, the links could then be craned into position upon rubber Maurer thermal expansion bearings, and their TMDs were installed. One of the final steps prior to completion was the physical testing and calibration of these dampers to verify their efficacy.

Conclusion

The interdisciplinary approach applied to the design, analysis and fabrication of this project was extremely successful. By operating within a shared 'master model' environment, the architectural, engineering and fabrication teams were able to swiftly iterate through multiple designs options and realise this unusual mixed-typology structure.

Harnessing advanced digital tools and workflows such as Reakt was critical for many aspects of the project – particularly in accurately simulating and resolving the complex local and global dynamic behaviour that occurs in the asymmetrical islands and their cluster arrangements. The results of these tests were looped directly back into the model to control multiple other aspects such as the layout and design of internal structural supports, and the specification of TMDs.

The synchronised master model was also vital in pursuing a prefabrication strategy that shortened the assembly period on site, yet maintained a high build quality. It allowed potential issues with the prefabrication sequencing and details to be highlighted and resolved in advance, and made economically feasible the scheduling and production of hundreds of uniquely shaped steel plate elements.

As a result, the project realised the initial vision laid out by Diller Scofidio + Renfro and Neiheiser Argyros, while also being completed on time and with minimal disruption to one of the busiest construction zones in London. Both they and the rest of the design team are excited to see subsequent phases of The Tide emerge across Greenwich Peninsula in future years.

8. Fabrication of mock-up used to test internal plate arrangement. © AKT II.

9. Completed Islands, ready for pre-assembly, testing and shipping. © AKT II.

10. Barge transportation and lifting schemes had to consider the unique shape and weight distribution of each island. For kind concession of Cimolai S.p.A.

11. Completed Islands arriving at the Peninsula. © AKT II.

12. Offloading on to remote-operated SPMTs. For kind concession of Cimolai S.p.A.

10

11

12

Acknowledgements

We would like to acknowledge and thank the rest of The Tide design team for their passion and expertise that helped realise this ambitious project:

Client: Knight Dragon
Architectural Designer (Lead): Diller Scofidio + Renfro (Ben Gilmartin, Elizabeth Diller, Charles Renfro, Ricardo Scofidio, Anthony Saby, Bryce Suite, Ning Hiransaroj, Alex Knezo, John Newman, Swarnabh Ghosh, Erioseto Hendranata)
Architectural Designer: Neiheiser Argyros (Ryan Neiheiser, Xristina Argyros, Giorgio Piscitelli, Eleni Vagianou, Danae Haratsis, Nikolas von Schwabe, Athina Zafeiropoulou, Catarina de Almeida Brito, Thalia Chrousos, Chris Yuan, Kevin Larson)
Structural Engineer: AKT II (Emmanuel Verkinderen, Daniel Bosia, Wai Pang, Camille Guyader, Diego Cervera de la Rosa, Edoardo Tibuzzi, Jeg Dudley, James Magbanua)
MEP engineers: AECOM
Landscape Architect: Gross Max
Lead Contractor: Mace
Specialist Fabricator: Cimolai S.p.A (Federico Siriani, Claudia Pavan, Mattia Tofanelli)

References

Diller, L., Scofidio, R. and Renfro, C. (2016) 'The Tide' Planning Application, Design Statement Part 1, p4, https://planning.royalgreenwich.gov.uk/online-applications/files/2CE78273DCCB273423334826767C0620/pdf/16_4183_R-PART_1_DESIGN_STATEMENT_15-12-2016__5_.-390275.pdf. (Accessed 8 January 2020]

Bachmann, H. and Ammann, W. 1987. *Vibrations in Structures: Induced by Man and Machines*, Zurich, Switzerland: IABSE.

Beg, D., Kuhlmann, U., Davaine, L. and Braun, B. 2011. *Design of Plated Structures: Eurocode 3: Design of Steel Structures, Part 1-5: Design of Plated Structures*, Chichester: Wiley.

British Standards. 2003. NA to BS 1991-2 National Annex to Eurocode 1: *Actions on Structures - Part 2: Traffic Loads on Bridges*.

Hicks, S. J., Feldmann, M., Heinemeyer, C., Lukic, M., Caetano, E., Cunha, Á., Goldack, A., Keil, A., Schlaich M., Smith, A., Hechler, O., Obiala, R., Galanti, F. and Waarts, P. (2010). *Human-Induced Vibrations of Steel Structures* (HIVOSS), Luxembourg: Publications Office of the European Union. (doi: 10.2777/79056)

Kingman, J., Dudley, J. and Baptista, R. 2017. 'The 2016 Serpentine Pavilion: A Case Study in Large Scale GFRP Structural Design and Assembly' in Menges, A., Sheil, B., Glynn, R. and Skavara, M. (eds), *Fabricate 2017: Rethinking Design and Construction*, London: UCL Press, pp. 138-145.

Tibuzzi, E. 2016. 'Interweaving Practice' in Kara, H. and Bosia, D. (eds), *Design Engineering Refocused*, Chichester: John Wiley & Sons, pp. 214-233.

Živanović, S., Pavić, A. and Reynolds, P. 2005. 'Vibration serviceability of footbridges under human-induced excitation: a literature review', *Journal of Sound and Vibration*, 279(1-2), pp. 1-74. (doi:10.1016/j.jsv.2004.01.019)

MAKING FORM WORK
EXPERIMENTS ALONG THE GRAIN OF CONCRETE AND TIMBER

SASA ZIVKOVIC / LESLIE LOK
CORNELL UNIVERSITY

Research Aims and Objectives

Ashes Cabin is a small building comprising a 3D-printed concrete substructure and a robotically fabricated Structural Insulated Panel (SIP)-panel envelope of irregular wood logs. The cabin has a footprint of 3 x 3 metres and lifts off the ground on 3D-printed legs which adjust to the sloping terrain. The concrete structure is characterised by three programmatic areas: a table, a storage seat element, and a 6.5m tall working fireplace. The project aims to reveal 3D printing's idiosyncratic tectonic language and examine preconceived notions about material standards in wood. The custom 3D printing process explores how the layering of concrete, the relentless three-dimensional deposition of extruded lines of material, and the act of corbelling can suggest new strategies for building. Built without formwork, concrete 3D printing eliminates substantial construction waste. The cabin aims to demonstrate the architectural and tectonic potential of concrete 3D printing by fabricating components on a self-built large-scale 3D printer. For its envelope, the cabin utilises wood which is widely considered as 'waste'. The invasive Emerald Ash Borer threatens to eradicate nearly all of the 8.7 billion ash trees in North America. Most of these trees cannot be processed by regular sawmills and are therefore regarded as unsuitable for construction. Mature ash trees with irregular geometries present an enormous untapped material resource. Through high-precision 3D scanning and robotic fabrication on a custom platform, this project aims to demonstrate that such trees constitute a valuable resource and present architectural opportunities.

From the ground up, digital design and fabrication technologies are intrinsic to the making of this architectural prototype and facilitating fundamentally new material methods, tectonic articulations, and forms of construction. The cabin's performance, structure, and architectural expression are inherently derived from its digital construction protocols and design logics at various scales. First, this research paper will outline challenges and opportunities – material, computation, fabrication, and logistic – associated with developing a multi-material and thermally-insulated building that utilises novel construction techniques and methods. Second, the paper will briefly outline the custom 3D printing process developed for this project with a focus on architectural detailing and material corbelling. Third, the main body of the research paper will focus on the design and development of a smart SIP system based on natural log

geometries. The developed panels are fully functional (insulated, waterproof, lightweight) and use high precision 3D laser scanning and custom robotic fabrication protocols to process irregular tree geometries which are normally not used in construction.

Research Context

The invasive Emerald Ash Borer threatens to eradicate most of the 8.7 billion ash trees in North America. Since its discovery in the United States in 2002, the ash borer has killed tens of millions of ash trees and has drastically transformed entire forest ecosystems in the process (Herms and McCullough, 2014). In New York State, ash trees constitute about 10% of the tree population. The Emerald Ash Borer was first discovered in 2009 and has since spread rapidly across the southern half of the state (USDA, 2019). Infested ash is often comprised of mature growth which includes many trees with irregular trunk and fork geometries. While such trees could be used for construction, they are typically regarded as economically 'invaluable' (worth about US$ 0.25 per tree) as they cannot be processed by regular sawmills. Most of the dead ash trees end up as firewood or perish without purpose while releasing carbon dioxide into the atmosphere. The project borrows strategies from traditional wood building and manufacturing (Blondeau and Du Clairbois, 1783) and aims to increase the yield of tree usage in construction. Currently, only around 35% of the wood of a tree is estimated to be used in construction (Ramage et al., 2017), mainly straight tree trunks and generally omitting curved timber altogether.

Ashes Cabin expands on research projects such as the Wood Chip Barn (Mollica and Self, 2016) at Hooke Park (Self, 2016), Limb at University of Michigan (Von Buelow et al., 2018), Log Knot at the Cornell Robotic Construction Laboratory (Hilburg, 2018) or industry applications developed by companies such as WholeTrees Structures (WholeTrees LLC, 2019). The process and design methodology shared by these projects constitutes a paradigm shift in the design and construction of wood structures: rather than first mass-standardising an irregular product (a tree) to subsequently mass-customise a design from the standardised components (plywood, 2x4s, etc.), each project starts with the available natural timber geometry and capitalises on its idiosyncrasies. This reciprocal design process fosters synergies and feedback between material, fabrication, digital form, and full-scale construction.

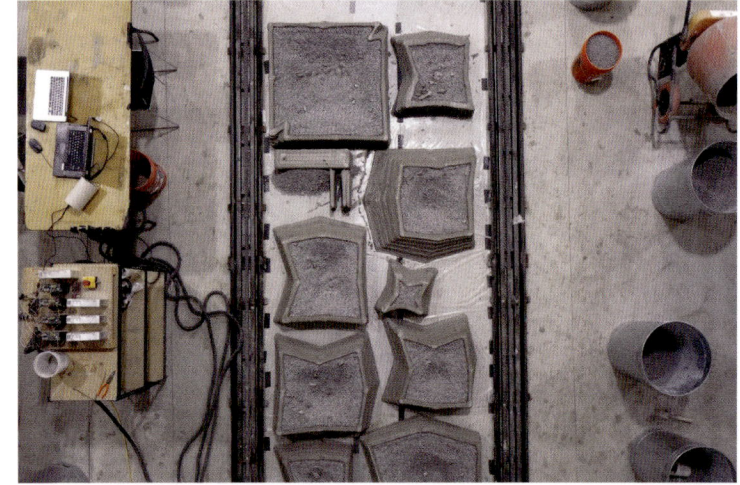

2

3

4

5

Dead ash trees form an enormous and untapped material resource. This project proposes to take advantage of the Emerald Ash Borer's carnage and appropriate irregularly shaped ash trees for construction. By implementing high precision 3D scanning and robotic-based fabrication technology, 'waste wood' is transformed into an abundantly available, affordable, and sustainable building material. No longer bound to the paradigm of industrial standardisation, this project revisits bygone wood craft and design based on organic, found and living materials. Architecturally, the naturally bent wood planks create enclosure and are strategically assembled to create window openings, framed views, awnings, door handles or entrances.

Research Questions

Most projects which use irregular and natural wood geometries for construction focus on leveraging round wood and its structural capacity. Ashes Cabin questions whether irregular and natural wood geometries can be used to create surface structures. Initial studies were conducted which test the feasibility of the idea both at the scale of study models and in initial single-surface full-scale prototypes. Technical research questions emerged during this process: What are the necessary computational protocols that enable toggling between physical material and digital model? What are the material behaviours of ash wood when cut into curved boards and assembled into surfaces? How thinly can boards be sliced, and what are the limits of log geometries? What fabrication tools and end-effectors are necessary to conduct this type of research? What fabrication processes need to be developed or advanced and what fundamental logistic processes are required?

One of the main research objectives of this project is the translation from fabrication concepts and prototypes into a fully-functional building as well as embracing all the constraints attached to such an enterprise. This significantly broadens and complicates any research questions. Beyond the prototypes, can a building be built using the two self-developed fabrication processes – high-corbel concrete 3D printing and robotic wood slicing? Can irregular timber geometries be used to create a fully-functioning, ventilated, waterproof and insulated high-performance building envelope? How does the envelope turn corners and how does it meet the roof? How are windows integrated into the SIP panel surface? What are the detail connections between wood and concrete?

A less quantifiable yet critically important research question is: What are the design possibilities of such an approach? Windows, doors, roof connections, awnings, roof drainage, foundations, floors, chimneys, and all associated details have to be re-thought through the lens of new technology and fabrication processes. In their radical and consequential architectural application lies the real potential of developing novel construction methods.

Research Methods

Cantilevered Concrete Printing
The concrete structure of Ashes Cabin was printed on an open-source large-scale three-axis gantry 3D printer, developed at the Cornell Robotic Construction Laboratory (Zivkovic and Battaglia, 2017). In horizontal layer concrete 3D printing, geometric surface complexity and sectional transformation are achieved through corbelling – an incremental offset of toolpath trajectories. To enable steep

1. Full scale surface test prototype. Image: Sasa Zivkovic.

2. Daedalus 3D printer by RCL, with printed cabin components.

3. Finished concrete structure with scale figure. Image: Reuben Chen.

4. Curved logs sliced at various and varying thicknesses. Image: Leslie Lok.

5. Robotic slicing of a curved log using the KUKA KR200/2 platform with a custom 5HP band saw. Image: Sasa Zivkovic.

cantilevers of up to 60° for printed geometries, a re-usable gravel support material method was developed to provide necessary structural support during the concrete printing process. The 3D-printed components function as sacrificial zero-waste formwork for the main structural system, a cast-in-place concrete structure with custom rebar cages (Lok and Zivkovic, 2018). The printed formwork was designed in small sectional modules to be transported and assembled manually without the use of any heavy machinery at the remote construction site.

Harvesting

The cabin's wood envelope was constructed from ten mature ash trees, infested by the Emerald Ash Borer, which were harvested from the Cornell Arnot Teaching and Research Forest. Trees were selected based on log diameter and curvature features; the selection presents a normal cross-section of available geometries which are not specialised but fall within regular parameters of tree growth. The project utilises both straight and curved logs to reduce waste and dependency on highly specialised trees. From the ten selected ash trees, 45 smaller logs were cut, catalogued and matched to the curvatures of the initial cabin design. A Skanect 3D Scanning iPad Kit was utilised for all fabrication and the cataloguing of timber stock inventory.

Design Process

Geometric form finding and custom assembly protocols from form-to-log and log-to-form were developed for this project. To construct the wood envelope, the research team harvested available ash trees, 3D scanned their log geometries, robotically sliced those logs into boards, and strategically assembled the boards to form a variety of surface conditions. Aggregated surface board yield relates to board thicknesses as well as the overall diameter of the log. As the board width changes with the log diameter, a custom script was developed in Grasshopper to lay out the boards in the 3D model and parametrically manipulate design relationships. The custom protocols and scripts enabled the design team to easily toggle between design concept, material reality and fabrication constraints. To fully utilise the available tree geometries, three surface-layering conditions were developed: (1) planar surfaces based on straight log geometries; (2) curved surfaces based on curved logs; and (3) double-curved surfaces based on curved or straight logs. The robotically-carved timber boards can be assembled into double-curvature surfaces by strategically adjusting the thickness of the band saw cut.

Robotic Log Slicing

Utilising a KUKA KR200/2 with a custom-built 5HP band saw end effector with a 25mm blade and 1.3 teeth

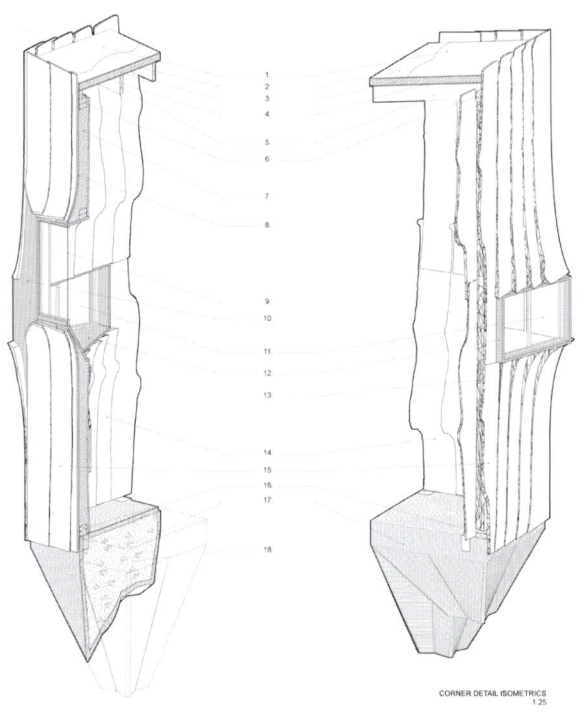

6

CORNER DETAIL ISOMETRICS
1.25

7

6. SIP panel detail. Image: HANNAH.

7. Window frame and undulating wood surface. Image: Andy Chen.

8. Cabin interior with windows that frame views in different directions. Image: Andy Chen.

9. View of cabin exterior and corner window. Image: Andy Chen.

10. Exterior view of cabin within the context of the site. Image: Andy Chen.

11. Bird's eye view of the finished project on site. Image: Sasa Zivkovic.

per inch, the research team could saw irregular tree logs into naturally curved boards of various and varying thicknesses (up to 2mm thickness). Logs were first mounted on a custom-built log-mounting system and then scanned in place to determine their position relative to the robot. The slicing process was relatively swift with the robot moving at a cutting speed of 10mm per second.

Panel Assembly and Detailing

A modular SIP panel façade was assembled from the robotically-sliced boards. The SIPs were insulated using a two-component closed-cell foam (for which a fully biodegradable option is also available). The façade assembly was fully ventilated and detailed to manage shrinkage and transformation of wooden boards to offset the air-drying process, and to not require an additional rain screen. The boards were arrayed into interlocking SIP façade panels and solid off-cuts could be structurally integrated in the assembly, resulting in a minimum waste fabrication method (this step was omitted due to time constraints and the team's limited resources). Minimal wooden frames were first built to hang the outer skin and subsequently apply ventilation strips, followed by 10cm of spray foam, and then install the inner wood skin to create a solid and structurally sound assembly. The entire project was pre-assembled in the team's research space before being installed on site over a two-week period. Custom window frames, a door, and a kitchen counter were designed and fabricated using plywood and single-pane glazing. The exterior envelope of the cabin was left untreated and will turn grey over time to naturally protect the exterior from environmental conditions.

Material Parameters

Ash wood is very conducive to this type of fabrication process due to its relatively low moisture content compared to other types of wood. After harvesting, the moisture content of the ash logs was 20%, close to the ideal moisture content of 10 – 15%. The low moisture content reduces warping once the boards are cut and ensures the geometric stability necessary to construct the envelope. Although additional time for drying would be preferable, the cut boards were assembled into façade panels two weeks after robotic slicing and remained stable throughout the fabrication process.

Research Evaluation

The mass-customised fabrication process developed for the Ashes Cabin project calls for constant feedback between material and digital realms. Fully leveraging the opportunity gap between the physical materiality of the wood and its digital design parameters remains one of the

8

9

10

most challenging aspects of such a project. In order to complete the cabin envelope within a challenging time frame and with limited resources, the research team had to cease the development of more ambitious surface geometries, the advancement of full zero-waste protocols, expedient detail connections between panels, and the evolution of computational design protocols that fully automate the process from 3D scanning to fabrication. Future investigations will focus on the further development of these aspects of the project. Furthermore, future investigations will focus on utilising more complex log geometries which can help generate a broader variety of surface conditions. Such surface conditions could be optimised for structural performance in a vertical or a horizontal assembly. Additionally, further research and testing is necessary to evaluate whether this fabrication method can be applied to other types of wood with a higher moisture content.

Overall, the project managed to fulfil most of its research objectives and demonstrates that irregular ash tree boards can be used to create a high-performance envelope for a fully-functional small building. It presents a pathway to address the massive environmental problem caused by the Emerald Ash Borer in North American Forests.

Conclusion

New techniques of construction are needed to address the world's prevalent environmental, economic, and social challenges. Simple technologies such as 3D scanning, a 5HP band saw robot, and custom computational protocols can assist in the development of much needed new ecological and architectural paradigms. Along with other projects, Ashes Cabin demonstrates that wood which is otherwise considered 'waste' can be used in construction and new technologies afford a different utilisation of materials. This approach challenges the current logics of mass-standardisation and their associated systemic inefficiencies. Design opportunities within this new ecological paradigm are tremendous. Architecturally, Ashes Cabin walks the line between the familiar and unfamiliar. Stark and bold black geometries pierce the wooden fabric-like envelope. The undulating wooden surfaces accentuate the building's programme and yet remain reminiscent of the natural log geometry which they are derived from. While transformed, the natural tree remains legible in the design.

Ashes Cabin is a fully functional building constructed from concrete and wood. Its architectural expression and function are profoundly derived from the digital design and fabrication technologies developed for this project.

By addressing the complex realities of building and construction, the authors believe that this project contributes to closing the gap between digital modelling, conceptual design development, and physical realisation – advancing a research discourse that increasingly focuses on full-scale implementation of new fabrication techniques in architectural projects (not installations) across scales.

References

Blondeau, E-N. and Vial Du Clairbois, H-S. 1783. *Encyclopédie méthodique. Marine*. Paris: Chez Panckoucke.

Herms, D.A. and McCullough, D.G. 2014. 'Emerald ash borer invasion of North America: history, biology, ecology, impacts, and management', *Annual Review of Entomology*, 59, pp. 13-30.

Hilburg, J. 2018. 'Knotted installation proposes ways to reduce timber waste', *Architect's Newspaper*, 29 October, https://archpaper.com/2018/10/cornell-log-knot. (Accessed 6 October 2019)

Lok, L. and Zivkovic, S. 2018. 'CORBEL CABIN: 3D Printed Concrete Building', in *ACADIA 2018: Re/calibration: on Imprecision and Infidelity* [Project Catalogue of the 38th Annual Conference of the Association for Computer Aided Design in Architecture (ACADIA)].

Mollica, Z. and Self, M. 2016. 'Tree Fork Truss', in Adriaenssens, S., Gramazio, F., Kohler, M., Menges, A. and Pauly, M. (eds), *Advances in Architectural Geometry 2016*, Zürich: Hochschulverlag, pp. 138-153.

Ramage, M. H., Burridge, H., Busse-Wicher, M., Fereday, G., Reynolds, T., Shah, D. U., Wu, G., Yu, L., Fleming, P., Densley-Tingley, D., Allwood, J., Dupree, P., Linden, P. F. and Scherman, O. 2017. 'The wood from the trees: The use of timber in construction', in *Renewable and Sustainable Energy Reviews*, 68(Part 1), pp. 333-359.

Self, M. 2016. 'Hooke Park: application for timber in its Natural Form', in Menges, A., Schwinn, T. and Krieg, O. D. (eds), *Advancing Wood Architecture: A Computational Approach*. London: Routledge, 2016.

USDA Forest Service and Michigan State University, *Emerald Ash Borer Information Network*, http://www.emeraldashborer.info. (Accessed 6 October 2019)

Von Buelow, P., Torghabehi, O. O., Mankouche, S. and Vliet, K. 2018. 'Combining parametric form generation and design exploration to produce a wooden reticulated shell using natural tree crotches', in *Proceedings of International Association for Shell and Spatial Structures (IASS) Annual Symposia* 2018, (20), pp. 1-8.

WholeTrees. Research and Development, *WholeTrees*, https://wholetrees.com/technology/. (Accessed 18 June 2019)

Zivkovic, S. and Battaglia, C. 2017. 'Open Source Factory: Democratizing Large-Scale Fabrication Systems', in *ACADIA 2017: Disciplines and Disruption* [Proceedings of the 37th Annual Conference of the Association for Computer Aided Design in Architecture (ACADIA)], pp. 660–69.

ADDITIVE FABRICATION OF CONCRETE ELEMENTS BY ROBOTS
LIGHTWEIGHT CONCRETE CEILING

GEORG HANSEMANN[1] / ROBERT SCHMID[1] / CHRISTOPH HOLZINGER[1] / JOSHUA TAPLEY[1] / HOANG HUY KIM[2] /
VALENTINO SLISKOVIC[3] / BERNHARD FREYTAG[3] / ANDREAS TRUMMER[1] / STEFAN PETERS[1]
[1] INSTITUTE OF STRUCTURAL DESIGN, GRAZ UNIVERSITY OF TECHNOLOGY
[2] INSTITUTE OF STRUCTURAL CONCRETE, GRAZ UNIVERSITY OF TECHNOLOGY
[3] LABORATORY FOR STRUCTURAL ENGINEERING, GRAZ UNIVERSITY OF TECHNOLOGY

Reinforced Concrete – The Building Material of the Century

For the last 150 years, engineers and designers have been choosing reinforced concrete as the material to use for load bearing structures. Over the decades it has proven itself as a robust composite material. It is versatile and has insulating and fire proofing properties. Reinforced concrete has become indispensable as a building material, both for the elements which come in contact with the ground and for the structural elements which transfer horizontal or vertical loads. Concrete is not only used in multi-storey buildings but also applied in infrastructure. Over the course of time, two production processes have established themselves, in-situ concrete construction and prefabricated construction. The latter can be further divided into fully precast elements and elements that are completed once they have been filled with in-situ concrete. Over the years, the cost of producing concrete elements has shifted between material and labour costs and this has effected the appearance of concrete constructions. Originally, the cost of the materials was high and the labour costs low and this led to lean, filigree designs. Nowadays, however, to save on the expensive labour costs and make use of the cheap material costs, bulky, thick walled components are very common. This development is also accompanied by the demands of recent building standards which include, for example, the necessary concrete cover for durable components. Fundamentally and above all else, there is an enormous demand for building materials due to current urbanisation trends and this, in turn, pushes us to rethink material efficiency. This is especially necessary as there are a large number of multi-storey buildings being built where the efficiency of the structure is ignored. They are responsible for a large amount of the building materials being used. In the light of the fact that the production of cement for reinforced concrete accounts for about 5% of global man-made CO_2 annually (Worrell et al., 2001), the question may be asked whether the way in which our reinforced concrete structures are built is in need of urgent review and revision. Although the composite material has seen many changes and improvements over the years in the area of concrete's properties, rebar manipulation and formwork production, one thing has barely changed and that is the pouring of the concrete. This article presents the research project COEBRO which dealt with using concrete printing to produce an alternative to a poured flat slab ceiling (Fig. 1).

Concrete 3D Printing as a Building Method

The vision of printing houses using a 3D printer was presented around 13 years ago (Khoshnevis et al., 2006). As far as the technology is concerned, an extrusion process has become established for a mortar-like mass. Nevertheless, the process is considered printing with concrete and not printing with mortar. Predominantly, the material is transported through the system using a worm pump and this restricts the maximum grain size of the aggregates. This makes it possible to place the concrete exactly and reduce the formwork needed to produce filigree components with complex geometries. In this way, the production of additional formwork is no longer necessary.

The low tensile strength of the concrete means there is a requirement for the integration of appropriate reinforcement, and the entrainment of wire or roving looks promising (Tapley, 2018). The mechanical requirements of the building elements, whether it be to prevent collapse or usability, defines the amount of necessary reinforcement. Presently, the uses for printed concrete are limited to plain concrete objects.

Based on these technical fundamentals, uses are being found. They include the appearance as part of the formal design. Examples include panels for building interiors (Kopper, 2019) or plant pots (Baumit GmbH, 2018). There are numerous large format installations which show the shaping potential and the boundaries between material and machine (David, 2018).

As far as the application of the technology for elements in building construction is concerned, there are prototype buildings that have been produced on site (Hager et al., 2016). They are usually twin-wall structures with minimal reinforcement. In these cases, the reach of the robot defines the size of the objects. The Chinese company WinSun produce precast elements for building construction that act as a lost formwork. The load bearing requirements are then achieved by adding standard concrete.

Concrete and the Question of Material Efficiency

The 3D printing process opens new doors for precise and sparse placement of material. Slender concrete elements with a thin wall could finally be produced at great speed and with little effort. This argument often becomes relevant when discussing the environmental aspects of concrete structures. A significant portion of concrete is used to produce flat slabs. For this reason, the question can be asked how can 3D printing improve the material efficiency of flat slabs.

Waffle slab ceilings and ribbed ceilings as planned by engineers such as Nervi or Favini, and architects such as Mangiarotti in the 1960s and 1970s, have become trademarks of buildings such as the Palazetto della Sport. But there are also large numbers of these types of material-efficient ceilings dating from the same period hidden behind suspended ceilings, some of which are being re-exposed after revitalisation. These ceiling use at least 30-40% less material compared to the equivalent flat slab ceiling, if not more. If shell effects are also used, such as in the projects from the ETH Zurich (Liew et al., 2017) then the material saving can be increased to 70%. This method was replaced by point supported flat slabs as the cost of the formwork outweighed the savings from the material. The waffle slab is due for a comeback as the CO_2 performance of construction becomes ever more important. Can 3D printed concrete formwork support conventional methods and offer long overdue solutions to lighter concrete construction?

3D Printing – A Machine-Material Depending Process

The developed process comprises of: (i) robotic control unit, (ii) automatic mixing pump, (iii) industrial robot with additional 7th axis, (iv) accelerator piston pump, (v) printing head. The hopper of the pump is filled from a Bigbag, which in turn is filled with dry premix. Once the concrete has been mixed it is pumped to the nozzle. Here an accelerator is injected into the concrete and mixed into an homogenous material. All of the necessary control values are supplied to the main computer and this passes the information to several different components. The industrial robot, the automatic mixing pump, and the accelerator piston pump are all linked to each other.

The concrete is required to stay in place instantaneously upon extrusion and to be strong enough to sustain the weight of the layers placed subsequently on top of it. The optimisation of the rheological and physical properties of fresh concrete are crucial for the printing process. Concrete must be optimised to obtain: (i) a good consistency involving high open time for pumping and extrusion, and (ii) a good structural build-up for non-deformed printed elements during vertical placement of concrete layers.

Premixed concrete is the best choice for an homogenous fresh concrete with a simple mixing process and can be mass produced in a factory.

High powder volume with a low cement content and a high inert/reactive ultrafine powder content must be developed to obtain a good structural build-up concrete. The most suitable accelerators must be tailored.

1. Suspended full scale experimental prototype. Image: Robert Schmid.

2. The layout of the ribs according to the principal stress trajectories. Graphic: Georg Hansemann

3. The placed and fixed forms before the insertion of the rebar cage. Image: Georg Hansemann.

4. The rebar after being shaped and placed in the formwork. Image: Georg Hansemann.

2

3

4

A good consistency for a concrete without an accelerator which has high open time for pumping and extrusion should be longer than 60 minutes.

The accelerator is injected directly into the stream of liquid concrete as it passes through the nozzle. The amount of accelerator that is introduced into the mixture is controlled by changing the injection pressure and the duration. The amount of accelerator that is necessary can be amended according to the printing geometry.

3D Printed Lost Formwork for Smarter Ceiling-Systems

In order to evaluate the performance of a mass-optimised flat slab, a full-scale case study was carried out (Fig. 2). The experiment was designed to show both the feasibility of the manufacturing method and the structural capability with respect to sustainable alternatives to conventional flat slabs. The aim of the experiment was to develop a largescale prototype where the material and weight was minimised compared to a standard flat slab alternative by using the developed production method of printing lost formwork.

The basis of the experiment was a 30cm-thick flat slab on a grid of columns with 8m spans and a characteristic service load of 5 kN/m² including superimposed dead and live loads. In a preliminary design, the required reinforcement for this common slab was determined.

This flat slab was then converted to a ribbed slab, where the ribs follow the trajectories of the inner forces of the flat slab. The thickness of the ribs stayed at 30cm. The final full-scale specimen represented a characteristic part of the point-supported ribbed slab between two columns. It was 8m long and 3m wide. The maximum dimensions of the lost formwork elements were based on the weight that two people could carry. Ribs were printed on to the formwork elements to increase the resistance to the forces which occur during movement, transportation and the hydrostatic pressure during the pouring process. No reinforcement was entrained in the printed concrete lines.

The exact amount of longitudinal reinforcement required, which was determined for the common flat slab, was then built into the new prototype, concentrated in the ribs as beam reinforcement with stirrups. The printed formwork was used as concrete cover. Another calculation was carried out in order to check the ultimate limit strength and the serviceability limit strength considering the same service load.

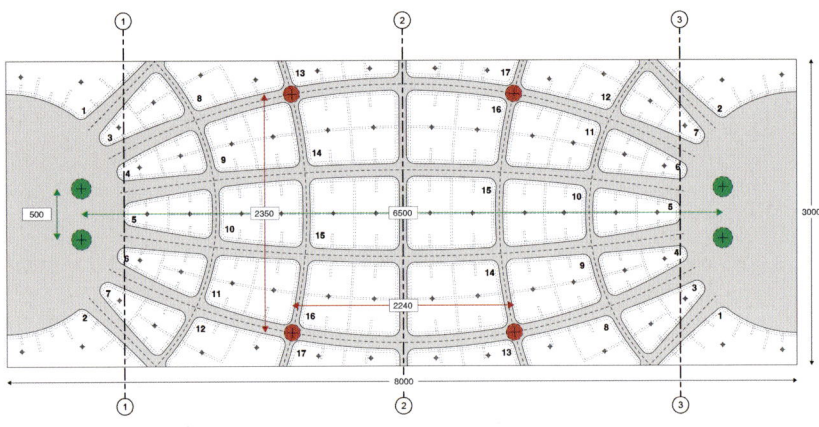

5

6

5. Ground view of the full-scale specimen – green: supporting points; red: loading points. Graphic: Bernhard Freytag, Georg Hansemann.

6. Bottom view of the final prototype during the bending test. Image: Bernhard Freytag.

7. COEBRO 3D printing team on the prototype before bending. (l-r) Georg Hansemann, Hoang Huy Kim, Robert Schmid, Dominik Schraml. Image: Andreas Trummer.

8. Bottom view of the final prototype before the bending test. Image: Robert Schmid.

9. 3D printed concrete formwork with additional supporting ribs. Image: Robert Schmid.

Using the developed 3D concrete printing facility, 34 forms were produced in effectively 4 hours. The nozzle moved at a speed of 250mm/s and an average form took 7 minutes to print (Fig. 9). The individual machine code scripts were created using an automatic software script. The input parameters were the contours of the object as well as the position and size of the ribs.

The finished forms were placed in the correct position, upside-down on a table form in the Rauter factory (Fig. 3). To prevent the forms from shifting during the pouring process they were fixed with a silicon sealant. The rebar was bent in the correct radii, connected as reinforcement cages and lifted into the correct spaces within the form (Fig. 4). After the edge formwork was positioned and fixed, the concrete slab was poured. The hardened slab was transported back to the Graz University of Technology to undergo plate bending tests (Figs 7, 8).

Due to the fact that the ribs met at the massive circular area around the columns, the carrying mechanisms of punching shear and hogging moments did not change compared to conventional flat slabs, only the punching load was smaller due to the reduced weight. Nevertheless, the experiment focused on the bending behaviour of the spans and the bond behaviour between the printed parts and in-situ concrete. The specimen was supported at four points close to the line of zero-bending-moment in the basic slab. The load was introduced at four points, the locations of which were chosen to achieve the best approximation of the bending moment distribution with respect to the distributed service load (Fig. 5).

The structural behaviour of the specimen was recorded using 26 strain and displacement sensors as well as a non-contact measuring system and crack microscopes (Fig. 6). The bending behaviour under service loads met the limits of the EC 2 in both regards, crack width (0.25mm < 0.4mm) and deflection (24mm < 26mm). The load bearing capacity is far beyond the capacity needed. The tensile strain of the rib-concrete and the printed concrete next to it did not differ from each other. One can conclude that the bond between these two parts was very strong. This was also confirmed by the observation of cracks, which occurred straight through both materials. Regarding the T-beam behaviour, the measurements of compressive strains at the top of the ribbed slab showed that the 10cm thick plate works as a fully activated compression zone.

Conclusion

The paper investigated the potential for 3D concrete printing. The key consideration is the use of 3D-printed elements in conventional concrete structures for a higher rate of resource efficiency. A 3D printing facility was presented. The promising prototype, the ribbed slab, proved that the assembly process works and showed the determined mechanical behaviour. Using this system, the goal of reducing the amount of concrete used was achieved. Future work will focus on two aspects. The first aspect is the search for applications that make concrete structures more efficient. This will require more flexibility for the concrete's properties, such as the density and strength, within the printing process. The second aspect is the need for a robust reinforcing system.

7

8

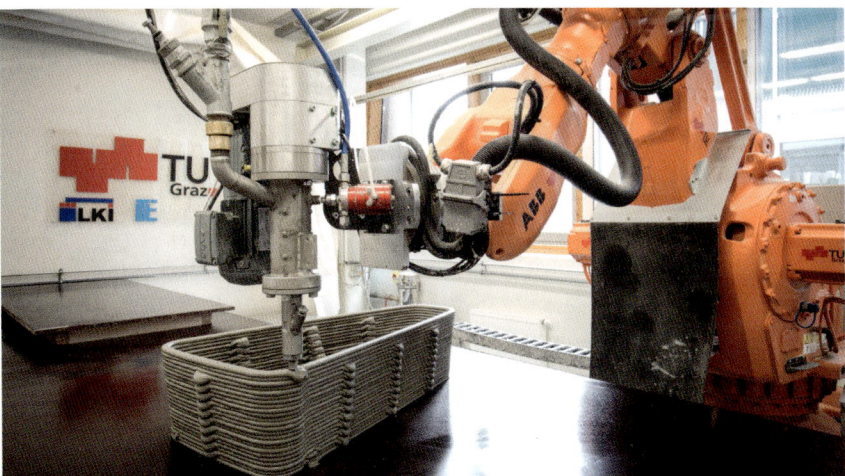

9

References

David. 2018. 'Digital Chaiselongue: Incremental3d and Philipp Aduatz 3D print innovative concrete chair', *3ders.org,* http://www.3ders.org/articles/20180405-digital-chaiselongue-incremental3d-and-philipp-aduatz-3d-print-innovative-concrete-chair.html. (Accessed 7 October 2019)

Hager, I., Golonka, A. and Putanowicz, R. 2016. '3D Printing of Buildings and Building Components as the Future of Sustainable Construction?' *Procedia Engineering* 151. pp. 292–299. (doi: 10.1016/j.proeng.2016.07.357)

Khoshnevis, B., Hwang, D., Yao, K. and Yeh, Z. 2006. 'Mega-scale fabrication by Contour Crafting', *International Journal of Industrial and Systems Engineering* 1(3), pp. 301–320. (doi: 10.1504/IJISE.2006.009791)

Kopper, T. 2019. 'Mit Druck in die Zukunft'. *Bauzeitung,* https://www.bauforum.at/bauzeitung/mit-druck-die-zukunft-186088. (Accessed 7 October 2019)

Liew, A., López, D., van Mele, T. and Block, P. 2017. 'Design, fabrication and testing of a prototype, thin-vaulted, unreinforced concrete floor', *Engineering Structures* 137, pp. 323–335. (doi: 10.1016/j.engstruct.2017.01.075)

Tapley, J. P. 2018. 'Carbon und Textilbewehrung für 3D-gedruckten Beton', in *10. Carbon und Textilbetontage: Tagungsband*, Trade fair, 25-26 September, Dresden: C³ - Carbon Concrete Composite e.V., pp. 28–29. https://www.carbon-textilbetontage.de/wp-content/uploads/2018/09/Final_C3_Tagungsband_CTBT2018_web.pdf. (Accessed 14 November 2019)

Worrell, E., Price, L., Martin, N., Hendriks, C. and Ozawa Meida, L. 2001. 'Carbon Dioxide Emissions from the Global Cement Industry', *Annual Review of Energy and the Environment* 26(1), pp. 303–329. (doi: 10.1146/annurev.energy.26.1.303)

DFAB HOUSE
A COMPREHENSIVE DEMONSTRATOR OF DIGITAL FABRICATION IN ARCHITECTURE

KONRAD GRASER / MARCO BAUR / ALEKSANDRA ANNA APOLINARSKA /
KATHRIN DÖRFLER / NORMAN HACK / ANDREI JIPA / ENA LLORET-FRITSCHI /
TIMOTHY SANDY / DANIEL SANZ PONT / DANIEL M. HALL / MATTHIAS KOHLER
ETH ZURICH / NCCR DIGITAL FABRICATION

Introduction

This paper describes the making of DFAB HOUSE, a multi-technology demonstrator of digital fabrication in architecture, engineering and construction (AEC). While most individual digital fabrication technologies used to build DFAB HOUSE have been presented independently at conferences and in journal articles, this paper describes how, in concert, they amount to an architectural achievement that is more than the sum of its parts. To do this, the paper does three things: it describes the process of conceiving and delivering the overall project; secondly, it highlights challenges in implementation; and finally it discusses the significance of DFAB HOUSE in the context of a rapidly transforming architectural research and practice.

Research Context

Project Setting and Objectives

DFAB HOUSE is an architecture project with a unique purpose: to learn about the possibilities of digital fabrication in a real-world setting. The initial idea originated at ETH Zurich within the Swiss National Centre of Competence in Research (NCCR) Digital

Fabrication, an interdisciplinary research initiative involving architecture, structural design, materials science, computer science, control systems engineering and robotics. The NCCR's founding in 2014 coincided with the launch of NEST by Empa (Swiss Federal Laboratories for Materials Science and Technology), a modular innovation incubator. NEST is a four-storey 'backbone' providing construction sites for experimental NEST Units, co-funded by Empa, research partners and industry. NEST Units are fully code-compliant buildings and follow strict performance standards (Richner et al., 2018).

The vision for DFAB HOUSE was to combine research from seven NCCR-affiliated ETH professorships in a single NEST Unit and realise it in collaboration with more than 40 industry partners. The three-and-a-half-year project timeline included: 1) investigating the application potential of NCCR research; 2) synthesising research into novel building processes, termed Innovation Objects; 3) conceptualising their role in the overall architectural project; 4) upscaling to application-ready state; and 5) constructing the building.

State of Digital Fabrication Demonstration

Architectural demonstrators allow research to be turned into a technically mature application outside of market constraints. Prior to DFAB HOUSE, digital fabrication research demonstration has largely been limited to single-storey pavilion structures focusing in-depth on one digital fabrication system. Seminal examples are the University of Stuttgart's ICD research pavilions, including the LAGA exhibition hall (Schwinn et al., 2016), Elytra Filament Pavilion (Prado et al., 2017), and the recent BuGa Wood and Fibre Pavilions (icd. uni-stuttgart.de). In addition, there is a trend towards construction demonstrators of additive manufacturing by industry. Examples are the Chicon House by ICON 3D, housing prototypes by Apis Cor, and 3D Housing 05 by CLS Architects and Arup (Valente et al., 2019). Few full-scale construction projects have integrated digital fabrication, among them the Sequential Roof at ETH Zurich (Apolinarska et al., 2016) and the Théâtre Vidy in Lausanne (Robeller et al., 2017). Otherwise, industry adoption of digital fabrication is currently very limited despite the need for AEC to embrace digitalisation (McKinsey & Co., 2016), and to improve efficiency, waste reduction, on-site safety, and productivity (Bock, 2015; World Economic Forum, 2016; Agustí-Juan et al., 2019). In this context, DFAB HOUSE, a three-storey, permitted and inhabited building, positions itself as today's most comprehensive multi-technology demonstrator of digital fabrication in architecture.

Research Questions

Digital fabrication research today is developing a growing number of tools and methods. However, little research has looked at integrating these technologies in the complex process of planning and constructing fully functional buildings. With respect to DFAB HOUSE, a two-fold research gap remains. First, there is currently no comprehensive description of the process of conceptualising, planning and implementing such a complex architectural demonstrator. Second, there is a lack of critical reflection on the overall project, evaluating both its significance to the field and its challenges. To address this gap, this paper seeks to answer two questions. First, how can a complete habitable building be designed and built primarily using multiple digital fabrication processes? This includes: how can research be scaled up from the lab to real-world 1:1 application? How can several new construction methods be integrated and interfaced? How can research and industry combine their resources and expertise? Second, what lessons are learned from such a project? This includes: how do new possibilities stand up to realistic constraints? How can risk and uncertainties, in terms of budget and schedule, be mitigated? What new forms of collaboration arise in this diverse multi-disciplinary space? This paper presents how DFAB HOUSE delivered an exemplary answer to the first question. It then addresses the second question, reflecting on its larger implications.

Realisation of DFAB HOUSE

Project Scope

DFAB HOUSE subsumed three parallel challenges under a holistic process: design integration, upscaling, and execution. For these tasks, the NCCR established a dedicated project management team.

Design integration included evaluation of the NCCR's evolving body of research in joint workshops with the research groups, Empa, and industry which assessed technology readiness, performance and future market potential. A deliberately open and inclusive design process shaped the overall project, where accommodating unknowns and changes was paramount. The project design intentionally kept interfaces between Innovation Objects simple to contain risk, yet made these interdependencies a subject of study. The use of parametric interfaces to link computational design and structural evaluation helped synthesise the stand-alone technologies into a comprehensive system.

Upscaling was the task of turning research at vastly different levels of development into construction-ready applications. Consortia were assembled early on by

2

3

engaging each research group's pre-existing network of industry partners and approaching new partners for DFAB HOUSE. Partnership contracts and agreements were set up to formalise responsibilities and liability. This push to add industry knowledge and expertise enabled full-scale co-development of technically mature applications. Physically proving that regulations, structural requirements and quality standards could be met was essential for approval by the client and authorities, so a dedicated budget was established to cover labour and material for structural tests, material samples and full-scale prototypes.

For execution, digital fabrication workflows were integrated into the reality of the construction practice. This included system design and engineering, technical detailing, design coordination through a central model, and the generation of construction data. Digital fabrication was performed both on site and off site. Importantly, construction contractors, not only researchers, were substantially involved in the execution of DFAB HOUSE. This led to previously untested levels of collaboration, knowledge transfer and risk mitigation between research and executing firms.

1. Site installation of Smart Slab segment. Photo: digital building technologies, ETH Zurich / Xijie Ma.

2 & 3. Exterior view of completed DFAB HOUSE. Photo: Roman Keller.

4. Innovation Objects in DFAB HOUSE, diagram. Image: NCCR Digital Fabrication / Konrad Graser.

Innovation Objects
DFAB HOUSE combines six new digital building technologies, termed Innovation Objects (Fig. 4).

1. The In-situ Fabricator (Fig. 4A) is a generic, context-aware, mobile fabrication robot. Its on-board sensing and computation system allows for autonomous repositioning, end effector localisation, and in-process fabrication

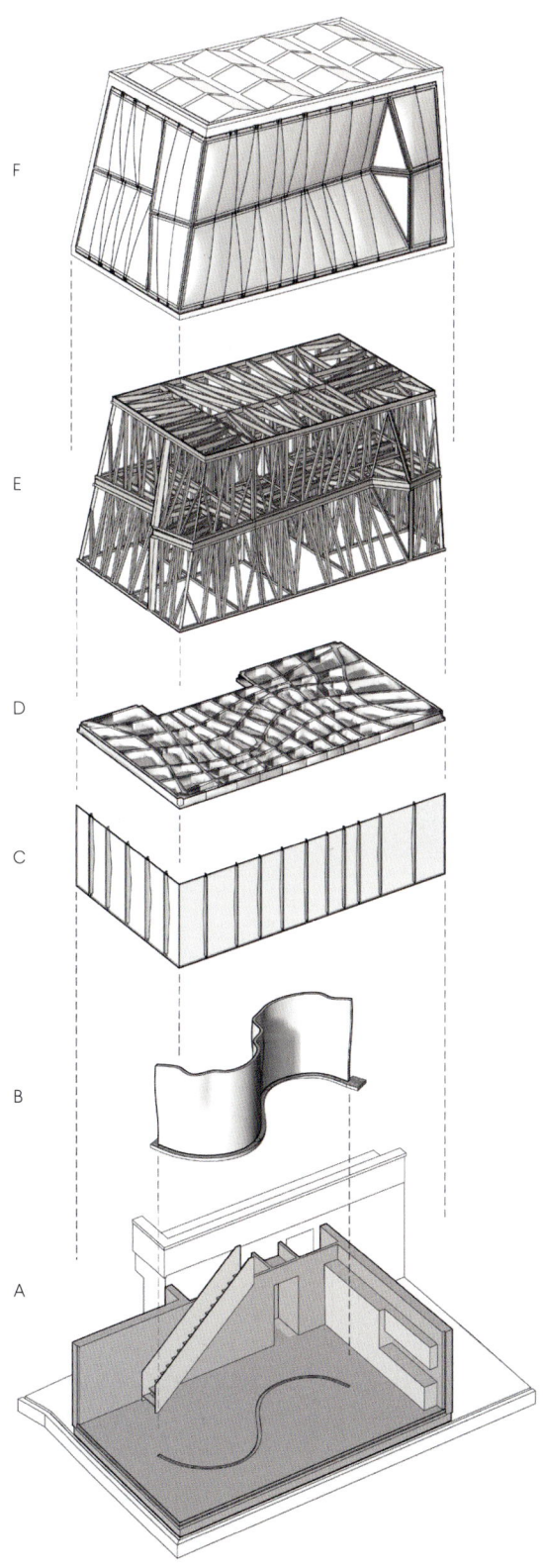

F

E

D

C

B

A

4

surveying using camera feedback. A long-term ETH research project, it serves as an instrument to explore robotic on site construction processes. By deploying the In situ Fabricator, DFAB HOUSE is the first construction project presenting robotic in situ fabrication not merely as a future vision but as a reality (Dörfler et al., 2019; Buchli et al., 2018; Lussi et al., 2018; Giftthaler et al., 2017) (Fig. 6).

2. Mesh Mould (Fig. 4B) is a robotically fabricated stay-in-place formwork and reinforcement for waste-free non-standard concrete construction. In DFAB HOUSE, Mesh Mould was implemented as a twelve-metre long undulating load-bearing wall. The In situ Fabricator was equipped with an application-specific end effector. It fabricated a three-dimensional welded rebar mesh sufficiently dense to contain fresh concrete, using manually fed 8 and 6mm standard steel rebar. Added fibres controlled the concrete flow while it was pumped in laterally and then manually trowelled. A 20mm finish layer of shotcrete was applied for fire protection (Hack, 2018; Hack et al., 2017; Kumar et al., 2017; Wangler et al., 2016) (Figs 6, 7, 9, 11).

3. Smart Dynamic Casting (Fig. 4C) is an automated robotic slip-forming process for prefabrication of material-optimised reinforced concrete structures. A small dynamic formwork continuously moves along a vertical axis, shaping the concrete during the critical phase when it changes from a soft to a hard material. The enabling material technology consists of a batch of retarded, self-compacting concrete which is then accelerated in a mixing reactor just before deposition into the moving formwork. 15 individually shape-optimised façade mullions were prefabricated for DFAB HOUSE with Smart Dynamic Casting (Lloret-Fritschi et al., 2018; 2016; Reiter et al., 2018; Scotto et al., 2018; Lloret et al., 2015) (Fig. 11).

4. Smart Slab (Fig. 4D) is a custom pre-cast concrete ceiling slab fabricated with 3D-printed formwork. It adopted large-scale binder jet sand printing to fabricate formwork elements. Eleven post-tensioned segments form a cantilevering slab supported by a grid of curved ribs. The high resolution and geometrical freedom of additive manufacturing broadened the design possibilities of architectural prefabricated concrete. The design was optimised to reduce material volume, resulting in a structure significantly lighter than a comparable conventional concrete slab. The slab integrates electrical and sprinkler systems, as well as sensors for long-term structural monitoring (Aghaei Meibodi et al., 2018; 2017) (Figs 1, 8, 9, 11).

5

5. Spatial Timber Assemblies (Fig. 4E) is a robotic prefabrication process for non-standard spatial timber structures. The upper two storeys of DFAB HOUSE were fabricated in the Robotic Fabrication Lab at ETH Zurich using two gantry-mounted robot arms, a CNC controlled table saw, and an automated tool changer. Two robots cooperated by alternately placing timber members and acting as temporary support to the three-dimensionally assembled structure. This assembly sequence ensured stability during construction. The pick-cut-scan-place workflow included custom cutting of standard cross-section timber, pre-drilling of screw channels, and spatial assembly. Screw connections were applied manually (Thoma et al., 2018; Adel et al., 2018; Gandía et al., 2018) (Figs 5, 10).

6. Lightweight Translucent Façade (Fig. 4F) is a double-layer pre-stressed membrane envelope system with a compressed aerogel insulating filling, developed specifically for DFAB HOUSE. The system allowed for continuous, non-planar membrane panels, up to eight metres in length, without thermal bridging. The inner membrane was pre-installed on the timber modules off-site while the outer layer was installed in situ before pneumatically filling the cavity with granulated aerogel. The system exemplifies how novel construction systems, such as Spatial Timber Assemblies, can trigger additional development of innovative concepts and constructive solutions (dfabhouse.ch) (Figs 2, 3).

5. Spatial Timber Assemblies at ETH Zurich Robotic Fabrication Lab. Photo: Roman Keller.

6. On-site fabrication of Mesh Mould by in situ Fabricator. Photo: Gramazio Kohler Research, ETH Zürich.

7. Mesh Mould wall after concreting. Photo: Gramazio Kohler Research, ETH Zürich.

Implementation Challenges

Due to the lack of technological precedence, Innovation Object development and integration did not follow a linear process. The following examples detail several challenges that shaped the project.

Mesh Mould best illustrates the challenges of meeting performance goals. The In situ Fabricator's reach limitations and weight predetermined the wall's ground level location. This resulted in high structural loads, calling for extensive load tests with standardised material samples. Rebar cross-sections increased, requiring a challenging full redesign of the robotic end-effector (Kumar et al., 2017). Production time was also an issue. The fabrication sequence was changed from a horizontal to a vertical build-up to reduce time-consuming repositioning steps. In addition, increasing the mesh size reduced the welding point count, cutting production time significantly over earlier versions. In the end, Mesh Mould achieved a high level of application maturity and inspired additional follow-on studies as the case studies for productivity (García de Soto et al., 2018) and sustainability impacts (Agusti-Juan et al., 2019; Mata-Falcón et al., 2019) of digital fabrication in construction.

In applying Smart Dynamic Casting, new problems arose regarding adjustments to the technology for material optimisation. Minimising mullion cross-sections increased material friction due to a greater ratio of formwork surface to concrete volume (Szabo et al., 2018). In addition, structural reinforcement was required. This combination required a highly fluid material to avoid void zones in the final structures. Variations in the raw materials further heightened the challenge. The resulting

need for material adaptations required new research. This research continues with observation of the long-term behaviour of the newly developed material by sensors installed in DFAB HOUSE (Lloret-Fritschi et al., 2018; Marchon et al., 2018; Reiter et al., 2018).

The design integration of Smart Slab and Spatial Timber Assemblies exemplifies the challenge of coordination across system interfaces. To achieve an optimal structural system, the systems were linked parametrically in an early design stage. While driven by different research groups, technologies and material constraints, both systems were structurally and architecturally co-developed. This complex design interdependence required a time-intensive iterative process involving researchers, project engineers and executing parties, highlighting a need for more efficient workflows for optimisation across multiple non-standard structural systems.

In addition to these technical intricacies, DFAB HOUSE also faced organisational challenges. During fabrication, schedule and budget were more easily met by highly integrated processes such as Mesh Mould or Spatial Timber Assemblies. However, Smart Slab presented a greater challenge as it paired high complexity with more discrete production steps by independent suppliers. This shows that questions of process organisation and integration, not just technology, need to be addressed for digital fabrication to be effective.

Permit issues also posed limits. The fire code, for example, was a governing factor in the dimensioning of all primary building elements. However, performance testing of digitally fabricated components could help push structural efficiency beyond the level achieved in DFAB HOUSE.

8

Communication challenges and conflicting priorities were present throughout the project, both between disciplines and between academic research and professional practice. Many formats of close collaboration helped overcome them, resulting in new forms of shared practice between the more than one hundred project participants, including over forty ETH researchers and technicians. Follow-up research by García de Soto et al. (2019) and Graser et al. (2019) has drawn early conclusions from this experience and pointed out vast future research potential.

Research Evaluation and Discussion

DFAB HOUSE has implications on multiple levels. First, DFAB HOUSE exposed digital fabrication to reality. It built upon the premise that full-scale construction in a real environment is a necessary step to better understand what digital fabrication enables us to do – and what its limitations are. It tested technical feasibility, structural safety and durability of digitally fabricated systems, building trust in their applicability. Perhaps more important, DFAB HOUSE exposed research to building regulations and both production and management limitations. Embedding 'boundless' research in the

context of practice in this way is the first step to moving demonstrated technologies from research to innovation and thus broader adoption. In addition, it has raised new research questions.

Second, DFAB HOUSE required new forms of collaboration. Its management encompassed multilateral negotiation but also focused on architectural design integration and collective solution-finding on many levels, generating interdisciplinary and inter-organisational shared knowledge in the process. The forms of collaboration and co-authorship that emerged over the course of the project indicate the integration processes needed to implement digital fabrication successfully in the future: breaking down information silos, both in research and practice; developing a common language to communicate across discipline boundaries; including new stakeholders from outside AEC and their knowledge; and establishing new networks and communities of practice.

Third, DFAB HOUSE and its underpinning research aimed to rethink the process of design and building on a fundamental level, rather than adhering to business as usual. It shows how the collective development of

8. Smart Slab during installation. Photo: digital building technologies, ETH Zurich / Andrei Jipa.

9. Completed project lower level – interface of Mesh Mould wall and Smart Slab.

10. Completed project upper level – Spatial Timber Assemblies.

9

10

processes by multiple disciplines in academia and industry can change the quality of research and practice, and create new, original solutions. Creating a physical building showed digital fabrication to be a viable concept for construction (Figs 9, 10, 11). It reframed the discourse on digital fabrication, refocusing it from a debate about technical feasibility to broader concerns about integrating its processes, its consequences in the workplace, and its value to both the AEC community and society more broadly.

The findings of this single case require additional investigation. Open questions remain in four areas in particular. First, DFAB HOUSE indicates resource saving potential on a conceptual level, but designing for digital fabrication to achieve optimal sustainability performance remains a future challenge. Second, all Innovation Objects combine digital with manual tasks but these examples hardly exhaust the theoretical possibilities. The topic of cost-benefit of automation and potential new models of man-machine collaboration offer vast opportunities for future research. Third, digital fabrication effectivity depends not on technology alone, but also on organisation and workflows. More research is required to better understand this relationship. Fourth, DFAB HOUSE offered practical lessons in interdisciplinary collaboration for digital fabrication, but important questions remain about how to best codify and preserve the resulting collective knowledge.

Conclusion

This paper summarises the interdisciplinary research and development of DFAB HOUSE and the role digital technologies played in its realisation. In addition, it describes the process of the project's realisation and details constraints, challenges and forms of collaboration. It discusses implications and limitations of this single case. It concludes that DFAB HOUSE offers new perspectives on how to implement digital fabrication in the AEC domain and opens up avenues for further research.

Acknowledgements

DFAB HOUSE and the research it demonstrates were funded by the Swiss National Science Foundation, ETH Zurich and Empa, and supported by more than 40 industry partners. DFAB HOUSE is the collective achievement of many project collaborators.

Principal investigators:
Prof. Dr Jonas Buchli, Prof. Dr Benjamin Dillenburger, Prof. Dr Robert Flatt, Prof. Fabio Gramazio, Prof. Dr Guillaume Habert, Prof. Dr Walter Kaufmann, Prof. Matthias Kohler, Prof. Dr Joseph Schwartz

Project collaborators:
Giulia Adagazza, Dr Mania Aghaei Meibodi, Arash Adel, Isolda Agustí Juan, Julio López Alonso, Dr Aleksandra Apolinarska, Dr Marco Bahr (DRSC AG), Marco Baur, Dr Mathias Bernhard, Pascal Breitenstein (ERNE AG Holzbau), Gonzalo Casas, Tanja Coray, Prof. Dr Kathrin Dörfler, Philippe Fleischmann, Hans Flückiger (Zühlke Group), Reto Fischer (Empa), Lukas Fuhrimann, Augusto Gandía, Rena Giesecke, Dr Markus Giftthaler, Florian Goecke (Seele Cover AG), Konrad Graser, Prof. Dr Norman Hack, Matthias Helmreich, Blanca Hren, Dr René Jähne, Andrei Jipa, Orkun Kasap, Dr Thomas Kohlhammer, Dr Nitish Kumar, Alexander Kummer, Matthias Leschok, Dr Andrew Liew, Dr Ena Lloret-Fritschi, Michael Lyrenmann, Dr Russell Loveridge, Manuel Lussi, Dr Jaime Mata-Falcón, Enrico Marchesi, Jesus Medina, Melina Mezari, Dr Ammar Mirjan, Matteo Pacher, Samuel Rebelo García, Dr Lex Reiter, Andreas Reusser, Heinz Richner, Dr Peter Richner (Empa), Daniel Rönz (ERNE AG Holzbau), Nicolas Ruffray, Dr Timothy Sandy, Dr Daniel Sanz Pont, Maximilian Seiferlein, Sarah Schneider, Fabio Scotto, Dr Linda Seward, Demetris Shammas, Lukas Stadelmann, Andreas Thoma, Nicola Vasic, Alexander Walzer, Dr Timothy Wangler, Thomas Wehrle, as well as many others who have contributed their skills and support.

References

Adel, A., Thoma, A., Helmreich, M., Gramazio, F. and Kohler, M. 2018. 'Design of robotically fabricated timber frame structures', in Anzalone, P., Del Signore, M. and Wit, A. J. (eds), *ACADIA 2018: Re/Calibration: On Imprecision and Infidelity*, Mexico City, Mexico: ACADIA, pp. 394-403.

Aghaei Meibodi, M., Bernhard, M., Jipa, A. and Dillenburger, B. 2017. 'The Smart Takes from the Strong', in Menges, A., Sheil, B., Glynn, R. and Skavara M. (eds), *Fabricate 2017: Rethinking Design and Construction*, London: UCL Press, pp. 210-17.

Aghaei Meibodi, M., Jipa, A., Giesecke, R., Shammas, D., Bernhard, M., Leschok, M., Graser, K. and Dillenburger, B. 2018. 'Smart Slab', in Anzalone, P., Del Signore, M. and Wit, A. J. (eds), *ACADIA 2018: Re/Calibration: On Imprecision and Infidelity*, Mexico City, Mexico: ACADIA, pp. 320-27.

Agustí-Juan, I., Glass, J. and Pawar, V. 2019. 'A Balanced Scorecard for Assessing Automation in Construction', *Creative Construction Conference 2019*, Budapest, Hungary.

Agustí-Juan, I., Müller, F., Hack, N., Wangler, T. and Habert G. 2017. 'Potential Benefits of Digital Fabrication for Complex Structures: Environmental Assessment of a Robotically Fabricated Concrete Wall', *Journal of Cleaner Production*, 154, pp. 330-40.

Apolinarska, A., Bärtschi, R., Furrer, R., Gramazio, F. and Kohler, M. 2016. 'Mastering the "Sequential Roof": Computational Methods for Integrating Design, Structural Analysis, and Robotic Fabrication', in Adriaenssens, S., Gramazio, F., Kohler, M., Menges, A. and Pauly, M. (eds), *Advances in Architectural Geometry*, Zurich: ETH Zurich, pp. 240-258.

Bock, T. 2015. 'The future of construction automation: Technological disruption and the upcoming ubiquity of robotics', in *Automation in Construction*, 59, pp. 113-121. (doi: 10.1016/j.autcon.2015.07.022)

Buchli, J., Lussi, M., Giftthaler, M., Dörfler, K., Sandy, T., Hack, N. and Kumar, N. 2018. 'Digital in situ fabrication – Challenges and opportunities for robotic in situ fabrication in architecture, construction, and beyond', *Cement and Concrete Research*, 112, pp. 66-75.

dfabhouse.ch, project website: https://dfabhouse.ch/lightweight-translucent-facade/. [Accessed 27 September 2019]

Dörfler, K., Hack, N., Sandy, T., Giftthaler, M., Lussi, M., Buchli, J., Gramazio, F. and Kohler, M. 2019. 'Mobile robotic fabrication beyond factory conditions: Case study Mesh Mould wall of the DFAB HOUSE', *Construction Robotics*, 3(1-4), pp. 53-67. (doi: 10.1007/s41693-019-00020-w)

Gandía, A., Parascho, S., Rust, R., Casas, G., Gramazio, F. and Kohler, M. 2018. *Towards Automatic Path Planning for Robotically Assembled Spatial Structures*. Cham: Springer.

García de Soto, B., Agustí Juan, I., Joss, S. and Hunhevicz, J. 2019. 'Implications of Construction 4.0 to the workforce and organizational structures', in *International Journal of Construction Management*. (doi: 10.1080/15623599.2019.1616414)

11. Completed lower level interior. Ensemble of Mesh Mould, Smart Slab and Smart Dynamic Casting.

García de Soto, B., Agusti-Juan, I., Hunhevicz, J., Joss, S., Graser, K., Habert, G. and Adey, B. 2018. 'Productivity of digital fabrication in construction: Cost and time analysis of a robotically built wall', *Automation in Construction*, 92, pp. 297-311. (doi: 10.1016/j.autcon.2018.04.004)

Giftthaler, M., Sandy, T., Dörfler, K., Brooks, I., Buckingham, M., Rey, G., Kohler, M., Gramazio, F. and Buchli, J. 2017. 'Mobile Robotic Fabrication at 1:1 scale: The In situ Fabricator', *Construction Robotics*, 1(1-4), p. 314. (doi: 10.1007/s41693-017-0003-5)

Graser, K., Wang, Y., Hoffman, M., Hall, D. M., Bonamoni, M. and Kohler, M. 2019. 'Social Network Analysis of DFAB HOUSE: A Demonstrator of Digital Fabrication in Construction', in *EPOC Engineering Project Organization Conference 2019*, Vail, CO: EPOC. https://img1.wsimg.com/blobby/go/19ec593e-0c9c-4cf8-a445-b774ad9dacfa/downloads/Graser_Wang_Hoffman_Bonanomi_Kohler_Hall.pdf?ver=1573652083291 (Accessed 2 January 2020)

Hack, N., Wangler, T., Mata-Falcón, J., Dörfler, K., Kumar, N., Walzer, A., Graser, K., Reiter, L., Richner, H., Buchli, J., Kaufmann, W., Flatt, R. J., Gramazio, F. and Kohler, M. 2017. 'Mesh Mould: An on site, robotically fabricated, functional formwork', in *Second Concrete Innovation Conference (2nd CIC)*, Tromsø, Norway.

Hack, N.P. (2018). 'Mesh Mould: A Robotically Fabricated Structural Stay-in-Place Formwork System', PhD Thesis, ETH Zurich.

https://icd.uni-stuttgart.de/?p=22287 and https://icd.uni-stuttgart.de/?p=22271. (Accessed 27 September 2019)

Kumar, N., Hack, N., Doerfler, K., Walzer, A., Rey, G., Gramazio, F., Kohler, M., Buchli, J. 2017. 'Design, Development and Experimental Assessment of a Robotic End-effector for Non-standard Concrete Applications', in *IEEE International Conference on Robotics and Automation (ICRA)*, pp. 1707-1713. (doi: 10.1109/ICRA.2017.7989201)

Lloret-Fritschi, E., Scotto, F., Gramazio, F., Kohler, M., Graser, K., Wangler, T., Reiter, L., Flatt R. J. and Mata-Falcòn. J. 2018. 'Challenges of Real-Scale Production with Smart Dynamic Casting', in Flatt, R. J. and Wangler, T. (eds), *First RILEM International Conference on Concrete and Digital Fabrication – Digital Concrete 2018*, Cham: Springer.

Lloret-Fritschi, E., Reiter, L., Wangler, T., Gramazio, F., Kohler, M. and Flatt, R. J. 2016. 'Smart Dynamic Casting – Slipforming with Flexible Formwork - Inline Measurement and Control', in *Second Concrete Innovation Conference (2nd CIC)*, Tromsø, Norway.

Lloret, E., Shahab, A. R., Mettler, L., Flatt, R. J., Gramazio, F., Kohler, M., Langenberg, S. 2015. 'Complex concrete structures: Merging existing casting techniques with digital fabrication', *Computer Aided Design*, 60, pp. 40-49. (doi: 10.1016/j.cad.2014.02.011)

Lussi, M., Sandy, T., Dörfler, K., Hack, N., Gramazio, F., Kohler, M. and Buchli, J. 2018. 'Accurate and Adaptive in Situ Fabrication of an Undulated Wall Using an on-Board Visual Sensing System', *2018 IEEE International Conference on Robotics and Automation*, Brisbane, QLD: ICRA, pp. 3532-3539. (doi: 10.1109/ICRA.2018.8460480)

Marchon, D., Kawashima, S., Bessaies-Bey, H., Mantellato, S. and Ng, S. 2018. 'Hydration and rheology control of concrete for digital fabrication: Potential admixtures and cement chemistry', in Flatt, R. J. and Wangler, T. (eds) *Cement and Concrete Research – Special Issue Digital Concrete*, 112, pp. 96-110. (doi: 10.1016/j.cemconres.2018.05.014)

Mata-Falcón, J., Bischof, P. and Kaufmann, W. 2019. 'Exploiting the potential of digital fabrication for sustainable and economic concrete structures', in Flatt, R. J. and Wangler, T. (eds), *First RILEM International Conference on Concrete and Digital Fabrication – Digital Concrete 2018*, Cham: Springer, pp. 157-166. (doi: 10.1007/978-3-319-99519-9_14)

McKinsey & Company 2016. 'Imagining Construction's Digital Future', Technical Report. Available online at https://www.mckinsey.com/industries/capital-projects-and-infrastructure/our-insights/imagining-constructions-digital-future#. (Accessed 27 September 2019)

Prado, M., Dörstelmann, M., Menges, A., Solly, J. and Knippers, J. 2017. 'ELYTRA FILAMENT PAVILION', in: Menges, A., Sheil, B., Glynn, R. and Skavara M. (eds), *Fabricate 2017: Rethinking Design and Construction*, London: UCL Press, pp. 224-231.

Reiter, L., Wangler, T., Roussel, N. and Flatt, R. J. 2018. 'The role of early age structural build-up in digital fabrication with concrete', in Flatt, R. J. and Wangler, T. (eds), *Cement and Concrete Research – Special Issue Digital Concrete*, 112, pp. 86-95. (doi: 10.1016/j.cemconres.2018.05.011)

Richner, P., Heer, Ph., Largo, R., Marchesi, E. and Zimmermann, E. 2018. 'NEST – A platform for the acceleration of innovation in buildings', *Informes de la Construcción*, 69(548), pp. 222-229. (doi: 10.3989/id.55380)

Robeller, C., Gamerro, J. and Weinand, Y. 2017. 'Théâtre Vidy Lausanne – A Double-Layered Timber Folded Plate Structure', in *Journal of the International Association for Shell and Spatial Structures*, 58(4), pp. 295-314. (doi: 10.20898/j.iass.2017.194.864)

Schwinn, T. 2016. 'Landesgartenschau Exhibition Hall', in Menges, A., Schwinn, T., Krieg, O. (eds), *Advancing Wood Architecture – A Computational Approach*, Oxford: Routledge, pp. 111-124.

Scotto, F., Fritschi, E. L., Gramazio, F., Kohler, M. and Flatt, R. J. 2018. 'Adaptive control system for smart dynamic casting: Defining fabrication-informed design tools and process parameters in digital fabrication processes', in *Learning, Adapting and Prototyping-Proceedings of the 23rd CAADRIA Conference, Tsinghua University, Beijing, China (CAADRIA)*, Beijing: CumInCAD, pp. 255-264.

Szabo A., Reiter L., Lloret-Fritschi E., Gramazio F., Kohler M. and Flatt R.J. 2018. 'Adapting Smart Dynamic Casting to Thin Folded Geometries', in Flatt, R. J. and Wangler, T. (eds), *First RILEM International Conference on Concrete and Digital Fabrication – Digital Concrete 2018*, Cham: Springer, pp. 81-93.

Thoma, A., Adel, A., Helmreich, M., Wehrle, T., Gramazio, F. and Kohler, M. 2018. 'Robotic Fabrication of Bespoke Timber Frame Modules', in Willmann, J., Block, P., Hutter, M., Byrne, K. and Schork, T. (eds), *Robotic Fabrication in Architecture, Art and Design 2018*, Cham: Springer, pp. 447-458. (doi: 10.1007/978-3-319-92294-2_34)

Valente, M., Sibai, A. and Sambucci, M. 2019. 'Extrusion-Based Additive Manufacturing of Concrete Products: Revolutionizing and Remodeling the Construction Industry', In *Journal of Composites Science*, 3(3), p. 88. (doi: 10.3390/jcs3030088)

Wangler, T., Lloret, E., Reiter, L., Hack, N., Gramazio, F., Kohler, M., Bernhard, M., Dillenburger, B., Buchli, J., Roussel, N. and Flatt, R. J. 2016. 'Digital Concrete: Opportunities and Challenges', in: *RILEM Technical Letters*, 10, pp. 67-75. (doi: 10.21809/rilemtechlett.2016.16)World Economic Forum 2016. 'Shaping the future of construction: A breakthrough in mindset and technology', Report, Switzerland: *World Economic Forum*. http://www3.weforum.org/docs/WEF_Shaping_the_Future_of_Construction_full_report__.pdf. (Accessed 27 September 2019)

FABRICATION AND APPLICATION OF 3D-PRINTED CONCRETE STRUCTURAL COMPONENTS IN THE BAOSHAN PEDESTRIAN BRIDGE PROJECT

WEIGUO XU / YUAN GAO / CHENWEI SUN / ZHI WANG
TSINGHUA UNIVERSITY

Since the introduction of 3D concrete printing technology about two decades ago (Khoshnevis et al., 1998), it has received increasing attention from people in both academia and the construction industry. This growing attention coincided with the advent of digital design and intelligent construction in the building construction industry; the latter was developed to address the challenges of labour shortage, increased structural complexity, low efficiency, and sustainability in building construction. However, at present, 3D printing technology is primarily used for the fabrication of decorative building components or prototypes in the laboratory only. This is because some technological improvements are still required before 3D-printed concrete can be widely used for fabrication of primary load-bearing building structures (Bos et al., 2016). One notable example of the use of 3D-printed concrete structures in practice is the bridge in the Netherlands which was built by researchers at the Eindhoven University of Technology (TU/e) in 2017. For the construction of the bridge, they used cable reinforced concrete and the whole structure was enhanced with steel tendons. The bridge proves the feasibility and safety of 3D-printed concrete structures for public use (Salet et al., 2018); however, the use of 3D-printed concrete as the sole structural material in large-scale building projects still poses questions in regard to efficacy and safety of such buildings.

The objective of our present research is to study the use of 3D-printed concrete in real-world projects, including those involving large-scale structural components and building systems. Accordingly, a pedestrian arch bridge was built using only 3D-printed concrete components, including structural units, handrails, and decorative deck panels; the bridge is composed of 44 units of 3D-printed concrete voussoirs, which was the result of a synthetic solution of material, design and an original-designed printing system.

Materials

For this study, a special composition of fibre reinforced concrete was developed which can meet the requirements of both structural strength and printability. In particular, our concrete consists of sulpho-aluminous cement (SAC), sand, polyvinyl alcohol (PVA) fibre, water, and multiple additives. Two types of sand are used with particle diameters of 0.2-0.4mm and 0.4-0.7mm. Furthermore, the additives include a retarder, thickener, water reducer, and early strength agent.

To apply the 3D concrete printing technique in a real-world project, the mechanical properties of the printed concrete (C_{mp}), including its resistance strength, flexural strength, and elastic modulus among others, should be appropriate for such a project. Although the concrete could be influenced by the dosage of all constituent materials, its mechanical properties are primarily affected by the dosages of cement (D_c), sand (D_s), fibre (D_f), and water (D_w); in particular, the water-cement ratio is the key determining factor for resistance strength, while the PVA fibre dosage affects flexural strength. The following expression can be used to represent the relationship between the abovementioned materials and mechanical properties of concrete:

$$C_{mp} \approx a_1 D_c + a_2 D_s + a_3 D_f + a_4 D_w + a_5 D_a$$

$$a_n \in R, a_1, a_2, a_3, a_4 \gg a_5, D_a = \text{dosage of the additives}$$

Moreover, to ensure the printability of concrete, two basic characteristics should be focused on, namely extrudability and buildability. The first characteristic is associated with the ability of the material to be extruded through a nozzle of a 3D-printing system, while the second characteristic reflects the strength of the printed mortar for layering without falling apart. The extrudability and buildability of cement can be adjusted by suitably modifying the proportion of the additives. The key factors that affect extrudability (C_e) include dosages of water reducer (D_{wr})

and thickener (D_t). The water reducer improves the fluidity of concrete which, in turn, makes it easy to be extruded. In contrast, the thickener increases the viscosity of the concrete which makes it harder for the concrete to be extruded to some degree; however, it also helps maintain the shape of the printed concrete. In contrast, the key factors that affect buildability (C_b) include dosages of retarder (D_r) and early strength agent (D_{es}). The retarder prevents the concrete from hardening in the printing system, while the early strength agent imparts strength to the concrete before it sets, which is useful for layering during the 3D printing process. In addition, the water reducer also has a retarding effect on the concrete similar to a retarder. Moreover, the buildability of concrete can be influenced by environmental factors, especially temperature (T). For example, with reduction in temperature, concrete hydration will slow down; accordingly, the dosages of additives will have to be adjusted. The following expression represents the relationship of extrudability and the additives, and buildability and the additives:

$$C_e \approx b_1 D_{wr} + b_2 D_t + b_3 D_r + b_4 D_{es} + b_5 T$$

$$b_n \in R, b_1, b_2 \gg b_3, b_4, b_5$$

$$C_b \approx c_1 D_r + c_2 D_{es} + c_3 D_{wr} + c_4 D_t + c_5 T,$$

$$c_n \in R, c_1, c_2, c_3, c_5 \gg c_4$$

2

1. Detail of the printing handrails.

2. Photo of the completed bridge.

3. Full view of the bridge with more than 200 pedestrians.

3

Thus, if a project involving 3D concrete printing is undertaken in winter, the entire printing process could be affected by changes in temperature. Therefore, in this study, different compositions of the printing material based on temperature were proposed and tested. The ratio of cement-sand-fibre-water is kept constant to ensure consistency of the mechanical properties. To test the effect of different material compositions on the resulting concrete, all test units were printed in the shape of standard test units instead of casting the concrete in the moulds. Since there were gaps between printed layers, the surface of the printed test units was uneven, which may cause deviation in the tests. Therefore, the crusts of these test units were cut off to minimise the influence of uneven surfaces. Aside from the compression, bending, and elasticity modulus tests, we conducted an anisotropy test for the printing unit as well. For our tests, a series of units were compressed parallel to and perpendicular to the layering direction. Our test results show that the maximum pressure resistance strength of the test units was 65MPa, while the maximum flexural strength was 15MPa; the average pressure resistance of the 12 test units

and flexural strengths of 6 test units were 46MPa and 10MPa, respectively. Furthermore, no significant anisotropy difference was observed in the case of resistance strength. Moreover, there are no significant differences in the mechanical properties of the units fabricated at different temperatures.

Design

The bridge constructed for our study using 3D-printed technology is located in a comprehensive industrial park in the Baoshan District of Shanghai, China. It is placed on top of a 14.4m-wide pool, and is part of the pedestrian walkway of the industrial park as well as a scenic spot. Based on the material performance test data, the fibre reinforced concrete is confirmed to be the best material to resist compressive stress; thus, an arch structure is proposed to fit the material characteristics. The structural design of our bridge is also inspired by a traditional Chinese stone arch bridge, the Anji Bridge in Zhaoxian, China, which is one of the oldest existing arch bridges in the world.

4

5

The typology of the arch used for our bridge is designed considering the following parameters:

1. According to the local geology, an abutment was set on each side of the pool, based on which the span and maximum side thrust of the bridge were determined;
2. Bridge gradient is limited to less than 8% considering pedestrian comfort;
3. Material performance data;
4. Preliminary design of handrails and deck panels is developed first to estimate the dead load of the bridge;
5. Width of the bridge is determined based on the surrounding roads.

Considering that the scale of the bridge is small, while the bearing capacity of abutments is relatively high, a circular arch is adopted; the rise and thickness of the arch were balanced as per the arch load conditions and limitations on the gradient. Thus, our final structure is a circular arch with uniform sections; the rise, span, width, and thickness of the arch structure are 2.17m, 14.47m, 3.6m and 0.9m respectively. Digital structure simulation and verification were conducted to optimise the design of the arch and its voussoirs using the Grasshopper and Midas software. Furthermore, the capability of the printing system was also accounted for, leading to a final structure with 44 voussoirs staggered in 4 rows that were assembled on site. Based on stress analysis, the voussoir sections were also topically optimised by removing material from inside the blocks. Our final analysis results indicate that there is redundancy in some triangular section areas when resisting the stress, so they were subtracted and left two X-shape crosses inside the rectangular margin. This truss structure can reduce the amount of material and save

printing time while also retaining strength. Based on calculation results obtained using the Midas software, a physical model is printed on a 1:4 scale to verify the obtained calculation results. The 44 scaled voussoirs were printed and assembled on a steel support in the laboratory. Two groups of vertical downward concentrated forces were applied near the centre of the arch until damage was observed. The test results indicate that the full-size structure could withstand a force of more than $120kN/m^2$.

Printing System

The printing system consists of several parts: the mixer, the pump, the six-axis robotic arm, the printing tool head, the controller, and the programming and controlling system. The printing hardware has four primary elements, including a concrete mortar mixer and a screw pump to convey the concrete mortar, a six-axis robotic arm to execute the printing program, and self-developed extrusion tool head. The extrusion tool head has a cylindrical storage silo with an auger flight inside. Concrete mortar was pumped into the silo and stirred again after being mixed in the mixer to avoid the material from hardening before printing; aside from mixing the mortar, the auger flight can also provide extra pressure for extrusion. This system ensures continuity of the mortar during printing because there is a relatively small chance of clogging in the printing head because of the auger movement as well as more buffering for any unexpected problem in the pumping system.

The printing program includes codes for both the movement of the robotic arm as well as the process control system. The digital model of each component

4. Printing process of concrete components.

5. Printed handrail component.

6. Structure test of the 1:4 scaled structure.

7. Compressive test of the 1:4 scaled structure.

is transformed into a printing path through an integrated program available in the Grasshopper software. Key printing information including the thickness of each layer and movement speed of the robotic arm are coded in the control program of the printing tool head and embedded pump. Though these codes are input into the robotic arm before operation, the speed of the robotic arm can be adjusted manually using the control display after printing begins. The quality of the final products can be examined by measuring their dimension and comparing them with the digital models.

In particular, the 900mm × 900mm structure component is an arch-like piece, which means that it has a 6.52° angular gradient in a total of 68 layers in this project. The printing speed closer to the outer edge should be slower, consequently forming relatively thicker layers; this cannot be achieved using three-axis printing machines. Moreover, two different types of tool paths were alternatively used during the printing process to improve the total structural strength of the printed structure.

Like the movement and speed of the robotic arm, the control signal for the auger flight was integrated into the process control system. In our study, though most of the control signal for the equipment used in the printing system were integrate into the printing program through the I/O module and open-source platforms owing to the instability of concrete mortar, some manual labour was required during the printing process. This included mixing of concrete dry mash and transportation of concrete mortar from the blender to pump. However, these steps can be automated by redesigning the equipment and integrating these steps into the hardware, thus reducing the cost of labour.

Construction

Besides the 44 voussoirs, 68 handrail components and 64 patterned deck panels were printed together using two sets of printing hardware mentioned earlier. We printed all voussoirs, which took 200 hours, while all other components were printed in another 250 hours. The dimensions of all the printed components were inspected, after which they were moved to the final site and assembled using a crane. Four arch steel angles were installed on the pre-constructed bridge piers, which were used as temporary support for assembling the voussoirs before the arch was completed and self-supporting. A real-time monitoring system with vibrating wire stress sensors and a high-precision strain monitor is installed to collect force and deformation data of the bridge in real time.

Compared with a concrete bridge of similar size built in a conventional manner, the cost of our 3D-printed bridge is only two-thirds that of a conventionally built one; this difference can be attributed to the fact that during the printing and construction of our bridge, no templates or reinforcing bars were used, leading to significant cost reduction.

Conclusions

The work performed in the present study successfully demonstrated the use of 3D-printed concrete structural components in a real-world project. Through the comprehensive design of materials, structural design, architectural design, and printing system, the printing of these structural components streamlines the workflow from digital design to intelligent fabrication, thus leading

8

to time and cost savings compared to conventional methods. The contributions of our study can be summarised as follows:

1. An innovative composition of materials for fibre reinforced concrete that is suitable for mass 3D printing was developed. In addition, an expression was established to summarise the relationship between the material composition and mechanical and printable properties. However, more research is needed to modify and refine the established expression.

2. The project shows that 3D concrete printing is a typical intelligent construction process. In this process there are two flows, a digital flow and a material flow, that control the printing process and results. Digital flow refers to the process from product design to printing control files, including the process of generation, addition, feedback, and optimisation. Material flow refers to the transfer and handling of material. The digital flow controls the

progress of the material flow, and the result of the material flow is the product. From this point of view, the process can be improved in two ways: the digital flow of the printing system in feedback optimisation and the material flow can improve feedback on digital flow.

3. A new 3D concrete printing system is developed with the following features: it can print spatially-curved objects; it can work continuously for a long time with high precision up to ±0.5cm. However, there are still problems in our system that need to be addressed. First, there are two software used in the printing process: one is the software to convert the design model to printing path, the other one is the control of the hardware. The two software can be integrated on one platform to form a smoother digital flow. Second, the hardware system consists of five parts and they can be integrated together in the next upcoming research. For example, the mixer and the pump can be combined into one, and it can even be integrated with the robotic arm to form a single

8. Hoisting of the structure units.

9. Workers assembling the handrails on the structure.

10. Workers assembling the deck panels.

9

10

machine. Thus, the mobility of the system can be enhanced significantly. Lastly, our proposed printing system is not entirely automated and thus still involves some manual labour. In the next version, if the software system and the hardware system are further combined with intelligent technology, a more automated printing process can be realised which will further reduce construction costs.

Nevertheless, to the best of our knowledge, our constructed bridge was the largest concrete bridge made of 3D-printed components when it was completed; it drew attention from both the industry and media because it showed the possibility of using 3D printing techniques in the construction and architecture industries in the future. The printing of structural concrete components has great potential for the production of construction components and even entire buildings both in prefabricated factory settings and on site. High freedom of the printing system allows the production of complex forms that are considerably difficult or expensive to produce using conventional methods; furthermore, as previously indicated, the 3D concrete printing technology can lead to structural optimisation and reduced material and labour costs as well as shorter construction times. Thus, an improvement in this technology can lead to an evolution in the architecture industry.

Acknowledgements

The research presented here is part of a research project conducted at the Tsinghua University (School of Architecture)-Zoina Land Joint Research Centre for Digital Architecture, and is supported by the Wisdom Bay Industrial Park.

Project 51538006 supported by National Natural Science Foundation of China.

References

Khoshnevis, B., Dutton, R. 1998. 'Innovative rapid prototyping process makes large sized, smooth surfaced complex shapes in a wide variety of materials', *Materials Technology*, 13(2), pp. 53–56.

Bos, F., Wolfs, R., Ahmed, Z., Salet, T. 2016. 'Additive manufacturing of concrete in construction: potentials and challenges of 3D concrete printing', *Virtual and Physical Prototyping*, 11(3), pp. 209–225.

Salet, T., Ahmed, Z., Bos, F., Laagland, H. 2018. 'Design of a 3D printed concrete bridge by testing', *Virtual and Physical Prototyping*, 13(3), pp. 222–236.

Q&A

Q&A 1
ANTOINE PICON WITH
JULIA BARFIELD AND KAI STREHLKE
MODERATED BY JENNY SABIN

Jenny So why don't we just kick off with the first question that I posed, which is where is your work heading right now? What are the key ideas and questions driving it?

Kai Blumer Lehmann is a company with a 144-year tradition in wood processing. The company tries to be at the cutting edge of woodworking and to achieve the balancing act between tradition and the latest state of the art construction. We are working with universities on projects to find out what is possible in timber construction today and what will come in the future. We try to be at the forefront of what is possible in the field of wood today without losing the craft traditions and values.

Julia Marks Barfield is a relatively young practice in comparison. We've been going 30 years. And, you know, we've always had a great variety of projects of different sectors and sizes, and we don't have any kind of house style. Our designs are always very site-specific and respond to a particular brief, particular client and a particular set of circumstances. So, all of our projects are really quite unique and unexpected in some way. We never quite know where we're going to end up when we start the design process. But in terms of the mosque, which is the project that brought us together with Blumer Lehmann, very happily, it's really an example of how we like to work with specialist subcontractors, people who really understand how to make things or the particular things that we're wanting to develop. We did that on the London Eye and with our Brighton i360 project and certainly on the mosque. We brought Blumer Lehmann on board at a very early stage, even before we had planning permission, just so that, you know, if you're trying to do something that is relatively innovative, you do need to work with the people who know how to build it. So that's a point about how we work. But in terms of what's happened this year, as far as I'm concerned, the world has completely changed in the last year in terms of the realisation of climate emergency.

1   2

And so, I think going forward, I would say we are going to focus all of our efforts to ensure that all of our projects respond appropriately to the emergency that is facing us all. We've always tried to do sustainable buildings ever since we started, and the mosque was no exception. I think the use of timber, in particular, has been a part of that, and I certainly see a future where we will do more buildings in timber because that's one of the most sustainable materials that we can use going to the future.

Antoine I'm not a designer, but a theorist and an historian. The first thing to say is that, for me, the digital even more than new technology is a culture. One of the things I'd say is to understand how fabrication is linked to these broad cultural stakes; well, that's one big set of questions. Then another question for me is how do we reconnect the architectural scale with the urban sphere and especially dealing with things like fabrication, robotisation, etc. So that is for me a source of enquiry.

And you know, I published a few years ago a book on Smart Cities. I'm interested in how do we jump from the architectural to the urban scale. And even more, like Julia, I think the question of climate change, the environmental crisis has risen in the past years and has become really the top priority. So how do we reconcile the use of digital tools with questions of sustainability and resilience, which are not completely evident? For me, this might be the most important thing at stake in years to come.

Jenny Well, let's pick up on some of these important points, because I think they relate to the second question in the sense that all three of you have brought up the topics of craft, of making, of areas of expertise in making and fabrication but then, importantly, how that is connecting to pressing issues

around climate change. So in that context, in terms of considering relationships between industry and practice and academia, do you see a greater convergence between research and academia and industry now compared to a decade ago? Are there perhaps exciting models or examples that are addressing issues of climate change as they relate to fabrication and craft that form bridges between research and academia and practice?

Kai I worked for ten years at ETH Zurich, ten years in an architectural office and now for five years at Blumer Lehmann. During my time at the university, the research projects were published, but rarely found their way into industry. Research that takes place in an ivory tower is still a big problem in my opinion. At Blumer Lehmann we have projects like the Urbach tower, which we built with ICD Stuttgart. This is an example where the leap from academia into industry has taken place. This is an important step. I see more convergence between science and industry. At Blumer Lehmann, we have many connections to universities. I have only been working in the company for five years and I am curious to see which research projects will prevail in the next ten years.

Julia Well, from my point of view, sadly, we're not really as involved in academia as I'd like us to be. I mean, I've been an external examiner at Queen's University, Belfast and currently Bath University. But that doesn't really involve working together. I would really love to get involved with research and, I mean, that's partly why I contacted The Bartlett in parallel to being asked to do this keynote speech, because I was very impressed with the Cork House. I was the chair of the Stirling Prize jury this year and so I was lucky enough to go and visit all of those shortlisted projects, one of which was the Cork House where the architects worked very closely with The Bartlett on developing cork as a potential regenerative material

1. Two workers prepare one of the pieces to be milled to shape, using a 5-axis CNC router. © Blumer Lehmann.

2. The tree crown containing the circular trimming beam for the dome being lifted into position. © Blumer Lehmann.

and part of the whole circular economy, and that's very interesting. I think we really should be doing more of that and making sure that we're developing regenerative approaches to building and, if possible, new materials that can have a low carbon footprint and ideally are, as I say, regenerative, so it eliminates any waste or even recycling.

Jenny Antoine, do you have anything to add to these comments, and the question I posed?

Antoine Yeah. The problem with the connection between academia and industry seems to me a structural problem. So, first I would like to note that within academia itself, we need to have more collaboration. For example, I'm often struck by the fact that you have some kids in schools of architecture playing on issues of resilience in one corner and others with an algorithm in another, and they do not always speak to each other. I think before connecting with the industry, we should connect with ourselves within academia and find more common goals. I think climate change is definitely something that should push us towards that.

Secondly, we need more research in design school. It's already much better – I would say the biggest difference from ten years ago might not be the connection yet with the industry, but might be the fact that we do have more research in design school. And having research in design school is a prerequisite if you want to have connection with the industry because you must have something to put forward. I think it's not a coincidence ETH was mentioned. I think the GSD, Harvard has definitely improved a lot in terms of creating a platform for research. Remaining on the question of institution structures, I think we need to think about what kind of hybrid structure-partnership we can build between academia and the industry. So, once we have the flows of ideas and research, how do we create structures that enable people to really communicate between what's happening in industry and what's produced in academia? I think that, for me, is the third point: how to be more inclusive and more coherent within academia to continue fostering research, and finally to create consortium or whatever, it can take a lot of forms. I think this is definitely what is on the table if we want to improve significantly the state of things in years to come. Anyway, we don't have the choice: we need to connect with industry more than in the past.

Jenny Yeah, I completely agree. Antoine, you mention that fragmentation and silos that we self-generate in academia; people working on algorithmic design versus resiliency versus building technology and so on. Are we seeing a similar fragmentation in practice, Julia? Is the discipline and practice of architecture holding on to a general practice as its core identity, or are we seeing it fragment into areas of specialisation, especially in this context of climate change

and emerging technologies and the need for a high level of expertise and precision to push this forward? What are your thoughts on this?

Julia Kai, do you want to talk?

Kai Yeah, I can start. I worked on architectural projects on the design side and now I work on the production side. In the case of the Cambridge mosque, I think the early contact between the architect and the contractor was a major factor in the success of the project. This enables the specialist to support the architect during the design phase. The more difficult and complex a task is, the better architects and specialists have to communicate and the earlier this process has to start.

For us a mock-up is a recipe for success. The best way to build a mock-up is to build it before the call for tenders, in order to really understand the difficulties of a design. A mock-up is the best way to verify that a design can be realised efficiently and cost-effectively. It gives security to the client, the architect and the contractor.

In Germany and Switzerland, architects and contractors are not allowed to have any contact before the bidding phase for public buildings. With complex architecture, this is too late. For successful projects, we have to establish good communication and trust between project partners at an early stage. Only in this way can entrepreneurial knowledge flow into the design. During my time in the architectural office, it was much easier for us to successfully implement private rather than public projects, because we were not bound to adhere to the prescribed work phases in private projects. Back to the question, I do not see any fragmentation. I still see the architect as a generalist who has a clear idea and concentrates on his design from a bird's eye view. The specialists should come on board early on to support the architect in implementing his ideas.

Julia I agree with a lot of that, but not all of it. As I said, we really like to work very early with subcontractors. I see it more of a partnership rather than us having the overview. We like to keep involved all the way through, and it was really helped by the common language of computer-aided design because we were able to pass 3D models back and forth because, as a practice, we've always made sure that we're right at the cutting edge of computer technology. So, we were able to develop the idea of the geometry, and then it was passed back and forth and I think that's a very fruitful and creative process that makes things that are quite unusual be able to happen. It's that conversation that is so important.

We tend to want to work on a whole variety of projects. We're working now on a mixed-use project. We're working on a bridge design. We're designing a drinking water fountain.

3

4

3. The completed prayer hall of Cambridge Central Mosque. © Morley von Sternberg.

4. One of the structural trees assembled on site, ready to be lifted into position. © Blumer Lehmann.

We like to work at lots of different scales and types of projects as an office, but we like to also get down to the detail. We want to be able to see the whole thing through. That's the way we like to work, and we resist being pigeonholed, I suppose.

Jenny So it sounds like the overarching theme is the necessity of collaboration?

Julia Absolutely. Absolutely, collaboration. So important.

Jenny Collaboration starting at the early phases of the design process, whether that is in academia or in practice.

Antoine I believe there is a tendency towards fragmentation in a complex technological world. But I think the discipline needs at the same time to still be in dialogue with its various constituencies. We need still to have a core preoccupation of concerns that sort of glide from specialist to generalist. I think that's actually still one of the tasks of academia, which is to explore what is the common ground of the discipline.

Jenny And Antoine, in terms of design and production, does the 21st century have more in common with the world of 500 years ago or 50 years ago?

Antoine There has been a tendency at the beginning to say that the digital is bringing us back to a kind of pre-modern, almost medieval or we're living a kind of Ruskinian condition. Actually, I don't believe that. I believe we have far more in common with 50 years ago than 500 years ago. One of the reasons is that we have moved past modernity as we know it, but we're still it's immediate children. And I think actually the legacy of modern media very often says that the fabrication is almost never trying to understand better its relation to industrialisation, to what the 20th century called

industrialisation. I would say there are still many connections between the two projects, whatever one says. So I think it's more urgent to know what your relation is to what happened 50 years ago than 500 years ago. I think, basically, we have more in common, but let's not forget Mark Twain had this famous saying that history doesn't repeat itself, it rhymes. So, it's, at most, a rhyme.

Kai I rather see a connection between the present time and the time 500 years ago. Standardisation is a characteristic of the industrialisation era. MDF is a product of that time. You destroy wood by destroying the fibres and then gluing them together again to create a standardised homogeneous product. Similar to the craftsmen 500 years ago, today we try to activate the fibres in the wood again. One example is the Cambridge mosque. In this project, we bent and glued the wood according to the load-bearing structure in order to align the fibres according to the flow of forces.

The Urbach tower is another project we built together with Achim Menges. In this case, very wet wood was glued crosswise with very dry wood. By adjusting the wood moisture content, a natural curvature is obtained, which has been specifically exploited architecturally in this project. Both projects consciously use the anisotropic properties of the wood fibre. Here I see a similar usage of the natural wood as 500 years ago. In current timber construction, I would reinterpret the motto 'form follows function' as 'form follows material'.

Antoine I think the nostalgia of the past is a deeply modern feeling. I'm not suggesting we should go back to modernity as we knew it, but I think in many respects, even your nostalgia of an improbable middle age is actually a modernist still very much indebted to modernism. it's like a British anthropologist Tim Ingold kind of argument: we're not trying to restore sympathy with matter and materials. I'm not saying that we should go back to what happened 50 years ago. I'm saying we should understand more carefully what is the relation we have with it, just like you don't want to imitate your parents. But you need to understand what is your relation. And actually, to realise that, even if you think you're behaving very differently, you're very often within the frame that your parents define.

Julia I've got a slightly different take. It's not really related to time, but more our connection with nature. I think one of the things that was so incredible about the detailed design of the Cambridge mosque, and you just alluded to it Kai, was that you were able to construct a material that absolutely was aligned with the structure or needs of that particular piece of the structure, much in the way that a spider's web is constructed in nature, where each element of the web is constructed in a slightly different way because it needs to perform differently structurally. So it's almost like we're getting to a kind of future where we're able to construct a material that is performing precisely as it needs to. And that's what we need to do in order to confront the climate emergency: design new materials that can meet the necessity of our low carbon future. I think timber is one of the very top ones, and I'm quite excited by the idea of developing the use of bamboo, for example, which is very fast growing. And I would love to do some research with academia into how we can make better use of bamboo. I mean, a tree takes 40 years to grow where bamboo can grow in 10 years. That's the kind of thing that would excite me about how academia and practice can work together.

Jenny Excellent. These are all really fantastic points. I'm going to bring together the last two questions because I think they do relate, especially in the context of what we've been discussing around climate change and fabrication. How do you see the FABRICATE community contributing meaningfully to the complexities of a changing world and, related to that, what do you each hope to get out of FABRICATE 2020? What do you hope to see transpire during the conference? The discussions?

Julia Well, I would just come back to what I've talked about, really. I think we do need to develop new low carbon materials and, obviously, timber is one of the best. But something like bamboo and, as you know, there's new types of materials and bricks made out of sand, and I think we can learn a lot from nature.

Kai FABRICATE is a conference where people meet every few years and see how technology, in the field of digital fabrication, has evolved in academia and industry. FABRICATE publications provide a chronology of the technology over a longer period of time as well as a testimony of the different focuses during this time.

I agree with Julia on the subject of carbon footprint. In our climate debate, wood is an excellent and sustainable material. In architecture, we keep seeing the emergence of hype versus trends. The climate crisis is definitely not a hype but a reality that we will have to deal with permanently in the future. Wood will certainly play an important role in this context. With my background at Blumer Lehmann, I am particularly interested in FABRICATE to learn about the current state of research and practice in the context of wood.

Antoine I'm in perfect agreement with what was said. It's clear that climate is the big issue and it's not a trend. It's a new condition. I would simply say that for me, FABRICATE is a forum, and I think part of what is constitutive of architecture is that it's not a fixed set of principles; it's an ongoing conversation. What I'm expecting is to see where the conversation is going. And I think this is what FABRICATE brings: what is the current state of the conversation? I think one of the advantages is that it's broad enough, big enough as it's not only trades, it's really a chance to see what is the state of affairs. What are we talking about these days? And I'm pretty convinced that climate will be extra present, as will wood and many recycled materials.

5

5. Prefabricated roof panels were lifted into place, and temporary platforms were built within the structural trees to allow the rooflights and linings to be installed.
© Blumer Lehmann.

6. The prayer hall tree structure nearing completion.
© Blumer Lehmann.

7. One of the completed pieces, pre-assembled in the factory.
© Blumer Lehmann.

6

7

Q&A 2
MONICA PONCE DE LEON
WITH CRISTIANO CECCATO
MODERATED BY JENNY SABIN

Jenny Our first question is, where is your work heading right now and what are the key ideas and questions that are driving it?

Monica Because of the nature and physical location of my practice in the US, I have become more and more interested in what I would call low-end construction and the tension between it and digital fabrication. The issue of precision is key – how to embed precision within the design so that it can work well despite the imprecision of labour. What aspects of the design can be defined through digital fabrication which allow for the messiness that actually happens when the project is enacted on site with low budgets and without access to high-end technology.

Cristiano It seems there's an interesting and natural complement in the conversation between what Monica is doing and what I've been engaged in. I have been working deeply in practice in recent years, with the odd foray into a more academic context providing an opportunity to zoom out and reflect on things, which is a good thing to do. The work that I've been doing is driven by the necessities of practice, and there's an issue there of breadth versus depth; there's a breadth of typologies and types of projects you could do, and the depth which is needed to understand a particular subject matter in greater detail.

A lot of the work I've been doing over the last decade has been in the field of aviation, which is probably the most complex type of architectural project an architect can do, given the sheer complexity of systems that we coordinate, the many stakeholders and, at times, conflicting technologies that we have to use to make something like an airport work. When we are the prime consultant or lead designer or the lead consultants on a project of this kind, it's really about solving

1

2

1. Aerial view of Beijing Daxing International Airport under construction (2018). Designed by Zaha Hadid Architects and ADP Ingénierie with BIAD and CACC. Image courtesy of BNAH.

2. Space frame roof assembly of Beijing Daxing International Airport (2017). The main building spans 700,000 sqm. Designed by Zaha Hadid Architects and ADP Ingénierie with BIAD and CACC. Image courtesy of BNAH.

multi-variable equations. We just opened the new airport in Beijing and we're working in India and Australia, and we have a whole bunch of other things in the pipeline. That means we have to confront how we design things from the general to the particular whilst understanding a local construction industry and its maturity in terms of the interaction between human endeavour and mechanical or physical or digital fabrication.

Solving that human-technical problem and overcoming it in a particular cultural or commercial situation becomes an interesting challenge because the way you work in one country is going to be very different to the way you work in another; the level of and type of technology, including design technology and design solution, is going to be different too. Being confronted with such work and being able to participate in events such as FABRICATE means you can take a step back and reflect on the fact that the work is really driven by solving what is ultimately a human problem: building things through technologies that express themselves in very different ways around the world.

Jenny So it seems there's a direct set of relationships between scale and where you're working in the world that impacts these outcomes, which I think relates to the second question; so do you think we are seeing a greater convergence between research in academia and industry now compared to a decade ago? Are the demands and problems we face in the context of construction and building made more prescient in terms of forming bridges between research and industry and practice compared to a decade ago?

Monica This is an important question. A decade ago, in my opinion, the use of digital technology in academia was more of a counterculture. And all of us, I would argue, were trying to provide an alternative to the corporate model. It came from an

idea of advancing the architect as an expert DIY; some of us are still doing that, perhaps. And of course, we are naive to think we could completely bridge the gap between drawing and making or design and making or even eliminate the concept of the gap. For me, it has been interesting to see the twists and turns that technological advances have taken, especially in fabrication.

Cristiano, I think that you occupy a very rare position because you have been able to maintain some of the edge of counterculture through your work. I would say that Frank Gehry's and Zaha Hadid's offices, and your work with them, stands as that counter distinction to the corporate norm. It has been interesting for me to see your work and your thinking evolve over time. But in general, I think that academia has lost some of that edge, some of that idea of being an alternate to the corporate model.

Cristiano Those are very kind words. I haven't thought about counterculture in a while because of the daily grind of things, but I do see where you're coming from with that idea. The office certainly maintains a culture of experimentation and the culture of wanting to rethink things. And that goes back to the teaching days, starting from Zaha, Patrik Schumacher, and a lot of other people who were engaged in education; then having the luxury and privilege of being able to try these things out in practice and see what works and what doesn't. In the UK, there is this notion of education versus training: the institutions educate you and then you go on the job and get trained. And this is true whether you're studying architecture or studying computer science, which I also did. Universities don't only teach you coding in a computer science course, they teach you deductive formal logic which is closer to the way lawyers work, and then it's up to you to apply this meaningfully. And so, in that sense, you're cultivating a kind of educated generalist.

3

4

What I find right now is that there is a new generation of people who are taking advantage of the omnipresence of technology and a kind of a digital culture in practice that allows you to almost say this is second nature. I'm no longer the digital wizard, or the computer specialist. Everybody here knows how to script and how to use it. I mean, my kids are better computers than I am now. And so suddenly, this is something that is very different to our countercultures, as Monica describes it; it is now something that has become, I don't like the word mainstream, but it's become understood. It's become something that people can leverage and take to a new level and actually employ in practice as the main driver of your work. I think that's really where this convergence of academia and industry is coming to fruition in a very interesting way. Whichever scale of operation you choose to work at, small project, large project, it doesn't really matter; it's the way of thinking that has been shaped that I think is so powerful.

Jenny Monica, you alluded to the fact that we've somehow lost an edge or an air of experimentation that was in place a decade ago, and I wonder if we could dwell on that for a moment in terms of the convergences that we're seeing and how that encourages or maybe opens up different types of experimentation that perhaps we have yet to open up in research and in the academy.

Monica It used to be that in the academy we would see ourselves as those seeing alternatives to the status quo. And by that same definition, we didn't necessarily hope to go mainstream. What I think has happened is that a lot of the research and experiments that we have been working on for a decade have become not only commonplace, but the very tools that large corporations now use to deploy work globally. So, if we think of convergence between academia and industry, it feels a little bit as if industry perhaps has swallowed

academia. Now, it's easy to generalise; there is plenty of work out there that stands as a counterpoint, that's why I was curious as to how you would answer that question, because I think your work is so unique and it shows so many possibilities that it's actually hard to consume, it's hard for it to become consumable. And that to me is really what was interesting about the promise of the use of technology at the outset.

Jenny I thank you for that, Monica. It's an amazing compliment. I mean, I agree, and it makes me think about dear colleagues, friends, heroes of mine, such as Bernard Cache, who very purposefully 'left the conversation', because he was so frustrated and almost disgusted by where we took things. In the 1990s he was coining terms that are now commonplace, 'the non-standard', his 'workshop Objectile', and leveraging what I think he saw as a critical practice around digital fabrication that was very, very political also; he was interested in the democratisation that it would afford. He was the first person to do the file-to-factory, mass-customized CNC machining of plywood panels, and so when he saw his famous panels in every other boutique hotel, I think he became discouraged by that. So, I wonder if the consuming – to use your word Monica – of what was experimental and cutting edge has something to do with the technology itself, and the bloodlines that can be quickly stylised if we're not careful. I guess for me and my work, we author the tools and a lot of the uniqueness comes from the experimentation with materials and collaboration across disciplines. But maybe you both could talk a little bit more specifically about tools and style and how that operates in your work, both from a research perspective, but also when it comes to fabrication and construction at large scale production.

Cristiano I have a severe aversion to the word 'style'. Style implies that you have ring-fenced a certain type of work, or a

3. Strand jack lifting of modularised spaced frame super structure. Designed by Zaha Hadid Architects and ADP Ingénierie with BIAD and CACC. Image © Zaha Hadid Architects.

4. Central support mega-column with skylight supporting space-frame shells. Designed by Zaha Hadid Architects and ADP Ingénierie with BIAD and CACC. Image © Zaha Hadid Architects.

certain type of visual outcome, that somebody can recognise as a particular appearance, a look and feel or belonging to a particular classification of work. And when you do that, you could argue that it's sort of dead, right? You have a style. It's not evolving. You're working in the style. That's the end of it, which I think is not only limiting and not very exciting, but also extremely dangerous because it implies that there's no evolution in the work that you do.

I'm more interested in something that comes from the work we did with people like John Fraser back at the AA. We were given an investigative approach, and defined a problem, whether it's a logical problem, a spatial problem, a functional problem; in its own definition, the problem would present you with the approach and the solution. And then it becomes a very powerful mechanism of coming up with something that, in many cases, is unexpected. If you look at some of the larger projects that our firm has been doing recently, you can say they have a certain look and feel or appearance; but they also respond very, very functionally in a pragmatic way to particular technical issues. It all comes from the same cultural line of thinking; it's just that the conditions and the context of the work has manifested itself in another way.

Hence the word 'style' becomes self-limiting, and as a practitioner who comes from a background of research this idea is disturbing to me, as it invalidates our daily effort to try and think things afresh. It's important that we don't lose that aspect of searching for the right solution in practice, even in some things that may be considered mundane at times, we should always strive for that kind of intellectual excellence to produce something that is outstanding and particular to the problem that we have.

Monica I, of course, completely share Cristiano's aversion to the word 'style', because I associate it a little too much with the idea of the master architect-creator that develops his/her own signature; of course, signatures are often not avoidable. We are who we are, and we have the tendencies that we have. But maybe it's the work of the architect to avoid regurgitating their own work over and over again. So, I think part of my answer would be one of scale. Scale in the end does influence one's work quite a bit. How we understand tools changes radically, whether we're working in an enormous scale or in a tiny scale. And the relationship to budget and labour changes dramatically depending on the scale and context that one is operating under. So, don't think of tools without thinking of those two things: budget and labour.

How does digital technology allow for greater complexity within a very low budget? I know that the myth is in the opposite direction, that digital fabrication is expensive. I actually have found it to be cheaper than regular construction,

and its relationship to labour actually makes certain tools redundant. One cannot think of digital fabrication without thinking of pre-fabrication. And again, the relationship of where something is fabricated and then brought to site. So, I share with Cristiano the idea that the approach is important, because it is really what allows you to structure this relationship.

Cristiano I think one of the things that's important, which Monica alluded to eloquently, goes back to what I said before: ultimately, the design and the construction remains a human problem. Technology is there to liberate us, to explore efficiently in terms of time and capabilities, and help bring the issues of fabrication, pre-fabrication and labour together.

If you embark on a project, the first question is whether it is even conceivable. And so, before you can go down the path of 'what am I going to design', or 'can I create something amazing', you must consider the material or geometric limitations which may condition your thinking, so the budgetary limitations in a sense become a creative challenge to overcome. What can I do with what little that I have? And what is it that I need to prioritise so that the building actually does what it has to do? And then perhaps consider if the functional solution that we've found also makes the building work as a piece of architecture. So it is a really profound question, because when you attempt to do a project in practice, you have to ask yourself all these questions and consider whether there is an opportunity to take something that could be described as 'applied research' and put it into practice.

Here is an example from something we're working on right now: the layout of a passenger terminal is quite a complex thing to do. We are testing certain generative techniques that go back to some early assessments of applying re-configurable self-similar features to find a very efficient solution for solving what is a mundane problem: parking aircraft at the terminal. Had we not done that research, we would not get involved in this kind of work. Had we not been able to combine two unrelated fields of work, you wouldn't be able to look for new solutions in this way. That, I think, is where those abstract research elements suddenly find expression in a real project. That is also true when you get to the issue of fabrication; you look at the budgets, what do they allow you to do in a particular location? Is there a way of automating certain processes? What work can be done automatically that then perhaps allows you to employ human labour where it adds more value and apply the machinery where it makes more sense. Sometimes that's the difference between making a project in a design concept possible and not being able to do it at all.

And ultimately, Monica as a practitioner will understand this very well: you have to maintain the confidence of your client that what you're doing is going to work and isn't just a wild escapade. So, you always have to think about how what you're doing will result in something that is not just fulfilling the contract but is actually doing it in a way that couldn't have been done before. That is really the value that you bring to the profession.

Jenny So in these contexts, how do you both look at practice? Is the discipline of architecture holding on to general practice as a core identity? Or are we seeing it fragment into specialisations? I think you both have an interesting take on this question, given the nature of your practice and research.

Monica I think that architecture has always been fragmented into specialisations, at least starting in the 20th century. I remember when I was little, I was asked: what kind of architect are you going to be? Are you going to build houses or do you want to do office buildings? In a way, the industry of building has always pushed architecture towards specialisation. What has been interesting, however, in the last five to ten years is how digital fabrication, digital technology, has actually become a subset. Now we have offices that do what is called 'design assist' or 'design assist and fabrication' where they provide digital technology services that may or may not have been used in the past. I find that interesting, that there's almost a technique, a specialisation that is happening within practice that I would not have predicted ten years ago.

Cristiano In a certain sense, we are all trained as architects, we all know how to draw, hopefully, we all know how to understand the basics of designing, composing and putting buildings together. And then people go down a specialist path. I did that for many years, to be honest. I studied computer science and always was very interested in it, even before I became an architect, and I spent many years working on the fabrication side of complex forms, learning how to do that right down to how you develop instruments of contract based on digital information. All those stepping stones meant I developed a very specific knowledge first, and then let it re-converge on a bigger picture of what it means to be a practicing architect, which includes everything from developing business, writing contracts, to work with clients and contractors; and then that particular understanding of how things need to come together, how to shape a team and need to work with specialists for a particular type of building to come to fruition. I can say very easily I could not do the work I do today had I not done the research that I did. But it also wouldn't be possible if I had not worked on the technical side of practice for many years.

Monica I would argue you are an exception. And I think that the firms you have been embedded within have been the exception. Today there is a whole industry that has sprung up of digital technology specialists that can be hired and un-hired by any architectural firm out there as yet another consulting business to provide the kind of services that you have integrated within your practice. I mean, you have written very well in the past, and quite early, about the notion of the architect as one who can synthesise and digital technology enabling this further, providing an alternative to the idea of the sub-consultant and the architect needing all of these sub-consultants working with them. It has been a surprise to me to see the emergence of digital technology as another area of 'sub-consulting'. It's very different to the trajectory that can be drawn through your work at Zaha's or at Gehry's, where integration was the idea, integration is the goal, and where integration is done successfully at a very large scale. What did you think of digital technology taking an unexpected turn and becoming yet another sub-consulting business?

Cristiano You know, knowledge is ultimately a commodity, right? And you can always buy at a price. Take the Swiss company Design-To-Production. They get hired, at times by architects, at times by fabricators, at times by contractors, at different positions within the contractual food chain, whether it's a general contractor or a specialist, and then take and execute somebody else's shape. They will perhaps re-think and re-rationalise it into fabricate-able components. and then go as far as providing the actual machine instructions and the G-codes to mill or produce the particular piece in question. You know, they inform the processes, they work directly with the design teams, bringing this knowledge as a consultant to teams that maybe don't have it.

I was part of an early such endeavour, the Gehry Technologies spin-off, and one of the projects we were involved in was advising on the modelling and creation of the information for projects like the Bird's Nest Stadium in Beijing. It is clearly something that was done by another architectural practice, we just had the know-how of how you translate that into digital component techniques.

So, you can bring that level of knowledge to others who, shall we say, may not have that readily available, they don't have the time or the resources, or the means to invest in a long-term development programme. Some people say they just need it to be solved now; it's just one thing and I need to get it done. And that's understandable.

I think what you're saying, if I'm understanding it correctly, is that you're going back to an issue of culture. Is there a culture of questioning, a culture of developing ideas, a culture of true research, where combining knowledge that exists with knowledge that's being developed results in something new? Then yes. And I can say definitely that I am very lucky, in a way privileged, to have worked in the firms that I have, to have had mentors along the way.

5

5. Main orientation space showing central dome and international departure bridges. The main building spans 700,000 sqm, making it one of the largest passenger terminals in the world. Designed by Zaha Hadid Architects and ADP Ingénierie. Image © Zaha Hadid Architects.

Monica Digital projects came to my office very early on and that opened up our practice exponentially. I think it's an interesting moment; specialisation is an interesting question right now in the discipline.

Jenny Let me segue to our last question. I think in many ways it builds upon what we've been discussing around issues of identity as it relates to specialisation of culture, the relationships between research, experimentation and practice. How do you see the FABRICATE community – the mentors and the pioneers from the 90s, like Cache and others, and the newcomers – contributing meaningfully to the complexities of a changing world and, related to that, what are you each hoping for or what do you hope to get out of FABRICATE in 2020?

Monica What is great about the FABRICATE conference and community is that there is a very generous spirit. Open source is alive and well, not only sharing ideas, but sharing techniques, sharing approaches. That I think is something that is distinctive to FABRICATE. Every time I am delighted to see that is still alive and well.

Cristiano The technology we have available to aggregate information and control that information means that for the first time, probably since we built cathedrals and castles, the architect is becoming something of a master builder through a digital medium. That means you can control the dissemination and the development of that design information right to the fabrication aspect of it. In a way, you're liberating yourself to reclaim the territory that previously had become lost to the profession where, in the words of Rem Koolhaas, the architect has become a glorified decorator.

I think this paradigm shift is important because a lot of us occupy many different segments of the very broad spectrum of work. We can't all be full-time professionals and academics, working on giant projects or researching how you code a machine or what the properties of a material can do. So, in a way, FABRICATE becomes a collective; a group of like-minded thinkers who can share different shades of work that is intimately interrelated, but manifests itself in many different ways. What I'm hoping to get out of participating in FABRICATE 2020 is inspiration, hearing about the new ideas out there, and keep evolving as somebody who wants to stay active in the field.

Q&A 3
CARL BASS WITH PHILIPPE BLOCK
MODERATED BY JANE BURRY

Jane So, Carl, where's your work heading right now? What are the key ideas and questions that are driving it?

Carl That's a good question. Well, I'm a little different from many of the participants who are architects by training. I continue to be really interested in the question of generative design and how we can use computing to help us co-design things and then how we can go from there to digital fabrication. And, given the complexity of the forms that we're able to create, what we can do with digital fabrication to help facilitate the creation of these forms.

I'm trying to use every opportunity I have to design things that have both an aesthetic and a functional use and trying to use generative design in them. Right now, I'm turning an old pickup truck electric. All the structures that I'm putting in the motors and batteries are generated by the computer. And then I'm figuring out ways to fabricate these easily.

Jane Philippe, what are the top things that you're working on and big questions that you're asking at the moment?

Philippe Well, I see opportunities or, more than that, necessities in using computation and digital fabrication to realise some of the things that we strongly believe in. They combine two key ideas: one is strength through geometry, and the second is material effectiveness. So, strength through geometry has to do with good structural form. In our case, we often look back to the beautiful Gothic vaults that formed stable, resilient structures that are still standing today – despite being made from very humble materials – because of their geometries; we can really learn something from that.

Material effectiveness is not the same as material efficiency. For the longest time engineering has focused on trying to do

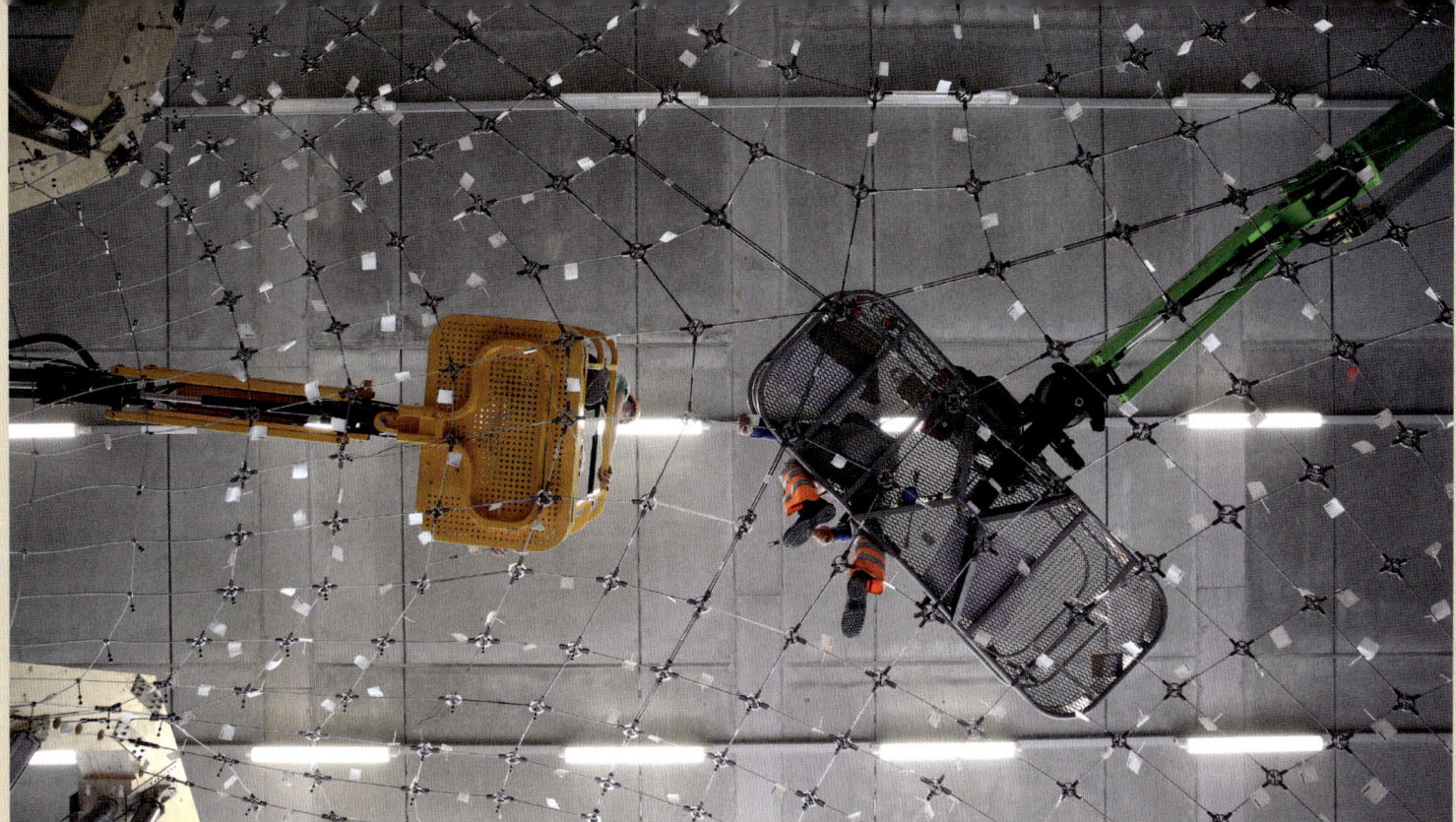

1

things with less, for example more lightweight. But, this can be absolutely irrelevant when this 'efficiency' is achieved, for example, through the use of very polluting, high-strength materials; thus, the issue is not efficiency as you would typically define it like a structural engineer. We try to argue that one would want to use materials for what they do best. Bamboo, for example, is happy in tension but concrete happens to be happy in compression.

That is directly related to rediscovering and reviving these structural geometries from the past, as structural form indeed had to be congenial to simple materials (locally) available. But, in order to integrate these geometries in modern design practices and also overlay other, often competing, performance criteria like acoustics, thermal comfort, or the integration of mechanical systems and so on, I believe this can no longer be solved just intuitively or by hand; particularly not when one is adding the layer of structural geometry, which – and Carl will agree with this – is absolutely not a standard, straight geometry that is easy to fabricate. So, if we don't find clever ways to realise these elegantly performing forms that allow the material to be used for what it's good for, such as concrete in compression, then all of these ambitions are just an academic discourse. We need to get them to a point where they start to rival even the economic reasons why we have resorted for the last 100 years to geometries that are absolutely wasteful and disrespectfully using our world's resources.

What drives me is the urgency that we need to do better because our world is not in the best shape and, unfortunately, our industry is largely responsible; for example, generating 40 percent of the man-made greenhouse gases; uncontrolled depletion of natural resources; and the creation of so much waste, most of it doomed to end up as landfill. Now, why I, as a structural designer, specifically care about those issues is that unfortunately most of the volume of material goes into the structures of multi-storey buildings, particularly into the floors. So, if one can do just a bit better there, by reducing the structural volume through better form, then this would make a huge impact. But, it's not enough; we need to do much better. We need to better activate the materials we use. We need to use recycled materials, even alternatives such as grown materials and so on. And as I said before, all this is possible by combining the key ideas of strength through geometry, learning from the past in a way, bringing the elegance and the resilience of these good structural forms back, and using materials for what they're good for. Everyone seems to be saying lately that we should no longer build in concrete because that's the evil of the world now. Well, in fact, per unit mass, it's actually the material with the least embodied energy, even better than timber. Rather than using that material in an inappropriate way (i.e. in bending, so that one needs reinforcements), what about we start using it only in areas of the structure where the compressive forces want to go? Then, we might offset things dramatically and very quickly.

1. Construction flexible formwork of full-scale prototype NEST HiLo roof, ETH Zurich, 2017. © Naida Iljazovic.

2

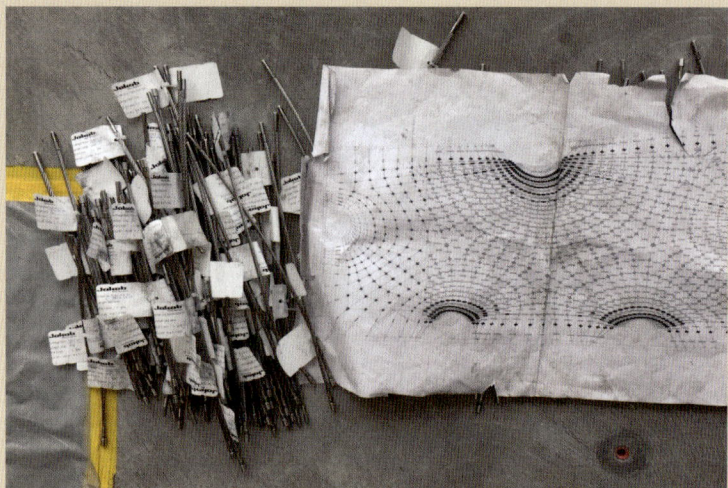

3

Jane Philippe, you were saying this just all becomes academic. Do you feel that there is this convergence between academia and practice at the moment, or are we spinning off into endless multiple disciplines?

Philippe Well, I think there are different aspects to that question. I feel increasingly that there is a clear and shared sense of urgency, but also that clients are starting to demand that our industry partners really tackle sustainability targets head-on. For this, I believe academic research has something to offer. I feel that lately there is an increasing keenness from industry to reach out to academia, wanting to collaborate and help find solutions; we do need to come together to tackle these wicked problems, I think. But on the other hand, Jane, well, perhaps it also has something to do with my personal evolution. Ten years ago, I had just started as an assistant professor at ETH Zurich; I didn't have this context, understanding and maturity then – I was naively fresh, just out of grad school.

But I want to be optimistic. Yes, today I feel a shared understanding of this urgency and this will to do better. Maybe it is driven by corporate strategies where sustainability needs to be one of those points, which is a more cynical take on it. But I nonetheless believe that more people actually understand that we need to work together to find solutions. I learnt to understand (and appreciate) that in academia we sometimes have approaches that are very foreign to practice. The building and construction industry cannot afford to approach things so dramatically differently, since profit margins are so small, and the risk is too high. So, serious investments of research in practice are very rarely realistic. And that is why and where industry sees us potentially as an ally.

Carl I think there's always this divergence between what happens in academia and what happens in real practice. I actually think it's a good thing. I know some people talk about it as though that split shouldn't occur, but I think there are commercial concerns and I think there are things that are further out on the horizon and worthy of study and exploration that take longer. If you think of the sciences, technology companies commercialise things. The basic science for many of the things that we're enjoying today was pioneered 20 to 50 years ago. Sometimes the underlying maths for them was done 50 to 200 years before. I don't think we should be so judgmental that just because something isn't immediately relevant that it doesn't serve as a spark of creativity and imagination and find its way in. And I think the reverse is true, when academic ideas become too impractical. I think both complement the other, and there's really a role for each. I think it would be detrimental if you homogenised it.

Philippe That's a fair point. But, nonetheless, in my personal journey, I did get frustrated by the fact that if you stick to fundamental research, you might have an impact at a certain point. But, praxis and the building industry need help right now; we also need to focus on finding solutions for the current environmental crisis.

Carl I couldn't agree more that the building industry desperately needs help. But it still needs people pioneering things that may not become relevant for five or ten years. I mean, one of the problems with the construction industry that I see is that it is such a low margin industry and it's constrained in a way to be incredibly low risk. I'll use the analogy of technology companies. You know, if you talk about venture capitalists, they talk about their portfolio in which two or three companies succeed wildly and maybe the other seven fail. The portfolio of most construction companies does the complete opposite.

2. Carbon-fibre reinforcement for the ultra-thin concrete shell placed on the fabric shuttering. © Naida Iljazovic.

3. Re-usable kit-of-parts of the cable-net falsework. © Naida Iljazovic.

It's organised so no project fails or no project loses money. That very cautious and conservative approach means adopting new ideas, materials, processes after they're proven as opposed to being willing to take more risks early on.

Philippe Well, I'm happy you talk about risk, because that is something that I think increasingly becomes the real bottleneck for introducing the necessary disruptive innovation. Someone needs to bridge that gap; someone needs to take that risk. And, as you are pointing out, the building industry doesn't have the margins to allow themselves to take that risk.

A couple of years ago, I would say: Why is industry not picking this up, or what is wrong with them? Do they not understand or don't want to? While, recently, I've been continuously surprised by the openness and willingness of industry to try out new things. But it always comes back to the same thing; it needs to be reasonable with respect to risk on their end. And so someone needs to bridge that gap. And that is a type of research that here at ETH Zurich we are lucky to be able to do, that we have a school board that is fully supportive; rather than making claims on how our ideas would change and/or save the world and doing the first eighty five percent in thinking, we are also being pushed to do fully-applied research and to transfer new concepts into practice. I am not saying that this is the only model, but someone needs to reduce the risk and bridge that gap. Otherwise, no innovation happens fast enough, or entirely different industries with different, more venture capitalist kinds of models, are going to take over and introduce new ideas very dramatically and shortcut the entire building industry and its traditional patterns, right?

Carl Yeah. I mostly see construction companies being willing adopters of technology. But as you point out, only willing to adopt relatively well-proven technologies. You know, in other industries people do it out of curiosity and they recognise it's an investment in the future. Unfortunately, the economic structure of the industry doesn't allow people to do that. I think to your other point, I've been involved lately with a number of things on both the design and the construction side that challenge some of the fundamentals that are not coming from within the industry. I'm involved with a number of companies that are using what essentially you would call robots to do construction work. One is doing autonomous construction equipment like backhoes and bulldozers. Another one is doing plasterboard and painting and finishing applications with robots. And so I think that's an interesting way to optimise what's being done. The ones that I find even more interesting are where people are completely rethinking the entire material and processes used and doing different forms of factory-built construction. I think the materials that they're able to use in the process, they're able to bring to bear, may upend the entire industry.

Philippe Actually, I think another aspect of risk has to do with the reality of building codes and liability and so on. Part of disruptive innovations and where significant new margins and efficiencies might occur is when we work together in different kinds of constellations. Currently I see a huge barrier to that in this sequential passing on of responsibility, as in: I am responsible that the clients are satisfied with it and that it has a funky geometry; I am responsible for not killing anyone – that might be the structural engineer; I'm responsible for trying to cram in all the building systems that are needed, and I will try to build it as cheaply as possible. If we don't find more integrated ways to bring all those requirements together, then we have no chance to reduce risk because then no one wants to cross these borders. And maybe, if I may jump ahead to one of the questions that you sent us in advance, Jane, where you asked in terms of design and production, does the 21st century have more in common with the world 500 years ago or 50 years ago.

I think it should be more like 500 years ago where we had master builders, where we had integration of skill, basically we had a core team. Now we have more requirements, so that cannot be one genius mastermind, but it needs to be a team of people. And we try to demonstrate that computation can be the glue of all of these performance requirements coming together so that we go towards a digital master builder or this digital master builder team, where liabilities, risks and authorship are being treated in a much more communal way. I think 50 years ago was when things were indeed going very badly because anything was becoming possible and there was only new computation, new materials, no constraints, and everyone was happy to do their part in the chain. And now we can no longer do that.

Carl I would agree. The over-segmentation and specialisation that has occurred over the last century has been to the detriment of having well-integrated holistic designs. I think it's been efficient in some way to parcel out the work to the particular professional. I think that system adds up to each of them minimising the risk of the participants, as opposed to if you go back to the Master Builder concept of 500 years ago, they were way out on the risk profile. Some of the structures they were able to put together had never been done before. I like the idea of a digital master builder.

When we started with generative design ten years ago, much of it was saying that the spaces that we're trying to solve problems in are too complex and multivariant for any individual. If we could understand aesthetic concerns, scheduling and cost concerns, structural concerns, heating and cooling concerns, then we could start to better understand these things in a way that was more similar to the way a master builder could understand it.

I used to do this interesting experiment: I would go to practitioners who would say they were very concerned about the energy usage of their building. I would do this thought experiment and ask them, if I took your building and I rotated it 20 degrees on your site, would you use more or less energy to heat or cool? And I cannot tell you how many blank stares I got back, where people who really thought they fully understood this really did not at all to the degree necessary. And then you couple that with other concerns like the cost and schedule, and you realise that there are literally hundreds of millions of solutions to what is the best building. I think we can move to a place where we use amazing amounts of computation that actually help us solve some of those problems and it may be that we end up with a digital replica of the master builder.

Philippe Well, here we may not entirely align. I do agree that we will be able to expect things that we never imagined before to come out of Machine Learning, Artificial Intelligence, all kinds of data-driven strategies. But, I also believe that we have to be careful. Part of the reason that we are where we are now is that the only thing all this so-called sophistication and computational power has done is allow people to forget or not fully grasp the core principles anymore. They believe too much in what these simulations give us, which often leads to a sense of misplaced sophistication and complexity. It often obstructs clarity of thinking and of development. I don't think common sense and intuition can be entirely replaced.

Carl I would say three things. One is that unless your digital simulations are good, all bets are off. If you have simulations with low fidelity to reality, no Machine Learning or Artificial Intelligence, none of this makes any sense. The second thing is I don't want to get rid of what's valuable about human insights. I think it's incredibly important that we maintain the human part of this. The last thing I'd say is just on this question of intuition. One of the things that I think would be really important in this day and age is to use tools to give designers immediate feedback. I think if I was working on a building and I changed the glazing or the eaves or the insulation, if I got instantaneous feedback, I believe that builds intuition. Right now, what happens is I do something, I pass it off to another professional; three weeks later, I get an answer that, you know, says something about heating or something about structure. That is not in the moment, it doesn't lend itself to building intuition.

Philippe I regret that I used the word intuition. That's not really what I meant to say because I agree with that. I am talking more about the danger of something that is entirely blackbox versus something that has at least aspects of whitebox, or a little bit more transparency, so that one can start to couple input and output and to understand the causalities between things. As structural engineers, for good reason, we have safety factors.

Most of these safety factors are to compensate for the entirely flawed models and simulations that we do. To share an example that my former advisor, John Ochsendorf, likes to give, one that he in turn learned from his advisor at Cambridge, Jacques Heyman: you are designing a four-legged stool with a point load precisely in the middle. If you design it in a computer, then it's going to take four equal reaction forces, you have a quarter of the forces on every leg, which seems to make total sense. But, you also know that if you're sitting on any kind of uneven surface, on a little terrace in Paris or so, your four-legged stool will be rocking, there will be always a leg not touching, which means that the leg opposite can also not carry any force. That means that you designed a stool to take four equal forces from that load, while in reality two lengths are taking half of the load, and there goes your safety factor anyway. What I want to say with this slight digression is that many simulations, many approaches in computation, assume perfect world conditions and don't acknowledge what will be in reality, what will be built certainly on the skills that we are talking about. In construction, you will have these key deviations. And so, we should also really question if we are not fooling ourselves with all these simulations. That's why I used this simple example of the four-legged stool, because quickly you can miss the obvious things and not acknowledge that the real world is not your perfect simulation. And that is the difference between the precision and the optimisation that makes sense for mechanical parts and scaling this up to building sites where (and this will not go away soon) we have these tolerances and crazy imprecisions that mean we have deviations where our models make absolutely no sense.

Jane Can I switch the topic a little bit here? How do you see the FABRICATE community contributing meaningfully to the complexities of a changing world? And what are each of you hoping to get from FABRICATE 2020?

Carl One of the things I'm really looking for from fabrication in general is how do we take advantage of a world in which we have microprocessors and sensors that can drive the fabrication process and help us both design better materials and processes, but also help in the actual fabrication. I think in some ways it's incredibly strange that we use all these digital tools. You know, we come up with things that are ideal or perfect. And then we go out and you look at a construction site and there's 17 concrete trucks that have pulled up all with different mixes, and we have no idea exactly what's in them. Or you watch people stringing wires and pulling them through holes, and it's nothing like we imagined when we had a perfect digital model. I think many of those things are fixable. I've seen examples in which we can now do things off site that will radically change the cost and quality of the things that we're able to build. And I think if we recognise we're in a world where skilled labour is more scarce and more expensive, our ability to

4

5

control things in factory-like environments will lead to higher quality, lower cost buildings in the future.

Philippe Well, first, I would strongly agree that the future of improved construction is most likely through off-site fabrication, beyond pre-fabrication even, and more integrated panellised systems and design-for-manufacturing automation and so on. I want to present one caveat though, which is that there are still many contexts in the world where we actually want to engage as much labour as possible. But, I think in combination with the precision that we can get off site, that is a very elegant combination.

What I hope from the FABRICATE community and from the FABRICATE conference is not to go back constantly to the sense of urgency and my frustration that we are not being more proactive and so on, but that is indeed what I want to see from FABRICATE. That there is more global awareness and a trend in a community of people who are extremely clever and have computational skills, fabrication insights, and are starting to steer all of this knowledge, expertise and drive to the big-scale challenges that our world is facing and where our industry is responsible to a lot of its challenges. I believe the FABRICATE community is impressive. Not only academics, but also people from industry who actually think about how to change and how to do things better. What I also hope is that the community starts to be less self-referential, because I think they are not aware of the extent to which computational fabrication experts are key to the solution. I find it absolutely crazy that if you go to conferences or events that talk about disaster relief and help, these are totally different people than the typical crowd that goes to FABRICATE. And so I think we need as a community to reach out and to use our brains and skills to achieve much, much more. That's what I hope from FABRICATE: a call for action and a realisation that we are part of the solution or we should be.

References

Block, P., Van Mele, T., Rippmann, M., Ranaudo, F., Calvo Barentin, C. and Paulson, N. 2020. 'Redefining Structural Art: Strategies, necessities and opportunities', The Structural Engineer, 98(1), pp. 66-72. [Available: https://block.arch.ethz.ch/brg/files/BLOCK_2020_Structural-Engineer_Redefining-structural-art_1578310555.pdf]

Block, P., Van Mele, T., Rippmann, M. and Paulson, N. 2017. *Beyond Bending: Reimagining Compression Shells*, Edition DETAIL, Munich.

4. Spraying of the 3cm-thin concrete surface.
© Naida Iljazovic.

5. One-to-one prototype for NEST HiLo's flexibly formed, textile-reinforced concrete roof built at ETH Zurich, 2017.
Photo: Mike Lyrenmann.

Q&A 4
METTE RAMSGAARD THOMSEN
WITH MEEJIN YOON
MODERATED BY JANE BURRY

Jane Meejin, where is your work heading right now? What are the key ideas and questions driving it?

Meejin Lately, I've been working on issues of perception and how techniques, tectonics and technologies affect our awareness of stories and public histories. It sounds vague, but in the last couple of years, because of the work we have done on the Collier Memorial at MIT and the UVA Memorial to Enslaved Labourers, I've been thinking about how tectonics and techniques can convey a story that is maybe much longer in time, whether it's historical or more about historic technologies and structures or construction; how attempts at representation and storytelling through visual cues – both pronounced and subtle – can sometimes surprise you. This is all based on techniques of digital craft that utilise computation, custom tool paths, and robotics to create textures and representations that play with our ability to read images as we move around a surface – possibilities I would not have expected maybe five, ten years ago.

Jane How do you think you've got there? Is it a surprise?

Meejin It is a surprise because, as an architect, I have been trained to work abstractly and have a certain level of discomfort working with metaphors – I prefer to work didactically with the tools and the technologies we have to express not what something is like, but rather what something is. I designed the Collier Memorial at MIT in memory of the police officer Sean Collier who was killed in the aftermath of the Boston Marathon bombings of 2013. It engaged so many different publics who were looking for different meanings or metaphors in the project. Despite resisting metaphors, it was clear they were going to be applied anyway. And so that project became about finding multiple meanings, some through the form of the memorial, some through the technical aspects of the project,

some through the spatial experience of the project, and others through subtle differences between surfaces.

The UVA memorial for enslaved labourers was also based on community engagement and input. The campus community really wanted a visual representation of slavery, whether it was a sculpture of an enslaved person or child, and what we found is that it is, of course, very hard to represent slavery pictorially. With artist collaborator Eto Otitigbe, we looked at photographic documentation and used an early photograph of Isabella Gibbons, an enslaved woman who was freed but stayed in the community and became a teacher. We took her eyes and blew them up to a colossal scale and carved them into blocks of stone using a technique that translated the photograph into custom tool paths of linear routing that allow images to become subtly visible. This required technological translation because the lines are the same width; it's just the depth of the carved lines in the stone that allows the eyes to be perceived from a certain distance and vantage point. I did not think my interests in digital technology and architecture would take me down this route from where I started 15 years ago with more literal-interactive technologies vs. these more visual-perceptual techniques.

Jane Were you very involved in the stories you wanted to tell like Sean Collier, and did you read a lot of slave stories?

Meejin A very close friend of Sean Collier was on the MIT committee that was constituted as the client group for the memorial, so I learnt a lot about Sean from him, and also his colleagues, the other police officers. They felt the memorial had to convey the things he loved and he cared about most. And so it was a process where stories were shared with me and I then had to synthesise them into some form of representation. With the UVA project, we worked with incredible historians and members of the community. The story of slavery is horrific and for the most part impossible to really process now. The humanity of each enslaved labourer was taken away, and so what we had from the archives is more a record of accounting than stories, because enslaved people were considered property. Out of the approximately four thousand enslaved labourers at UVA during that period, we know only about 13 percent of the individuals' names. And the vast majority of them are only partial names. How do you represent every person with a memorial that acknowledges their humanity?

Jane Thanks Meejin. Mette, where's your work heading? And maybe you could pick up on some of those storytelling points. I think that's something that's close to you too.

Mette The thing I'm most concerned with right now, and the way that I think my work is changing, is a stronger and stronger sense of urgency around questions of sustainability. I think they have always been part of an argument for our work. We have long been considering ideas of optimisation, not in a sort of positivist sense, but in terms of what happens when we start considering the way we are working with materials, working in a lighter framework, work smarter with less. What happens to the way we think about what architecture can be and the expression and potential of what spatial identity can become?

1. Collier Memorial, solid stone vault. © Höweler + Yoon Architecture.

2

3

So not only how to optimise structures, that's part of it, but there is also embedded criticality and curiosity for a new identity of what architecture could be.

I think that space of thinking is being provoked into maturity by the present context. The world is changing, we are on this exponential curve and we're sitting on the most accelerated point of it. Maybe part of that acceleration is that I am being asked to be part of new kinds of networks that allow me to engage with these questions in very different ways and also more political ways. And I find it an interesting expansion of my remit, my perception. We're working on the United International Architects (UIA) Congress where we're trying to structure this global research outreach, trying to figure out what are the dialogues that architecture should take responsibility for or be part of within the Sustainable Development Goals. How do we consider our contribution? What is the impact that we as a field can have? This is the overarching political engagement.

I think what we have in common, Meejin, is a desire that within the worlds of the institution and within the worlds of facilitating for others, there's also a real need to touch, a need to be part of the technologies, a need to understand all this.

Over the last 10, 15 years we've been considering where our field could go; we've been prototyping methods to reconsider what our processes of design and fabrication and production could be. So, at every conference we see a new method of designing, specifying, fabricating a timber structure, a concrete shell – the research practice we are part of has been iterating these experiments for quite a while. And if we look back over the catalogue of work, not only our own but our field, to an external eye it can seem repetitive. I think what is happening now is that the work is maturing and getting ready to take on

larger questions. Coming back to the story of the material, this trickles down in concrete terms to changes of perception of what materials are. CITA has been working a lot over the years with timber, steel, fibreglass, textiles. These traditional materials of architecture are part of the geosphere. If we understand the geosphere as being a place of resource scarcity and taking materials from that sphere exhausts supply, then if we move into the biosphere, we become part of a cyclical way in which materials are something co-produced. The question then becomes how do we actually engage this and how can that intelligence be used, but within a new bio-based material paradigm. So it is very different from what you were saying, Meejin.

Meejin What's interesting is that concerns related to the built environment are triggered by increased awareness of climate change and how our resource extraction, as well as the act of building itself, creates such high CO_2 emissions. And so going from high energy emission construction and fabrication to – I am assuming when you're talking about bio-base it's research into these new materials and organic materials like mushrooms? I think work in this area is important and fascinating, and that architecture should actively be innovating in the area of biological and organic systems and materials.

In the last few years, I've rediscovered solid stone and I try to approach building in a way that thinks not of a 30- or 50-year lifespan, but a 100-, 200-, 300-year lifespan. Rediscovering and integrating some of these ancient techniques and re-evaluating historic structures and solid materials for approaches to design and construction that don't require an excess of layered systems, plastics, silicones and synthetic composites in order to achieve what they need to as buildings has been an interesting direction.

2. Collier Memorial, block fabrication. © Höweler + Yoon.

3. Isoropia at Venice Biennale, The Danish Pavilion, CITA, 2018.

Mette It's a really good way of bridging because I think it's exactly the temporality of the material that is interesting. We're working with biopolymers, we're also working with mycelia, but the core interest right now is moving across this spectrum of bio-materials. How do we work within a very broad framework and understanding of what the new requirements are that we have to work with and conceptualise? And, of course, the central thing is durability; we know timber can last, but if we start working with biopolymers, their durability is an issue which we can't control. But control is a perception. Rather than changing it, why don't we change us? Instead of saying I can't work with biopolymers because they rot after eight months, why not change our practices of inhabitation and return to more active processes? I mean, years ago in my geographical sphere, it would be natural to chalk your buildings every year. You're part of reconstructing your building all the time. And so with these materials, how can we be part of practices of continual rebuilding?

Meejin I think, Mette, the similarity is that there is a desire to design for specific material, whatever that material may be. If it's mycelium, then you start to think of a different temporal period of design, different tectonics. I mean, I want to design almost everything with one material. For stone structures, like the Collier Memorial, we were so invested in not making it post-tension, not embedding steel, and trying to figure out: could you produce a structure purely of that one material by working with its capacity?

Jane Are we seeing a greater convergence between research in academia and industry now compared with a decade ago?

Mette I think it is an interesting question. When we did Smart Geometry in 2011, I remember the discussion lay around how academia could keep up with practice. The perception was that research in practice was way ahead. But I wouldn't say that's true anymore. I think there is a stronger established dialogue, but also a stronger established sense of what it is that we are contributing to.

I think that academic research has real contribution to make to the way we understand and think about what technology should be about. Even if there's no direct uptake in industry, it still has great importance. I think it's that we are maturing a research culture across the field. When I did my PhD, which was just before coming to MIT in 2005, I was the fourth PhD person in my programme. It was a very young culture. I feel that there's a lot happening and we're finding out what it is that we can know and what the important impact of that knowledge can be.

Meejin Thinking about the Smart Geometry moment, it felt like for that to be really rigorously tested it needed the profession, or the practice, to test it across many types of buildings, many kinds of geometry, larger geometries, different tectonic systems. In the academy, most things have been limited to the scale of the pavilion, or programmatically or environmentally simple structures. The relationship between the academy and industry is productive and complimentary because the academy can test ideas and speculate at a small scale, and industry can test at a larger scale, and literally scale innovations. I think the difference we're seeing now is that much of the interesting research going on in the academy does not yet seem useable to the profession. And so the kind of bio-based material research going on seems very 'far out' to the building industry, which might be looking at material innovation in a shorter timeframe.

And, I agree, I'm not sure we can use the word ahead, but I do think the curiosities within academia, because of issues around resources and climate change and sustainability, can be much more speculative in terms of a timeline than industry, which has a scalar and practical threshold which limits thinking through, let's say, compostable bricks. Industry standards are still for durability, 30-year warranties. And, the interface with construction, this is where academia has real potential – but, I have seen only limited success within the US context in partnerships between construction industries and material industries. I think a more direct line between the two could help impact the profession in ways we're currently unable to do because there's a big gap between the architecture profession's interest and, let's say, ours in the academy.

Jane Do you think that the discipline of architecture is holding on to general practice at the moment, as its core identity? Or are we beginning to see that fragment into specialisations?

Meejin I think we saw over a significant period, at least the last decade, every large company with the financial capability start their own advanced research group, within the corporate firms, and within the big design firms. At MIT, where I was for the last 18 years, I would say it's distributed into specialisations already – research and the sub-disciplines around architecture as a field of scholarship and research is very distributed. Now that I'm at Cornell, I feel like I've entered a different world where it is still very much about generalised professional education. I think we need both general practice and specialisation. I think there is value to both the generalist perspective and research expertise.

Mette I also come from an institution that adamantly holds on to the generalist perception of what an architect can be or what architectural education is. And yet I teach within a highly-specialised Master's programme, so we do a programme on computational design and fabrication where we ask students to use their general design sense, their general understanding of what design is and their knowledge of criticality from general education to re-address what these technologies are.

I was visited by the Danish Minister for Science and Education a year ago and I realised that what was important to communicate was why this kind of research cannot happen in an engineering education. We sit in the Academy so we have such a different context and tradition of what we're doing. The research is technical in outset – it probes the technologies of design fabrication – but it also always returns to architecture, asking what are the spatial differences these technologies make. How can we change what architecture can be? I don't want to leave behind a criticality of design thinking or the methodologies of architecture, I think they are absolutely central to our identity. It is that which crosses the scales. By giving students the permission or the possibility to delve into things and find their own critical practice within a narrow field, allows them to find their identity. So it is not a straightforward answer. I think what you were saying, Meejin, is that it is not about leaving behind generality and saying let's make these very splintered master's groups that are cutting up the cake. It's more, what are we actually taking with us as an aperture into our practice and how does this practice meet the world, which has many different contexts?

Jane That's really interesting. I will move on to the next question because we have limited time. In terms of design and production, does the 21st century have more in common with the world 500 years ago or 50 years ago?

Mette This is an interesting question. When you sent it to us, I was thinking 500 years ago? 1600s? The start of Enlightenment? So you're at the discovery of the world, categorising and mapping of the world. Yesterday, I was reading a text called *The Shift on Glass* and the author is talking about the dawning of the second machine age in 1935, the ability to reconnect man to nature. Here we sit in the fourth machine age, and we are focusing on new materials and social responsibility. I felt there's a sort of slightly positivistic single-mindedness about it, which maybe had greater depth in the latter part of the 20th century with critical theory. There is something about how the conditions of what happened, not 50 or 500, but 100 years ago, to what's happening now that's radically different.

100 to 200 years ago, we were developing these processes which were fundamental parts of rebuilding society and lifting us out of the slums. However, here we sit 100 years later readdressing industrialisation – through paradigms such as Industry 4.0. Yet the scope is so different now. Industrialisation comes with a disregard for waste and overproduction, the belief being that if manufacturing is cheap enough then waste is a necessary by-product of efficiency and optimisation. Waste appears in many forms: in over-production and wasteful manufacture; in fundamentally subtractive fabrication technologies; in over-engineering; and in our inability to re-extract materials on disassembly. However, as we enter a new economic era in which our finite resources limit our potential for growth, this disregard is no longer possible. So, I don't think that we are discovering the world as we did 500 years ago – instead I think we are part of very large upheaval readdressing our methods of producing and consuming materials. To instigate a real breakthrough in material thinking we need to move from a modernist perception of resource as infinite and available without consequence, to an ecological understanding of resource as a shared global reserve to be balanced between the needs of the environment and that of humanity. We need to fundamentally rethink what materials are and how we work with them. We are now in the 'decade of action' – the ten years leading up to the fulfilment of the sustainability goals. We need to rethink our way of living, of building and designing in a very new context.

Jane Meejin, what do you reckon? 50 or 500?

Meejin Maybe it's more like a 150. If we are now in the fourth industrial age, we have inherited a discipline that grew up and blossomed in the industrial age. And so, as you were saying Mette, mass manufacturing created a building industry that is about additive components and layering of systems. That's how we were trained and educated, how we learnt to put a building together. But our intellectual training around how to make architectural form is probably not about putting components together to arrive at architecture, it's more about carving space out of solids or the abstraction of the planar chipboard on our desks when we were growing up in architecture school.

I would say that this moment feels to me like somewhere between 250 and 150 years ago, when they were testing glass in the first industrial revolution. Now we're testing shrimp shells and mushrooms and all kinds of other bio-materials. But I think it's similar in that there is a kind of desire to invent another way of building again that challenges the economic and labour assumptions of the last century. And maybe that's the confluence of automation or robotics with the bio-material interest or resuscitating old material interests that's simultaneous right now. And I think that convergence feels a little more like alchemy or chemistry than it does of industrial production for the assembly line.

Jane I wonder if we need to curb our urge to build a little bit? How do you see the FABRICATE community contributing meaningfully to the complexities of this changing world? And what are you both hoping to get from FABRICATE 2020?

Mette Well, in response to the first question then, absolutely. I think that the research culture, the community around FABRICATE, are maturing very fast. We are seeing our community able to attract funding, to create, to be the

4

5

creators and instigators, of very large research undertakings. So, for instance, dFAB at ETH, The New Centre of Excellence at the University of Stuttgart and Innochain, they're able to consolidate, but also be the drivers of very large research undertakings. And what I find so interesting is that they are also starting to split up our community.

It's like so-called 'echo chambers'; it sounds negative but I don't mean it like that. I mean how in your own practice, you keep repeating the same drawing, the same drawing, and then you're allowed to jump. I feel like that's what we've been doing as a community. We've been repeating the same kinds of projects, and now the thing is blossoming and we've seen quite big differences. Achim Menges' project is quite tied to industry. The deal is his ambition is within the remit of industry 4.0. dFAB is quite tied to concrete. It is a quite specific material practice. There is also timber research in it, but it is still quite single-focused. So it seems to me that rather than answering 'yes, I've seen a building that makes a lot of sense'. I would say, 'yes, we are driving a research culture, we're driving research agendas, which attracts national and international attention at the cusp of research.' That's fantastic.

What I dream of for 2020 is to stop seeing some of these more probe-like things, to see the consequence of them. Not just technological solutions that can be implemented within buildings tomorrow or even the day after tomorrow, but also to consider where is it that our field should go to establish a dialogue about the spreading of factors and opening up of directions, then what are the territories that we should cover and how? How do we establish languages that are different from each other rather than similar?

Meejin For me, I think of the FABRICATE community not necessarily as solvers, but searchers – searching out questions through an active, iterative testing model at certain scales. And I've always appreciated that, even though, like in other disciplines, it's important to clearly state the problem. I think almost everyone who participates in FABRICATE can state the problem that they're trying to 'solve'. But I don't know if that's really the problem. The curious questioning and interrogation of the topic, or the investigation, is at least as important if not more than the 'solution' because it's about the methodologies and being able to deploy those methodologies in other enquiries as well. This is what I value about the FABRICATE community.

And then in terms of 2020, I would be really excited to see people speculate on scaling current research interests in compostable materials, bio-materials, artificial intelligence, automation, and how those things are going to converge in a way that actually has impact. I was reading that 5 percent of CO_2 emissions come from concrete, and that it is the second most used material in the world. As we rapidly urbanise, concrete is still going to be the choice material, but how could we imagine changing our usage of concrete? Or, perhaps reconfigure the proportions of what it's made of and how it's formed? Or, how could we change our approach to thinking about permanence and temporality and embrace compostable materials and organic materials in mainstream construction. Reflecting on what you were saying earlier, Mette, how do we change our value system, our time-based assumptions about building, our economic assumptions about durability, to rethink how we build in a rapidly urbanising context? Those are questions we are all trying to answer now.

4. PCM façade modelling thermodynamics to predict the performance of phase changing materials, CITA with Kieran Timberlake, KADK, 2017.

5. UVA Memorial, exterior surface detail. © Höweler + Yoon.

Q&A
BIOGRAPHIES

Antoine Picon

Antoine Picon is the G. Ware Travelstead Professor of History of Architecture and Technology, and Director of Research at the GSD, Harvard Department of Architecture. Trained as an engineer, architect and historian, Picon works on the history of architectural and urban technologies from the eighteenth century to the present. He has published extensively on this subject. He is, amongst others, the author of *French Architects and Engineers in the Age of Enlightenment* (1988, English translation 1992), *Claude Perrault (1613-1688)* (1988), *L'Invention de L'ingénieur moderne* (1992), *La Ville territoire des cyborgs* (1998), *Les Saint-Simoniens* (2002), *Digital Culture in Architecture* (2010), *Ornament: The Politics of Architecture and Subjectivity* (2013), *Smart Cities: A Spatialised Intelligence* (2015), and *La Matérialité de l'architecture* (2018). He has edited many other volumes, in particular *L'Art de l'Ingénieur* (1997), and *La Ville et la Guerre* (1998). Picon is also Chairman of the Foundation Le Corbusier, and a member of the French Academy of Architecture and the French Academy of Technology.

Julia Barfield

Julia Barfield founded Marks Barfield Architects in 1989 with husband and partner David Marks (1952-2017), the firm known as both the designers and the creative entrepreneurs behind the London Eye and the British Airways i360 in Brighton. Marks Barfield Architects is a multi-award winning practice with a portfolio of work across many sectors including: culture and education; bridges and transport; sports and leisure; and workplace and mixed use developments. The most recently completed project is the Cambridge Central Mosque which opened in April 2019.

Barfield chaired this year's Stirling judging panel, was on the National RIBA awards panel until 2018, sits on several quality and award judging panels and examines at the University of Bath. She lectures on sustainability in architecture and is on the steering group of Architects Declare.

Kai Strehlke

Kai Strehlke joined Blumer Lehmann AG in 2015, where he is working on the interface between digital data and CNC manufacturing of large scale timber structures. Parallel to this, he has taught Design and Digital Processes since 2016 at the Department of Architecture at Bern University of Applied Sciences. Between 2005 and 2015 he built up and led the Department of Digital Technologies at the architectural office Herzog & de Meuron in Basel. From 1997 to 2004 Strehlke researched and lectured at the chair of CAAD at the Swiss Federal School of Technology in Zurich and submitted his PhD with the theme of 'The Digital Ornament in Architecture, its Generation, Production and Application with Computer-Controlled Technologies'.

Monica Ponce de Leon

Monica Ponce de Leon is the founding principal of MPdL Studio and Dean and Professor at Princeton University School of Architecture. Her highly acclaimed and broadly published work has received 13 Progressive Architecture Awards, 13 awards from the American Institute of Architects, and the Harleston Parker Medal.

A dedicated educator, Ponce de Leon was previously a professor and director of the Digital Lab at Harvard's Graduate School of Design (1996–2008) where she was one of the first researchers who investigated the use of robotics in fabrication for buildings. She then served as dean of University of Michigan's Taubman College (2008–2015) where she developed a state of the art student-run digital fabrication lab, integrating digital fabrication into the curriculum of the school. Largely due to Ponce de Leon's pioneering work, the use of digital tools is now commonplace in architecture schools across the country.

Cristiano Ceccato

Cristiano Ceccato is a Director at Zaha Hadid Architects (ZHA) in London, having previously worked for Frank O. Gehry Partners in Los Angeles. Trained as an architect and computer scientist, he engages across all levels of design and technical development, with worldwide project delivery experience on a wide range of typologies. Cristiano is also an accomplished software developer, having previously co-founded the BIM company Gehry Technologies in California.

Cristiano has spearheaded ZHA's entrance into the aviation market since 2010. He is the Project Director for the Beijing Daxing Airport (72mppa) in China; the Navi Mumbai International Airport (70mppa) in India; and the Western Sydney Airport (82mppa) in Australia. Cristiano is a graduate of the Architectural Association and Imperial College in London. He is a Fellow of the Royal Society of Arts and a Fellow of the Royal Aeronautical Society, where he sits on the Air Transport Specialist Group board.

Carl Bass

Carl Bass designs and builds things – robots, boats, electric cars – in his Berkeley, CA workshops. Bass serves as Chairman of the Board of Zoox and Velo3D as well as the lead director of Zendesk Inc. He also serves on the board of directors of Planet Labs, Built Robotics, Formlabs, Bright Machines, Dyndrite, and nTopology; on the board of trustees of the Smithsonian's Cooper-Hewitt National Design Museum, Art Center College of Design, and California College of the Arts; and on the advisory boards of Cornell Computing and Information Science, UC Berkeley School of Information, and UC Berkeley College of Engineering.

Carl Bass was president and CEO of Autodesk from 2006-2017. He spent 24 years at Autodesk where he held a series of executive positions including chief technology officer and chief operating officer. Bass co-founded Ithaca Software and Buzzsaw. He holds a BA in Mathematics from Cornell University.

Philippe Block

Philippe Block is Professor at the Institute of Technology in Architecture at ETH Zurich, where he co-directs the Block Research Group (BRG) together with Dr Tom Van Mele. He is also the director of the Swiss National Centre of Competence in Research (NCCR) in Digital Fabrication, and founding partner of Ochsendorf DeJong & Block (ODB Engineering). Block studied architecture and structural engineering at the VUB, Belgium, and at MIT, US, where he earned his PhD in 2009. Research at the BRG focuses on computational form finding, optimisation and construction of curved surface structures, specialising in unreinforced masonry vaults and concrete shells. Within the NCCR, BRG researchers develop innovative structurally informed bespoke prefabrication strategies and novel construction paradigms employing digital fabrication. With the BRG and ODB Engineering, Block applies his research into practice on the structural assessment of historic monuments in unreinforced masonry and the design and engineering of novel shell structures.

Mette Ramsgaard Thomsen

Mette Ramsgaard Thomsen is Professor and Head of CITA (Centre for Information Technology and Architecture) at the Royal Danish Academy of Fine Arts, Schools of Architecture, Design and Conservation. Her research examines how computation is changing our material cultures: the way we design through the new information rich paradigm; the way we fabricate through new robotically-steered processes; and the way it changes the remits and spatial potential of architecture. In 2005 she founded the Centre for IT and Architecture research group (CITA) at the Royal Academy of Fine Arts. By investigating advanced computer modelling, digital fabrication and material specification in projects including Predictive Response, Complex Modelling and Innochain, she has been central to the formation of an international research field examining advanced modelling methods that integrate simulation and predict material behaviour. In 2016 she was awarded the Elite Research Prize for outstanding researchers of international excellence, and in 2018 she was appointed General Reporter for the UIA2023 world congress 'Sustainable Futures'.

Meejin Yoon

Meejin Yoon is an architect, designer, artist, educator, and co-founding principal of Höweler + Yoon. She is currently the Dean of Cornell University's College of Architecture, Art and Planning. Previously, she was Professor and Head of the Department of Architecture at MIT where she began teaching in 2001. Yoon's design work and research investigate the intersections between architecture, technology and public space. She is the author of *Absence* and co-author of *Public Works: Unsolicited Small Projects for the Big Dig*.

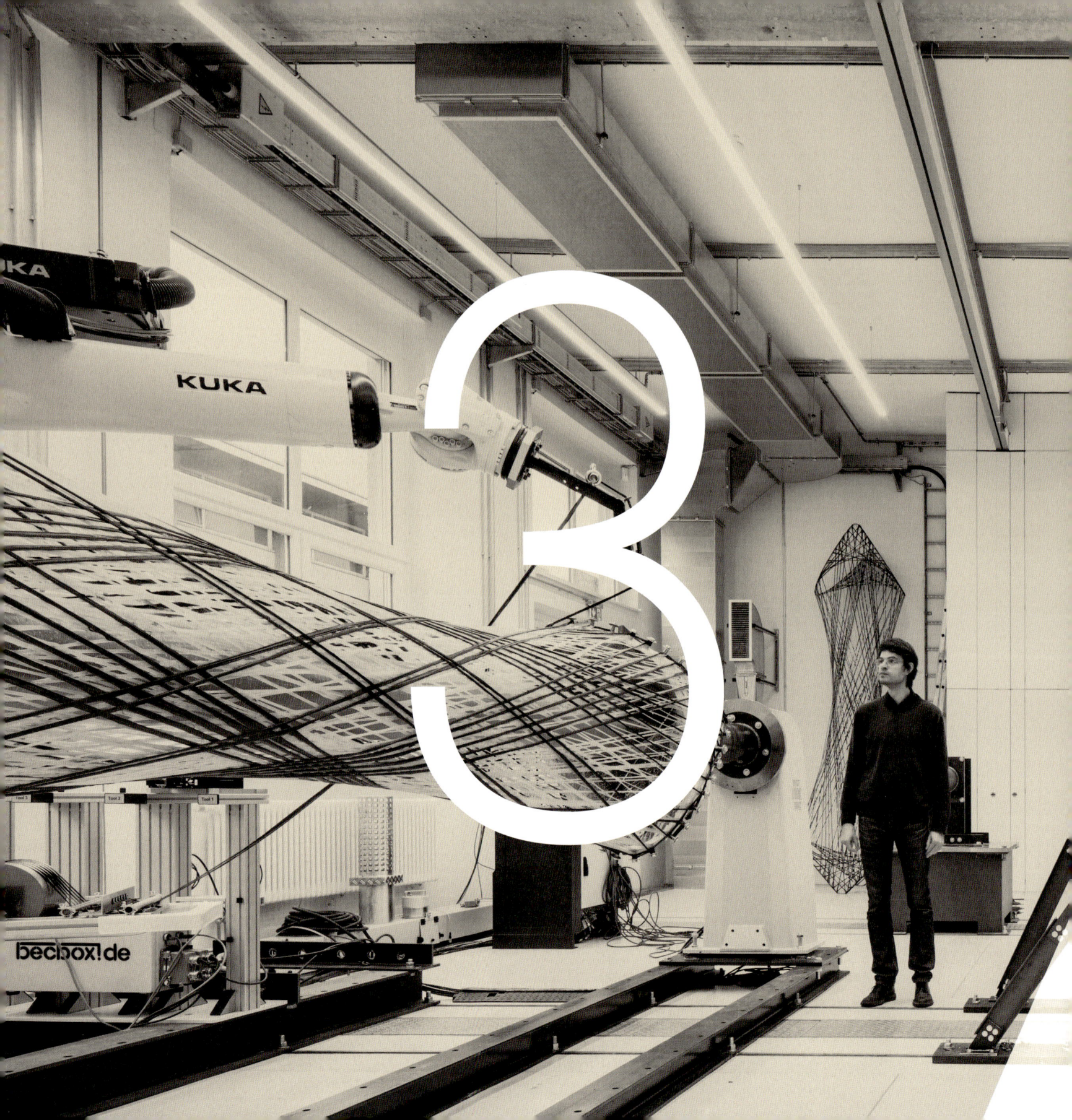

OPTIMISATION
FOR A CHANGING
WORLD

1

ARCHITECTURAL SCALE KAGOME WEAVING
DESIGN METHODS AND FABRICATION CONCEPTS

PHIL AYRES / SORAYA BORNAZ
CITA / KADK
ADAM ORLINSKI / MORITZ HEIMRATH
BOLLINGER+GROHMANN INGENIEURE
ALISON GRACE MARTIN
INDEPENDENT

Research Aims and Objectives

In this paper, key challenges regarding the design and fabrication of Kagome weaves at architectural scale are addressed. The motivation for seeking to transfer this basket making strategy to architectural production is that it provides a clear set of principles for achieving a broad range of complex, doubly-curved morphologies (including freeform and high-genus) while only using straight strips of material in fabrication. In contrast to milling, casting and forming approaches for realising complex geometric designs, using straight strips in combination with Kagome principles can offer key advantages without constraining the morphological design space.

In this study, two research questions are defined:
1) How can existing representational methods, found in the literature, be extended to support design analysis and fabrication at architectural scale?
2) What are the fabrication strategies for realising large scale woven structures that preserve the principle of material interlacing?

In answering these research questions, the principles governing Kagome weave are described, as are the methods of integrating these principles into digital tools for design exploration and analysis – with clear extensions to the state-of-the-art. A novel and scalable fabrication concept for realising Kagome weaves at architectural scale is also described. This concept utilises strips of geo-synthetic cementitious composite mat and has been tested in the context of a one-week workshop resulting in a full-scale prototype. The merits and drawbacks of this approach are critically assessed, and perspectives on further developments to both the design tools and fabrication methods are provided.

Kagome Principles

The topological principles underlying Kagome weave have long been tacitly understood and exploited by the craftsperson to realise functional and art objects with complex morphologies at modest length scales (Fig. 2). In common with all weave logics, Kagome is based on a strategy of material interlacing. However, in contrast to biaxial plane weave variations, Kagome is a tri-axial system. In this system, triangular material crossings produce local reciprocal frames. Therefore any Kagome weave can be understood as a network of reciprocal frames and this network gives rise to the redundancy,

resilience and versatility of this weave form. The combined action of friction and locking (resulting from the action of neighbouring reciprocal frames) alleviates the need for any fixings.

A regular network is the simplest configuration. This produces a planar hexagonal tessellation. However, manipulation of the underlying weave topology, by introducing singularities, gives rise to double curvature. This is due to the creation of out-of-plane stresses in the weave material. Simple topological rules govern the type and degree of curvature (Fig. 3). Positive Gaussian curvature is created by replacing a hexagon with a lesser-sided polygon. The greater the number of edges removed – from hexagon (-6) to pentagon (-5), to square (-4), to triangle (-3) – the more pronounced the curvature. For negative Gaussian curvature, the number of sides is increased – from hexagons (-6) to heptagons (-7), octagons (-8) and so on. The greater the number of edges, the more pronounced the curvature (Ayres et al., 2018; Martin, 2015).

This rationale for controlling double curvature, combined with the ability to achieve complex and arbitrary geometrical targets using only straight strips of material, makes Kagome a particularly attractive target of exploration for transfer to architectural scale (Fig. 4). However, this transfer presents fabrication challenges for realising load-bearing structures using a material interlacing strategy. In conventional basket weaving, the base material is chosen to provide a balance between pliability and bending stiffness. Pliability is necessary to

work the material into local interlaced conditions and, as the weave progresses, bending stiffness develops properties of self-bracing – especially in conditions of double curvature. In conventional weaving materials, this places limits on cross-sectional sizes which generally lie orders of magnitude below architectural scales and required performance profiles.

State of the Art

The affinity between Kagome patterns and computational tri-meshes has been documented and demonstrated in the literature using variations of the Medial Construction method. In Mallos, the Kagome pattern is generated without the constraint of straight strips or 'weavers' as they are also known (Mallos, 2009). In Ayres et al., a variation of the Medial Construction method is applied to the dual of a tri-mesh (Ayres et al., 2018). The dual provides a valence 3 n-gon topology, with the Kagome pattern derived through vertex truncation. The pattern is then relaxed to produce straight weavers. As clear extensions to the state of the art, we demonstrate how the orientation property of mesh face edges is used to efficiently identify individual weavers and is a product of modelling the weave's geometric interlacing. We also integrate a structural analysis method into the modelling workflow.

In terms of fabrication approaches, the hexagonal tiling pattern that acts as the basis of Kagome weave has been exploited to potent aesthetic effect in a number of projects by Shigeru Ban, including the Nine Bridges

2

1. Detail of the material interlacing. Photo: © Fluid Bodies Team.

2. Examples of complex morphologies in Kagome weave using only straight strips of material. Credit: Alison Grace Martin.

3. Simple topological principles govern the generation of curvature in Kagome weaving. These are represented in the design mesh through altering the valence of specific vertices.

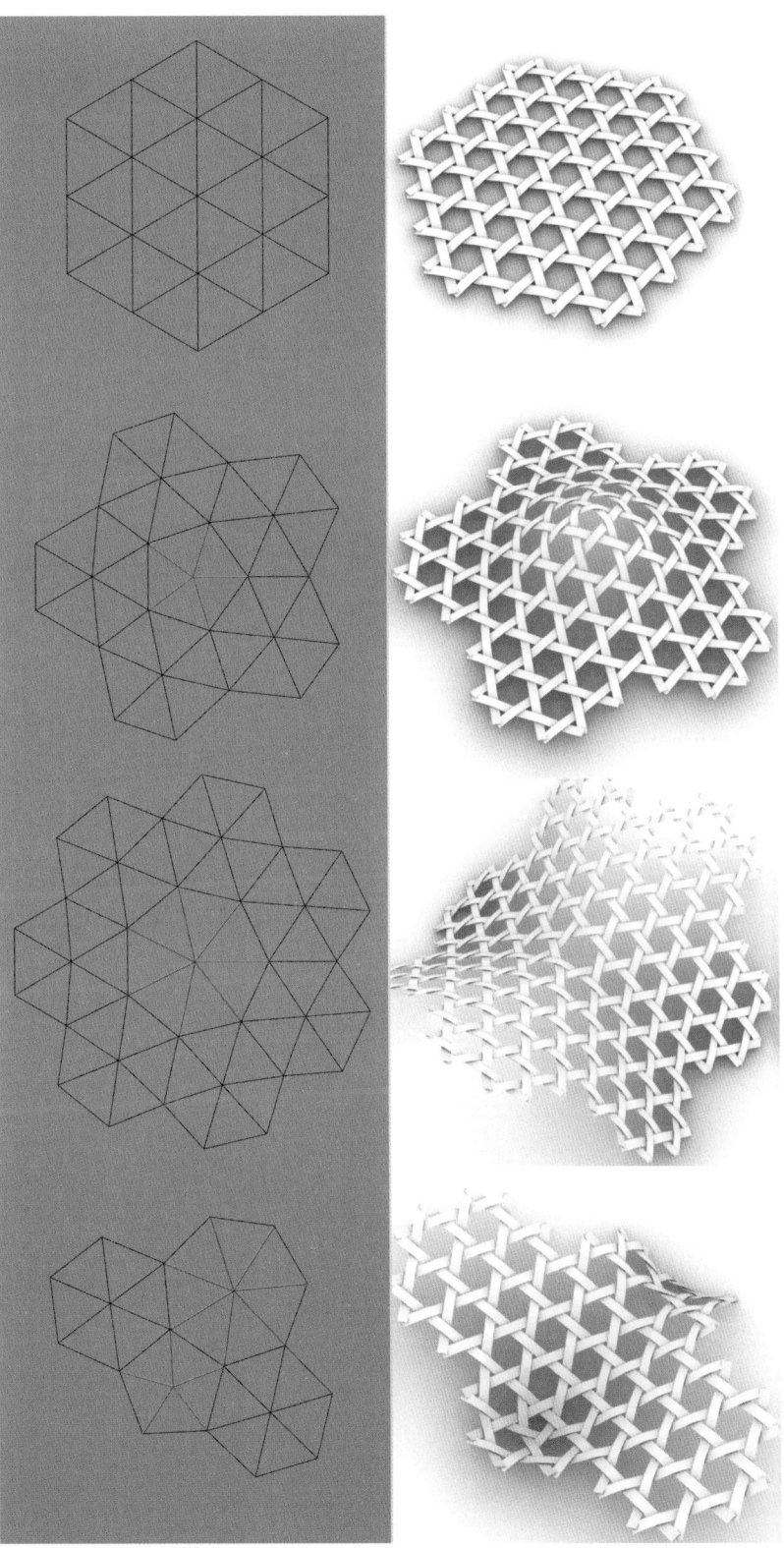

Golf Clubhouse and Centre Pompidou-Metz. However, the interlacing property of weave is sacrificed due to the sizing of members and assembly logic. In addition, the design geometries are developed as a projection of the hexagonal tiling onto a design surface (Scheurer et al., 2013). This has implications on fabrication as curvature has to be manufactured into the members rather than being a property emerging from controlled topology in interaction with mechanical properties of the material, as in the case of conventional woven artefacts. Principled interlacing at architectural scale has been demonstrated in the context of elastically bent structures such as the temporary CODA Jukbuin pavilion (CODA, 2013). In this case, curvature is induced in a hexagonal network of straight strips through boundary constraints. This approach deforms the hexagonal network and places limits on the amount of generated curvature. Without the introduction of topological singularities, highly localised curvatures cannot be achieved and remain global in character. A further motivation for exploring physical Kagome systems at architectural scale is provided by experimental simulation results that indicate Kagome grid shells outperform quadrilateral grid shells (Mesnil et al., 2017).

In summary, and to the best of the authors' knowledge, it can be stated that a viable and scalable fabrication approach that allows for material interlacing, and a principled topological approach for achieving curvature with straight strips of material, has yet to be demonstrated at architectural scale for load-bearing structures.

Research Context

A one-week workshop at the École nationale supérieure d'architecture de Versailles (ENSA-V) provided the framework for testing a novel approach to weaving at architectural scale and producing a proof of concept woven concrete composite shell structure. The fabrication concept originated from the art-based research project 'fluid bodies' at the University of Applied Arts, Vienna. The aim of this project was to explore potential applications of concrete canvas – a proprietary geo-synthetic cementitious composite mat – in the context of furniture and shell design. Geo-synthetic cementitious composite is a prefabricated material composite that exists in two states with different structural behaviours: state A as a flexible geo-synthetic fibre matrix that contains dry cement; and state B as a hardened cement (by the addition of water) that bonds the textile fibres into a solid composite structure.

The workshop commenced with a two-day design competition in which students probed different designs revolving around strategies of cutting and weaving. The final three days focused on fabrication and resulted in an 8 x 8 x 2.5m shell structure, together with three vertical sculptures ranging from 2.5 to 6m in height. Although the design targets were not predetermined, pre-developed digital tools helped to conceptualise weaving patterns on top of different design inputs, as well as balance physical model building with digital design development. Furthermore, the digital tools supported the simulation of the woven structure's tensile hanging behaviours in their flexible condition, and the analysis of their structural strength in their solid state.

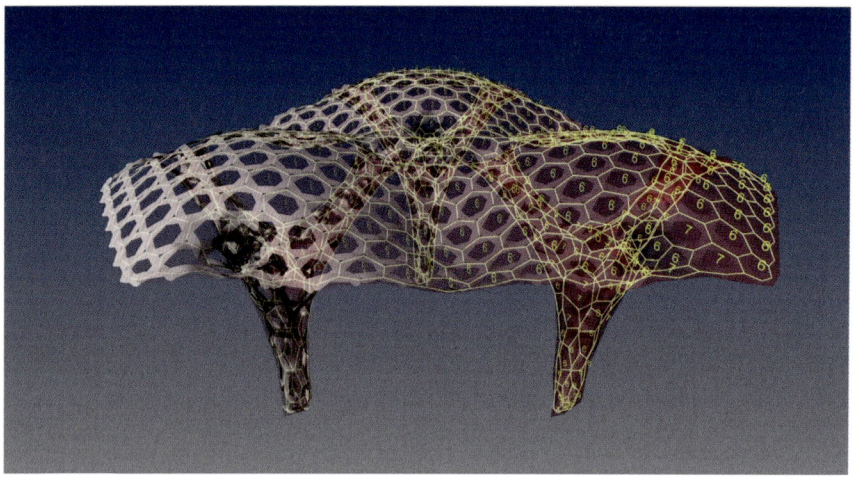

4

Research Methods

Representational Approach

The basis of the weave representation method is a manifold triangular-faced mesh. To act as a design mesh, it must embody a weave pattern topology that corresponds to the curvature of the design target. Topology alteration is achieved by altering the number of incident edges on mesh vertices, otherwise known as altering the mesh valence. With the correct topology created, the Kagome pattern is then generated by connecting the mid-points of each face edge to construct its medial triangle. This defines a new mesh face representing a reciprocal triangle of the weave. Repeating this for each face in the original design mesh results in a new mesh that is not 'watertight', as only the reciprocal triangles are explicitly represented. A preliminary relaxation is applied to this weave topology to generate conditions of straightness for what will become the interlaced weavers. The weavers are determined as a by-product of the process for modelling the interlaced geometry. This process exploits the mesh edge orientation property governed by the 'right-hand-rule', and simply requires that start vertices of each mesh face edge are translated along the vertex normal to the required interlacing height. A new line joins this modified vertex to the unmodified end vertex (Fig. 5). This creates sequences of lines with a saw-tooth configuration. These are joined and reconstructed with a spline curve to represent the interlaced geometry of each weaver. With weavers now identified and interlaced, they can be skinned to represent the dimensions of the weave material and interrogated to extract fabrication information.

Once this geometry is obtained, a linear structural analysis is carried out using Rhino/GH plugin

Karamba3D (Preisinger, 2013). The objective of this analysis is to ensure that the hardened interlaced structure is self-sustaining and not subject to excessive deformations under loading. In the case of the workshop, the load-case was considered to be the weight of a workshop participant. The simulation is modelled to reflect the fabrication procedure, with weavers tied at their intersections. A key implication of this is that the simulations do not need to consider friction. This is a key difference from conventional woven systems which are primarily friction based. The complete computational design workflow for the workshop prototype is presented in figure 6.

Fabrication Approach

The fabrication process begins with two pre-weaving production stages. The first stage is the assembly of a low resolution triangular cable net mounted between boundary edges. The network of cables provides a minimal formwork that pre-defines the intended geometry. The triangular net also embodies the directions of the tri-axial weaving pattern and serves as a three-dimensional weaving map. In the second stage, geo-synthetic cementitious composite mats are cut into straight strips and are re-sealed at the edges. The weaving work occurs in three stages corresponding to the three sets of weavers. The first set of weavers follow one direction of the triangular cable network and is laced with the net. The second set of weavers follows a second direction in the net and is laid upon the first set of weavers. Lacing both layers with the cable structure allows the position of strips to be fixed in space. The introduction of the third set of weavers is where the weave system becomes interlaced, locking all three directions into a tri-axial structure. The Kagome pattern is woven dry and then pre-tensioned

4. Speculative architectural study for a Kagome woven branching structure. The underlying topology of the weave shown on the right as the dual of the design mesh.

5. Steps in the Kagome representation approach. The approach exploits properties of meshes and mesh faces.

6. Computational design workflow for the workshop prototype.

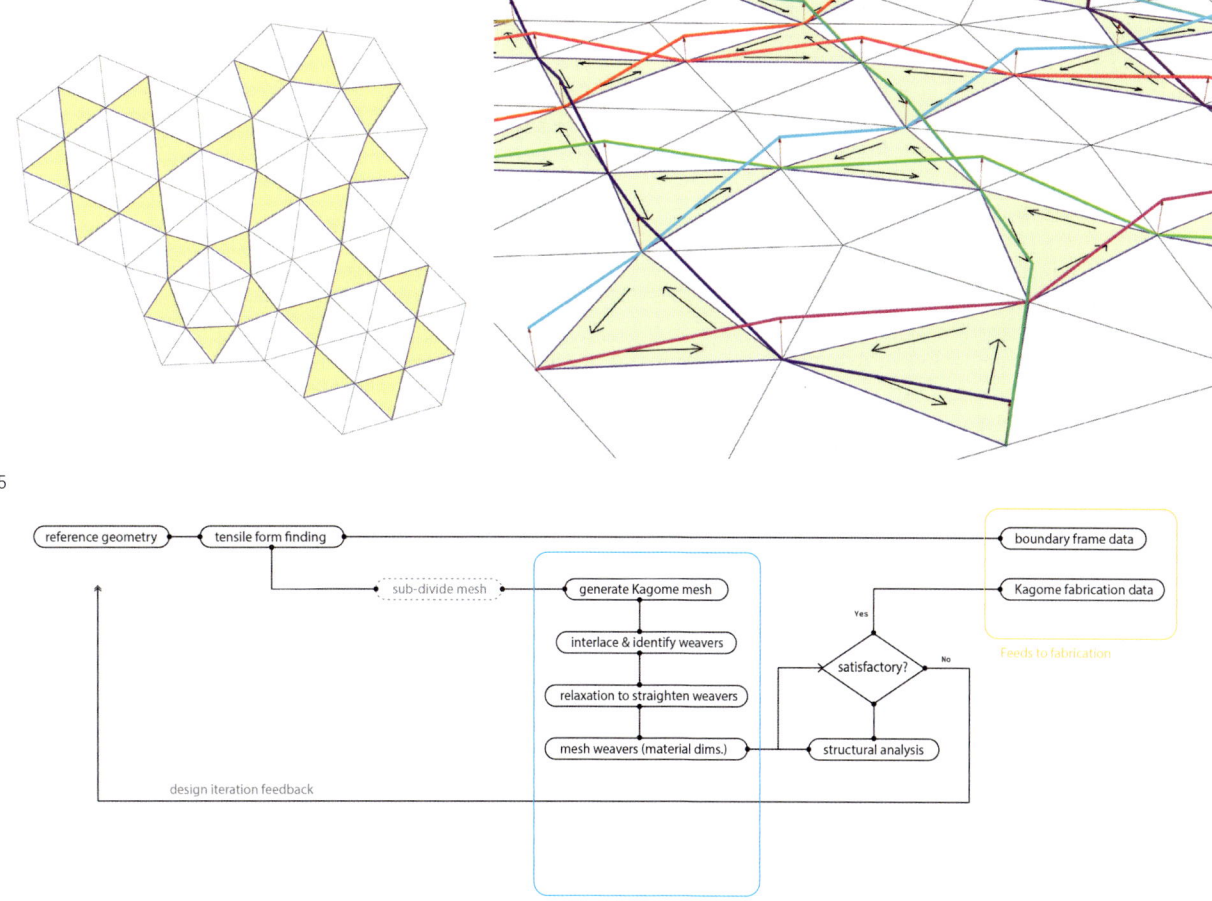

into the target geometry. The benefit of this material is that it is very pliable which allows it to be closely interlaced, resulting in locally interlocking joints. However, in contrast to basket making where the emerging artefact exhibits self-bracing properties, cement impregnated weaving needs temporary support mechanisms due to its lack of bending stiffness. The woven structure is then hydrated to activate cementitious bonding. This transforms the hanging tensile structure into a shell capable of resisting compression as well as bending forces.

Weaving tri-axial patterns in space at architectural scale requires a set design that serves as navigation and provides orientation as well as organisation within the execution process. The critical link between the digital model and the physical object is established via the low resolution triangular cable network. Individual mesh edge loops are cut and marked. Zip ties snap three edge loops into a vertex knot that is easily fixed in position at corresponding cable mark-ups. Through this approach, the geometric formwork, as well as the tri-axial pattern, can be translated between the digital and physical realm with a high level of control (Fig. 7).

Research Evaluation

This section offers a brief critical evaluation of the processes and results spanning design and production.

The digital design tool has successfully integrated a structural analysis procedure, providing explicit information for the production and interlacing of weavers. However, the design environment does not yet generate curvature informed topologically principled meshes from design targets. The implication is that the production of meshes needs to be done by hand and this can be a complex task, especially for new users, as in the context of the workshop. As such, the final geometry of the workshop prototype relies on generating curvature through deformation of a regular hexagonal topology and self-weight, rather than the judicious introduction of singularities.

The mechanical properties of the cementitious strips demand alternative assembly strategies to those conventionally employed by the craft weaver. The lack of bending stiffness and self-weight necessitates the pre-fabrication of temporary formworks which, in this case, were boundary restraints for anticlastic surfaces. The processing and preparation of strips from the proprietary cementitious mat proved to be a significant task which, in future work, should be produced to size by the manufacturer. Finally, the investigation met its primary measure of success – to produce a free-standing, load-bearing, woven structure that approximates the digital design model (Figs 8, 9).

Conclusion

In conclusion, this investigation has set out to address key challenges in the design and fabrication of Kagome weaves at architectural scale. Two complementary lines of enquiry have been reported: 1) the further development of digital design tools tailored to the investigation and representation of Kagome patterns, their materialisation, their principled organisation and their structural performance; and 2) the development of a novel fabrication concept using strips of geo-synthetic cementitious composite mat that allows for material interlacing. The viability of the fabrication concept was tested through the production of a large scale (8 x 8 x 2.5m) load-bearing weave in the context of a one-week workshop. This fabrication approach resulted in a bonded and hardened material interlacing as opposed to friction-based interlacing that characterises conventional

Kagome woven systems and artefacts (Fig. 1). While further testing is required to fully determine the merits and drawbacks of this approach, the physical prototype establishes the viability of the construction concept and validates the integrated digital design workflow. This represents a success in the transfer of Kagome weave concepts for application at scales beyond conventional woven artefacts. In turn, this promises to enrich the vocabulary of architectural construction systems with a novel methodology that offers potent and complex spatial potentials through material continuity, particularly in the relationship between volume and surface as shown in figure 4. In contrast to the elastically bent and temporary Jukbuin pavilion, the use of cementitious composite mat offers a vector towards permanence and, potentially, sufficient load-bearing capacity to support environmental enclosures. In contrast to the Nine Bridges Golf Clubhouse and Centre Pompidou-Metz projects, the principles of Kagome weave offer a rationalised approach to element pre-fabrication predicated on linear material geometries, but without constraint to the morphological design space. However, the required shift in assembly logic, from an assembly of highly discretised sub-elements to a materially continuous interlacing, is likely to be the principle challenge to practical feasibility facing the weave concept – particularly as length scales increase.

Immediate open challenges that frame future developments include: the development of a 'topology-finding' method for the automatic generation of principled meshes with curvature informed valence; manufactured strip production of the composite mat to specified weaver dimensions; and the extension of the net formwork procedure to support the realisation of geometries with positive Gaussian curvature.

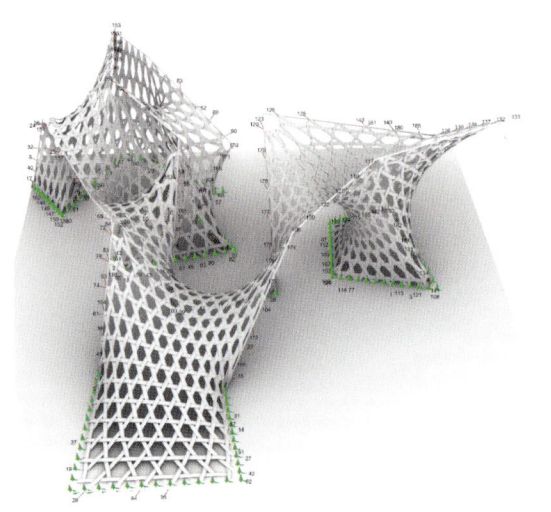

7

7. Overall comparison between the digital model (left) and the cured weave with boundary frames removed (right). Photo: © Fluid Bodies Team.

8. The completed weave accommodating an impromptu point-loading test. Photo: © Fluid Bodies Team.

9. The completed weave, free-standing. Photo credit: © Fluid Bodies Team.

8

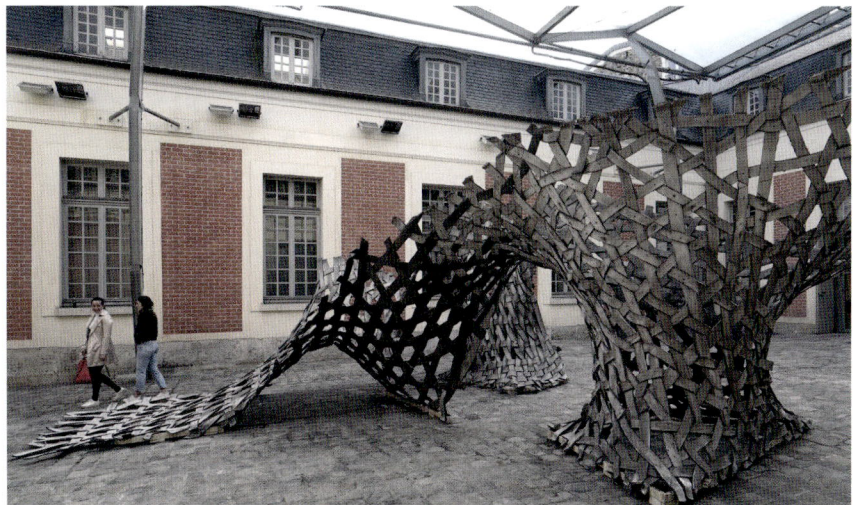

9

Acknowledgements

This paper is based on research conducted by a multitude of people operating in different circles and domains of expertise that gravitated in the context of a workshop held at ENSA-V, Paris in May 2019.

FLUID BODIES / Intelligent Fabrication workshop by MADAME Architects & Bollinger + Grohmann Ingenieure by invitation, and together with, Klaas De Rycke at ENSA-V Paris.

FLUID BODIES Research Team: Klaus Bollinger, Quirin Krumbholz, Rupert Zallmann, Adam Orlinski, Anna Rademacher, August Kocherscheidt, Moritz Heimrath.

Supported by CITA: Phil Ayres, Soraya Bornaz.

Special thanks are extended to Daniel Piker for counsel and assistance with aspects of the Kangaroo 2 relaxation implementation for the Kagome weave representation.

Special thanks are also extended to all the student workshop participants from ENSA-V.

FLUID BODIES is an art based research project located at the University of Applied Arts, Vienna and funded by: www.fwf.at (PEEK Programme).

References

Ayres, P., Martin, A. G. and Zwierzycki, M. 2018. 'Beyond the Basket Case: a principled approach to the modelling of Kagome weave patterns for the fabrication of interlaced lattice structures using straight strips', in *Advances in Architectural Geometry 2018*, Chalmers: Chalmers University of Technology, pp. 72-93.

CODA, Jukbuin Pavilion, http://coda-office.com/work/Jukbuin (accessed 4 October 2019)

Mallos, J. 2009. 'How to weave a basket of arbitrary shape', in *ISAMA* 2009, Albany, NY: University of Albany, pp. 13-19.

Martin, A. G. 2015. 'A basketmaker's approach to structural morphology', in *Proceedings of the International Association for Shell and Spatial Structures*, Amsterdam: (IASS) Symposium.

Mesnil, R., Douthe, C., Baverel, O. and Léger, B. 2017. 'Linear buckling of quadrangular and kagome gridshells: a comparative assessment', in *Engineering Structures*, 132, pp. 337-48.

Preisinger, C. 2013. 'Linking Structure and Parametric Geometry', *Computation Works: The Building of Algorithmic Thought*: *Architectural Design – Special Issue*, 83(2), pp. 110-113. (doi: 10.1002/ad.1564)

Scheurer, F., Stehling, H., Tschümperlin, F. and Antemann, M. 2013. 'Design for assembly – digital prefabrication of complex timber structures', in *Beyond the Limits of Man*, Proceedings of the IASS 2013 Symposium, Wroclaw.

1

RETHINKING EFFICIENT SHELL STRUCTURES WITH 3D-PRINTED FORMWORK

XIANG WANG / CHUN PONG SO / LIMING ZHANG / ZHEWEN CHEN / PHILIP F. YUAN
TONGJI UNIVERSITY

Introduction

Advanced fabrication technique such as additive manufacturing provides the ability for designers to create much more complicated geometries with novel materials than their ancient counterparts. This opens up new perspectives on efficient design and construction methodology based on the performance of structures. Ongoing research at Tongji University related to the application of 3D printing in construction focuses on the feasibility of using 3D-printed formworks for thin shell structures to enable a pure eco-friendly and efficient construction process. Based on the characteristic and restrictions of the material as well as the fabrication technique, the presented method shows the overall design procedure including the structural logic, fabrication and assembly process.

The two presented shell projects show a progressive development of the ideas and the applications of their variations in large-scale shell projects (Figs 1, 2). They started from a collaborative research project of bending active formwork with an experimental pavilion as a demonstrator and were later developed and reformulated in a large-scale brick shell with a new structural solution.

Structural logic is generated based on the material's behaviour, and also with respect to their natural and artificial usage in structures and craftworks.

Additive Manufacturing as Formworks with Complicated Geometry

Additive manufacturing techniques have been applied widely in rapid prototyping by the production manufacturing industry in the last decade (Campbell et al., 2012). Its extension in the architecture industry, which is represented mostly by the large-scale FDM 3D-printing technique, has greatly enlarged the possibilities of fabrication and materialisation of parametric-defined geometry (Ou et al., 2015).

Compared to the 3D printing of traditional building materials such as cement and concrete, a significant application of 3D-printed plastic or polymer in the architectural industry is the customised formwork for complex structural components (Jipa et al., 2017; Jipa et al., 2016). The material efficiency derived from this technique provides an answer to the serious concerns regarding the vulnerable state of the environment and a future with sustainable building processes.

This paper explores such advantages that are well-suited to the construction of complex shells which rely on the complicated structural actions of three-dimensional equilibrium. In the past, efficient shells usually required large falsework to control the form and to take the load of the partial shell before they completed their shape. This would, in turn, cause great waste of materials as well as human labours, making the construction inefficient. The main target of this work is to set up a design-fabrication-assembly framework of such method and to apply that in real thin shell projects.

3D-Printed Bending-Active Formwork – A Research Project

In Spring 2019, a joint workshop between ETH, MIT and Tongji University was organised to explore the feasibility to 3D print lightweight and stable formwork for unreinforced shell structures with traditional masonry and concrete (Yuan and Philippe, 2019). The target was to utilise the large deformation of bending-active structures to enhance the structural stability by introducing curvature through bending. For this research, a design framework was made from the initial form-finding of compression-only funicular shell structures to the bending simulation based on the dynamic relaxation method in Grasshopper, as well as the explicit-dynamic analysis in FEM software such as Abaqus (Fig. 3). The form-found doubly-curved geometry was further optimised to develop a surface that could be unrolled as a planar pattern for 3D printing. The global geometry was then stabilised with the V-shape cross-section from the corrugation of the bent plates (Fig. 4) and hence gained safety as well as redundancy.

Shell Geometry and the Form-Finding of the 'Red Pavilion' Shell

Based on the success of the research pavilion during the joint workshop, a similar design workflow was later applied and reformulated in another, larger, thin shell project. In the 'Red Pavilion' brick shell, the form-finding process employed two different popular methods and software to find the possible compression-only form for the shell while controlling the geometry based on specific design requirements. Both the Thrust-Network-Analysis (TNA) method (Rippmann, 2016), via RhinoVAULT plugin for Rhinoceros, based on the Graphic Statics, and the

2

1. Experimental Pavilion as demonstrator of the MIT/ETH/Tongji Workshop.

2. The 'Red Pavilion' Brick Shell Project for the Wuzhen World Internet Conference.

3. Design strategy and the specific techniques in the research of bending active 3D-printed formwork for unreinforced thin shells (Left: Form-finding and optimisation; Right: Simulation and analysis of the bending process).

4. Construction Process with the bent 3D-printed formwork.

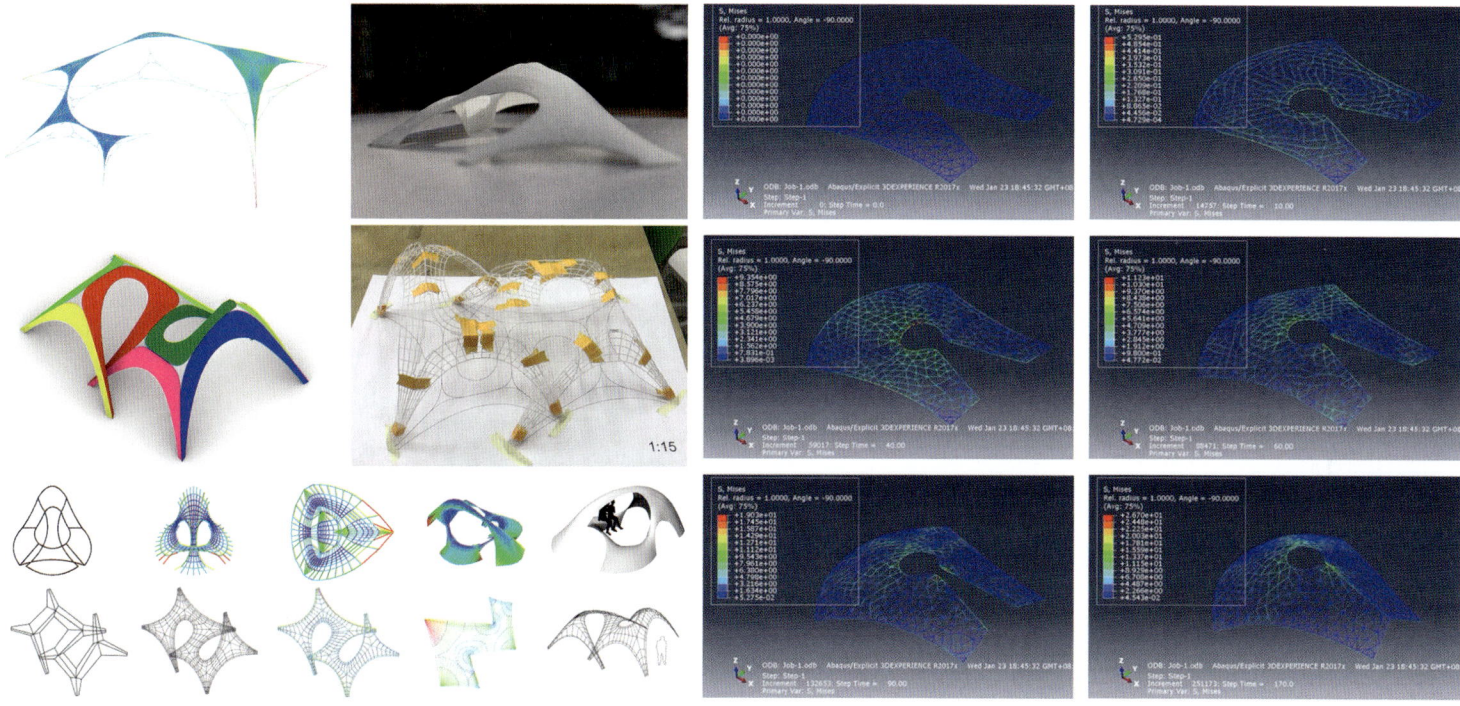

3

4

Particle-Spring (PS) method via Kangaroo2 plugin for Grasshopper, based on the dynamic analysis of the equilibrium state, were applied to find the final shell geometry. The global geometry was further manipulated to control the distribution of internal forces in shells by controlling the force edge length for local elements in the TNA method and the local spring stiffness in the PS method. This method enabled a special area with concentration of compression which worked as the walkable roof area, as well as the tilted-up free edge area with significant double curvature which provided much more structural redundancy for the large-scale thin shell. As a result, the final shell reached a maximal span of 40m with a cross-section of only 150mm (three layers of bricks; section-span ration 1:267).

Design of the Formwork System

The initial concept and guide of design was to use the 3D-printed elements as the formwork of the thin shell as well as part of the structure in its long-time life cycle. With this consideration, the insulation material, such as polyurethane in this case, was also included in the formwork system and worked together with the 3D-printed blocks. After the printing of the lattice-formed elements of the formwork, a thick layer of polyurethane was cast on top and milled with the robotic arm according to the designed doubly-curved surface of the shell (Fig. 5).

The pattern design of the 3D-printed blocks was based on the original UV quadrilateral mesh of the form-found shell, and reformulated to a reciprocal structure with a so-called 'nexorade' pattern. This is mostly due to the low Young's modulus of the ABS plastic so that the reciprocal structure can provide better stiffness than the quad-mesh. Meanwhile, as the reciprocal pattern would bring the eccentricity of the adjacent edges that made the interior surface rugged, the 'nexorade' could decrease the extent of such eccentricity and also align the direction of new edges better along the original force vectors (Mesnil et al., 2018) (Fig. 6). Geometrically, as the FDM 3D-printing technique required a flatbed surface to avoid the tilting problem caused by the temperature difference, a planarisation optimisation process was also applied on the initial mesh. Rather than a conical-mesh optimisation method which relies on the small deformation of mesh nodes and will change the structural behaviour of the shell, the optimisation of pattern was realised simply by relocating the diagonals of every quadrilateral to the polygon centre and creating a new planar bottom surface (by allowing discontinuity at adjacent blocks). As 3D-printing techniques have no limit on the geometry of the side walls of the building blocks, a smoothen process was applied on the nexorade mesh by interpolating curved surfaces in both the UV direction of the formwork (Fig. 6). After the whole optimisation process of the pattern, 1500 blocks were generated to compose a large reciprocal formwork structure and the maximum deviation of adjacent blocks in the vertical direction was decreased from 7cm to less than 3cm.

Robotic Fabrication Techniques

For the fast prefabrication of the 1500 building elements, a semi-automated robotic-aided fabrication procedure was applied by combining multiple techniques such as the 3D printing, milling and drilling. The 3D printing was finished by the KUKA KR120 robot arm with a plastic extruder as end-effector. After that, the PU layer was cast manually in the prefabrication factory to about 15cm with a layer of glass fibre fabric as isolation. A second KUKA KR180 robot arm with a large milling end-effector finished the top layer of the PU according to the geometry of the shell surface. With the same machine, the next process was finished by the robot, drilling the side wall holes to connect the adjacent blocks.

On-site Assembly and Accuracy Control

With the help of the 3D-printed geometry and the pre-drilled holes in the side wall of the building blocks, the on-site assembly of the huge shell formwork was

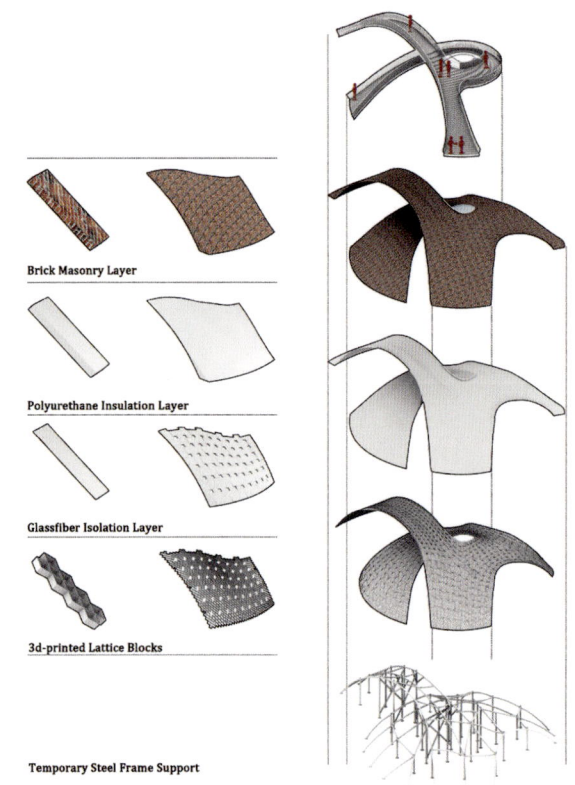

Brick Masonry Layer

Polyurethane Insulation Layer

Glassfiber Isolation Layer

3d-printed Lattice Blocks

Temporary Steel Frame Support

5

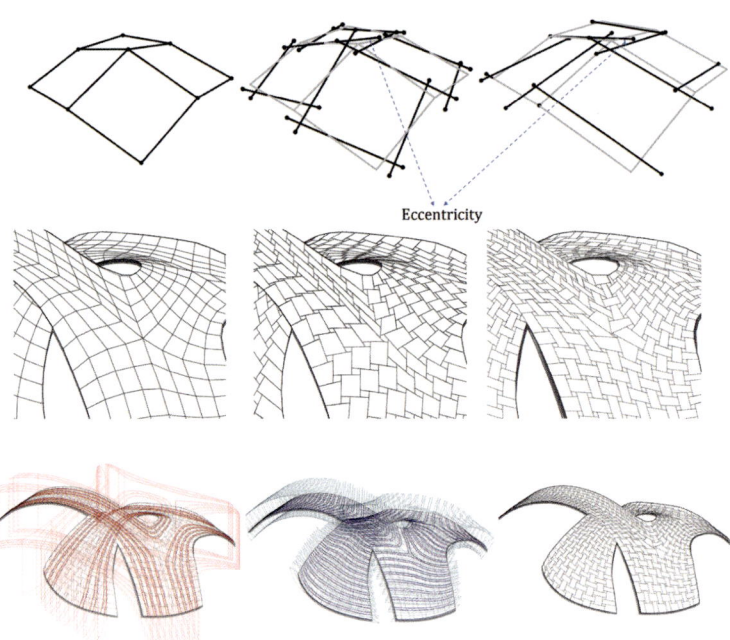

Eccentricity

6

5. Diagram of the construction details and fabrication sequence of the formwork system.

6. Design of the reciprocal structure pattern of the 3D-printed formwork system.

7. 3D scanning and rematch analysis for the accurate positioning of the formwork.

8. Loading test to check the structural response and the safety of the shell.

simplified through the positioning and connecting of the corresponding holes. However, small inaccuracies happened due to the tolerance of the robotic fabrication process. Like a similar shell project, the Armadillo masonry shell in Venice (Block et al., 2017), a temporary supporting steel frame was introduced to help the positioning and tuning of the soft and flexible plastic formwork. The mesh of the steel frame was designed with a 12cm inward offset of the original shell surface. Thread-rod shims were welded on the steel frame to provide an adjustable support for the accurate positioning of the formwork system. According to the FEM analysis, the maximum edge length of the steel frame mesh at about 5 metres and a minimal frame thickness of the printed blocks at 3cm was determined to guarantee an acceptable small deformation for the load of two layers of bricks.

The on-site adjustment of the formwork system was finished by simply tuning the shims according to the computational model of the formwork design. After the first adjustment, a full 3D scan of the work was done to check the geometry (Fig. 7) and the maximum tolerance was controlled in the range of ±2cm which provided enough accuracy for the final masonry work of the brick shell.

7

8

Structural Analysis and Load Test

Structural analysis of the shell is finished by the FEM analysis which considered different load cases including the dead load, full live load and half live load. Furthermore, a final in-situ loading test was also done to check the safety and its correspondence to the analysis result (Fig. 8). The loading test lasted a day and a half to check the structural response to the different loading cases of the shell and, finally, 90 tonnes of sand bags were added on the walkable area of the shell. After a one-night loading procedure for the safety test, the untouched temporary supporting frame was demolished to finish the final process of the construction.

Conclusion

Both projects presented in this paper show the new efficient building technique that can be derived from the advanced manufacturing technique with the marriage of computational design methods. They show also a successful result of the structural-performance-based design framework where both the fabrication technique as well as the structural behaviour are taken into consideration. The fast and accurate construction of the red pavilion provides a future for the green construction of large-scale complex shells with an optimised formwork system and the application of eco-friendly materials and fabrication techniques. In the collaboration between the designers and structural engineers, not only a digital modelling strategy but also a wrap-around construction system was developed to fulfil the energy-saving and sustainable building future of the efficient shell structures.

Acknowledgements

The authors would like to thank the contribution of the following people on the joint workshop and the 'Red Pavilion' shell.

ETH/MIT/Tongji Joint Workshop 'Robotic Force Printing' (pre-research for Red Pavilion)
Prof. Philippe Block, Prof. Philip F. Yuan, Dr.-Ing. Xiang Wang, Kam-Ming Mark Tam, Gene Ting-Chun Kao, Zain Karsan, Alex Beaudouin, Ce Li, Ben Hoyle, Molly Mason, Weizhe Gao, Weiran Zhu, Zhe Guo, Dalma Foldesi, Hyerin Lee, Jung In Seo, Anna Vasileiou, Youyuan Luo, D, Xiao Zhang, Liming Zhang, Hua Chai.

'Red Pavilion' Brick Shell
Prof. Philip F. Yuan, Wen Zhang, Dr.-Ing. Xiang Wang, Xiangping Kong, Chun Pong So, Liming Zhang, Zhewen Chen, Xuwei Wang, Yong Peng, Bin Jiang, Zhun Zhang (AND Office).

This research is funded by the National Natural Science Foundation of China (Grant No.51578378), the Special Funds for State Key R&D Program during the 13th Five-year Plan Period of China (Grant No.2016YFC0702104) and the Sino- German Centre Research Program (Grant No.GZ1162).

References

Block, P., Rippmann, M., Van Mele, T., & Escobedo, D. J. F. 2017. 'The Armadillo Vault Balancing Computation and Traditional Craft', in Menges, A., Sheil, B., Glynn, R. and Skavara, M. (eds), *Fabricate*, London: UCL Press, pp. 286-293.

Campbell, I., Bourell, D. and Gibson, I. 2012. 'Additive Manufacturing: Rapid Prototyping Comes of Age', *Rapid Prototyping Journal*, 18(4), pp. 255-258.

Jipa, A., Bernhard, M., Dillenburger, B., Ruffray, N., Wangler, T. and Flatt, R. J. 2017. 'skelETHon Formwork: 3D Printed Plastic Formwork for Load-Bearing Concrete Structures', in *Proceedings of the 21st Congreso Internacional de la Sociedad Iberoamericana de Gráfica Digital, 2017*. São Paulo: Blucher, pp. 345-352. (doi: 10.5151/sigradi2017-054)

Jipa, A., Bernhard, M., Meibodi, M. & Dillenburger, B. 2016. '3D-printed stay-in-place formwork for topologically optimized concrete slabs', in *Proceedings of the 2016 TxA Emerging Design + Technology Conference, 2016*. Texas Society of Architects, pp. 97-107. (doi:10.3929/ethz-b-000237082)

Mesnil, R., Douthe, C., Baverel, O. and Gobin, T. 2018. 'Form finding of nexorades using the translations method', *Automation in Construction*, 95, pp. 142-154.

Ou, J., Cheng, C.Y., Zhou, L., Dublon, G. and Ishii, H. 2015. 'Method of 3D printing micro-pillar structures on surfaces', in *Adjunct Publication of the 28th Annual ACM Symposium on User Interface Software and Technology*. New York: ACM, pp. 59-60. (doi: 10.1145/2815585.2817812)

Rippmann, M. 2016. *Funicular Shell Design: Geometric approaches to form finding and fabrication of discrete funicular structures*. Zurich: ETH Zurich.

Yuan, P. F. and Philippe, B. 2019. *Robotic Force Printing: A Joint Workshop of MIT/ETH/Tongji*, Shanghai, China: Tongji University Press.

9. The 'Red Pavilion' Brick Shell Project for the Wuzhen World Internet Conference.

KNITCANDELA
CHALLENGING THE CONSTRUCTION, LOGISTICS, WASTE AND ECONOMY OF CONCRETE-SHELL FORMWORKS

MARIANA POPESCU / MATTHIAS RIPPMANN / TOM VAN MELE / PHILIPPE BLOCK
BLOCK RESEARCH GROUP, INSTITUTE OF TECHNOLOGY IN ARCHITECTURE, ETH ZURICH

This paper describes the design, development, computational workflow, digital fabrication and construction of KnitCandela, a thin, undulating, concrete waffle shell built using a flexible formwork system featuring a custom, prefabricated knitted textile as shuttering and a form-found cable net as the main load-bearing formwork. The shell was developed by the Block Research Group at the Institute for Technology in Architecture of ETH Zurich in collaboration with the Computational Design Group of Zaha Hadid Architects (ZHCODE) as part of the first exhibition of Zaha Hadid Architects in Latin America. It was exhibited at the Museo Universitario Arte Contemporáneo (MUAC) in Mexico City between October 2018 and July 2019.

Designed as an homage to the Spanish-Mexican shell builder Félix Candela (1910-1997), the curved geometry of the shell is reminiscent of Candela's iconic restaurant in Xochimilco, while its fluid form and colourful interior surface are inspired by the traditional Jalisco dress. Candela relied on hyperbolic paraboloids to efficiently build curved concrete shells with reusable straight formwork elements. The design of KnitCandela breaks free of the constraints of ruled or developable surfaces. Instead, it demonstrates that complex concrete structures can be built at low economic and environmental cost through the strategic use of computational design and fabrication, combined with craftsmanship.

The five-tonne concrete shell (Fig. 1), with a surface area of 50m², was cast on a flexible cable-net and knitted fabric formwork, weighing just 55kg. Following a digitally-generated knitting pattern, the fully shaped, double-layered 3D-knitted shuttering of the formwork was produced in just 36 hours on a commonly available CNC knitting machine. Due to its lightness, it was easy and compact to transport to site. The load-bearing cable-net and knitted formwork was tensioned in a temporary timber/steel frame and coated with a special stiffening cement paste, developed at the Chair of Physical Chemistry of Building Materials at ETH Zurich. Fibre-reinforced concrete was manually applied to the formwork to realise a 3cm-thick shell with a quadrilateral grid of stiffening ribs with a height of 4cm.

Flexible Forming of Concrete

Doubly-curved, rib-stiffened shells offer an efficient load-bearing capacity but have complex geometry. As a result, their non-standard shapes can be challenging,

1

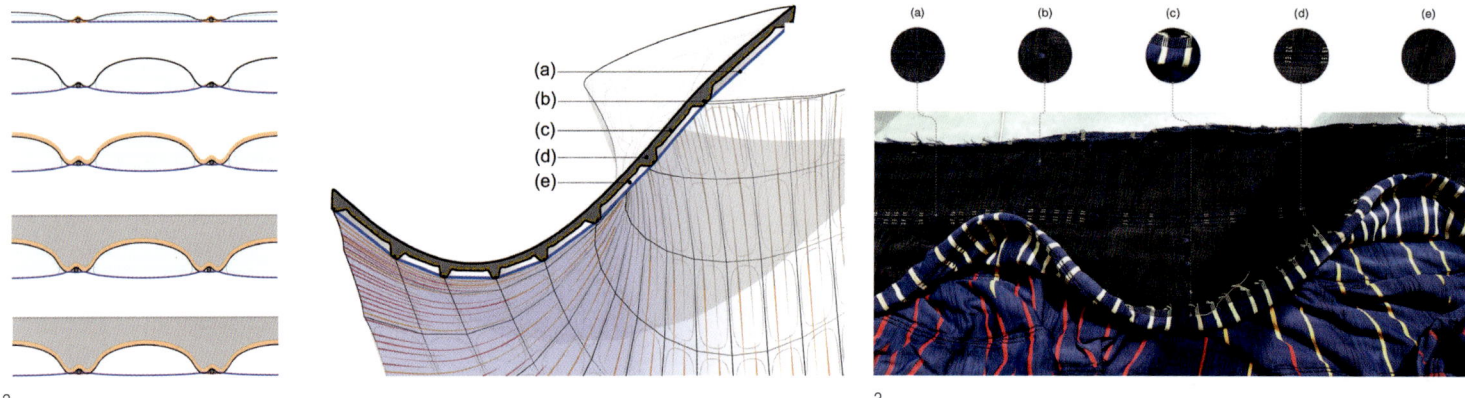

2

3

expensive, wasteful and time-consuming to build with traditional formwork methods that rely on single-use cut timber or milled foam. These custom-fabricated formwork constructions account for approximately half to as much as two-thirds of a structure's cost (García de Soto et al., 2018) and take a lot of time to manufacture, requiring months of carpentry or CNC milling (Søndergaard et al., 2018). Additionally, these rigid and often heavy moulds have to be held in place by scaffolding, needing foundations. As such, traditional approaches are not economically and ecologically viable for non-standard and doubly-curved structures.

Using a membrane or fabric can offer an alternative flexible forming system that needs minimal or no scaffolding (Veenendaal et al., 2011). As textiles are compact and light, they can be effortlessly transported to the construction site and have proven to be a waste-reducing solution to formworks for a wide range of building components (Hawkins et al., 2016). To achieve the desired geometry, textiles need to be tensioned into shape using rigs, frames or external supports (West, 2016). Tensioning may also be done using hybrid approaches where a cable net (Veenendal and Block, 2014; Méndez Echenagucia et al., 2019), bending-active elements (Lienhard and Knippers, 2015; Cuvilliers et al., 2017; Ramsgaard Thomsen et al., 2018) or inflatables (Ahlquist et al., 2017) form a self-supporting system with the textile. Fabric formwork systems generally use single-layered, woven fabrics with uniform texture and structural properties. To avoid wrinkles, their shaping and the integration of other features relies on the extensive tailoring and joining of different flat sheets of material.

In contrast to woven textiles, knitted materials can be tailored to non-developable and three-dimensional shapes, allowing for functional integration and the design of very specific properties without the need for gluing, welding or stitching. Therefore, using weft-knitted textiles as part of these flexible systems broadens the geometric possibilities and offers the opportunity for functional integration, which may result in simplified logistics on site.

Constraining the Design Space

The structure was designed as a 3cm-thick, anticlastic concrete shell with 4cm-high stiffening ribs in both directions, thus resulting in a doubly-curved waffle shell. The design of the structure's geometry was informed by the formwork system and resulting fabrication constraints. The formwork system behind KnitCandela was made up of a timber and steel tensioning frame, a load-bearing steel cable-net falsework, and a custom 3D-knitted textile shuttering.

The system sought to investigate construction opportunities in terms of material and weight saving, streamlining logistics on- and off-site and exploring new aesthetic opportunities offered by using knitting. To demonstrate the integration and shaping possibilities of spatial knitting at an architectural scale, the knitted shuttering was designed to have channels and openings providing guidance and alignment for the load-bearing cable net; additionally, pockets were included to shape voids in the finished concrete structure to achieve material and weight savings. These cavities were obtained by inflating modelling balloons in the pockets. The construction steps and resulting waffle shell are shown in figure 2.

The densities of the knitted textile on both layers were carefully tailored to control to which side of the formwork the pocket would inflate and into what precise shape. The edge details were created by inserting steel rods into the edge-boundary channels and held up by laser-cut wooden profiles. The double-sided textile used as shuttering presented a decorative and technical layer, including

1. KnitCandela is a concrete waffle shell built using a lightweight, stay-in-place, cable-net and knitted fabric formwork. Photo: Angélica Ibarra.

2. Steps for creating the KnitCandela's concrete waffle-shell section (from top to bottom): (a) tensioning the two-layered knitted textile, and cable net; (b) inflating of the pockets; (c) coating the knitted shuttering with a fast-setting cement-paste layer; (d) casting of the concrete waffle shell; and (e) deflating of the pockets to form the voids.

3. Double-layered knitted textile produced in one piece, featuring an aesthetic front face and a technical back face that includes for controlling the position of cables, inflatables and edge detailing: (a) openings for the cable-net nodes; (b) openings for inserting balloons; (c) textile border for joining pieces together; (d) channels for cables; and (e) variable loop densities and sizes.

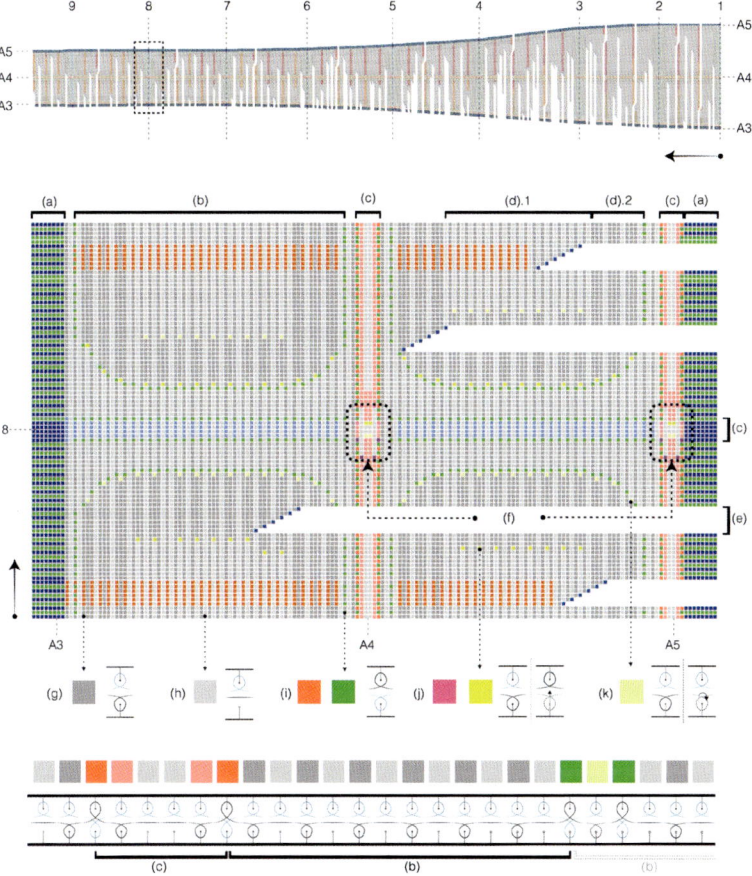

4. Generated knitting pattern for Strip 2 showing the features and functions needed to achieve them: (a) seam detail; (b) pocket; (c) vertical and horizontal channels; (d) varied loop densities; (e) short row; (f) openings in channels at their intersection; (g) knit front and back (yarn 1 and yarn 2); (h) float front and knit back (yarn 1 and yarn 2); (i) knit front and back (yarn 2 and yarn 1); (j) knit front and back, then transfer front to back; and (k) knit front and back, then drop front stitch.

features for inserting, guiding and controlling the position of cables and inflatables, and is shown in figure 3.

From a fabrication point of view, the textile was only limited by the needle-bed width (1.3m) of the knitting machine (Steiger Libra 3.130). Taking advantage of the knitting machine's ability to create infinitely long pieces, the geometry was split into four long strips (16m-26m in length), resulting in a total of four seams over the entire surface.

The cable-net and knitted shuttering formwork, defining the final shell, was form-found using a target geometry that was defined through a series of design iterations with the goal of balancing the aesthetic and structural targets of the project. To keep the detailing of the formwork clean and simple, the topology of the cable net was restrained to a quad pattern, with closed continuous ring cables in the 'horizontal' and boundary-to-boundary cables in the 'vertical' direction.

Computational Knitting

A digital workflow was established for the project, which aided the iterative design and engineering process, the generation of the informed geometry (based on the fabrication and formwork system constraints), and the production of all needed manufacturing instructions and data. The entire workflow was developed using the COMPAS framework, an open-source computational framework for research and collaboration in architecture, engineering, fabrication and construction (Van Mele et al., 2017).

For producing a knitted textile, a knitting pattern is needed to drive the CNC machine. *compas_knit* (Popescu, 2019), a digital pipeline developed to automatically generate knitting patterns from a given 3D geometry, was used to produce the textile shuttering of KnitCandela. The generated knitting patterns were informed by the knitting direction and a target loop width and height, which for this project were determined to be 3.5mm and 2mm, based on pre-stressing tests. Patterns were generated in patches matching the quadrilaterals formed between cables. This not only made for a computationally less intensive process, but also naturally aligned the patterns to the cable directions which made the fabrication of their channels simpler and cleaner. After all 2D patch patterns were generated for a given strip, they were combined into one single pattern and the locations of the cables and decorative colour lines were automatically mapped on the combined pattern and marked with a colour code. Then a BMP-format pixel image was exported with each colour representing a predefined function (knit, transfer, drop stitch etc.) for the machine to perform (Fig. 4). Finally, the BMP image was imported into the machine's proprietary software, Model 9, where each colour was assigned a symbol from a library developed for this project.

Enhancing Craftsmanship

The concrete shell was constructed on site over a period of four weeks. The elements needed for the construction were fabricated in Mexico and Switzerland. The textile shuttering was fabricated at ETH Zurich, vacuum-packed and transported to Mexico in two suitcases, as regular checked luggage. The timber and steel frame for tensioning was fabricated in Mexico City.

To assemble the formwork, the four strips of textile were sewn together into one wider strip, and the cables inserted in the corresponding channels of the textile. Turnbuckles were attached to the ends of the cables and all nodes were

5

6

temporarily fixed in place with zip ties. This package was then attached to the frame and tensioned into shape by gradually tightening the turnbuckles around the outer perimeter.

Given the tight schedule of the project and fabrication limitations, the tensioning rig was custom-designed to be easily manufactured with traditional methods and effortlessly assembled into a self-contained frame. The planar timber arches, built only out of standardly available profiles, were tilted into position and then braced by in-situ welded tubular steel profiles. The waffle shell's weight-saving cavities were created by inserting and inflating standard modelling balloons into the pockets of the double-layered textile. Laser-cut plywood edge profiles were attached to the cables (Fig. 5), then the fabric was folded over and the boundary spline was fixed to the profiles, ensuring a clean edge detail and a reference for the concrete thickness. The entire textile was sprayed with a thin, fast-setting cement-paste coating (Fig. 6). The Calcium Aluminate Cement (CAC) coating was designed to harden within two hours in ambient conditions, stiffening the textile to minimise local deformations when concrete was applied (Reiter, 2019).

With the formwork surface realised, glass-fibre-reinforced concrete was applied in three layers. First, all ribs were filled in; then, a second layer built up the thickness of the shell (Fig. 7); and, finally, a third finishing layer was applied and hand rendered smooth (Fig. 8). Finally, once the concrete cured, the cables were released from the frame to let the shell stand unsupported. The frame was dismantled and removed, while the pockets were deflated, leaving the textile in place and visible on the intrados of the structure (Fig. 10).

Increasing Productivity

Prototyping, design, engineering, fabrication and construction was carried out by multiple teams in Europe and Mexico over a period of three and a half months. The timber and steel frame was fabricated and assembled by construction workers in two weeks. In the meantime, once designed and generated, the knitted textile took only 36 hours of machine time to produce, with each of the four strips being a two-layered, weft-knitted textile produced in one manufacturing process. Due to the low weight (25kg) and compactness, the textile could be easily transported to the worksite. Installing the formwork in the frame and casting concrete took a total of two weeks, of which one week was dedicated to assembling the textile shuttering and cable-net falsework and an additional three days were dedicated to preparing the formwork for coating (tensioning, inserting and inflating balloons, and attaching and fixing the edge details). The cement-paste coating was sprayed onto the textile in two sessions of four hours. Finally, three layers of fibre-reinforced concrete were applied over the course of three days.

The digitally designed and fabricated textile provided integrated features for inserting and guiding elements such as cables and inflatables that helped shape the sophisticated mould. This not only made it possible to shape a mould that would otherwise require extensive milling (more than 750 hours or 3 months for a similar surface area, according to Gardiner et al., 2016) but also significantly simplified on-site logistics. An example of this being the pockets of the textile which shape individual cavities of different shapes and sizes using the same standard element (balloon). In this case, the standard balloons produced varied solutions through the

5. Attaching the laser-cut edge profiles to the steel cables of the tensioned formwork. Photo: Maria Verhulst.

6. Spraying the cement-paste coating on to one side of the tensioned formwork. Photo: Mariana Popescu.

7. Hand rendering of the concrete of the waffle shell. Photo: Mariana Popescu.

8. Fibre-reinforced concrete manually applied in layers and rendered smooth. Photo: Mariana Popescu.

9. Tensioned cable-net and knitted textile formwork needing minimal scaffolding. Photo: Maria Verhulst.

7

8

9

10

embedded properties of the textile. By including the construction intelligence within the custom textile, the need for extensive labelling could be avoided, placement errors reduced and the construction of the mould drastically sped up.

Realising a complex concrete structure in a short period of time was possible because of a streamlined design process complemented by a robust production pipeline such that the development could be pushed close to the start of construction. Moreover, on-site logistics was kept simple, drawing upon existing craftsmanship and bridging computational design, digital fabrication and crafts.

Relying on a computational approach using the open-source framework COMPAS, numerous structural and constructional iterations could be simulated digitally and physically prototyped thanks to the smooth connection to fabrication. This uncompromised digital chain allowed for an intense development cycle between multiple collaborating teams, resulting in the efficient structural design, engineering, digital fabrication, and construction of KnitCandela. The demonstrated design-to-production process presents an outlook towards a more integrated, research-driven architectural and engineering practice with increased productivity.

Discussion and Outlook

The KnitCandela prototype demonstrated that with an appropriate computational design and digital fabrication pipeline, knitted textiles can be easily produced.

Furthermore, when combined with load-bearing elements, knitted textiles can be used to shape complex geometries at an architectural scale. Tensioning the cable-net and textile formwork in a timber frame removed the need for dense scaffolding to support heavy moulds from below (Fig. 9). Because of time and site constraints, the frame used for tensioning was custom-designed and fabricated for this project. However, a system relying on standard scaffolding elements could be developed, making the tensioning frame a reconfigurable and reusable part.

As a thoroughly efficient, ecologically conscious construction system, the stay-in-place mould for this complex structural geometry produced almost no waste. The minimal foundations and scaffolding required to realise KnitCandela's formwork give a glimpse of how the formwork for such expressive forms of significant size (50m²) can be designed, fabricated and realised with a minimal footprint, in a very short period of time (three and a half months) and at low cost (EUR 2,250, excluding labour and the external frame). The computationally designed, materially- and waste-efficient approach demonstrated in KnitCandela targets all those areas where project timelines and budgets often get out of control – transport and on-site logistics, manual labour (for the formwork fabrication and construction), installation costs, etc. – while also being an elegantly designed structure that embraces the aesthetic opportunities offered by the knitted textile. The system takes a step in confronting the challenges faced by the building industry today and offering practical, easily realisable solutions for a more sustainable way of building.

10. Top view of the KnitCandela pavilion showing its radial symmetry. Photo: Leo Bieling.

Acknowledgements

Design and engineering

Block Research Group (BRG), ETH Zurich: Mariana Popescu, Matthias Rippmann, Andrew Liew, Tom Van Mele, Philippe Block [detailed design and structural engineering]

Zaha Hadid Architects Computation and Design Group (ZHCODE): Filippo Nassetti, David Reeves, Marko Margeta, Shajay Bhooshan, Patrik Schumacher [sketch design]

Fabrication and construction

BRG: Mariana Popescu, Matthias Rippmann, Alessandro Dell'Endice, Cristian Calvo Barentin, Nora Ravanidou [knitted formwork and fabrication data]

Architecture Extrapolated (R-Ex): Alicia Nahmad Vazquez, Horacio Bibiano Vargas, Jose Manuel Diaz Sanchez, Asunción Zúñiga, Agustín Lozano Álvarez, Migue Juárez Antonio, Filiberto Juárez Antonio, Daniel Piña, Daniel Celin, Carlos Axel Pérez Cano, José Luis Naranjo Olivares, Everardo Hernández, Ramiro Tena. [on-site construction and coordination]

Concrete development

Chair of Physical Chemistry of Building Materials, ETH Zurich: Lex Reiter, Robert J. Flatt [cement-paste coating]

Holcim Mexico: Jose Alfredo Rodriguez, Carlos Eduardo Juarez, Delia Peregrina Rizo [fibre-reinforced concrete]

The research presented in this paper was supported by the Swiss National Centre of Competence in Research (NCCR) Digital Fabrication, funded by the Swiss National Science Foundation (NCCR Digital Fabrication Agreement # 51NF40-141853)

The authors would like to dedicate this paper to their late co-author, colleague and friend, Dr Matthias Rippmann, whose contributions were essential to this work as to numerous other projects from the Block Research Group at ETH Zurich

References

Ahlquist, S., McGee, W. and Sharmin, S. 2017. 'PneumaKnit: Actuated Architectures Through Wale- and Course-wise Tubular Knit-constrained Pneumatic Systems', *ACADIA 2017: Disciplines & Disruption, Proceedings of the 37th Annual Conference of the Association for Computer Aided Design in Architecture (ACADIA)*, pp. 38–51.

Cuvilliers, P., Douthe, C., Peloux, L. D. and Roy, R. L. 2017. 'Hybrid structural skin: prototype of elastic gridshell braced with a concrete envelope', in *Proceedings of IASS Annual Symposia, International Association for Shell and Spatial Structures (IASS)*, pp. 1–10.

García de Soto, B., Agustí-Juan, I., Hunhevicz, J., Joss, S., Graser, K., Habert, G. and Adey, B. T. 2018. 'Productivity of digital fabrication in construction: Cost and time analysis of a robotically built wall', *Automation in Construction*, 92, pp. 297–311.

Gardiner, J.B., Janssen, S. and Kirchner, N. 2016. 'A realisation of a construction scale robotic system for 3D printing of complex formwork.', In *ISARC 2016 – 33rd International Symposium on Automation and Robotics in Construction*, pp. 515-521.

Hawkins, W. J., Herrmann, M., Ibell, T. J., Kromoser, B., Michaelski, A., Orr, J. J., Pedreschi, R., Pronk, A., Schipper, H. R., Shepherd, P., Veenendaal, D., Wansdronk, R. and West, M. 2016. 'Flexible formwork technologies – a state of the art review', *Structural Concrete* 17(6), pp. 911-935.

Lienhard, J. and Knippers, J. 2015. 'Bending-active textile hybrids', *Journal of the International Association for Shell and Spatial Structures* 56(1), pp. 37-48.

Mendez Echenagucia, T. M., Pigram, D., Liew, A., Van Mele, T. and Block, P. 2019. 'A cable-net and fabric formwork system for the construction of concrete shells: Design, fabrication and construction of a full-scale prototype', *Structures*, 18, pp. 72-82. [https://doi.org/10.3929/ethz-b-000302717]

Popescu, M., Rippmann, M., Van Mele, T. and Block, P. 2017. 'Automated generation of knit patterns for non-developable surfaces', *in Humanizing Digital Reality – Proceedings of the Design Modelling Symposium 2017,* Paris: Springer, pp. 271–284.

Popescu, M. 2019. 'KnitCrete: Stay-in-place knitted fabric formwork for complex concrete structures', PhD thesis, Department of Architecture, ETH Zurich.

Ramsgaard Thomsen, M., Tamke, M., La Magna, R., Fragkia, V., Längst, P., Lienhard, J., Noel, R. and Sinke Baranovskaya, Y. 2018. 'Isoropia: An Encompassing Approach for the Design, Analysis and Form-Finding of Bending-Active Textile Hybrids.' In *IASS Symposium 2018: Creativity in Structural Design*.

Reiter, L. 2019. 'Structural build-up for digital fabrication with concrete - Materials, methods and processes', Department of Civil, Environmental and Geomatic Engineering, ETH Zurich.

Søndergaard, A., Feringa, J., Stan, F. and Maier, D. 2018. 'Robotic abrasive wire cutting of polymerized styrene formwork systems for cost-effective realization of topology-optimized concrete structures', *Construction Robotics*, 2(1-4), pp. 81–92.

Van Mele, T., Liew, A., Mendéz, T., Rippmann, M. and others 2017. *COMPAS: A framework for computational research in architecture and structures*, http://compas-dev.github.io/. (Accessed 2 January 2020)

Veenendaal, D. and Block, P. 2014. 'Design process for prototype concrete shells using a hybrid cable-net and fabric formwork', *Engineering Structures* 75, pp. 39–50.

Veenendaal, D., West, M. and Block, P. 2011. 'History and overview of fabric formwork: Using fabrics for concrete casting', *Structural Concrete* 12(3), pp. 164–177.

West, M. 2016. *The fabric formwork book: Methods for building new architectural and structural forms in concrete*, London: Routledge.

PRINTED ASSEMBLAGES
A CO-EVOLUTION OF COMPOSITE TECTONICS AND ADDITIVE MANUFACTURING TECHNIQUES

ROLAND SNOOKS
RMIT UNIVERSITY / STUDIO ROLAND SNOOKS
LAURA HARPER
MONASH UNIVERSITY / STUDIO ROLAND SNOOKS

This research explores the integration of carbon fibre structural networks within large-scale 3D-printed polymer architectural skins. The approach is developed through a lineage of iteratively designed projects that establish a co-evolution of fabrication technique and tectonic logic. Within this lineage, the paper is focused on two projects, Cloud Affects and B515 Studios, which experiment with the algorithmic generation of structural networks and their fabrication through sacrificial formwork strategies. The research demonstrates a co-dependent relationship developed through the feedback of generative design processes and the refinement of large-scale fused deposition modelling (also known as Big Area Additive Manufacturing, or BAAM). The implications of this co-evolution are explored here in terms of form, structure and detailing.

This fabrication research has emerged from a trajectory of algorithmic design focused on the generation of intricate geometries and the compression of tectonics into a single heterogeneous assemblage. Embedding carbon fibre structural networks within polymer printed architectural skins enables a shift from cladding to an integration of form, surface and structure – an expression of the synthetic negotiation of complex systems. This enables architecture to fully leverage the geometric possibilities of 3D printing to reify the complexity of algorithmically generated architecture and reveal a new set of formal and topological possibilities. Specifically, Cloud Affects explores the formal and topological possibilities enabled by improved functionality of BAAM printing, while B515 Studios has advanced the jointing and detailing logic to create a continuous integration of carbon fibre structural ribs within thin skins. This paper details specifically the challenges and opportunities presented by the material characteristics of polymer and carbon fibre. However, as discussed in the conclusion, the techniques and construction methods developed throughout this process have broader applications extending to other materials including 3D-printed metals and concrete.

AgentBody Generative Algorithms

The algorithmic processes that underlie this research agenda form a methodological approach described here as Behavioural Formation. This methodology, which has been in development since 2002, draws on the logic of swarm intelligence and operates through multi-agent algorithms (Snooks, 2020). Swarm intelligence describes the collective behaviour of decentralised systems, in

1

2

3

which the non-linear interaction of its constituent parts self-organise to generate emergent behaviour (Bonabeau et al., 1999). Repositioning this logic as an architectural design process involves encoding architectural design intention within computational agents. It is the interaction of these agents that leads to a self-organisation of design intention and the generation of emergent architectural forms and organisational patterns. These architectural behaviours establish local relationships between architectural elements and are driven by either direct criteria such as structural or programmatic requirements, or more esoteric concerns relating to the generation of form or pattern.

The specific behavioural algorithm deployed in the projects presented here, the agentBody algorithm, draws on the logic of ant-bridges, where it is the interconnected geometry of the ants' bodies that forms architectural or structural matter. Their logic of connection leads to highly intricate assemblages that have been leveraged in these projects for their ornamental and structural potential. AgentBodies are inherently architectonic, consisting of a geometric skeleton within which behaviours, material properties and fabrication limitations can be encoded within agents, operating as control points of the skeleton. This topological structure establishes a type of digital materiality. Empirically derived material behaviour, including the geometric limitations of robotic fabrication such as printing draft angles, can be encoded within the geometry of the skeleton.

Constructing the compressed tectonics integral to the generative logic of these behavioural algorithms requires the fabrication of porous geometries and embedded lattice

systems. This requires specific technical capacity and innovations including the ability to 3D print complex surface topology at a large scale, and the seamless integration of structure and jointing into the formal articulation of the project.

Cloud Affects

Cloud Affects is a gallery-scale architectural installation designed through an agentBody algorithm which integrates form, structure and ornament within topologically-complex lattices and surfaces. The lattice becomes a continuous series of hollow formwork conduits within which carbon fibre is infused, creating a structural skeleton. A second independent surface forms a translucent skin which encloses the structural lattice. The inner and outer geometries periodically laminate to create sufficient structural rigidity between the two.

Each assembly is divided into approximately twelve printed components sized to correspond to the limitations of the printing bed. The project has been designed to be pre-fabricated with the capacity to be disassembled. Consequently, joints between components are resolved using mechanical fixing through laser-cut steel plates cast within the carbon fibre.

B515 Studios

B515 Studios consists of two self-contained volumes which sit within a larger open-plan floorplate containing workshops and maker spaces for RMIT University. The studios are designed with 105m² of translucent polycarbonate 3D-printed walls embedded with a carbon

1. Cloud Affects: Shenzhen Biennale. Photo: RMIT University.

2. SensiLab Studio: robotic 3D printing process.

3. SensiLab Studio. Photo: Peter Bennetts.

4. B515 Studios: fabrication photograph, 3D printed polymer panels. Photo: Roland Snooks.

5. NGV Pavilion: sacrificial formwork structural skeleton.

fibre structural skeleton. The two studios are positioned with adjacent translucent polycarbonate skins creating a canyon-like space between them. Similar to Cloud Affects, B515 Studios uses an agentBody algorithm to generate a complex lattice which is translated into a structural skeleton. However, in B515 studios, the geometry of structure and enclosure are further integrated, with the external skin crimped or pinched to allow a single line of polycarbonate to define and enclose hollow conduits to be later infused with carbon fibre. This results in an overall reduction of polycarbonate material, shorter tool paths and lighter components while achieving a similar structural integrity.

The structural skeleton creates a defined larger scale pattern within the polycarbonate walls, a pattern which is translated firstly into window mullions and then panel articulation to enable it to be continued over the perimeter of the studios. A secondary, finer scale pattern within the polycarbonate skin creates both additional patternation as well as establishing points of lamination between the inner and outer skin of the polycarbonate to create local stiffening of the surface. The carbon fibre of the primary skeleton is infused through multiple adjacent components, creating continuous structural ribs. The project is due for completion in February 2020.

Context

This research contributes to a larger milieu of advanced architectural fabrication research in which robotic deposition of fibre composites and 3D printing of permanent formwork are being increasingly explored, most notably at the ICD Stuttgart, ETH Zurich and Politecnico di Milano. The carbon fibre winding projects of the ICD, including the Elytra Filament Pavilion, leverage the capacity of formwork jigs to define ruled and minimal surface geometry (Prado et al., 2017). Permanent formwork strategies are adopted in the gluing of fibre composites to the inflatable formwork explored by the ICD (Dörstelmann et al., 2015) and the 3D-printed surfaces developed by the DBT Lab at ETH (Hyunchul et al., 2018), which establishes a sequential relationship of surface and structure. Alternatively, the development of continuous fibre pultrusion 3D-printing techniques at Politecnico di Milano establish an entirely integrated relationship of surface and 3D-printed form (Invernizzi et al., 2016). These approaches all explore the deposition of structural material without the use of moulds and in doing so create new possibilities and limitations.

The strategy posited here of printing structural conduits within architectural skins differs from the approaches described above in that it enables substantial carbon fibre structural members to be infused within the skin of the projects. In particular, Cloud Affects demonstrates an approach where structure is not subservient to the geometry of the skin (such as taping to inflatable or printed surfaces) or the convergence to physically efficient forms (such as minimal surfaces), but instead structure and skin negotiate a nuanced interrelationship with the capacity to generate complex and intricate form. Printing conduits for carbon fibre infusion enables detailed control of the profile of the structural members and an efficient process for embedding fibre composites without the use of moulds.

Methodology: The Co-evolution of Fabrication and Tectonics

This research has been developed through a methodology of iterative practice-based research in which the strategies evolve through, and in response to, a sequence of projects. The key projects in this evolution are: the NGV Pavilion (2015-2016), which initiated a strategy for concrete reinforced 3D polymer printed sacrificial formwork; SensiLab Studio (2017), which is a polymer 3D printed studio located within an open-plan research space; and Floe, commissioned by the National Gallery of Victoria for its Triennial Extra programme (2018), which is an architectural installation that draws on the atmospheric effects of the Antarctic landscape. These projects demonstrate ways in which innovation in fabrication technique can create new architectural design possibilities, while design projects and generative design processes can catalyse the development of fabrication techniques – with the two engaged in a recursive loop. Fabrication processes define many of the limitations and biases in the design of architectural form, structure and detailing of these projects. Through the evolution of this lineage of projects, the functionality of the RMIT Architecture BAAM robotic cell has developed, refined and expanded in parallel to advancing the sophistication of tectonic approaches and their attendant generative algorithms.

Form

The 3D printing for Cloud Affects and B515 Studios required the development of improved BAAM functionality to enable the fabrication of complex topology and form with substantial directional freedom. This expanded functionality includes: the development of reliable and accurate start-stop printing; methods for printing temporary support material; and printing non-parallel/non-horizontal layers. This functionality, while modest in terms of technical development, has significant design implications. Start-stop printing is essential to enable topological diversity, as the printed form no longer needs to be designed from a continuous surface. This development required the full-integration of the extruder controls to the robot IOs and path planning techniques to minimise the string-pull of the polymer. Printing support material enabled a greater diversity of lattice geometries, as it was no longer necessary to cantilever the entire print directly from the build plate. Non-horizontal printing, utilising the six-axis capacity of industrial robotics, enabled more complex and less directional formal possibilities as complex forms can be segmented into smaller parts that have limited draft-angle requirements while enabling complexity at the macro-

6

scale. While developed specifically for the parameters of plastics, many of the techniques presented here are applicable to other materials and are currently being further explored at RMIT through robotic 3D printing of metals.

The multi-agent algorithmic methodology used on these projects, where architectural intent is embedded within the behaviour of each agentBody, also enabled the integration of rules and limitations of the material and printing process. For example, maximum draft angles were designed into the behaviours of agentBodies, ensuring that forms generated through algorithmic processes corresponded to printable geometries rather than being post-rationalised. The formal potential of these projects is also integrally tied to their structural capacity. The integration of carbon fibre to support structurally difficult cantilevering geometries propelled experimentation with new BAAM functionality and the development of compressed tectonics.

6. Cloud Affects: detail.

7. Cloud Affects: prototype detail.

Structure

A key question for the resolution of complex algorithmic geometries in 3D-printed skins is how to embed structure. The methods for achieving this have developed and became more sophisticated over the chronology of these projects. In Sensilab, a kind of extruded truss was created through the separation and corrugated profile of three interconnected polymer skins which produced sufficient structural capacity to support the weight of the 2.8m high wall. Agent behaviours were designed to respond to both aesthetic/formal concerns and structural logic, with behaviours generating corrugation frequency and depth in response to adjacent structural support. Larger projects such as Floe (6m tall) experimented with the agentBody generation of a structural lattice. The final installation was constructed from laser-cut and CNC brake-press folded steel interwoven through a swarm of 70 overlapping 3D-printed polymer panels. The lattice was refined and individually sized through feedback from a Finite Element Analysis (FEA) model developed by engineers Bollinger+Grohmann, but limitations in BAAM functionality at the time prevented the full integration of this lattice into the skin.

The decision to experiment on Cloud Affects with carbon fibre infused structures was developed in collaboration with Boeing, as part of the ongoing RMIT Boeing Alliance and Mike Xie's Centre for Innovative Structures and Materials at RMIT University. Carbon fibre offers the benefit of a high strength to weight ratio in contrast to the identified challenges of casting concrete including shrinkage, hydrostatic pressure on the formwork prior to curing, and difficulties in logistics after casting off site. The topological complexity made possible by advancements in BAAM techniques enabled a structurally efficient agentBody lattice to be generated within the polymer skin of Cloud Affects. A FEA model enabled structural analysis to inform the recalibration of agent behaviours. For example, behaviours were designed to separate vertically to create greater structural depth in the skeleton where there was excessive deflection, establishing a process for conditioning the generative process based on structural analysis.

The implications of the carbon fibre structure were then further developed in B515 Studios where the rigidity of the carbon fibre skeleton enabled a shift from a triple skin polymer that is highly corrugated to a thinner double skin with less deviation in plan. Structural conduits were also designed to be continuous across joints, allowing the carbon fibre to be infused through multiple components to create continuous structural ribs from floor to ceiling and reducing the reliance on mechanical fixing.

7

Detailing

A key challenge for BAAM polymer printing is the requirement for multiple components, and therefore joints, produced by the limitations of the printing environment. While materials such as concrete can be printed continuously on site, the sensitivity of polymer to temperature during cooling requires the implementation of a heated base plate and a controlled temperature environment. These challenges increase when printing in polycarbonate – a polymer that provides increased strength, fire-rating and acoustic functionality while at the same time requiring higher temperatures and having greater susceptibility to warping, particularly in the vertical joint, which impedes high-precision connections.

The first attempt to solve these issues in a constructed project (SensiLab) de-coupled the vertical joint from the algorithmic structural pattern, creating an overlapping detail which allowed adjacent panels to slide past each other for the required tolerance. However, the expressed joint interrupted the continuity of the generative surface pattern and imposed a secondary reading that interfered with the original design intention. A second iteration (Floe, 2018) used an overlapping shingle-like detail where polymer components were fixed to a steel frame rather than each other. This avoided the issue of tolerance but also failed to satisfy the intention of integrating structure and skin.

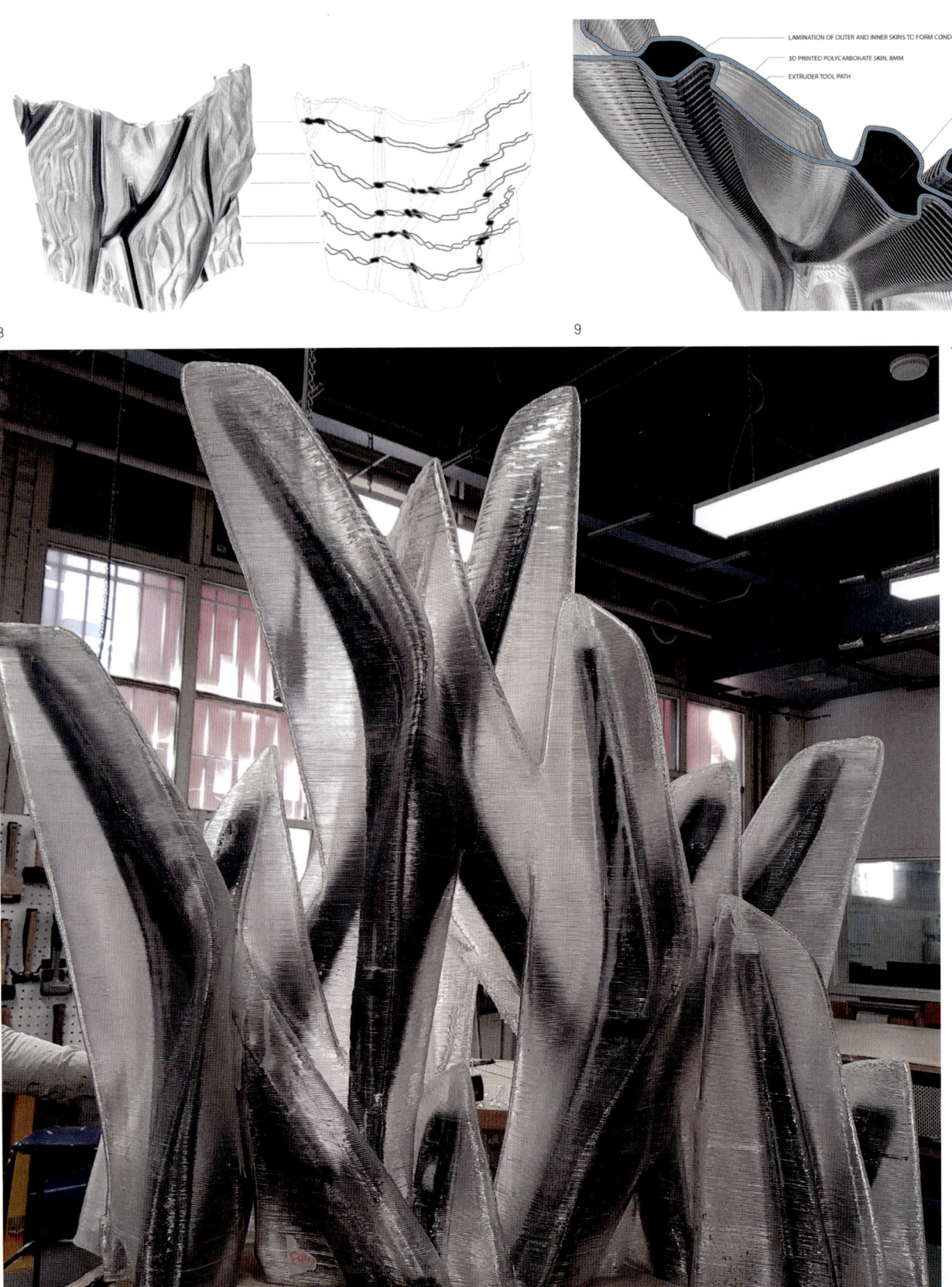

8   9   10

Labels on diagram 9:

LAMINATION OF OUTER AND INNER SKINS TO FORM CONDUIT

3D PRINTED POLYCARBONATE SKIN, 8MM

EXTRUDER TOOL PATH

CARBON FIBRE REINFORCED CONDUIT

CARBON FIBRE REINFORCED CONDUIT, SPLIT AT PANEL JOINT

8. B515 Studios: carbon fibre reinforcement digram.

9. B515 Studios: section detail.

10. Cloud Affects: fabrication photograph. The embedded carbon fibre structural members are silhouetted within the polymer skin. Photo: RMIT University.

An innovation that enabled the overlap of component joints and embedded structure was developed in the B515 Studios project. A set of parameters based on logical component sizes (maximum of 2000mm relating to heated base plate and minimum of 1200mm related to efficient toolpath times) were embedded within the agentBody algorithm used to generate the structural lattice. This allowed a logic of reasonable and workable component division to be overlaid on the structural network without the imposition of a new joint logic. A set of 'twin' details were developed for structural conduits which enabled some to act as tolerance joints between components while appearing with a similar profile and size, and allowing for the same structural capacity as adjacent unified structural ribs.

Conclusion

The research presented here developed from an architectural ambition to reify the complex geometry generated through behavioural processes of formation through a material and physical compression of surface, structure and ornament. Critical to achieving this is the development of strategies for embedding structural logic into surfaces. The research presented here progresses this through three identifiable methods: integration of structural heuristics within algorithmic behaviours; strengthening of a thin and lightweight surface with corrugation and curvature; and finally the integration of composite materials to create a structural lattice intertwined within the surface itself.

The projects presented here are realised with polymers and composites which has allowed for efficient and rapid experimentation. However, the broader research aim is to explore and expand the potential of geometries created through a variety of materials within additive manufacturing, and to reveal inherent strengths and characteristics of this construction which cannot be achieved through other means. The research has progressed: the integration of structure and services through conduits embedded within skins; the use of complex printed skins as sacrificial formwork; and printing of structurally-optimised complex form which allows for the use of less material in construction. These techniques challenge how building skins are envisaged and speculate on the potential evolution of construction systems in response to additive manufacturing.

References

Bonabeau. E., Theraulaz G. and Dorigo M. 1999. *Swarm Intelligence: From Natural to Artificial Systems*, Oxford: Oxford University Press.

Dörstelmann, M., Knippers, J., Koslowski, V., Menges, A., Prado, M., Schieber, G. and Vasey, L. 2015. 'ICD/ITKE research pavilion 2014–15: Fibre placement on a pneumatic body based on a water spider web', *Architectural Design* 85(5), pp. 60-65.

Kwon, H., Eichenhofer, M., Kyttas, T. and Dillenburger, B. 2018. 'Digital Composites: Robotic 3D-Printing of Continuous Carbon Fiber-Reinforced Plastics for Functionally-Graded Building Components', in Willmann, H., Block, P., Hutter, H., Byrne, K. and Schork, T. (eds), *Robotic Fabrication in Architecture, Art, and Design*, Cham: Springer, pp. 363-376.

Invernizzi, M., Natale, G., Levi, M., Turri, S. and Griffini, G. 2016. 'UV-Assisted 3D Printing of Glass and Carbon Fiber-Reinforced Dual-Cure Polymer Composites'. *Materials*. 9(7), p. 583. (doi: 10.3390/ma9070583)

Prado, M., Dörstelmann, M., Solly, J., Menges, A. and Knippers, J. 2017. 'Elytra Filament Pavilion: Robotic Filament Winding for Structural Composite Building Systems', in Menges, A., Sheil, B., Glynn, R. and Skavara, M. (eds), *Fabricate: Rethinking Design and Construction*, London: UCL Press, pp. 224–233.

Snooks, R. 2018. 'Sacrificial Formation', in Wit, A. and Daas, M. (eds), *Towards a Robotic Architecture*, Novato, CA: Oro Editions.

Snooks, R. 2020. *Behavioral Formation: Volatile Design Processes and the Emergence of a Strange Specificity*, New York: ACTAR.

Project Credits

Cloud Affects (RMIT Architecture | Snooks Research Lab)

Design Team: Roland Snooks (design lead), Philip Samartzis (sound artist), Hesam Mohamed, Charles Boman, Nic Bao, Gavin Bufton, Caitlyn Parry, Marc Gibson, Dasong Wang. Structural Engineering: RMIT CISM (Director Mike Xie). B515 Studios (Studio Roland Snooks + Paul Morgan Architects + Zilka Studio) Polymer Wall Design Team: Roland Snooks, Laura Harper, Dasong Wang, Stella Yang.

LARGE-SCALE FREE-FORM TIMBER GRID SHELL
DIGITAL PLANNING OF THE NEW SWATCH HEADQUARTERS IN BIEL, SWITZERLAND

HANNO STEHLING / **FABIAN SCHEURER** / **SYLVAIN USAI**
DESIGN-TO-PRODUCTION

This case study discusses the realisation of the new headquarters for Swatch in Biel (Switzerland), designed by Shigeru Ban Architects, which was inaugurated in October 2019.

The four-storey office building has a 'snake-like' floor plan and an arched cross section. The building height ranges from 8 to 26m. Structurally, it consists of concrete core and slabs enclosed by a timber grid shell with a total area of 11,000m², subdivided into 2,800 quadrilateral fields of roughly 2 x 2m each.

This grid shell supports a façade composed of a variety of elements ranging from ETFE domes to glass and solid elements (Fig. 4). Due to the free-form shape of the building, none of these elements are identical throughout the whole structure. The same holds true for the 4,500 glue-laminated timber beam segments forming the primary façade/roof structure which remains visible on the inside. This paper focuses on the timber structure and highlights key aspects of the parametric planning process ranging from reference geometry through execution planning to on-site assembly.

State of the Art

Enabled by the renaissance of timber as a construction material and technological progress both in CAD modelling and CNC-fabrication, timber grid shells have become a viable option to execute free-formed building structures. As opposed to preceding generations of timber grid shells such as the famous *Multihalle Mannheim* by Frei Otto (Mannheim, 1975), these 21st-century grid shells do not find their shape based on material properties but exploit the possibility to CNC-mill curved timber beams in order to follow almost any given design shape while being stiff enough to act as primary structure even for wide-spanning roofs and façades (Chilton and Tang, 2017).

Shigeru Ban has been pioneering free-formed timber grid shells since the construction of his Centre Pompidou Metz, [Metz, 2010]. From there, a direct line can be drawn to the building presented in this paper, with each project adding complexity and advancing the state of the art. While the timber beams of the Centre Pompidou merely touch each other at crossings, the following Nine Bridges Golf Club [Yeoju, 2009] – which was planned later but opened earlier than the Centre Pompidou – has beams intersecting each other, resulting in a visually single-

2

layered shell. In the concert hall Seine Musicale, [Paris, 2017], the grid shell supports a glass façade following its shape and resting solely on the timber structure. Finally, the Swatch Headquarters, [Biel, 2019] introduces technical installations running in one level with the grid shell, penetrating beams at every crossing. As a result, this can be marked as the first time a free-formed timber grid shell integrates a full-featured office façade.

Definition and Optimisation of Reference Geometry

Reference Surface

Free-form timber structures such as the one described here consist of CNC-manufactured continuously curved glue-laminated timber beams. As fabrication data for gluing and CNC-machining is directly derived from the 3D model, a precise and continuous reference surface is a mandatory basis for all subsequent models (Scheurer et al., 2013).

In this case, an iterative optimisation process was employed, generating a NURBS surface from a series of highly continuous NURBS curves and checking it against spatial requirements like floor plan outlines as well as structural requirements such as curvature. Initially, a total of 8 cross sections at key positions of the

building were drawn as degree 7 NURBS curves with only 10 control points each. Using the predefined ridge curve of the building, these control points were interpolated into a field of 126 x 10 points which was then used to define a surface. The ensuing optimisation algorithm moved control points within the cross-section planes in order to reach spatial and structural requirements. The result is a highly continuous 'light-weight' NURBS surface describing the free-formed geometry with no more than 1,260 control points (a low control point count reduces local geometric disturbances and eases geometric operations on the surface).

An interesting side effect of the optimisation process can be seen at the 'head' of the building. The eaves of the building leave the ground to reach over the street. Due to its strictly rectangular topology, the surface still covers the full building height, leading to larger 'unused' surface parts below the eaves. Here, the optimisation lacked restrictions or goals, leading to a 'wrinkled' and less continuous result (Fig. 5).

Reference Beam Axes

The axis grid is the result of a spring-mass relaxation optimisation aiming at a uniform edge length of 2.1m with

1. Grid shell during on-site assembly (May 2017). © Thomas Rohner.

2. View from the bridge over Nicolas G. Hayek Street towards the 'head' of the roof structure resting on the neighbouring 'Omega 2' building. © Swatch.

a field diagonal of 2.97m to reach rectangle-like shapes on the free-formed surface. During the relaxation process, some nodes could be restricted to movement along certain curves (such as sill or ridge curves), or even entirely fixed in position (to synchronise predefined balcony or door positions with the grid). This allowed balance of conflicting requirements until an overall satisfactory result was found.

The local anomalies of the balcony openings, a key feature of Shigeru Ban's grid design, were applied retroactively. The 3 x 3 façade-fields around each balcony were trimmed out of the axis grid and replaced by the intersection results of predefined ellipsoids and the reference surface. A subsequent curve blending process ensured geometric continuity with the original curves.

Local Cross-Section Optimisation

Structurally, the grid shell is a very diverse system ranging from structurally beneficial arch-like regions to very function-driven regions starting near vertical at the sill and ending in a flat ridge. Hence, dimensioning the whole structure by its most loaded members would have led to a highly over-dimensioned structure. Furthermore, façade depth was to be minimised in office areas in order to improve light incidence and general user experience, while the same was less relevant for areas such as storage. Therefore, different cross section heights ranging from 760 to 925mm were defined for different regions of the building. As the structure forms one continuous surface, cross sections could not simply be stepped but had to continuously morph from one height into another. This was done by defining a map of fixed-height regions on the reference surface and inserting height transition zones between them. To create offset surfaces, a network of isoparametric curves was first defined on the reference surface. Each curve was then split and offset according to the fixed-height regions, interpolating between the offset parts in the transition zones. From the variable-offset curve networks, new NURBS surfaces were generated. With this approach, no less than 87 variable-distance offset surfaces were generated and used as geometric references for all parts of both grid shell and façade.

Ensuring Assemble-Ability

Assembly Concept

Structurally, the grid shell consists of double-layer beams in one direction and single-layer beams in the other. The latter do not reach the full height of the shell but are sistered with filling parts spanning only from one node to the next.

The building was divided into 13 assembly sectors along the spine. Within these, the beam segments were assembled from inner to outer layer and from sill to ridge. The inner layer was assembled on a setting jig, also made from timber. After assembling the outermost layer, the jig could be removed in an assembly sector. In all prefabricated structures, ease of assembly is a key factor in detail development. Many common assembly concepts for regular structures stop working when in a free-form project every connection is pointing in a different direction. In the structure at hand, all beams are curved and twisted and follow a reference surface with convex and concave regions, necessitating complex and individualised details to allow assembly of all parts. This shall be exemplarily demonstrated by the two most important details of this project: cross joint and butt joint.

Cross-Joint

The grid shell is based on a traditional woodworking cross-joint, the lap joint, which cuts away half of the cross section of both beams so that they appear to run through each other after assembly, transferring load along both directions. This joint, however, can only be mounted from the direction defined by its vertical faces, making it impossible to mount a curved beam with several lap joints pointing in different directions (Stehling et al., 2017).

To overcome this limitation, a 'skewed' lap joint was developed for the project, where all 'vertical' faces open towards the assembly direction by a defined angle, thereby extending the range of possible assembly directions to a cone-shaped region, the 'assembly cone' (fig. 6). A curved segment can be assembled if and only if there exists an assembly vector that lies within the assembly cones of all its cross joints. The larger the overlap between the cones, the more margin can be allowed during assembly. In extreme cases, a segment would allow exactly one assembly vector, keeping allowable margin to the tolerances designed into the joint, in this case 1mm of distance between the faces of the crossing beams.

Technically, the skew angle could have been individualised for every crossing, reverse-calculating it from the desired assembly vector of each segment. But this would have created a rather turbulent pattern of wide angles at segment ends and narrow angles around the centres, which was not desired for aesthetical reasons. Instead, a set of four different skew angles (6°, 9°, 12°, and 14°) was defined and applied to whole regions of the building according to structural requirements. The segment lengths were then defined based on the given assembly cones. Having fewer different angles also eased quality control in production.

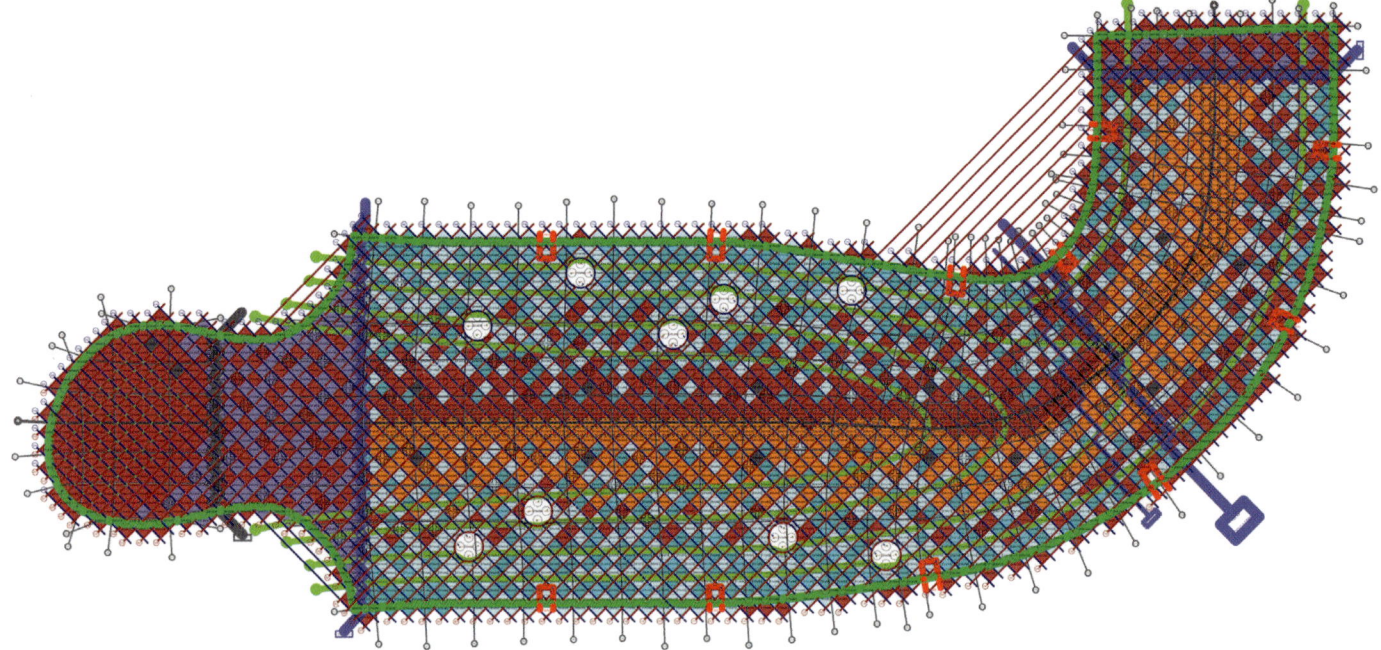

3

It is fair to say that this joint has a large impact on the visual appearance of the grid shell, as the skewed faces stay partly visible (Figs 2, 7). This fact was embraced by the architect who then took an active role in defining the skew angles of the joints.

Butt Joint

The butt joint between beam segments uses the common slot plate detail, where a steel plate connects both beam segments via steel dowels. Usually, the plate is preassembled in one segment and then connected to the other one by inserting the dowels during on-site assembly.

Having a steel plate stick out of the beam segments before on-site assembly would have restricted assembly direction to the plane of the steel plate. This would have greatly reduced the assembly freedom gained by the previously described skew lap. For the keystone segments at the ridge, assembly would have been downright impossible due to the torsion between both ends of the segment.

Therefore, a variation of the joint was developed where steel plates were preassembled in both segments but were not exceeding beyond the ends of the timber beam. After on-site assembly, these plates were connected by a third steel plate. This third plate was of conical shape and therefore self-positioning after being inserted into the slot.

An additional factor had to be taken into account in the concave regions of the structure. Here, the angle between both ends of a segment would close towards the outside rather than open, making assembly from the outside impossible. This was avoided by skewing the cutting plane between segments similar to the skew lap. This, in turn, meant that the assembly order had to be fixed early in the process, as the skew direction of the detail depended on it directly.

Segmentation

Since the innermost segments were positioned on an assembly jig, their segmentation did not have to respect geometric assembly constraints and thus was targeted at an optimal transport and handling length of 13m. For the middle and outer layers, the maximum possible segment length was defined by the directions and opening angles of its skew lap joints, which led to an average segment length of about 7.5m.

The final segmentation was achieved by first defining 'hard' segmentation points at assembly sector boundaries and at sudden curvature changes such as around the balconies; and then running an iterative optimisation process aiming at segments not necessarily of similar length but of similar margin in their assembly directions.

3. 'Flat Grid' drawing. Beam axes (diagonal grid), façade elements (coloured squares), balcony openings (white circles), fire exit doors (red) form a regular grid, while building axes and concrete edges (thick green) are distorted. © Design-to-Production.

4. Aerial view of the finished building with its 'mosaic' of different façade element types. © Swatch.

3D Coordination

Integrated Office Façade

The timber structure supports a full-featured office façade comprising glass elements with electrically-operated shades, ETFE cushions, heating and cooling elements, sprinklers and ventilation. The required electrical wiring and air/water piping runs along or, in case of the air piping, within the beams of the grid shell. Therefore, the installations penetrate crossing beams at every node, further weakening the cross sections already reduced by the lap joint. To control this in a structured way, rules were established as to what kind of piping could run in which direction and at which level of the grid shell.

3D Coordination Based on 2D Planning

The integrated office façade necessitated a detailed 3D-coordination between several planners. Due to the sheer complexity and free-form nature of the project, it was not feasible to have the planners construct their own 3D models and bring them together for review and clash detection. Instead, a mapping technique was developed, reproducing the structure as an 'unrolled' 2D drawing where straight beam axes form a very regular grid and instead the building axes and concrete edges are distorted (Fig. 3).

This so-called 'flat grid' allowed planners to draw installations on a schematic level and then automatically map them into the 3D model space based on their topology in 2D and the predefined parametric rules for precise positioning relatively to the beam. Likewise, changes made in the 3D model could be unrolled and mapped back into the 2D representation. This bidirectional mapping process in fact allowed for the 2D planning of a complex 3D structure.

Digital Fabrication

Parametric Detail Model

The 4,500 glue-laminated timber beam segments of the grid shell are affected by a multitude of detailing, ranging from the described cross- and butt-joints to shear connectors, installation cut-outs and supports. More than 140,000 screws, bolts and connectors had to be present in the detailed 3D model in order to be included in order lists, fabrication data and collision control. It goes without saying that such a model could only be done parametrically, i.e. by defining rules for detail families and applying them to the model algorithmically, automatically adapting to each individual geometric situation.

However, a model of this size and complexity cannot be achieved using a 'generator' approach where, after changes, the entire model would be recomputed. Next to

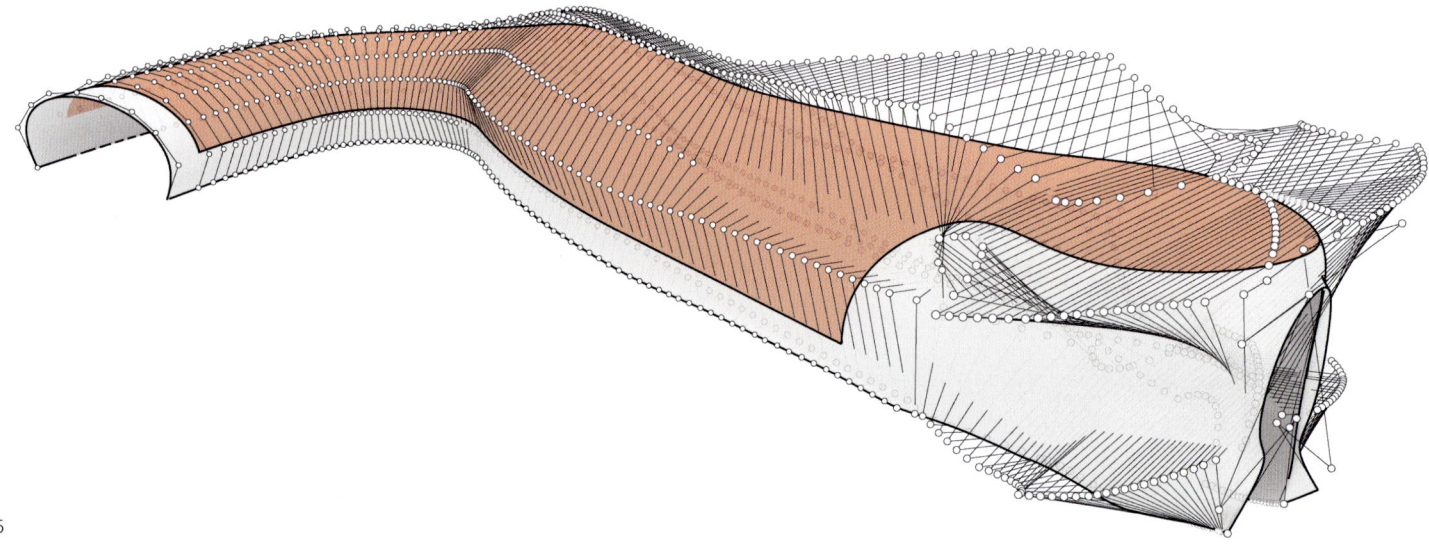

5

the sheer computation time each step would require, there are qualitative and practical problems. Parts that already went into fabrication must not be changed in the model anymore, and the system must be able to handle exceptions – it is not efficient to complicate a parametric definition working for 3,999 nodes just to automate the 4,000th as well. It is important to keep in mind that, while the parametric framework can and will be reused between projects, the building itself is a one-off and each individual situation has to be solved exactly once.

Hence, a 'step-by-step' approach was established, allowing to run tasks only on parts of the model or to intervene with manual modelling in exceptional situations and still be able to feed the result back into the following parametric process steps, including automatic quality control of the manually modelled parts. This allowed for a very controlled, efficient and secure modelling process.

Model-Based Approval

Quality control is an essential part of modelling for digital fabrication. As the model will be rendered into reality by computer-controlled machinery and even manual post-processing in the workshop only handles single parts out of context, possible errors might only be noticed on site where their effect on both schedule and cost is highest.

In this project, a three-tier quality control process was employed. First, the parametric model was checked during generation both algorithmically and manually.

6

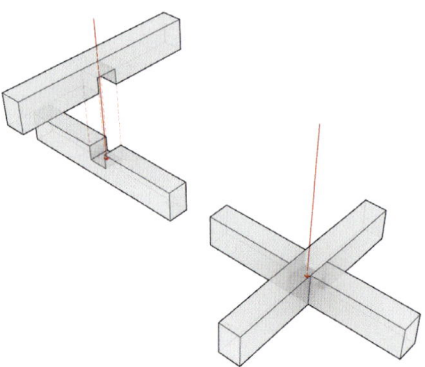

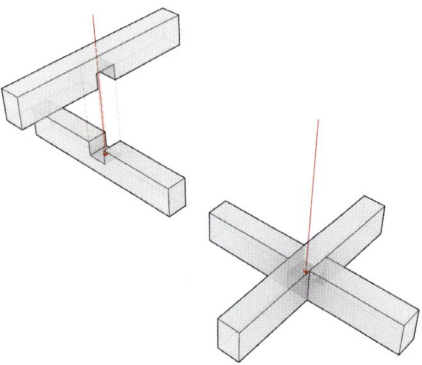

5. Reference surface with control points, area relevant for the grid shell shown in red. © Design-to-Production.

6. The traditional lap joint (top) can be assembled from exactly one direction. The skew lap joint (bottom) extends this into a cone-shaped region around the joint axis. © Design-to-Production.

7. Inside view of the foyer. At beam crossings, the skewed lap joints make it possible to 'read' the primary and secondary beam directions. © Swatch.

7

Conclusion

This case study shows a successful example of digital planning and fabrication of a structure that is very complex both in geometry and in its functions and interfaces. Main contributors to the process presented here were Shigeru Ban Architects (Europe) as design architect, Itten Brechbühl as local architect, Hayek Engineering representing the client, Création Holz as timber consultant, SJB Kempter Fitze as structural engineer, Blumer Lehmann as timber contractor and Design-to-Production providing the digital planning process.

It must be noted that such a seamless digital process from a pre-tender design stage to post-tender fabrication and assembly is still exceptional today. The so-called 'tender-divide' often also marks a point where fabrication-models are re-created from scratch by the contractors. Building Information Modelling (BIM) as of 2019 mainly aims at problems of 3D-coordination and conventional on-site building processes. The information and quality requirements of off-site pre-fabrication and assembly are largely ignored – which prevents architecture, engineering and construction (AEC) from adopting a more industrialised production process and catching up with productivity (and low error rates) of other industries (Scheurer, 2017).

We need to re-define the requirements and re-structure the planning process from the perspective of realisation: by defining a lightweight but precise reference geometry as the basis for all models already before tender; by including execution knowledge earlier in the planning process; by establishing better technical and conceptual interfaces from one building phase to the next. BIM to fabrication!

References

Chilton, J. and Tang, G. 2017. *Timber Gridshells – Architecture, Structure and Craft*, London: Routledge.

Scheurer, F., Stehling, H., Tschümperlin, F. and Antemann, M. 2013. 'Design for Assembly – Digital Prefabrication of Complex Timber Structures', in: Obrębski, J. B. and Tarczewski, R. (eds), *Beyond the Limits of Man: Proceedings of the International Association for Shell and Spatial Structures (IASS) Symposium 2013*.

Scheurer, F. 2017. 'BIM to Fabrication – Durchgehende Digitale Planungsprozesse bis zur Montage', in *23. Internationales Holzbau-Forum IHF 2017*.

Stehling, H., Scheurer, F., Roulier, J., Geglo, H. and Hofmann, M. 2017. 'From Lamination to Assembly – Modelling the Seine Musicale', in Menges, A., Sheil, B., Glynn, R. and Skavara M. (eds), *Fabricate 2017: Rethinking Design and Construction*, London: UCL Press, pp. 258-263.

Second, list exports were made showing amounts and dimensions of parts which could be cross-checked with calculations and other data sets independently from the actual 3D geometry. Third, and most importantly, a six-eyes-approval process was established between the parametric planner, the timber contractor and the structural engineer. Export models of the parts to be approved along with all relevant surrounding parts were generated and commented on by all three parties in the form of issue lists. Only when all issues on a part were resolved and approved, did it go into fabrication. As a result, the error rate on the whole grid shell could be held well below one percent, and no 'blocking' on-site issues were experienced.

OPTIMISATION OF ROBOTIC PRINTING PATHS FOR STRUCTURAL STIFFNESS USING MACHINE LEARNING

ZEYNEP AKSÖZ
UNIVERSITY OF APPLIED ARTS VIENNA
SAMUEL WILKINSON / GIANNIS NIKAS
FOSTER + PARTNERS

Introduction

This paper describes a distributed design and optimisation strategy which is tested in a case study concerning robotically-printed spatial structures. Through robotic printing, structures can be optimised by generating complex geometries with local morphological differentiations with a constant unit topology, while accommodating variable large-scale geometries. The design problem can be approached from top down or bottom up design and optimisation strategies. Separating the top-down and bottom-up design in two isolated processes limits the flow of feedback between both design scales, resulting in investigation restrictions in design space exploration. The top down approach to the design problem results in late consideration of the bottom up properties for structural enhancement, while bottom up strategies consider the global appearance of the design in a later stage. The ideal approach for a design workflow is continuous feedback between these two processes by simultaneous exploration and reaction. This project describes a computational method that enables the exploration of design space simultaneously as a top-down and bottom-up process by exploiting the potentials of meta-heuristic search and machine learning. Top down design is concerned with optimisation of the global form regarding global parameters, whereas the bottom up design is concerned with the optimisation of local modules that share the same topology but differ in morphology to suit the local structural requirements.

Research Context Programming Structural Properties in Materials

Recent research at the Specialist Modelling Group (SMG) at Foster + Partners, where this experiment took place, focuses on programming local structural properties in load bearing elements. The research investigates changes in the structural behaviour of beam elements through differentiated material distribution, informing intrinsic structural properties. The team working on the research had already experimented with the large-scale 3D-printed steel elements, however these elements were extruded using layered printing, hence a differentiation of the material densities was only achieved in two dimensions.

The many axes of freedom that the industrial robotic arm offered, as well as the combination of it with 3D printing procedures, enabled a deeper exploration of spatial printing for lattice structures. Instead of depositing it

1

on a layer basis, the material is extruded along the axis of the struts without the need of additional supports. This methodology has advantages in the speed of printing and in the strength of the structure compared to the conventional layered method, but comes with its own challenges. One of the challenges is the material behaviour which is influenced by the set-up of the robot. This setup influences the maximum extrusion length. Furthermore, a continuous printing path is preferred to save fabrication time, though this path should not intersect itself to avoid collisions during the printing process with already deposited material.

For the beam experiment, the setup consists of a seven-axis robotic arm with a custom-made end-effector tool. The end-effector uses a polymer plastic filament (in this case ABS) which is pushed through a 3x filament feeder to a custom heat block. The heat block has to melt the filament at a temperature of 250°C and extrude the matter through the nozzle.

The star-shaped section of the nozzle geometry increases the surface area of the material exposed to the air after it is extruded, allowing for quicker cooling and setting. Additionally, the extruded material is also cooled mechanically by six blower fans that speed the process of lowering the material temperature and render the liquefied plastic once again into solid filament.

The fabrication of the optimised 2.5m beam structure was printed in approximately 40 robot hours of print time and used roughly 8-9kg of ABS filament.

Approaches to Spatial Printing and Optimisation

Spatial printing of lattice-like structures is a widely-researched field. Mesh Mould project (Hack, 2015) counts as one of the primary publications on this subject. In Mesh Mould, tooling and workflow for robotic spatial printing with polymer and metal is investigated for load-bearing spatial structures which function as formwork for concrete structures. The project analyses the structural capacities of different mesh topologies where different regular topologies are evaluated. The students of Gilles Retsin and Manuel Garcia at UCL further investigated spatial printing using a design-to-production strategy which they called 'Discrete Fabrication'. This method proposes to discretise the geometry into voxels where the printing path in each voxel calibrates itself within a given range of different possible topologies in consideration of the

2

1. The beam was 3D printed in 8 separate pieces, which were connected by zip ties.

2. The plastic filament is pushed through a 3x filament feeder to a custom heat block.

3. The structural setup consists of a cantilevering beam with a point load on the cantilevering end. To simulate the stresses in the beam, the overall shape of the beam is analysed as a shell element using the FEA tool Karamba. (top) From FEA, the stress lines are extracted to generate the input for the ANN, the distribution of the stress lines are depicted in the diagrams (middle and bottom).

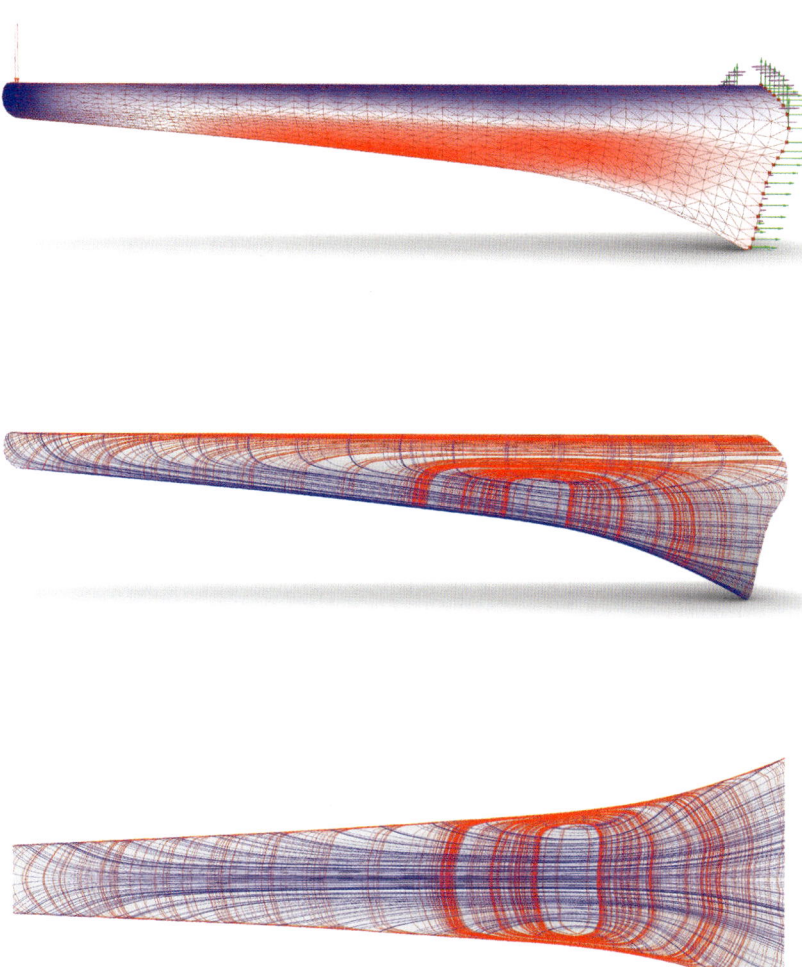

connections to the other voxels. In so doing, the computational simulation of the toolpath is reduced and the computational process becomes more efficient (Retsin et al., 2017). Through variability of the connection combinations for each voxel, this process can execute differentiating spatial densities in the printed lattice, however the density is not informed by the structural behaviour of the global form.

At a smaller scale, Sean Hanna investigates optimal printing patterns for 3D printing of small-scale structures which are informed from the local stress distribution of a given global shape. The research uses a subsampling strategy, which they call 'unit cubes', to generate optimal lattice topologies considering the stress pattern corresponding to the location of each unit cube. Machine learning is applied to execute optimised lattices. Consequently, long computation periods that emerge with iterative optimisation of complex spatial structures are avoided (Hanna, 2007). The application of machine learning as an alternative to iterative optimisation is further investigated in the Lace Wall project. In this project, a form of active hybrid structure is generated using cable rods. Again, the global form is subsampled in cells where different topologies of cable rods which aggregate in these cells are developed. The structural properties of each topology are analysed and an ANN is trained to indicate the distribution of different topologies in different cells regarding the structural behaviour of the global geometry in the corresponding region (Tamke et al., 2017).

All these mentioned projects are concerned with the modular structures and the handling of the diversity in between the modules. However, so far there has not been a synergy between the global design and the modular design where both processes, namely top-down and bottom-up, inform each other simultaneously. Current research further expands the scope of computational workflows in handling the complexity, taking the flexibilities that come with spatial printing as an advantage to test the workflow starting from design up to fabrication.

Problem Setup

Arcangeli has been determined from classical plate theory; the continuous rib structures that are constructed from the isostatic curves of the same continuous body would have identical structural behaviours under identical loading and support conditions (Halpern et al., 2017). A continuous body can be converted to a lattice structure that is generated by orienting the dements in the lattice

3

4

to structural patterns whose geometries are linked to intrinsic properties of the surface. Thus, solid structural elements like beams can be converted to lattice-like structures where the material mass can be reduced while maintaining similar structural performance.

The present case study focuses on the design of a cantilevering beam element, which will be fabricated as a lattice structure. The design problem involves parameters in two different scales. The top-down approach considers the cantilevering beam not just as a structural member but also an element of architectural design involving parameters that define the overall geometry of the element while addressing the spatial requirements, such as reducing the cross-section height. The bottom-up approach concerns the development of the lattice structure that is optimised for the load bearing capacities of the beam considering local cross-section forces of the lattice and the distribution of principal stresses. The local optimisation of the bottom up approach further informs the global geometry, enabling the generation of solutions that can accommodate thinner beam cross sections.

For the purposes of elementary experimentation, a basic structural setup was selected where only a point load of 500kN was applied at the cantilevering end of the beam. However, this is only a demonstrator experiment which is conducted to test the workflow from design to fabrication. A more complex architectural and structural problem would limit the initial testing, introducing far more parameters resulting in a more complex problem setup.

Computational Workflow

A distributed design strategy was applied, where design variables and design requirements are coupled in independent subgroups (Hajela and Berke, 1991). The design problem was subsampled in global and local optimisation problems. The local optimisation problem was handled by an ANN that is trained to extrapolate local rules for the enhancement of the lattice structure. The overall geometry of the lattice was iteratively generated and evaluated by a meta heuristic solver that controls the global design parameters, yet considers the global and local optimisation processes to evaluate the solutions.

The global and local optimisation processes, where global optimisation is concerned with top-down design goals and local optimisation is concerned with bottom-up design goals, ran simultaneously allowing the design team to conduct a top down design exploration while optimising the structural properties via the bottom up process. Both processes manipulate the same computational model synchronously.

The top down process produced two outputs, a continuous body representing the shape of the beam and a regular lattice, both of which were used to formulate the optimisation problem handled by the ANN. The bottom up approach was informed from the stress distribution in the continuous body that was dependent on the global geometry and the structural setup.

4. The local optimisation using ANN results in a lattice with variable densities along the beam, which is driven by the stress distribution.

5. (top) The beam lattice before optimisation; (middle) the principal stress distribution; (bottom) optimised lattice.

The overall computational workflow followed a five-step iterative process, that was automated.

1. Initialise the global parameters to generate a new solid for the beam.
2. Simulate the stress distribution in the solid using FEA program Karamba3d, output principal stress lines.
3. Convert the beam to a regular lattice and simulate cross section forces using Karamba3d.
4. Input the local structural properties of the regular lattice and principal stress lines to ANN, output the printing path.
5. Input the solution to the evolutionary solver calculate the structural deformation and mass to evaluate.
6. Iterate.

Local and Global Optimisation for 3D Printing

The top down process focuses on the global geometry of the beam element while considering the structural deformation, material mass and cross-section height of the beam as optimisation criteria. Furthermore, the overall appearance of the beam element is a qualitative measure of evaluation that is conducted by the designer's selection. The bottom up process focuses on the generation of an optimal 3D printing path that is informed by local stresses. Directly printing the stress lines is not possible, since the lattice produced by the stress lines results in a rectangular subdivision pattern which might not accommodate shear forces. Furthermore, some of the sections of the lattice contain distances that exceed the maximum or minimum print distance without support. The design of the lattice must consider the support less printing distances while preventing the occurrence of shear forces. Therefore, the lattice must be adjusted locally regarding the stress distribution and fabrication constraints.

In order to simultaneously optimise the global geometry and the local density of the lattice, local and global variables have to be integrated into the same optimisation setup. Introducing all parameters concerning both scales results in a high complexity problem that results in time-expensive optimisation processes. Handling the local optimisation by an ANN reduces the complexity of the problem while allowing real-time feedback to integrate in the multiple criteria optimisation procedure.

Local Optimisation and Learning

The local optimisation was handled by an ANN trained to execute optimal local morphologies. In the local optimisation procedure, the global parameters are kept fixed. The surface representing the global geometry was

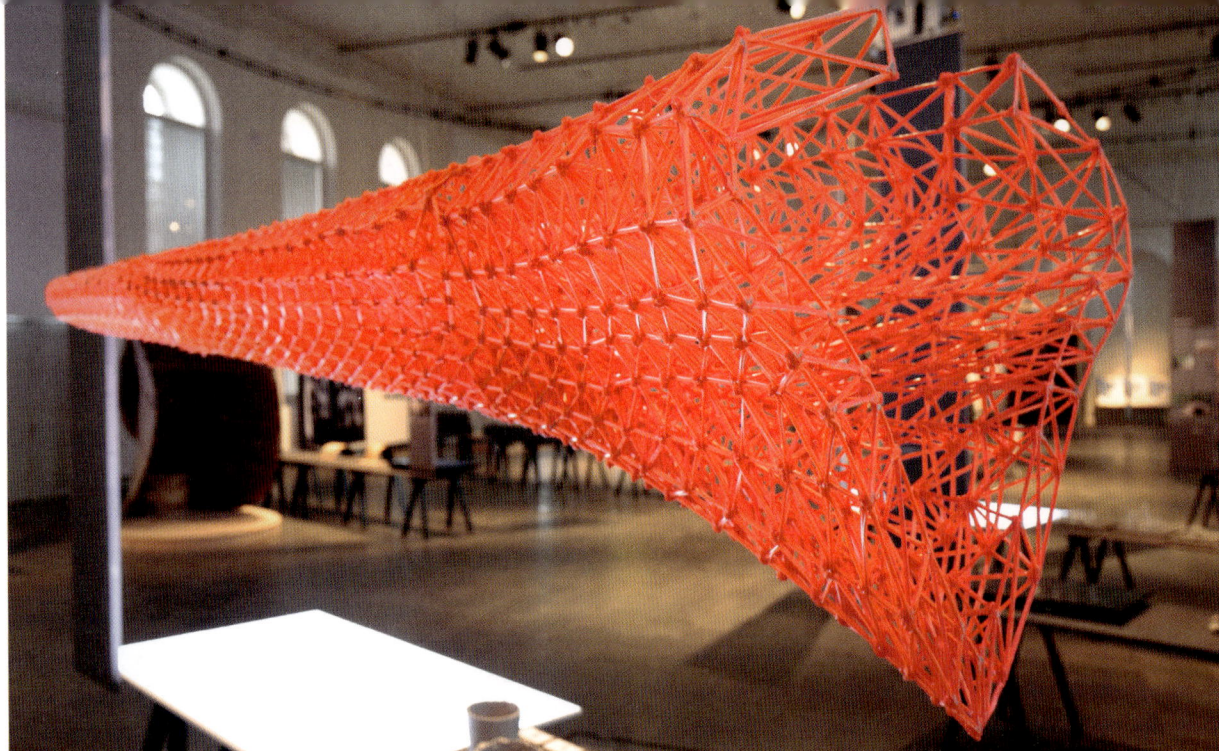

6

subsampled into modules that share the same topology but can differentiate in morphology. These modules represent the maximum sizes accommodated by 3D printing, but were adjusted considering the optimisation criteria between maximum and minimum printable distances.

The maximum and minimum printable distances are related to the material used for 3D printing. In this case ABS, a plastic polymer, was used. Understanding the material properties was crucial for the spatial printing process to succeed. The process of defining these restrictive distances includes several parameters that have to be defined in order to achieve the desired material behaviour. Some of these parameters are extrusion temperature and extrusion speed, as well as the speed of the robotic arm itself.

The ANN receives a subsampled geometry and implements a simple optimisation rule on each sample. The selected optimisation rule is represented as a beam with two supports, where a GA is used to find the ideal location of the supports. The optimisation criteria are selected as minimisation of the deformation of the given beam and minimisation of the distance to the nearest stress line. The encountered locations of the supports were used to generate the printing path from the given lattice. In this case, only the horizontal path is informed from the stress distribution, while the vertical print layers are kept constant. In several runs of optimisation, best solutions are recorded to train the ANN.

The training process requires a large solution set. Each global geometry contains nearly 450 subsamples. The training set was obtained through the generation and optimisation of ten distinct solutions using the evolutionary solver. This still is a computationally expensive process. However, once trained the ANN can be implemented in different 3D printing processes, without additional iterative optimisation processes.

Global Design Search Using Meta-Heuristics

For the global optimisation procedure, multiple criteria solver Albert is used. Albert is developed along the scope of the PhD research by Zeynep Aksöz, which this case study is a part of. Albert uses a genetic algorithm to explore the design variations, while enabling the user to interact with the exploration process at four different levels (Aksöz, 2019):

- Passive interaction by visually exploring the solutions.
- Interaction with the objective function by changing the weights of the selected optimisation criteria.
- Interaction through user-induced mutation to establish diversity.
- Interaction through selection to guide the GA towards preferred solutions.

6. Final printed beam.

At the top-down level, the ideal and desired global geometry for the beam was explored by changing the global parameters. The evolutionary solver is informed from the criteria considering global and local optimisation procedures. On the one hand, the global parameters control the height and width of the beam at both ends as well as the geometric properties of the curves that generate the beam by a loft. The feedback from the ANN was the final printing path which was used to simulate the deformation and the material mass of the lattice. The optimisation criteria were set to minimise the height of the beam, and minimise the mass and deformation.

In the graphical user interface of Albert, the designers are able to access the distinct solutions representing the final printing path visually and guide the optimisation process by selecting desired solutions. The design procedure was informed from the interaction of the top-down and bottom-up processes that was further inspected by the designer.

Conclusion

This project demonstrates a design space exploration procedure that accommodates intuitive creative exploration while implementing a multi-modal optimisation procedure from early on. Conventionally in the creative exploration process, further steps such as fabrication or structural optimisation are poorly considered, since the consideration of all the criteria drastically increase the complexity of the design problem. The design solutions are usually an abstraction of the design problem, lacking information of further procedures of optimisation and realisation.

The 3D-printed beam case study emphasises a multimodal approach to design optimisation, where complex optimisation criteria which emerge in later design stages are integrated in the initial design process. Accordingly, it is aimed to break the linearity of the design process, enabling information to travel from former experiences to the early design stage to construct more sustainable workflows. The simultaneous information feedback regarding the fabrication constraints enables a seamless workflow where these complex criteria can be considered from the initiation of the project. The ANN, in this case, allows simultaneous integration of the local objective function in the early design exploration, which is achieved by disassembling the design problem in sub-parts. This distributed design strategy enables the reduction of the problem's dimensionality, resulting in a less complex iterative optimisation procedure.

This methodology can be applied in diverse multimodal optimisation problems, and the designer and the computer interact with different parts of the design problem simultaneously. In this case, the ANN is assigned to handle a generic part of the problem that can be encountered in distinct projects, where the same trained ANN model can be applied to optimise the generic problems.

On the other hand, the global design problem can be reformulated in each project. The meta-heuristic process is an extension of the creative exploration, enabling the user to explore the design solutions without any abstraction. Finally, creative exploration becomes a unified process integrating information from all stages of the design.

References

Aksöz, Z. 2019. *Reflections on Multiple Criteria Optimization in Early Design Phase Through Applications of AI and Machine Learning for Human Machine Collaboration*. Vienna: University of Applied Arts, Vienna.

Hack, N., Lauer, W.V., Gramazio, F. and Kohler, M. 2015. 'Mesh Mould: Robotically Fabricated Metal Meshes as Concrete Formwork and Reinforcement', in Brameshuber, W. (ed), *Proceedings of the 11th International Symposium on Ferrocement and 3rd International Conference on Textile Reinforced Concrete*, Aachen, Germany: Rilem Publication, Pro 98, pp. 347-358.

Hajela, P. and Berke, L. 1991. 'Neural Network Based Decomposition in Optimal Structural Synthesis', *Computing Systems in Engineering*, 2(5/6), pp. 473–481.

Halpern, A. B., Billington, D. P. and Adriaenssens, S. 2017. 'Nervi's isostatically inspired ribbed floors: From the ribbed floor slab systems of pier luigi nervi', in Cruvellier, M., Sandaker, B. and Dimcheff, L. (eds), *Model Perspectives: Structure, Architecture and Culture*, London: Routledge, pp. 123–131. (doi: 10.4324/9781315091105)

Hanna, S. 2007. 'Inductive machine learning of optimal modular structures: Estimating solutions using support vector machines', *Artificial Intelligence for Engineering, Design, Analysis and Manufacturing*, 21(4), pp. 351–366. (doi: 10.1017/S0890060407000327)

Retsin, G., Jimenez Garcia, M. and Soler, V. 2017. 'Discrete Computation for Additive Manufacturing', in Menges, A., Sheil, B., Glynn, R. and Skavara, M. (eds), *Fabricate: Rethinking Design and Construction*, London: UCL Press, pp. 178-183.

Tamke, M., Zwierzycki, M., Deleuran, A. H., Baranovskaya, Y. S., Tinning, I. F. and Thomsen, M. R. 2017. 'Lace Wall: Extending Design Intuition Through Machine Learning', in Menges, A., Sheil, B., Glynn, R. and Skavara, M. (eds), *Fabricate 2017: Rethinking Design and Construction*, London: UCL Press, pp. 98-105.

THE ANATOMY OF A SKELETON
HYBRID PROCESSES FOR LARGE-SCALE ROBOTIC FABRICATION

EMMANUEL VERCRUYSSE
THE BARTLETT SCHOOL OF ARCHITECTURE, UCL

Research Aims and Objectives

The aim of the research – which ran in parallel to teaching within the Design and Make course – is twofold. The primary objective is the application of a design strategy driven by the fundamental preoccupation of the relationship between drawing and making, which set up an attitude that required oscillating between intuitive acts and precise operations. This was explored through embedding digital tools within established timber fabrication processes. By exploring design at the point of physical production, new protocols are created that foster an attitude towards making architecture which allows tacit knowledge and intuitive acts of design to work hand-in-hand with technological innovations, such as precision 3D scanning and the coded protocols of robotics. Secondly, the research seeks to introduce a morphologic innovation within conventional glulam typologies through the production of the closed geometry glulam component. The geometry of this component is informed by performance requirements within a larger structural system and attempts to maximise the inherent strength of timber by aligning the grain orientation into a closed configuration and thus explore a territory into non-standard glulam geometry.

The design and fabrication of a library provides the vehicle to conceive, test and implement an advanced and bespoke set of system operations. Central to the investigation is the skeleton structure that acts as an articulated armature to support the library's envelope and accommodates its internal workings (Fig. 1). By hybridising a diverse set of technologies and processes, an innovative fabrication methodology is developed that combines highly bespoke glue-lamination strategies with digital machining processes.

The timber forming process merges aspects of conventional glue-lamination with the technique of cross-laminated timber (CLT), allowing for the production of large-scale volumetric frames. This composite is seen as a new type of blank, the raw stock material on which a number of operations are performed which lead to a final timber component. The blank is no longer a neutral or uniform object; it is bespoke as its geometry is prescribed and codified by specific design information.

Within the sequenced workflow, the blank is calibrated in the robot cell as 'bespoke stock material' and operated upon by the robotically-controlled band saw to produce delicately sculpted components, carved precisely by the

2

robot arm to meet at complex three-dimensional angles to form a cohesive structural system (Fig. 2).

Scanning technologies are strategically deployed throughout the project to provide a continuous assessment as they interrogate the accuracy of the machined components, reveal material behaviour and crucially facilitate the various phases of assembly. This methodology was fundamental to facilitate the mating of the second phase of the project – the skin – to the erected skeleton structure as it provided accurate build data rather than the simulation data of the digital model space.

Through developing this design to production workflow, the research endeavours to challenge the conventions of existing methodologies and ultimately bring about a morphologic innovation in timber construction.

Research Context

The location of the research – Hooke Park – plays a central role within the project as it offers an extraordinary opportunity for experimental fabrication with timber. The working woodland provides the raw material and is simultaneously the design studio, fabrication space and building site.

Previous research undertaken at Hooke Park sets the tone for a focus on largely under-explored aspects of timber. A critical analysis into material efficiency led to varied applications of wood that is generally perceived as waste material within the production of timber. In the Workshop by Frei Otto/ABK, thinnings from the woodlands provide the main structure. In the Wood Chip Barn, the inherent form of naturally forked trunks – discarded by timber production – was employed to configure the structural Vierendeel-truss (Self et al., 2017).

The skeleton component of the project endeavours to deploy this attitude of efficiency within the current developments of engineered timber such as glulam and cross-laminated timber. The advantages of these products are well known as larger and longer components can be produced than would be possible with traditional solid sawn timber. These products can facilitate a higher material efficiency but the processes are often plagued by the production of large quantities of waste through subtractive machining operations. Whilst both glulam and CLT apply processes of ordering timber to obtain a large level of homogeny, the project investigates this process and how material could be reconfigured to optimise usage and introduce a new geometric strategy for the fabrication of building components.

Through merging aspects of conventional glue-lamination and CLT techniques, an optimised alignment is achieved by configuring the grain-structure according to the structural requirements of the components. The research of Tom Svilans of Innochain/Blumer Lehmann explores a similar territory through the discretisation of components into triangular or tetrahedral elements and a multi-scalar approach which links together the digital model of the architectural element with the digital model of the timber assembly from which it is machined (Svilans et al., 2018).

This forming strategy of the stock material outlines the first act of a bespoke workflow for the fabrication of these components. Several digital processes are nested within the processes, such as CAM templates and photogrammetry, to facilitate the delicate operations of the robotically-controlled band saw to produce the sculpted components of the skeleton.

Many of the most advanced glulam projects are fabricated in the production facilities of Blumer Lehmann. This timber company worked closely with architects Marks Barfield to form the timber structure of the recently completed Mosque in Cambridge (Wilson, 2019). The logic underlying the fabrication of the structure for the Cambridge Mosque carries an important relevance to the skeleton project. Infinitely more complex, the project consists of more than 6,000 joints reduced to just 145 different types of components and 23 different types of glulam timber blanks (Bau.Werk, 2018). The rationalisation of the structure into different types and components had a large significance as it assisted in composing the logic of the workflow to fabricate the skeleton. Different scanning strategies were applied and continued beyond the production phase as they featured heavily in matching the design of the skin to the built skeleton structure as the process fundamentally negated the digital data with the discrepancies of the build structure (Fig. 3).

Research Questions

The larger territory explored in the research deals with the interrelationship of intuitive acts – inherent within drawing and craft – with the precise and predefined procedures of digital technologies in the production of architectural constructs.

Can new protocols be established that foster an attitude towards making architecture which allows tacit

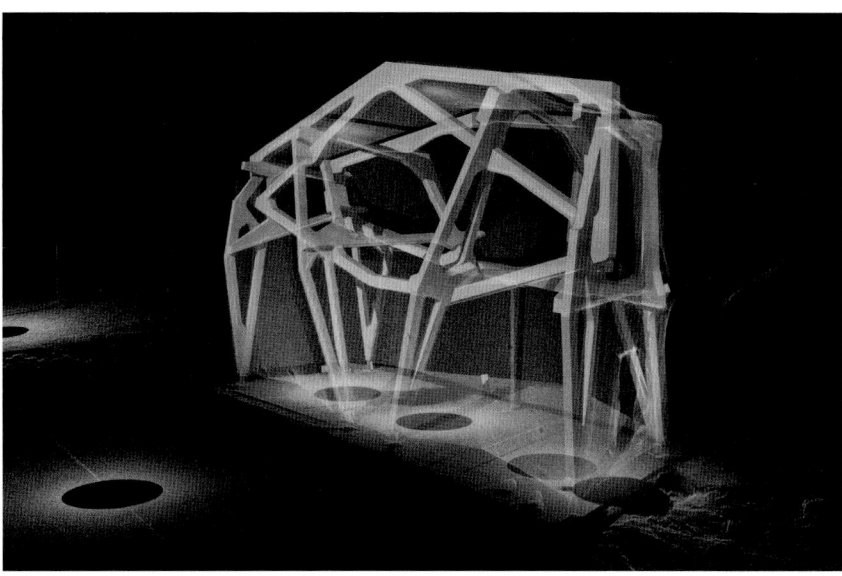

3

knowledge and intuitive acts of design to work hand-in-hand with digital technologies, such as precision 3D scanning and the coded protocols of robotics? And is there scope to enrich the dexterous craft of traditional timber methodologies through a careful integration and placement of digital tools?

The investigation into fabrication methodologies takes a closer look at the current advancements in timber construction and specifically into the processes of engineered timber products. The forming procedures of glue lamination and cross laminated timber are dissected to reveal opportunities to advance existing processes. Is it possible to establish an innovative approach by breaking down the various sub processes and cross referencing methods that belong to each category?

CLT generally produces panel geometries while conventional glulam-fabricated components are divided into three categories: straight elements; single-curved elements; and double-curved elements. These types inherently present an increasing complexity in production and consequently cost. Can a new category be established within these traditional morphologies?

More complex geometries generally require multiple machining operations that generate significant redundancy within the stock material. Can a higher material efficiency be achieved through the development of bespoke stock that approximates the desired geometry? And can a high level of material

1. Complex timber geometry enabled by bespoke workflows. Image: Johnny Blayney.

2. Dimension verification and manual finishing processes applied to the sculpted glu-lam components after they left the robot cell. Image: Veda Barath.

3. Digital capture of the assembled skeleton structure. Image: Thomas Parker.

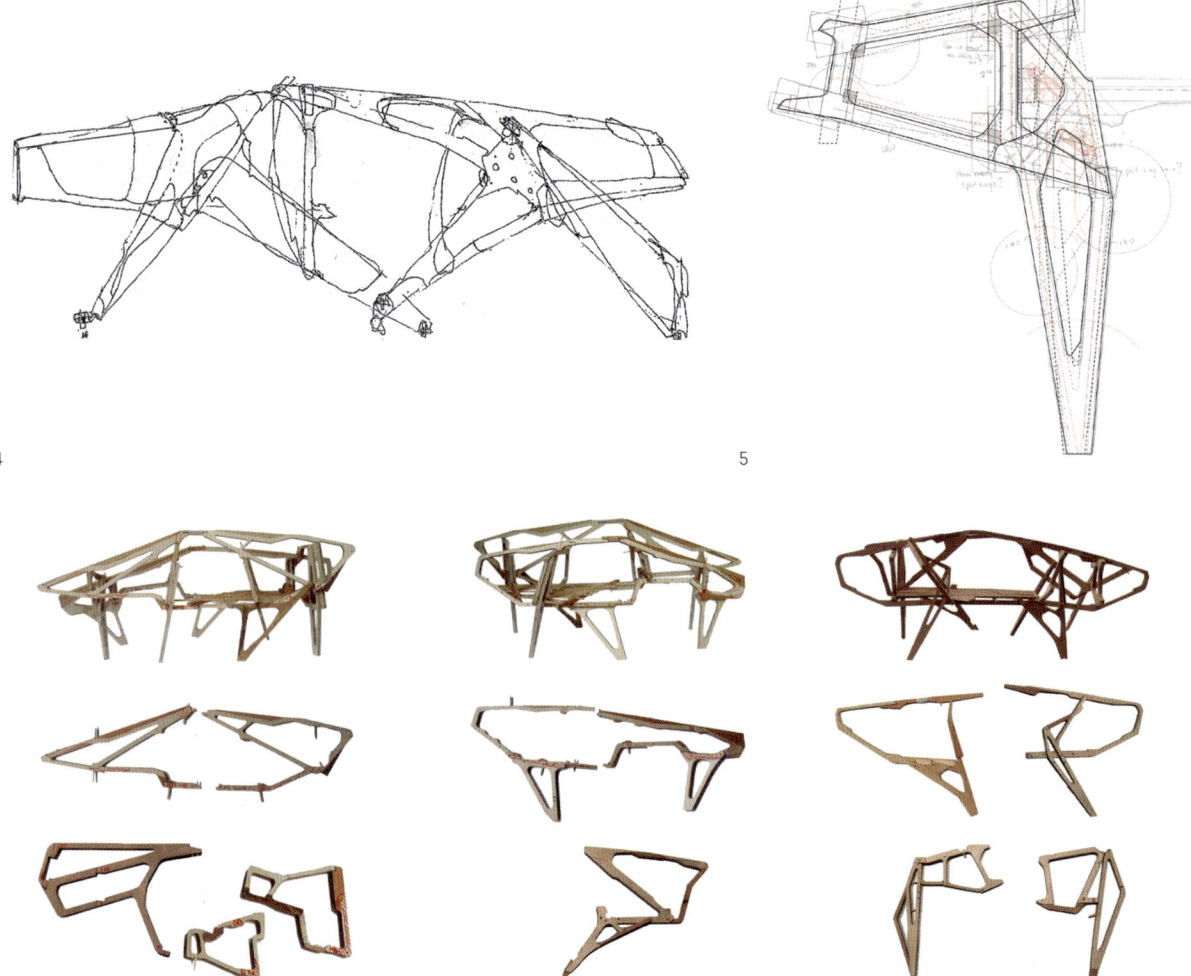

4

5

6

homogeny be reached by configuring and aligning grain patterns into a closed geometry component?

Scanning technologies played an important role in the developed workflow as they mediated between the digital and physical space and looked to answer questions in relation to extending the role of digital technologies beyond the design and fabrication processes.

Research Methods

Oscillating between intuitive acts and precise operations, the initial design sketches provided the underlying structure for CAD data and, subsequently, g-code for the flat bed router (Fig. 4).

As an instinctive activity is encapsulated in the gestural nature of the sketch, this intuitive act is diluted by the translation into the digital realm and often completely absent by the time fabrication data is produced. The project strived to maintain the presence of the hand drawing throughout the design and production stages (Fig. 5).

The early processes were highly iterative; CAM models were analysed and annotated by drawing directly on the components. This assessment instructed the digital redrawing, beginning the process of translation from sketch to code once more (Fig. 6). This method of iterative processes aims to negotiate the overly deterministic nature of digital designs, a challenge eloquently described in 'The Death of Determinism' by Jordan Brandt (2012).

4. The key structural strategies were extracted from this intuitive sketch which functioned as the most significant driver to inform the skeleton construct.

5. Drawing illustrating all the revisions and alterations of the leg component/ iterations.

6. Three generations of CAD/CAM models with hand drawn annotations to inform subsequent iterations of the components.

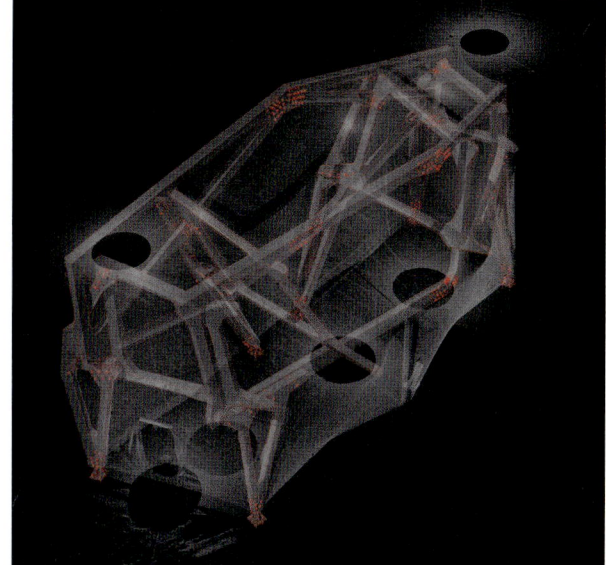

7

8

7. Inspecting the spatial alignment of the tool and the blank stock material in correlation with the programmed positions and robotic motions. Image: Michael Arnett.

8. Data overlay in search of divergence between the digital model and the 'as-built', using information from the Lidar scan. Image: Thomas Parker.

These particular interrelationships between the made and the drawn allowed the design to incrementally advance towards larger scale constructs and eventually a final translation towards 1:1 robotic fabrication while extending the role of the drawing deep into the fabrication process. As such, the precision inherent within the digital drawing is formally located within the intuitive act of the hand drawing.

Moving into the production of the individual frames, the potential of the closed geometry was explored as a new typology to add to the existing glulam categories. This geometry requires a change of direction and the grain orientation plays a fundamental role in achieving structural consistencies. The structural behaviour was enhanced by applying a cross lamination and further improved by the closed geometry as the components are made stiffer through their composition. The cross-laminated glulam frame is seen as a new type of blank: no longer neutral or uniform, instead its geometry is prescribed by specific design and structural parameters.

A digitally-produced jig guided the forming process of this bespoke blank and formed the first digital control mechanism. The jig performed a strategic role within the workflow as it acted as the confluence of the analogue phases and the digital data that would guide the robotic processes. Marcations defined points which the robot could re-reference in order to construct the plane rotation of the frame within the cell. This constructed a verification method linking the analogue assembly process with the robotic machining. This logic created an adaptable machining environment where the stock material could quickly be moved to new positions to machine additional faces which were originally out of reach (Fig. 7).

This bespoke fabrication workflow deployed a reconfigured band saw mounted on the robot arm. This set-up has been applied to timber fabrication within a number of projects, most notably 'Bandsawn Bands' by Ryan Luke Johns and Nicholas Foley (Johns et al., 2014), and 'Robotic Wood Tectonics' by Philip Yuan and Hua Chai's (Yuan & Chai, 2017). The re-appropriation of the band saw plays an important role as it explores robotic processes alongside a technique that is firmly rooted within traditional fabrication methodologies. The ways in which the tool can be used has been fundamentally altered: the relationship between band saw and material is reversed as the saw, animated by the robotic arm, travels towards the stock rather than the other way around.

Photogrammetry proved essential to minimise slippage or divergence between the digital (design and operation) models on one hand, and the material behaviour inherent to timber and the physicality of machining on this scale on the other. This direct feedback loop allowed for a continuous assessment of components and an ongoing revision of the digital model space.

Different scanning strategies were applied and continued beyond the production phase as they featured heavily in matching the design of the skin to the built skeleton

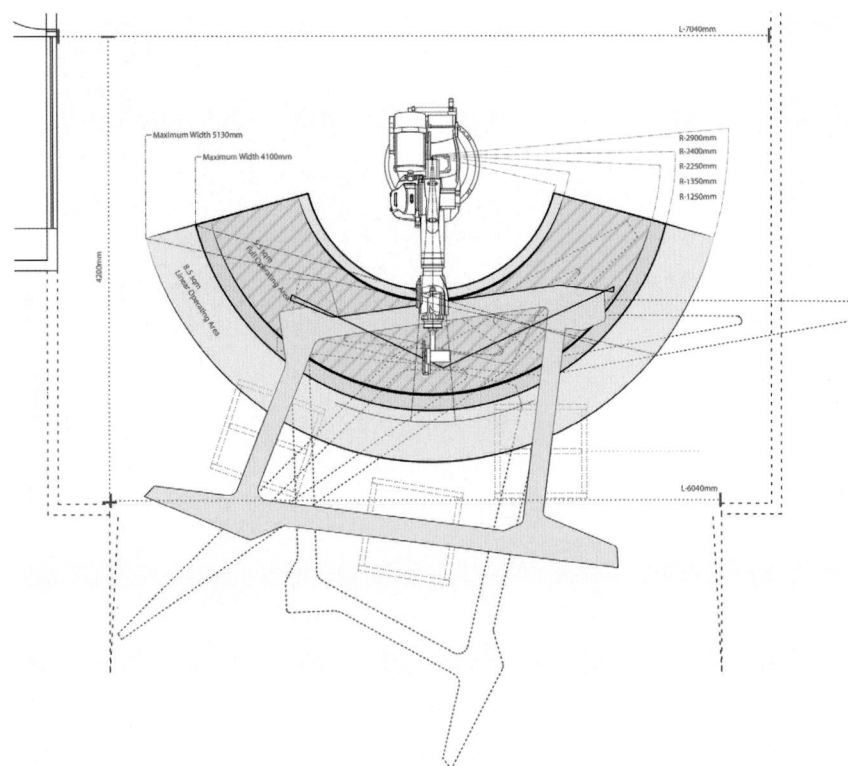

Maximum Width 5130mm
Maximum Width 4100mm

L-7040mm
R-2900mm
R-2400mm
R-2250mm
R-1350mm
R-1250mm

L-6040mm

9

9. Simulating highly
choreographed
manoeuvres in order
to maintain positional
accuracy between the
robotic band saw and
the glulam blank frame.
Image: Michael Arnett.

10. A test assembly of
the skeleton to verify
dimensional precision
and component alignment.
Image: Kevin Kim.

At first glance, our digital workspace appears to contain an absolute precision. The process of physical production operates within a different dimension as material behaviours and aspects such as gravity distort this precise world (Fig. 10). Next to the CNC templates, scanning technologies form the connective tissue between the digital space of simulation and the physical realities of material production. They provide not only a highly-calibrated work space, but crucially allow for precise interrogations of the freshly-machined components. As such, photogrammetry and LIDAR scanning proved essential to minimise any slippage or divergence as it creates a direct feedback loop between the digital (design and operation) models on one hand, and the material behaviour inherent to timber and the physicality of machining on this scale on the other. This allowed for a continuous assessment of components and an ongoing revision of the digital model space.

The fabrication of the individual frame component of the skeleton incrementally advances conventional processes within engineered timber. The bespoke blank managed to combine concepts of material efficiency, aligned grain direction and increased stiffness while at the same time maintaining a sophisticated sculptural aesthetic.

Conclusion

This project regards intuitive design processes as the main driver and looked to use digital tools lightly, applying them not to negotiate the formal language but instead to take up a strategic position that facilitates the materialisation of the components. The final form of the frames responds to an evolution of the language that began with a highly intuitive sketch which was enriched along the design trajectory by architectural, structural and technical input.

Through exploring and developing this design-to-production workflow, this project sought to embed digital tools – the robotically-controlled band saw and the digitally-produced jigs – within established timber fabrication processes. The bespoke workflow and tooling tested the technical feasibility and aesthetics of sculpted glulam and was successfully applied in the production of the skeleton structure. The strategy also challenged the conventions of existing digital methodologies by ensuring the technique remained firmly rooted within traditional fabrication methodologies.

The closed geometry glulam component adds a typology within existing engineered timber strategies. Its structural and fabrication logic utilises the uncomplicated

structure as the process fundamentally negated the digital data with the discrepancies of the built structure (Fig. 8). This provided moments where the different data sets and thus different model spaces collapsed to provide insights in the deviant behaviour of both realms.

Research Evaluation

Attempts to extend the role of the physical drawing into the scripted protocols of robotic fabrication seemed flawed at an initial reading. Unlike traditional craftsmen, the robotic arm has no need to set out its cuts as it enacts the invisible instructions which have been endlessly rehearsed through digital simulations.

This reference system cannot disappear completely though, especially with the immediate need to machine from multiple positions, as the robot operated upon large scale closed frames. Therefore, a logic was devised that carefully considered the physical orientation of both tool and glulam blank. This required a method of stock-holding that allowed for the relocation of the frames within the robot cell while maintaining a positional accuracy and addressing the need for both work-piece stability and maximum access (Fig. 9).

10

production processes of standard straight components and combines it with the optimised grain direction, an aspect borrowed from CLT components. This combination offers exciting opportunities within timber construction as straightforward forming processes are deployed to achieve geometric complexity.

The scanning technologies further reinforce a fundamental attitude towards the digital – that it be understood very much as an augmentation of the analogue, rather than a substitute. The project is driven by a desire to explore the production of architecture intuitively through iterations of drawing, craft and code. In this way, it employs the tacit knowledge of a material on which craft relies while exploring the possibilities afforded by the pinpoint precision of the technological eye and hand of scanner and robot.

References

Bau.Werk. 2018. 'Paradise garden made of wood'. In Holzbau-Schweiz, https://www.holzbau-schweiz.ch/de/first/magazine-online/detail/magazin-artikel/paradiesgarten-aus-holz/magazin-backlink/58/. (Accessed 23 December 2019)

Brandt, J. 2012. 'The death of determinism', in: Ayres, Phil (ed.), *Persistent modelling: Extending the role of architectural representation*, England: Routledge, pp. 105-116.

Johns, R.L. and Foley, N. 2014. 'Bandsawn bands: feature based design and fabrication of nested freeform surfaces in wood', in Mcgee, W. and Ponce de Leon, M. (eds), *Robotic Fabrication in Architecture, Art and Design*, Switzerland: Springer International Publishing, pp. 17-32.

Self, M. and Vercruysse, E. 2017. 'Infinite Variations, Radical Strategies', in Sheil, B., Menges, A., Glynn, R. and Skavara, M. (eds), *Fabricate 2017: Rethinking Design and Construction*, London: UCL Press, pp. 30-36.

Svilans, T., Poinet, P., Tamke, M. and Thomsen, M. R. 2018. 'A Multi-scalar Approach for the Modelling and Fabrication of Free-form Glue-laminated Timber Structures', in de Rycke, K., Gengnagel, C., Baverel, O., Burry, J., Mueller, C., Nguyen, M.M., Rahm, P. and Thomsen, M.R. (eds), *Humanizing Digital Reality*, Singapore: Springer, pp. 247-257.

Wilson, R. 2019. 'Defining the English mosque: Marks Barfield's Cambridge Central Mosque', *Architects' Journal*, 11 July 2019, p. 52.

Yuan, P.F. and Chai, H. 2017. 'Robotic Wood Tectonics', in Sheil, B., Menges, A., Glynn, R. and Skavara, M. (eds), *Fabricate 2017: Rethinking Design and Construction*, London: UCL Press, pp. 30-36.

BUGA FIBRE PAVILION
TOWARDS ROBOTICALLY-FABRICATED COMPOSITE BUILDING STRUCTURES

SERBAN BODEA / **NICCOLO DAMBROSIO** / **CHRISTOPH ZECHMEISTER** / **ACHIM MENGES**
INSTITUTE FOR COMPUTATIONAL DESIGN AND CONSTRUCTION, UNIVERSITY OF STUTTGART
MARTA GIL PEREZ / **VALENTIN KOSLOWSKI** / **BAS RONGEN** / **JAN KNIPPERS**
INSTITUTE OF BUILDING STRUCTURES AND STRUCTURAL DESIGN, UNIVERSITY OF STUTTGART
MORITZ DÖRSTELMANN / **ONDREJ KYJANEK**
FIBR GMBH

Synergy between academia and industry stands at the core of the BUGA Fibre Pavilion (Fig. 1), a research-driven project focused on a novel, robotically-fabricated composite building system suitable for long-span architectural applications. Lightweight, load-bearing elements were fabricated entirely out of Glass and Carbon Fibre Reinforced Polymers (G/CFRP), to complete this large-scale composite structure at the Bundesgartenschau 2019 in Germany, the first building of this kind. Accelerating development in the field of research into composite building structures at the University of Stuttgart, the project integrated design-engineering that conceptually and technically transferred biological principles from natural fibre morphology into architecture.

In this paper, the authors present a pre-fabrication method built on recent industrial-scale advances into robotic coreless filament winding. Improved fabrication procedures are complemented with advancements in structural design methods, contributing to this building system's applicability and showcasing the architectural qualities inherent to fibrous morphology.

Novel Fibre Composite Building System for Long-Span Structures

In January 2018, The Institute for Computational Design and Construction (ICD) and The Institute of Building Structures and Structural Design (ITKE), together with industry partner FibR GmbH and client Bundesgartenschau Heilbronn 2019 GmbH formed a research consortium for the development of the BUGA Fibre Pavilion. This is the first building where the entire load-bearing structure was robotically fabricated out of G/CFRP (Fig. 1). Inter-disciplinary work enabled the development of novel computational design and numerical structural evaluation methods along with integrated automated fabrication and construction processes.

The novel fibre composite building system integrated and interfaced with a hierarchy of subsystems adapted to structural and functional needs. The building component, a load-bearing hyperboloid fibrous body, succeeded in being both light-weight and large-scale, balancing morphological complexity of the fibrous lattice with economic feasibility through pre-fabrication.

1

2

Sixty building components of twelve types, assembled by means of variable-angle steel connectors, articulated into distinctive nodal configurations. The composite load-bearing structure transferred loads directly to concrete foundations, embodying efficient load induction and eliminating unwanted discontinuities in the composite fibrous body. The building envelope consisted of a transparent ETFE membrane. This pre-tensioned membrane integrated a cable net structurally supported by the composite structure.

State-Of-Technology and Preliminary Work on Composite Building Structures

The presented contribution to the state of technology builds upon over fifty years of international research on filament-wound structures. Research includes anisotropic grids (anisogrids), a system of continuous unidirectional, densely-wound, helical, circumferential and axial ribs fabricated from composite materials. Anisogrid lattices are efficient fibre-wound structures, a reason for the extensive research into their development. Huybrechts et al. (1999) provides a comprehensive report on anisogrid history from The United States of America and The Soviet Union.

One of the best examples of anisogrid structures originated at the Central Institute of Special Machine Building in Moscow (1981-1985). Interstage components of spacecraft were fabricated through automated filament winding of carbon fibre tows into grooves machined in foam coating applied to a mandrel. Integrated design, manufacturing and testing, highlighting the lattice's self-stabilisation behaviour under axial compression, were central to the research (Vasiliev et al., 2001).

The next step in automation was robotic filament winding. Sorrentino introduced research where an industrial robot replaced the kinematic system utilised by Vasiliev. Here too, foam coating applied to a mandrel was used to ensure fibres were wound at specified angles (Sorrentino et al., 2017).

In aerospace, efficient and cost-effective composite trusses were developed for the design and construction of Gamera II (Woods et al., 2016). Geometric complexity of the aircraft's structure demanded the development of a novel coreless filament winding process. The high structural performance of the design, at multiple scales, was demonstrated in laboratory and flight-tests at the 2012 AHS Sikorsky Prize competition.

The 'ultra light fibre placed truss', was developed utilising the weight to strength ratio advantage of composite materials. This design is highly compatible with efficient, long span, construction systems. Filament winding on a mandrel enabled customisation of the truss' cross-sections. The high stiffness of these elements matches their ability to incorporate variable densities and contributes to an enlarged design space (Langone et al., 2016).

Consequential research on composites and coreless filament-wound structures has been conducted at the University of Stuttgart since 2012. The ICD/ITKE Research Pavilion 2012 (Reichert et al., 2014) proposed a monocoque FRP structure translating biological fibrous morphology into a pavilion-scale installation. Longer spans and increased efficiency in load distribution were achieved with the ICD/ITKE Research Pavilion 2013-14. Here, a freeform segmented shell was built out of light-weight hyperboloid components (Dörstelmann et al., 2015). The project implemented robotic pre-fabrication: two synchronised robotic arms carrying winding scaffolds wound G/CFRP by orienting about a stationary fibre source.

Throughout these examples, the scalability and adaptability of the material and building systems were major challenges. The Elytra Pavilion (Prado et al., 2017) showed that fibre structures can be designed for efficiency and scalability. The pavilion integrated structure and function for an over ten-metre span enclosure and remains a milestone for the implementation of coreless wound composite building systems in site-specific installations.

Based on the experience from the above-mentioned academic work, FibR GmbH was established in 2017 to transfer the underlying computational design and robotic fabrication strategies into architectural applications, enabling their implementation on an industrial scale. FibR offers integrated design, construction detailing, robotic fabrication and on-site installation services for high-performance, lightweight structures with projects ranging from façades and load-bearing structures, to modular lightweight systems for exhibitions, fairs, architectural interiors and furniture.

Drawing from the academic background in cross-disciplinary research of its team, FibR perfectly fit the research consortium's agenda of inter-disciplinary collaboration, thus enabling a novel, explorative design and construction repertoire.

Towards Robotically-Fabricated Composite Building Structures

The BUGA Fibre Pavilion is illustrative of the co-design framework through its operational loops: the first, design-engineering-to-construction involves computational design methods and building logistics while the second, material-to-fabrication, works at element-material-system level. Fabrication processes, material systems and engineering methods are thus inherently interdisciplinary (Fig. 5).

Design Methods

Historically, long-spanning domes proved a suitable typology for architectural production, given their ultra-efficient volume to surface area ratio. For the BUGA Fibre Pavilion, multiple design iterations utilised the qualities of the building system to enable an open, bright space ideal for semi-outdoor events. Of upmost importance for the design process was the ratio of different component types over the total number of components. A hemisphere, as underlying surface for the dome, was geodetically discretised into five identical sectors and the resulting three-dimensional grid, subsequently structurally optimised (Rongen et al., 2019). This resulted in an optimisation of the ratio, greatly simplifying fabrication.

Simulation and Fibre-Syntax Development

The components' fibre morphology consisted of continuous multi-performative layers geometrically encoded as 'syntaxes', encompassing structural demands, material properties and architectural requirements. In coreless filament winding, fibres span freely in space under tension, anchored around winding pins. When fibres are laid over existing ones, they deform at intersections. Over many iterations, the result is a structural lattice. Understanding the behaviour of thousands of fibre strands proved challenging as conventional geometrical means hardly offer robust ways of constructing surfaces arising from such reciprocal deformation of free-spanning fibres. ICD/ITKE-developed dynamic-relaxation simulation tools were integrated into the computational design workflow to form-find the geometry of the components. This resulted in the

1. Interior impression of the BUGA Fibre Pavilion's characteristic fibrous node configurations: the dome structure exhibits five axes of symmetry. Image © Roland Halbe.

2. Industrial fabrication process featuring robotic core-less filament winding and the already fabricated composite component pieces. FibR GmbH, Stuttgart, Germany. Image © FibR GmbH.

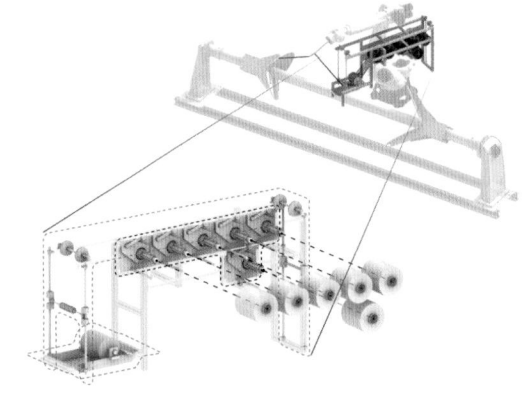

a

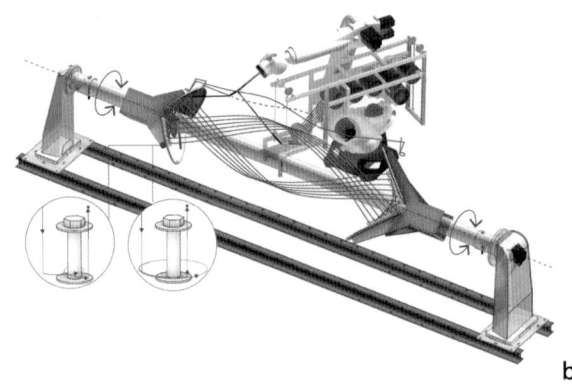

b

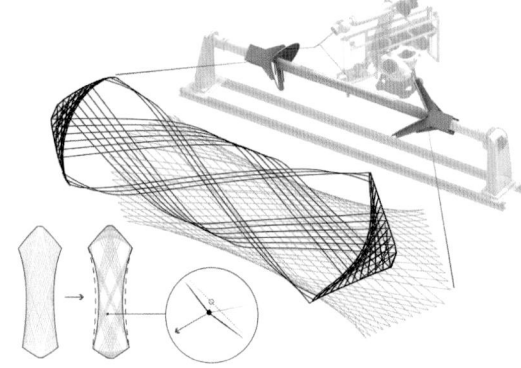

c

3

benchmarking of multiple winding approaches (Fig. 3c), ensuring efficient material use and optimal fibre interaction (Zechmeister et al., 2019).

Material System Research and Development

Robot programming tools developed at the ICD contribute to the well-established industrial planning practice for technical composites presented in Bock (2007) and Peters (2011). Developments include adaptive motion planning methods for robotic coreless filament winding. Fabrication simulations allowed the efficient mapping of all robot-targets inside the working envelope of the standard KUKA Robot210-R3100, which was equipped with a custom winding effector and controlled an external kinematic system, a mechanically-synchronised standard 1-axis positioner. Performing a combination of automated wrapping and travelling motions, the robot sequentially added fibres, pulling them through a drum-type epoxy-resin bath (Fig. 3a) and anchoring them around winding pins fixed to an open winding scaffold, attached to the external kinematic system. The motion instructions for the robot setup were based on the specific fibre syntaxes of each layer. These fibre syntaxes served as blueprints for generating the machine code (Fig. 3b).

The physical manifestation of the digital syntax, the fibrous bodies, were fabricated from three materials: the translucent glass-fibre lattice, the black carbon-fibre reinforcement, bound together by an epoxy-resin matrix. Glass-fibre was wound first, physically form-finding an initial surface and performing as an elastic 'lost mould'. Carbon-fibre was wound next and constituted the structural material, primarily considered in all structural engineering and verification. Figures 4 and 5 illustrate the precise tailoring of carbon-fibre directions to structural force-flow resulting in the distinctive aesthetics of the completed structure.

Engineering Methods

Numerical structural analysis (Fig. 5) allowed the modelling of loads from the pre-stressed membrane and cables-net into a set of forces, informing fibre layup and steel connection design. The components' fibre bundles were modelled and evaluated for buckling while bundle thicknesses and buckling lengths required for stability were also computed. A particularly consequential evaluation was performed for the components' edge conditions; here, an 'edge reinforcement ring syntax' was implemented, to successfully induce loads generated by the ETFE membrane.

3. Research and Development of the BUGA Fibre Pavilion: (a) Integrated fibre impregnation system and roving tension control; (b) 7-Axis Kinematic System; (c) G/CFRP filament form-finding for multistage winding procedure. Image © ICD/ITKE, University of Stuttgart.

4. Research and Development of the BUGA Fibre Pavilion – Robotic core-less filament winding: Modular winding scaffold – winding preparation; Glass fibre – winding process; Carbon fibre – winding process. Image © ICD/ITKE, University of Stuttgart.

5. Engineering methods – Global model, digital environment merging different types of information: (left) detailing; (middle) finite element analysis (red indicates zones of higher stress); (right) abstract geometrical description. Image © ICD/ITKE, University of Stuttgart.

  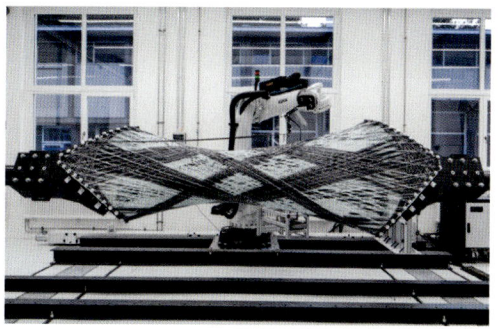

4

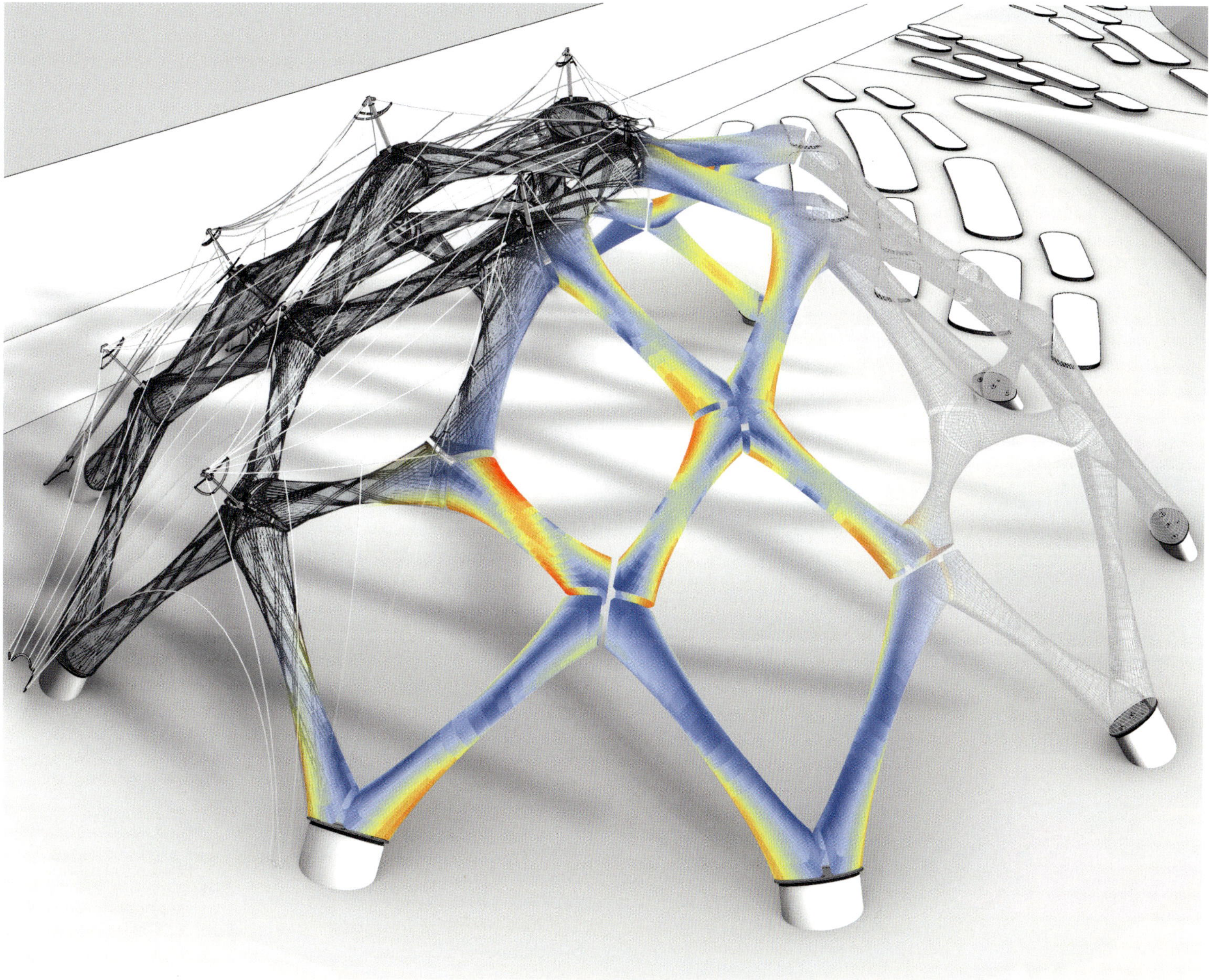

5

6

Additional engineering development involved component connections which were optimised through a set of structural tests on robotically-fabricated fibre specimens. Load transfer between steel connectors and the fibrous body was thus successfully modelled. A computational tool was developed to compute the alignment angle of fibre bundles to component edge condition – parallel to loading direction (Gil Pérez et al., 2019). Factors influencing the failure modes of fibre composite structures were identified, evaluated and optimised, thus enhancing feedback between structural modelling, testing and fabrication, enabling lighter, more efficient designs.

Experimental Validation

As compared to steel, wood or concrete structures, there exist limited engineering codes for structural composites. Therefore, this project developed its own experimental validation methodology. Structural evaluation methods developed in collaboration with the Baden-Württemberg building authorities informed the work of all involved partners (Fig. 6). According to the structural validation methodology, all twelve component types were non-destructively tested to resist 60 to 80 KN. Thus, structural implications and fabrication constraints could be simultaneously evaluated. Subsequently, three destructive structural tests were performed and successfully passed, at 250KN per component. Complete data sets of geometrical and structural failure data were generated. The results were subsequently used to verify the structural capacity for all component types.

Industrial Fabrication

At FibR, sixty components were fabricated using reconfigurable, modular winding scaffolds that allowed all twelve different component geometries ranging from three to five metres to be efficiently pre-fabricated. The winding scaffold was composed of a central shaft with two steel clamps equipped with removable metric bolts that served as anchor pins. Each anchor pin was additionally equipped with thin-walled aluminium spacers that remained embedded in the cured composite. The function of the spacer was twofold: to create a precise interface between the anchor pin and the composite and to serve as interface for the component-component connections of the completed structure.

After the necessary quantity of fibres was applied, the central shaft was decoupled from the positioner. The composite cured together with the shaft and the winding scaffold in a non-pressurised oven, according to a curing profile for constant high strength and thermal stability of the composite. Once cured, each composite component was removed from the reusable winding scaffolds (Fig. 2).

The curing temperature, ambient temperature and humidity during the winding process were recorded for each component and subsequently compiled in a quality-assurance protocol.

6. Experimental validation of fabrication prototypes at the ICD Computation and Construction Laboratory, Stuttgart, Germany. Image © ICD/ITKE, University of Stuttgart.

7. Research and Development of the BUGA Fibre Pavilion at the ICD Computation and Construction Laboratory. Top row: Robotic core-less filament winding; Bottom row: Fibre impregnation system and quality control. Image © ICD/ITKE, University of Stuttgart.

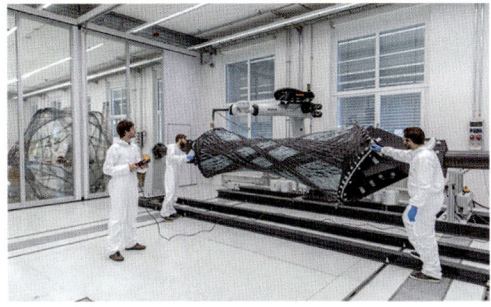

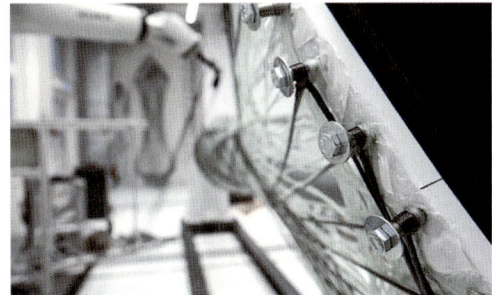

Development of the BUGA Fibre Pavilion 2019

Design-engineering methods supported automated fabrication processes which, in turn, enabled a research-driven material system. All solutions incorporated evaluations of structural capacity, while informing architectural and spatial implications early in the development (Fig. 5).

Utilising Finite Element Analysis, the composite structure could be improved to better align with requirements coming from the wind-loaded membrane. The structural optimisation resulted in a 27% reduction of critical forces while complying with all fabrication and architectural constraints (Rongen et al., 2019).

Concomitant to research and development of building component types and building system details, fabrication of the composite load-bearing structure was carried out between November 2018 and March 2019, at FibR GmbH (Fig. 2). ICD and ITKE adopted a scientific-support and quality-control role, thus all sixty components were produced on schedule, by 5th March. The efficiency of the process gradually increased, achieving an eight-hour fabrication time per component, with five to six hours of effective winding time.

The successful technology transfer from academia to industry underlines the importance of application-oriented research in architectural fabrication methods and its testing in 1:1 demonstrator projects (Fig. 7).

Advancing Industry Standards for Automated Composite Construction

Compared to previous composite building systems, the ratio winding scaffold perimeter to distance between winding scaffolds was reduced. The Elytra Pavilion exemplified a ratio close to 20. For the BUGA Fibre Pavilion, this ratio is equal to 1. This translated to fewer winding points, simpler connections, longer spans and a more efficient structural utilisation of fibres. Furthermore, while previous systems could only scale up through significant component-number increase, the BUGA Fibre building system scales through its components.

The composite load-bearing structural elements, weighed on average 7.6Kg/m², resulting in a load-bearing composite structure of only 4.8 tonnes. Spanning 23 metres and covering an area of 400m², the building offered an immersive experience of the sinuous landscape of the Horticultural Show (Figs 1, 8). From April to October 2019 the BUGA has been visited by over 2.3 million visitors and was considered a showcase for the State of Baden-Württemberg's digital transformation through innovation in building integrative design and construction processes.

The Pavilion demonstrated the potential of fibre composite lightweight structures fabricated through coreless filament winding for building industry applications, for the first time at large-scale outside an academic experimental context (Figs 2, 7).

8

During the course of the project, the coreless robotic filament winding process was proven to be robust, efficient and scalable. Quality control measures contributed to process stability. The project offered a unique opportunity to improve fabrication and automation efficiency (Figs 2, 3, 4) and paved the way for further applications in construction projects that are currently under research at the University of Stuttgart and being commercially developed at building-scale at FibR GmbH.

Finally, the building exemplified differentiation in performance through the local tailoring of geometry and physical properties, from component to load-bearing structure. Each robotically wound element utilises finely calibrated fibre pre-tension in form-found lattices to achieve structural equilibrium and usher in new aesthetic possibilities (Fig. 9).

Through the use of the latest computational technologies and fabrication methods, the project offers an insight into lightweight architecture that, only a few years ago, would have been impossible to design or build.

Acknowledgements

The authors would like to thank the Bundesgartenschau Heilbronn GmbH, the State of Baden-Württemberg and the University of Stuttgart for generous support and trust in the project. In addition, the authors express their sincere gratitude to the Baden-Württemberg Stiftung, GETTYLAB, Forschungsinitiative Zukunft Bau and Leichtbau BW for their support. The research has also been partially supported by the Deutsche Forschungsgemeinschaft (DFG, German Research Foundation) under Germany's Excellence Strategy – EXC 2120/1 – 390831618. The authors are grateful to the scientific development and robotic fabrication teams, including students and support staff, who helped to complete the BUGA Fibre Pavilion.

PROJECT PARTNERS

ICD – Institute for Computational Design, University of Stuttgart
Prof. Achim Menges, Serban Bodea, Niccolo Dambrosio, Monika Göbel, Christoph Zechmeister
ITKE – Institute of Building Structures and Structural Design, University of Stuttgart
Prof. Jan Knippers, Valentin Koslowski, Marta Gil Pérez, Bas Rongen

With support of: Rasha Alshami, Karen Andrea Antorvaeza Paez, Cornelius Carl, Sophie Collier, Brad Elsbury, James Hayward, Marc Hägele, You-Wen Ji, Ridvan Kahraman, Laura Kiesewetter, Xun Li, Grzegorz Lochnicki, Francesco Milano, Seyed Mobin Moussavi, Marie Razzhivina, Sanoop Sibi, Zi Jie Tan, Naomi Kris Tashiro, Babasola Thomas, Vaia Tsiokou, Sabine Vecvagare, Shu Chuan Yao

FibR GmbH, Stuttgart
Moritz Dörstelmann, Ondrej Kyjanek, Philipp Essers, Philipp Gülke
with support of: Leonard Balas, Robert Besinger, Elaine Bonavia, Yen-Cheng Lu

Bundesgartenschau Heilbronn 2019 GmbH
Hanspeter Faas, Oliver Toellner

PROJECT BUILDING PERMIT PROCESS
Landesstelle für Bautechnik
Dr Stefan Brendler, Dipl.-Ing. Steffen Schneider
Proof Engineer
Dipl.-Ing. Achim Bechert, Dipl.-Ing. Florian Roos
DITF German Institutes of Textile and Fibre Research
Prof. Dr-Ing. Götz T. Gresser, Pascal Mindermann

PLANNING PARTNERS
Belzner Holmes Light-Design, Stuttgart
Dipl.-Ing. Thomas Hollubarsch
BIB Kutz GmbH & Co.KG, Karlsruhe
Dipl.- Ing. Beatrice Gottlöber
Transsolar Climate Engineering, Stuttgart
Prof. Thomas Auer
Frauenhofer-Institut ICT
Dipl.-Ing. Elisa Seiler

PROJECT SUPPORT
State of Baden-Wuerttemberg, University of Stuttgart, Baden-Württemberg Stiftung, GETTYLAB, Forschungsinitiative Zukunft Bau, Leichtbau BW, Pfeifer GmbH, Ewo GmbH, Fischer Group

References

Bock, T. 2007. 'Construction Robotics', *Autonomous Robots* 22(3), pp. 201-209.

Dörstelmann, M., Knippers, J., Menges, A., Parascho, S., Prado, M. and Schwinn, T. 2015. 'ICD/ITKE Research Pavilion 2013-14 – Modular Core-less Filament Winding Based on Beetle Elytra', *Architectural Design*, 85(5), pp. 54-59. (doi: 10.1002/ad.1954)

Dörstelmann, M., Knippers, J., Koslowski, V., Menges, A., Prado, M., Schieber, G. and Vasey, L. 2015a. 'ICD/ITKE Research Pavilion 2014–15: Fibre Placement on a Pneumatic Body Based on a Water Spider Web', *Architectural Design*, 85(5), pp.60-65.

Gil Pérez, M., Dambrosio, N., Rongen, B., Menges, A. and Knippers, J. 2019. 'Structural optimization of core-less filament wound components connection system through orientation of anchor points in the winding frames', in *Proceedings of the IASS Annual Symposium 2019*, 7-10 October 2019, Barcelona, Spain. Huybrechts S.M., Hahn S.E., Meink T.E. 1999. 'Grid stiffened structures: A survey of fabrication, analysis and design methods', *International Conference on Composite Materials (ICCM) Proceedings*.

Koslowski V., Solly S. and Knippers J. 2017a. 'Structural design methods of component based lattice composites for the Elytra Pavilion', in Bögle, A. and Grohmann M. (eds) *Proceedings of the IASS Annual Symposium 2017 Interfaces: architecture engineering science*, September 25-28th, 2017, Hamburg, Germany.

Koslowski V., Solly S. and Knippers J. 2017b. 'Experimental investigation of Failure modes of lattice GRID composites for building structures based on case studies', in *Proceedings of the SAMPE Europe Conference 2017*. November 15-16th, 2017, Stuttgart.

Langone R.J., Silver M.S. & ADC Acquisition Company. 2016. *Ultra light fibre placed truss*, US 9404249 B2.

Menges, Achim. 2006. 'Michael Hensel; Frei Otto', *Techniques and Technologies in Morphogenetic Design: Architectural Design, Special Issue*, 76(2), pp. 78-87. (doi: 10.1002/ad.243)

Menges, A., Knippers, J. 2015. 'Fibrous Tectonics', *Architectural Design*, 85(5), pp. 40-47. (doi: 10.1002/ad.1952)

Peters, S.T. (ed.) 2011. *Composite Filament Winding (First edition)*, Materials Park, Ohio: ASM International.

Prado, M., Dörstelmann, M., Solly, J., Menges, A., Knippers, J., 2017. 'Elytra Filament Pavilion: Robotic Filament Winding for Structural Composite Building Systems', in Menges, A., Sheil, B., Glynn, R. and Skavara, M. (eds), *Fabricate 2017: Rethinking Design and Construction*, London: UCL Press, pp. 224-231.

Prado, M., Dörstelmann, M., Schwinn, T., Menges, A. and, Knippers, J. 2014. 'Core-Less Filament Winding', in McGee W. and, Ponce de Leon M. (eds), *Robotic Fabrication in Architecture, Art and Design*, Cham: Springer International Publishing, pp. 275–289. (doi:10.1007/978-3-319-04663-1_19)

Reichert S., Schwinn, T., La Magna, R., Waimer, F., Knippers, J. and Menges, A. 2014. 'Fibrous Structures: An integrative approach to design computation, simulation and fabrication for Lightweight, Glass and Carbon Fibre Composite Structures in Architecture based on Biomimetic Design Principles', *CAD Journal*, 52(July), pp. 27-39. (doi: 10.1016/j.cad.2014.02.005)

Rongen, B., Koslowski, V., Gil Pérez, M. and Knippers, J. 2019. 'Structural optimization and rationalization of the BUGA fibre composite dome'. In *Proceedings of the IASS Annual Symposium 2019*, 7-10 October 2019, Barcelona, Spain.

Sorrentino, L., Marchetti, M., Bellini, C., Delfini, A. and Del Sette, F. 2017. 'Manufacture of high performance isogrid structure by Robotic Filament Winding', *Composite Structures*, 164, pp. 43-50.

Van de Kamp, T., Dörstelmann, M., Dos Santos Rolo, T., Baumbach, T., Menges, A. and Knippers, J. 2015. 'Beetle elytra as role models for lightweight building construction', in *Entomologie heute*, 27, pp. 149-158.

Vasey, L., Baharlou, E., Dörstelmann, M., Koslowski, V., Prado, M., Schieber, G., Menges, A. and Knippers, J. 2015. 'Behavioral Design and Adaptive Robotic Fabrication of a Fibre Composite Compression Shell with Pneumatic Formwork', in Combs, L. and Perry, C. (eds), *Computational Ecologies: Design in the Anthropocene, Proceedings of the 35th Annual Conference of the Association for Computer Aided Design in Architecture (ACADIA)*, Cincinnati, OH: University of Cincinnati, pp. 297-309.

Vasiliev V.V., Barynin V.A. and Rasin A.F. 2001. 'Anisogrid lattice structures – survey of development and application', *Composite Structures*, 54(2-3), pp. 361-370. (doi: 10.1016/S0263-8223(01)00111-8)

Woods, B. K. S., Hill, I. and Friswell, M.I. 2016. 'Ultra-efficient wound composite truss structures', *Composites Part A: Applied Science and Manufacturing*, 90, pp. 111-124.

Zechmeister, C., Bodea, S., Dambrosio, N. and Menges, A. 2020. 'Design for Long-Span Core-Less Wound, Structural Composite Building Elements', in Gengnagel, C., Baverel, O., Burry, J., Ramsgaard Thomsen, M. and Weinzierl, S. (eds), *Impact: Design with All Senses*, Cham: Springer International Publishing, pp. 401-415.

8. Exterior night time impression of the BUGA Fibre Pavilion at the Bundesgartenschau2019, Heilbronn, Germany. Image © Roland Halbe.

9. Interior night time impression of the BUGA Fibre Pavilion dome structure, featuring the light-conductivity of the transparent fibreglass body exposed by the integrated lighting installation, Bundesgartenschau2019, Heilbronn, Germany. Image © Roland Halbe.

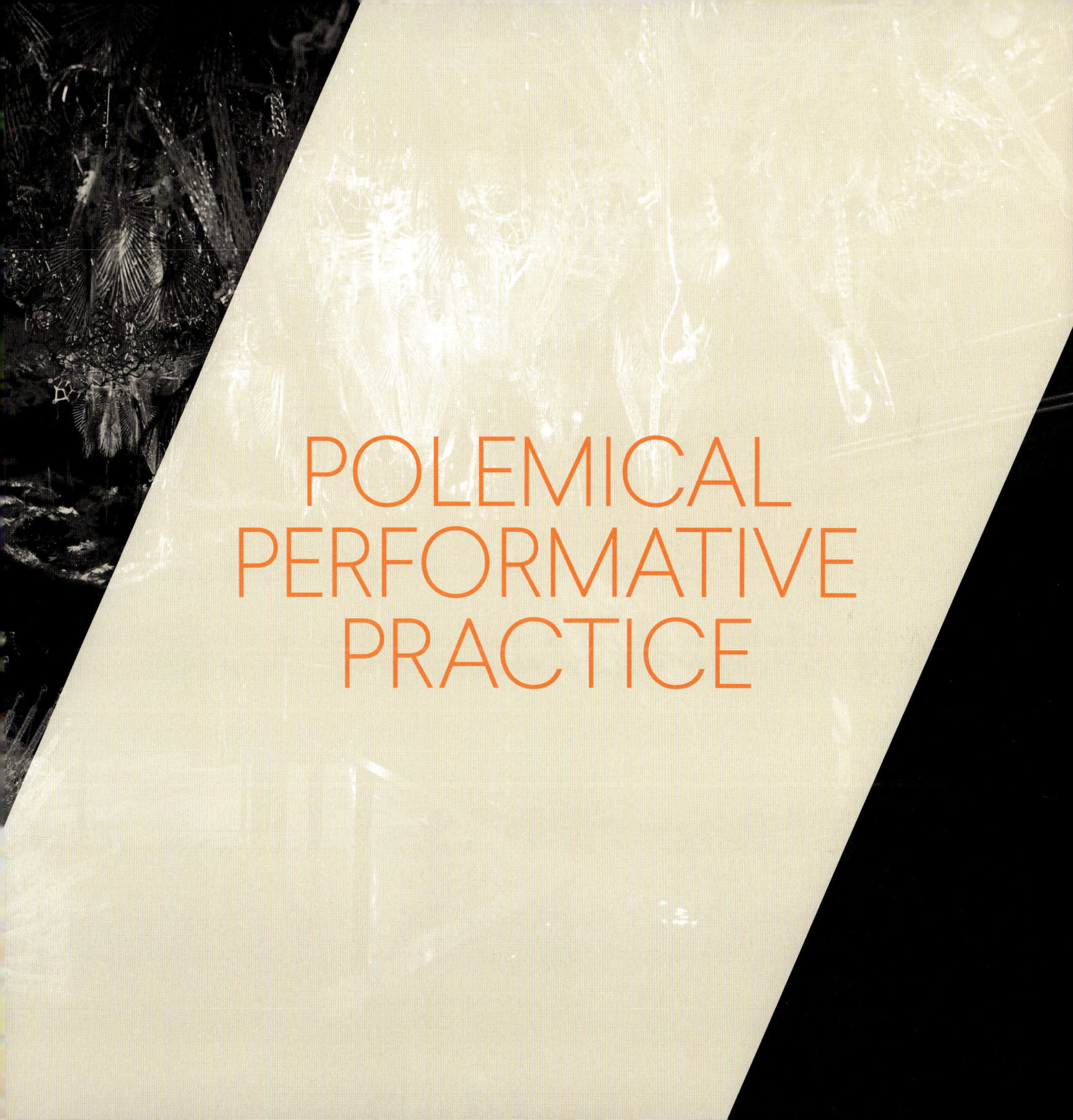

POLEMICAL PERFORMATIVE PRACTICE

EMBEDDED ARCHITECTURE
ADA, DRIVEN BY HUMANS, POWERED BY AI

JENNY E. SABIN
JENNY SABIN STUDIO / CORNELL UNIVERSITY
JOHN HILLA
JENNY SABIN STUDIO
DILLON PRANGER
JENNY SABIN STUDIO / CORNELL UNIVERSITY
CLAYTON BINKLEY
ARUP / ODD LOT DESIGN
JEREMY BILOTTI
JENNY SABIN STUDIO / MASSACHUSETTS INSTITUTE OF TECHNOLOGY

Introduction

Named after the polymath, mathematician, first computer programmer, and early innovator of the computer age, Ada Lovelace, Ada is a collaborative project by Jenny Sabin Studio for the Artists in Residence Program at Microsoft Research, 2018-2019. The first architectural pavilion project to incorporate AI, Ada is a lightweight knitted pavilion structure designed with Microsoft Research which embodies performance, material innovation, human-centred adaptive architecture and emerging technologies, including artificial intelligence and affective computing. An external rigid experimental shell structure assembled from a compressive network of 895 unique 3D-printed nylon nodes and fibreglass rods holds Ada's form in continuous tension. Working with researchers and engineers at Microsoft Research, Ada is driven by individual and collective sentiment data collected and housed within the Microsoft Research Building 99. A network of sensors and cameras located throughout the building offer multiple opportunities for visitors and participants to engage, interact with, and drive the project. The data include facial patterns, voice tones and sound that are processed by AI algorithms and correlated with sentiment. Three scales of responsive and gradated lighting, including a network of addressable LEDs, a custom fibre optic central tensegrity cone, and five external PAR lights respond in real time to continuous streams of sentiment data. These data are correlated with colours, spatial zones within the project, and responsive materials.

An important aim of the project was to expand and inspire human engagement. While artificial intelligence powers the project through the precise narrowing and statistical averaging of data collected from individual and collective facial patterns and voice tones, the architecture of Ada augments emotion through aesthetic experience, thereby opening the range of possible human emotional engagement. In turn, the project opens new pathways for fundamental research on the use of AI to correlate connections between human sentiment and local environment. Ada will be used as a platform for researchers to test their data and machine learning algorithms at Microsoft Research.

Suspended from three points and hovering above the ground floor of the atrium, Ada is a socially and environmentally responsive structure that is interactive and transformative. This environment offers spaces for

2

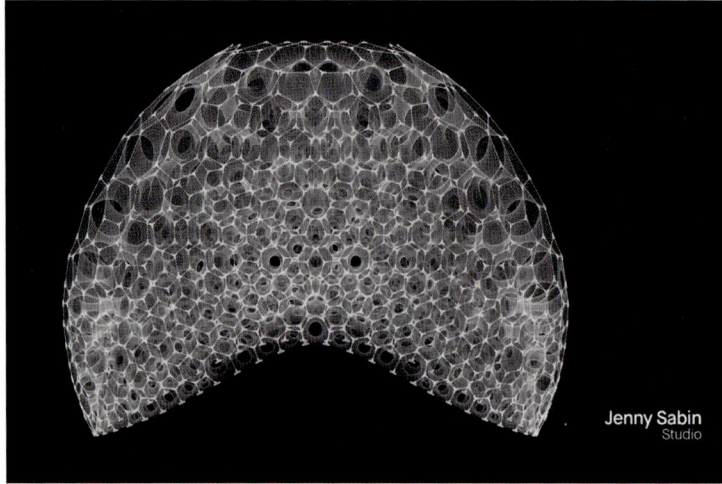

Jenny Sabin
Studio

3

Background

The history of modern computing may be traced back to an uncanny meeting between two disparate inventions that were simultaneously emerging: the punch cards that mechanised the Jacquard loom through stored memory, and Babbage's steam-driven calculator, the Analytical Engine. Credited with being one of the first computer programmers, Ada Lovelace intuited the revolutionary impact that Jacquard's punch cards would bring to Babbage's computer, launching the precursors of modern-day scientific computing. As Lovelace stated, 'The Analytical Engine weaves algebraic patterns, just as the Jacquard loom weaves flowers and leaves' (Lovelace, 1843). In this project, the textile as an information-mediating surface architecture builds upon this history with forward-looking integration of artificial intelligence and affective computing. In the last decade, knitting and high-tech fabric structures have been explored for their responsive and versatile material behaviour in architecture (Sabin et al., 2018). For example, Active Textile Tailoring is a new project at the Self-Assembly Lab where they are exploring changes in fibre shape and structure in response to heat and moisture for custom fit. In parallel, affective computing has found itself embedded in prototypical architectures at the scale of the human body as wearables in fashion. Behnaz Farahi's recent work embeds human sentiment as data into responsive fibre systems (Farahi, 2018). Many data-driven responsive projects are now incorporating data as an

active and evolving overlay of spatial information. For example, Jason Kelly Johnson of Future Cities Labs employs techniques to inscribe and translate data collected from local sites and environmental analysis, such as ambient sound, into materials and spatial fields, creating novel configurations and lighting effects (Johnson and Gategno, 2018). Asif Khan's MegaFaces installation for the Sochi Winter Olympics also integrates light and image to generate a responsive façade of visitors' faces scanned and updated every 20 seconds (Frearson, 2014). Drawing synergies with this body of international research, Ada builds upon 13 years of design development at the intersection of knitted textiles, bio-inspired design, computation, and architecture.

Methods

Generative Design and Structural Analysis
The design of Ada commenced with a series of collaborative conversations between Jenny Sabin and Microsoft Research on topics spanning artificial intelligence, adaptive and embedded architecture, affective computing and personalised space. Initial design studies were later informed by a 3D-scanned model of Microsoft Building 99, the location for Microsoft Research in Redmond, Washington where the installation would ultimately be housed. This approach allowed for precision modelling within a detailed and accurate representation of the site. A series of ellipsoidal and spherical 3D models were generated in Rhinoceros as an iterative study that primarily considered the overall form of Ada in relation to lines of sight, opportunities for interaction, circulation paths, and material and structural qualities. These initial studies would ultimately inspire the form of the exoskeleton as a concave shape that lifts along

curiosity and wonder, individual and collective exchange, and rigorous research experimentation as the pavilion filters light, casts dynamic shadows, and changes in response to participants' input.

1. The first architectural pavilion project to incorporate AI, Ada is a lightweight knitted pavilion structure composed of digitally knit responsive and data-driven tubular and cellular components held in continuous tension via a 3D printed semi-rigid exoskeleton shell. Photo: Jake Knapp for Microsoft.

2. Ada, designed and built by Jenny Sabin Studio for Microsoft Research Artist in Residence Programme 2018-2019, fills an airy 3-storey corner in building 99 on Microsoft's Redmond, Washington campus. Ada translates data into colour and light. Photo: John Brecher for Microsoft.

3. Generative study of Ada with form-found fabric structure and exoskeleton. Lines of sight, opportunities for interaction, site conditions, circulation paths, and material and structural qualities are considered as primary design constraints. Courtesy Jenny Sabin Studio.

the short axis at the bottom to allow inhabitants to enter the space underneath. The polygon grid structure that makes up this surface was generated using parametric computational tools developed as Grasshopper definitions that are based on graph theory. The process of form-finding was based on particle spring systems and implemented via Rhinoceros, Grasshopper and plugin Kangaroo developed by Daniel Piker. The NURBS surfaces were discretised into the mesh network M_0 with defined grid spacing and grid shape based on the final digital knitting fabrication process. Nodes of the mesh triangular faces are considered as particles connected by edges which are calculated as elastic springs. We input mechanical properties of the knit fabric by assigning axial stiffness and a damping coefficient to each edge of M_0. The form found mesh M_1 is then generated from the node coordinates and their connectivity. From mesh M_1, we used the dual graph method to reconstruct a new mesh representation M_2 which is tessellated by polygonal cells and cones.

The size and density of the cells in this network were manipulated according to the geometry of the exoskeleton, specifically the angles of curvature in the concave form. Once generated, the exterior cells were pulled inward to create an inner surface with an adjacent polygon grid that has a soft materiality and reciprocal structural behaviour. The cells on both the exoskeleton and inner surface were filled with either circular panels or conical forms that connect the two surfaces which are referred to as windows and cones respectively.

The structural concept of Ada builds upon previous work by Jenny Sabin Studio, with engineering design by Arup, where structures display the balance of tensile and compressive forces as a means for generating lightweight

4

4. Jenny Sabin and her team installing the knit fabric structure to the exoskeleton. The size and density of the cells in this network were manipulated according to the geometry of the exoskeleton, specifically the angles of curvature in the concave form. Precise tolerances between the transfer of the forces in the tension net and the compressive outer 3D printed nodal shell, were simulated and incorporated as variable parameters in the digital fabrication process such as a stretch factor. Photo: John Brecher for Microsoft.

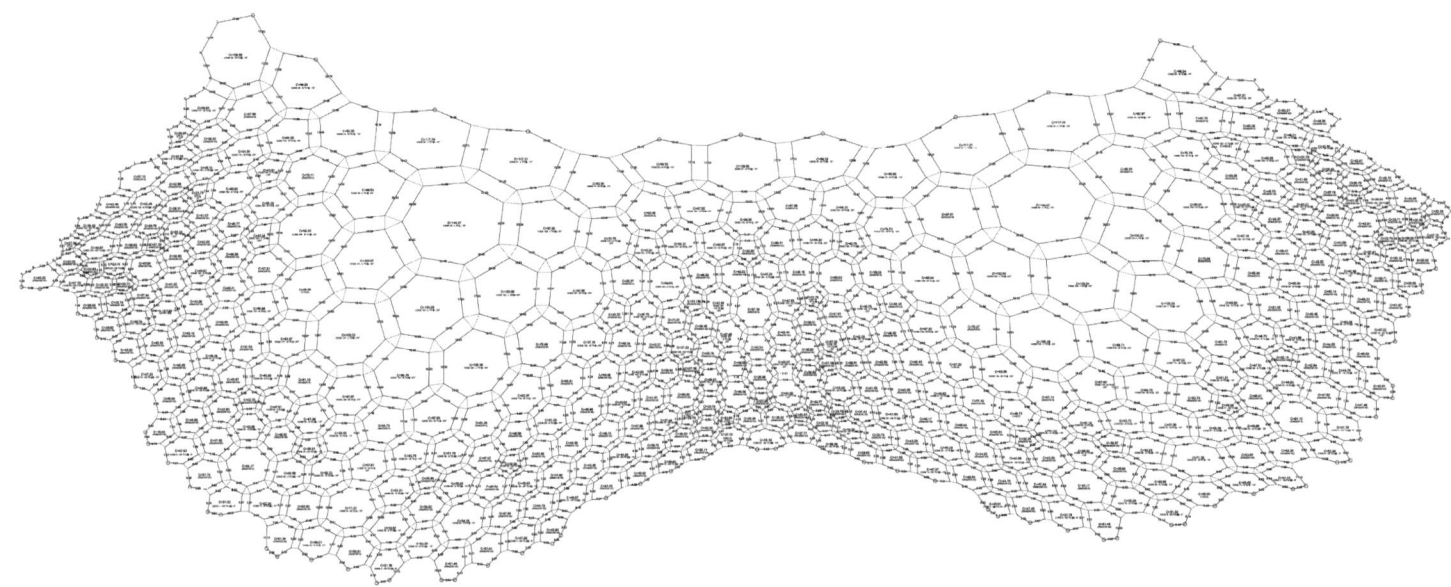

5

and expressive forms. The generative question for the design was how to create a convex surface (an ovaloid) of knitted tensile elements. Early in the process, we identified that a compressive, shell-like structure was required to achieve this form, and developed the idea for a hexagonal mesh, grid shell structure. In order to achieve this, we developed the concept of a lightweight three-dimensional cable truss or, more accurately, a cable-stiffened hybrid grid shell consisting of an outer compressive layer (the grid shell) and an inner tensile layer (a 'cable net' of nylon webbing), connected together by tension elements (the digitally knitted 'cones'). The pretension in the webbing net applies a uniform load to the grid shell which stabilises it against deformation that would lead to elastic buckling. The capacity and stability of the structure was confirmed via explicit finite element analysis, accounting for non-linear geometric effects using the analysis software Oasys GSA.

When the net form-finding process was complete, each cell and cone received a unique ID that followed each component through the entire fabrication and production process. The circumference of each of the cells when slack and when fully elastically prestressed was entered into an excel spreadsheet to aid in knit fabrication planning. The knit materials include a high-tech responsive yarn and a white fire retardant 'fill' yarn called Drake. The photoluminescent fibres emit light after the absorption of electromagnetic radiation from, for instance,

the sun or UV lights. This causes the light emission or glowing effect across the fabric structures.

The free edge of the hybrid grid shell was stiffened using a custom-fabricated aluminium edge ring that also serves to transfer tensile and compressive reactions between the webbing net and outer exoskeleton. Over the flattest part of the shell edge, the ring splits into two pieces which creates a more expressive separation between the tensile and compressive surfaces, but also results in a stiffer element to resist out-of-plane buckling at this location with low inherent geometric stiffness. Working in conjunction with the exoskeleton, the upper and lower metal rings were designed to establish terminal conditions. This provided both structural stability and weight, and a framework for establishing key points of attachment for the exoskeleton at the top and bottom of the installation.

3D-printed Nylon Nodes and Exoskeleton
The complex composition of cellular units that aggregate to make up the exterior surface of Ada required an exoskeleton that can synchronously define both the shape of each cell and the overall geometric form. This network contains an irregular combination of convex polygons that have between four and seven edges. We were interested in further exploring the use of pultruded fibreglass rods that had been used in previous work for the grid shell members; using them as bending-stiff struts rather than an active-bending spline. While the structure

5. Sewing pattern drawing for inner net surface showing distribution of 'cones' and 'cells'. The tension elements or 'cones' connect the inner surface to the outer surface, behaving as springs. Courtesy Jenny Sabin Studio.

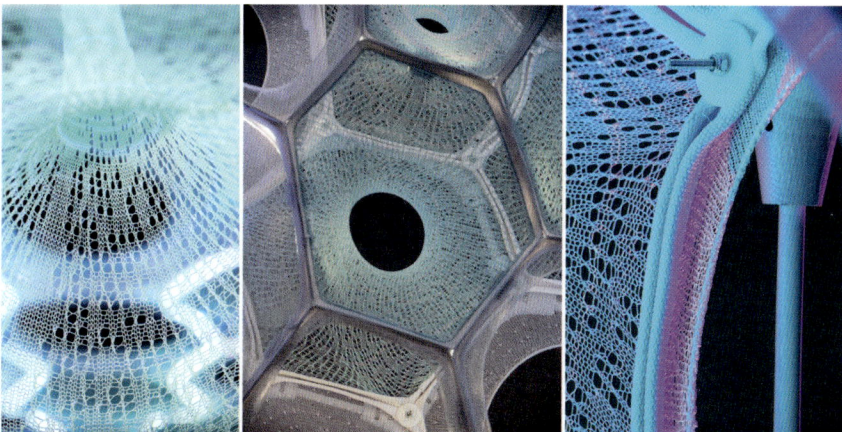

6

7

is 4-way symmetrical, there are 895 nodes due to the variable patterning and size gradient of the mesh. For this reason, mass-customisation via 3D printing was an obvious fabrication choice. A node typology was developed by generating a tubular end fitting around each of the three rods coming into a node and then meshing together. In order to allow for the assembly of the structure, a number of the nodes were split along the mid-surface and clamped together using stainless steel cable ties. Each node was required to transfer compression and flexure between all the rods coming into it. Interference fits, aided by the pre-compression in the shell, created these positive connections between the nodes and rods without use of adhesive. Several materials were considered for these nodes, including PLA, ABS, and nylon. After mechanical testing, according to ASTM D638-14 standard methodologies on an Instron 5900 Series Universal Testing Instrument, Multi-Jet Fusion (MJF) printing in nylon was determined to have the most appropriate performance characteristics for handling the significant bending forces created by the rods at each node. MJF by GoProto is a new technology that heat-fuses parts at the voxel (volumetric-pixel) level, resulting in rapidly manufactured parts with both superior finishes and mechanical strength.

Central Tensegrity Cone

The central tensegrity cone is a cable net forming a simple hyperboloid of one sheet stretched between a pair of circular rings. The system is pretensioned by means of a central flying strut and radial cables connecting the mast ends to the rings and resulting in an extraordinarily lightweight armature for the custom fibre optic fabric skin. The central tensegrity cone comprises a finely tuned steel structure wrapped in a semi-transparent fabric that is embedded with fibre optics. The sleeve contains panels of the fibre optic fabric that were designed to conform to the dimensions of the interior tensegrity cone and sewn and finished together with alternating strips of elastic material. A zipper that runs the vertical height of the cone is also sewn into the fabric as a means of joining the two ends of the sleeve. Seven programmable LED strips run the vertical length of the cone to connect a series of diodes directly to bundles of fibre optic strands within the fabric sleeve. Light from these diodes is transmitted across the strands and is visible through a subtle glow of the fibres and bright emissions through curated breaks in the surface of the fibres.

Brain Ring Hardware

Ada's Brain Ring is a bespoke yet simple assembly of laser-cut stainless-steel parts with strategic voids for ventilation and channels for wiring. It accommodates

6. Material details of Ada. (left) Responsive photoluminescent yarns activated by 3-tiered lighting system driven by real-time sentiment data collection; (middle) detail of responsive interior knit surface connected by the 'cone' tension elements to the 3D-printed exoskeleton. The primary tension forces are taken through the nylon webbing. The LED network nests in the fold of the webbing between the two surfaces; (right) connection detail of the knitted fabric surface to a 3D-printed node in the exoskeleton. Photos: Jake Knapp for Microsoft.

7. Tensegrity cone with embedded fibre optics. Situated at the centre of Ada, the tensegrity cone is an independent structure that was designed to showcase additional innovations in AI-driven responsive materials and interactive lighting technology. Seven programable LED strips run the vertical length of the cone to connect a series of diodes directly to bundles of fibre optic strands within the custom-designed and fabricated fabric sleeve. Photo: John Brecher for Microsoft.

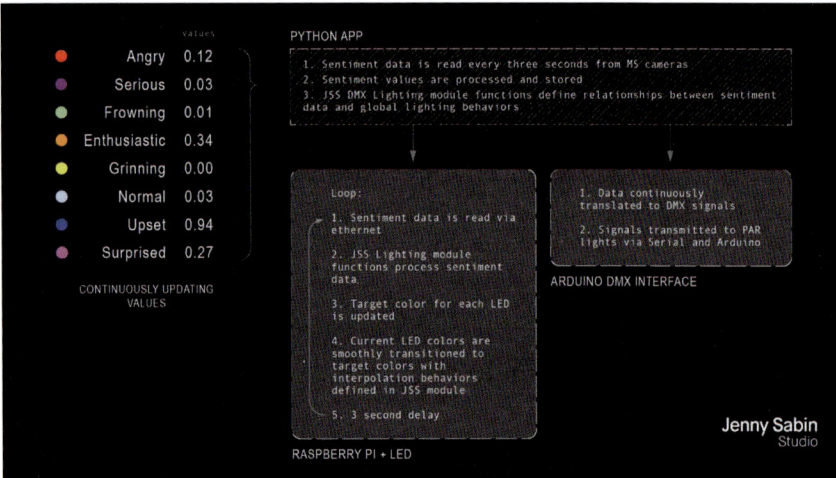

		values
●	Angry	0.12
●	Serious	0.03
●	Frowning	0.01
●	Enthusiastic	0.34
●	Grinning	0.00
●	Normal	0.03
●	Upset	0.94
●	Surprised	0.27

CONTINUOUSLY UPDATING VALUES

PYTHON APP

1. Sentiment data is read every three seconds from MS cameras
2. Sentiment values are processed and stored
3. JSS DMX Lighting module functions define relationships between sentiment data and global lighting behaviors

Loop:
1. Sentiment data is read via ethernet
2. JSS Lighting module functions process sentiment data.
3. Target color for each LED is updated
4. Current LED colors are smoothly transitioned to target colors with interpolation behaviors defined in JSS module
5. 3 second delay

RASPBERRY PI + LED

1. Data continuously translated to DMX signals
2. Signals transmitted to PAR lights via Serial and Arduino

ARDUINO DMX INTERFACE

Jenny Sabin
Studio

8

9

all of the electronics and networking hardware used to process, display and spatialise sentiment data read from an on-site PC. It discretises the data into streams depending on spatial, contextual conditions. The brain ring contains Raspberry Pi 3B+ microcontrollers, custom PCBs (printed circuit boards) for PWM (pulse width modulation) addressable LED control, Ubiquiti 10X Ethernet Switches, power supplies, and ethernet and power cables. Working collaboratively, Jenny Sabin Studio and Microsoft Research designed and programmed the software architecture for two programs which allow Ada to interface with human sentiment in her environment: a program running on the on-site PC, and a program running on each Raspberry Pi in the Brain Ring.

PC & Raspberry Pi Software

The PC software continually queries data from the network of MSR cameras which analyse user facial expressions. These expressions are classified using Microsoft researcher Daniel McDuff's platform, which drives Ada. McDuff works at the intersection of psychology and computer science to design hardware and algorithms for sensing human behaviour at scale in order to build technologies to improve human experience and daily life. AI algorithms turn this data into numeric gradients of sentiment which are then passed to the PC in the form of probabilities, each representing the program's certainty that a given expression is being observed. Expression data is cross-referenced by the programs to check for patterns such as:

1. Global average of all sentiment values
2. Local averages of sentiment in close physical/spatial proximity within Ada's site
3. Sentiment values with global maximum probability
4. Sentiment values with local maximum probability in close physical/spatial proximity within

Ada's site

A table of colour values represented as three-component vectors (red, green, blue) was designed to correspond to real-world facial expressions and voice tones. Colour vector transformations are applied through a series of functions which augment or inter-relate spatial zones based on [1]-[4] above. Finally, colour vectors are transmitted to their respective spatial zones on Ada's exoskeleton and knit structure through a local network connecting Raspberry Pis to the external PC, and through a PC-DMX interface to Elation SIXPAR PAR lights. When data are received, the program instantiates a specified number of LED pixel-objects, passing a colour vector to each one as its colour attribute. The pixels are illuminated through a series of animation frames which update each pixel's colour attribute. The animation occurs at an interval of 3 seconds,

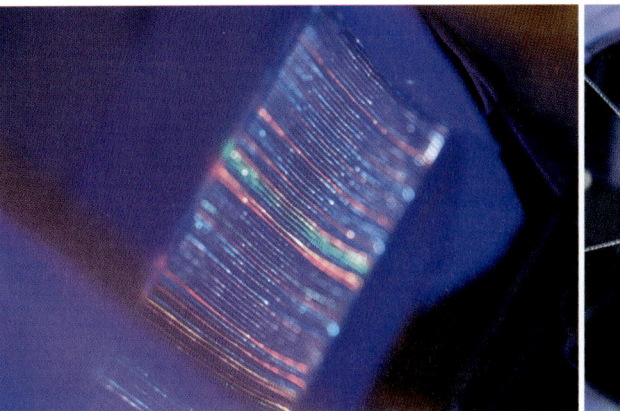

with 100 frames per second. Lighting software and hardware systems work in tandem to continually update the display colour of the LED network, which uses addressable LED strips in lengths varying from 1.26m to 6.46m. Strips are partitioned into zones on Ada's overall form, each corresponding to a camera located in Ada's site. A single 360-degree camera is housed on the interior of Ada at the centre of the tensegrity cone. This acts as a cycloptic eye through which inhabitants can experience a direct and personal interaction with Ada from within. Strips are connected to data and power through Ada's Brain Ring. Ada's three-tiered lighting system – PAR lights, LEDs, photoluminescent fibres, and fibre optics – provides critical and emergent experiential effects in relationship to human behaviour in Ada's context.

Results and Discussion

Generative Design, Exoskeleton, and Tensegrity Cone

The final digitally-fabricated result of a generative design process within a 3D-modelling environment is dependent on an accurate representation of physical and material conditions. As discussed, a physics engine was developed in Grasshopper to simulate the built form of all non-rigid elements (knit surfaces, nylon webbing systems, etc.) under accurate force conditions. Traditional techniques and machinery require that 3D forms in the Rhinoceros space must be projected, flattened, or unwrapped into a legible 2D representation. For complex geometries and double curvature there is an inherent approximation that is necessary in order to make this translation possible, and this carries a variable level of inaccuracy due to the challenge of simulating the physical material behaviour and elasticity. Additionally, standardisation of elements was desirable for easier fabrication and assembly which encouraged dimensional rounding in order to maximise homogeneity. Often these errors in translation and rounding were either absorbed into a

8. Embedded system diagram highlighting sentiment-to-colour translation. Courtesy Jenny Sabin Studio.

9. View from above, participant interacting with Ada through the central camera. Photo by Jake Knapp for Microsoft.

10. (left) Illumination of the optical fibres embedded in the central tensegrity cone; (right) interactive camera located at the bottom of the central tensegrity cone. Photos by John Brecher for Microsoft.

stretch factor associated with non-rigid materials or accounted for within established tolerances.

The exoskeleton, in co-action with several other key elements in the project, is a major contributor to the structural infrastructure of Ada. Moreover, these characteristics added an interactive haptic feature to Ada that would shake, ripple and bounce when touched and pushed by inhabitants.

Fabric Structure and Base/Upper Ring

Due to the high level of precision needed for the key attachment points, fabrication techniques of three-dimensional freeform aluminium tube-bending allowed for variable radius profiles to be produced in the base ring. The fabric structure was produced using four distinct cones lengths of 20.3cm, 30.5cm, 48.7cm, and 61cm with the assumption that the inherent elasticity of the knit fibre in each cone would be able to accommodate the 182 unique lengths that composed the entire network of cones within the canopy.

Conclusion

Ada builds upon 13 years of collaborative work and innovation across architecture and science, where projects embrace and are informed by technology, non-standard and bio-steered concepts, and the hidden spatial structures within data. These projects have the capacity to facilitate and reveal human expression and emotion in the built environment (Sabin et al., 2018). Through ten built projects commencing with the myThread pavilion in 2012 and, most recently, with Lumen for MoMA and MoMA PS1 YAP 2017, Jenny Sabin and her team have explored generative design and digital fabrication in knit and woven structures through multi-sensory responsive environments. Drawing synergies with current work at the intersection of data-driven cyber-physical assemblies, digitally knit structures, and textile architecture, Ada celebrates, integrates, and materialises AI, affective computing, responsivity, and material performance as can also be seen in work by Ahlquist, CITA, Farahi, Johnson, Khan, and Scott.

However, in contrast to these projects, Ada breaks new ground in scale, in the intricacy of embedded systems, and fine-scale design and manipulation of fibre material, resulting in the first architectural pavilion structure to be driven by human sentiment data in real time and powered by artificial intelligence. This platform would not have been possible without the unique collaboration with Microsoft Research. Unlike the pioneering work of Mark Sagar, such as his BabyX project that seeks to humanise

11

AI through 'more symbiotic relationships between humans and machines', Ada does not appear lifelike (Vance, 2017). Instead, Ada offers subtle and abstract interactions with humans through space, material and form to augment and expand our emotional range in a specific context – an office environment – which, in turn, affects the probable sentiment data being collected as new information. The spaces and environments that we inhabit influence and partially shape who we are and how we are feeling.

Through the integration of responsive materials and emerging technologies including artificial intelligence, Ada offers an interface for personalising architecture, to make it more human and reflexive. At the same time, Ada expands human emotional engagement through beauty and materiality. Ada has the capacity to promote and, hopefully, increase wellbeing through direct engagement with the architecture that we inhabit and encounter.

Ada's form, software functionality, and relationship to its physical and social context inform one another as a result of a rigorous design process in which materials, data and light are programmed. Installation challenges, due to variable tolerances and the precise transfer of forces across the complex structural system of Ada, present productive areas to refine for future projects. The introduction of fibre optics and finer scale manipulation and programming of a 3-tiered lighting system also present important leaps and openings for future permanent projects featuring embedded architectural systems. Finally, Ada opens up dialogue around important and pressing issues concerning personal data acquisition and privacy as well as justifiable concerns with AI. Ada is a project that celebrates AI, an architecture that is 'happy to see you' and 'smiles back at you'.

11. Ada, view from above with reflection in glazed surface. Ada incorporates responsive digitally-knit textiles as an information mediating surface architecture to materialise human sentiment data captured live and processed through artificial intelligence algorithms and affective computing. Photo by John Brecher for Microsoft.

Acknowledgments and Credits

Jenny Sabin Studio Team
Jenny E. Sabin – Architectural Designer and Artist
Dillon Pranger – Project Manager
John Hilla, Jeremy Bilotti, William Qian – Design, Production, Installation
Clayton Binkley and Judy Guo; Arup – Design Engineer

Fabrication and Manufacturing
GoProto, Dazian, Avatar Knit, Fabric Images, Accufab

Microsoft Research Ada Core
Technical Fellow and Director: Eric Horvitz
Director of PM and Special Projects: Shabnam Erfani
Principal Research Designer/Fusionist: Asta Roseway
Principal Design Director: Wende Copfer
Principal Electrical Engineer: Jonathan Lester
Principal Researcher: Daniel McDuff
Partner Director/Ethics: Mira Lane

Special Thanks to Allison Linn, Kiesha Clayton, John Roach, John Brecher, Cornell AAP, Henry Honig, Evelina Barhudarian, Christopher O'Dowd, Ahishek Udupa, Gregory Lee, Kathleen Walker, Stef Letman, Vaishnavi Ranganathan, Lex Story, Todd Jurgenson, Teresa LaScala, Tracy Tran, Trey Bagley, Jin Kim, Nicolas Villar, Chris Lovett, and the Blank Family. Thanks also to Jane Burry for her insightful input on this paper.

References

Ahlquist, S. 2015. 'Social Sensory Architectures: Articulating Textile Hybrid Structures for Multi-Sensory Responsiveness and Collaborative Play', in *ACADIA 2015: Computational Ecologies – Design in the Anthropocene, Proceedings of the 35th Annual Conference of the Association for Computer Aided Design in Architecture*, Cincinnati: ACADIA, pp. 263-273.

Ahlquist, S. 2016. 'Sensory material architectures: Concepts and methodologies for spatial tectonics and tactile responsivity in knitted textile hybrid structures', *International Journal of Architectural Computing*, 14(1), pp. 63-82.

Baranovskaya, Y., Prado, M., Dörstelmann, M. and Menges, A. 2016. 'Knitflatable Architecture – Pneumatically Activated Pre-programmed Knitted Textiles', in Herneoja, A., Österlund, T. and Markkanen, P. (eds), *Complexity & Simplicity – Proceedings of the 34th eCAADe Conference - Volume 1*, Oulu, Finland: University of Oulu, pp. 571-580.

Farahi, B. 2018. 'Heart of the Matter: Affective Computing in Fashion and Architecture', in *ACADIA 2018: Recalibration – On imprecision and infidelity*, Mexico City, Mexico: ACADIA, pp. 206-215.

Frearson, A. 2014. 'Asif Khan designs a "Mount Rushmore of the digital age" for the Sochi Winter Olympics', *Dezeen*, January 2014, https://www.dezeen.com/2014/01/10/asif-khan-mount-rushmore-of-the-digital-age-sochi-winter-olympics/. (Accessed 4 December 2019)

Johnson, J. K. and Gattegno, N. 2018. Future Cities Lab, http://www.future-cities-lab.net/. (Accessed 2 January 2020).

Lovelace, A. 1843. 'Sketch of the Analytical Engine Invented by Charles Babbage, Esq. by L.F. Menabrea, with Notes upon the Memoir by the translator,' in Taylor, R. (ed) *Scientific Memoirs Selected from the Transactions of Foreign Academies of Science and Learned Societies*, vol. 3, London: Richard and John E. Taylor, pp. 666-731.

Moorman, A., Liu, J. and Sabin, J. E. 2016. 'RoboSense: Context Dependent Robotic Design Protocols and Tools', in Velikov, K., Ahlquist, S., del Campo, M. and Thün, G. (eds), *ACADIA 2016: Posthuman Frontiers: Data, Designers, and Cognitive Machines, Proceedings of the 36th Annual Conference of the Association for Computer Aided Design in Architecture*, Ann Arbor: ACADIA, pp. 174-183.

Sabin, J. E., Pranger, D., Binkley, C., Strobel, K. and Liu, J. L. 2018. 'Lumen', in *ACADIA 2018: Recalibration – On imprecision and infidelity*, Mexico City, Mexico: ADADIA, pp. 445-455.

Sabin, J. E. 2013. 'myThread Pavilion: Generative Fabrication in Knitting Processes', in Beesley, P., Kahn, O. and Stacey, M. (eds), *ACADIA 2013: Adaptive Architecture*, Cambridge: ACADIA, pp. 347-354.

Sabin, J. and Jones, P. L. 2017. *LabStudio: Design Research Between Architecture and Biology*. London & New York: Routledge Taylor and Francis.
Scott, J. (2013). 'Hierarchy in Knitted Forms: Environmentally Responsive Textiles for Architecture', *ACADIA 2013: Adaptive Architecture*, Cambridge: ACADIA, pp. 361-366.

Thomsen, M. R., Tamke, M., Karmon, A., Underwood, J., Gengnagel, C., Stranghoner, N. and Uhlemann, J. 2016. 'Knit as bespoke material practice for architecture', in Velikov, K., Ahlquist, S., del Campo, M. and Thün, G. (eds), *ACADIA 2016: Posthuman Frontiers: Data, Designers, and Cognitive Machines, Proceedings of the 36th Annual Conference of the Association for Computer Aided Design in Architecture*, Ann Arbor: ACADIA, pp. 280-289.

Vance, A. 2017. 'Mark Sagar Made a Baby in His Lab. Now It Plays the Piano', *Bloomberg Businessweek*, 7 September 2017, https://www.bloomberg.com/news/features/2017-09-07/this-startup-is-making-virtual-people-who-look-and-act-impossibly-real. (Accessed 4 December 2019)

Wang, A. and Ahlquist, S. 2016. 'Pneumatic Textile System', in Velikov, K., Ahlquist, S., del Campo, M. and Thün, G. (eds), *ACADIA 2016: Posthuman Frontiers: Data, Designers, and Cognitive Machines, Proceedings of the 36th Annual Conference of the Association for Computer Aided Design in Architecture*, Ann Arbor: ACADIA, pp. 290-297.

Yunis, L., Ondřej, K., Dörstelmann, M., Prado, M., Schwinn, T. and Menges, A. 2014. 'Bio-inspired and fabrication-informed design strategies for modular fibrous structures in architecture', in Thompson, E. (ed.), *Fusion – Proceedings of the 32nd eCAADe Conference – Volume 1*, Newcastle-upon-Tyne: Department of Architecture and Built Environment, pp. 423-432.

DIAGRAMS OF ENTROPIC FORCES
DESIGN FOR NEW DISSIPATIVE FABRICATION

PHILIP BEESLEY

LIVING ARCHITECTURE SYSTEMS GROUP / UNIVERSITY OF WATERLOO & EUROPEAN GRADUATE SCHOOL

He sees efflorescences in fragments of ice, imprints
of shrubs and shells yet so that one cannot detect
whether they be imprints only, or the things themselves.
Gustave Flaubert, *The Temptation of Saint Anthony*

Introduction

This discussion explores precarious *entropic* and
dissipative qualities within new architectural scaffold
systems. 'Meander', an immersive fabrication project
that integrates these qualities, is described. Dissipative
energy-shedding component systems create a form-
language supporting fertile and sustainable architecture.
The paper includes descriptions of individual components,
joint and scaffold design, and fabrication methods.
Entropy can imply that the universe is a soulless machine
lapsing into disorder. Similarly, classical architectural
design can be seen as dominated by resistance to decay.
In terms borrowed from contemporary physics, historical
architecture in the West has tended to follow conservative
forces that pursue low entropy and high order. Within
energy conservation-dominated classical models, free
citizenship is made possible by the finite *urbs* and
fundamental *firmitas* where stable fortified enclosing
walls and ground surfaces of the city provide resistance

and hardened boundaries (Vitruvius, 15BC). In contrast,
non-conservative forces dominated by entropy and
dissipation connote loss of civility. However, must entropy
inevitably mean 'disorder', leading to death and decay?
New conceptions reveal refreshing qualities of entropy
embedded within intermeshed dynamic topologies. New
voices extending the mid-twentieth century chemist and
physicist Ilya Prigogine's preceding insights, and
applying them to open systems, state that entropy makes
fundamental contributions to living systems (Prigogine,
1977). Recent writing on evolutionary dynamics by Jeremy
England has contributed to further reform of the meaning
of entropy (England, 2018). Instead of 'disorder', entropy
can be redefined as a force that seeks a maximum of
diverse freedom and potential. Those optima form the
basis for living systems to arise and flourish. This renewal
can contribute to new kinds of architectural fabrication.

New form-languages for architecture can foster mutual
relationships and interaction. Components that integrate
entropy can open their boundaries, pursuing precarious,
reactive qualities. Qualities following these renewed
conceptions can be seen within physical component
systems shedding and exchanging forces with their
surroundings, maintaining durability and coherence

2

while at the same time generating entropy and exchange. Instead of resistance to decay, this new approach offers dissipative adaptation of the vast forces passing through the world.

Order

Ernst Schrödinger's mid-20th century treatise *What is Life?* asserted that the essential ingredient of life is negentropy, an ordering force that opposes the decay and disorder of the world (Schrödinger, 1992). Conservation of energy is implicit within that conception. If we follow the second law of thermodynamics which declares that entropy inexorably increases, we might agree that our fate is disease and death. This conception has influenced the form-languages of architecture in fundamental ways (Beesley, 2018).

Seen today, classical architectural design has been dominated by the pursuit of low entropy. The Roman writer Vitruvius described *firmitas*, an essential core of permanent, durable, inert substance (Vitruvius, 15BC). Closed boundaries sheltering interiors from the exterior with dense, concentrated building materials of stone and brick create low entropy within their bounded territories. In contrast, high entropy tends to be created outside enclosed buildings. Rebounding in response to dense enclosing boundaries, forces to the exterior tend to be amplified. To the outside turbulent wilderness may freely play, in counterpoint to the calm and stable sanctuaries inside.

While the human interpretations that underlie the term are ancient, the word entropy is modern. The root of the word was coined amidst industrial revolution searches for efficient work. Entropy was coined in the early 18th century as the amount of energy lying within physical materials that is not available for 'work'. Taken from *tropos*, Greek for turning and transformation, this original interpretation denotes the cost of energy needed to change material from one state to another. Where the objective is yielding maximum work from a machine, entropy can be positioned as an emphatically negative word.

A strikingly new conception of entropy was offered by Prigogine in his 1978 Nobel address. He asserted that the closed systems of classical science differ from the conditions of the natural world. Upending conceptions of inevitable decay within the world, he described realms of dissipative forms formed by energy shedding – the barred, clumping textures of cumulus clouds, rolling standing waves in the ocean and in constantly shifting dunes – holding their forms steady amidst fluxing exchanges (Beesley, 2018). Prigogine argued that these forms are a natural result of far-from-equilibrium forces in the world. Dissipative forms might seem ephemeral, but they are in reality tenacious and durable, holding their organisations in dynamic balance while materials and energy constantly cycle through them. Building from Prigogine, the MIT-based physicist Jeremy England now proposes that life itself epitomises entropic production (England, 2018). Cycling of materials orchestrated in the metabolisms and perturbations fostered by life yield a maximum of entropy.

With this, the word entropy needs redefinition. Instead of disorder, entropy can be redefined as a distinct force that seeks diverse freedom and maximum potential. With such a fundamental shift, assumptions guiding the boundaries of architecture have reasons to shift in turn. Within conceptions guiding classical architecture, free citizenship was made possible by the conservative *urbs* where the city's stable fortified enclosing walls provide resistance and hardened boundaries, gathering and retaining energy. Might an alternative architecture construct constantly shifting, open thresholds that seek exchange? An experimental canopy and shell construction developed in 2019 by the Living Architecture Systems Group demonstrates potential approaches. The group is an international partnership of designers and researchers directed by the author and hosted by the University of Waterloo, Canada.

Meander

Meander is a new experimental interactive architectural work of halo-like shells and mechanical veils that are formed like rivers and clouds. The 2019 work is a permanent test-bed within a cultural centre in Cambridge, Ontario, Canada. Paradigms of precarity and diffusion guide Meander's design and fabrication. In contrast to the protection of wall-building, these structures draw

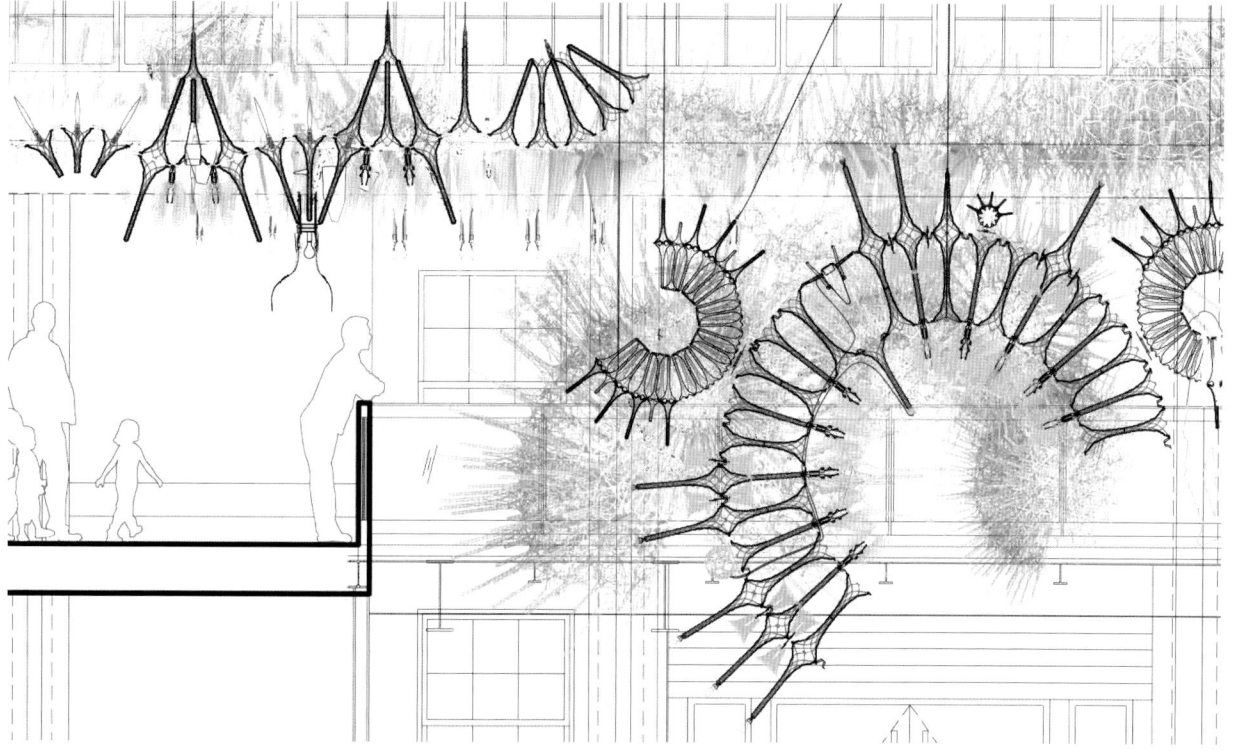

3

1. Noosphere, Toronto, 2018, showing expanded shell topologies. Philip Beesley/ LASG.

2. Amatria, Amatria, Bloomington, 2018, showing shell, canopy and cloud topology. Philip Beesley/ LASG.

3. Partial section of Meander, Cambridge, 2019 with bridge, space-truss and shells. Philip Beesley/LASG.

impulses inward and outward, shedding forces in rippling oscillations of exchange.

The structures are organised as a series of reticulated scaffolds. A threefold architecture is created of shell, canopy and veil sections organising the whole. The structural series includes mounded hollows enwreathed by river-like canopies and outer cloud-like veils. The structures within this project offers minimal material consumption achieved with automated cutting, and thermal and mechanical forming of expanded arrays of filamentary structures. Hovering filters composed of hundreds of thousands of laser-cut thermally-formed transparent polymer and mylar, glass and expanded sheet steel components creates diffusive thresholds. Sensors embedded throughout the environment trigger vibrating motions, pulsing lights and whispering sounds in undulating peristaltic waves. The design and fabrication of these openwork scaffolds suggest methods for creating full-scale resilient and responsive architecture capable of integrating distributed control systems, diverse kinetics, and evolving component functions.

Shells

Meander contains first generations of a new shell and vaulting system made from interlinking expanded-mesh hollow struts. Hexagonal tiles are interlinked at their corners using triangular elastic coupling plates. Rings of face-attached equilateral hexagons create convex clusters surrounding pentagonal cores. Following classical primary polyhedron patterns described by Archimedes, these clusters are assembled into icosahedral spheres each containing twelve pentagon and hexagon ring clusters. Orchestrated voids and concave fragments within these shells create spaces for gathering and shelter.

Projection of tile centre-points inward and outward create varying pyramidal units that range from shallow spider forms to elongated trumpet-like spines. Acrylic and stainless steel spars employ thin sheets of mechanically-formed stainless steel and thermally-formed acrylic and PETG (Polyethylene Terephthalate, Glycol modified) transparent polymers, formed with polar arrays of concentric overlapping slitting patterns. Forming expands these digitally machined patterned sheets into hyperbolic shells providing efficient lightweight branching structures. Spine-struts make a bubbling, porous massive building system full of interlinking voids, akin to the spaces of sinuses or termite mounds.

4. Exploded detail view of Meander, showing LED Cluster with Vibrating Fronds. Philip Beesley/ LASG.

5. Meander Lexicon, Shell and River. Philip Beesley/ LASG.

4

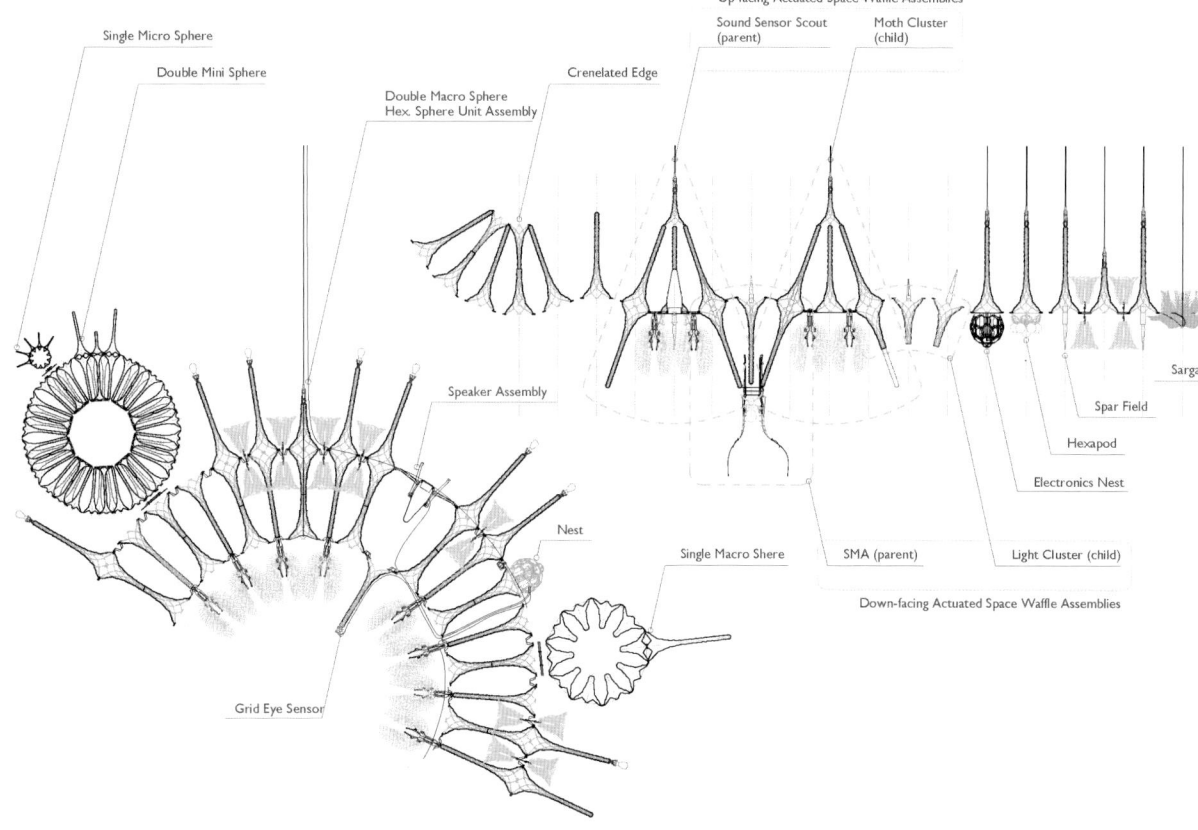

Single Micro Sphere

Double Mini Sphere

Double Macro Sphere
Hex. Sphere Unit Assembly

Crenelated Edge

Up-facing Actuated Space Waffle Assemblies

Sound Sensor Scout
(parent)

Moth Cluster
(child)

Speaker Assembly

Nest

Sarga...

Spar Field

Hexapod

Electronics Nest

Single Macro Shere

SMA (parent)

Light Cluster (child)

Down-facing Actuated Space Waffle Assemblies

Grid Eye Sensor

Components

Components are designed with reactive, poised dispositions. Kinetic functions that offer trembling and vibrating movement are enhanced by design that brings materials close to their limit of spanning and stability, creating subtle precarity. Flexure and elasticity are retained by voiding out large surfaces and volumes, opening components for deflection and compliance. Mesh-works of relatively long tensile filaments are embedded with small compressive struts, creating tension-integrity networks carrying gentle pre-stressed forces.

Scaffolds are designed for resilience and force-shedding. Material is laid along axial paths using fused deposition and digital cutting. By interlinking multiple components, the accumulation of large force-concentrations in adjacent assemblies tends to be mitigated. Chains of individual compressive details are linked together into overlapping diagonal arrays. Detailing methods derived from textile crafts include gussets, seams and folds that blend and distribute force. Where rigid assemblies of components

are required for protection of delicate electronics or iquid chemical solutions, layers are added to cushion accumulated forces.

Covering the inner surfaces of the skeletal scaffolds are polar arrays of mechanisms and lighting instruments. The massed lining of each hemispherical shell responds to feather-light variations of air movement in the surrounding environment, responding with shimmering cyclical motion. Reticulated long-fingered fronds of stiffened laser-cut polyester sheet give resonating cowls that enclose small glass vials holding salt and oil liquids.

Fissured fronds are fitted with spinning weight-offsetting miniature motors that impart vibrating movement. Tapered glass vessels carry high-powered custom LED lights, concentrated by narrow-beam reflectors creating axial beams shining through the cores of structural components. Cradling each light and surrounded by frond-clusters are cellular manifolds made from multiple glass vessels. Combinations of oil and inorganic chemicals in aqueous solutions create chemical skins within these prototype cells.

6

Tile-shaped components lining these manifolds are designed for reversible reactive behaviours. Thin sheets of durable polymer are shaped in tapered filamentary comb filters. Rows of filaments are tested in cycles, finding the maximum possible lengths that avoid collapse while maintaining maximum reaction faces. Capacity for heat exchange serves as a practical measure of this capacity for reaction.

Canopies

Spherical shell forms at the core of the test-bed act as templates generating outer layers of tessellated membrane skins. Akin to multiple layers of moulted outer parchment skins in onions, spheres support extended cowl membranes whose surfaces swell, ripple and then subside into extended horizontal membranes. Incremental hollow struts bridge between these cowl layers and inner spheres, supporting interstitial spaces saturated with delicate glass flasks and frondworks. Triangular arrays of peaks and valleys organise extended river surfaces. Similar to the component groups seen within the central cluster of shells, concave and convex hyperbolic ring-clusters of

face-attached hexagonal spars make up this fabric. By organising those component groups in alternating upward and downward orientations, a triangular waffle space-truss is created. Tensegrity coupling employs compressive metal rod cores surrounded by the tensile jackets contained within interlinked hyperbolic shell clusters. This resilient structure is stiffened by expanded-mesh hexagonal struts that support telescoping posts and spires.

Veils

Billowing skeletal canopies intersecting with the edges of the space-grid layers extend the outer surfaces of Meander. Skeletal hexagonal frames follow tiled arrangements harmonised with the inner cores. Sections of the outer membrane show additional chiral organisation. In these sections, each tile contains a rotated core encircled with alternating upward and lower-reaching flexible curved arms. Matching triangular couplers extend this quasiperiodic spiralling matrix. Curved skeleton arms carry curving fronds with extended combs. Comb tines are extended close to their cantilevered span limit. These

6. Upward view of Astrocyte Detail, Toronto, 2017, showing manifold of clustered liquid cells and vibrating fronds.

7. Detailed view of central hemispherical shell cluster, Meander, Cambridge, 2019.

8. Elevation view of central shell structures, Meander, 2019.

9. Panoramic view of central shell cluster and flanking canopies, Meander, Cambridge, 2019.

7

8

9

react with trembling vibration to slight shifts in the surrounding atmosphere. The composite structure performs as a gentle mechanical pump. Intersecting combs create a toothed valving structure tending to close against downward drafts of air while amplifying upward currents. The nested spiral fabric membrane is elastic, accommodating large displacements within its hung tentwork placement, gently stretching and contracting in response to air movements.

Conclusion

These experimental works imply form-languages for designing buildings. Instead of valuing resistance and closure, new form-languages for architecture can foster mutual relationships and pluripotent interaction. Stable enclosing walls of the city provide resistance and hardened boundaries that provide local sanctuaries, but those same walls create turbulent disjunctions. Instead of closed boundaries, an alternative architecture can construct dynamic, constantly shifting open thresholds that invite constantly renewed exchange. Far from weakness and vulnerability, this exchange can be seen to directly support thriving living structures. Dissipative forms founded upon a renewed definition of entropy can be translated into new component systems supporting contemporary architectural practice. To restate the biologist D'Arcy Wentworth Thompson's famous maxim 'natural form is a diagram of forces' (Thompson, 1917): dissipative architectural forms can be diagrams of entropic forces.

References

Beesley, P. 2018. 'Precarious Living Reactions: New Paradigms for Robotic Architecture', in Daas, M., & Wit, A. (eds), *Towards a Robotic Architecture. Framework and Processes*, Novato, CA: ORO Editions.

England, J. 2018. 'Why Trees Don't Ungrow', *Aeon*, https://aeon.co/essays/does-the-flow-of-heat-help-us-understand-the-origin-of-life. (Accessed 23 December 2019)

Flaubert, G. 1911. *The Temptation of St. Anthony*, (trans. Hearn, L.), New York: Boni and Liveright.

Prigogine, I. 1977. 'The 1977 Nobel Prize in Chemistry, Ilya Prigogine', Nobel Media AB, http://www.nobelprize.org/nobel_prizes/chemistry/laureates/1977/press.html. (Accessed 23 December 2019)

Schrödinger, E. 1992. *What is Life?: The Physical Aspect of the Living Cell; with Mind and Matter and Autobiographical Sketches*, Cambridge: Cambridge University Press.

Thompson, D. W. 1917. *On Growth and Form*, Cambridge: Cambridge University Press.

Vitruvius, M. ~ 15BC. *De Architectura (The Ten Books on Architecture)*, Morgan, M. H. (trans.) (1914), Cambridge, Mass.: Harvard University Press.

DISCRETE TIMBER ASSEMBLY

GILLES RETSIN
THE BARTLETT SCHOOL OF ARCHITECTURE, UCL

Digital Materials

Using a number of built demonstrators, this paper describes a computational design and fabrication method for timber assembly, based on the notion of discreteness. This research attempts to combine aspects of the field of Digital Materials and Programmable Matter with the architectural field of Prefabrication and Modularity. While these two fields are at opposing ends of the spectrum in terms of scale and functional operation, this research proposes that many of the properties and challenges are transferable.

Neil Gerschenfeld and the Centre for Bits and Atoms at MIT have developed the notion of 'Digital' Materials, which can be understood as an approach to Programmable Matter. Programmable Matter is a wider field that straddles robotics, computer science, material science and engineering, and focuses on the creation of materials whose properties can be adapted and coded (Gerschenfeld et al., 2015). This includes MetaMaterials, certain Soft Robotics, Self-Assembly and Self-Reconfiguring Modular Robotics.

Digital materials can be precisely defined as a discrete set of parts, which are reversibly joined with a discrete set of relative positions and orientations (Cheung, 2012). These can then be assembled into larger scale wholes with functional performance, such as robots, aeroplanes or infrastructure. Gerschenfeld proposes that 'digital fabrication' is a process that compiles these discrete building blocks, whereas analogue fabrication is based on continuous subtraction or deposition of matter. For example, 3D printing and robotic milling are considered analogue fabrication methods.

Some of the challenges digital materials attempt to tackle in robotics and mechanical engineering are highly relevant to architecture and construction. Digital Materials and Programmable Matter aim to automatically or autonomously manufacture functional machines or infrastructures from smaller base units. Architecture in its most basic sense attempts the same: assembling functional buildings from smaller parts. However, programmable matter is more focused on the active and immediate performance of a whole, its mechanical operation. In architecture, the functionality is concerned with change over a long period of time. Adaptability, assembly and disassembly are processes taking place over weeks, months or years, rather than seconds. Primarily, the transferable aspects from programmable matter and digital materials are a short and integrated production

chain, the potential for automation and the concept of limited modular parts establishing vast variation, complexity, versatility, adaptation and re-assembly over time.

Programmable Matter and Modularity

Digital materials attempt to overcome the discontinuity present in analogue fabrication where unrelated processes have to be combined. These result in expensive, time-inefficient and inflexible production chains, where every machine needs its own customised fabrication process (Langford, 2019). Just like robotics and manufacturing, architecture and construction suffers from a similar analogue syntax with resulting discontinuities, unrelated processes and errors. On average, buildings are composed of over 7000 different parts and processes which need to be assembled together into a functional whole. This makes construction slow, expensive and difficult to automate. To achieve full automation, every part and process would need its own unique species of robot.

In a context of increasing cost of labour and decreasing robot cost, this so called 'Automation Gap' (Claypool, 2019) leads to an ever-decreasing productivity in construction. The construction industry has flat-lined since 1947, whereas manufacturing has radically increased its productivity through higher degrees of automation (McKinsey, 2017). As building is slow and expensive, only a limited number of actors can take the risk to construct. This in turn keeps the market limited and scarce in supply of housing and puts the decision-making of housing construction in the hands of the few – government and large developers. Cooperative efforts to construct housing have proven difficult to scale, again partially as a result of complicated construction and procurement.

In response to the housing crisis and flat-lined productivity, there is a renewed interest in Modularity and Prefabrication as an alternative. For example, Design for Manufacturing and Assembly (DfMA) and modular timber construction aim to take as much labour off site as possible. However, these approaches can't radically

2

3

improve productivity as the production chain is still discontinuous, analogue and difficult to automate. Moreover, the associated business model is reactive and service-based. Modules are one-offs that have to be redesigned for every site and every project.

An approach based on a digital understanding of parts and assembly offers a promising alternative. The work of Alfred Bemis and Leonardo Mosso present a historic precedent of a voxel-based architecture (Botazzi, 2018), as well as Frank Lloyd Wright's Textile Block houses. More contemporary, Philippe Morel (EZCT) developed the Universal House as a discrete voxel-based building system (Morel, 2011), while Jose Sanchez' Polyomino project proposed discrete building blocks as platforms for collaborative design (Sanchez, 2018). The interest in this approach is reinforced by the theoretical and historical work on Discreteness and Computation by Mario Carpo (Carpo, 2014).

Digital Modularity

This research attempts to transfer some of the core-concepts of 'digital materials' to architectural modularity, establishing a short, integrated, continuous production chain based on generic, serialised versatile building blocks cut from two-dimensional sheet materials, with limited connection possibilities and passive error correction. These building blocks are function-agnostic – function is only established after assembly. The parts therefore exist independent of an actual building and should be able to construct a complex variety of outcomes. This idea is often compared to molecular biology, where

all of life is assembled from just 20 standardised amino acids as modular building blocks (Langford, 2019).

The notion of digital fabrication is then redefined as the assembly or compilation of these building blocks into a functional structure. An example of an actual 'digital' fabrication method could be, for example, Jonathan Hiller's and Hod Lipson's proposal for 3D-Voxel Printing, where physical voxels are defined as 'physical, self-aligning, fundamental units' (Hiller and Lipson, 2009) that are assembled by a printer. Can the construction of buildings become like an additive manufacturing process, based on the continuous assembly of discrete parts? This process allows for a high degree of automation, both in the prefabrication of the parts and in the assembly of the parts into buildings.

This research further questions a cost-effective, scalable method of production, the scale of the building blocks themselves and the amount of variation within sets of elements. The large-scale, 1:1 prototypes aim to test the use of two-dimensional base material, limited connection possibilities, repeating units which are invariant to rotation, complexity and variability from repeating units, structural capabilities, tension joints and the potential for automation.

Tallinn Architecture Biennale Installation

The question of an organic assembly of serialised, digital-material like hollow timber building blocks was first framed with the Diamonds House, a 2015 project for a multi-family dwelling in Belgium by Gilles Retsin Architecture (Fig. 3). In collaboration with the UCL Design Computation Lab

1 & 2. Gilles Retsin, Tallinn Architecture Biennale Pavilion, 2017. Photo: NAARO.

3. Gilles Retsin, Diamonds House, Belgium, 2015.

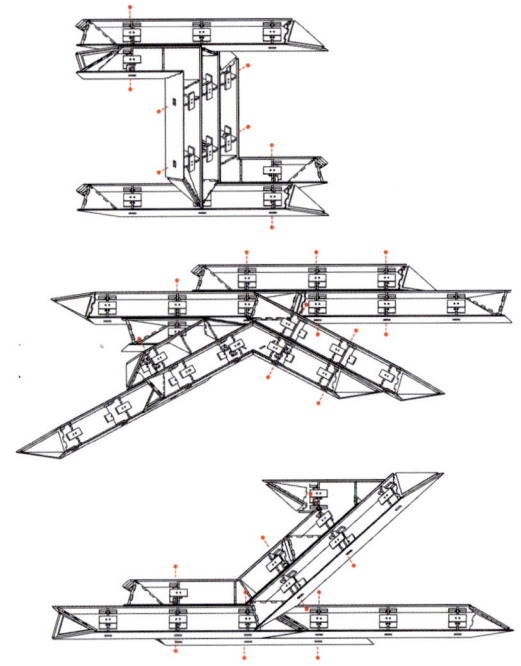

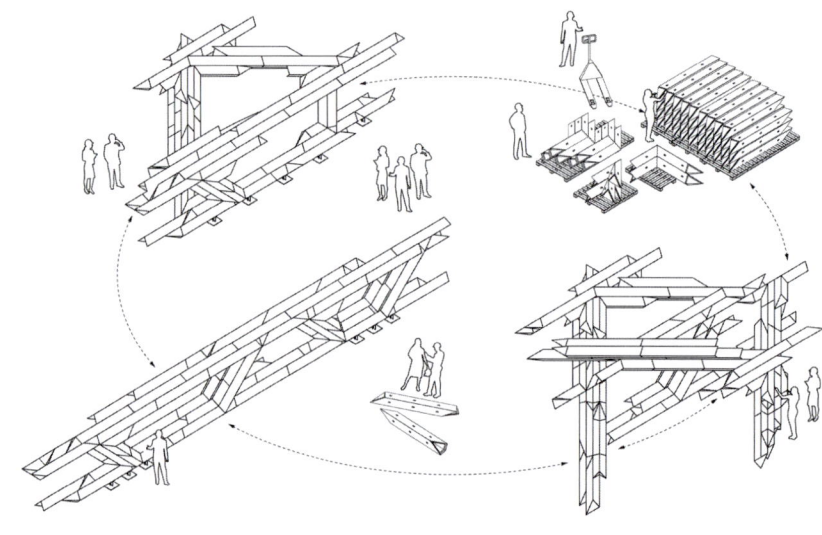

4

5

(DCL), an installation for the Tallinn Architecture Biennale (TAB) in 2017 formed the opportunity to prototype and test this idea on a 1:1 scale. The installation is a fragment of an abstract larger housing block, a fragment of which was then selected and further detailed (Figs 1, 2).

A family of discrete building blocks was developed: a straight element, a 90° corner element, a 45° corner element and its inverse, a 135-degree corner element. The straight element's proportions are derived from one sheet of exterior plywood (3300 x 1350 x 18mm). All toolpaths were designed assuming a simple 3-axis CNC machine, using a standard and 45° drill bit. The toolpath was kept as simple as possible, to allow for quick cutting. The decision was made to avoid any visible finger joints or notches, details typical for CNC plywood projects. While there are internal notches, the sides of the elements are cut under 45° and connected with PVA glue and a series of 30mm nails. The part is designed as a box beam-like element, consistent of a skin and three interior frames to stiffen the box. The interior frames are notched in the skin and hold a small plate with two 14mm-diameter circular openings. These function as inserts for mild steel threaded rods (M10), which connect the parts laterally. The rods are fixed with polymer-insert lock nuts, to resist turning which could result from vibrations during the assembly. The internal stiffening frame coincides with the position of the rods, forming a continuous stiffening frame throughout multiple elements. These stiffening frames set out the modular rhythm and limited connection possibilities for the building blocks. The overall tolerance for the installation is defined by the 4mm difference between the circular opening for the steel rods and the rod diameter. A 36mm-thick shear-key element is inserted in the opening left for the rods, preventing lateral movement between building blocks.

The male-female endings of the building blocks have no mechanical connectivity, but together with the tension rods and stiffening frames allow for passive error correction throughout the installation. Moreover, by alternating the orientation of the 45° element, a substantial amount of geometric interlocking is achieved. The different corner elements follow a similar build-up, but also incorporate an additional internal stiffening frame, a continuous piece of plywood orientated in the long direction of the part. This frame allows load-paths to shift and establishes structural continuity (Fig. 4).

All elements are flip-invariant and appear multiple times in different load cases and positions throughout the installation. By staggering and overlapping the parts, the combination of steel rods and shear keys combines the initially discrete building elements in a continuous monolithic structure.

4 & 5. Gilles Retsin, Tallinn Architecture Biennale Pavilion, 2017.

6. Gilles Retsin, Tallinn Architecture Biennale Pavilion, 2017. Photo: NAARO.

7. Gilles Retsin, *Real Virtuality*, Royal Academy of Arts, 2019.

6

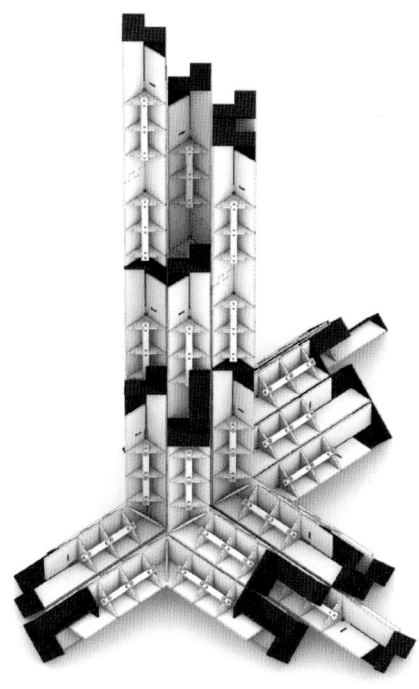

7

Cost-efficiency, variation and complexity

The TAB installation negotiates the challenges of building complex, variegated large-scale structures out of serialised, function-agnostic, discrete building blocks. It presents a method for building discrete parts from a single, two-dimensional base material, using only one machine. The installation suffered minimal deflections and deformations and was completed with an overall tolerance of 4mm along a maximum length of 12.5m. Large cantilevers of up to 4.5m were achieved, without notable deflection (Fig. 6). The biggest difference with digital materials is that the elements are not regular, space-filling polyhedra or sphere as in most examples of digital materials, but are asymmetrical. The decision for a beam-like element has certain advantages on a large, architectural scale: it allows for staggering and overlapping and it reduces the number of joints.

The seriality of the elements and their properties of self-alignment and error correction allowed for a quick and efficient assembly, with only a small crew of four people in a space of five days – including site-preparation and finishing. Automation of on-site assembly is a long-term possibility, but doesn't appear as an absolute necessity. If the scale of the parts is large enough, pre-assembly with a simple crane could be more efficient. The seriality also enabled adaptation on site.

It was decided to deviate from the design model and move one element on site to reinforce a cantilever which displayed deflection.

Another installation at the Royal Academy (2019) questions the structural topology of the building block and the amount of material required (Fig. 8). Parts are designed as a 12mm plywood internal stiffening frame in three directions, connected to a light external skin of 9mm plywood (Fig. 7). This significantly reduced the weight of the elements. A Hololens was used to stream instructions to the build crew, further reducing the assembly time.

In both cases, the lack of mechanical connection in the male and female endings of the elements is problematic and ultimately resulted in the need for the additional corner-elements to transfer forces between different planes. While the corner elements are efficient and of architectural interest, they do complicate the process. A subsequent installation developed for Tongji University in Shanghai (2019) introduces this connection, reducing the total number of elements to just one. If only one element is used, it's worth investing in robotically pre-fabricating the part.

This was tested with the project ALIS, developed in the context of the Architectural Design MArch (B-Pro) Programme at The Bartlett School of Architecture with

8. Gilles Retsin,
Real Virtuality, Royal
Academy of Arts, 2019.
Photo: NAARO.

Master's students Joana Correia, Evgenia Krassakopoulou, Akhmet Khakimov, Kevin Saey and Estefania Barrios. Two industrial robots were used to pre-assemble a box-like element. The robots pick and place pre-cut material from a pre-cut stack of components and assemble these on a central pedestal using a nail gun. This process could be further improved with the use of press-fit joints, as demonstrated by the research of Christopher Robeller et al. (2017).

Towards discrete automation

This research reveals a new notion of the architectural part as a discrete building block, combining aspects of digital material and programmable matter with architectural prefabrication and modularity. Discrete timber assembly offers multiple potential answers to falling construction productivity, the housing crisis and global climate crisis.

Once discretised, construction is more integrated and assembly becomes a continuous and organic process, similar to additive manufacturing. The part hierarchies and types commonly associated with assembly disappear. Physical and digital reality overlaps completely, there is no more representational gap between both. What is computed is what is assembled, and what is assembled in return computes. This method therefore enables increased automation of construction, requiring potentially no minimal handling off site and only minimal manual handling on site.

By using timber, we make optimal use of large-scale industry for the fabrication of sheets and localised, small-scale manufacturing for the customisation and assembly of building elements and buildings. Each building could be assembled differently, to a granular level, without increasing the production chain. This can happen at no extra cost, as the customised placement of elements is merely an informational task. Compared to modernist and current modular prefabrication, the function-agnostic, serialised parts demonstrate increased variability, versatility. This short production chain, only based on sheet-materials, is in turn agile and easy to customise to different building blocks. It does not propose a centrally controlled, universal, objective building block as a single solution.

The small-scale infrastructure needed to construct building blocks and assemble buildings could make construction more accessible, faster and therefore less capital intensive, opening the market to a larger group of house-builders. Housing could be assembled, disassembled and adapted much faster, which in turn puts into question modes of ownership, forms of domesticity and procurement. The possibility to disassemble, moreover, has important ecological implications, where building blocks can be continuously recycled into other buildings.

As a further outlook, building blocks could become 'smart bricks', integrating mechanical functionality such as the transfer of heat, air, water or electricity. These could then be continuously assembled into fully-functional buildings. Mechanical functionality then becomes emergent and decentralised. Ultimately, the aspects presented here are the easiest part of construction, most labour is consumed on the fit-out of technical devices. However, it's with this initial abstraction that automation begins. Without first redefining the syntax of how we build, any attempt to automate is futile.

References

Carpo, M. 2014. 'Breaking the Curve: Big Data and Design', *Artforum*, 52(6), pp. 168-173.

Claypool, M. 2019. 'Discrete Automation', *e-flux*, https://www.e-flux.com/architecture/becoming-digital/248060/discrete-automation/. (Accessed 5 October 2019)

Cheung, K. 2012. 'Digital Cellular Solids: Reconfigurable composite materials', PhD Thesis, MIT, Boston.

Gerschenfeld, N., Carney, M., Jenett, B. Calish, S. and Wilson, S. 2015. 'Macrofabrication with digital materials', *Architectural Design* 85(5), pp. 122-127.

Langford, W. 2019. 'Discrete Robotic Construction'. PhD Thesis, MIT, Boston.

McKinsey Global Institute. 2017. *Reinventing Construction: A Route to higher Productivity*, https://www.mckinsey.com/~/media/McKinsey/Industries/Capital%20Projects%20and%20Infrastructure/Our%20Insights/Reinventing%20construction%20through%20a%20productivity%20revolution/MGI-Reinventing-Construction-Executive-summary.ashx. (Accessed 5 October 2019)

Hiller, J. and Lipson, H. 2009. 'Design and analysis of digital materials for physical 3D voxel printing', *Rapid Prototyping Journal* 15(2), pp. 137-149.

Robeller, C., Helm, V., Thoma, A., Kohler, M., Gramazio, F. and Weinand, Y. 2017. 'Robotic Integral Attachment', in Menges, A., Sheil, B., Glynn, R. and Skavara, M. (eds), *Fabricate 2017: Rethinking Design and Construction*, London: UCL Press, pp. 92-97.

Morel, P. 2011. 'Sense and Sensibilia', *Architectural Design* 81(4), pp. 122-129.

Sanchez, J. 2018. 'Platforms for Architecture: Imperatives and Opportunities of Designing Online Networks for Design', in: Anzalone, P., Del Signore, M. and Wit, A. J. (eds), *ACADIA 2018: Recalibration on Imprecision and Infidelity – 38th Annual Conference of the Association for Computer Aided Design in Architecture*, 18-20 October 2018, Mexico City: ACADIA.

1

TOWARDS DISCRETE AUTOMATION

MOLLIE CLAYPOOL
THE BARTLETT SCHOOL OF ARCHITECTURE, UCL

'Discrete Automation' is presented here as a novel means to problematise existing contexts and prevailing social practices in architecture and construction around digitisation and automation in housing production, offering with it an alternative way of organising architectural production which utilises automation and digital production techniques and technologies. The Discrete – a 'new digital architecture' that emphasises part-to-whole relationships as described in the work of Gilles Retsin (Retsin, 2016; 2019) and others (Sanchez, 2017; 2019; Kohler, 2016) – is further articulated in design research developed with students of Architecture MArch Unit 19 and Architectural Design MArch Research Cluster 4 in the Design Computation Lab (DCL), directed by Mollie Claypool, Manuel Jimenez Garcia, Gilles Retsin and Vicente Soler at The Bartlett School of Architecture, UCL over the last several years.

The three projects – Semblr (Ivo Tedbury, Architecture MArch Unit 19, 2017), Chamfer (Alessandro Conning-Rowland, Architecture MArch Unit 19, 2018) and ALIS (Estefania Barrios, Joana Correia, Akhmet Khakimov, Evgenia Krassakopoulou, Kevin Saey, Architectural Design MArch Research Cluster 4, 2019) – are part of a multi-year research agenda around automation and

housing. As such, they are prototypes for the materialisation of Discrete Automation in housing production. Discrete Automation provides an alternative framework for building assembly utilising automated technologies such as industrial and modular robots, as well as a 'customisation-in-assembly' strategy for building parts that can anticipate changes in context over time.

Part-to-whole relationships customised in assembly enables a re-articulation of architecture's ontology away from a Modernist, deterministic and hierarchical ontology. In a Discrete ecology, the meaning and value of the relationships between different agents emerges through their appearance rather than through a top-down approach; as an accumulation of self-similar parts into heterogeneous assemblies. Retsin has argued that the Discrete 'asserts that a digital form of assembly, based on [discrete] parts that are as accessible and versatile as digital data, offers the greatest promise for a complex yet scalable, open-ended and distributed architecture' (Retsin, 2019). This suggests a new understanding of the ecology between things, where the relationship between individuals, society and nature (Kohler, 2016) should not be fixed or predetermined but can instead respond to changing requirements.

Automation takes the Discrete a step further, by articulating an approach that can deal with part-to-whole architectural relationships as well as how these relationships may change, using logics from automation in response to their contextualisation in society, in real time, across scales. Automation is not just a technical problem to be solved, but a much wider political framework (Frase, 2016; Winner, 1980). Automation is a mechanism for the distribution of power (Eubanks, 2018; Benjamin, 2019), and therefore an apparatus for the cross-scale coordination of resources in different contexts. It can also enable the questioning of the material hegemony of architectural production through revealing the inefficiencies of existing practices in design and construction. The three projects included here demonstrate the potential of Discrete Automation to enable a discussion about what building practices – from design to construction – could begin to look like when Discrete Automation is therefore both a form of architectural politics and a technique for digital production.

If automation is a design problem (Claypool et al., 2019), Discrete Automation must be inclusive to the politics of design. Problematising the wider socio-political status quo of architectural production in an age of automation forces questions such as: How do we automate already? Why should we automate? When should we automate? How should we automate? Automation is a platform where social and economic issues and questions can come together (Inglewood and Youngs, 2014) in order to be impactful in the reimagining of relationships of design, manufacturing, politics and space.

Problematising Architectural Production

As in all Design Computation Lab research, housing is chosen as it is the most highly politicised typology. This has been demonstrated in the work of sociologists Saskia Sassen (2012), Mary Pattilo (2013) and other writers (Srnicek and Williams, 2015) who show how the instrumentalisation of housing as a commodity, rather than a human right, is problematic. As Sassen has written, 'housing has become ... a financial instrument that has lengthened the distance between itself and the underlying asset (housing) to an extreme' (Sassen, 2012). This displacement of people and their needs over time away from the centre of any discussion around housing creates an asymmetrical relationship between housing production and people. It denies the recognition that evolving social practices are embedded in domestic environments (Colomina, 2006; Hester, 2017) and removes agency from those who inhabit domestic spaces to inform how these spaces are designed, constructed, used or changed.

Architecture, manufacturing and construction have been complicit in these asymmetries in power and production, amplifying the financialisation of the housing market with difficult and precarious labour models. (FLEX and Stride, 2018) Construction has also taken a very slow pace in terms of industry-wise digitisation, remaining one of the most analogue industries worldwide (Oesterreich and Teuteberg, 2016). Yet digitisation in other industries has provided more efficient and accessible pathways for these services and industries to reach more people, quickening processing time with ever-increasing computational power and surpassing human capacity in many forms of labour (Benjamin, 2019).

Digitisation in architectural production has largely remained in the virtual environment. 'Digital design' in the first digital turn enabled the reimagining of architectural form utilising computational techniques (Carpo, 2012; 2017), allowing both an emphasis on digital architecture's aesthetics as signified by 'blobitecture' (Lynn, 1998) as well as the notions of 'procedurality, flexibility, variability, correlation and interdependency' to be embedded in the digital design processes and operations (Poole and Shvartzberg, 2015).

The ability to produce many different variants of the same object efficiently was not translated to building practices. This disparity between how buildings are designed and how they are manufactured and assembled resulted in the extension of existing production chains to deal with the physical challenges and complexities of realising 'digital architecture'. This differs greatly in comparison to other industries from automobile manufacturing to agriculture and food manufacturing that have transformed their practices using automation.

When automation has been utilised in construction, it has oft resulted in task-specific robots for jobs such as bricklaying by Gramazio and Kohler Research, ETH Zurich with The Programmed Wall (2006) or companies such as Construction Robotics with the Semi-Autonomous Mason (2015). Task-specific robots effectively replace existing analogue forms of labour but do not negate the wider issues of coordination found on construction sites. While Japan and other Asian countries have made developments towards on-site construction reflecting the coordination found in factory settings with the notion of an 'integrated automated construction site' (Bock and Lagenberg, 2014), automation has oft been used to deal with problems within existing traditions in building delivery, eg. the development of design software such as building information modelling (BIM) and project management tools by addressing issues of

1. Automated assembly into a small house using mobile robots. Image: Ivo Tedbury, Semblr, Architecture MArch Unit 19/Design Computation Lab, UCL, 2017.

2. Aggregation glossary of space and parts. Image: Alessandro Conning-Rowland, Chamfer, Architecture MArch Unit 19/Design Computation Lab, UCL, 2018.

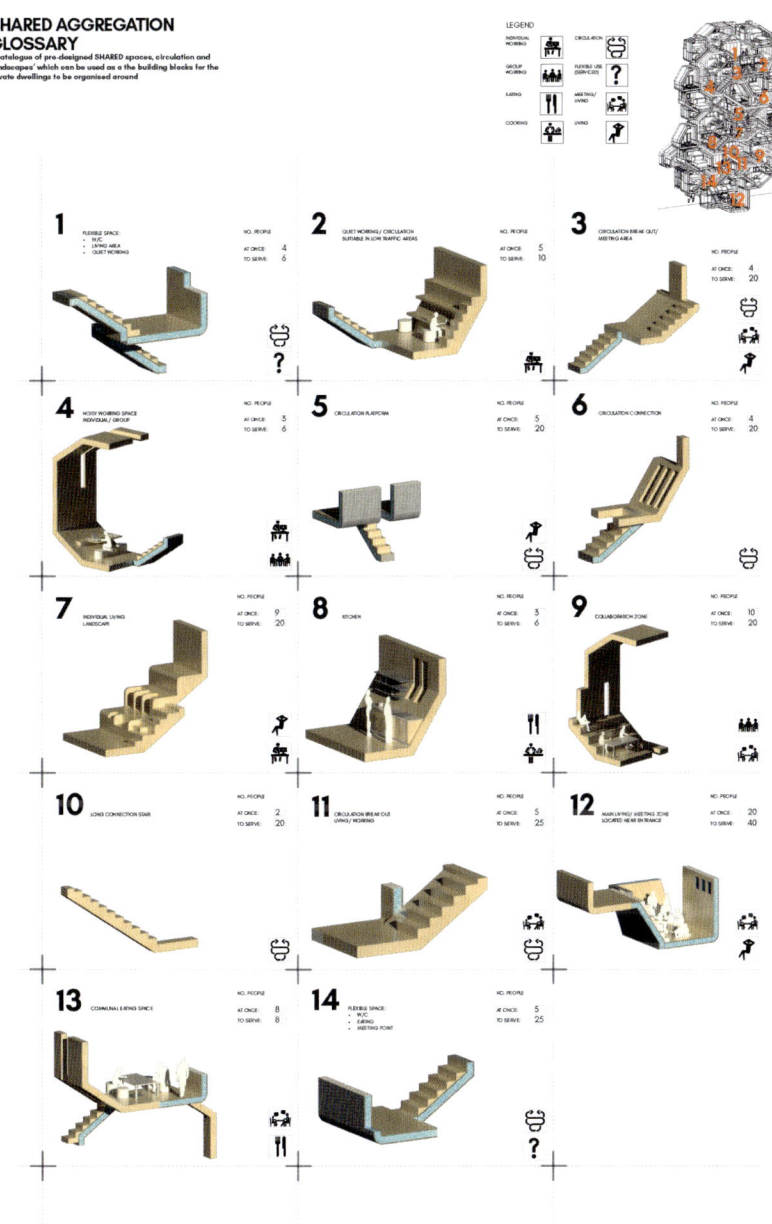

SHARED AGGREGATION GLOSSARY
A catalogue of pre-designed SHARED spaces, circulation and 'landscapes' which can be used as a the building blocks for the private dwellings to be organised around

communication, responsibility and oversight between project stakeholders.

It has been pointed out that automated construction must 'consider the need for customisation of an increasingly individual society, as well as the intrinsic conditions of architecture' (Bock and Lagenberg, 2014). This is increasingly important when universal or standardised building systems are inadequate in societies that need to adapt to changes in available resources. Captured in the work of all three Design Computation Lab projects included below, this problematising of the limitations of current strategies for digital design, digital fabrication and automation has proved a fertile ground for Discrete Automation.

Frameworks of Anticipation in Discrete Automation

Discrete Automation provides an opportunity to consider how changing social practices – in construction and in domesticity – can be reflected in housing production. To further this point, the notion of 'frameworks of anticipation' is useful in relationship to the Discrete, as anticipatory frameworks aim to meaningfully engage an extended group of agents in production processes. Anticipatory practices act in bundles that 'move between different spaces and translate expectations from the local to the global' (Alvial-Palavicino, 2016), ensuring scalability of practices.

In Design Computation Lab projects, anticipatory practices are embedded in several ways. Frameworks of anticipation are found in the ways in which the Discrete parts are bounded by social practices (eg. forms of labour or domestic use/function), manufacturing practices (eg. digital fabrication techniques) and assembly practices (eg. construction techniques). It is also considered in terms of the patterns of use and function built into each Discrete assembly. This is enabled by a framework of coordinated automation. Each anticipatory practice takes into account the expectations or boundaries of the other.

As has been argued by Retsin and others, the Discrete aids in streamlining production chains. Due to the self-similarity, seriality and repetition of each building part in a particular organisation, there is no need to lengthen production chains in order to achieve a wider variety of possible assemblies (Retsin, 2019). Discrete Automation takes this one step further, enabling customisation-in-assembly to anticipate possible change in a given assembly over time. This is different to 'customisation-in-fabrication' or 'customisation-in-design' as common to previous generations of digital designers (Carpo, 2017).

2

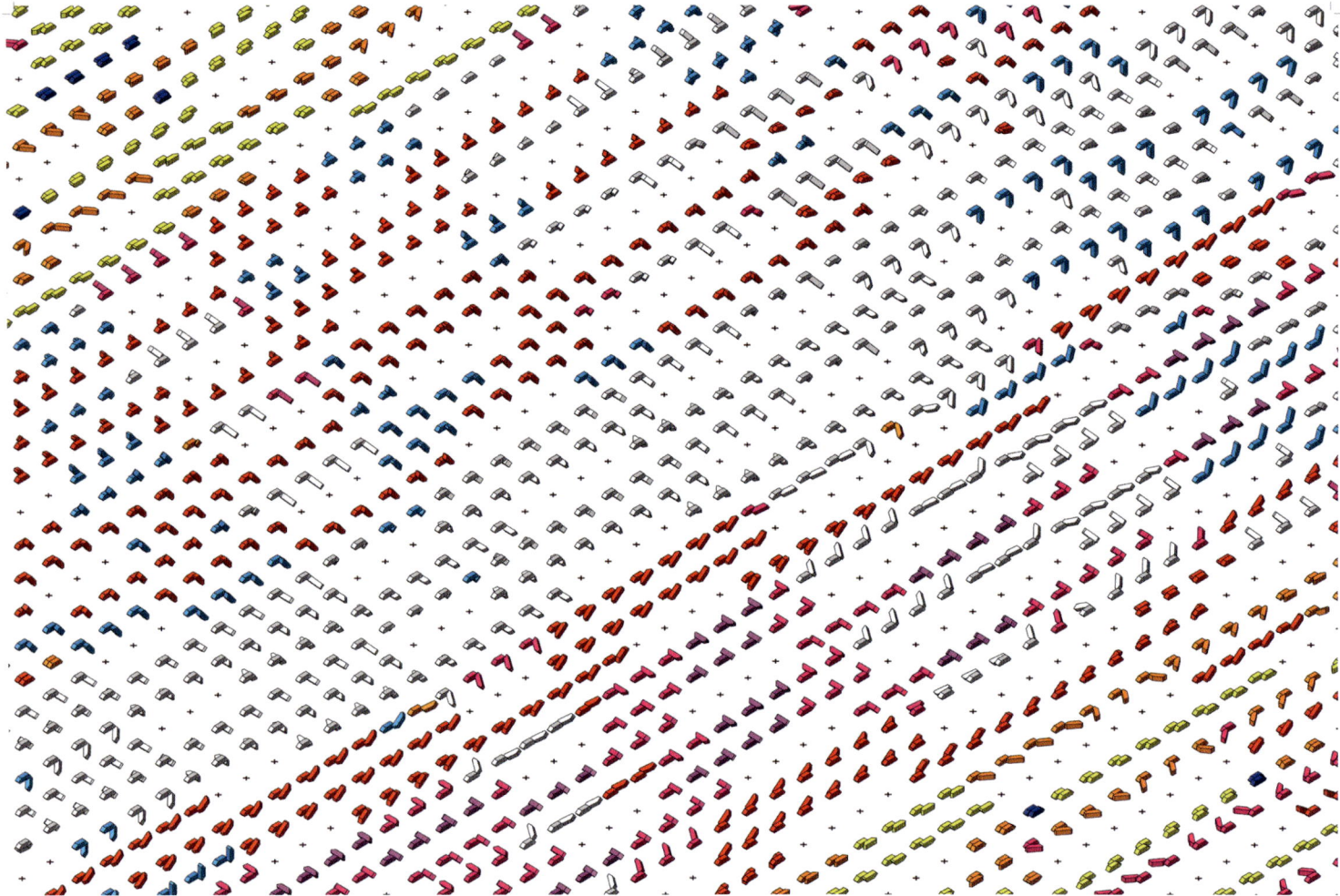

3

Discrete Automation also considers what is technologically possible now, in the contemporary moment, as well as what will be possible in the future due to further accessibility of technology (eg. Moore's Law), and more widely, due to increased computational and technological capacity and cost reduction. This anticipatory practice is embedded in the tectonic articulation of Discrete building parts as an assemblage of space, material and structure. But it is also articulated in the forms of labour used – analogue or automated or a combination of both – in each project. This takes into account a need to address issues of resistance and scepticism in construction and the wider public towards automation – eg. a fear of automated feudalism (Ford, 2015) – in the built environment. Discrete Automation aims to shift the Overton Window of what are acceptable possible uses for automation in digitising construction and prompting consultation on the new forms of labour that can be created using automation (Mean, White and Lasota, 2017).

The Implications of Discrete Tectonics

As Discrete architectural approaches for automated housing production, each of the three projects here – Semblr, Chamfer and ALIS – rethink basic building blocks of architecture from a fixed-function set of elements, eg. 'column', 'beam', 'staircase', 'slab'. This is done using an anticipatory framework for the re-articulation of architectural tectonics, materiality and scale. Each project uses an approach to automation that acts on the scale of manufacturing techniques and as a wider effort of coordination of analogue and digital labour.

A Discrete architectural tectonics reduces the number of thousands of building parts in a typical building to a few parts based on the concept of digital materials (Gershenfeld et al., 2015). In the case of Semblr (Fig. 1) and ALIS there is one part, and in Chamfer there are 4 different parts (Fig. 2). The parts are streamlined in their design for efficient manufacturing and assembly. Similar to WikiHouse (2011-) the bed of a computer-numerical control (CNC)-machine is used as the maximum boundary of material that can be used for each building part, but with the aim to reduce material waste to a minimum and tool calibration time as the same parts can be cut repeatably. A CNC-machine is a digital fabrication tool that is relatively accessible and can be made mobile as it fits in a standard Luton van. Sheet material – timber – is also chosen for each project as it is the best material for using with a CNC-machine for the efficient fabrication of serially repeated parts as it only requires a 2-axis tooling pattern. It is also a renewable resource. In the case of Chamfer, cardboard – an affordable, easy-to-manipulate and easy-to-manufacture material that can be made from recyclable materials – is also used to gain rigidity on the interior of each building part as the building parts are designed to be 'open' on one or two sides depending on the part. However, in Semblr and ALIS, the building parts are 'closed' on every side and sheet timber is only used to form the base of each building part.

In the case of each of the three projects, matrixes of possible building part combinations are created. These combinatoric matrices are constrained by building part geometry. In the case of Chamfer, a set of 4 different building parts are edited in width, depth and height to create sixteen different self-similar building part types. In Semblr, there is one building part – a polygonal volume (Fig. 3) that is rotated on its end surfaces – while in ALIS there is a rectangular volume (Fig. 4). These types are able to be combined in different ways to create a possible combinations matrix of one hundred possible different combinations. As demonstrated in Chamfer (Fig. 2), the matrix of tectonic possibilities is simultaneously evaluated for their potential as structural parts, service connections, spatiality – eg. for private spaces or shared spaces – and circulation spaces (Fig. 5) as well as how the parts can be used to create façades, roofs, walls and floors. In each project, parts can be combined according to different needs across buildings or sites, enabling customisation-in-assembly.

Automation and Labour

Automation here functions in several ways. In all three projects, digital fabrication technologies, such as CNC-machines, are used to produce the pieces that make up building parts. In the example of ALIS, industrial robots are used to assemble the pieces into building parts. Discrete Automation provides an alternative framework for building assembly utilising

3. Generated combinations of discrete parts. Image: Ivo Tedbury, Semblr, Architecture MArch Unit 19/ Design Computation Lab, UCL, 2017.

4. Detail of assembly of discrete parts. Image: Estefania Barrios, Joanna Correia, Akhmet Karkhimov, Evgenia Krassakopoulou, Kevin Saey, Automated Living System (ALIS), Architectural Design MArch, Design Computation Lab, UCL, 2019.

5. Interior view of shared spatial landscape of parts. Image: Alessandro Conning-Rowland, Chamfer, Architecture MArch Unit 19/ Design Computation Lab, UCL, 2018.

4

5

digital production technologies such as industrial and modular robots – as in Semblr and ALIS – for the automated fabrication and assembly of building parts, as well as a 'customisation-in-assembly' strategy of these building parts into demonstrators for housing that can change over time.

Key to Discrete Automation is the development of architectural parts which can be managed by human labour, as in Chamfer, or automated labour, as in Semblr and ALIS, anticipating future shifts towards the digitisation of construction on a wider scale. Parts are light, small and easier to handle. A single part can be made using digital fabrication technologies or conventional making tools like table saws, or assembled into parts using analogue labour (1-2 people) or automated labour (1-2 robots) (Fig. 6). On a larger scale, as in Semblr, parts can be constructed together into larger assemblies using analogue or digital labour such as mobile robots (Fig. 7), without the necessity for larger conventional construction machinery. Patterns of construction follow algorithmically-designed digital assembly logics, allowing for ease of access to parts in order to change, replace or remove them. This makes initial capital investment in housing have a much longer lifecycle, able to adapt and change without huge implications on the Discrete ecology of resources, labour and technology.

As such Discrete Automation presents an ecology for production in which architectural labour and spatial practices can be computed, and recomputed, and computed again and again without extending production chains. Discrete Automation does not project a post-anthropocene world without humans where technologies and spaces inhabit dark worlds entirely their own (Young, 2019). Architectural production for housing has great consequence to the wellbeing of many people. Thus, the material hegemony inherent to the architecture and construction disciplines need to be re-articulated. Discrete Automation is an approach that seeks to take the first step in developing a more critical, anticipatory and optimistic approach to the automation of architectural production.

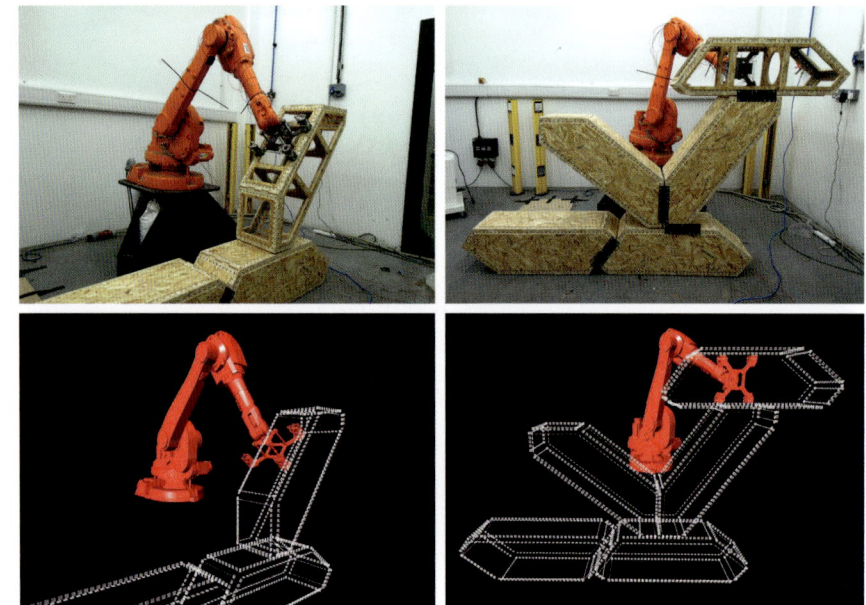

6

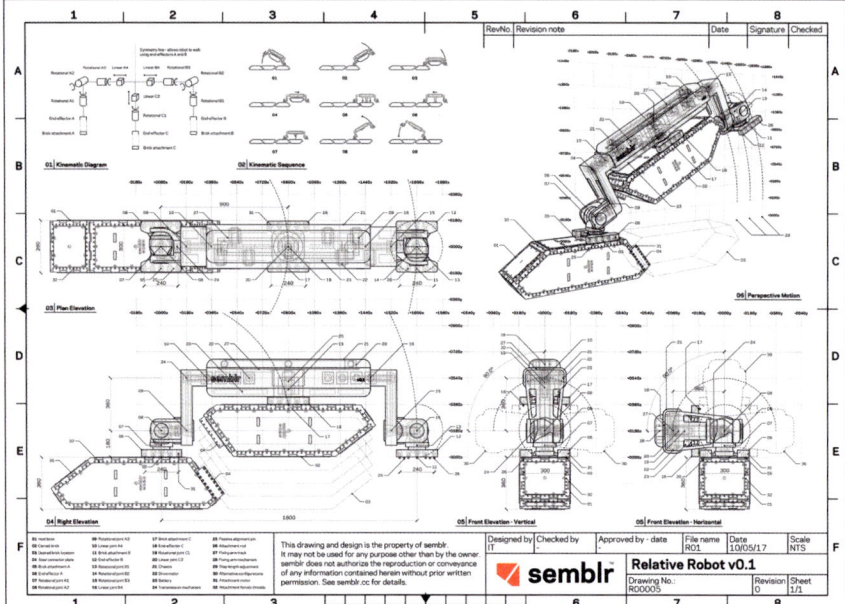

7

References

Alvial-Palavicino, C. 2018. 'The future as practice: A framework to understand anticipation in Science and Technology.' *TECNOSCIENZA Italian Journal of Science & Technology Studies*, 6(2). Open Journal Systems 2.4.2.0.

Retsin, G. (ed.) 2019. *Discrete: Reappraising the Digital in Architecture – Architectural Design Special Issue*, 89(2), Oxford: John Wiley & Sons.

Benjamin, R. 2019. *Race After Technology: Abolitionist Tools for the New Jim Code*. Cambridge, UK; Medford, MA: Polity Press.

Bock, T., Langenberg, S. 2014. 'Changing Building Sites: Industrialisation and Automation of the Building Process', in *Robots: Challenging Architecture at a Larger Scale – Architectural Design*: Special Issue, 84(3), Oxford: John Wiley & Sons, pp. 88-99.

Carpo, M. 2012. *The First Digital Turn: 1992-2012*. Oxford: John Wiley & Sons.

Carpo, M. 2017. *The Digital Turn: Design Beyond Intelligence*. London: MIT Press.

Claypool, M., Garcia, M., Soler, V. and Retsin, G. 2019. *Robotic Building: Architecture in the Age of Automation – Detail: Special Edition*. Munich: Detail Edition.

Colomina, B. 2006. *Domesticity at War*. Boston, Mass.: The MIT Press.

Eubanks, V. 2018. *Automating Inequality: How High-Tech Tools Profile, Police, and Punish the Poor*. New York: St Martin's Press.

FLEX & Stride, J. 2018. 'Shaky Foundations: Labour Exploitation in London's Construction Sector FLEX 2018', https://www.labourexploitation.org/publications/shaky-foundations-labour-exploitation-londons-construction-sector. (Accessed 10 August 2019)

Frase, P. 2016. *Four Futures: Life After Capitalism*. London: Verso.

Ford, M. 2015. *Rise of the Robots: Technology and the Threat of a Jobless Future*. Grand Haven, Mich: Brilliance Audio.

Hester, H. 2017. 'Promethean labors and domestic realism', *e-flux*, https://www.e-flux.com/architecture/artificial-labor/140680/promethean-labors-and-domestic-realism/. (Accessed 20 December 2019)

Inglewood, L. and Youngs, G. 2014. 'Designing the Digital Economy, a report by the Design Commission', 14 May 2014, https://www.designcouncil.org.uk/sites/default/files/asset/document/Design%20Commission%20report%20-%20Designing%20the%20Digital%20Revolution.pdf (Accessed 20 October 2019)

Gershenfeld, N., Carney, M., Jenett, B., Calisch, S. and Wilson, S. 2015. 'Macrofabrication with Digital Materials: Robotic Assembly', *Material Synthesis: Fusing the Physical and Computational – Architectural Design: Special Issue*, 85(5), Oxford: John Wiley & Sons, pp. 122-127.

Köhler, D. 2016. *The Mereological City*, Bielefeld: transcript Verlage.

Mean, M., White, C. and Lasota, E. 2017. 'We Can Make: Civic Innovation in Housing', https://kwmc.org.uk/projects/wecanmake/. [Accessed 15 September 2019]

Oesterreich, T.D. and Teuteberge, F. 2016. 'Understanding the implications of digitisation and automation in the context of Industry 4.0: A triangulation approach and elements of a research agenda for the construction industry', *Computers in Industry*, 83, pp. 121-139.

Pattillo, M. 2013. 'Housing: Commodity versus right', *Annual Review of Sociology*, 39, pp. 509-531.

Retsin, G. 2016. 'Discrete and Digital: A Discrete Paradigm for Design and Production', *TxA Emerging Design + Technology Proceedings*, 3-4 November 2016, Texas Society of Architects.

Retsin, G. 2019. 'Bits and Pieces', *Discrete: Reappraising the Digital in Architecture – Architectural Design*: Special Issue, 89(2), Oxford: John Wiley & Sons, pp. 38-45.

Poole, M. and Shvartzberg, M. 2015. 'Introduction', in *The Politics of Parametricism: Digital Technologies in Architecture*. London: Bloomsbury, pp. 1-18.

Sanchez, J. 2017. 'Combinatorial Commons: Social Remixing in a Sharing Economy.' *Autonomous Assembly: Designing for a New Era in Collective Intelligence, Architectural Design*: Special Issue, 87(4), Wiley & Sons, pp. 16-21.

Sanchez, J. 2019. 'Architecture for the Commons: Participatory Systems in an Age of Platforms', *Discrete: Reappraising the Digital in Architecture – Architectural Design*: Special Issue, 89(2), Oxford: John Wiley & Sons, pp. 22-29.

Sassen, S. 2012. 'Expanding the Terrain for Global Capital When Local Housing Becomes an Electronic Instrument', in Aalbers, M.B. (ed), *Subprime Cities: The Political Economy of Mortgage Markets*, Hoboken, NJ: Blackwell Publishing Ltd, pp. 74-96, http://www.saskiasassen.com/PDFs/publications/expanding-the-terrain-for-global-capital.pdf (Accessed 10 August 2019)

Srnicek, N., Williams, A. 2015. *Inventing the Future: Postcapitalism and a World Without Work*. London; New York: Verso.

Winner, L. 1980. 'Do Artifacts Have Politics?', *Modern Technology: Problem or Opportunity?: Daedalus*, 109(1), Boston, Mass: The MIT Press, pp. 121-136.

Young, L. 2019. 'Neo-Machine: Architecture Without People', *Machine Landscapes: Architectures of the Post-Anthropocene, Architectural Design*: Special Issue, 89(1), Oxford: Wiley & Sons, pp. 6-13.

6. Robotic assembly test using custom end-effector. Image: Ivo Tedbury, Semblr, Architecture MArch Unit 19/ Design Computation Lab, UCL, 2017.

7. Robotic schematic arrangement. Image: Ivo Tedbury, Semblr, Architecture MArch Unit 19/ Design Computation Lab, UCL, 2017.

HOUSE #05
INCREMENTAL CONSTRUCTION IN DIGITAL PRACTICE

PAUL LOH
UNIVERSITY OF MELBOURNE
DAVID LEGGETT
LLDS / POWER TO MAKE

House #05 explores the integration of custom moulds with a proprietary construction system for in-situ concrete casting (Fig. 2). The project foregrounds a design methodology that allows the fabrication procedure to drive the design process, primarily using tooling and construction procedures as agents to inform the architectural design.

The design methodology is made possible through the setup of LLDS's practice, where the architectural studio also fabricates building components. The project devises a unique digital workflow that incorporates feedback and evaluation of as-built information into the live design data to incrementally modify the fabrication information for construction. The aim is to overcome the challenges of integrating highly precise digitally-fabricated components to suit the on-site condition, specifically the interfaces between different work packages (Denari, 2012). The project asks: Can this very pragmatic desire allow digital fabrication to challenge the design through making?

In studying the making of tools in archelogy, Lambros Malafouris (2016) proposed that the prehistoric man makes tools, such as an axe head, without picturing the shape of the tool in the flint stone. Instead, the design of the axe head emerges through a continuous process of shaping the material to eventually produce a useful form that is fit for purpose. Every strike on the flint by the maker informs the following strike until the stone is incrementally shaped. It implies that design is a process that develops through the act of making and requires a positive feedback loop (Johnson, 2001).

House#05 adopts Malafouris's notion of material engagement into practice, whereby the making and digital fabrication techniques lead the design through a continual process. That is to say that the tooling and making procedure are deliberately privileged above other criteria to inform the design. Here, the project demonstrates a methodology of designing in which digital fabrication is much more akin to a traditional sense of craftmanship (Pye, 1968) where construction constraints and opportunities are fed back into the making procedure. The research asks: If tooling can inform the design process, then how can the construction procedure produce feedback that can also shape the design?

1

2

3

Context and Background

House#05 is a single dwelling situated in a narrow four-metre-wide leftover site in the inner suburbs of Melbourne, Australia. The house is conditioned by the existing terrace typology with two boundary walls. Responding to the lack of garden space for the dwelling, the roof of the house is conceived as an elevated 'plant pot', which is raised eight metres above the ground so that it receives natural daylight and is not overshadowed by neighbouring buildings. The void below the roof becomes the dwelling. The roof is supported by two concrete boundary walls that are anchored to the ground, forming a three-metre-deep concrete plinth. The plinth contains the most private spaces of the dwelling: the snug, bedrooms, utilities and bathrooms. In this project, digital fabrication is utilised across multiple packages of work. This paper will focus on the in-situ concrete package to examine the workflow of incremental construction.

LLDS has a unique setup. Alongside its architectural practice, it operates a 500m² micro-manufacturing workshop with a three-axis CNC router and a seven-axis robotic arm (Fig. 3). The parallel mode of making and designing allows for a fluid dialogue, from experimentation to the integration of research into construction workflow. It allows the practice to fabricate construction components and integrates them into a standard building contract for the project. The integration of digitally-fabricated components with a proprietary construction technique enables the practice to manage the level of complexity associated with the construction. It allows for a more natural adaption of such techniques by small-scale contractors that predominantly operate within the bespoke housing market in Australia.

Design Intent

The boundary of the terrace typology set up a condition where the parallel walls create a flutter echo effect in the open plan interior. To reduce the echo effect, the design intent is to texture the surfaces of the off-form concrete to scatter the sound (Brady and Olesen, 2010). While the effect is simulated in digital model using a ray-tracing methodology, the physical acoustic test has not yet been performed at the time of writing. The fair-faced concrete is exposed internally, providing thermal mass to regulate the environment, especially useful with Melbourne's extreme temperature changes.

To achieve the textured concrete, CNC-fabricated moulds are inserted into a proprietary formwork system. The pattern for the concrete formwork is produced by generating a series of parallel lines as toolpath in Grasshopper 3D, which is visually simulated in RhinoCAM. The tooling is performed on a polyisocyanurate (PIR) panel coated with a two-part polyurethane coating that forms a hard impact-resistant surface. The thickness varies depending on whether the mould is applied to the interior wall or external retaining wall. The coating provides a smooth and gloss finish to the cast as well as acting as a release agent. The PIR is re-used as insulation for the cavity wall and screeded floor.

LLDS partnered with an off-form concreter to develop the fabrication procedure. The off-form concreter proposed the use of the PERI™ DUO system – a modular formwork that does not require a crane and provides a self-supporting scaffolding system; the requirement for this was also partly driven by the tight site constraints. The design team integrated the associated procedural knowledge into

1. MDF mould of the vaulted soffit tightly fitted on site. Image: LLDS.

2. House #05 in-situ concrete soffit and wall using robotic milled formwork. Image: LLDS.

3. Robotic milling of House #05 building component and various prototypes. Image: LLDS.

4. Prototypes are used to assess buildability and milling time to reduce the cost of the mould. Image: LLDS.

5. Resulting pleated visual effect to the concrete wall. Image: LLDS.

6. Visualisation of the entire toolpath for the concrete mould for House #05. Image: LLDS.

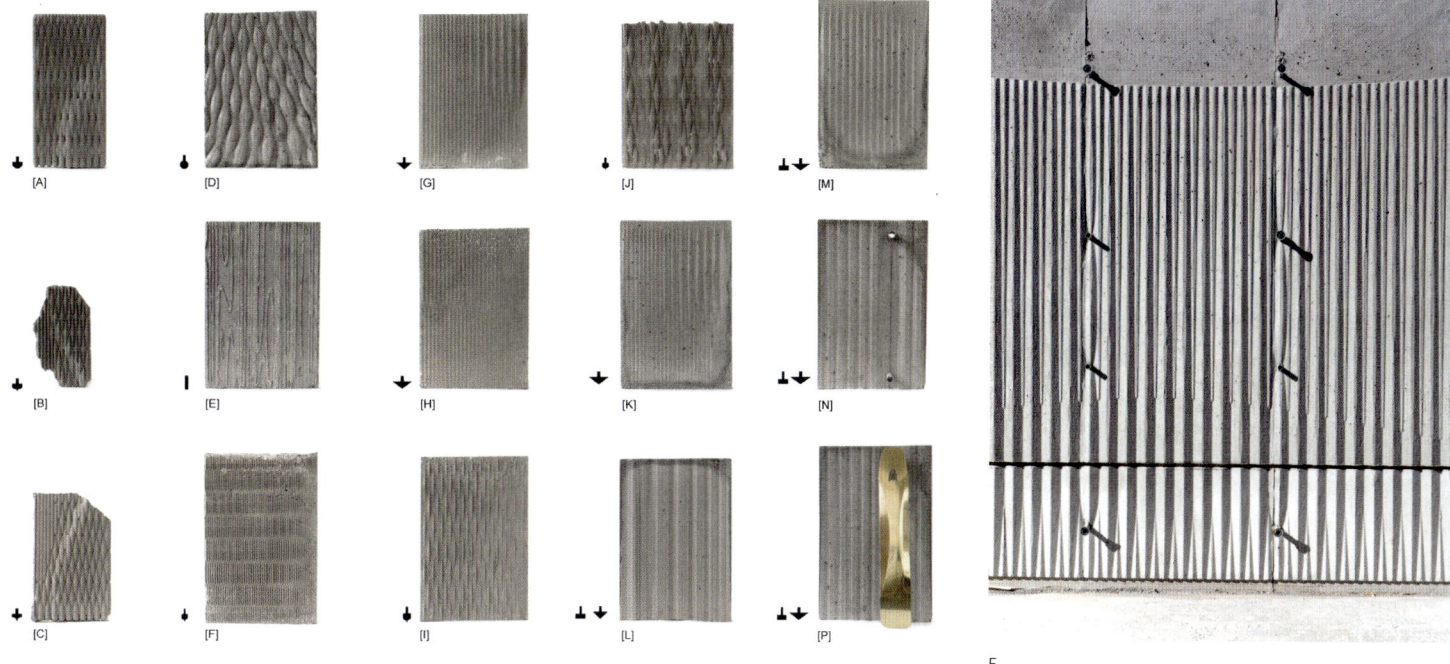

4

5

the design and production of the PIR mould, such as splitting the panels for site assembly, and the day joint associated with the pour sequence. The project used a self-compacting concrete by Holcim™ to avoid vibration which could otherwise damage the mould.

Designing Through Tooling

Prior to engaging with the concreter, the practice developed over 15 prototypes (Fig. 4). In the experiment, a standard concrete mix was used. The texture is based on a standard tool profile with variation to the depth of the toolpath. Early prototypes (Figs 4A–4J) explored the textural potential of the surface. The marking left by the tool produces depth to the surface. Of the tools tested, only a small portion proved to be feasible, as some formed undercuts which made the mould challenging to remove (Figs 4B & 4C). Some created an extrusion that was too fine and easily damaged when the mould was struck (Figs 4F–4I). The tool's profile, cut depth and width conditioned the pattern but at the same time provided a series of unique aesthetics that were useful for the design process. The resulting pleated pattern (Figs 4K, 4M, 4N) was developed based on an interference of two sets of toolpaths which produced variable pleating across the surface (Fig. 5).

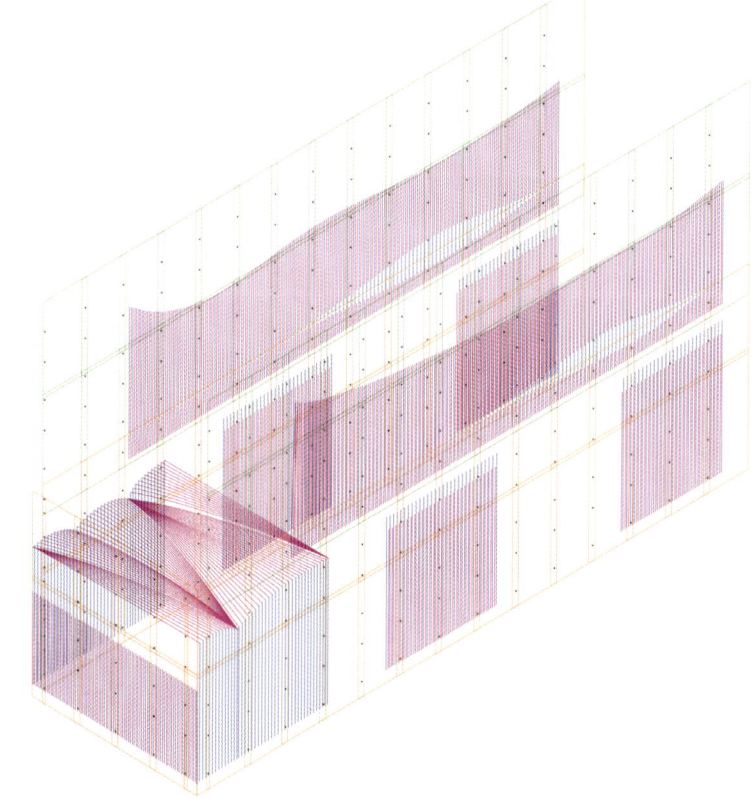

6

Tooling Geometry

To understand the constraints of the tooling, the toolpath was tested on several geometric scenarios. The linear motion of the toolpath produced an unresolved design when applied to a radial layout. However, the transition of depth works best when the linear toolpath is maintained, and variation in height is used to deliver a transverse or diagonal shift across the topography. This technique is applied to the concrete soffit. For the final iteration of the soffit design, the tool paths converge into a series of vaults. Figure 6 visualises the toolpath for the entire project for fabrication.

The vaulted soffit is a design response to the engineer's requirement to add two 300mm-deep down stand beams to take the load of the green roof. For the soffit, a medium-density fibreboard (MDF) mould coated with a high gloss polyurethane is used instead of the PIR, as the mould needs to support the weight of reinforcement bars prior to pouring the concrete. The mould is first milled using the three-axis CNC router and is finished with a final set of toolpaths using the Kuka KR120 robotic arm (Fig. 7). The two-step process helps reduce excessive waste, but critically allows the layer of MDF that makes up the mould to be screw-fixed from the underside. As each mould weighs up to 180kg, when the concreters strike the formwork, the mould is removed in layers from the underside to ensure the full weight does not collapse on the workers.

The fabrication workflow uses tooling and construction procedures to inform the design and deals with the practical demands of the mould. It integrates the constraints and opportunities of the proprietary system within a self-contained digital workflow (Fig. 8). Lessons learned from the various prototypes feedback into the detailing, such as the articulation around cast-in power sockets, and the alignment of the toolpath around the tie points and its interface at the joint line. The tie holes are plugged with brass plates which are sometimes used for handrails, coat hooks and picture hangers to support the inhabitation of the room.

Negotiating As-Built Tolerance to Construct Feedback

When the PIR mould panels were installed on-site, each being 4 metres tall and 0.9 metres wide, the main tolerance issue was caused by the proprietary modular formwork panels, which varied in width by up to +/- 1.5mm. This led to creep in the tie hole positions along the 13-metre long wall, resulting in misalignment with the corresponding holes within the PIR mould panels.

7

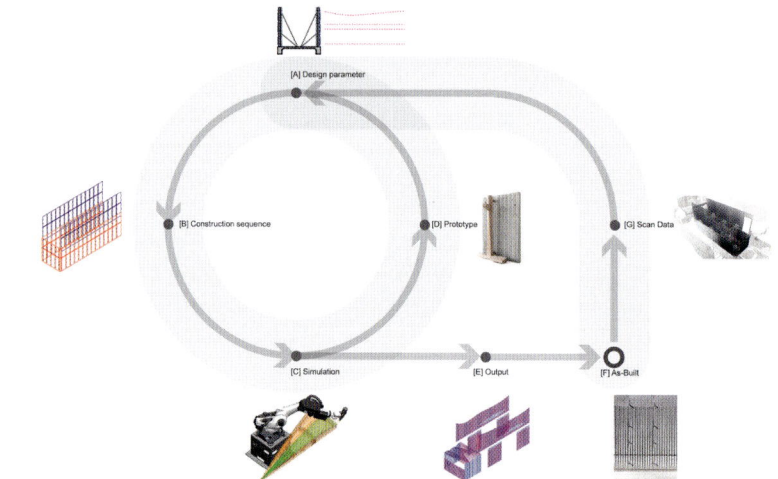

8

9

Following the first pour of the wall, the as-built information was captured using a high-resolution environment scanner. The point cloud model was aligned with the Rhino 3D model to re-evaluate the fabrication data. As the PIR panel had shifted along the length, the pattern and tie bars in the upper level were misaligned – in some areas by up to 10mm. As the tie bar position is the primary interface between the PIR and the formwork, only the holes and the vertices of the toolpath were re-aligned to allow the pattern to remain continuous (Fig. 9). The point cloud identified areas of discrepancy and error, such as edges where the vaulted soffit rests were found to be 5 to 10mm out of plumb. While this is within the tolerance of the concrete structure, it would cause the soffit mould to misalign and create large gaps between the mould (Fig. 1). The two-step milling procedure of the mould allowed the final geometry of the soffit to be adjusted and trimmed by the robotic arm to match the as-built geometry (Fig. 10).

Incremental Construction in Practice

In this project, LLDS put into practice a 'just-in-time' method of fabrication in which the fabrication data was aligned with the site information. The research highlighted the importance of looping in the as-built information as part of the file-to-production protocol. The use of fabrication information as a live data set to incrementally inform the design and construction also helps to avoid the contractor manually hacking precise components for them to fit on site.

The practice set-up and the partnership with the concreter provided a unique opportunity in this project to design, fabricate, construct, survey and readjust the fabrication data to account for site discrepancy. The two layers of feedback allow the practice to challenge the design through making. First, using iterative prototypes, both physical and digital, the tooling and making procedure informs the design process. Second, the scanned as-built data informs the fabrication process and allows the practice to be nimble in responding to site tolerance and error. These feedback loops are rare in construction as it's time-consuming and not often cost-efficient. However, the feedback processes create an agile workflow that begins to address the messy nature of on-site construction. The result is an incremental construction methodology that enabled LLDS to embed architectural detailing within the digital workflow, encoding craft into the algorithms.

7. Robotic milling of the soffit mould at LLDS workshop. The set-up of the practice allowed for an integrated workflow from design to production. Image: LLDS.

8. Digital workflow incorporating two layers of feedback to the final design. Image: Paul Loh.

9. Point cloud scan of the as-built data overlay with the machine toolpaths. Image: Paul Loh.

10. The concrete soffit after striking. Image: LLDS.

10

Acknowledgements

Architects: LLDS – Paul Loh, David Leggett and Yuanye Huang
Concrete Structural Engineer: Bollinger + Grohmann Ingenieure – Sascha Bohnenberger and Bernhard Waschl
Off-form Concreter: Roniak Construction – Nick Angelopoulos
Formwork Fabricator: Power to Make

References

Brady, P. and Olesen, T. 2010. 'Integrating Sound Scattering Measurements in the Design of Complex Architectural Surfaces: Informing a parametric design strategy with acoustic measurements from rapid prototype scale models', in *FUTURE CITIES, 28th eCAADe Conference Proceedings.* Zurich: ETH Zurich, pp. 481–491.

Denari, N. 2012. 'Precise form for an imprecise world.', in Marble, S. (ed.) *Digital Workflows in Architecture.* Basel: Birkhäuser, pp. 28–43.

Johnson, S. 2001. *Emergence: The connected lives of ants, brains, cities, and software.* New York: Scribner.

Malafouris, L. 2016. *How Things Shape the Mind.* Cambridge, MA: The MIT Press.

Pye, D. 1968. *The Nature & Art of Workmanship.* Chippenham, UK: A & C Black.

CONCRETE CHOREOGRAPHY
PREFABRICATION OF 3D-PRINTED COLUMNS

ANA ANTON / PATRICK BEDARF / ANGELA YOO / BENJAMIN DILLENBURGER
DIGITAL BUILDING TECHNOLOGIES, ETH ZURICH
LEX REITER / TIMOTHY WANGLER / ROBERT J. FLATT
PHYSICAL CHEMISTRY OF BUILDING MATERIALS, ETH ZURICH

This paper introduces the cutting-edge 3D Concrete Printing (3DCP) process which stands at the core of the project *Concrete Choreography*, a family of nine prefabricated concrete columns. By simultaneously overseeing technological development, computational design and robotic fabrication, an interdisciplinary research team was able to reframe the challenge of large-scale high-resolution 3DCP.

The prefabricated columns set the stage for the summer season of the Origen Festival of Culture, held annually in the awe-inspiring alpine setting of Riom, Switzerland (Fig. 1). Design and fabrication of the columns was formulated as a studio course brief for the Master of Advanced Studies in Architecture and Digital Fabrication at ETH Zurich (ETHZ). Framing the latest research in 3DCP within the context of the performing arts, the project liberated design thinking from conventional concreting techniques and fostered an holistic approach to the conception and realisation of a novel, multi-layered material system.

Towards an Additive Materiality

Due to their rich formal and cultural history, columns were the perfect archetypical testing ground for computational design tailored to innovative fabrication. The research investigated the characteristics of a new concrete column typology emerging from properties of 3DCP. While previous work in the field of generative design has focused on the procedural articulation of form (Hansmeyer and Dillenburger, 2013), Concrete Choreography merged design and fabrication methods. The main research aim of this project was to demonstrate the remarkable architectural qualities achievable through 3DCP, but impossible with any other printing method or conventional casting technique.

A key objective was to deliver fine print resolution as a result of high production speed, process stability and robustness. The specific fast-setting 3DCP process using a low yield stress mortar developed at ETHZ pushes the limits of conventional prefabrication of structural elements. Another objective was to investigate the extrusion layer as a design instrument for high-resolution and multi-scalar material articulation. The column typology fulfilled the geometric criteria to test the fast, vertical build-up rate of the fabrication method, demonstrating the targeted qualities along significant element heights. It also provided the opportunity to assess the robustness of the recently developed 3DCP

1

prefabrication platform. The challenge was to find out whether new formal expressions and material qualities could be produced by directly 3D printing exposed concrete elements without the need of post-processing.

A New Context for Building with Concrete

Aiming to reduce the ecological footprint of concrete (Orra et al., 2019), digital fabrication explores ways to decrease the amount of concrete used and to remove the additional work sequences or unnecessary materials used in temporary scaffolds and formworks. This inherently challenges the rationalisation and serialisation dogmas at the core of the economic motivation to reuse the formwork, and thereby limiting the design space. In this effort, 3DCP provides an opportunity to build lean structural elements by placing concrete only where needed (Khoshnevis, 2004). Combining the ecological advantages of no-waste constructions with shape customisation of digitisation, mould-less shaping of concrete shifts the focus of concrete research from formwork production to controlling the properties of fresh paste during its transition to cured concrete. Thus, the transition from indirect – formwork-based manufacturing – to direct fabrication of 3D printed components triggers a radical paradigm shift in concrete technology.

Intense competition to materialise the first 3D printed house has shaped the 3DCP start-up scene (Labonnote et al., 2016). Succeeding in the development of a substantial body of work, the majority of house prototypes focused on simple, low-resolution elements which materialised in somewhat modest architectural products, both in terms of spatial quality and engineering ambition. In order to achieve the promised efficiency of additive manufacturing in construction, designers must free themselves from conventional serialised production and investigate differentiation as a method of performance optimisation. Although the many economic and environmental benefits of 3DCP inevitably lead to its quick adoption in industry, the process can achieve much more than simply inheriting the approaches and aesthetics of conventional concreting. To realise the full architectural potential of 3DCP, research in method-specific explorations is essential. In support of the freeform concept, a fabrication-driven classification of 3DCP building systems was proposed by Duballet. This marks a necessary step forward to create a comprehensive catalogue of possible fabrication strategies that encourage geometric explorations in 3DCP (Duballet et al., 2017).

The challenges in delivering high-quality objects and spaces are motivated by an almost exclusive focus on material and process development rather than on design methods. When it comes to building tall elements quickly and without process interruptions, a set on-demand material strategy, introduced for 3DCP by Gosselin et al. in 2016, proves to be the most promising approach to date. Hydration control of cementitious materials or setting on-demand is the method on which these processes rely in most cases (Reiter et al., 2018).

Two successful examples of 3DCP developed to industrial standards are the Sika 3D-printing technology (Liard et al., 2019) and the BauMinator from Baumit (Karaivanov et al., 2019). Both systems use set on-demand material processing and deliver robust fabrication at fast printing speeds. However, the proprietary nature of these technologies largely limits explorations in material formulation and processing. Even if the issue of material deposition were solved using a process that controls cement hydration, 3DCP poses immense challenges regarding structural integrity, reinforcement and durability (Wangler et al., 2019). Such challenges are more easily addressed if tackled in an open-source prefabrication set-up.

Research Focus

Relying on the aesthetics of cast concrete, the majority of realised large-scale 3DCP constructions contextualise the need for design methods more suited for the new fabrication process. Targeting a meaningful materialisation of layered extrusion processes, several research questions sharpened the project focus. 3DCP should successfully balance hardware specifications, print resolution, print speed and strength capacity of fresh mortar paste. Defining a process-specific set of parameters quantitatively describes the geometric affordances of the fabrication technique. Hence, the research asked: what was the set of parameters which define the fabrication space of 3DCP?

Fast production of on-demand, materially-efficient and geometrically-complex architectural elements are some of the obvious advantages that can increase the quality of concrete products. The geometric freedom provided by 3D printing enabled the inclusion of internal features, facilitating a high degree of functional integration, such as space for reinforcement, alignment details, lighting channels and rainwater drainage. Site-specific customisation and porous interiors, as well as surface ornamentation, contribute to a novel design language for concrete prefabrication. Therefore, the research investigated how design space for the column typology could be enhanced by 3DCP.

Research and Prototyping

The proposed research methodology materialised in experiments that mapped out fabrication space and design space with the aim of identifying quantitative and qualitative architectural principles for 3DCP. Prototyping started with specimens investigating material and fabrication limits. The resulting parameter set informed a custom computational design tool allowing an early evaluation of print feasibility, fast design iterations and immediate output of fabrication instructions.

Fabrication Space: Quantitative Parameters

All columns were entirely prefabricated at the Robotic Fabrication Lab (RFL) of the ETHZ, using one ABB IRB 4600 industrial robot mounted on a Güdel three-axis gantry system (Fig. 6). The print-tool was mounted at a 45° orientation on the sixth robot axis to reach the component height without changing the robot working configuration during printing. In this setup, the robot could print multiple 3.2-metre-high artefacts, aligned to the Y axis of the gantry. Production was executed in automatic mode to ensure safety at necessary print-speed. In automatic mode, a laser-fence enclosed the production area separating it from the material handling and control areas. Columns were printed next to each other and moved outside the safety enclosure 24 hours after printing.

In accordance to prefabrication setup affordances, each column geometry was discretised into 540 printable cross-sections at a layer-height of 5mm. This resulted in approximately 250,000 robot-targets per column, more

data than the RFL ABB IRC5 controller could store as an executable file. This questioned the feasibility of printing large objects at high resolutions. The realisation of the project benefited from COMPAS FAB (Rust et al., 2019) and an ABB communication library developed by Fleischmann et al. for the RFL. This custom software continuously streamed online data directly to the robot controller at a sufficient data transfer rate for the required print speed. This communication system simplified the workflow by eliminating the necessity to split the file into modules and procedures. Since every process interruption translates to imperfections in the column structure, real-time communication allowed the printing of one column in a continuous process.

A robotic end-effector was specifically developed for the set on-demand 3DCP process in a collaboration between the chairs of Digital Building Technologies and Physical Chemistry of Building Materials at ETHZ. Through this tool, it is possible to initiate concrete strength build-up, resulting in vertical building speeds of up to 3000mm/hour. As an example, a hollow cylindrical column of 300mm diameter and 1000mm height was built in just 20 minutes. The concrete mix consisted of calcareous sand with an ordinary Portland cement-based binder containing 15% limestone and 8% microsilica substitution, at a water-to-powder ratio of 0.4. Superplasticiser and a viscosity modifier were dosed to get proper printing rheology, and a retarder extended the open time. The retarded concrete was pumped to the mixing reactor of the print tool where a calcium aluminate cement activator was intermixed just before extrusion, initiating the strength build-up. The activator was dosed as a suspension at

2

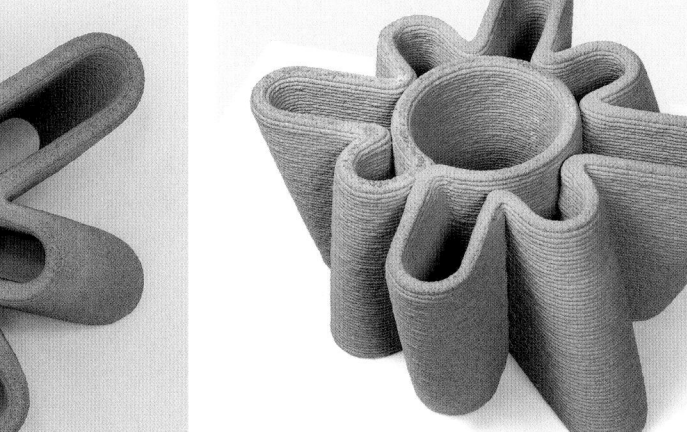

1. Concrete Choreography at The Origen Festival of Culture. Photo: Benjamin Hofer.

2. Overhang capacity: print tests show the maximum overhangs for good quality printing between [-20; 20] degrees Photo: Axel Crettenand.

approximately 2% of the amount of Portland cement. Progressive cavity pumps, numerically controlled through the robot interface, delivered concrete and accelerator to the mixing reactor.

A particularity of this mortar is its initial low-yield stress. In geometric terms, the mortar fluidity limits the overhang capacity. The maximum overhang angle was experimentally determined: a central cylinder supported truncated cones that alternate interior and exterior inclinations at angles between 5° and 20°, in 5° angle increments (Fig. 2). Only those cones with an angle too big for the overhang would collapse, thus indicating the expected range of possible overhangs. This experiment essentially contains all elements of the column typology: a vertical cylindrical core that supports the overhanging outer surface.

Design Space: Qualitative Parameters

Two procedural computational design engines based on trigonometric functions and mesh subdivision were developed and utilised in the design process (Anton et al., 2019) (Figs 3, 4). Features like macro-porosity, self-intersecting print-paths and gradual overhangs exemplify the versatility and significant aesthetic potential of 3DCP when employed in large-scale concrete structures. For instance, features of the column could be distinguished by whether a print-path was self-avoiding or self-intersecting.

Each column was designed as a double shell composition with structural internal bracing. The outer shell dimensions ranged from 250 to 600mm with a highly differentiated ornamental exterior, whereas the inner shell, housing a cavity for traditional reinforced concrete, was kept as rational as possible for increased stability (Fig. 5). Within each layer, these shells were connected by minimal print-paths. Consequently, this internal bracing structurally supported the adjacent shell layers of freshly printed material and increased the achievable overhang for the column geometry, as well as providing a closed core for partial concrete casting.

Trigonometric functions were also used to drive print-path deviations creating material-driven ornamentation. This procedural ornament was calibrated at the limit of material stability from layer to layer. The characteristic dripping behaviour of concrete became a powerful design tool, helping to subvert the horizontal layer aesthetics. This feature was used selectively and to dramatic effect at the base and capital of the columns to emphasise their ornamental purpose and to distinguish them from the shaft (Fig. 9).

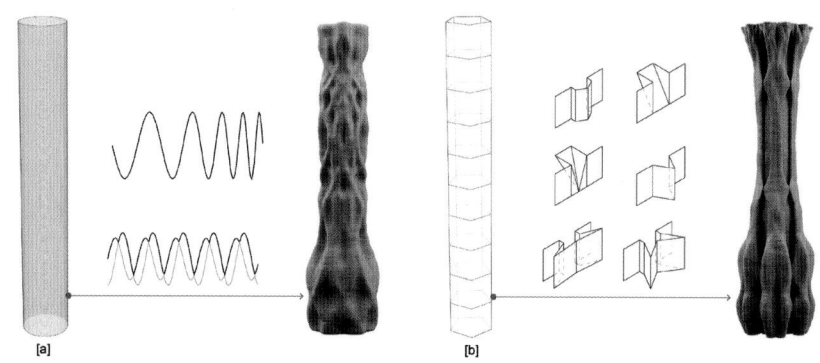

3

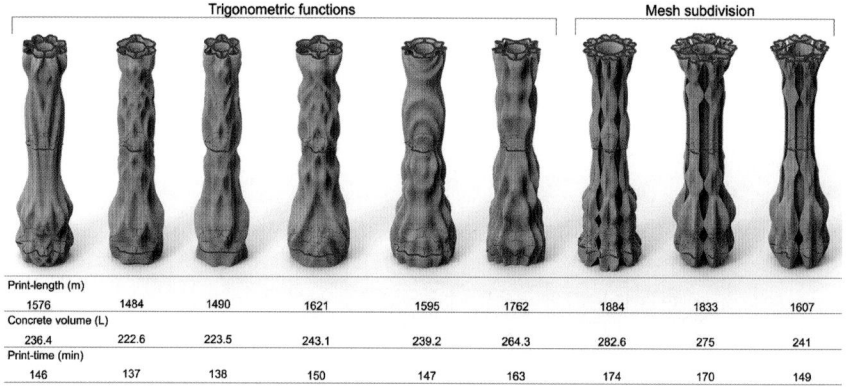

4

Print-length (m)								
1576	1484	1490	1621	1595	1762	1884	1833	1607
Concrete volume (L)								
236.4	222.6	223.5	243.1	239.2	264.3	282.6	275	241
Print-time (min)								
146	137	138	150	147	163	174	170	149

3. Design engines:
(a) trigonometric functions;
(b) mesh subdivision.

4. Fabrication metrics for the nine columns.

5. Printed geometries exhibit hollow structures enabled by 3D printing. Photo: Keerthana Udaykumar.

6. Fabrication set up. Photo: Axel Crettenand.

5

6

Designing for 3DCP questions if accurate geometric representation is indeed needed for the generation of precise fabrication instructions. As demonstrated by the high accuracy with which surface ornaments emerge solely from print-path manipulation, the fabrication technique affords the creation of complex surfaces previously only achievable with extremely complex moulds or as a result of elaborate craftsmanship. This represents a research turning point: from designing the variation in geometry generation to mastering variation in the fabrication process.

Successful Prefabrication of Nine Columns

The resulting nine, individually designed, 2.7-metre-tall columns were delivered in just ten weeks. Four weeks were dedicated to design and prototyping, followed by five weeks of fabrication and design development. During the final week of the project, concrete cores were cast and the columns were transported to site.

Transportation and site conditions influenced the structural requirements for the prefabricated columns. Situated in an alpine village at an altitude of 1,257m, the columns were subject to significant wind-induced dynamic loads. First, a reinforced concrete foundation – 1.20 x 1.20 x 0.2m – provided a base for the column printed on top. To ensure the robustness of the base to column connection, a vertical rebar cage was inserted through the hollow cavities of the inner shell and base. Next, fresh concrete was cast into the reinforced core making the ensemble monolithic and ready for transportation only 24 hours later. Using a central hook attached to the rebar cage, each column could be lifted into position on site with a crane. Lastly, the timber deck and lighting were executed in-situ by a local carpenter (Figs 7, 8, 1).

Filament cross-section of 25mm x 5mm and print-speed of 180mm/s were the characteristic fabrication metrics. For a column fabricated to Concrete Choreography project specifications, these translated to an effective print-time of 2.5 hours per column.

A column was considered fully fabricated once the targeted 2.7 metre-height was reached, if the rebar cage could be inserted, and if visual inspection revealed no major defects. From a total of twelve columns printed at full height over a period of five weeks, nine became part of the final installation. Thus, the 3DCP process registered a success rate of 75%, calculated for the fabrication period and excluding prototyping. An early evaluation of the 3DCP also led to the conclusion that efficiency and process stability increased with every printing iteration.

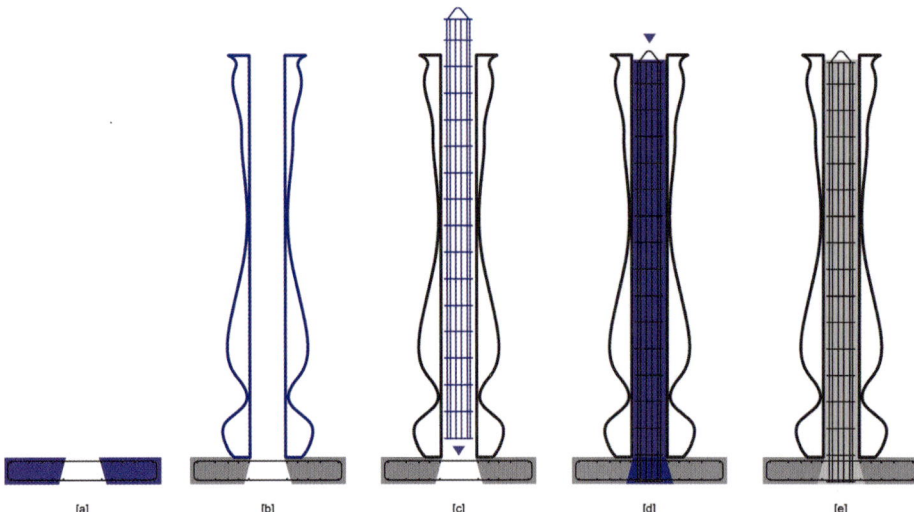

[a]   [b]   [c]   [d]   [e]

7

From Shaped to Shaping

The research environment at ETHZ is proof that interdisciplinary collaboration in the field of digital fabrication can immediately yield tangible results. In just eighteen months, researchers developed a viable 3DCP system that included material formulation and processing as well as computational design and robotic fabrication. Furthermore, as an immediate step to nurture this open and collaborative mindset, research was disseminated into education culminating in the realisation of Concrete Choreography.

The project literally provides a set design. What differentiates it within the tradition of stage design is precisely the permanence of its construction material. The manifest decision to work with a structural building material is based on the hypothesis that for the first time, concrete is as easily directed and formable as, for example, plaster or foam. In addition, the performing arts context exposed the general public to new ways of building with and experiencing concrete. Digitisation no longer exclusively belongs to the exact sciences; its social impact is equally relevant in shaping a digital building culture validated by the end-user.

Within the emerging field of large-scale on-demand 3DCP, the project sets a new standard for high-quality architectural building elements. The shift in perception of concrete as an inert material and passive recipient of form – through formwork – towards directly organising the material into the final artefact allows for an unprecedented geometric richness and material articulation. This research extends previous work in the field through specifically designing for a layer-based material system which addresses multiple scales: from complexity of overall form, to structural integrity during build-up and high resolution surface textures. Thus, architects may claim responsibility for designing the entire printed element, not only a component's boundary representation. The fabrication-driven project also showcases an upscaling strategy for 3DCP. Since fabrication data results directly from the design process, intermediate steps like construction drawings are no longer required. The designer/fabricator thus gains valuable time to invest in design development. In less than a day from design completion, the 1:1 concrete column is prefabricated and ready to be manipulated, consequently elevating the fabrication technology from rapid-prototyping to direct-fabrication. The successful completion of the project, integrating computation and fabrication, showcases the shifting roles and responsibilities of the designer/fabricator as demonstrated by the short process chain. Moreover, the quality of execution, level of detailing and high printing speeds exemplify the contribution of automated 3DCP to digital concrete.

To conclude, the presented project not only proves transformative from an ecological and economical perspective, but demonstrates that a design-oriented approach to concrete printing research can yield spectacular results that challenge building convention. This approach is necessary to realise the full architectural potential of 3DCP in its adoption to industry.

7. Fabrication and reinforcement sequence: (a) reinforced concrete base with central hole detail; (b) direct 3DCP of a double shell column; (c) vertical reinforcement cage insertion; (d) central core casting; (e) final column.

8. Transportation: loading the columns from ETH Zurich. Photo: Benjamin Hofer.

9. Details: (a), (b), (d), (f) material ornament – print-path distortion using trigonometric functions; (b), (d) macro-porosity; (c) seam resulted from self-intersecting print-path; (a), (d), (f) gradual overhangs. Photo: Sofia Michopoulou.

8

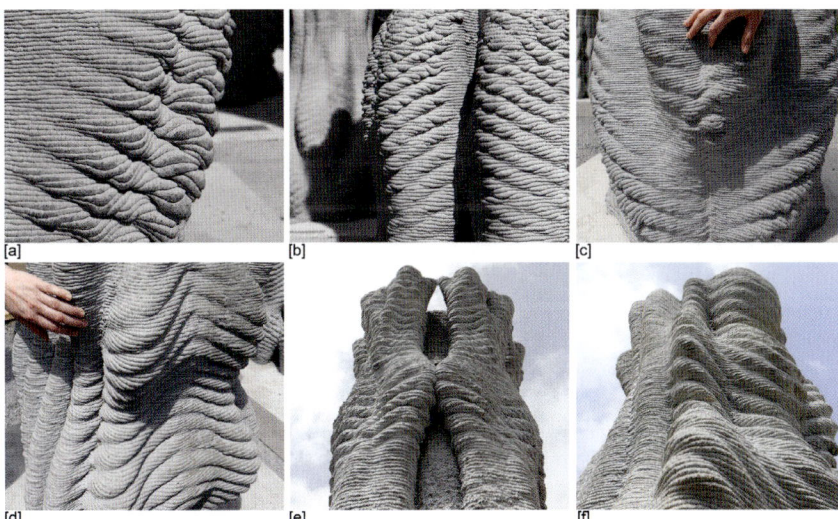

[a] [b] [c]

[d] [e] [f]

9

Acknowledgements

This research was supported by the NCCR Digital Fabrication, funded by the Swiss National Science Foundation (NCCR Digital Fabrication Agreement #51NF40-141853).

We recognise the commitment and passion of our students from the MAS D-fab, ETH Zurich 2018/2019 as well as the support from The Origen Foundation and in particular that of Giovanni Netzer. We acknowledge the contribution of Philippe Fleischmann et al. (RFL) to the development of the custom ABB communication library used in the robotic fabrication process. Our sincere gratitude goes to Michael Lyrenmann, Tobias Hartmann (RFL), Heinz Richner and Andreas Reusser (Concrete Lab) for the knowledge invested in the realisation of Concrete Choreography.

References

Anton, A., Yoo, A., Bedarf, P., Reiter, L., Wangler, T. and Dillenburger, B. 2019. 'Vertical Modulations: Computational design for concrete 3D printed columns', *ACADIA 2019 – Ubiquity and Autonomy* conference proceedings, Austin Texas.

Duballet, R., Baverel, O. and Dirrenberger, J. 2017. 'Classification of building systems for concrete 3D printing', *Automation in Construction*, 83, pp. 247-258.

Gosselin, C., Duballet, R., Roux, P., Gaudillière, N., Dirrenberger, J. and Morel, P. 2016. 'Large-scale 3D printing of ultra-high performance concrete – a new processing route for architects and builders', *Materials and Design*, 100, pp.102-109.

Hansmeyer, M. and Dillenburger, B. 2013. 'Mesh Grammars: Procedural Articulation of Form', *Open Systems: Proceedings of the 18th International Conference on Computer-Aided Architectural Design Research in Asia (CAADRIA 2013)*, pp. 821-82.

Khoshnevis, B. 2004. 'Automated Construction by Contour Crafting: Related Robotics and Information Technologies', *Automation in Construction*, (13), pp. 5-19.

Karaivanov, A., Balog, O., Weissmann, P., Steinbrecher, B., Materna, H. and Baumit Beteiligungen Gmbh [AT]. 2019. 'Nozzle for Concrete, Mortar Or Similar And Its Use'. EP3431172 (A1).

Labonnote, N., Rønnquist, A., Manum, B. and Rüther, P. 2016. 'Additive construction: state-of-the-art, challenges and opportunities', *Automation in Construction* (72), pp. 347-366.

Liard, M, Lootens, D., Schumacher, M. and Sika Tech AG [CH]. 2019. 'Method for the 3D-printing of Mineral Binder Compositions'. WO2019030255 (A1).

Orra, J., Drewnioka, M. P., Walker, I., Ibell, T., Copping, A. and Emmitt. S. 2019. 'Minimising Energy in Construction: Practitioners' Views on Material Efficiency', in *Resources, Conservation & Recycling* (140), pp. 125-136.

Reiter, L., Wangler, T., Roussel, N. and Flatt, R.J. 2018. 'The role of early age structural build-up in digital fabrication with concrete.' *Cement and Concrete Research*, 112, pp. 86-95.

Rust, R., Casas, G., Parascho, S., Jenny, D., Dörfler, K., Helmreich, M. and Gandia, A. 2018. 'Gramazio Kohler Research'. *COMPAS FAB*. https://github.com/compas-dev/compas_fab [accessed 23 December 2019].

Wangler, T., Roussel, N., Bos, F. P., Salet, T. and Flatt, R. J. 2019. 'Digital Concrete: A Review', *Cement and Concrete Research*, 123, pp. 2-17.

LITTLE ISLAND
SCULPTURAL STRUCTURE THROUGH DIGITAL DESIGN AND FABRICATION

YONG-WOOK JO / DAVID FARNSWORTH / JACOB WIEST
ARUP
ROSARIO GALLO
ACCESS ANVIL / SCOTT SYSTEM

Project Introduction and Challenges

Project Vision

Little Island is an artificial island that is being built on the Hudson River, west of Manhattan, to provide a unique park experience for the New York public. It will be owned and maintained by the public agency, Hudson River Park Trust, and be operated by Little Island, a special organisation established for the park.

Over the years, Hudson River Park Trust has successfully renovated old piers into public parks, recreational facilities or office and retail complexes. Little Island, a completely new structure on the river, will revitalise this section of Hudson River Park with almost three acres of new public park space featuring lush greenery and a diverse array of world-class arts, educational and community programming (Little Island, 2019).

Under the overall design management by the prime consultant Mathews Nielsen Landscape Architect and in collaboration with the U.K.-based designer Heatherwick Studio, Arup was selected to realise the project vision for most engineering and consulting disciplines. Standard Architects is the executive architect.

Fort Miller Company (FMC) is the precast concrete manufacturer; Tymetal, a sister company of FMC, is the steel fabricator; and Access Anvil / Scott System, another sister company of FMC, is the foam formwork fabricator and smooth formliner manufacturer.

Design Features and Challenges

The signature design of Little Island, featuring irregular, unique and complex undevelopable curved surfaces with few repetitions, sets it apart from other pier structures, but also imposes the most significant challenges for design, documentation, fabrication and erection. The geometry was not possible or practical to convey via conventional 2D documentation, so the team adopted an open approach to 3D modelling where we quickly realised that the only way to ensure geometry of construction would align on site would be a common design and construction model with the use of direct-to-manufacturing digital fabrication techniques for all the complex geometry elements.

Design

Architecturally Exposed Structural Precast Concrete Structure

Construction on the Hudson causes challenges because

of the marine environment which typically push designs towards prefabrication to remove the need for falsework. Pier construction generally consists of piles placed in the river bed, topped with precast pile caps and planks, and tied together with a cast-in-place concrete slab. These constraints made precast the right choice for this project, and the architect desired to use structural precast elements that would be exposed with architectural quality finishes. The precast technology would need to push past current convention to meet this vision. Also, a unique structural system has been proposed which is structurally effective, constructible and, at the same time, visually intriguing.

Pots

The deck structure consists of a unique module called 'Pots', tulip-shaped assembly of precast concrete elements. Typically, a pot is 4.5m tall and approximately 37m² on plan area. A pot is supported by a 900mm diameter cylinder pile.

Each pot is composed of four to six 'petals', with thickened side struts and bottom edge beams, that sit on a central 'column head'. The column head seamlessly transitions from the pot's bulbous curved shape to the cylindrical pile geometry. The centre of the column head acts as a vertical support for planks and 'star beams' above, which span radially from the centre to the pot corners. Petal interiors typically transition from sloped to vertical moving away from the column head. Stainless steel embedded plates and welded external plates connect the petals to each other and the column head.

Pot Geometry Generation

The outside surface geometry of the pot is generated by the architect through a parametric script. Base rules of geometry are defined through discussions between architect and engineer to balance complexity with architectural vision. For example, the petal outer surface generally has a one-way curved surface except edges where it rolls up to make the petal joint smooth, so the

2

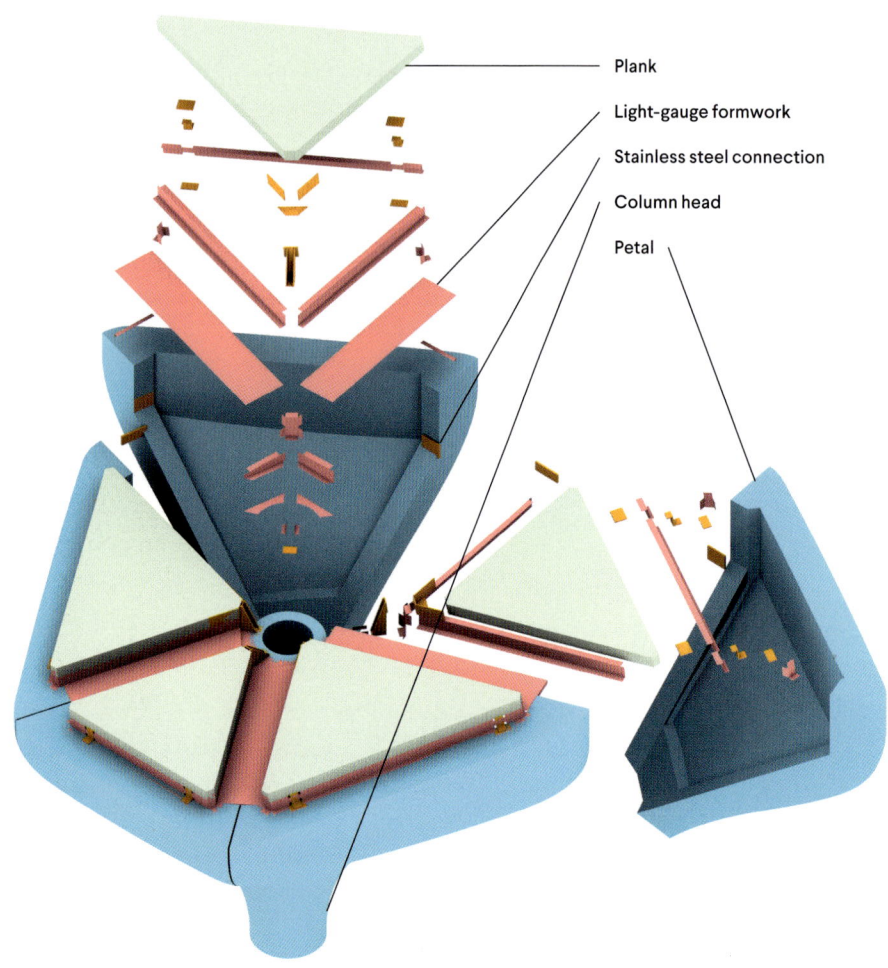

Plank

Light-gauge formwork

Stainless steel connection

Column head

Petal

1. Pier 55 during Construction. Photo: Timothy Schenck.

2. Exploded view of a 'Pot'.

3. Detailed 3D rebar model.

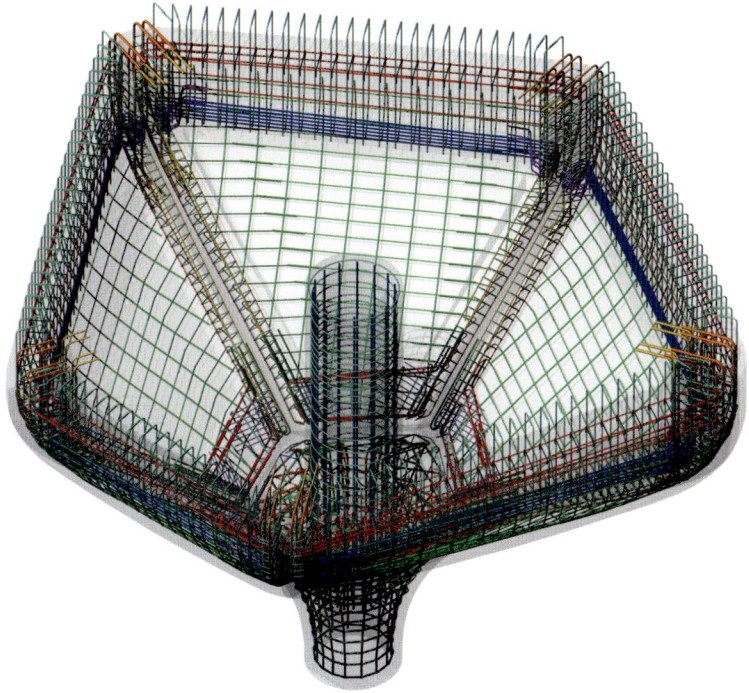

horizontal rebars can be straight with splicing edge bars that are hooked and anchored in the cages of the strut bars. Internal surfaces are generated by Arup using another set of parametric algorithms added to the architect's scripts to meet the required structural criteria and are geometrically simple to facilitate the conventional formwork fabrication for the interior surfaces. The joint between the column head and the petals is also defined making sure the connection using steel plates is feasible and the drainage of incidental water inside the pot is considered.

Rationalisation
Although the overall layout and the plan shape of pots follow a specific pentagon pattern called the Cairo-Pentagon, fitting them into an overall square plan with relatively straight edges and providing varying elevations across the top surface resulted in many different pot shapes. 39 different pot types resulted in 39 column head forms and 192 unique curved petal forms used to generate 132 pots and 656 petals. The curved exterior faces at the bottom portion of the pot are typical within pot types and the elevation variation required to meet the topography of the pier are achieved through pouring varying height 'extension walls'. So, while each pot and each petal

are unique, repetition of formwork was possible to a great extent. A few very special and complex pot types, particularly in areas over the southern access way and near the amphitheatre, are only used once.

Structural Analysis Model Generation
On top of the scripts that generated pot geometries, another set of algorithms is added to generate a highly-detailed analysis model in GSA, needed to design the rebar for all precast elements as well as connection plates and embeds. All design elements are explicitly modelled and custom final member design post-processing tools were created to calculate the required rebars, steel plate sizes, and the number of studs, using model force outputs directly and quickly to generate the results.

Stainless Steel Connections and Light-Gauge Sheet Metal Formwork Geometry Generation
Pot precast elements feature seven distinct connection types with multiple instances of each type based upon petal and plank geometry. This resulted in an average of 35 pieces that may have unique set-out, unique geometry, and unique plate size and weld prep definitions, dependent upon overall pot geometry and loading. Over 15,000 plates are defined and set-out parametrically. The light-gauge sheet metal formwork features 12 distinct elements to form the star beam elements. Slab geometry, which drives plank and star beam geometry, is essentially unique across all pots resulting in over 7,700 elements in total that are defined and set-out parametrically. The light-gauge includes bolt hole locations and cut-outs to avoid conflict with the steel connections.

Rebar Detailing Model Generation
Also generated in 3D using parametric scripts are the rebar models for petals and column heads. A completely detailed model includes all information needed for cutting and bending, including the clear cover, development and splice length, bending radius, etc. This was the major enabler for the realisation of the complex precast elements.

Deliverables in 3D
All surfaces of precast elements, exact shape and dimensions of stainless steel components, bent shape of light gauge stay-in-place formwork steel, and rebars in the complex petals and column heads are completely generated by the scripts with little manual adjustment. The resulting Rhino models, both the 'as-in-place' format in which all components are in their final locations in 3D, and the 'arrayed' format in which all components are laid out on a 2D surface, are provided to the precast and steel fabrication contractors with full geometry for use in shop drawing production and final fabrication.

4

5

Coordination in 3D Environment

All design team members worked in 3D using either Rhino or other BIM software, and coordinated trades in 3D as well. A Navisworks model was created by importing each team member's 3D components for coordination, clash detection and for contractor's information and reference.

Fabrication

Digital Fabrication

The fabrication team implemented new production processes to accommodate the 3D delivery of the construction documents in order to produce the complex geometric shapes. In an environment where tape measures, people, wood and steel are the norm, the utilisation of CAD/CAM technology, automatic equipment and script writing was a very novel concept that had to be implemented in order to fabricate the unique shapes within tolerance, work within a budget and meet the timeline of the project.

Fabrication Challenges

The doubly curved surfaces of the unique shapes presented the most significant challenge on the project. For the formwork, traditional mediums like wood and steel do not bend in doubly curved directions, urethane formliner lead times exceeded 48 months, carpentry requirements far exceeded current capacity and the formwork construction could not be quality controlled. Through the implementation of CAD/CAM subtractive manufacturing techniques in a production sequence, fabrication methodologies were created to build the formwork. The process included reverse engineering

of the models and scripts generated during the design process for digital input of the geometry within CAD software to create the negative shape. Once created, the parts underwent a digital design process.

Model to as Built

The employment of digital fabrication for formwork production of complex architectural shapes allowed us to bridge the gap between architectural concept and the built environment. To build the formwork for curved concrete elements, CAD/CAM subtractive manufacturing techniques, utilisation of foam and polyurethane as new production mediums, and the employment of automatic equipment in a production sequence were the only means for fabrication. Large foam billets were cut on a CNC wire cutter into profiles to maximise yield of material and to fit within the parameters of the CNC five-axis milling machine. Once cut, some assembly and prep work to the foam was required prior to placement on the CNC router.

Programming Methods

The engineering process included utilising CAM software programming to direct and control the CNC cutting sequence and part verification software to ensure part fabrication feasibility prior to reaching the CNC machine. Prior to the part making it on to the machine, the fabrication team built a program that verified the toolpath developed by the engineer. The program provided data about the tool path and verified planned production run times for the team to utilise when planning a production schedule. In addition to building a production schedule, the program provided other information to the team allowing them to run parts through the night without supervision.

4. Applying coating to milled foam formwork.

5. Rebar placement on formwork actual.

6. Access Anvil's Concrete Form Post Coating. Photo: Timothy Schenck

7. The Fort Miller Company's Production Line Assembling Rebar on the Concrete Form. Photo: Timothy Schenck.

6

7

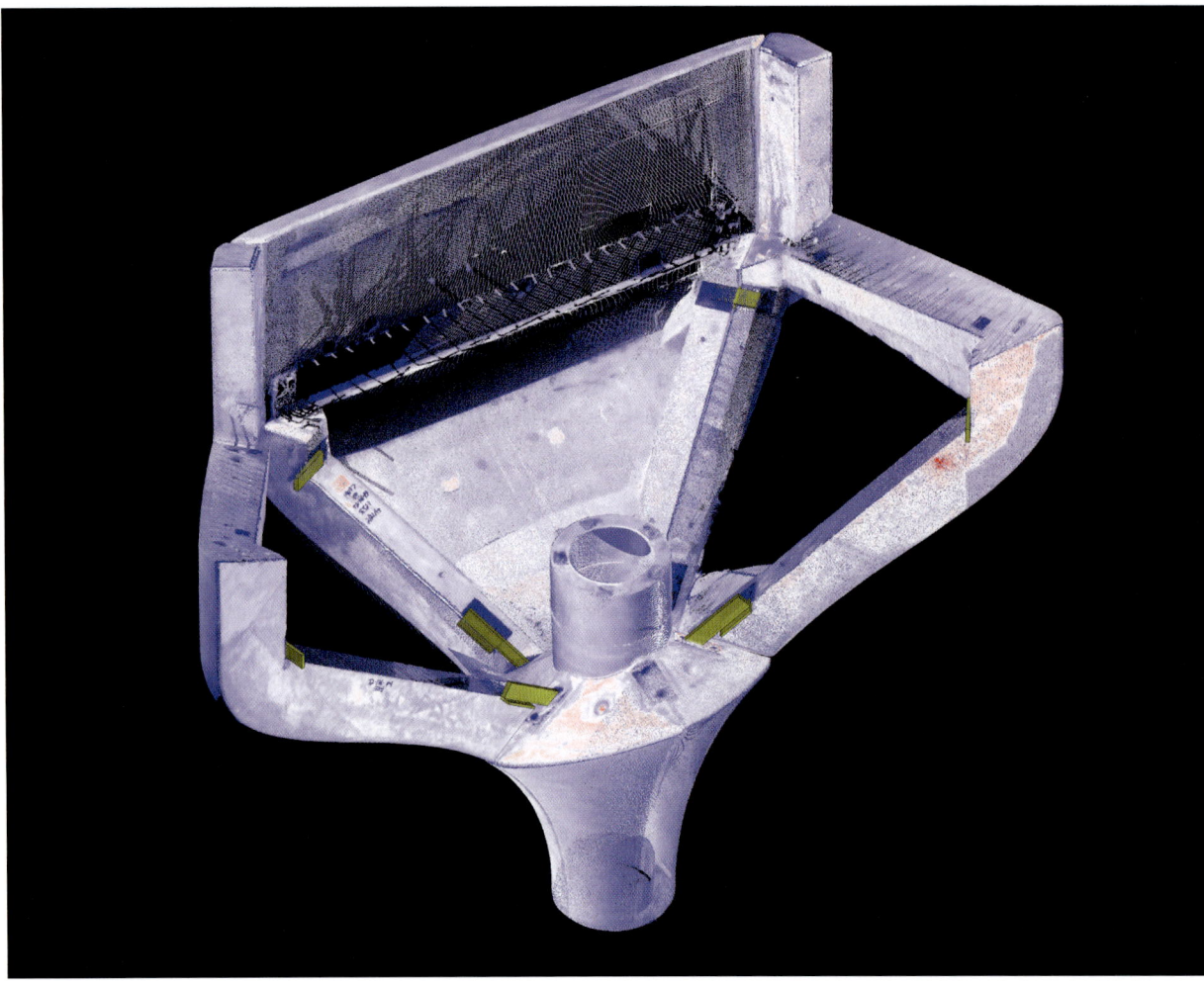

8

New Surface Treatment

After the parts were milled and assembled, the surface aesthetic was applied. Traditional products such as architectural grade plywood or formliners are utilised to achieve the concrete finishes on various construction projects. Due to the nature of the shapes and long lead times, a new method had to be implemented on a large scale that allowed the team to turn forms over quickly, achieve a surface aesthetic required by the design team, and be used repeatedly for design economy. A high pressure polyurethane product was applied to the foam that met all of the design criteria.

Automation of Shop Drawings Generation

The development of the form was the first challenge to overcome for the fabrication team, and the challenges continued to pressure traditional construction methods. Parametric programming software allowed the team to address other issues associated with the construction of the concrete shapes. The custom programs and scripts generated by parametric programs automated the process of creating 2D cross sections and views from 3D models of each pot to be used in the development of precast concrete shop drawings. Tables were developed for each rebar used in the production process from the 3D scripts that were generated from the design team's scripts. The net effect of the scripts to produce shop drawings significantly reduced the amount of engineering time to develop 2D drawings manually for production. Data from the scripts had to be translated in an understandable way for the manufacturing purposes. The use of custom programs converted the massive amounts of data into readable .txt and .csv files for manufacturing.

Digital Information Transfer

Manual methods of digital information transfer were not feasible. Equipment acquired had to speak the same language relative to the 3D models. The fabricators relied

8. Virtual assembly of 3D scanned precast elements.

9. Pier 55 during Construction. Photo: Timothy Schenck.

9

heavily on the tolerances of the CNC equipment to mill the forms, automatically bend the rebar and laser-cut the various embed plates connecting petal to petal within a pot and unique steel geometry for stay-in-place formwork to hold the pots together. The sharing of information and connectivity between three different companies allowed the fabrication team to trust and verify each part was built to tolerance, would fit in its location and be set as needed, a unique communication experience.

Quality Control Using Digital Tools
The quality control procedures also relied on digital processes. Since the architectural shapes were undulating and not orthogonal, we digitally scanned the as-built part, downloaded the scan into CAD software and overlaid the scan on the 3D model to verify the results of the part compared to the 3D model. The process provided a sense of tolerance control and further verification of the process.

Construction

Assembly
All concrete and steel components fabricated at Fort Miller Company and Access Anvil were transported by lorry the one-hour drive to the assembly site at Port of Coeymans on the Hudson river edge. A total of eight assembly stations were set up by the marine contractor to

meet the tight schedule. Completely assembled pots were placed into the hopper barge that could store a maximum of four pots. A total of four barges operated in turns for delivery of the assembled pots to the project site.

Site Erection
Pots arrived at the site in the barge and were dragged by tug boat to be erected by a floating crane on to piles. A well-planned erection procedure meant one pot was erected in a few hours.

Topping Slab
Finally, the cast-in-place topping slab was poured to tie all the pots and the flat pier together and create a monolithic, highly indeterminate moment-frame pier structure.

Conclusion

Little Island is a ground-breaking departure from conventional pier construction and utilises the latest advances in digital design and fabrication technology to successfully deliver a structure that is both functional and playfully sculptural at the same time. The major challenge of generating, engineering, communicating and fabricating the complex geometry was overcome with intensive use of parametric scripts, automation and digital data communication in the design phase, and the use of milled foam formwork and bending rebar using a detailed 3D model in the fabrication phase. The collaboration between all parties to deliver this project was critical in achieving a successful outcome for future generations to enjoy. When complete, Little Island will be a new icon of the west side, and a visible reminder of what can be achieved when the conventional scoping boundaries of contractors and designers are blurred and project participants come ready to collaborate.

Acknowledgements

The authors are thankful for the opportunity to participate in the design and fabrication of this unique and challenging project in New York City, and the collaboration with exceptionally talented clients, designers and contractors.

References

Little Island. 2019. https://littleisland.org. (Accessed 23 December 2019)

GSA. 2019. Oasys software, https://www.oasys-software.com/products/structural/gsa/. (Accessed 23 December 2019)

Navisworks. 2019. *Autodesk* https://www.autodesk.com/products/navisworks/overview. (Accessed 23 December 2019)

McNeel, R. & Associates. 2019. *Rhinoceros, 3D computer graphics and CAD software*, https://www.rhino3d.com. (Accessed 23 December 2019)

HUDSON YARDS VESSEL, NEW YORK

EDOARDO TIBUZZI / JEG DUDLEY
AKT II
PABLO ZAMORANO / PETER ROMVARI
HEATHERWICK STUDIO

Heatherwick Studio was invited to design a public centrepiece for Hudson Yards, a new district built above a working rail yard on Manhattan's West side. This is a short depiction of the journey the studio embarked on and the collaboration with structural engineering firm AKT II to design a three-dimensional, explorable space through the vehicle of simple steps.

Human Interaction as Generator of Form

Climbing the Vessel is a unique experience. Composed of 2,500 steps, 154 flights, 80 landings and 16 storeys, the new public centrepiece for Hudson Yards is a new public centrepiece for Hudson Yards is designed to lift people up and offer views across the Hudson River, Manhattan, and of other visitors. As a centrepiece to a new development, the design team wanted to create something that visitors might be able to touch and use, not just to look at. Drawing inspiration from the ancient stepwells of India the aim was to create an experience at a human scale, in a location that is surrounded by tall towers. The focus on a human level was maintained throughout the design and the fabrication process.

Geometric Principles

The footprint of the Vessel is small (15m diameter) and it gets wider as the stairs climb upward (46m diameter at the top). This gesture minimises the space it takes away from the urban realm and maximises the space it creates above, while also seeking to create a memorable silhouette and a new public attraction in the area. There is a sequence of exploration, from the intimate entrance to the ascending journey as the space expands upwards.

From a pure geometric point of view, the Vessel is a lattice of ramps and landings forming a monolithic rigid diagrid of a structure. This is characterised by inner and outer hoops of ramps connecting two levels of landings in a vertical zigzagging pattern. An interlayer is generated by the shifting of the inner and outer hoops of ramps towards each other, creating a structural overlap. This interlayer constitutes the primary vertical support to the Vessel, and the inner and outer hoops of ramps act as rigid tie rings contributing to its lateral stiffness.

Towards the base of the structure the depth of the ramps and landings increase, offering an enhanced strength and stiffness, while towards the top these reduce to minimise

1

weight. This structural diagrid is wrapped into the shape of a large cup geometrically resolved into a vertical spine element.

Simple Strategies into Complex Form

The aim was to create a place that inspires discovery while using simple strategies to make the project viable, both in terms of design and fabrication. Early in the design process an attempt was made to make the platform size similar on all levels. The smaller lower rings held fewer platforms than the bigger higher ones. This brought the challenge of gradually reducing the number of platforms and resulted in a loss of symmetry. In the end, the team found that a platform size that grows with the shape can add to the interest of the project and, as such, the same number of platforms can be achieved on every level. The new approach allowed the form to be considered as a single segment that is mirrored and repeated around the circumference. This ensured the design team could focus on designing a perfect segment rather than spreading their effort across myriad elements. The resulting symmetry is also visually more appealing and

2

1. Full scale mock-up at the Cimolai yard, prior to shipping to US. © Heatherwick Studio

2. Example of an Indian stepwell. © Wym Arys.

3. The evolution of Vessel from 2D to 3D. © AKT II.

4. Vessel, a new centrepiece for Manhattan's Hudson Yards. © Evelyn Akhmerov.

3

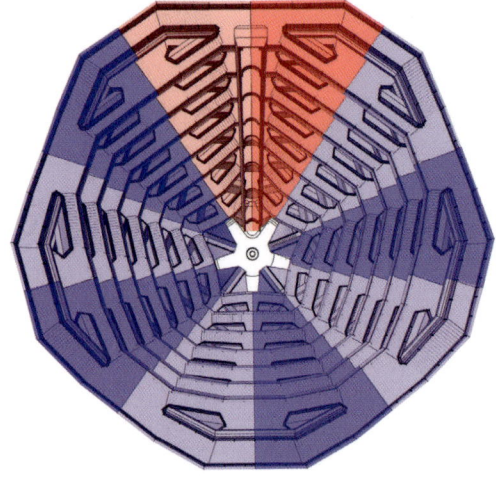

5

6

communicates the design idea more clearly.
One segment is used as a symmetrical spine that
hosts the elevator, using inclusive design to enrich
the design ambitions and to bring geometrical clarity.

Geometry as Enabler of Performance

The top-heavy configuration of the geometry makes
the project inherently wobbly – imagine a wine glass
perched on its stem without the wide base. Additionally,
the zigzagging staircases cause the structure to effectively
behave like a giant spring – 'lively' in engineers'
terminology. The combined force of all the visitors
walking on the steps – whose movements sometimes
could be synchronised to a live band – cause vibrations
to travel through the structure. It was clear from the
beginning that brute force wouldn't resolve the structure;
geometry and new digital techniques would have to be
combined to resolve an elegant solution.

Design Process Based on Human Experience

The design process involved the refinement of a formula
that captures the logic of generating the geometry of the
Vessel. The interconnecting parameters were limited by
many factors – including the city code for step size,
minimal headroom and structural capacity. Any one
decision would influence many aspects of the design.
For example, while in search of the optimal inclination
of the stairs, the width also changed due to headroom
affecting the overall shape. The design was an organic
process that required a great deal of collaboration
between Heatherwick Studio and AKT II. The design
team thoroughly investigated each line of thought and

interrogated the end result, asking simple questions:
does this achieve our intent; what emotions does it evoke;
could a more appealing form be created by altering other
priorities like the number of landings and their sizes?
This was not a linear journey and involved exploring
many avenues of thought in tandem.

Design Tools

During concept design, the design team used hand
sketches, 3D modelling software and visual scripting.
Digital techniques were always complemented with
hands-on exploration through maquettes and 1:1 mock-
ups. It is difficult to judge the reality and scale of a virtual
design just by looking at a drawing or a model on a screen.
To replicate the experience key elements were produced in
1:1 using a variety of tools: a plywood model to replicate
the steps or tape to mark out the platform footprint on
Heatherwick Studio's main courtyard. A range of scales
were used for the models to best judge the outcome
throughout the design stages.

Parametric Flow

While physical processes vitally informed the design,
the Vessel would be impossible to conceive without
close digital collaboration across the team. The primary
objective of setting up the design workflow was to unlock
the design potentials by connecting form to performance
and discovering the hidden relationships and forces that
drove the design to its final configuration. AKT II's
Re.AKT toolkit provided the link between the geometric
environment and the various specialist structural analysis
packages used during the design phase. The toolkit

5. A rotationally
symmetrical structure.
© Heatherwick Studio.

6. Resolving the base.
© Heatherwick Studio.

7. Re-AKT, Interoperable
design toolkit, from shape
to performance. © AKT II.

8. Dogbone, the
DNA of Vessel. ©
Heatherwick Studio.

required only one input (the curve defining the sectional profile of the Vessel from Heatherwick Studio) and a set of numerical parameters that can be controlled through a single excel file.

A series of checks and validation algorithms were included to allow a responsive design process. Step gradient ratios, minimum height constraints and minimum ramp width values were visualised in real-time to provide a constant feedback to all team members. The production process was also automated, with plans, sections and details extracted dynamically from the grasshopper definition, together with setting-out data such as point coordinates and plate flattening and tagging.

The output was a fully controllable, organised model with structural and material proprieties embedded within the Rhino surfaces. The parameters were defined and shared between AKT II and Heatherwick Studio to control the setting out of both architectural and structural models using a single strategy. Once the 3D model was created, data could be extracted or grouped to enable simple selection of individual plates or portions of the Vessel. This then allowed greater control in the structural design when the selection of plates or portions of the Vessel was required in order to assess the results and allow for optimisation.

Dogbone as DNA of Vessel

The pattern generated by the geometrical zigzag, combined with the load distribution across the section and the willingness of using off-site fabrication as much as possible, very quickly defined a highly unusual shape as the 'best fit' to achieve all the targets. While the size of the grid, flight of steps and platforms were influenced by the relation to the context, construction code and visitor experience, the portioning of each unit was optimised for ease of transport. The decision of where to split the structure had a vital impact on the overall aesthetic of the finished structure, and it was also beneficial to avoid locations where forces are concentrated. Therefore, the platforms were kept as one piece, with the split halfway through the stairs, resulting in units resembling 'dogbones'.

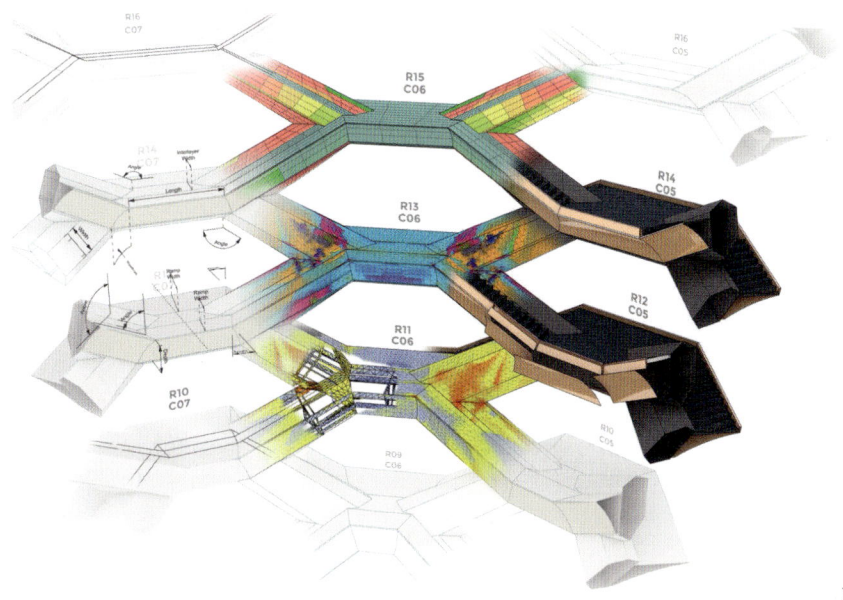

The elongated 'x'-shape form quickly started to inherit a central role in the project. It virtually stored every single parameter related to the geometric setting out, the structural performance and the use of the Vessel, and thus became the central core of the whole project. The dogbones' corners defined the inclination of the ramps as well as functioning as surfaces for connecting one piece to the next; its centre of mass defined the best way of lifting the piece on site.

Human-Centred Performance

As the structure's purpose was designed for maximum human interaction, the number of people that can access the Vessel at any one time was a major design consideration. With no predetermined function, the structure encourages each individual to explore the structure at their own pace, making it difficult to predict how people were going to move and what the dynamics would be as a result. AKT II therefore had to make certain assumptions as to the number of people that could use the Vessel, and then decide on the proportion of them that

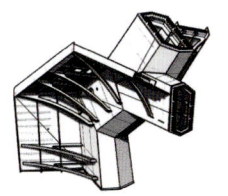

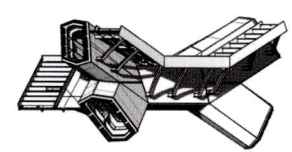
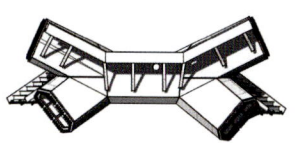
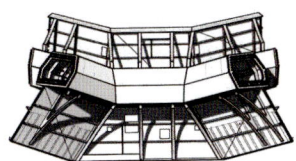

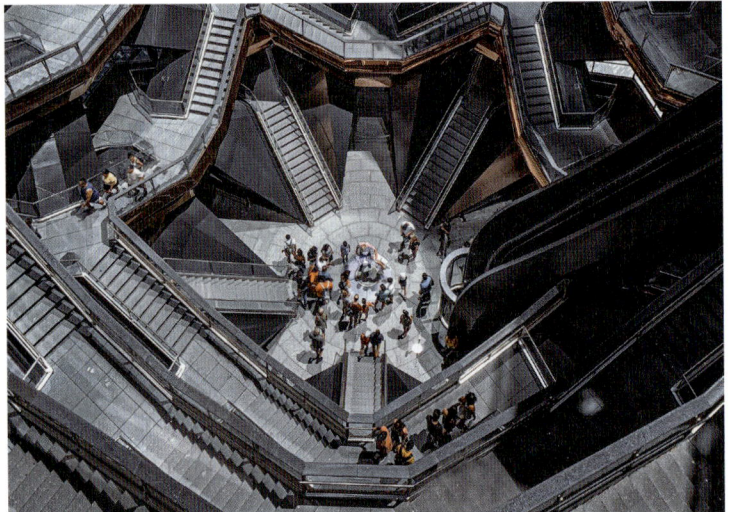

9

10

are likely to synchronise their step. Two scenarios were considered: typical day-to-day usage and a special event, for example a concert in the plaza.

Dynamic Analysis

The particular focus on people's usage of the structure required a very detailed dynamic assessment. The magnitude of this movement can be relatively small, however the rate at which the movement takes place can be comparable to a large stadium or sports venue where people are exiting the structure, causing the structure to accelerate and then harmonise into a certain frequency. Every structure has a certain frequency at which it vibrates. It was interesting to discover that neither increasing the mass nor increasing the vertical stiffness had a significant impact on the structure dynamics. From a strength point of view, Vessel can accommodate a relatively large number of visitors. Nevertheless, a limit was set due to the dynamic behaviour, requiring structural vibrations to be kept at an acceptable level. The structure could withstand five times the load but the comfort of the people on it determined its capacity.

Damping Technology

The Vessel is a complex mix of different degrees of freedoms that are generating non-symmetric modes which are causing high accelerations both horizontally and vertically. To damp those frequencies, the design team proposed to install several Tuned Mass Damper (TMD) devices. A TMD device consists of a moving mass connected to springs and damping elements. The mass reacts to an imposed movement of the

structure to which it is connected and the two masses (structure and inertial mass) start to move relative to each other. The passive damper is stretched and compressed, reducing the vibrations of the structure through increasing its effective damping. TMD systems are typically effective over a narrow frequency band and must be tuned to a particular natural frequency. A dynamic time history analysis was performed at this stage to test the allowable occupancy of the Vessel and the number and location of dampers required. The proposed tuned mass dampers were then tuned to limit the response of the Vessel to within the allowable limits. Several iterations of the design were required to find the right harmonic frequency of the structure and the level of damping required.

The devices were carefully located at the point where a significant vibration was occurring (the top two rows of landings) and connected to the structure in the landing decks where they could be concealed in the shell of the interlayer whilst remaining accessible through custom-made openings in the structure for maintenance purposes.

Materials

The human experience is the central touchstone to Heatherwick Studio's design intent. If a place is valued by its users, it is less likely to be redeveloped in the short term, leading to a more sustainable period of use appropriate to its materials.

The materials used on the project echo the design intent of an elevated urban space. When looking down from the top of the Vessel, the urban material pallet of dark precast pavers prevails, linking it to the typical street materiality

9. View from the top, looking inwards.
© Scott Gummerson.

10. Assembling on site.
© Ondel Hylton, CityRealty.

of the city. When looking up from the plaza, the polished copper-coloured steel underside brings the structure to life with reflections of the surrounding city and of the movement of the people. The playful PVD coating to the steel cladding was chosen because it is very hard and more corrosive resistant, and is more environmentally friendly than traditional coating processes like electroplating. Between the outer and inner ring of shiny polished steel panels lies the architectural framework that contrasts with its raw welds and rough painted steel, showcasing the story of the robust nature of the structure that holds the platforms up. In the modern manufacturing process, the honesty of materiality and the joy in the way structure has been made is often lost. The design team believes that putting the materiality at the heart of the design process elicits stronger intuitive emotional responses from the people who experience it.

Prefabrication

Prefabrication was the obvious choice for a structure of this complexity. The engineer on record Thornton Tomasetti worked closely with the design team through design assist, fabrication and construction. Although the critical setting out and 'templating' of the 'dogbone' main elements was determined through the parametric model, almost all of the internal stiffeners, diaphragm plates, et cetera within the interior of the structure had to be manually positioned and welded to achieve the desired build tolerance. The macro steel elements forming the Vessel included 5 pedestals, 10 'special dogbones' (S Shape), 65 dogbones and 8 spine elements. It required over 6,300 shop drawings to fabricate the Vessel entirely in the specialist Cimolai workshops in Italy. The manual welding required high craftsmanship skills which is celebrated by the visible welds on the framework. To achieve the tight tolerances, geometry checks were performed at every major welding stage using laser trackers. A very tight tolerance was required at the connection points of the dogbones to enable the pieces to fall in place. A thick connecting plate was welded at the four ends of each dogbone that was milled down by a CNC milling-boring machine complemented with a calibration system. Before shipping the dogbones, the fabricators pre-assembled the bottom third of the structure to test achievable tolerances, prior to their finishing touches of sandblasting, painting and applying waterproofing. To save time on site, a number of elements were installed in the factory before shipping. These included MEP items – such as the drain and cable conduit, cladding rails and most of the shiny cladding. At this stage, in order to handle the dogbone elements, it was necessary to design a cradle, bale to support the

weight of the pre-assembled element, and special moving equipment to transport it into the desired location. The balustrades, floor paving and lift were installed on site after the pieces reached their destination following a 15-day journey across the Atlantic.

Interoperable, Multidisciplinary Design

In the traditional implementation of a conventional project, architecture and engineering exist in a rigid binary without overlap. But increasingly, that disciplinary line becomes blurry, especially in projects where the design is challenging form, performance and fabrication. Engineers are now not just refining and testing architectural compositions but working alongside design teams to generate them with close attention to abstract concepts such as structural honesty and human experience. Heatherwick Studio are not a conventional architectural practice and AKT II are not conventional engineers, allowing both to break conventional boundaries. This was essential to describe, control and model a unique structure such as the Vessel, that was both fundamentally engineering-based and yet simultaneously entirely governed by the limits of human movement. The result can be considered a testament to what is possible when engineering and architecture are thoroughly immersed in a collaborative process.

References

Kara, H. and Bosia, D. 2016. *Design Engineering Refocused*. London: John Wiley & Sons.

Kingman, J., Dudley, J. and Baptista, R. 2017. 'The 2016 Serpentine Pavilion. A case study in large-scale GFRP structural design and assembly', in Menges, A., Sheil, B., Glynn, R. and Skavara, M. (eds), *Fabricate: Rethinking Design and Construction*, London: UCL Press, pp.138-145.

Rabagliati, J., Janssen, J., Tibuzzi, E., De Paoli, F., Casson, P. and Maddock R. 2017. 'Bloomberg Ramp: Collaborative Workflows, Sharing Data and Design Logics', in De Rycke, K., Gengnagel, C., Baverel, O., Burry, J., Mueller, C., Man Nguyen, M., Rahm, P. and Ramsgaard Thomsen, M. (eds), *Humanizing Digital Reality, Design Modelling Symposium Paris 2017*, Singapore: Springer Nature Singapore Pte Ltd, pp. 153-166.

Tibuzzi, E. and Marzev, D. 2017. 'Multi-Performative Skins', Menges, A., Sheil, B., Glynn, R. and Skavara, M. (eds), *Fabricate: Rethinking Design and Construction*, London: UCL Press, pp. 280-285.

EDITORS
BIOGRAPHIES

Jane Burry

Jane Burry is an architect, professor and Dean of the School of Design at Swinburne University of Technology, Melbourne, Australia. She is lead author of *The New Mathematics of Architecture* (Thames & Hudson, 2010), editor of *Designing the Dynamic* (Melbourne Books, 2013) and co-author of *Prototyping for Architects* (Thames & Hudson, 2016), and has over a hundred other publications. Burry has practiced and taught internationally, including involvement as a project architect in the technical office at Antoni Gaudí's Sagrada Família Basilica with partner Mark Burry. She is co-curator of the 2018 International Exhibition 'Dynamics of Air'. Recent funded research explores the opportunities for leveraging digital fabrication with simulation and feedback to create better, more sensitive, human-centric spaces; and manipulating geometry and materiality of architecture to fine tune the acoustic, thermal and air flow aesthetics for higher quality environments. Other partnered research investigates rich environmental data gathering and its application to designing better urban environments.

Jenny E. Sabin

Jenny E. Sabin is an architectural designer whose work is at the forefront of a new direction for 21st century architectural practice – one that investigates the intersections of architecture and science and applies insights and theories from biology and mathematics to the design of responsive material structures and adaptive architecture. Sabin is the Arthur L. and Isabel B. Wiesenberger Professor in Architecture and Associate Dean for Design at Cornell College of Architecture, Art, and Planning where she established a new advanced research degree in Matter Design Computation. She is principal of Jenny Sabin Studio, an experimental architectural design studio based in Ithaca and Director of the Sabin Lab at Cornell AAP.

Sabin holds degrees in ceramics and interdisciplinary visual art from the University of Washington and a Master of Architecture from the University of Pennsylvania. She was awarded a Pew Fellowship in the Arts 2010 and was named a USA Knight Fellow in Architecture. In 2014, she was awarded the prestigious Architectural League Prize. Her work has been exhibited internationally including at the FRAC Centre, Cooper Hewitt Design Triennial, MoMA, and most recently as part of Imprimer Le Monde at the Centre Pompidou. Her book *LabStudio: Design Research Between Architecture and Biology*, co-authored with Peter Lloyd Jones, was published in 2017. Sabin won MoMA & MoMA PS1's Young Architects Programme with her submission, *Lumen* (2017).

Bob Sheil

Bob Sheil is Professor in Architecture and Design through Production at The Bartlett School of Architecture UCL, and has been Director of School since 2014. He is the author of multiple book chapters, refereed papers and articles on design, making and technology. He has co-designed and built six artefacts/built works, and his work has been exhibited internationally on eleven occasions. He has edited seven books, including three issues of *Architectural Design*: *Design through Making* (2005), *Protoarchitecture* (2008), and *High Definition: Negotiating Zero Tolerance* (2014); an AD Reader, *Manufacturing the Bespoke*, published in 2012; and *55/02: A sixteen*(makers) Monograph* (also 2012). He is a Co-Founder of the FABRICATE conference and book for which he was Co-Chair and Co-Editor in 2011 (London) and 2017 (Zurich).

Marilena Skavara

Marilena Skavara is a London-based architect and interaction designer. She is a co-founder and partner at Codica Ltd., a London-based digital product design practice focused on outcome-driven innovation. She has led and contributed to transformational projects for Mercedes Benz, UCL, M&S, HM Government and several leading start-ups in fintech, automotive, AI, health, femtech and media. She has also been involved in social impact projects for non-profits in the US, UK and EU.

Prior to that, she ran physical computing workshops for The Bartlett, UCL, the Architectural Association (AA) in London, Ecole Speciale d' Architecture in Paris, and other universities in Sweden and Denmark. Skavara is one of the founding members and editors of FABRICATE — a triennial international peer-reviewed conference and publication, which explores the progressive integration of digital design with manufacturing processes, and its impact on design and making in the 21st century. She holds a MSc (Hons) degree in Architecture from the National Technical University in Athens and a MSc (Hons) Adaptive Architecture & Computation (AAC) from The Bartlett, UCL. Her MSc graduate project 'Adaptive fa[ca]de' was extensively exhibited, published and presented at conferences and publications.

CONTRIBUTORS
BIOGRAPHIES

1: BIO-MATERIALITY

MUD Frontiers

Virginia San Fratello with her partner Ronald Rael, draws, builds, 3D prints, teaches and writes about architecture as a cultural endeavour, deeply influenced by craft traditions and contemporary technologies. Through their studio, RAEL SAN FRATELLO, they speculate about the social agency of design, particularly along the borderlands between the USA and Mexico. Their drawings, models and objects are in the permanent collections of the Museum of Modern Art, the Cooper Hewitt Smithsonian Design Museum, and the San Francisco Museum of Modern Art. They are founding partners of the Oakland-based make-tank Emerging Objects.

Ronald Rael, with his partner Virginia San Fratello, draws, builds, 3D prints, teaches and writes about architecture as a cultural endeavour, deeply influenced by craft traditions and contemporary technologies. Through their studio, RAEL SAN FRATELLO, they speculate about the social agency of design, particularly along the borderlands between the USA and Mexico. Their drawings, models and objects are in the permanent collections of the Museum of Modern Art, the Cooper Hewitt Smithsonian Design Museum, and the San Francisco Museum of Modern Art. They are founding partners of the Oakland-based make-tank Emerging Objects.

The Design and Fabrication of Confluence Park

Andrew Kudless is a designer based in Houston, Texas where he is the Bill Kendall Memorial Endowed Professor at the University of Houston's Hines College of Architecture Design and Director of the Advanced Media Technology Lab. In 2004, he founded Matsys, a design studio exploring the emergent relationships between architecture, engineering, biology and computation. The work of Matsys has been exhibited internationally and is in the permanent collections of the San Francisco Museum of Modern Art, the Centre Pompidou in Paris, and the FRAC Centre in Orleans, France. His work on Confluence Park has won a number of awards including a 2019 AIA Honor Award.

Joshua Zabel is the Vice President of Business Development at Kreysler & Associates, a world-class composites fabrication facility in the Bay Area, San Francisco. He has been at K&A since 2005 and has filled many roles. As Director of Digital Fabrication he was involved in the digital aspects of nearly every project to pass through K&A's shop. Projects have ranged widely: architectural façades, submarine hulls, giant bat skeletons, and dark matter satellites, to name a few. He has developed an expert understanding of composites, and is at the forefront of AEC and the composites industry's efforts to maximise their architectural potential.

Chuck Naeve is Founding Principal of Architectural Engineers Collaborative. Naeve has managed structural engineering projects and business activities of engineering firms for over thirty years. He has practiced extensively in the United States, as well as internationally. Naeve is known for creating architectural structures in support of building architecture, and for developing sustainable building structures in harmony with the natural environment. Chuck Naeve has been recognised with honorary membership of the American Institute of Architects, Austin and Texas chapters, for his significant contributions to the field of architecture and to the built environment.

Tenna Florian is a Partner with Lake|Flato Architects in San Antonio, Texas. She was drawn to Lake|Flato because of their place-based approach to sustainable design. As a leader of the Eco-Conservation studio at Lake|Flato, her focus is on highly sustainable projects that integrate into the natural environment. Florian has been active in developing green initiatives for her firm and for the city of San Antonio. Her work includes: Naples Botanical Garden in Naples, FL; the Dixon Water Foundation Josey Pavilion in Decatur, TX – the ninth certified Living Building Challenge project in the world; and an AIA Honor Award winning project, Confluence Park.

The Role of Robotic Milling in the Research and Development of the Cork Construction Kit

Oliver Wilton is Director of Technology and Lecturer in Environmental Design at The Bartlett School of Architecture, UCL. He contributes to developing, augmenting and leading the school's strategy for technology in architecture. His research and teaching covers design, habitation, material technology, environmental and energy performance, and new forms of construction. Wilton is a director at architecture practice WW Studio. He has over two decades of experience, including involvement in a range of innovative award-winning built projects and consultancy ranging from technical assessment for the Ashden Awards to co-delivering Sustainable Urban Development consultancy to the Taiwanese government.

Matthew Barnett Howland is Director of Research and Development at CSK Architects in Eton, where he is responsible for developing a life-cycle approach to making buildings. He led on the research, design and construction of the multi-award winning Cork House, a pilot project for an innovative solid cork construction kit with outstanding whole life performance. Howland is an architectural tutor, and has taught diploma units at the Architectural Association, University of Cambridge and London Met, where he was awarded the RIBA Tutor Prize in 2004.

Peter Scully is the technical director of B-made, The Bartlett Manufacturing and Design Exchange, and Technical Director of The Bartlett's Design for Manufacture Master's programme. He has worked in bespoke manufacturing for 25 years, developing a special focus on design at the interface between disciplines, and has run companies that play a key role in the realisation of bespoke architectural and artistic works. Scully has worked with architects, engineers and artists, deploying holistic project stakeholder understanding throughout the full process to curate workflows toward buildable outcomes. He has contributed to a range of built projects internationally, utilising procedural and tacit knowledge within design.

Pulp Faction: 3D printed material assemblies through microbial biotransformation

Ana Goidea is a PhD candidate at Lund University, where she investigates the potentials of additive manufacturing in architecture through computational design. She received her Master's of Architecture from CITAstudio at The Royal Danish Academy of Fine Arts, after which she has been teaching and working at studios with different strategies for digital fabrication. Her research combined with industry through the design and co-fabrication of one of the first 3D-printed buildings in Europe. Her interests are at the intersection between living systems, complex geometries and material performance, currently manifested through a project on bio-hybrid materials for 3D printing.

Dimitrios Floudas is a researcher at the Biology Department of Lund University. He is a fungal biologist who received his doctorate in evolutionary biology and systematics of fungi at Clark University, Massachusetts. His research interests are centred on the function, versatility and evolution of metabolic processes in fungi. In his current project, Floudas is using a series of experimental approaches and techniques such as spectroscopy to explore the diversity of decomposition mechanisms in fungi involved in plant-based materials. A deeper understanding of these mechanisms will facilitate their use in innovative applications and products.

David Andréen is a senior lecturer at Lund University where he leads a research group exploring the intersection of biology, computation and architecture. He completed his doctorate at UCL as part of an international and transdisciplinary team studying termites and their mounds as a model for architectural design. Andréen's expertise includes large scale additive fabrication, self-organised construction, agent design, and the interaction of complex geometries and building physics. He is the director of the master's programme in architecture at Lund University, and over the past decade has explored computational design and the changing roles of architects together with students at universities including Lund and The Bartlett School of Architecture.

From Machine Control to Material Programming: Self-shaping wood manufacturing of a high performance curved CLT structure – Urbach Tower

Dylan Wood is a designer and researcher at the Institute for Computational Design and Construction (ICD), University of Stuttgart where he leads the Material Programming Research Group. His team's research focuses on developing intelligent design and fabrication principles for smart materials that can be utilised for material robotics, building systems, construction and manufacturing. He holds a ITECH, MSc. with distinction from the University of Stuttgart, and a B.Arch from the University of Southern California. Professionally, he has worked as a designer and computational fabrication specialist at Barkow Leibinger Architects in Berlin and DOSU Studio Architects Los Angeles.

Philippe Grönquist is a research assistant in the Wood Materials Science lab at the Institute of Building Materials, ETH Zurich. His research about wood includes both a fundamental aspect where scale-dependent structure-property relations are explored and an applied aspect for employing such knowledge in timber engineering and architecture. He is specialised in mechanical behaviour and theoretical and applied computational mechanics for materials simulations. Grönquist has worked with research partners from ICD, University of Stuttgart on the development and application of self-shaping wood for timber structures. He holds a BSc. and MSc. in civil engineering from ETH Zurich.

Simon Bechert is a structural engineer and research associate at the Institute of Building Structures and Structural Design (IKTE) at the University of Stuttgart. His research focuses on the development of building systems, connection strategies and integral structural design processes for segmented timber shell structures. Bechert researches structurally informed lightweight timber plate structures within projects that explore advanced computational design strategies for resource effective and robotically fabricated building systems. Applying this research, he led the structural design effort of innovative lightweight structures such as the BUGA Wood Pavilion 2019 in Heilbronn, Germany and the Urbach Tower at the Remstal Gartenschau 2019, Germany.

Lotte Aldinger is a structural engineer and holds a Master of Science with distinction from the ITECH master's programme

at the University of Stuttgart. As a research associate at the Institute of Building Structures and Structural Design in 2018 to 2019, she contributed to the structural design of two innovative lightweight timber structures: the BUGA Wood Pavilion 2019 in Heilbronn, and the Urbach Tower at the Remstal Gartenschau 2019, Germany. Aldinger's primary interest lies in an integrative process for the structural design of shell structures with informed fibre layouts by applying computational design.

David Riggenbach is Project Leader in the Timber Construction and Engineering team at Blumer-Lehmann AG since 2008. As a timber construction engineer, he is responsible for the structural design and implementation of timber construction projects with a number of internationally-known designers. He continuously explores the limits of timber engineering and testing the possibilities of the material. Riggenbach's most notable realised projects are the mountain inn Chäserrugg, 2'262 m.a.s.l., designed by Herzog & de Meuron, the origami folding structure of the Théâtre de Vidy in Lausanne, and the Hotel Kulm in St. Moritz by Foster + Partners.

Katharina Lehmann is the CEO and Delegate of the Board of Directors of the Lehmann Group in Gossau, Switzerland. The family business of the Lehmann Group, now in its 5th generation, has been dealing exclusively with the material wood for over 140 years; the group of companies are based in Switzerland, Germany and Luxembourg. Lehmann is known for her commitment to the Swiss timber industry and timber construction and contributes her knowledge to numerous projects in the timber industry as well as research. She is also committed to the sustainable management of tropical forests. For her, wood is the epitome of sustainability.

Markus Rüggeberg is Senior Scientist at the Institute for Building Materials at ETH Zurich, and at Empa, Dübendorf, Switzerland. He received his PhD in Biology from the University of Freiburg, Germany and worked at the Max-Planck-Institute of Colloids and Interfaces, Potsdam, Germany. He has positioned his research on wood at the interface of engineering, material science and molecular biology, covering fundamental and applied research on structure-mechanics-relationships and wood-water-interaction. A focus of Rüggeberg's work is re-thinking the materiality of wood by turning its drawbacks into new capacities, for example utilising dimensional instabilities and its affinity to water for developing self-forming manufacturing processes for architecture and construction.

Ingo Burgert studied Wood Science and Technology at the University of Hamburg, Germany and received his diploma in 1995. He obtained a doctoral degree from the same University in 2000. From 2000-2003 he was Postdoc at BOKU, Vienna, Austria, and from 2003-2011 research group leader at the Max Planck Institute of Colloids and Interfaces, Potsdam, Germany. Since 2011, Burgert has been Professor for Wood Materials Science at ETH Zurich and group leader at EMPA, Dübendorf.

Jan Knippers is a practising consulting engineer and, since 2000, head of the Institute for Building Structures and Structural Design (ITKE) at the University of Stuttgart. His interest is in innovative and resource-efficient structures created at the intersection of research and development, and practice. From 2014 to 2019 Knippers was the coordinator of the DFG collaborative research centre Biological Design and Integrative Structures. Since 2019, he has been Deputy Executive Director of the Cluster of Excellence Integrative Computational Design and

Construction for Architecture and Vice-rector for Research of the University of Stuttgart. He is author of several books, numerous scientific publications, and member of various advisory boards.

Achim Menges is an architect in Frankfurt and full professor at the University of Stuttgart, where he is the founding director of the Institute for Computational Design and Construction (ICD) and the director of the Cluster of Excellence Integrative Computational Design and Construction for Architecture (IntCDC). In addition, he has been Visiting Professor in Architecture at Harvard University's Graduate School of Design and held multiple other visiting professorships in Europe and the United States. His work focuses on integrative design at the intersection of computational design methods, robotic manufacturing and construction, as well as advanced material and building systems.

Bending the Line: Zippered Wood creating non-orthogonal architectural assemblies using the most common linear building component (the 2x4)

Blair Satterfield is Associate Professor and Chair of the architecture programme at the University of British Columbia, where he also directs the UBC SALA HiLo Lab. The lab is an internationally published research initiative that reckons with the energy and material efficient use of second stream materials in analogue and digital design fabrication processes, especially as they apply to architectural construction. Satterfield is a co-founding principal with Marc Swackhamer of HouMinn Practice. HouMinn's work is widely published and exhibited, and has been awarded multiple *Architect Magazine* R+D Awards, an *ID Magazine* National Design Award, and a Core77 National Design Award.

Alexander Preiss is a recent graduate from the Master of Architecture programme at The University of British Columbia and holds a Bachelor of Architectural Studies from Carleton University. He is a research assistant at UBC SALA HiLo Lab, where he develops innovative processes that translate between material behaviour, digital simulations, and robotic fabrication. Preiss's personal research pursues alternative structures in design methodologies that deploy computation to enrich design intent. He currently works and lives in Ottawa.

Derek Mavis is a M. Arch candidate at the University of British Columbia, in Vancouver, Canada and has been a research assistant in UBC's HiLo Lab since May 2018. He earned his BA in Greek and Roman studies from Carleton University in Ottawa, Canada. He enjoys working in both the digital and analogue environments of the lab's research. Mavis has a background in carpentry and robotic design and fabrication. He is interested in the development of novel fabrication methods and tools, and how they can be exploited by designers.

Graham Entwistle is a workshop and digifab technician at the University of British Columbia's School of Architecture and Landscape Architecture. He has a background as a furniture designer/maker and has a BFA in Industrial Design from Rhode Island School of Design. He is interested in the interplay between the experience of making and understanding.

Marc Swackhamer is Professor and Chair of the School of Architecture at the University of Colorado, Denver, where he also directs the LoDo Lab. His research practice, HouMinn, is a partnership with Professor Blair Satterfield. Together, they challenge broadly accepted approaches to design agency through interdisciplinary partnerships, unconventional making, and material misuse. HouMinn is widely published, exhibited, and has been recognised with numerous international design awards. Swackhamer is also a recognised and award-winning educator, and former Head of the Architecture programme at The University of Minnesota. Swackhamer co-authored the book *Hypernatural: Architecture's New Relationship with Nature* with Blaine Brownell.

Matthew Hayes is a M.Arch student at The University of Colorado Denver and a research assistant working in the LoDo Lab. He earned both his A.A. and B.S. in Architecture along with minors in Landscape Architecture and City and Regional Planning from The Ohio State University. Hayes has a background in museum display design, residential architecture, and is interested in prototyping and holistic design, with specific focus on mining opportunities generated when working between analogue and digital craft.

Biocomposites from Annually Renewable Resources Displaying Vision of Future Sustainable Architecture: Design and fabrication of two 1:1 demonstrators

Hanaa Dahy is a registered architect, engineer and material developer. Through the frame of her professorship, in 2016 she established the research department BioMat (Bio-based Materials and Materials Cycles in Architecture) at ITKE (Institute for Building Structures and Structural Design), the Faculty of Architecture and Urban Planning in the University of Stuttgart. Dahy established her office in 2003 in Cairo before moving to Germany in 2009 to complete her doctoral studies and to merge her experience with European architecture and industry. She owns a number of patents in the biocomposites field and has won a number of international awards.

Jan Petrš is an architect and research associate at the Department of Bio-based Materials and Materials Cycles in Architecture (BioMat) at Institute of Building Structures and Structural Design (ITKE), University of Stuttgart. He obtained his master's degree at Faculty of Architecture at Czech Technical University in Prague where he has continued as a doctoral candidate. His research focuses on the integration of soft actuators and smart systems into bio-based materials, parametric design, and self-assembly systems. In 2010 Petrš co-founded Archistroj Design Studio, focusing on digital and computational design, adaptive urban systems and robotics.

Piotr Baszyński is a research associate at the department of Bio-based Materials and Materials Cycles in Architecture (BioMat) at Institute of Building Structures and Structural Design (ITKE), University of Stuttgart. He earned his master's degree at the Faculty of Architecture at Warsaw University of Technology. He gained professional experience while working on projects of complex geometry buildings and landscapes at the office of L-A-V-A Stuttgart, and on his own projects of public utility spaces as a co-founder of [winkle] design group. His current research focuses on the application of natural long-fibre bio-composite materials in housing architecture.

Cellulosic Biocomposites for Sustainable Manufacturing

Stylianos Dritsas is Associate Professor in Architecture and Sustainable Design at the Singapore University of Technology and Design. His research interests are in design computation, digital fabrication and sustainable manufacturing. He developed the Computer Aided Design and Manufacturing software as well as the robotic 3D-printing Material Extrusion system for large-scale FLAM

bio-composites. In the past he has taught at the Harvard Graduate School of Design, Ecole Polytechnique Federale in Lausanne, the Architectural Association in London, and practiced architecture in KPF London.

Yadunund Vijay was a Graduate Research Assistant in Engineering Product Development at the Singapore University of Technology and Design. His background is in Mechanical Engineering and he earned his dual master's degree from SUTD and MIT for the study of industrial process control optimisation, including work on the development of FLAM 3D-printing.

Samuel Halim was an Undergraduate Research Assistant in Architecture and Sustainable Design at the Singapore University of Technology and Design. He contributed in the design, analysis, testing and fabrication of Natural Composite Pillar prototype.

Ryan Teo was an Undergraduate Research Assistant in Architecture and Sustainable Design at the Singapore University of Technology and Design. He contributed to the FLAM 3D rapid prototyping and the development of the Natural Composite Pillar prototype.

Naresh Sanandiya is a Post-Doctoral Research Fellow at the SUTD-MIT International Design Centre at the Singapore University of Technology and Design. His background is in chemistry and his research is on chemical modification of biopolymers for their application in biomimetic adhesives in wet environments, thixotropic and stimuli-responsive hydrogels.

Javier G. Fernandez is Assistant Professor in Engineering Product Development at the Singapore University of Technology and Design. His research is on the study of biological materials. At SUTD, he designed FLAM, a cellulosic bio-composite for large-scale manufacturing; at the Harvard Wyss Institute he designed Shrilk, a biocompatible material inspired by the insect cuticle; and at MIT, he developed MicroMasonry, a technology to assemble artificial organs. He was awarded the world's most outstanding young researcher in materials science by the Bayer Foundation, the Zwick Science Award for his studies on Mechanical Testing, and best PhD thesis at the University of Barcelona.

2: SYNTHESISING DESIGN AND PRODUCTION

Kuwait International Airport Terminal 2: Engineering and fabrication of a complex parametric megastructure

Lucio Blandini studied structural engineering at the Universities of Catania and Bologna before moving to the University of Stuttgart. There he obtained his PhD at the Institute for Lightweight Structures and Conceptual Design (ILEK). In this context, he developed and built the so-called Stuttgart Shell, a filigree glass-only shell structure spanning 8.5m. After completing a master's degree in architecture at the University of Pennsylvania, he took up a position as project manager at Werner Sobek. He has been partner as well as managing director since 2018. As of spring 2020 he is head of ILEK and full professor at the University of Stuttgart.

Guido Nieri studied structural engineering at the University of Pisa before starting to work as a project engineer for a major glass manufacturer in Switzerland. Since 2016, he has been project manager at Werner Sobek in Stuttgart, Germany. Nieri's professional focus lies on complex geometries and parametric design, and program scripting (VBA, C#, Grasshopper).

A Factory On the Fly: Exploring the structural potential of cyber-physical construction

Asbjørn Søndergaard is founding partner and Chief Technology Officer in Odico Construction Robotics, a technology enterprise dedicated to large scale architectural robotic formwork fabrication. Founded in 2012 through a joining of research trajectories following the Fabricate 2011 conference, Odico Construction Robotics has embarked on a mission to revolutionise global construction. In daily work, Søndergaard heads the software development and industrial research and development within the company. This work entails several high-profile research efforts to develop novel fabrication technologies within architectural construction, such as Robotic Hot-Blade cutting, Abrasive Wire-cutting of EPS-optimised formwork; and automation of non-repetitive robotic manufacturing.

Radu Becus is a computational design specialist at Odico Construction Robotics. Educated as an architect at Universitatea Tehica din Cluj-Napoca, Romania, his work centres on digital robotic production and technology R&D, with an emphasis on workflow optimisation and system representations within Odico's development work. Drawing on background studies mining social media data as the basis for urban analysis, as well as a maker-oriented passion for advanced digital production, Becus's work is situated at the overlap between computer science, robotics and design.

Gabriella Rossi is a researcher and computational architect at the Centre of IT and Architecture (CITA) KADK Copenhagen, and teaches the master's programme in Computation in Architecture. She has worked as a computational design specialist at Odico Robotics and has assisted research projects at Politecnico di Milano. Rossi's work focuses on the field of Robotics and Machine Learning, exploring how interdisciplinary computational processes and robotic fabrication change the way we design and manufacture buildings. She holds a Computation MA degree from KADK, and an Architecture BSc from Politecnico di Milano. Rossi is a member of the Danish Association of Architects.

Kyle Vansice is an architectural designer, working in the Chicago office of Skidmore, Owings & Merrill. He also leads a design research group at SOM: Blackbox, focused on leveraging advanced computation and fabrication methodologies to foster greater interdisciplinary collaboration. He holds graduate degrees in both architecture and structural engineering, and has lectured at the School of the Art Institute, the University of Michigan, and Iowa State University.

Rahul Attraya holds a Master of Arts from University of Michigan, Taubmann College. Living and working in Chicago as an architectural assistant at Skidmore, Owings & Merrill LLP, he is contributing to the work of Blackbox as well as design work of SOM.

Austin Devin holds a PhD in structural engineering from the University of Dublin. As a structural engineer at Skidmore, Owings & Merrill, he has assumed responsibility as design engineer on several high-profile projects conducted from SOM's practice.

Direct-to-Drawing: Automation in extruded terracotta fabrication

Scott Overall is associate, Computational Design, at SHoP Architects. He holds a Bachelor of Science in Civil Engineering from the University of Kentucky and a Master of

Architecture from Columbia University. His work focuses on applied computation in design and construction, as seen on projects such as the Botswana Innovation Hub, and Syracuse National Veterans Resource Complex. He has taught Virtual Design and Construction at Columbia University.

John Paul Rysavy is a Senior Associate at SHoP Architects. He received a Master of Architecture from The University of Texas, Austin following study at L'École nationale supérieure d'architecture de Versailles and Illinois School of Architecture. He has worked notably on the Botswana Innovation Hub and Uber Headquarters. Rysavy has held teaching positions at the University of Texas and has served as a guest critic at several academic institutions.

Clinton Miller is Director, Computational Design, at SHoP Architects. He received a Bachelor of Science in Architecture and a Bachelor of Arts in Mathematics from the Ohio State University, and a Master of Architecture from the Columbia GSAPP. Miller has worked on many of SHoP's projects, including Atlantic Yards B2, Pier 17, and the Uber Headquarters.

William Sharples is Principal, SHoP Architects. He holds a Bachelor of Engineering from Pennsylvania State University, and a Master of Architecture from Columbia University. He has led SHoP's major institutional and commercial work with clients such as Columbia University, Fashion Institute of Technology, Botswana Innovation Hub, and Google Inc. He lectures widely at academic institutions and has held teaching positions at Cornell University, Yale University and the Parsons School of Design.

Christopher Sharples is Principal, SHoP Architects. Christopher holds Bachelor of History and Bachelor of Fine Arts degrees from Dickinson College, and Master of Architecture from Columbia University. He has taught at Cornell University, Parsons School of Design, The City College, City University of New York, Columbia University, and the University of Virginia. Sharples has served as Principal on many significant projects including the Barclays Center, SITE Santa Fe gallery expansion, Google Headquarters Offices and, currently, Uber Headquarters in San Francisco.

Sameer Kumar is Director, Enclosure Design, SHoP Architects. Kumar holds a Bachelor of Architecture from CEPT University and a Master of Architecture from the University of Pennsylvania. He has led façade direction on many of SHoP's most high-profile projects including 111 West 57th Street, South Street Seaport, and Domino Sugar Refinery Development. Kumar currently serves as Visiting Lecturer at Princeton University and the University of Pennsylvania.

Andrea Vittadini is Project Director, SHoP Architects. He received a Bachelor of Architecture from Politecnico di Milano in Milan, Italy, and a Master of Architecture from Yale University. Vittadini has played a key role as project director on several important projects including the Botswana Innovation Hub, a master plan for the LaGuardia Airport, Orlando International Airport, Konza Technology City Master Plan and Pavilion in Nairobi, and 447 Collins Street in Melbourne. Vittadini has co-taught at Cornell University with William Sharples.

Victoire Saby is Senior Associate, SHoP Architects. She holds a Master of Architecture from ENSAPLV, Paris and a Master of Engineering from École des Ponts et Chausses. Saby has worked on several of SHoP's high-profile jobs including the Hudson's Site Project in Detroit, and the SITE museum in Santa Fe. She specialises in interdisciplinary design that spans across architecture, engineering, computation and construction. Saby has taught and lectured at institutions in France and the US.

The Tide [Phase 1]: Greenwich Peninsula, London

Emmanuel Verkinderen is a Technical Director at the London-based engineering firm AKT II. After graduating from École Centrale de Nantes, he worked in the aircraft and spacecraft industries, designing fuselage structures and engines attachments. In 2007, Verkinderen moved into the construction industry where he has since designed a number of complex buildings, bridges, sculptures and large scale industrial masts. From his time in industry, he has gained insight into cutting-edge materials and substantial experience at the forefront of monocoque and stressed skin design.

Bryce Suite is a designer currently residing in London. He received his master's degree in 2012 from Columbia University Graduate School of Architecture, Planning, and Preservation after earning a bachelor's degree in architecture from the University of Kentucky in 2007. He has previously worked at studios in Chicago, New York City, and is currently an Associate at Diller Scofidio + Renfro. Suite has been a guest critic and lecturer at the Architectural Association, Royal College of Art, Pratt Institute, and is a former Associate in Architecture at Columbia.

Ryan Neiheiser is a principal at architecture studio NEIHEISER ARGYROS. He received his master's degree in 2008 from Princeton University after earning a dual bachelor's degree in Engineering and Art from Swarthmore College in 2001. Neiheiser has worked at a number of award-winning firms, including OMA, Rotterdam, and Diller Scofidio and Renfro, New York. Neiheiser has taught master's level thesis at Princeton University and, since 2014, taught design studio at the Architectural Association. He is co-founder of the architecture publication, *Another Pamphlet*, was a co-editor of the book, *Agenda: Can We Sustain Our Ability to Crisis?* (Actar, 2010), and has published articles in *New Geographies*, *Bidoun*, and *Pidgin*.

Edoardo Tibuzzi is a designer and researcher based in London with over 14 years' experience in delivering complex geometry projects. During his work at AKTII, he has completed various projects, including the UK Pavilion (Shanghai 2010 Expo), BMW Pavilion and Coca-Cola Beat-box (London 2012 Olympic Park), Bloomberg's London Headquarter (2012-2017). He collaborates with several academic institutions such as the AA School, the RCA and UCL in London, KTH and Chalmers University in Sweden and the NYIT in New York, running various lectures and workshops. He published several papers and co-authored *Design Engineering Re-Focused*, (Wiley, 2016) and the *Nexus Network Journal*, (Springer, 2018).

Jeg Dudley is a computational designer and Associate within the Parametric Applied Research Team (P.art) at engineering firm AKT II. He received architecture degrees from the University of Bath before working for companies across the design spectrum, including RoboFold, Heatherwick Studio and Atmos. Dudley has extensive industry experience in the design, optimisation and construction of complex geometries. He has run workshops and lectured at several academic institutions, including the Royal College of Art, UCL and the University of Westminster, where he is a Visiting Lecturer.

Making Form Work: Experiments along the grain of concrete and timber

Sasa Zivkovic is assistant professor at Cornell University Architecture, Art, and Planning where he directs the Robotic Construction Laboratory (RCL), an interdisciplinary research group investigating robotic-based construction technology. Zivkovic is a co-principal of HANNAH, an architecture practice based in Ithaca, New York. HANNAH's work focuses on the architectural implementation of contemporary building practices and utilises novel material applications as well as innovative digital construction methods to address subjects of architecture and urbanism. In collaboration with the building industry, HANNAH and RCL explore the implementation of construction techniques such as additive concrete manufacturing and robotic timber construction.

Leslie Lok is assistant professor at Cornell University College of Architecture, Art, and Planning. She is also a cofounder at HANNAH, an award-winning experimental design practice for built and speculative projects. HANNAH's work focuses on the architectural implementation of contemporary building practices and utilises novel material applications as well as innovative digital construction methods to address subjects of architecture and urbanism. In collaboration with the building industry, the office explores the implementation of construction techniques such as concrete additive manufacturing and robotic timber construction. Lok's research and teaching explore the intersection of housing, urbanisation and mass-customised construction methods at multiple scales.

Additive Fabrication of Concrete Elements by Robots: Lightweight concrete ceiling

Georg Hansemann has been a project assistant at the Institute of Structural Design since 2015. He graduated in architecture at Graz University of Technology in 2014. Since 2015 he has been working on the research project COEBRO: Additive fabrication of concrete elements by robots, investigating robotics, programming, plant as well as application development; it was successfully completed in 2019 and is the basis of his ongoing dissertation 'COEBRO (ceiling)'. He is currently working on reinforcement concepts for 3D-printed concrete, application potentials of this new technology, and a research project with foam concrete.

Robert Schmid has been a project assistant at the Institute of Structural Design since 2016. He studied architecture at the Graz University of Technology and at the NTNU in Trondheim. Since 2015 he has been working on the research project 'COEBRO: Additive fabrication of concrete elements by robots', with a focus on robotics, programming, plant and application development. After successfully completing the COEBRO research project, he started working on further developments and applications of this new technology in his dissertation 'COEBRO (façade)'.

Christoph Holzinger has been scientific assistant at the Institute of Structural Design since 2017. He studied civil engineering at the Carinthia University of Applied Sciences. From 2011 to 2017 he worked as a structural engineer and later as a technical project manager at Werner Sobek Stuttgart on various national and international projects and competitions where he specialised in the field of structural optimisation (MVM). He worked on projects including Okmeydani and Göztepe Training and Research Hospitals in Istanbul and Stuttgart 21 Main Station. He is currently working on the research project '3DWelding – Additive Manufacturing of Structural Steel Elements'.

Joshua P. Tapley studied civil engineering and economics at *Graz University of Technology*, specialising in structural engineering. He is currently working as a research assistant at the Institute for Structural Design. After completing his Master's thesis which investigated numerical calculations for centrally load steel T profiles, he started working as a scientific assistant and worked on the successful research projects 'STELA – Smart Tower Enhancement Leoben Austria' and 'COEBRO: Additive Fabrication of Concrete Elements by Robots'. His ongoing dissertation investigates modern methods of reinforcing printed concrete elements.

Hoang Huy Kim is a scientific assistant in the Institute of Structural Concrete at Graz University of Technology (TU Graz). He received his doctorate at TU Graz in 2017, publishing his PhD thesis, 'A Systematic Mix Design Approach for Ultra-High Performance Fibre Reinforced Concrete'. He has been working in the field of cement and concrete research since 2004, focusing on the development and application of innovative concrete technology for sustainable construction. He was responsible for material development on the project 'COEBRO'.

Valentino Sliskovic graduated in Civil Engineering from Graz University of Technology in 2015. His Master's thesis was part of a research project and dealt with biaxial load carrying capacity of UHPC shell structures. Between 2015 and 2019, Sliskovic worked as a project assistant at the Laboratory for Structural Engineering. During this time, he was part of several research projects, including 'Shell-structures made of UHPC', 'QUICKWAY' and 'COEBRO'. Since 2019 he has worked as a structural engineer at Vatter&Partner ZT-GmbH.

Bernhard Freytag is the head of the Laboratory for Structural Engineering at Graz University of Technology. He studied civil engineering at Graz University of Technology, graduated with his diploma in 1997 and concluded his doctoral thesis titled 'The Glass-Concrete Composite Method of Construction' in 2002. His present main focus of research is on Experimental Methods in Structural Engineering and Design and Construction of Ultra High Performance Concrete Buildings. He successfully completed his teaching habilitation in 2014. Prof. Freytag was awarded 1st prize at the 2008 Wolfgang Houska Awards as well as 1st prize at the 2008 Österreichischen Baupreises.

Andreas Trummer is Associate Professor for Structural Design and Robotic Fabrication at Graz University of Technology. He studied Structural Engineering at TU Graz and at EPFL Lausanne and earned his PhD at the BOKU Vienna in 2002. He published his habilitation treatise *Structural Robotics* in 2014. He established the Roboter Design Labor in 2009. His research and teaching is focused on questions of materials and resources for structures and digital fabrication of load carrying building elements. The contribution to prefabricated concrete shell-elements was awarded with the nomination for the Austrian state-prize. The Ceramic Shell Project presented the collaboration with the GSD Design Robotics Group. The ongoing project is about the future of concrete 3D printing processes.

Stefan Peters is Professor at the Institute for Structural Design at Graz University of Technology. He studied Civil Engineering at the University Stuttgart and, since 1998, has been working as a structural engineer. After working as project engineer at the Ingenieurbüro and at Werner Sobek Stuttgart, he became a Scientific Assistant at the Institute of Building Structures and Structural Design. He received his doctorate from Jan Knippers on the subject of the structural application of GFK and glass. In 2007 he founded, together with Stephan Engelsmann, the civil engineering company Engelsmann Peters Beratende Ingenieure with branches in Stuttgart and Graz.

DFAB House: A comprehensive demonstrator of digital fabrication in architecture

Konrad Graser is a PhD candidate at the Chair of Innovative and Industrial Construction at ETH Zurich. He was the project manager and design lead of the DFAB HOUSE, a full-scale architectural demonstrator of interdisciplinary research at the Swiss National Centre for Competence in Research Digital Fabrication. Previously, Graser worked as project manager at Werner Sobek Stuttgart, and as design associate and VDC manager at SHoP Architects, New York. He has been a teaching assistant at Yale School of Architecture and adjunct professor at California College of the Arts, and holds a Diploma in Architecture from ETH Zurich.

Marco Baur studied architecture with a focus on the development of material systems and digital design methods under the leadership of Prof. Achim Menges and Prof. Jan Knippers, at both the Institute for Computational Design and the Institute for Structural Design at the University of Stuttgart. After his studies, Baur worked as a project engineer at Werner Sobek, Stuttgart, and later as a project manager at Werner Sobek, New York on the technical development of complex building envelopes. In 2016, Baur joined the NCCR Digital Fabrication as the Deputy Project Manager for the DFAB HOUSE.

Aleksandra Anna Apolinarska is a computational designer, architect and researcher focused on complex geometries and coding. She holds a Dr.sc. from the Institute of Technology in Architecture at ETH Zurich where she is now a Postdoctoral Fellow at Gramazio Kohler Research, conducting research on robotically assembled discrete timber structures and developing innovative methods that address complex interrelations between geometry, structural performance and robotic fabrication. Apolinarska is a registered architect with extensive experience in computational design of geometrically complex buildings, gathered through several years of her professional career working on challenging signature projects in offices across Europe including Foster + Partners, UNStudio and designtoproduction.

Kathrin Dörfler is an architect and researcher in the field of robotic fabrication. Her research focuses on on-site robotic and mixed-reality fabrication. She holds a Master's degree in Architecture from TU Vienna, and a PhD degree in Digital Fabrication from ETH Zurich. Together with Romana Rust, she co-founded the Architecture studio dorfundrust. Dörfler was postdoc at Gramazio Kohler Research at the National Centre of Competence in Research (NCCR) Digital Fabrication. In summer 2019, she joined TU Munich as a Tenure Track Professor to establish a research group at the TUM Department of Architecture and the TUM Department of Civil, Geo and Environmental Engineering.

Norman Hack is an architect and a researcher in the field of digital fabrication. He holds a degree in architecture from Technical University Vienna and the Architectural Association in London. Following his graduation, he worked as a programming architect in the Digital Technologies Group at Herzog & de Meuron. His interest in seamless digital design and fabrication processes led him to pursue a doctorate with Gramazio Kohler Research at ETH Zurich. Hack currently holds a Tenure Track Professorship for Digital Building Fabrication at the Institute of Structural Design at Technische Universität Braunschweig.

Andrei Jipa has previously taught computational design at the University of Westminster, London and collaborated with Aedas, Mamou-Mani, Loop.pH, MAD, DUS and Exploration before becoming a PhD candidate at DBT, ETH Zurich, supervised by Profs Benjamin Dillenburger, Skylar Tibbits and Ştefana Parascho. He focuses on 3D-printed formwork for functional concrete building components. Jipa had a key role in the design and fabrication of the Smart Slab formwork system.

Ena Lloret-Fritschi is an architect with a strong interest in searching for innovative ways of processing and shaping concrete without the need for traditional formwork. She is currently a PostDoctoral researcher in a bridge position between the Chair of Gramazio Kohler Research and the Chair of Physical Building Chemistry of Prof. Robert Flatt. Her work is embedded in the research strand Mouldless Shaping with concrete within the DFAB or the NCCR, ETH, where she guides PhD students and coordinates projects. Lloret-Fritschi was awarded her PhD on Smart Dynamic Casting: A Digital fabrication method for concrete structures in 2016.

Timothy Sandy received his PhD in Robotics from ETH Zurich in 2018 and is currently a post-doctoral researcher with the Robotic Systems Lab at ETH Zurich. His research is focused on developing sensor fusion, visual tracking and control algorithms for high accuracy mobile manipulation and augmented reality manipulation task guidance.

Daniel Sanz Pont is a postdoctoral researcher at the Physical Chemistry of Building Materials Group, Institute for Building Materials of ETH Zurich and NCCR Digital Fabrication since March 2016. In February 2016 he obtained his international PhD from Polytechnic University of Madrid, Spain (PUM), partially developed at ETH (since July 2014) with the thesis entitled 'Thermal and Mechanical Behavior of Gypsum with Silica Aerogels'. He currently conducts research on aerogel building elements via digital fabrication, starting from material development and processing, up to its application into elements for the building enclosure, including all aspects of the performance and building physics.

Daniel M. Hall is Assistant Professor of Innovative and Industrial Construction at the Department of Civil, Environmental and Geomatic Engineering of ETH Zurich. Hall holds a Doctor of Philosophy (2017) in Civil and Environmental Engineering (CEE) from Stanford University. He also holds a Master of Science (2014) in Civil and Environmental Engineering with an emphasis in Sustainable Design and Construction from Stanford University and a Bachelor of Science (2008) in Architectural Engineering from the College of Architecture and Environmental Design at California Polytechnic State University San Luis Obispo. He is founder and organiser of the Stanford Industrialised Construction Forum since 2014.

Matthias Kohler is Professor of Architecture and Digital Fabrication at the Department of Architecture of ETH Zurich where he co-directs the Gramazio Kohler Research group (2005) with Fabio Gramazio. He is a principal of the architecture practice Gramazio Kohler Architects (2000), which realised award-winning projects such as the living lab building NEST (Next Evolution in Sustainable Building) for the Swiss Federal Laboratories for Material Science and Technology (2016). In academia, he initiated and directed the Swiss National Centre of Research (NCCR) Digital Fabrication (2011-2017) and headed the DFAB HOUSE project (2019). He currently engages in architectural research on augmented computational design and fabrication with artificial intelligence and extended reality.

Fabrication and Application of 3D-Printed Concrete Structural Components in the Baoshan Pedestrian Bridge Project

Weiguo Xu is a pioneer and leader in digital architectural design and digital fabrication in China. He has promoted the rapid development of digital architecture here through teaching, curating, publishing and engineering projects. He is professor at Tsinghua University, the founder of XWG Archi Studio, and one of the initiators of DADA (Digital Architecture & Design Association). Professor Xu launched the 'Parametric Architectural Design Course' at Tsinghua University in 2003. Since 2004, he has curated the Digital Architecture Biennale five times. In recent years, his research has focused on intelligent construction based on robotic arms.

Yuan Gao is an architect and a researcher working at the Tsinghua University (School of Architecture)-Zoina Land Joint Research Centre for Digital Architecture. She holds a Bachelor degree in Architecture from Tsinghua University and a Master's degree in Architecture from Cooper Union. Her research is focused on digital fabrication with robotic arms, especially 3D printing concrete with robotics.

Chenwei Sun is an architect, designer, engineer and programmer. He studied architecture in Tsinghua University and TU Delft. Now as a core member of the research team at Tsinghua University (School of Architecture)-Zoina Land Joint Research Centre for Digital Architecture, he explores the boundary of digital construction which is a multidisciplinary subject combining design, engineering, materials and programming. Recently he and his team accomplished several experiments and practices in robotic 3D concrete printing, ranging in scale from urban furniture to architecture.

Zhi Wang is a researcher at Tsinghua University (School of Architecture)-Zoina Land Joint Research Centre for Digital Architecture, where he focuses on the study and application of concrete 3D printing. He is also a designer who has been engaged in architecture practice and vernacular architecture research in rural areas of western China. He studied architecture at Tsinghua University, China.

3: OPTIMISATION FOR A CHANGING WORLD

Architectural Scale Kagome Weaving: Design methods and fabrication concepts

Phil Ayres is an architect, researcher and educator. He is Associate Professor at CITA, which he joined in 2009 after a decade of teaching and research at The Bartlett, UCL. His research primarily focuses on the design and production of novel bio-hybrid architectural systems that couple technical and living complexes, with the development of complimentary design environments. Ayres has pursued this research in the context of two EU funded Future and Emerging Technology (FET) projects – 'flora robotica' and 'Fungal Architectures' – acting as Principle Investigator on both. He is editor of *Persistent Modelling – extending the role of architectural representation*, published by Routledge.

Adam Orlinski studied at the University of Applied Arts Studio Prix in Vienna and graduated in 2011 with the Honorary Prize of the Austrian Ministry of Science and Research. He is currently working at Bollinger + Grohmann Vienna and is part of the developer team of 'Karamba3D' – an interactive parametric finite-element plugin for Grasshopper. Both professionally and in academia, his research focuses on interdisciplinary digital design strategies and their possible fabrication methods in the context of structural design.

Moritz Heimrath studied architecture at the Academy of Fine Arts in Stuttgart and finished his studies at the University of Applied Arts in Vienna in 2010. He is currently Partner at Bollinger + Grohmann Vienna and part of the developer team of 'Karamba3D' – an interactive parametric finite-element plugin for Grasshopper. His work and research focuses on the relationship between computational strategies, structural design and architecture. He is specialised in parametric workflows for structural designs and uses them in his daily office practice.

Soraya Bornaz is a research and development engineer and scientist based in Paris. She has been involved in several high technology innovation projects across different industries including oil and gas, and architecture. In 2019, she joined the Flora Robotica project team at CITA as a research assistant to provide her expertise in structural design and material modelling. She is currently working at MOMA, a French firm specialised in scientific innovation, integrated tool development, and research strategy consultancy. Bornaz also holds a master's degree in computational design and digital fabrication from the École des Ponts in Paris, France.

Alison Grace Martin is a weaver and independent researcher. She studies weaving techniques, based around the principles of pattern, tension and repetition. Martin's work aims to push expectations of traditional fibre work in order to expose relationships with complex surface visualisation and structural morphology. She believes that the necessarily slow and painstaking process of hand-building physical models allows unexpected connections to be made and provides tactile understanding and practical insights into spatial concepts.

Rethinking Efficient Shell Structures with 3D-Printed Formwork

Xiang Wang is a post-doctoral researcher at the College of Architecture and Urban Planning (CAUP) at Tongji University. He is also a member of WG21 of the International Association of Shell and Spatial Structures (IASS). His research focuses on innovative structural design with digital tools (especially of shell structures and spatial structures) and robotic fabrication technology. His work includes the development of computational design workflow and software of structural design as well as completing the corresponding fabrication technique with robotics.

Chun Pong So started his master's study in Architectural Design at Tongji from 2018, with specialisations in construction and timber joints. He is a researcher at Fab-Union. His interests cover mass timber structure, prefabrication and erection, robotic arms and discrete architecture. Within the Fab-Union, So's research focuses on timber joints, wanting to rebuild the system of traditional mortise and tenon connections and turn it into a modern construction process.

Liming Zhang is a PhD candidate at the College of Architecture and Urban Planning (CAUP) at Tongji University. He has many years of research experience in robot fabrication and robot 3D printing. Zhang served as digital fabrication team leader on projects including the 2018 Venice Biennale China Pavilion outdoor exhibition pavilion 'Cloud Village' project and Shanghai Artificial Intelligence Conference spatial printed service kiosk.

Zhewen Chen is a graduate student at Tongji University College of Architecture and Urban Planning. Her research focuses on the integration between structural topological

optimisation and robotic 3D printing, especially in the material of plastic.

Philip F. Yuan is Professor at the College of Architecture and Urban Planning (CAUP), Tongji University; Visiting Professor 2019 at Massachusetts Institute of Technology (MIT); and Thomas Jefferson Visiting Professor 2019 at University of Virginia. His research mainly focuses on the field of performance-based tectonics in architecture as well as robotic fabrication. Yuan has published more than 10 books on this work and related fields in both English and Chinese. His research and projects have received many international awards, have been published and exhibited worldwide and have formed parts of several renowned museum collections including the permanent collection of the Museum of Modern Art (MoMA) in New York.

KnitCandela: Challenging the construction, logistics, waste and economy of concrete-shell formwork

Mariana Popescu is a post-doctoral researcher at the Block Research Group (BRG) at ETH Zurich, involved in the NCCR Digital Fabrication. Popescu is an architect with a strong interest in innovative approaches to fabrication processes and use of materials. She studied architecture at the Delft University of Technology, before obtaining her PhD at the BRG in 2019. Her research focuses on the development of KnitCrete, a novel, material-saving, labour-reducing, cost-effective formwork system for casting doubly-curved geometries in concrete using 3D knitting. She is the main author of the award-winning KnitCandela shell and was included in the MIT Technology Review Innovator Under 35 list in 2019.

Matthias Rippmann was a senior scientist at the Block Research Group (BRG) at ETH Zurich. He was a key author of numerous BRG projects and had more than 10 years of research and teaching experience in the field of digital methods in architecture. His PhD (2016) was awarded the ETH medal for outstanding doctoral dissertation. He developed the award-winning software RhinoVAULT. From 2016 to 2018, he was post-doctoral researcher in the NCCR Digital Fabrication. Rippmann studied architecture at the University of Stuttgart and worked for renowned architectural offices, ILEK at the University of Stuttgart and Werner Sobek Engineering. Matthias passed away on 24 August 2019.

Tom Van Mele is co-director and head of research of the Block Research Group (BRG) at ETH Zurich, and lead developer of COMPAS, an open-source computational framework for research and collaboration in architecture, engineering, fabrication and construction. Van Mele studied architecture and structural engineering at Vrije Universiteit Brussel in Brussels, where he received his PhD in 2008. In 2010, Van Mele joined the BRG, where his technical and computational developments have formed the backbone of multiple flagship projects, including the Armadillo Vault (2016 Architecture Biennale, Venice), the NEST HiLo roof prototype (2017), and the NEST HiLo unit (under construction).

Philippe Block is a full professor at the Institute of Technology in Architecture at ETH Zurich, where he leads the Block Research Group (BRG). He is also Director of the National Centre of Competence in Research (NCCR) in Digital Fabrication. Block studied architecture and structural engineering at VUB in Belgium and at MIT in the US, where he earned his PhD in 2009. With the BRG, he applies research into practice on the design and engineering of novel shell structures. He has won numerous awards, including the

Rössler Prize for most promising young professor from ETH Zurich (2018) and the Berlin Arts Prize 2018 for *Baukunst*.

Printed Assemblages: A co-evolution of composite tectonics and additive manufacturing techniques

Roland Snooks is an Associate Professor at RMIT University, and director of the architectural practice Studio Roland Snooks. Snooks' design research explores behavioural processes of formation that draw from the logic of swarm intelligence and multi-agent algorithms. He has taught widely in the US including at Columbia University, University of Pennsylvania, SCI-Arc and the Pratt Institute. He received a PhD from RMIT and a Master in Advanced Architectural Design from Columbia University, where he studied on a Fulbright scholarship. Snooks' work has been exhibited widely and acquired for the permanent collections of institutions including the Centre Pompidou and the FRAC.

Laura Harper is a practicing architect with 20 years' experience in Europe and Australia where she has led award winning residential, public and urban projects. She is also a lecturer in the Monash University Urban Laboratory in Melbourne, Australia where her research considers material and construction through their systematic connection to wider processes and structures of the city. Harper is a graduate of RMIT University and received her PhD from Monash University.

Large-Scale Free-Form Timber Grid Shell: Digital planning of the new Swatch headquarters in Biel, Switzerland

Hanno Stehling is partner and head of software development at the digital building process consultancy Design-to-Production in Zurich, where he leads a team of architects and programmers developing digital tools for CAD-CAM workflows and general data management. He graduated with a diploma in architecture from University of Kassel, Germany. He focused his strong background in computer programming on the intersection between architecture and computer science, joining a research group focused on parametric design led by Prof. Manfred Grohmann of Bollinger + Grohmann and Oliver Tessmann. After graduating, Stehling worked as a freelance programmer and as computational designer for architects including Bernhard Franken before joining Design-to-Production in 2009.

Fabian Scheurer is co-founder of Design-to-Production and leads the company's office in Zurich. He graduated from the Technical University of Munich with a diploma in computer science and architecture and gathered professional experience as a CAD-trainer, software developer and new media consultant. In 2002 he joined Ludger Hovestadt's CAAD group at the ETH Zurich, where he co-founded Design-to-Production as a research group to explore the connections between digital design and fabrication. At the end of 2006, Design-to-Production teamed up with architect Arnold Walz and became a commercial consulting practice, supporting architects, engineers and fabricators in the digital production of complex design.

Sylvain Usai is a trained architect developing digital fabrication solutions for complex timber structures at Design-to-Production since 2014. He works in close collaboration with architects, engineers and contractors to precisely describe freeform buildings using custom-made software programs and allow for their realisation. Usai gathered experience on both programming and design for manufacture and assembly on freeform projects such as La Seine Musicale in Paris (2015-2017) and the Swatch Headquarters in Biel (2017-2019), as well as standard projects such as Krokodil Lokstadt Winterthur (2019).

Optimisation of Robotic Printing Paths for Structural Stiffness Using Machine Learning

Zeynep Aksöz is a partner in OpenFields studio//research. She is a Research Associate and Lecturer at University of Applied Arts Vienna, as well as a University Assistant in Technical University Vienna in Department for Structural Design. Aksöz has a Dr.techn. from University of Applied Arts Vienna, focused on applications of AI and Machine Learning in Early Design Phase. Through her ongoing research, teaching and practice, she explores generative design processes through the collaboration between human and machine intelligence. Aksöz is investigating design methodologies with Artificial Intelligence, critically reflecting on the current processes of optimisation.

Samuel Wilkinson is an associate within Foster + Partners' Specialist Modelling Group (SMG), the practice's multi-disciplinary research and development group. Since joining in 2014, he has been leading the group's collaborative research with universities and industry, primarily through EPSRC, InnovateUK, H2020, or private funding. Wilkinson has an EngD from UCL, in the use of machine learning for approximating computational fluid dynamics in the generative design of tall buildings, an MRes from UCL in Adaptive Architecture and Computation, and an MEng/BArch from the University of Nottingham in Architecture and Environmental Design.

Giannis Nikas is an Associate at Foster + Partners, where he works on computational design strategies, prototyping and fabrication strategies. He consults on a wide range of projects worldwide including Apple Stores and Battersea Power Station. Nikas collaborates on several research initiatives currently being developed by the firm, including robotic fabrication strategies. He specialises in the development of software and hardware for motorised robotic arm end-effectors and the integration of robotics in architecture. He has studied in Thessaloniki, Greece and at the Design Research Lab at the Architectural Association, London. His main interests lie in the integration of fabrication methodologies and their application to contemporary building practices.

The Anatomy of a Skeleton: Hybrid processes for large-scale robotic fabrication

Emmanuel Vercruysse is first and foremost a designer, with a deep interest in the relationship between drawing and making. He approaches design as a tacit process, and as a series of translations between drawings and objects that oscillate between intuitive acts and precise operations. This approach to design, combined with his in-depth knowledge of digital fabrication techniques, means that Vercruysse views the digital very much as an augmentation of the analogue, rather than a substitute and he continues to explore the production of architecture intuitively through iterations of drawing, craft, intuition and code. Vercruysse is Programme Director of the MArch course Design for Manufacture at The Bartlett, UCL.

BUGA Fibre Pavilion: Towards robotically-fabricated composite building structures

Serban Bodea is a Romanian-born architect and PhD candidate at the Institute for Computational Design and Construction (ICD). Bodea holds a MSc. in Architecture from Delft University of Technology and has collaborated with ONL, KCAP, IBA and AtelierPro on multiple interdisciplinary projects. His work integrates research and education; he was Researcher and Educator at Hyperbody TUDelft (2016), is alumnus of the The Norman Foster Foundation Atelier 2017-Robotics, and has taught Integrative Technologies and Architectural Design Research (ITECH) since 2017. His University of Stuttgart work spans design-engineering and fabrication for large-scale composite building systems, particularly applicable to lightweight, load-adapted Fibrous Morphology.

Niccolo Dambrosio is a Research Associate at the Institute for Computational Design and Construction at the University of Stuttgart. He holds a Master in Architecture degree from the Polytechnic University of Bari as well as an advanced degree as Master of Architecture from the Graduate School of Design at Harvard University. Dambrosio's current research focuses on the use of anisotropic fibre composite materials in additive production processes for high performance, lightweight structures.

Christoph Zechmeister is a research associate at the Institute for Computational Design (ICD) at the University of Stuttgart. He holds a Master of Science from Vienna University of Technology as well as a postgraduate Master of Advanced Studies in Architecture and Information from ETH Zurich. Before joining the ICD, Zechmeister worked as a Junior Architectural Designer at UNStudio, Amsterdam as well as in multiple offices in and around Zurich, Switzerland. With a deep interest in computational design and additive manufacturing, Zechmeister is currently involved in developing high performance lightweight structures in the Cluster of Excellence on Integrative Computational Design and Construction for Architecture.

Marta Gil Pérez is a Research Associate at the ITKE Institute of Building Structures and Structural Design, University of Stuttgart. She obtained a Master in Architecture at ETSAM, University Politécnica de Madrid (Spain). Afterwards, she was granted a full scholarship to study for a master's in Structural Engineering at Seoul National University (South Korea). For three years she worked at C.S. Structural Engineering in South Korea, participating in the structural design of projects in South Korea and the Middle East. Currently, Pérez's research focuses on the structural design and building system development of robotically-fabricated coreless wound fibre composite structures.

Valentin Koslowski is a structural engineer, researcher and teacher at Prof. Dr.-Ing. Jan Knippers' Institute of Building Structures and Structural Design (ITKE) at the University of Stuttgart. He specialises in designing load-bearing structures with fibre-reinforced composite materials. He worked on multiple, international projects with novel carbon and glass fibre composites and taught the Modelling and Simulation Seminar course at the University of Stuttgart. He holds a Master of Science in Civil Engineering from the Technical University of Munich and a Bachelor of Engineering in Civil Engineering from the University of Applied Sciences, Biberach.

Bas Rongen is a Research Associate at the ITKE Institute of Building Structures and Structural Design, University of Stuttgart. From Eindhoven University of Technology in the Netherlands, he obtained a master's degree in structural engineering and a master's degree in architecture. This interest in the synergy between architecture and structure led him to the ITKE at the University of Stuttgart. Rongen's research interests lie in the field of geometrical and structural optimisation of lightweight structures. In close collaboration with the Institute of Computational Design (ICD), University of Stuttgart, he focuses on robotically-fabricated lightweight composite structures.

Moritz Dörstelmann is managing partner of FibR GmbH (www.fibr.tech), a specialist company for computational design and robotic fabrication of bespoke fibre composite structures, which enables the exploration of a novel design and construction repertoire for expressive high-performance lightweight structures. His work on digital fabrication technology provides societally relevant solutions for resource efficient architectural construction. Dörstelmann is a registered architect. He developed the underlying digital design and robotic fabrication strategies of his work through seven years of research at the University of Stuttgart, Harvard University and as visiting professor for Emerging Technologies at the Technical University of Munich.

Ondrej Kyjanek is co-founder and CTO of FibR GmbH, a specialist company of bespoke filament structures, and a former research associate at the Institute for Computational Design and Construction (ICD) at the University of Stuttgart, where his research focused on advanced robotic automation and human-machine collaboration in the timber construction industry. He studied architecture and urban planning at the Czech Technical University in Prague (Bc.), followed by the Integrative Technologies and Architectural Design Research (ITECH) programme at the University of Stuttgart (MSc.).

Jan Knippers See page 312.

Achim Menges See page 312.

4: POLEMICAL PERFORMATIVE PRACTICE

Embedded Architecture: Ada, driven by humans, powered by AI

Jenny E. Sabin See Editor's Biographies page 310.

John Hilla is a Designer with Jenny Sabin Studio and a Research Associate in the Sabin Design Lab at Cornell AAP. As a graduate of the Master of Architecture programme at the University of Pennsylvania, Hilla was awarded the Henry Adams Medal and was a finalist for the Student of the Year honour from the American Institute of Architects. Additionally, he received the Outstanding Graduate Student Award and the Legacy Award for Academic Engagement at Syracuse University, where he earned a Master of Science degree in Engineering Management and a Bachelor of Science degree in Mechanical Engineering.

Dillon Pranger is a licensed architect and senior designer at Jenny Sabin Studio. His current research involves unconventional building materials and construction techniques. These explorations have been realised through his leadership roles on various Jenny Sabin Studio pavilion installations, including Ada for Microsoft Research, Lustre for House of Peroni 2018, and Lumen for the 2017 MoMA PS1 Young Architects Programme. In addition to practicing, Pranger has taught architecture at various institutions, including Harvard GSD, Cornell University, and Syracuse University. He holds a B.S. in Architecture from the University of Cincinnati (2012) and a M.Arch from Cornell University (2015).

Clayton Binkley trained as a sculptor and a structural engineer and practices as an artist, craftsman and multidisciplinary designer. He received his BA in sculpture from Yale University and his MEng in structural engineering from the University of Bath. Binkley has collaborated extensively with Jennifer Newsom and Tom Carruthers of

Dream The Combine, most recently on the 2018 MoMA PS1 Young Architects Programme installation, Hide & Seek. Working with Arup for over a decade, he has used his skills as a structural engineer to help open up new possibilities for artists and designers, including: Janet Echelman, Jenny Sabin, John Grade, Lead Pencil Studio and Jill Anholt.

Jeremy Bilotti is a graduate fellow at MIT's Design and Computation Group, and a dual-degree candidate in MIT's Department of Computer Science. He is also leading research projects at MIT's Self-Assembly Lab. As a designer at Jenny Sabin Studio, Bilotti led the development of software and hardware systems in collaboration with Microsoft Research for Ada. During his B.Arch at Cornell University, he was Senior Research Associate at the Sabin Design Lab, and contributed to groundbreaking work at Cornell's Robotic Construction Laboratory. Bilotti's work has been published by Routledge, RobArch, in ACADIA's peer-reviewed proceedings, and was exhibited in the 2019 Shenzhen Biennale.

Diagrams of Entropic Forces: Design for new dissipative fabrication

Philip Beesley is a multidisciplinary artist and architect. His research is recognised for its pioneering contributions to the field of responsive interactive architecture. Beesley directs Living Architecture Systems Group, an international group of researchers and creators. He is a professor at the University of Waterloo, Ontario and the European Graduate School. He represented Canada at the 2010 and 2020 Venice Biennale of Architecture. Beesley's collaborations with artists, scientists and engineers include diverse projects from haute couture to complex electronic systems that can sense, react and learn. This experimental work explores subtle phenomena and constantly changing boundaries at the outer edges of current technology.

Discrete Timber Assembly

Gilles Retsin is an architect and designer, who founded Gilles Retsin Architecture. He studied architecture in Belgium, Chile and the UK, where he graduated from the Architectural Association. His design work and critical discourse has been internationally recognised through awards and exhibitions at institutions including the Museum of Art and Design, New York and the Centre Pompidou, Paris. Retsin edited an issue of *Architectural Design* on the Discrete and has co-edited *Robotic Building: Architecture in the Age of Automation*. He is Programme Director of the M.Arch Architectural Design at The Bartlett, UCL. He co-founded the UCL Design Computation Lab which does high profile research into new design and fabrication technologies.

Towards Discrete Automation

Mollie Claypool is an architecture theorist and Co-Director of Design Computation Lab (DCL) at The Bartlett School of Architecture, UCL in London where she is also Coordinator of History & Theory in MArch Architectural Design. She is Managing Editor of *Prospectives*, a new open-source publishing platform to be launched in 2020 for research on computation and automation in architecture and design. She is Director of Automated Architecture (AUAR), a design and technology startup based in the UK and is co-author of the recent book *Robotic Building: Architecture in the Age of Automation* (DETAIL Edition, 2019). Claypool was awarded a Fellowship in Automation by the South West Creative Technology Network, funded by Research England, in 2019.

House #05: Incremental construction in digital practice

Paul Loh is an architect and senior lecturer at the Melbourne School of Design, University of Melbourne. His research focuses on the cognitive engagement of making in design practice with digital fabrication and robotics. He studied architecture at the University of Melbourne, University of East London (UEL), the Architectural Association (Design Research Lab) and gained his doctorate at RMIT University with a dissertation on Digital Material Practice: the Agency of Making. Loh has previously taught at UEL and the AA. He is a founding partner of LLDS / Power to Make.

David Leggett is a registered architect in Australia and the UK. Leggett studied architecture at the University of East London and the University of Westminster. He is a founding partner of LLDS / Power to Make, a new breed of architectural practice that integrates digital fabrication in the design of architecture. He established the Architectural Research Laboratory in 2017, which explores novel fabrication techniques and processes applicable to the construction industry. Leggett teaches graduate design Studio 15 at the Melbourne School of Design.

Concrete Choreography: Prefabrication of 3D-printed columns

Ana Anton is a PhD Candidate at the chair for Digital Building Technologies, ETH Zurich and associated to the National Centre for Competence in Research – Digital Fabrication, where she leads the research in concrete 3D printing. She received her architectural degree, cum laude, at TU Delft, in 2014 and continued her research until 2016 as part of the Hyperbody Research Group. While her scientific research addresses complexity and emergence in architecture, her designs exploit materiality encoded for digital fabrication. Her current thesis, 'Tectonics of Concrete Printed Architecture', focuses on robotic concrete extrusion processes for large scale building components.

Patrick Bedarf is a PhD researcher at the chair for Digital Building Technologies, Institute of Technology in Architecture at the Department of Architecture of ETH Zurich and recipient of the ETH research grant. After studying architecture at HTWK Leipzig and TU Delft, he gained experience internationally in offices including Zaha Hadid (London), Delugan Meissl (Vienna) and Henn (Berlin, Beijing). Bedarf lectured and tutored workshops in architectural schools throughout Europe (ETH Zürich, TU Delft, TU Berlin, Politecnico di Milano). His work challenges conventional building culture through innovative design and fabrication processes and currently investigates large-scale 3D printing with porous materials.

Angela Yoo is currently a Research Assistant at the chair of Digital Building Technologies, Institute of Technology in Architecture of ETH Zurich. Upon graduating with a Master's of Architecture (Prof. Hons) from the University of Auckland in 2014, she gained professional experience at Monk Mackenzie Architects based in New Zealand. Moving to Switzerland in 2017, she graduated from the MAS in Architecture and Digital Fabrication at ETH Zurich and has since been involved in research and teaching activities. Her recent projects have focused on design for robotically 3D-printed concrete and 3D-printed formwork for functional building components in architecture.

Lex Reiter is a post-doc researcher at ETH Zurich in the group Physical Chemistry of Building Materials. He works on early age strength build-up and its control for concrete extrusion 3D printing and similar digital fabrication processes with concrete. His research interest is in the physical and chemical processes that enable concrete to be shaped without formwork at high vertical rate, as well as the associated processing challenges.

Timothy Wangler is a senior researcher in the Physical Chemistry of Building Materials group, Institute for Building Materials, at ETH Zurich. He received his PhD in Chemical Engineering from Princeton University with an emphasis on organic-inorganic interactions in construction materials, with his recent research focusing on materials and processing applications in digital fabrication with concrete.

Robert J. Flatt became Professor of Physical Chemistry of Building Materials at Institute of Building Materials, ETH Zurich in September 2010. Before that he was Principal Scientist Head of Inorganic Materials in Corporate Research at Sika Technology AG, the R&D branch of Sika AG. Prior to joining Sika, he spent two and a half years as postdoctoral researcher at Princeton University in the Department of Civil and Environmental Engineering within the materials group of Prof. G.W. Scherer. He studied at the Swiss Federal Institute of Technology in Lausanne, where he obtained his masters in Chemical Engineering and a PhD from the Materials Science Department.

Architect **Benjamin Dillenburger** is Assistant Professor for Digital Building Technologies at the Institute of Technology in Architecture at the Department of Architecture, ETH Zurich. His research focuses on the development of building technologies based on the close interplay of computational design methods, digital fabrication and new materials. In this context, he searches for ways to exploit the potential of additive manufacturing for building construction. He previously was appointed as Assistant Professor at the John H. Daniels Faculty of Architecture, Landscape and Design at the University of Toronto. He obtained his PhD and worked as a senior lecturer in the CAAD group, at ETH Zurich.

Little Island: Sculptural structure through digital design and fabrication

Yong-Wook Jo is an Associate in the New York office of Arup, and leads the firm's multi-disciplinary team as the project manager for Little Island project. Trained in both architecture and engineering, he has collaborated with the world's top architects and contractors with shared understanding of iconic projects featuring complex and irregular geometries and unique technical challenges. Jo's portfolio includes retail, tall buildings, education, airport as well as marine and infrastructure projects. He received a bachelor's degree in architecture from Yonsei University, Korea, and a master's degree in structural engineering from the University of California, Berkeley.

Rosario Gallo leads the team at Access Anvil Corp. (AAC), a Fort Miller Group company, located in Greenwich, New York. AAC is an ISO 9001 certified company that specialises in the design and fabrication of custom concrete formwork and five-axis CNC milling techniques. In addition to its fabrication and milling capabilities, AAC acquired the Scott System product line located in Denver, Colorado to add fabrication of urethane formliners, plastic formliners and brick inlay products to its concrete forming line. Our team provides innovative solutions to complex construction problems.

David Farnsworth is a Principal with Arup's New York office. Farnsworth has a depth of experience in the design and management of projects both locally and globally. His experience includes tall buildings, piers, bridges, rail, airport and civil projects. Having successfully delivered projects through all types of procurement methods – including design bid build, design build, construction management, and direct work with contractors – Farnsworth enjoys collaborating with all project participants to deliver innovation and risk mitigation to each new project. He currently leads Arup's Americas Property Market Business and has designed some of the world's most iconic tall building structures.

Jacob Wiest is a Senior Engineer at Arup who has spent time in their New York and Sydney building structures teams, working on projects varying in typology and market. His proficiency in parametric and digital tools supports an interest in projects with complex geometry and data management requirements. Wiest attended the Pennsylvania State University where he received a Master's and Bachelor's of Architectural Engineering.

Hudson Yards Vessel, New York

Edoardo Tibuzzi See page 314.

Jeg Dudley See page 314.

Pablo Zamorano is Head of Geometry and Computational Design at Heatherwick Studio. He works across all projects providing expertise and guidance on new technologies and techniques, and the execution of challenging geometries. Since joining the Studio in 2015, Zamorano has also worked as Deputy Project Leader on Coal Drops Yard, an award-winning retail quarter and public space in King's Cross, London, where he oversaw all design packages into construction. Prior to working at the studio, Zamorano worked at SOM London, as well as New York City and Santiago. He has lectured widely, and his personal work has been published and awarded internationally.

Peter Romvari joined Heatherwick Studio in 2011. Since then, Romvari has made a significant contribution to a number of the studio's projects including Vessel – the landmark centrepiece for Hudson Yards in Manhattan's West Side. He played a crucial role in driving the overall geometry of the highly complex structure, from concept phase through to informing fabrication and construction. Most recently, Romvari has worked on a kinetic glasshouse, developing the geometry for a project that is as much a machine as a building. His background is architectural practice and the visual arts, having worked as a 3D artist at Atelier Peter Kis.

Fabricate 2020 Co-organisers

Platinum Partner

Gold Partners

Silver Partners

Bronze Partners

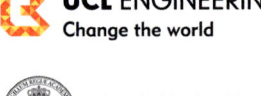

In collaboration with

Fabricate 2020

Editors
Jane Burry, Jenny Sabin, Bob Sheil, Marilena Skavara
Copyeditor
Clare Hamman
Design
Patrick Morrissey / Unlimited
Printing
Albe De Coker, Antwerp, Belgium

First published in 2020 by
UCL Press
University College London
Gower Street
London WC1E 6BT

Available to download free: www.uclpress.co.uk

ISBN: 9781787358126 (Hbk.)
ISBN: 9781787358119 (PDF)
DOI: https://doi.org/10.14324/111.9781787358119

North America Co-Publisher: Riverside Architecture Press
riversidearchitecturalpress.ca

Additional photography
p 1. BUGA Fibre Pavilion. © Roland Halbe; p 20. Cork House. © David Grandorge; p 82. Cambridge Central Mosque © Blumer Lehmann; p 176. ICD Computation and Construction Laboratory. © ICD/ITKE, University of Stuttgart; p 244. Meander, Cambridge, 2019.